The Juvenile Justice System

Delinquency, Processing, and the Law

DEAN J. CHAMPION
CALIFORNIA STATE UNIVERSITY, LONG BEACH

MACMILLAN PUBLISHING COMPANY
NEW YORK

MAXWELL MACMILLAN CANADA
TORONTO

To George A. Captain, who oversees the Roman Room on the Cumberland "Strip" and understands the ups and downs of textbook writing.

Editor: Christine Cardone
Production Supervisor: Andrew Roney
Production Manager: Sandra Moore
Text and Cover Designer: Blake Logan
Cover Illustration: photograph:
Photo Researcher: Diane Kraut
Illustrations: Monotype Composition Company
This book was set in 10/12 Meridien by The Clarinda Company and was printed and bound by Book Press Inc.
The cover was printed by Phoenix Color Corp.

Macmillan Publishing Company
866 Third Avenue, New York, New York 10022

Macmillan Publishing Company is
part of the Maxwell Communication
Group of Companies.

Maxwell Macmillan Canada, Inc.
1200 Eglinton Avenue East
Suite 200
Don Mills, Ontario M3C 3N1

Library of Congress Cataloging-in-Publication Data

Champion, Dean J.
    The juvenile justice system: delinquency, processing, and the law/
    Dean J. Champion.
        p.   cm.
    Includes bibliographical references and indexes.
    ISBN 0-02-320615-2
    1. Juvenile justice, Administration of—United States.
2. Juvenile courts—United States.   I. Title.
KF9779.C425   1992
345.73′081—dc20
[347.30581]   91-20923
                        CIP

Printing: 3 4 5 6 7   Year: 3 4 5 6 7 8

Preface

Juvenile justice systems in the United States have only recently been established. Until 1899 there were no juvenile courts. Juveniles had no constitutional rights or protection until the mid-1960s. Since then, the juvenile justice system has acquired an importance that rivals its counterpart for adults, the criminal justice system.

This book, *The Juvenile Justice System*, has been written to highlight major events that have provided form and function to the vast network of legal mechanisms available to juveniles through the juvenile justice process. Written for basic courses about the juvenile justice system, this book provides both instructors and students with the most up-to-date coverage of major problems and issues pertaining to youthful offenders and to how they are processed by police, prosecutors, the courts, and corrections.

Organization

This book consists of five parts. Part I shows how juveniles are legally defined. Because some youths commit serious crimes, they sometimes interface with the criminal justice system by various means. Several parallels between juvenile and criminal courts will be presented, because certain types of juvenile offenders may be processed by either system. Different kinds of juvenile offenses are described, and several key sources are illustrated that assist us in charting patterns of offending behavior. Guiding the conduct of different actors within the juvenile justice system are various philosophies that reflect alternative explanations for delinquent behavior as well as ideas on how best to manage it. Several theories of delinquent behavior are described, including a unique examination of how these theories have influenced our attitudes about the treatment and processing of juvenile offenders over the years.

Utilizing a systemic approach, Part II provides an overview of the juvenile justice system, including strategic points where important decisions about juveniles are made. Juvenile contacts with police officers and preliminary juvenile court processing are emphasized. The discretionary authority of law enforcement officers and prosecutors reveals the differential importance assigned to both legal and extralegal factors that directly affect a youth's life chances. A distinction is made between status and delinquent offenders, and the reactions of important juvenile court personnel to this distinction are examined. Crime seriousness, prior record, and an offender's age, race/

ethnicity, socioeconomic status, and gender are key elements that influence decision making at key points in the juvenile justice process.

Part III illustrates the procedures whereby the most serious juvenile offenders are waived or transferred to criminal courts where they might receive the harshest punishments. Interestingly, youths processed by criminal courts are often treated more leniently than if their cases had been adjudicated by juvenile courts. The roles of defense and prosecuting attorneys are described; so too are certain aggravating and mitigating circumstances that function to intensify or lessen one's punishment. Several landmark cases are illustrated that outline the constitutional rights that juveniles have been given by the U.S. Supreme Court. A unique summary of major juvenile rights is presented, together with legal citations where such cases may be read more extensively.

Part IV illustrates the broad range of sanctions that may be imposed on juvenile offenders. Nominal, conditional, and custodial punishments are described, including alternative dispute resolution, community-based probation projects and services, electronic monitoring and home confinement, shock probation and parole, and wilderness experiments. Recidivism rates of juvenile offenders who participate in these various programs are presented as one means of assessing a program's effectiveness.

Part V presents several unique comparative contrasts with the juvenile justice systems of Japan, Great Britain, and the Soviet Union. An elaborate chart compares key elements of the juvenile justice system of the United States with the systems of each of these countries so that students may appreciate how delinquency is defined and managed in several other countries. A concluding chapter summarizes numerous important trends in juvenile justice by focusing upon law enforcement, prosecution and the courts, and juvenile corrections.

Features

Student interest in juvenile justice is heightened through the inclusion of up-to-date examples, highlights, cases, and materials that accompany traditional text content and factual information. One case example is about Pamela Smart, a teacher who seduced a fifteen-year-old student and successfully convinced him to kill her husband. Convicted in 1991, Mrs. Smart was sentenced to life imprisonment without parole, while the youth received a similar life term for the murder he committed. Other special features have been included, such as the following:

• In-depth coverage of the discretionary powers of law enforcement officers, intake personnel, and prosecutors illustrates the high degree of subjectivity that persists throughout the juvenile justice system and many of the nonrational factors that adversely affect youths.
• The interrelatedness of theory, policies, and practices is featured throughout all chapters, as different types of treatment programs for youths and contrasting management perspectives are presented.

- Theories of delinquency are presented, as well as an assessment of their long-range impact on procedures and types of punishments imposed for various types of offenders.
- Throughout each chapter, "Juvenile Highlights" sections offer a lively array of boxed materials that correspond with and complement text materials. These Highlights are glimpses of current events and observations about the juvenile justice system that will heighten interest in the topics presented.
- Only the most current sources have been used, in order to provide the freshest scholarly materials in each topic area. The deinstitutionalization of status offenses is covered at length, including responses from law enforcement officials and the juvenile judiciary, which have not always been uniformly favorable.
- An extensive analysis of juvenile rights and of the transfer process is provided, as well as forecasts of likely developments in future years.
- The nature of juvenile offending has changed during the past few decades, and new offending patterns are described. Juvenile gangs, an escalation of juvenile violence, and greater rates of female offending are examined.
- Public expectations of greater accountability among juvenile offenders currently clash with more tranditional perspectives that seek to protect youths from the criminogenic juvenile courtroom atmosphere. This and other issues are highlighted and discussed.
- A comprehensive coverage of correctional options for juveniles is presented, including the most current intermediate punishments. Detailed analyses of current correctional programs are given, including alternative dispute resolution, intensive supervised probation, wilderness programs, electronic monitoring, shock probation and parole, and home confinement.
- Unique coverage is given to various classification systems designed to separate more serious juvenile offenders from less serious ones. Risk prediction and needs assessments are increasingly important methods for determining how different types of youths should be treated and managed.
- Detailed coverage of major landmark cases in juvenile rights is provided. The death penalty for juveniles is discussed in detail, and this discussion includes opposing views from professionals about whether it should be used.

Pedagogical Aids

Every attempt has been made to create a book that will convey material about the juvenile justice system in an interesting and informative way. Numerous short-answer discussion questions are presented at the end of each chapter to facilitate student review of important material. Key terms are listed as well, and a comprehensive glossary of these terms is provided in the Appendix.

Further, all legal cases are indexed, and the page numbers of their location throughout the book are indicated. A bibliographical listing includes over 1200 sources; a majority of these citations are post-1985. This bibliography also includes citations from papers presented at the most recent professional meetings of the Academy of Criminal Justice Sciences, the American Society of Criminology, and the American Sociological Association.

All parts are prefaced by part openers that explain chapter organization and content as well as the author's rationale for chapter choices and order. Each chapter includes summaries as well as suggested readings of mostly recent materials. Graphs, charts, and tabular materials in each chapter enable students to grasp materials more clearly and to understand trends that are depicted. The book contains many photographs in order to portray vividly many of the more important concepts and personalities that have helped to shape the course of juvenile justice.

An *Instructor's Manual and Test Bank* includes over 1,500 items, consisting of true–false, multiple-choice, and short-answer essay questions. Chapter outlines are presented, together with key terms and cases that deserve to be highlighted in lectures. The *Test Bank*, which is available on disk for the microcomputer, should enhance a professor's test construction and administration.

Acknowledgments

I would like to express my appreciation to the many persons at Macmillan who have developed this project. A special thanks is extended to Christine Cardone, my editor, who oversaw this project from beginning to end. I am grateful for her faith in my project and for the encouragement and assistance she has continuously provided. To Chris Migdol and Diane Kraut for their assistance in the illustration program, I also extend my appreciation.

A book's quality is improved greatly by the instructive comments, criticisms, and suggestions of other professionals who review various portions of the manuscript at different stages of the book's progress toward completion. My appreciation is extended to all reviewers who took their valuable time to help me make this a better book. These reviewers include: Gennaro Vito, University of Louisville; Sesha Ketlineni, Illinois State University; Lorie Fridell, Florida State University; and William Doerner, Florida State University.

Dean J. Champion

Brief Contents

Detailed Contents

CHAPTER 10

The Legal Rights of Juveniles   302

PART IV

The Juvenile Justice System: Corrections   333

CHAPTER 11

Nominal and Conditional Sanctions: Warnings, Diversion, and Standard Probation   336

Juvenile Delinquency: The Problem and Its Measurement

The juvenile justice system is the means by which most adolescents are judged or adjudicated when they are charged with violating laws or ordinances. The system, sometimes described as a process, is a somewhat fragmented network of agencies, organizations, and courts that deal with errant adolescents. Although local, state, and federal laws may be at variance concerning whose interests should be served by this system or process, it is generally accepted that the purpose of the system is the management and control of youthful offenders.

The array of actions or behaviors that come within the purview of this system are not always by definition illegal acts. If we designate certain behaviors as violative of our criminal laws, for instance, then those who allegedly violate these laws and engage in prohibited behaviors may be subject to criminal sanctions or penalties. But criminal penalties can only be sustained against those violators who are designated by the courts as adults, who are responsible for their ac-

deserving blame

tions, and who are proven guilty by the state beyond a reasonable doubt. For nonadults, a separate adjudicatory process exists for the purpose of deciding culpability and appropriate punishment. Therefore, two separate justice systems coexist—the adult and juvenile justice systems. While age is most often the determinant of which system is brought into play when violations of ordinances or criminal laws are alleged, some adolescents may become subject to the full range of adult penalties through judicial writ or legislative statute. This book focuses on the juvenile justice system predominantly, although certain parallels between the criminal and juvenile justice processes will be drawn.

Societal labeling has resulted in the emergence of loose terminology to depict the wide variety of adolescent conduct. The terms *juvenile delinquency* and *juvenile delinquent* are both frequently used and abused as behavioral descriptors. Applied to all youths who attract the professional interest of law enforcement agencies, "delinquent" and "delinquency" describe conduct that is both unfavorable and unlawful. Thus, a youth apprehended by police officers for "loitering" in a public place after 10:00 P.M. may be labeled "delinquent." Another youth apprehended by police officers for wielding a semiautomatic rifle and attempting to rob a convenience store by force may also be labeled "delinquent." These examples highlight at least one deficiency of this label—that is, radically different behaviors are depicted by the same term.

Part I includes three chapters that describe juveniles and the system of justice that is designed for them. Chapter 1 describes the emergence of juvenile courts in the United States and the particular philosophy that led to their creation and assigned them their various functions. In recent decades, numerous reforms have brought about modifications in virtually every dimension of the juvenile justice system. Furthermore, changing societal values and interests have led to reassessments of the ways in which youthful offenders are defined and treated. An integral feature of Chapter 1 will be a description of early conceptions of youths and their responsibilities under the law, as well as more modern conceptions of youths and their conduct. Included also are several philosophies, often competing, about how youths should be managed or controlled by societal agencies and organizations.

Chapter 2 examines different definitions of youthful conduct. It will become apparent that little consensus exists about how illegal youthful behavior should be codified, conceptualized, and/or treated. Official measures of delinquent and nondelinquent behaviors are presented. Their weaknesses and strengths are reviewed, particularly in relation to the ways specific juvenile behaviors have been categorized over time. Thus, both violent and nonviolent juvenile conduct is examined, together with assorted trends over time that might be attributable to differences in gender, race/ethnicity, and socioeconomic status.

Chapter 3 presents several explanations of youthful conduct, both lawful and unlawful. Although several popular theoretical explanations will be described, these descriptions are not intended to be extensive or elaborate. Rather, it seems relevant to examine certain explanations and theories that have influenced the nature and development of treatment programs for youths over the years, how certain unlawful conduct by youths has been punished, and how various agency and organizational policies have modified youthful client services, management, and control.

CHAPTER 1

Juvenile Justice: Origins and Issues

Introduction

ARE THESE QUOTATIONS CONTRADICTORY?

> *The jailing of juveniles must be viewed as cruel and unusual punishment* (Carlson, 1987).

> *Young citizens should be held strictly accountable for their actions* (Springer, 1987).

> *A study shows overwhelming support for a juvenile justice system with rehabilitation as its primary goal* (Steinhart, 1988).

> *There is a trend in the United States toward more punitive responses to delinquency* (Bishop *et al.*, 1989).

> *Changing laws and juvenile sentencing reforms show a pattern of continued lenient treatment of juveniles* (Harris, 1988).

> *The system of special courts for young people should be preserved, but not in its present condition* (Springer, 1987).

The above statements and expressions of opinion are all derived from the research reports of professionals in diverse fields who study or are concerned about the *juvenile justice system*. As the contrasting statements illustrate, attitudes toward youths who violate the law are extremely mixed. A clear and universally acceptable mandate about what should be done with delinquent youths, in the form of a consistent standard of punishment or treatment, does not exist.

Although it has been faulted by critics in many respects, the juvenile justice system is an essential component of American jurisprudence. *The* **juvenile justice system** *consists of a more or less integrated network of agencies, institutions, organizations, and personnel that process juvenile offenders.* This network is made up of law enforcement agencies; prosecutors and courts; corrections, probation, and parole services; and public and private community-based treatment programs that provide youths with diverse services. The definition is intentionally qualified by the phrase "more or less integrated," because the concept of juvenile justice means different things to the federal government on the one hand, which rarely involves itself with the juvenile offender, and to the states on the other. Even among states, differences exist. The juvenile justice systems of some states, for example, are much more highly centralized than those of others; some juvenile justice systems fall under the jurisdiction of the state's Department of Corrections, whereas the family courts oversee the system in other states; and the definition used to determine who falls under the jurisdiction of juvenile courts differs from state to state. Also, in some jurisdictions, the diverse components of the juvenile justice system are closely coordinated, while in other jurisdictions, these components are at best loosely coordinated, if they are coordinated at all.

Many criminologists and criminal justice professionals express a preference for the term "process" rather than "system" when they refer to juvenile justice. A major reason for this is that "system" connotes a condition of homeostasis, equilibrium, or internal balance among system components. "Process" focuses more on the different actions taken by and on the contributions of each of these components in dealing with juvenile offenders at various stages of "processing" through the juvenile justice "system." Furthermore, the term "system" implies coordination among elements in an efficient production process, but in reality, communication and coordination among juvenile agencies, organizations, and personnel in the juvenile justice system are often inadequate or nonexistent.

Further clouding the concept of juvenile justice is the fact that different criteria are used to define the broad classes of juveniles among local, state, and federal jurisdictions. Within each of these jurisdictions, certain mechanisms exist for redefining particular juveniles as adults so that they may be legally processed by the adult counterpart to juvenile justice, the criminal justice system. Despite these definitional ambiguities and systemic interfaces among jurisdictions, most scholars who investigate juveniles understand what is meant by juvenile justice. As with pornography, these scholars and investigators recognize the juvenile justice process whenever they see its components, even if they may not always be able to define it precisely.

This book is about the juvenile justice system. Because of the multifaceted nature of this system or process, the wide variety of characteristics of its intended clients, and its interrelatedness with the criminal justice system, we may acquire a better understanding of its nature, purposes, and development if we can place it within a historical framework. Thus, the first part of this chapter describes the historical emergence of juvenile justice in the United States. Key events are noted, and their significance and influence on contemporary juvenile agencies and organizations is discussed. Early versions of juvenile justice were affected by and patterned substantially after early English **common law** and the role of kings and their agents in public affairs; we will trace the origins of our system in English law. Interestingly, certain functions and objectives of contemporary juvenile justice systems have their origins in fifteenth-century England, although particular ideas about how youths of all ages were to be defined, judged, punished, or treated also existed in biblical times.

Following this historical introduction, the juvenile court will be described. This is a relatively recent concept. It is both pivotal and pervasive in most juvenile justice systems. Coexisting with juvenile courts are criminal courts designed to adjudicate adult offenders. Several important characteristics of both types of courts will be described, along with some of their differences. One feature that distinguishes these courts from one another is the age range of the clientele over which each exercises jurisdiction. The matters dealt with by these court systems vary as well. Some of these major differences will be highlighted.

Insinuating itself throughout the juvenile justice system in both Colonial and modern times is the doctrine of *parens patriae*. This doctrine originated in early English common law in the twelfth century. Meaning literally the "parent of the country," *parens patriae* referred originally to the fact that the king of England was both a sovereign and a guardian of persons under legal disability, including children (Black, 1979:1003). (*Parens patriae* will be discussed in greater detail later in this chapter.) This concept has been particularly influential with regard to juvenile court practices as contrasted with criminal courts. In recent decades, there have been numerous reforms throughout the juvenile justice system, and the *parens patriae* doctrine has become both transformed and limited as it applies to youths. This transformation will be described later in this chapter.

Finally, alternative managerial philosophies exist that favor various modes of juvenile control. Some of these philosophies are in direct conflict, and all have competing implications for affected juveniles. A description of these philosophies is in order at the outset, since all currently available juvenile services and programs have been variously influenced by them. As we will see, no consensus exists presently among juvenile justice scholars and researchers about which philosophy is best or most useful. The result is a programmatic Tower of Babel, replete with conflicting values, interests, and aims with regard to the goals and purposes of the juvenile justice system.

The History of Juvenile Courts

English Common Law and Juvenile Accountability. Juvenile courts are a relatively recent American creation. However, modern American juvenile courts have various, less formal European antecedents. In biblical times, Roman law vested parents with the almost exclusive responsibility for disciplining their offspring. Age was the crucial determinant of whether youths were subject to parental discipline or to the more severe penalties invoked for adult law violators. While the origin of this cutting point is unknown, the age of 7 was used in Roman times to separate infants from older children who were accountable to the law for their actions. During the Middle Ages, English common law established under the monarchy adhered to the same standard. In the United States, several state jurisdictions currently apply this distinction and consider all children below the age of 7 to be not accountable for any criminal acts they may commit.

Under the laws of England during the 1500s, **shires** (counties) and other political subdivisions were organized to carry out the will of the king. Each shire had a **reeve,** or chief law enforcement officer. In later years, the term

During the Colonial period, both juveniles and suspected witches were judged and punished for wrongdoings informally and quickly, without benefit of counsel or the right of due process. (Courtesy of the Library of Congress)

"shire" was combined with the term "reeve" ("shire-reeve") to create the word "sheriff"—a term that is now applied to the chief law enforcement officer of most U.S. counties. While reeves enforced both criminal and civil laws and arrested law violators, other functionaries, called **chancellors,** acted on the king's behalf and dispensed justice according to his wishes. These chancellors held court and settled disputes that included simple property trespass, property boundary disagreements, and assorted personal and property offenses, including public drunkenness, thievery, and vagrancy. The courts conducted by chancellors were known as **chancery courts** or **courts of equity.** Today, some jurisdictions in the United States, such as Tennessee, have chancery courts where property boundary disputes and contested wills may be adjudicated by chancellors. These courts have other powers as well, although they deal primarily with equity cases (e.g., breaches of contract, specific performance actions, and child custody cases).

In eighteenth-century England, no distinctions were made with regard to age or gender when punishments were administered. Youthful offenders age 7 or older were subject to the same harsh types of punishment imposed on adults. Stocks and pillories, whipping posts, branding, "ducking stools," and other forms of corporal punishment were meted out to juveniles as well as to adult male and female offenders for many different types of crimes. **Banishment** was used in some instances as a means of punishing serious offenders. The death penalty was invoked frequently, often for petty crimes. Incarceration of offenders was particularly sordid, as women, men, and youths were confined together in jails for lengthy periods. No attempts were made to classify these offenders by gender or age, and all prisoners slept on hay loosely thrown on wooden floors.

Bridewell Workhouse. These eighteenth-century jails were patterned largely after **workhouses** that were still common nearly two centuries earlier. In 1557, for example, **Bridewell Workhouse** was established in London. Although the manifest aim of such places was to punish offenders, Bridewell and other similar facilities were created primarily for the purpose of providing cheap labor to satisfy mercantile interests and demands. Interestingly, jailers and sheriffs profited greatly from leasing their inmates to various merchants in order to perform semiskilled and skilled labor (American Correctional Association, 1983). Authorities claimed that the work performed by inmates for mercantile interests was largely therapeutic and rehabilitative, although in reality the profit motive was the primary incentive for operating such houses. Exploitation of inmates for profit in these and other workhouses was perpetuated by jailers and sheriffs for many decades, and the general practice was accepted by an influential constituency of merchants and entrepreneurs.

Poor Laws. At the time Bridewell Workhouse thrived, English legislators had already created various statutes known as the **Poor Laws.** In part, these laws targeted relationships between debtors and creditors and prescribed sanctions for those unable to pay their debts. Debtors' prisons—a product of life during this period—were places where debtors were incarcerated until such time as they could pay their debts or fines. Debtors needed to work to earn the money required to pay off their debts—but imprisonment prevented them from doing so. Consequently, they would be incarcerated indefinitely—or until someone, perhaps a relative or influential friend, could pay their debts for them. Many died in prison because of their "failure" to pay their debts.

It is evident that the Poor Laws were directed at the poor or socioeconomically disadvantaged. In 1601, additional statutes were created that provided constructive work for youths deemed by the courts to be vagrant, incorrigible, truant, or neglected. In general, education was not an option for these youths—it was an expensive commodity available almost exclusively to children from the upper social strata, and it provided a major means of achieving still higher status over time. For the masses of poor, education was usually beyond their reach; they spent most of their time earning money to pay for life's basic necessities. They had little or no time to consider education as a viable life option (Sanders, 1945).

The Indentured Servant System and the American Colonies. Many youths during this time became apprentices, usually to master craftsmen, in a system of involuntary servitude. This servitude was patterned in part after the **indentured servant** system. Indentured servants entered voluntarily into contractual agreements with various merchants and businessmen to work for them for periods of up to seven years. This seven-year work agreement was considered by all parties to be a mutually beneficial way of paying for the indentured servant's passage from England to the colonies. In the case of youthful apprentices, however, their servitude, for the most part, was compulsory. Furthermore, it usually lasted until they reached adulthood or age 21.

During the Colonial period, English influence on penal practices was apparent in most New England jurisdictions. Colonists relied on familiar traditions for administering laws and sanctioning offenders. It is no coincidence, therefore, that much criminal procedure in American courts today traces its origins to legal customs and precedents inherent in British jurisprudence during the 1600s and 1700s. However, relatively little attention was devoted to the legal status of juveniles during this period or to how they might be handled.

In other parts of the world during the same era, certain religious interests were devising institutions that catered primarily to youthful offenders. For example, in Italy, a corrective facility was established in 1704 to provide for unruly youths and other young people who violated criminal laws. This facility was the **Hospital of Saint Michael,** constructed in Rome at the request of the Pope. The institution was misleadingly named, however, since the youths it housed were not ill. Rather, they were assigned various tasks and trained to perform semiskilled and skilled labor—useful tools which would enable them to find employment more easily after their release from Saint Michael. During rest periods and evening hours, youths were housed in individual cells (Griffin and Griffin, 1978).

Penal Reforms. Reforms relating to the treatment and/or punishment of juvenile offenders occurred slowly. Shortly after the Revolutionary War, religious interests in the United States moved forward with various proposals designed to improve the plight of the oppressed, particularly those who were incarcerated in prisons and jails. In 1787, the Quakers in Pennsylvania established the *Philadelphia Society for Alleviating the Miseries of Public Prisons.* This largely philanthropic society was comprised of prominent citizens, religious leaders, and philanthropists who were appalled by existing prison and jail conditions. Adult male, female, and juvenile offenders continued to be housed in common quarters and treated like animals. The **High Street Jail** in Philadelphia was one eyesore that particularly attracted the Society's attention. Because members of the Quaker faith visited this and other jail facilities regularly to bring food, clothing, and religious instruction to inmates, they were in strategic positions to observe the totality of circumstances in which those confined found themselves.

In 1790, the Society's efforts were rewarded. An older Philadelphia jail facility originally constructed in 1776 was overhauled and refurbished. It was named the **Walnut Street Jail.** This facility has considerable historical significance for corrections, since it represented the first real attempt by jail authorities to classify and segregate offenders according to age, gender, and seriousness of crime. The Walnut Street Jail was innovative in at least three respects. First, it pioneered what is now known as **solitary confinement.** Sixteen large solitary cells were constructed to house prisoners on an individual basis during evening hours. Second, prisoners were segregated from other prisoners according to the seriousness of their offenses. More hardened criminals were placed with others like them. First offenders or petty offenders were similarly grouped together. Third, women and children were maintained in separate rooms during evening hours, apart from their male counterparts.

Additionally, the Walnut Street Jail was, to a degree, rehabilitative. It sought to train its inmates for different types of labor, such as sewing, shoemaking, or carpentry. Unskilled laborers were assigned tasks such as beating hemp for ship caulking. Most prisoners received modest wages for their skilled or unskilled labor, although much of this pay was used to offset their room and board expenses. Finally, religious instruction was provided to inmates by Quaker teachers. This provision underscores the dramatic influence of religion in the shaping of prison policies and practices relating to inmate treatment and benefits.

The Child Savers. As more families gravitated toward large cities such as New York, Philadelphia, Boston, and Chicago during the early 1800s to find work, increasing numbers of children were "at large," most often left unsupervised by working parents who could not afford child-care services. Lacking familial controls, many of these youths committed acts of vandalism and theft. Others were simply idle, without visible means of support, and were designated as vagrants. Again, religious organizations intervened in order to protect unsupervised youths from the perils of life in the streets.

Believing that these youths would subsequently turn to lives of crime as adults, many reformers and philanthropists sought to "save" them from their plight. Thus, in different cities throughout the United States, various groups were formed to find and control these youths by offering them constructive work programs, healthful living conditions, and above all, adult supervision. Collectively, these efforts became widely known as the **child-saving movement.** Child savers came largely from the middle and upper classes, and their assistance to youths took many forms. Food and shelter were provided to children who were in trouble with the law or who were simply idle. Private homes were converted into settlements where social, educational, and other important activities could be provided for needy youths.

The New York House of Refuge. The **New York House of Refuge** was established in New York City in 1825 by the Society for the Prevention of Pauperism (Cahalan, 1986:101). Subsequently imitated in other communities, the House of Refuge was an institution largely devoted to managing **status offenders,** such as runaways or incorrigible children. Compulsory education and other forms of training and assistance were provided to these children. However, the strict, prisonlike regimen of this organization was not entirely therapeutic for its clientele. Many of the youthful offenders who were sent to such institutions, including the House of Reformation in Boston, were offspring of immigrants. Often, they rebelled when exposed to the discipline of these organizations, and many of these youths eventually pursued criminal careers as a consequence (Ferdinand, 1986). It would appear that at least some of these humanitarian and philanthropic efforts by child savers and others had adverse consequences for many affected juveniles.

Up until the late 1830s, there was little or no pattern to the division of labor between parental, religious, and state authority. As private interests continued to include larger numbers of juveniles within the scope of their supervision, various jurisdictions sought to regulate and institutionalize the assorted juvenile assistance, treatment, and/or intervention programs. In many communities, city councils sanctioned the establishment of facilities to accommodate youths who were either delinquent, dependent, or neglected. As more formal state control over youths evolved through legislation, it became increasingly clear that the early English concept of _parens patriae_ was becoming institutionalized.

In 1839, a decision in a state case invested juvenile authorities with considerable parental power. **Ex parte Crouse** (1839) was a case involving a father who attempted to secure the release of his daughter from the Philadelphia House of Refuge. The girl had been committed to the Philadelphia facility by the court because she was considered unmanageable. She was not given a trial by jury. Rather, her commitment was made arbitrarily by a presiding judge. A higher court rejected the father's claim that parental control of children is exclusive, natural, and proper, and it upheld the power of the state to exercise necessary reforms and restraints to protect children from themselves and their environments. While this decision was only applicable to Pennsylvania citizens and their children, other states took note

BOX 1.1

Juvenile Highlights

Can hard-core delinquents make good as adults? Former Massachusetts Senator Royal Bolling, Sr., has almost always believed that most delinquent youths, if given half a chance, can turn their lives around with the right opportunities. Much of his spare time has been devoted to working with delinquent youths, often gang members, who have had frequent run-ins with the law.

One of Bolling's "projects" was a youth named Billy Celester. Celester was born in a poor black inner-city neighborhood in Boston. A high school dropout, Celester eventually joined the Marseille Dukes, a youth gang that constantly fought with rival gangs in turf wars. Celester married in 1960 at age 16, after his girlfriend became pregnant. He worked at a low-paying job for a year before divorcing. One afternoon, he saw some of his former fellow gang members in a fight with another group. He attempted to intervene, but police officers came on the scene and arrested Celester on suspicion of being an active gang member. It was later determined that he was not an active gang member. However, authorities found that he had not paid child support, in direct violation of a previous court order. He spent six months in jail for nonpayment of child support, and when he was released, he had grown to hate the "racist" system that had jailed him. He turned back to the gang he had formerly left as a source of friendship and belongingness.

Through a community youth worker who had obtained the confidence of other gang members, Celester was put in contact with Senator Bolling, who became his father-figure and mentor. Bolling helped him land a high-paying job as a sandblaster in a naval shipyard. At age 22, Celester was encouraged by Bolling to take the Boston police examination. Certain that the police department would not want him, Celester needed considerable encouragement from Bolling before actually taking the exam. His high marks enabled him to join the Boston Police Academy, and in August, 1968, he became a Boston Police Department patrolman. Even then, however, his future was not secure. Many blacks in the Boston community rejected him as an "Uncle Tom" and labeled him a traitor. Yet he stuck it out, with Senator Bolling's encouragement. In 1985, he became area commander of his former neighborhood. In 1990, he became Deputy Superintendent of the Boston Police Department, and he works today with many inner-city youths who remind him of himself as a teenager. Having been turned around himself by someone who was willing to give him a chance, he believes that he can make a difference in the lives of the youths he now counsels.

(Some factual information obtained from Christopher Phillips, "How One Problem Kid Got a Chance," *Parade Magazine,* December 2, 1990, pp. 20–21.)

of it and sought to invoke similar controls over errant children in their jurisdictions. In effect, children (at least in Pennsylvania) were temporarily deprived of any legal standing to challenge decisions made by the state in their behalf.

Reform Schools. Throughout the remainder of the nineteenth century, different types of institutions were established to supervise unruly juveniles. At roughly mid-century, **reform schools** in several jurisdictions were created. One of the first state-operated reform schools was opened in Westboro, Massachusetts in 1848 (U.S. Department of Justice, 1976). By the end of the century, all states had reform schools of one sort or another. All of these institutions were characterized by strict discipline, absolute control over juvenile behavior, and compulsory work at various trades. Another common feature was that they were controversial.

The primary question raised by reform school critics was, "Do reform schools reform?" Since many juveniles continued their delinquent conduct after being released from these schools and eventually became adult offenders, their reform or rehabilitative value was seriously questioned. The Civil War exacerbated the problem of unruly youths, since many families were broken up. Orphans of dead soldiers were commonplace in the post-Civil War period. Such children were often committed to reform schools, regardless of whether they had committed criminal offenses. Many status offenders were sent to reform schools, simply because they were vagrants. Many of these children did not need to be reformed. Rather, they needed homes and noninstitutional care.

The First Juvenile Court. Because of the awesome power of the state and the control it exerted over childrens' affairs, few legal challenges of state authority were lodged by complaining parents. However, an Illinois case in 1870 paved the way for special courts for juveniles and an early recognition of their rights. A youth, Daniel O'Connell, was declared vagrant and in need of supervision and committed to the Chicago Reform School for an unspecified period. O'Connell's parents challenged this court action, claiming that his confinement for vagrancy was unjust and untenable. Existing Illinois law vested state authorities with the power to commit any juvenile to a state reform school as long as a "reasonable justification" could be provided. In this instance, vagrancy was a reasonable justification.

The Illinois Supreme Court distinguished between misfortune (vagrancy) and criminal acts in arriving at its decision to reverse Daniel O'Connell's commitment. In effect, the court nullified the law by declaring that reform school commitments of youths could not be made by the state if the "offense" was simple misfortune. They reasoned that the state's interests would be better served if commitments of juveniles to reform schools were limited to those committing more serious criminal offenses rather than those who were victims of misfortune. Three decades later, the Illinois legislature established the first juvenile court on July 1, 1899 by passing the *Act to Regulate the Treatment and Control of Dependent, Neglected, and Delinquent Children,* or the **Illinois Juvenile Court Act.**

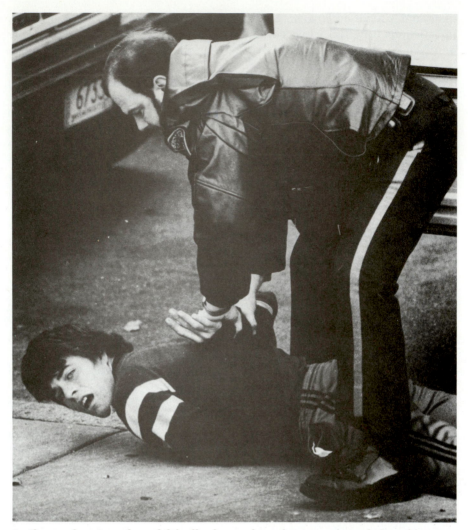

Swift apprehension of youthful offenders and tough treatment are believed by some critics to be effective deterrents to delinquency. (AP/Wide World Photos)

This act provided for limited courts of record, where notes might be taken by judges or their assistants, to reflect judicial actions against juveniles. The jurisdiction of these courts, subsequently designated as "juvenile courts," would include all juveniles under the age of 16 who were found in violation of any state or local law or ordinance. Also, provision was made for the care of dependent and/or neglected children who had been abandoned or who otherwise lacked proper parental care, support, or guardianship. No minimum age was specified that would limit the jurisdiction of juvenile court judges. However, the act provided that judges could impose secure confinement on juveniles 10 years of age or over by placing them in state-regulated juvenile facilities such as the state reformatory or the State Home for Juvenile Female Offenders. Judges were expressly prohibited from confining any juvenile under 12 years of age in a jail or police station. Extremely young juveniles would be assigned probation officers who would look after their needs and placement on a temporary basis.

During the next ten years, 20 states passed similar acts to establish juvenile courts. By the end of World War II, all states had created juvenile court systems. However, considerable variation existed among these court systems, depending on the jurisdiction. Not all of these courts were vested with a consistent set of responsibilities and powers. Some indication of the wide variety of court systems is shown in Table 1.1.

While Illinois is credited with establishing the first juvenile court system in the United States, an earlier juvenile justice apparatus was created in Massachusetts in 1874. This was known as the **children's tribunal,** and it was used exclusively as a mechanism for dealing with children charged with crimes; it was kept separate from the system of criminal courts for adults (Hahn, 1984:5). Some years later, in 1899, Colorado implemented an education law known as the Compulsory School Act. Although this act was primarily targeted at youths who were habitually absent from school, it also encompassed juveniles who wandered the streets during school hours, without any obvious business or occupation. These youths were termed "juvenile disorderly persons," and they were legislatively placed within the purview of truant officers and law enforcement officers who could detain them and hold them for further action by other community agencies (Champion, 1990a:402; Hahn, 1984). While both Massachusetts and Colorado created these different mechanisms specifically for dealing with juvenile offenders, they were not true juvenile courts equivalent with those established in Illinois.

Who Are Juvenile Offenders?

Juveniles Defined. Depending upon the jurisdiction, **juvenile offenders** are classified and defined according to several different criteria. According to the 1899 Illinois act that created juvenile courts, the jurisdiction of such courts would extend to all juveniles under the age of 16 who were found in violation of any state or local law or ordinance. About a fifth of all states, including Illinois, place the upper age limit for juveniles at either 15 or 16. In the remaining states, the upper limit for juveniles is 17 (except for Wyoming, where it is 18). Ordinarily, the jurisdiction of juvenile courts includes all children between the ages of 7 and 17 (Black, 1979:779). At the federal level, juveniles are considered to be persons who have not attained their eighteenth birthday (18 U.S.C., Sec. 5031, 1990).

The Age Jurisdiction of Juvenile Courts. While fairly uniform upper age limits for juveniles have been established in all U.S. jurisdictions (either under 16, under 17, or under 18 years of age), there is no uniformity concerning

TABLE 1.1   Organization of American Juvenile Courts

Court system	State(s)
Family and domestic relations court	Delaware, Hawaii, New York, Rhode Island, South Carolina
Juvenile and domestic relations court	New Jersey, Virgin Islands, Virginia
Independent juvenile court	Utah, Wyoming
Court of common pleas	Ohio, Pennsylvania
Juvenile division of probate court	Michigan
Circuit and district courts, concurrently	Alabama
Circuit and magistrate's courts, concurrently (the latter having limited jurisdiction and no authority to confine)	West Virginia
Independent juvenile court or superior court judge sitting as juvenile court judge	Georgia
County court	Arkansas
Trial division of high court	American Samoa
Juvenile division of district court plus juvenile court for specific counties (only Denver County in Colorado)	Colorado and Massachusetts
Each county chooses which court is juvenile court	Texas
Independent juvenile and county courts	Nebraska, Tennessee
Judges are assigned juvenile jurisdiction, plus there are separate provisions for specific counties	Wisconsin
Special juvenile courts or family courts in specific parishes; where these have not been established, district courts have jurisdiction in parishes within their districts and parish courts plus city courts have concurrent jurisdiction with district courts only within their constitutionally established jurisdictional boundaries	Louisiana
District court is juvenile court in specific counties; in counties of not more than 200,000 (and in St. Louis county), the probate court handles juvenile matters	Minnesota
Youth court division of the family court or the county court or the chancery court or certain municipal courts	Mississippi
Trial division of the high court or the district or community courts	Trust Territories
Juvenile cases are heard in district court by a judge or judges who volunteer to specialize in juvenile cases. Where no judge volunteers to specialize, the chief district court judge assigns individual judges to serve in juvenile court on a rotating basis.	North Carolina

SOURCE: U.S. Department of Justice, *A Comparative Analysis of Juvenile Codes* (Washington, D.C.: U.S. Government Printing Office, 1980), p. 7.

applicable lower age limits. As we have seen, English common law placed juveniles under age 7 beyond the reach of criminal courts, since it was believed that those under age 7 were incapable of formulating criminal intent. However, many juvenile courts throughout the United States have no specified lower age limits for juveniles within their purview. While no juvenile court will march a three-year-old before a judge for adjudication, many of these courts exert almost absolute control over the lives of young children or infants of any age. This control often involves placement of children or infants in foster homes or under the supervision of community service or human welfare agencies who can meet their needs. Neglected, unmanageable, abused, or other *children in need of supervision* (CHINS) are placed in the custody of these various agencies, at the discretion of juvenile judges. Thus, juvenile courts generally have broad discretionary powers over most persons under the age of 18.

The Treatment and Punishment Functions of Juvenile Courts. The idea that in order for juvenile courts to exercise jurisdiction over juveniles, these youths must be "offenders" and must have committed offending acts (conceivably illegal acts or crimes) is misleading. A significant proportion of youths who appear before juvenile judges have not violated any criminal laws. Rather, their status as juveniles renders them subject to juvenile court control, provided certain circumstances exist. These circumstances may be the quality of their adult supervision, if any. Other circumstances may be that they have run away from home, are truant from school, or loiter on certain city streets during evening hours. Runaways, truants, or loiterers are considered *status offenders,* since their actions would not be criminal if committed by adults. (A more extended treatment of types of juvenile offenders will be presented in Chapter 2.)

Additionally, children who are physically, psychologically, or sexually abused by parents or other adults in their homes may come within the scope of juvenile court authority. It is within the discretion of juvenile courts to place abused children in foster homes or to decide on other placements. Unruly children or other children in need of supervision might be obligated by the courts to receive therapy or treatment from one or more community agencies or services. In short, juvenile courts exercise both punitive and therapeutic options over minors.

Juvenile Delinquents Defined. The majority of youthful offenders who appear before juvenile courts have violated state or local laws or ordinances. These youths are most frequently termed **juvenile delinquents.** Federal law says that juvenile delinquency is the violation of any law of the United States by a person prior to his eighteenth birthday, which would have been a crime if committed by an adult (18 U.S.C., Sec. 5031, 1990). In law, juveniles are referred to as *infants.* A legal definition of a juvenile delinquent is *any infant of not more than a specified age who has violated criminal laws or engages in disobedient, indecent, or immoral conduct, and is in need of treatment, rehabilitation, or supervision* (Black, 1979:385).

It is evident from these definitions that juvenile courts may define juveniles and delinquency more or less broadly, and that for many jurisdictions, a delinquent act is whatever these courts say it is. This ambiguity is unsettling to many critics of the juvenile justice system, who feel that the authority of juvenile judges is too broad and ought to be restricted. The charge of incorrigibility, for instance, most often arises in everyday disputes between parents and children. The courts, thus far, have mediated these disputes largely in favor of adults.

At least some critics contend that juvenile courts should not intervene in less-than-life-threatening events that arise from normal parent–child relations (Guggenheim, 1985a). However, the vast bulk of incorrigibility charges that result in court-imposed sanctions on juveniles involve ordinary parent–child disputes. For some critics, these disputes are not appropriately a part of the business of American courts (Guggenheim, 1985a). Other experts contend, however, that society has thrust upon children a kind of pseudomaturity which, when coupled with the emerging rights of children, presents a compelling justification for greater state involvement in parent–child disputes (Leddy, 1985). The discretionary powers of juvenile judges will be examined more thoroughly in Chapter 2, but it is important at the outset to understand that much of this authority originated under the early English doctrine of *parens patriae.*

Parens Patriae

As indicated earlier in this chapter, **parens patriae** is a concept that originated with the English monarchy during the twelfth century. It means literally "the father of the country." Applied to juvenile matters, it means that the king is in charge of, makes decisions about, or has responsibility for all matters involving juvenile conduct. Within the scope of early English common law, parental authority was primary in the rearing of young children. However, as children advanced to age 7 and beyond, they acquired some measure of responsibility for their own actions. Accountability to parents was shifted gradually to accountability to the state, whenever youths 7 years of age or older violated the law. In the name of the king, chancellors in various districts adjudicated matters involving juveniles and the offenses they committed. Juveniles had no legal rights or standing in any court. They were the sole responsibility of the king or his agents. Their future often depended largely upon decisions of the chancellor. In effect, children were wards of the court, and the court was vested with the responsibility of safeguarding their welfare.

Chancery Courts. Chancery courts of twelfth- and thirteenth-century England and later years were charged with many tasks, including the management of the affairs of children, along with those of the mentally ill and incompetent. An early division of labor was created, involving a three-way relationship between the child, the parent, and the state (Blustein, 1983). The underlying thesis of *parens patriae* was that the parents were merely the agents of society in the area of child rearing, and that the state has a primary and legitimate interest in the upbringing of children. Thus, *parens patriae* created a type of fiduciary or trustlike parent−child relationship, with the state able to exercise the right of intervention to delimit parental rights (Blustein, 1983).

Because children could become wards of the courts, and subject to their control, a key concern for many chancellors was for the future welfare of children when they came under their jurisdiction. The "welfare" interests of chancellors and their actions led to numerous rehabilitative and/or treatment measures. Some of these measures included placement of children in foster homes or their assignment to various work tasks for local merchants. Parental influence in these child placement decisions was minimal. In the context of *parens patriae*, it is fairly easy to trace the influence of this early philosophy of child management to subsequent events in the United States, such as the child-saver movement, houses of refuge, and reform schools (Watkins, 1987). These latter developments were both private and public attempts to rescue children from their hostile environments and meet some or all of their needs through various forms of institutionalization.

Modern Interpretations of Parens Patriae

Parens patriae in the 1990s is very much alive throughout juvenile court jurisdictions in the United States, although some erosion of this doctrine has occurred during the past three or four decades. The persistence of this doctrine is evidenced by the wide range of dispositional options available to juvenile court judges and others involved in the earlier stages of offender processing in the juvenile justice system. Most of these dispositional options are either nominal or conditional, meaning that the confinement of any juvenile for most offenses is regarded as a last resort. As will be seen in Chapter 4, nominal or conditional options involve relatively mild sanctions (e.g., verbal warnings or reprimands, diversion, probation, making financial restitution to victims, performance of community service, participation in individual or group therapy, or involvement in educational programs), and these sanctions are intended to reflect the rehabilitative ideal that has been a major philosophical underpinning of *parens patriae* (Feld, 1987a).

Rehabilitation and Parens Patriae. However, the strong treatment or rehabilitative orientation inherent in *parens patriae* is not acceptable to some juvenile justice experts (Springer, 1987). Contemporary juvenile court jurisprudence stresses individual accountability for one's actions. Consistent with a growing trend in the criminal justice system toward "just deserts" and justice, a similar trend is being observed throughout the juvenile justice system (Champion and Mays, 1991). This "get tough" movement is geared toward providing law violators with swifter, harsher, and more certain justice and punishment than did the previously dominant rehabilitative philosophy of American courts.

BOX 1.2

Juvenile Highlights

Who should take the responsibility for dealing with runaways? The juvenile courts? Community agencies? Each year, over one million teenage youths take to the streets as runaways. Finding out that making ends meet is difficult, many of these youths turn to prostitution or trafficking in illegal drugs as ways of surviving on the streets. They hustle tricks from doorways, and many steal anything they might be able to pawn for food or drugs. Approximately 5,000 youths each year die on the streets; many of these are buried in unmarked graves when their identities cannot be determined.

Polk Street in San Francisco attracts thousands of runaways, although such streets are found in most U.S. cities. The motives of runaways are diverse, although the glitter and glamour of large cities suggests a life full of fun and excitement. Covenant House in San Francisco can accommodate about 40 youths at a time in its small facility. One problem is insufficient funding for such houses by the federal government and other sources. Only about $26 million is available annually to assist runaways, but the numerous clinics and community centers that must draw from these funds for their support quickly deplete these dollars.

Youths of all ages come to Covenant House. One girl ran away from home 13 times before she finally made it as far as San Francisco. Now she "tricks" with "johns" for a few dollars to pay for a place to "crash" from one night to the next.

Prostitution is the most direct means to the end. A steady supply of "johns" or customers means steady income for pimps. It also means steady exploitation of young children. Pimps say that many johns want them to find boys or girls without pubic hair as the most desirable sexual objects. Bus stations and railway stations are key contact points for obtaining new recruits. Incredibly, about a third of all runaways are lured into prostitution within 48 hours after leaving home. In most localities, juvenile courts have lost jurisdiction over runaways. It is questionable whether these courts could make a difference, even if they continued to exercise such jurisdiction. The alternatives often are placement in foster homes or homes for girls. But too many youths have negative experiences with adoption or foster home placement. They complain of being treated like merchandise—being chosen like clothes from a rack—and being treated accordingly by their ready-made families. There are no easy answers to the runaway problem.

(Some factual information adapted from Pete Axthelm, "Somebody Else's Kids," *Newsweek,* April 25, 1988, pp. 63–68.)

For juveniles, this means greater use of nonsecure and secure custody and incarcerative sanctions in state group homes, industrial schools, and reform schools (see Chapter 13). For juveniles charged with violent offenses (see Chapter 2), it frequently means being transferred to the jurisdiction of criminal courts for adults, where more severe sanctions such as life imprisonment or the death penalty may be imposed (see Chapter 7) (Bishop *et al.*, 1989). Not all authorities agree that this is a sound trend, however. Based upon selected public opinion polls, some experts suggest that while many people favor a separate juvenile justice system different from that for adults, they exhibit a strong preference for a system that sentences most juveniles to specialized treatment or counseling programs in lieu of incarceration, even for repeat offenders (Steinhart, 1988).

The Changing Rights of Juveniles. Influencing the *parens patriae* doctrine are the changing rights of juveniles (see Chapter 10). Since the mid-1960s, juveniles have acquired constitutional rights more in keeping with those enjoyed by adults in criminal courts. Some professionals believe that as juveniles are vested with greater constitutional rights, a gradual transformation of the juvenile court is occurring in the direction of greater criminalization (Challeen, 1986; Dale, 1987; Feld, 1987b; Orlando *et al.*, 1987). Interestingly, as juveniles obtain a greater range of constitutional rights, they become more immune to the influence of *parens patriae*. Quite simply, juvenile judges are gradually losing much of their former almost absolute autonomy over juveniles and their futures.

Juvenile and Criminal Courts: Some Preliminary Distinctions

While a more extensive description of the various dimensions of the juvenile court will be presented in Chapters 4 and 8, a preliminary comparison will be made here to highlight some of the major distinguishing features of juvenile and criminal courts. The intent here is not to describe both courts in depth, but rather, to identify major commonalities and differences. Because of the diversity of juvenile court organization among jurisdictions, some juvenile courts may be more formal or elaborate than others. Generally, the following statements about these different courts will hold true:

1. *Juvenile courts are civil proceedings designed exclusively for juveniles, whereas criminal courts are proceedings designed for alleged violators of criminal laws. In criminal courts, alleged criminal law violators are primarily adults, although selected juveniles may be tried as adults in these courts.* The civil–criminal distinction is important, because a civil adjudication of a case involving a juvenile does not result in a criminal record. In criminal courts, a judge or jury finds defendants either "guilty" or "not guilty." In cases of guilty verdicts, offenders acquire criminal records. These records of convictions follow offenders throughout

Civil proceedings — criminal proceedings

their lives, unless they are able to have their convictions overturned, set aside, or reversed on appeal to higher courts. However, juvenile court adjudications are sealed or "forgotten" once juveniles reach the age of majority.

2. *Juvenile proceedings are informal, whereas criminal proceedings are formal.* Attempts are made in many juvenile courts to avoid the formal trappings that characterize criminal proceedings. Juvenile judges frequently address juveniles directly and casually. Formal criminal procedures relating to the admissibility of evidence or testimony are not followed, and hearsay from various witnesses is considered together with hard factual information and evidence.

3. *In most states, juveniles are not entitled to a trial by jury, unless the juvenile judge approves. In all criminal proceedings, defendants are entitled to a trial by jury if they desire one,* and if the crime or crimes they are accused of committing carry incarcerative penalties of six months or more. The requirement of judicial approval of a jury trial for juveniles in most jurisdictions is one of the remaining legacies of the *parens patriae* doctrine in contemporary juvenile courts. At least eleven states have legislatively mandated jury trials for juveniles in juvenile courts if they are charged with certain offenses, and if they request such jury trials (U.S. Department of Justice, 1988).

4. *Both juvenile and criminal proceedings are adversarial.* Juveniles may or may not wish to retain or be represented by counsel (*In re Gault,* 1967). In

Juvenile courts in most states are informal proceedings where judges attempt to determine the facts and decide what is best for youthful offenders. (© J. P. Laffont/Sygma)

almost every case, juvenile court prosecutors allege various infractions or law violations against juveniles, and these charges may be rebutted by the juveniles themselves, by their parents, or by witnesses. If juveniles choose to be represented by counsel, their defense attorneys are permitted to present a reasonable defense of the charges alleged.

5. *Criminal courts are courts of record, whereas juvenile proceedings may or may not maintain a running transcript of proceedings.* Court reporters record all testimony presented in most criminal court actions. All state trial courts are courts of record, where either a tape-recorded transcript of proceedings is maintained, or a written record is kept. If appeals by either the defense or the prosecution are lodged with higher courts later, these transcripts may be consulted as proof of errors committed by the judge or either the prosecutor or the defense. Original convictions may be reversed or they may be allowed to stand, depending on what the records disclose about the propriety of the proceedings. In juvenile courts, in contrast, recorded transcriptions of proceedings are not required by law in most jurisdictions (*In re Gault*, 1967). However, some juvenile judges may have the resources and/or interest to provide for such transcriptions, particularly if serious offenses have been alleged.

6. *The standard of proof for determining guilt in criminal proceedings is ''beyond a reasonable doubt.'' The same standard is applicable in juvenile courts where violations of criminal laws are alleged and incarceration in a juvenile facility is a possible punishment. However, the less-rigorous civil standard of ''preponderance of the evidence'' is used in all other juvenile matters before the court (In re Winship,* 1970).

7. *The range of penalties juvenile judges may impose is limited, whereas in most criminal courts, the range of penalties may include life imprisonment or the death penalty in those jurisdictions where the death penalty is used.* The jurisdiction of juvenile judges over youthful offenders usually terminates whenever these juveniles reach adulthood. Under certain circumstances (for example, cases of mentally ill or mentally retarded juvenile offenders), juvenile judges may retain their jurisdiction over older offenders for longer periods, although this is relatively rare.

It should be apparent from this brief comparison that criminal court actions are more serious and have more significant long-term consequences for offenders than actions taken by juvenile courts. It is possible, for instance, for a particular juvenile to be adjudicated as delinquent ten times or more by the same juvenile judge within a relatively short time period. These delinquency adjudications are not necessarily additive in the sense that five or more of them will result in confinement to a state industrial school or group home. However, certain juveniles who appear before judges with frequency are likely to sustain more stringent punishments within the relatively lenient range of juvenile court sanctions. Many juveniles who are recidivists commit offenses of the petty variety. They tend to engage in petty theft, vandalism, or occasional drug use.

In the case of adult recidivists, legislative action in most jurisdictions has mandated that these offenders be subject to "habitual offender" statutes, wherein sufficient subsequent convictions will lead to one's being classified as a **habitual offender.** Under these laws, if adults are convicted of violating habitual offender statutes (e.g., they are convicted of three or more serious crimes at different times), they are subject to a mandatory penalty of life imprisonment. In practice, these habitual offender statutes are infrequently invoked, since incarcerating all habitual offenders would greatly aggravate the present prison overcrowding problem. In any case, the habitual offender penalty exists and can be imposed as a punishment for adult recidivists.

The juvenile court continues to be guided by a strong rehabilitative orientation in most jurisdictions, whereas criminal courts seem to be adopting more punitive sanctions for adult offenders. Although many critics see juvenile courts moving in a similar punitive or "just deserts" direction in the treatment and adjudication of juveniles, many youths are still directed toward treatment-oriented "punishments" rather than being incarcerated in secure juvenile facilities. Of course, overcrowding exists in juvenile facilities to almost the same extent as in most prisons and jails in the United States. Thus, it is in the best interests of the state to provide alternatives to incarceration for both adult and juvenile offenders. These alternatives are not necessarily the "right" alternatives, but they are expedient and practical ones under the present circumstances.

Alternative Philosophies of Managing Juvenile Offenders

As the various components of the juvenile justice process are presented in later chapters, it will become apparent that this process has been shaped at various points by varying philosophies about how juveniles should be treated and managed. In some respects, the contrasting philosophies tend to parallel several of the concepts applicable to the management and treatment of adult offenders. These include (1) *the medical model;* (2) *the rehabilitation model;* (3) *the community reintegration model;* (4) *the prevention/control model;* (5) *the "just deserts" model;* (6) *the reality therapy model;* and (7) *the justice model.*

1. *The Medical Model.* The **medical model** *assumes that juvenile delinquency is a disease subject to treatment.* It is otherwise known as the "treatment model." The treatment or medical model seeks to locate the cause of the disease (delinquency) and then to prescribe medication (a treatment program) as a cure. According to this model, incarcerating offenders is ineffective as a means of preventing future criminal behavior.

Interestingly, the medical model was officially recognized in 1870 by the Declaration of Principles promulgated by the National Prison Association (later known as the American Correctional Association) (McAnany *et al.,*

1984). At the time these principles were officially recognized, criminal justice authorities believed that criminals suffered from illnesses brought on by malnutrition and psychological maladies. Controlled diets and psychiatric treatments were used extensively as "medicine" to effect cures of criminal behaviors.

The medical model has much broader application than that associated with disease identification and an appropriate medical prescription. The "treatment" may be individual or group therapy and may be entirely unrelated to medicine. For instance, advocates of the medical model promote group encounters, family therapy, or individual therapy as "cures" for antisocial or delinquent behavior (Alexander *et al.*, 1988; Breunlin *et al.*, 1988; Lombardo and DiGiorgio-Miller, 1988; Schram and Rowe, 1987). However, purely medical remedies may be in order for adolescent sex offenders (Dembo *et al.*, 1987c; Jackson, 1984; Knopp, 1985). Psychiatric strategies such as Jungian therapy are also prescribed in selected instances involving the treatment of female adolescent prostitutes (Newton-Ruddy and Handelsman, 1986).

2. *The Rehabilitation Model.* The most common model for the handling of juvenile offenders is the **rehabilitation model.** Like the medical model, the rehabilitation model underscores the ineffectiveness of secure confinement for juvenile offenders. As an alternative, the rehabilitation model stresses experiences that enable youths to overcome various social and psychological handicaps that have placed them in their delinquent status. These experiences or strategies may be educational or social remedies (Greenwood, 1986b). Ideally, it would most favorable to isolate such problem children in their early years. Such "youths at risk" could be targeted for early intervention programs that would assist them in becoming integrated into school activities and social groups (Greenwood, 1986b; Gutknecht, 1988; Rydell, 1986; Stutt, 1986). In a sense, the rehabilitation model incorporates various aspects of the treatment or medical model, since the treatments ordinarily prescribed in the context of the medical model are analogous to various rehabilitative experiences (Rossum *et al.*, 1987; Steinhart, 1988).

3. *The Community Reintegration Model.* Some investigators believe that youths who commit delinquent acts have become alienated from their communities or estranged from society. Therefore, it is important to assist these youths to become reintegrated into their communities. Institutionalization is not the answer. Rather, an alternative to incarceration that will keep youths in their communities will be of greater value in helping them to overcome their delinquent propensities. **Community reintegration models** are designed to provide positive experiences for selected delinquent youths while they remain within their communities and participate in everyday activities such as attending school (Martin, 1987; Schram and Rowe, 1987). Temporary placement in residential treatment centers within communities preserves the general concept of community reintegration (Goldsmith, 1987).

4. *The Prevention/Control Model.* The **prevention/control model** attempts to deal with or repress delinquency before juveniles have an opportunity to

commit delinquent acts or to advance to more serious offenses (Packer, 1968). Using intervention strategies for youths at risk in their early years has been suggested as a delinquency prevention method (Greenwood, 1986b; Hurley, 1985). For juveniles who have already been adjudicated as delinquent, wilderness experiences and other outdoor educational programs are means whereby they may be subject to limited control by others. Under the close supervision of adults in a nonthreatening atmosphere, many youths may acquire skills to cope with their various problems and develop better self-concepts (Greenwood, 1986d). Residential placement programs introduce an element of control as well. For instance, Goodstein and Southeimer (1987) report the variable effectiveness of ten residential institutions for juveniles in a Pennsylvania jurisdiction. Recidivism appeared to depend upon the length of placement in such institutions. Over time, the propensity to engage in delinquent conduct decreases substantially for most juveniles. Thus, in this instance, such residential placements were deemed more or less useful, depending upon a youth's length of stay.

5. *The "Just Deserts" Model.* In recent years, juvenile justice critics have recommended that more stringent means be employed for dealing with juvenile offenders (Springer, 1987). The **"just deserts" model** stresses offender accountability, regardless of the offense committed (Treanor and Volenik, 1987; Watkins, 1987). Rehabilitation and treatment are not rejected outright, but they are secondary to punishment commensurate with the seriousness of the offense. Increasingly, juvenile courts and the juvenile justice process are subjecting juvenile offenders to more stringent treatments or corrective measures, reflecting the "just deserts" philosophy (Feld, 1987c; McDermott and Laub, 1987). Judges are increasingly inclined toward imposing probation as a sentence, but with conditions. These conditions may include community service work, victim restitution, participation in individual or group therapy, enrollment in drug or alcohol treatment programs, or some other constructive activity. Youths who are subjected to such experiences appear to be less inclined toward recidivism than those who are extended a large degree of leniency by the system (Harris, 1988; Rossum *et al.*, 1987).

6. *The Reality Therapy Model.* The **reality therapy model** appears to be the juvenile equivalent to the **shock probation** sometimes administered to adults as a sentence (Vito, 1984). Shock probation is an incarcerative sentence which involves a short stay in a jail or prison (up to 130 days). If offenders behave well during that period, they are brought back to court for resentencing. Judges will often sentence them to probation for the remainder of their statutory sentence. The "shock" of confinement, in some instances, functions as a "cure" for further criminal behavior. In short, these offenders have experienced what it is like to be confined. In a sense, they are shocked into conforming to the law to avoid further incarceration.

For juveniles, similar experiences, not necessarily incarcerative, are proposed in various programs. For example, in studies of juvenile offenders in Kansas and Maryland, youths have become heavily involved in visits to prisons, discussions with incarcerated offenders, and other reality experiences

(Locke *et al.*, 1986; Mitchell and Williams, 1986). Exposing these youths to the realities of prison life seemed to be helpful in decreasing recidivism rates among study participants. Some programs are designed to confine youths temporarily in secure juvenile facilities to achieve the same effect (Greenwood, 1986).

7. *The Justice Model.* A leading proponent of the **justice model** is Fogel (Fogel and Hudson, 1981). The justice model advocates fair and reasonable treatment of those convicted of crimes or adjudicated as delinquent. It does not reject rehabilitation, but rather it conceives rehabilitation as functional to the extent that participation in rehabilitative programs is voluntary. With an aim toward fairness in treatment, the justice model must necessarily embrace due process, which emphasizes safeguards extended to juveniles at all stages of their processing by the juvenile justice system.

Application of the justice model to juveniles is problematic. Although several significant constitutional rights have been extended to them as an important part of due process, juveniles have not as yet been granted the full range of rights, guarantees, and constitutional protections normally available to adults in criminal courts. The doctrine of *parens patriae* continues to influence what happens to youths as they face adjudicatory proceedings. *Parens patriae* and due process are to some degree incompatible. As Shireman notes, "It is not clear precisely how we are to move in the future in efforts to achieve essential and evident fairness and still retain the 'idealistic prospect' of an intimate, informal protective proceeding. There is much yet to be done" (Fogel and Hudson, 1981:148).

Each of these approaches toward or philosophies of juvenile treatment and management promotes certain aims as priorities. Increasingly important in the management of juvenile offenders is their acceptance of responsibility for offenses they commit. It is true that juveniles are being treated more like adults each year, as they are extended greater constitutional rights. However, the *parens patriae* doctrine is still quite influential in affecting their life chances in juvenile courts. In subsequent chapters, it will be apparent that each model has exerted some impact upon intervention programs and other strategies that are employed throughout the juvenile justice process as means of dealing with youthful offender behaviors. Of those presented above, the justice, "just deserts," and reality therapy models seem most frequently used in contemporary juvenile programs. No single theme is dominant, however, and many programs continue to provide a wide variety of therapy, group and individual counseling, and rehabilitation programs for many of the youths who enter the juvenile justice system.

Summary

The juvenile justice system is a more or less integrated network of agencies, institutions, and personnel that process juvenile offenders. In the twelfth century, the king of England established the doctrine of *parens patriae,* whereby he functioned as the father of the country and made decisions relating to juveniles and their welfare. Early English common law assumed that all infants under the age of 7 were not accountable for their actions. Parents had primary responsibility for maintaining discipline among their children.

The child-saver movement was strong during the 1800s. This movement promoted the belief that children could be rescued from societal circumstances that might otherwise cause delinquency and lead to lives as adult criminals. State authority eventually encroached on private interests and exerted extensive control over large numbers of errant juveniles. Parental authority over children decreased accordingly, as state interests became primary. Eventually, specialized courts called juvenile courts were created to further formalize the way youths would be managed and processed.

Juvenile courts are largely an American creation, with the first juvenile court having been established in Illinois in 1899. Currently, all jurisdictions throughout the United States have juvenile courts. These courts perform various functions, including adjudications of juveniles as either delinquent or nondelinquent. Some major differences between juvenile courts and criminal courts for adults are that juvenile courts are civil, and an adjudication as delinquent does not mean that a youth will acquire a criminal record. Compared with criminal courts, juvenile courts are less formal, are less likely to be courts of record and to keep running transcriptions of court proceedings, and have less severe penalties as punishments. Both types of courts are adversarial. Although the standard of proof in both types of courts is "beyond a reasonable doubt" whenever a person's freedom is in jeopardy, juvenile courts in many jurisdictions also utilize the civil standard, "preponderance of the evidence."

Alternative models for managing or treating juvenile offenders include the medical or treatment model, in which delinquency is considered a disease or illness. Prescriptions are provided to cure the illness. Closely related to the treatment or medical model is the rehabilitation model. The community reintegration model uses similar treatment strategies, although this model locates treatment facilities within the community to preserve a youth's identity with it. The prevention/control model strives to reduce or eliminate delinquent behavior by targeting "high risk" or "at risk" youths in their early years and instituting various interventions. The "just deserts" and justice models stress punishments that are commensurate with the wrongful acts committed by youths. Finally, the reality therapy model uses shock experiences, such as temporary incarceration in a prison or jail, to awaken youths to the realities of prison life.

Key Terms

Banishment (8)

Bridewell Workhouse (8)

Chancellors (8)

Chancery court (8)

Children's tribunal (15)
Child-saving movement (11)
Common law (6)
Community reintegration model (25)
Court of equity (8)
Ex parte Crouse (11)
Habitual offender (24)
High Street Jail (10)
Hospital of Saint Michael (9)
Illinois Juvenile Court Act (13)
Indentured servant (9)
"Just deserts" model (26)
Justice model (27)
Juvenile delinquents (17)
Juvenile justice system (5)

Juvenile offenders (15)
Medical (or treatment) model (24)
New York House of Refuge (11)
Parens patriae (18)
Poor Laws (8)
Prevention/control model (25)
Reality therapy model (26)
Reeve (7)
Reform schools (13)
Rehabilitation model (25)
Shire (7)
Shock probation (26)
Solitary confinement (10)
Status offenders (11)
Walnut Street Jail (10)
Workhouses (8)

Questions for Review

1. What is meant by the juvenile justice system? What are the different components of it? Why do some critics believe that it should be called a process rather than a system? Explain.
2. What is meant by *parens patriae?* How is this doctrine related to juvenile rehabilitation and treatment? What evidence is there that this doctrine continues to be influential in juvenile courts today?
3. Relate the following: chancellors, chancery courts, common law, and *parens patriae.*
4. What were some of the common punishments administered to both adult and juvenile offenders during Colonial times?
5. What were the Poor Laws? What were their functions?
6. Who were indentured servants? How were juveniles used origi-

nally within the indentured servant concept?
7. What is the significance for juveniles of the Walnut Street Jail in Philadelphia? Discuss.
8. What are houses of refuge? When were they first established in the United States? What do houses of refuge have to do with the child-saver movement?
9. Briefly identify several important developments occurring during the 1800s that led to the eventual establishment of juvenile courts.
10. What is a juvenile court? When and where was the first juvenile court established? What was the original jurisdiction of this juvenile court?
11. What is meant by juvenile delinquency? How are juveniles defined? What kinds of cases are likely to come before juvenile judges? Are these cases al-

ways connected with delinquency? Explain.

12. What is a status offender? How
do status offenders differ from
delinquent offenders?

13. How does acquiring greater
constitutional rights for juveniles conflict with the doctrine
of *parens patriae?*

14. Compare and contrast juvenile
courts with criminal courts.
What are their basic similarities? What are their major differences?

15. What similarities exist between
the medical model, the rehabilitation model, and the community reintegration model relating to treatment and
intervention programs for juvenile delinquents?

16. Identify some of the key characteristics of the following models: prevention/control, "just
deserts," reality therapy, and
justice.

Suggested Readings

BARNUM, R. (1987). *From Children to Citizens.* New York: Springer-Verlag.

BURCHARD, J. D., and S. N. BURCHARD (EDS.) (1987). *Prevention of Delinquent Behavior.*
Newbury Park, CA: Sage.

FABRICANT, M. (1983). *Juveniles in the Family Courts.* Lexington, MA: Lexington
Books.

MAHONEY, A. R. (1987). *Juvenile Justice in Context.* Boston: Northeastern University
Press.

RUBIN, H. TED (1985). *Behind the Black Robes—Juvenile Court Judges and the Court.*
Beverly Hills, CA: Sage.

WEISHEIT, RALPH A., AND ROBERT G. CULBERTSON (1985). *Juvenile Delinquency: A Justice
Perspective.* Prospect Heights, IL: Waveland Press.

CHAPTER 2

Measuring Delinquency: Types Of Juvenile Offenders

Introduction

Youths aged 13 to 18 make up about 9 percent of the U.S. population. However, members of this age group account for 20 percent of all arrests annually (Jamieson and Flanagan, 1989:484). This overrepresentation of juveniles among those arrested for crimes has attracted the attention and interest of many organizations and agencies. Is there currently a crime wave being perpetrated by youthful offenders? Are juveniles becoming increasingly violent in the acts they commit? What can or should be done to decrease or prevent juvenile offending behavior?

This chapter examines the concept of delinquency and how it is both officially and unofficially defined. Each jurisdiction has its own ways of defining juvenile offenders and classifying their behavior. We will describe the primary sources of information about juvenile offenders, including the *Uniform Crime Reports*. This official information source, though flawed in several respects, provides data on both adult and juvenile offenses in different jurisdictions. Such information is used by agencies and organizations as a measure or gauge of program effectiveness. The strengths and weaknesses of this and other data sources will be described, together with several criticisms of each.

Besides these official sources, unofficial information about juvenile offenses is provided by juveniles themselves through *self-reports*. Juveniles are questioned about their offending activities, and on the basis of anonymous responses, their self-report data are compared with data provided by official sources. The value of such self-reported information will be examined. An important distinction is made between youthful offenders who engage in serious offenses and those who are involved in less serious activities known as *status* offenses. Recently, several jurisdictions have attempted to separate the more serious offenders from the less-serious ones by removing certain types of less serious offenders from secure detention facilities such as jails and industrial schools, as well as from the dispositional authority of the juvenile courts; and as a result, the *deinstitutionalization of status offenses* has occurred. This process will now be described.

The final portion of this chapter will discuss the general question of whether juveniles who are adjudicated for minor offenses progress eventually to more serious offenses. Does *career escalation* occur among juvenile offenders, in which they progress from less serious to more serious crimes as they grow older? Also, are there major differences in juvenile offending behavior attributable to gender? These and related questions will be highlighted.

Delinquency: Preliminary Definitions and Distinctions

Juveniles. The jurisdiction of juvenile courts depends upon the established legislative definition of juvenile in each state. The federal government has no juvenile court. The infrequent federal cases involving juveniles are heard in federal district courts, but adjudicated juveniles are housed in state or local facilities if the sentences involve incarceration. Ordinarily, upper and lower age limits are prescribed. However, these age limits are far from uniform among jurisdictions. As was seen in Chapter 1, common law has been utilized by some jurisdictions to set the minimum age of juveniles at 7, although no state is obligated to recognize the common law as it pertains to youths. In fact, some states have no lower age limits that limit juvenile court jurisdiction. Table 2.1 shows upper age limits for most U.S. jurisdictions.

Those states with the lowest maximum age for juvenile court jurisdiction include Connecticut, New York, and North Carolina. In these states, the lowest maximum age for juvenile court jurisdiction is 15. Those states having a lowest maximum age of 16 for juvenile court jurisdiction are Georgia, Illinois, Louisiana, Massachusetts, Missouri, South Carolina, and Texas. The state having the lowest maximum age of 18 for juvenile court jurisdiction is Wyoming. All other states, including the federal government, use 17 as the

TABLE 2.1   Age at Which Criminal Courts Gain Jurisdiction of Young Offenders

Age of offender when under criminal court jurisdiction (years)	States
16	Connecticut, New York, North Carolina
17	Georgia, Illinois, Louisiana, Massachusetts, Missouri, South Carolina, Texas
18	Alabama, Alaska, Arizona, Arkansas, California, Colorado, Delaware, District of Columbia, Florida, Hawaii, Idaho, Indiana, Iowa, Kansas, Kentucky, Maine, Maryland, Michigan, Minnesota, Mississippi, Montana, Nebraska, Nevada, new Hampshire, New Jersey, New Mexico, North Dakota, Ohio, Oklahoma, Oregon, Pennsylvania, Rhode Island, South Dakota Tennessee, Utah, Vermont, Virginia, Washington, West Virginia, Wisconsin, Federal districts
19	Wyoming

SOURCE: "Upper age of juvenile court jurisdiction statutes analysis," Linda A. Szymanski, National Center for Juvenile Justice, March 1987.

lowest maximum age for juvenile court jurisdiction (Flanagan and Jamieson, 1988:94–95). Under the federal *Juvenile Delinquency Act of 1974, juveniles are persons who have not attained their eighteenth birthday* (18 U.S.C., Sec. 5031, 1990).

Juvenile offenders who are especially young (under age 7 in most jurisdictions) are often placed within the control of community agencies such as departments of human services or social welfare. These children frequently have little or no responsible parental supervision or control. In many cases, the parents themselves may have psychological problems or suffer from alcohol or drug dependencies. Children from such families may be abused and/or neglected, and may be in need of supervision and other forms of care or treatment.

Juvenile Delinquency. Federal law defines juvenile delinquency as *the violation of a law of the United States by a person prior to his eighteenth birthday, which would have been a crime if committed by an adult* (18 U.S.C., Sec. 5031, 1990). Of course, because of the variation in definitions of juveniles among the states, this federal definition may not apply. A broader, legally applicable definition of juvenile delinquency is *a violation of any state or local law or ordinance by anyone who has not yet achieved the age of majority* (adapted from Black, 1979:779). Of course, the "age of majority" depends upon the defining jurisdiction.

Probably the most liberal definition of juvenile delinquency is *whatever the juvenile court believes should be brought within its jurisdiction.* This definition vests juvenile judges and other juvenile authorities with broad discretionary powers to define almost *any* juvenile conduct as delinquent (Watkins, 1987).

To illustrate the implications of such a definition for any juvenile, consider the following three scenarios.

Scenario #1: A 13-year-old female has recently been apprehended and charged with murder. She is accused of being a serial killer who has murdered twelve elderly women in different parts of the community over a six-month period. These women lived alone and were dependent on others for various services. This female juvenile would run errands for these women, including trips to the store for food and medicines. She would use various rodent poisons mixed with different foods to kill her victims. The last woman she attempted to poison did not die, but rather became ill. Diagnosed by doctors as having ingested poison, the woman reported the female juvenile as the only subject likely to have had an opportunity to poison her. The juvenile was questioned by police and eventually admitted her guilt and involvement in the murders of the other elderly women. The juvenile has been examined by psychiatrists and awaits adjudication by the juvenile judge.

Scenario #2: A 14-year-old male has been reported to police several times by observant neighbors who claim that he wanders about the neighborhood daily unsupervised and without purpose. Investigations by authorities disclose that his parents are alcoholics, often in drunken stupors for much of the day, who exert little or no control over his behavior. The youth is supposed to be attending school, but school records indicate unusually large numbers of absences. He has appeared in juvenile court on six different occasions, largely because of his lack of school attendance and loitering behavior. The juvenile judge has formally ordered him to attend school during regular daytime hours, after repeated warnings to his parents to ensure his school attendance. He now faces the juvenile judge and is charged with violating this court order.

Scenario #3: A 12-year-old female has been taken into custody by authorities on a charge of lewd conduct. Neighbors and others visiting her neighborhood have complained that she has been deliberately exhibiting herself in the nude through a front-room window near the sidewalk. The passersby who inform police of her exhibitionist behavior include several adults, some with younger children. Police investigate and observe her nude in the front-room window. They arrest her and take her to juvenile hall for processing. She now faces the juvenile judge on lewd conduct charges.

These and a thousand other scenarios could be presented. Are all of these scenarios the same? No. Are all of these scenarios of equal seriousness? No. Can each of these scenarios result in an adjudication of "delinquency" by a juvenile judge? Yes. Whether juveniles are serial murderers, loiterers/truants, or exhibitionists, they may be lumped into one large "delinquent" category. This fact has caused many professionals and others who study the system to question whether juvenile courts are sufficiently discriminatory about the cases brought before them. Clearly, some juvenile offenses are more serious than others. This variability in the seriousness of juvenile offenses has prompted many jurisdictions to divert less serious cases away from juvenile courts and toward various interested agencies where the juveniles involved can receive assistance rather than punishment (Davidson *et al.*, 1987; DeAngelo, 1988; Osgood, 1983; Polk, 1984).

Today, the majority of U.S. jurisdictions restrict their definitions of juvenile delinquency to *any act committed by a juvenile which, if committed by an adult, would be considered a crime* (Rogers and Mays, 1987:566). This is the working definition we will use in this text, and it will apply to all subsequent chapters. However, we cannot ignore those jurisdictions in which juveniles are charged with "non-crimes," or behaviors that are considered offenses and are defined as such strictly on the basis of their status as juveniles.

Status offenses *are any acts committed by juveniles which would (1) bring the juveniles to the attention of juvenile courts and (2) not be crimes if committed by adults.* Common juvenile status offenses include running away from home, truancy, and curfew violations. Adults would not be arrested for running away from home, being absent from school without excuse, or walking the streets after 10:00 P.M. However, if juveniles in certain jurisdictions engage in these behaviors, they may eventually be included within the broad "delinquency" category together with more serious juvenile offenders who are charged with armed robbery, forcible rape, murder, aggravated assault, burglary, larceny, vehicular theft, or illicit drug sales.

Status Offenders and Delinquent Offenders

Status offenders are of interest to both the juvenile justice system and the criminal justice system. While status offenses such as **runaway** behavior, truancy, or curfew violations are not dangerous per se, many experts believe that there are several adverse concomitants of status offenses. For example, studies of runaways indicate that many of them have psychological problems and have been physically and sexually abused by their families (Janus *et al.*, 1987; Loeb *et al.*, 1986; McCormack *et al.*, 1986; Shaffer and Caton, 1984). Evidence suggests that many runaways engage in theft or prostitution to finance their independence away from home (Garbarino *et al.*, 1986). Some runaways join delinquent gangs to cope with the hostile environment (Alaska Senate Finance Committee, 1986). Although not all runaways are alike (Kufeldt and Perry, 1989), there have been attempts to profile them (Kaplan *et al.*, 1989; Shane, 1989). Runaway behavior is complex and difficult to explain (Schulman and Kende, 1988), although most researchers agree that runaways generally have severe mental health needs (Shaffer and Caton, 1984).

Some of the children who become runaways have been described by investigators as "chronically oppositional," meaning that they violate rules, disobey parents, and engage in other unruly behaviors such as fighting or making verbal assaults and threats (Wahler, 1987). Stages of runaway

Running away from home is a status offense, not a crime. But many runaways are eventually drawn into sexual exploitation, either willingly or unwillingly, as they attempt to survive on the streets alone. (© Dorothy Littell/Stock Boston, Inc.)

behavior include the "unsettling" stage, which occurs during the first few days away from home (Palenski, 1984); the "exploratory" stage, when the child makes the decision to stay away from home for a prolonged period; and finally, the "routinization" stage, when children develop social attachments with others, possibly other runaways (Palenski, 1984).

Depending on how authorities and parents react to children who have been apprehended after running away, there may be positive or adverse consequences. Empathy for runaways and their problems is important for instilling positive feelings in them (Grieco, 1984). Various shelters have been established to offer runaways a nonthreatening residence and social support system in various jurisdictions. Covenant House, which originated in New York City during the 1960s, provides various services to runaway youths (Ritter, 1987). Similar homes have been established in Houston, Fort Lauderdale, Toronto, and Guatemala. These shelters often locate particular services for runaways that will help meet their needs. Many children accommodated by these shelters report that they have been physically and sexually abused by family members (Janus *et al.*, 1987). Thus, there is some coordination of these homes with various law enforcement agencies to investigate these allegations and assist parents in making their homes safer for their children (Janus *et al.*, 1987; Ritter, 1987).

Other types of status offenders are **truants** and violators of curfew and liquor law. Some research shows that these offenders differ from runaways in that they are more serious offenders (Shelden *et al.*, 1989). Truants and liquor law violators may be more inclined to become **chronic offenders** and to engage in more serious, possibly criminal, behaviors (Clarke *et al.*, 1985; Shelden *et al.*, 1989). Truancy and violating curfew are regarded by some experts as indicative of "undisciplined offenses." A study of 863 youths referred to the Clarke County Juvenile Court in Las Vegas, Nevada, in 1980 was conducted to determine whether true differences existed among runaways, truants, and curfew violators with regard to their inclination to progress to more serious delinquent acts (Shelden *et al.*, 1989). Findings showed that male status offenders had a greater tendency than females to escalate to more serious delinquent offenses. Furthermore, runaways were not as likely as truants or **curfew violators** to escalate to more serious acts after their initial court referrals. However, analyses of self-reported information by juveniles in other studies suggest that escalation to more serious juvenile offenses does not necessarily occur. Rather, panels of boys studied over a long time period revealed a pattern of stable or constant juvenile misbehaviors rather than a progression to more serious juvenile offenses (Rankin and Wells, 1985).

Regarding status offenders, juvenile courts seem most interested in chronic offenders or persistent offenders—those who habitually appear before juvenile judges. Repeated juvenile court involvement may eventually be followed by adult criminality (Benda, 1987). Among many juvenile justice reformers, for instance, it is commonly assumed that status offenders will have low rates of recidivism. However, a study was conducted of 932 juveniles in Wisconsin correctional facilities during the period 1965–1967. Of these juveniles, 166 were status offenders. These subjects were studied as long as they remained in the juvenile justice system, and they were also observed for a ten-year period as adults. It was found that 33 percent were returned to training schools after their first releases, largely because of new delinquent acts. Furthermore, 38 percent were subsequently convicted as adults for serious felonies (Benda, 1987). Additional support for the Benda research has been reported by Greenwood (1986c) and Tonry and Morris (1986), who found a clear connection between juvenile criminal activity and adult criminal careers.

A factor considered quite influential in contributing to juvenile offender chronicity and persistence is direct contact with juvenile courts. Contact with juvenile courts, especially frequent contact, is believed by some researchers to "stigmatize" youths and cause them either to be labeled or to acquire

BOX 2.1

Juvenile Highlights

Is violent juvenile crime increasing or decreasing? At the 1989 Winter Conference of the American Correctional Association in San Antonio, Texas, Barry Krisberg, the president of the National Council on Crime and Delinquency, asked whether kids were getting "worse" nowadays. He said that about 80 percent of the public seems concerned with what they believe to be an epidemic of violent youth crime. But he noted that youth crime is down 20 percent from ten years ago. He concluded that kids aren't getting worse. Rather, a smaller group of hardcore offenders is becoming more violent.

Many state jurisdictions report contrary trends, however. In Tennessee, for instance, the number of youths referred to the state's juvenile courts for serious offenses against others jumped from 2,655 to 3,903, a rise of 1,248 referrals between 1984 and 1986. Patricia J. Garlock, a specialist working with the Tennessee Juvenile Justice Commission, says that referral rates indicate an alarming difference between the white and nonwhite pop-

ulations. Currently, there is an overrepresentation of minorities in Tennessee's juvenile justice system. Inadequate education, poverty, and a lack of job training are blamed as some of the more important factors that account for these statistics. One judge, Memphis Juvenile Court Judge Kenneth Turner, said that socioeconomic factors play a major part in whether one gets in trouble with the law, and that if one has the necessities of life, one is not inclined to steal.

Patricia Garlock cautions that the referral figures may be due not only to an increase in the number of offenses being committed, but also to an increase in the referral reporting from juvenile courts. Nevertheless, violent juvenile offenses seem to be confined primarily to heavily populated urban centers. Counties within the major urban areas of Tennessee have higher referral rates than the less densely populated counties.

(Some factual information adapted from an Associated Press article in *The Knoxville News-Sentinel,* December 28, 1987, p. A7 [No author].)

self-concepts as delinquents or deviants (Davidson *et al.,* 1987; DeAngelo, 1988; Frazier and Cochran, 1986; Pratt, 1983). (A more extended discussion of labeling theory is presented in Chapter 3.)

Many of the steps officials have taken to minimize juvenile contact with the juvenile courts have been geared toward preserving the discretionary authority of these courts over affected juveniles within the scope of *parens patriae.* Another measure that has received much attention in recent years as a major reform occurring throughout the juvenile justice process is removing certain types of offenses from the jurisdiction of juvenile judges (Blackmore *et al.*, 1988). Because status offenses are categorically less serious than criminal offenses committed by juveniles, they have been targeted by legislatures in various states for removal from the scope of juvenile court authority. The removal of status offenses from the discretionary power of juvenile courts is called the *deinstitutionalization of status offenses* or *DSO*.

The Deinstitutionalization of Status Offenses

What is DSO? The **deinstitutionalization of status offenses (DSO)** emerged in the mid-seventies after the *Juvenile Justice Act of 1974* was passed. Although some states had moved in the direction of adopting DSO before this time, it wasn't until the early 1980s that it really became popular.

In essence DSO means "the removal from secure institutions and detention facilities of youths whose only infractions are status offenses such as running away from home, incorrigibility, truancy, and curfew violations." (Schneider, 1984a:410–411). Three types of deinstitutionalization that may occur are described, depending on the jurisdiction.

The first form of deinstitutionalization is **decarceration,** in which juveniles charged with status offenses remain under court jurisdiction and are subject to the filing of petitions in juvenile court. While detention of these youths is prohibited, they may be removed involuntarily from their homes and placed in nonsecure facilities, put on probation, required to attend treatment or service programs, and subjected to other behavioral restraints.

A second type of deinstitutionalization deals with **dependent and neglected children** (Schneider, 1984a:411). While the juvenile court continues to exercise jurisdiction over some of these youths, **diversion programs** are established to receive status offenders directly from law enforcement officers, schools, parents, or even self-referrals. These diversion programs provide "crisis intervention" services for youths, and their aim is to return juveniles eventually to their homes. However, more serious offenders may need the more elaborate services provided by shelter homes, group homes, or even foster homes.

The third type of deinstitutionalization, according to Schneider (1984a:411), is **divestiture of jurisdiction.** Under full divestiture, juvenile courts cannot detain, petition, adjudicate, or place youths on probation for any status offense. Schneider (1984a:411) notes that under full divestiture, all services are provided by nonjustice agencies on a strictly voluntary basis. She indicates that by 1984, the states of Washington and Maine had legislatively mandated divestiture laws for all juvenile courts and had removed all status offenders from their jurisdiction. Since then, most other jurisdictions have enacted similar types of divestiture statutes (Colley and Culbertson, 1988).

Early proponents of DSO believed that custodial confinement of status offenders would "harden" them, thus increasing the likelihood of their committing more serious offenses in the future (U.S. Senate Judiciary Committee, 1984). As we have seen thus far, this belief has not received widespread support in the research literature (Datesman and Aickin, 1985; Logan and Rausch, 1985; Rankin and Wells, 1985). Another belief about DSO was that it would greatly diminish the number of cases brought before juvenile courts throughout the United States as well as the numbers of detainees in juvenile secure facilities (Schneider, 1984a; U.S. Senate Judiciary Committee, 1984). This belief too has been refuted to some degree by studies of DSO in selected jurisdictions.

Research About DSO and Its Impact. One of the most penetrating analyses of DSO is a report and review of the literature by Schneider (1984a). Schneider reviewed the findings of more than 70 studies of the multifaceted impact of DSO, including 38 programs underway in 19 different states. Schneider's conclusion is to the point: there appears to be no impact. Or if there is an impact, the literature is inconclusive about DSO's effects. However, Schneider does indicate assorted adverse effects of DSO that have been observed in different jurisdictions, and there is independent support for these negative implications of DSO. Five experiences with DSO have been highlighted by Schneider as significant.

1. *DSO has failed to reduce the number of status offenders in secure confinement, especially in local detention.* Supporting this experience is a study by Logan and Rausch (1985). They studied a DSO program implemented in Connecticut from December, 1976 to December, 1977. On the basis of a survey of the state's automated juvenile court data base, they found that the juvenile gross detention rate actually increased after DSO. Independently of the DSO program, juvenile courts appeared to switch from institutional to noninstitutional procedures for removing juveniles from homes to secure facilities.

2. **Net-widening,** *or pulling youths into the juvenile justice system who would not have been involved before, has increased as one result of DSO.* Schneider (1984b) notes that Washington, D.C., along with several other jurisdictions, drew larger numbers of status offenders "into the net" of the juvenile justice system after DSO was implemented. This net-widening occurred as follows: Originally, juvenile courts adjudicated both status and delinquent offenders. However, law enforcement officers seldom bothered to do much more than give status offenders verbal warnings and "wrist-slaps." Many juvenile court judges issued stern reprimands to status offenders and returned them to the custody of their parents. Once DSO was recommended, however, juvenile courts lost control over status offenders, and these offenders acquired a new legal definition. Various community agencies were then established to provide community-based services for these status offenders as noninstitutional actions. Because of the existence of these new services, many law enforcement officers directed youths to them for treatment. Many of these youths would have received only verbal warnings from police previously. In this way, DSO created a new class of juvenile offender as well as new action

alternatives for law enforcement officers to follow. The ultimate result was to drag more youths into the "net" to serve certain juvenile justice ends.

3. **Relabeling** *(e.g., adjudicating youths as delinquent or as emotionally disturbed who, in the past, would have been defined and handled as status offenders) has occurred extensively after DSO* (Schneider, 1984a:411). This particular consequence has been initiated, in part, by police officers who appear resentful over their loss of discretion relating to status offenders (Schneider and Schram, 1986). For instance, it is easy for a police officer to relabel a juvenile curfew violator a larceny or burglary suspect and hold the youth in detention for an extended period. Juvenile judges themselves have sometimes been resistant to these DSO reforms because of this effect of relabeling—that is, loss of discretion over status offenders (Colley and Culbertson, 1988).

4. *DSO has had little if any impact on recidivism rates among status offenders* (Schneider, 1984a:411). One rationale for deinstitutionalizing status offenders has been that since they will not be exposed directly to the potentially adverse "criminalizing" atmosphere of juvenile courts, they will not be as likely to recidivate (Benda, 1987; U.S. Senate Judiciary Committee, 1984). Recidivism among juveniles is perceived by some professionals as a symbolic gesture of defiance of adult authority inherent in the court system. Treating status offenders differently and less formally, it has been believed, might reduce a youth's propensity to show defiance of authority and "do it again."

Community-based services provide more informal, nonthreatening atmospheres for meeting youths' needs, and making them feel less rejected compared with arrest and detention in a jail or jail-like environment (Palenski, 1984). However, of those investigations that have focused on recidivism among status offenders, the findings are not promising. Benda (1987) reported a 33 percent rate of recidivism among a sample of 166 status offenders. And in two Washington jurisdictions, Seattle and Yakima, recontact rates between status offenders and police either remained the same or increased after DSO had occurred (Schneider et al., 1983).

However, a three-year study examined the influence of court appearances on juvenile recidivism for 907 subjects, of whom two thirds had participated in programs that diverted their status offense cases from juvenile court, and one third had received no special diversionary treatment (Stewart et al., 1986). The diverted youths were subjected to warning or dismissal, referral to appropriate community agencies, or unofficial probation. Those from the diverted sample had substantially fewer subsequent court appearances in a three-year follow-up compared with the nondiverted offenders. The researchers concluded that when youths were treated in a more humane way and encouraged to work out their problems through nonpunitive methods, there were substantial positive effects. But another study contradicts these findings and suggests that harsher treatments are more effective at reducing recidivism among juvenile offenders. In an investigation of 476 youths selected from Dauphin County (Harrisburg), Pennsylvania Probation Department files from

1960–1975, it was found that in general, those youths who were adjudicated on their first referral to juvenile courts had lower rates of recidivism than nonadjudicated, diverted youths who were either warned or granted informal probation (Brown *et al.*, 1987).

Conrad (1983) admits that there are certain interpretive, statistical, and methodological problems associated with studies of recidivism of youths relegated to both formal and informal programs. Although he acknowledges that certain studies show that incarcerating juveniles may be more effective than community-based punishments for reducing rearrest rates, he also indicates that the greater the severity of the punishment, the sooner youths are likely to be rearrested. He concludes that juvenile justice should be predictable, but not necessarily harsh. He believes that both social scientists and judges should be listening for answers from the community, the children who commit delinquent acts, their parents, and the professionals and volunteers who are trying to help.

5. *DSO has generated numerous service delivery problems, including inadequate services, nonexistent services or facilities, or a general inability to provide services within a voluntary system* (Schneider, 1984a:411). When DSO occurs and community-based service agencies are called upon to accommodate large numbers of youths diverted from juvenile courts by legislative mandate, these services may be inadequate or simply nonexistent. In some instances, status offenders with special problems may be rejected outright by more than a few of these agencies. For example, delivery services in 13 states under a National Runaway and Homeless Youth Program were examined in 1983. Three hundred and fifty-three staff members, youths, and parents were interviewed, and it was found that most of these programs did not accept youths who were or appeared to be psychotic, violent, or addicted to drugs or alcohol (U.S. General Accounting Office, 1983). Thus, it would seem that youths most in need of these services are being denied them by agency personnel.

This particular problem associated with DSO is widespread. Several studies suggest that many runaways, truants, and incorrigibles are psychologically disturbed and in need of mental health services (Bucy, 1985; Chinen *et al.*, 1986; Clarke *et al.*, 1985; Grieco, 1984; Schulman and Kende, 1988; Shaffer and Caton, 1984). In fact, studies of existing youth services in various jurisdictions report that these services often resolve the least serious problems, while more serious family and drug problems remain unresolved (California Department of the Youth Authority, 1985a; O'Connor *et al.*, 1984). A major contributing factor to these program failures is chronic overcrowding of facilities (Lerner, 1988; Wiebush *et al.*, 1985). (Chapters 12 and 13 will address in greater detail the overcrowding problem associated with both secure and nonsecure treatment programs and intermediate punishment alternatives.)

At least one observer regards DSO unfavorably. Kearon (1989) opposes DSO largely on theoretical grounds. He is particularly critical of the way runaways have been treated in the aftermath of DSO. Kearon contends that adolescent street abuse cannot be appreciably reduced as long as DSO is the prevailing philosophy of the state. The state must regain its legitimate control over runaways, asserts Kearon, in order to shield them from their most self-destructive urges. He encourages the use of secure detention facilities for short-term periods, especially for those youths who have run away from open facilities and require treatment in a secure setting. He believes that the state can mandate such treatment. He suggests up to three-day stays for some runaways to remind them of the court's authority. Longer stays of 30 days or more in intensive care would be needed for those offenders with drug or alcohol dependencies and psychological problems. And for many youths, he recommends long-term confinement for from 12 to 18 months to ensure that proper intervention treatment can be provided.

Kearon's admonitions about deemphasizing DSO and restoring the authority of juvenile courts over status offenders are supported, in part, by the juvenile judiciary, many of whom resist DSO reforms. However, such judicial opposition to DSO may not necessarily lead to the positive outcomes anticipated by Kearon. For instance, there is some evidence that juvenile judges have overreacted in response to their lost jurisdiction over status offenders. One form of overreaction may be manifested in the dramatic increase in the issuance of criminal contempt citations against juveniles who have engaged in noncriminal behaviors such as truancy and runaway behavior. If status offenders are ordered to attend school and elect not to attend, they are in direct violation of a court order and may be held accountable, and thus may be subject to criminal contempt charges. Thus, although judges may support a move to reverse the trend toward DSO, their reasons and motives may be different from those of Kearon.

Putting aside questions of the relative merits of DSO and the ambiguity of research results concerning its short- and long-term effects, there is no doubt that DSO is widespread nationally and has become the prevailing juvenile justice policy. DSO has set in motion numerous programs in all jurisdictions to better serve the needs of a growing constituency of status offenders (Blackmore *et al.*, 1988). This necessarily obligates growing numbers of agencies and organizations to contemplate new and innovative strategies, rehabilitative, therapeutic, and/or educational, to cope with these youths, who have diverse needs. Greater cooperation between the public, youth services, and community-based treatment programs is required to facilitate development of the best policies and practices (Farnworth *et al.*, 1988; Kearney, 1989; Krisberg, 1988; McCarthy, 1989).

Measuring Delinquency

The Uniform Crime Reports. A major source of information about both adult and juvenile offenders is the **Uniform Crime Reports (UCR).** The UCR is published annually by the Federal Bureau of Investigation (FBI) in

Washington, D.C. The UCR is a compilation of arrests for different offenses according to several time intervals. Reports of arrests are issued quarterly to interested law enforcement agencies. All rural and urban law enforcement agencies are asked to voluntarily submit statistical information on 29 different offenses. Most of these agencies submit arrest information, and thus, the UCR includes data from over 15,000 law enforcement agencies throughout the United States.

In coming years, the UCR will begin to change its methods of compiling and reporting data. Projections by the FBI are that future reports will include the circumstances of individual criminal events, offender, victim, and arrestee information, and data vital to the understanding of issues such as drug use,

TABLE 2.2   Uniform Crime Report, Part I Crimes and Their Definition

Crime	Definition
Murder and Nonnegligent Manslaughter:	The willful (nonnegligent) killing of one human being by another
Forcible Rape:	The carnal knowledge of a female forcibly and against her will; assaults or attempts to commit rape by force or threat of force are also included
Robbery:	The taking or attempting to take anything of value from the care, custody, or control of a person or persons by force or threat of force or violence and/or by putting the victim in fear
Aggravated Assault:	An unlawful attack by one person upon another for the purpose of inflicting severe or aggravated bodily injury
Burglary:	The unlawful entry of a structure to commit a felony or theft
Larceny-Theft:	The unlawful taking, carrying, leading, or riding away of property from the possession or constructive possession of another, including shoplifting, pocket picking, purse snatching, thefts from motor vehicle of parts or accessories
Motor Vehicle Theft:	Theft or attempted theft of a motor vehicle, including automobiles, trucks, buses, motorscooters, and snowmobiles
Arson:	Any willfull or malicious burning or attempt to burn, with or without intent to defraud, a dwelling house, public building, motor vehicle or aircraft, and the personal property of another

SOURCE: U.S. Department of Justice, *Crime in the United States 1989*, Washington, DC: U.S. Government Printing Office, 1990.

spousal and child abuse, and parental kidnapping. Logistical problems among the various reporting agencies have slowed the implementation of this new reporting format, but future reports are expected to be more accurate and enlightening.

Crime in the UCR is classified under two major categories, **Part I offenses** and **Part II offenses.** *Part I offenses are considered the more serious, and eight serious felonies are listed. These are murder and nonnegligent manslaughter, forcible rape, robbery, aggravated assault, burglary, larceny-theft, motor vehicle theft, and arson.* Table 2.2 lists the eight major **index offenses** (Part I offenses) and their definition.

The "index offenses" in Table 2.2 are major offenses known as *felonies. Generally,* **felonies** *are violations of criminal laws that are punishable by terms of imprisonment of one year or longer in state or federal prisons or penitentiaries.* These offenses are known as "index offenses" because they provide readers of the UCR with a sample of key or index crimes that can be charted quarterly or annually, according to different jurisdictions and demographic and socioeconomic dimensions (e.g., city size, age, race, gender, urban–rural). Thus, the crime categories listed are not intended to be an exhaustive compilation. However, it is possible to scan these representative crime categories to obtain a general picture of crime trends across years or other desired time segments.

Table 2.3 shows both Part I and Part II offenses nationally for 1988, according to age of arrestees. Part II offenses include (1) several felonies other than Part I felonies; (2) *misdemeanors,* and (3) selected status offenses. **Misdemeanors** *are violations of criminal laws that are punishable by incarcerative terms of less than one year in city or county jails or comparable facilities.* Those status offenses that are listed, including runaway behavior, truancy, and violation of curfew, are not crimes, *but they are reported together with selected criminal offenses to give a more complete picture of law enforcement arrest activity throughout the United States.* Neither Part I nor Part II offenses listed in Table 2.3 comprise an exhaustive compilation. Rather, the FBI's intent is to describe crime generally and to portray certain trends on the basis of arrests reported in selected offense categories.

Because of the age breakdown presented in Table 2.3, it is possible to examine juvenile arrest statistics for different offenses and age categories. For example, by inspecting Table 2.3, we can determine that juveniles under age 18 accounted for about 16 percent of violent crime arrests in 1988. For property crimes, juveniles accounted for about 32 percent of all arrests. Specific crime categories may be consulted as well. For instance, 1,765 juveniles under age 18 were arrested in 1988 for murder or nonnegligent manslaughter. Over 351,000 juveniles under age 18 were arrested in that same year for larceny-theft.

Besides this kind of factual information about juvenile offenders, the UCR may also be used to gauge the **incidence** of arrests across youthful age categories. We can inspect Table 2.3 and determine that for runaways, arrests increase for juveniles and peak between ages 13 and 14. For subsequent years, the numbers of arrests for runaway behavior decrease. For curfew

TABLE 2.3   Part I and Part II Offenses by Age of Arrestee, 1988*

	Offense Charged	Total All Ages	Ages Under 15	Ages Under 18	Ages 18 and Older	Under 10
	Total	10,149,896	526,421	1,634,790	8,515,106	45,597
	Percent[a]	100.0%	5.2%	16.1%	83.9%	0.4%
Part I Offenses	Murder and nonnegligent manslaughter	16,326	201	1,765	14,561	7
	Forcible rape	28,482	1,372	4,118	24,364	98
	Robbery	111,344	6,470	24,337	87,007	231
	Aggravated assault	304,490	11,345	38,536	265,954	809
	Burglary	331,758	42,376	111,284	220,474	4,204
	Larceny-theft	1,162,752	152,952	351,133	811,619	14,444
	Motor vehicle theft	153,016	15,870	61,301	91,715	279
	Arson	14,505	4,117	6,216	8,289	1,169
	Violent crime[b]	460,642	19,388	68,756	391,886	1,145
	Percent[a]	100.0%	4.2%	14.9%	85.1%	0.2%
	Property crime[c]	1,662,031	215,315	529,934	1,132,097	20,096
	Percent[a]	100.0%	13.0%	31.9%	68.1%	1.2%
	Total Crime Index[d]	2,122,673	234,703	598,690	1,523,983	21,241
	Percent[a]	100.0%	11.1%	28.2%	71.8%	1.0%
Part II Offenses	Other assaults	687,928	36,112	97,634	590,294	3,098
	Forgery and counterfeiting	73,465	937	6,125	67,340	40
	Fraud	260,848	4,740	12,135	248,713	123
	Embezzlement	11,699	110	949	10,750	3
	Stolen property; buying, receiving, possessing	125,092	8,015	31,435	93,657	302
	Vandalism	225,544	43,810	90,027	135,517	7,404
	Weapons; carrying, possessing, etc.	163,480	6,923	26,966	136,494	354
	Prostitution and commercialized vice	78,731	157	1,432	77,299	13
	Sex offenses (except forcible rape and prostitution)	78,239	6,247	12,585	65,654	632
	Drug abuse violations	850,034	10,077	76,986	773,048	219
	Gambling	18,106	131	774	17,332	5
	Offenses against family and children	51,035	730	2,363	48,672	176
	Driving under the influence	1,293,516	403	17,674	1,275,842	159
	Liquor laws	492,385	8,746	124,024	368,361	289
	Drunkenness	606,053	1,969	17,886	588,167	154
	Disorderly conduct	573,580	25,738	88,813	484,767	2,100
	Vagrancy	29,270	650	2,450	26,820	40
	All other offenses (except traffic)	2,217,116	69,209	243,622	1,973,494	6,828
	Suspicion	11,066	703	2,164	8,902	46
	Curfew and loitering law violations	55,327	15,418	55,327	X	362
	Runaways	124,709	50,893	124,709	X	2,009

TABLE 2.3 (continued)

10 to 12	13 to 14	15	16	17	18	19
130,473	350,351	291,045	364,780	452,544	499,454	480,274
1.3%	3.5%	2.9%	3.6%	4.5%	4.9%	4.7%
27	167	273	461	830	919	905
267	1,007	793	900	1,053	1,229	1,140
1,320	4,919	4,795	6,081	6,991	7,296	6,575
2,657	7,879	6,977	8,964	11,250	11,662	11,425
11,408	26,764	20,012	23,230	25,666	25,048	19,889
46,359	92,149	59,564	66,539	72,078	65,381	53,110
1,980	13,611	14,319	15,776	15,336	11,736	9,069
1,256	1,692	808	640	651	519	467
4,271	13,972	12,838	16,406	20,124	21,108	20,045
0.9%	3.0%	2.8%	3.6%	4.4%	4.6%	4.4%
61,003	134,216	94,703	106,185	113,731	102,684	82,535
3.7%	8.1%	5.7%	6.4%	6.8%	6.2%	5.0%
65,274	148,188	107,541	122,591	133,855	123,792	102,580
3.1%	7.0%	5.1%	5.8%	6.3%	5.8%	4.8%
9,866	23,148	17,080	20,020	24,422	24,766	25,218
174	723	915	1,579	2,694	3,616	4,050
919	3,698	3,554	1,278	2,563	5,224	8,111
24	83	80	271	488	635	648
1,502	6,211	6,210	7,566	9,644	9,831	8,292
13,839	22,567	14,335	15,377	16,505	13,374	10,408
1,462	5,107	4,911	6,508	8,644	9,792	8,697
19	125	185	329	761	2,124	3,196
1,721	3,894	2,122	1,978	2,238	2,372	2,317
1,055	8,803	12,589	21,304	33,016	43,839	44,559
20	106	169	198	276	320	312
136	418	482	538	613	1,349	1,373
49	195	633	4,159	12,479	29,578	37,497
671	7,786	15,487	35,872	63,919	81,745	71,864
156	1,659	2,572	4,666	8,679	16,196	17,245
6,276	17,362	15,252	20,212	27,611	30,027	28,313
120	490	474	554	772	1,167	1,159
15,559	46,822	40,810	56,319	77,284	99,360	104,024
179	478	445	547	469	347	411
2,387	12,669	12,636	15,156	12,117	X	X
9,065	39,819	32,563	27,758	13,495	X	X

TABLE 2.3 *(continued)*

Offense Charged	20	21	22	23	24	25 to 29
Total	448,723	430,639	419,466	419,160	421,568	1,864,134
Percent[a]	4.4%	4.2%	4.1%	4.1%	4.2%	18.4%
Part I Offenses						
Murder and nonnegligent manslaughter	845	794	786	717	668	2,995
Forcible rape	1,120	1,157	1,256	1,214	1,214	5,640
Robbery	5,810	5,543	5,273	5,178	5,178	21,386
Aggravated assault	11,487	12,132	12,393	12,910	13,019	60,943
Burglary	16,038	13,864	12,788	11,940	11,790	47,645
Larency-theft	43,882	39,871	37,940	36,736	36,091	161,687
Motorvehicle theft	7,213	6,211	5,575	4,744	5,050	18,781
Arson	407	387	415	398	375	1,706
Violent crime[b]	19,262	19,626	19,832	21,156	20,079	90,964
Percent[a]	4.2%	4.3%	4.3%	4.4%	4.4%	19.7%
Property crime[c]	67,540	60,333	56,718	54,124	5,300	229,819
Percent	4.1%	3.6%	3.4%	3.3%	3.2%	13.8%
Total Crime Index[d]	86,802	79,959	76,550	74,280	73,079	320,783
Percent[a]	4.1%	3.8%	3.6%	3.5%	3.4%	15.1%
Part II Offenses						
Other assaults	25,603	28,444	29,082	30,329	31,226	142,617
Forgery and counterfeiting	3,979	3,745	3,590	3,569	3,586	15,962
Fraud	9,172	10,759	11,513	11,971	12,441	58,131
Embezzlement	663	578	552	552	569	2,293
Stolen property; buying, receiving, possessing	6,625	5,923	5,317	4,983	4,713	18,847
Vandalism	8,679	8,383	7,709	7,457	7,135	29,900
Weapons; carrying, possessing, etc.	7,682	7,515	7,271	6,985	6,745	28,473
Prostitution and commercialized vice	3,557	3,908	4,672	5,137	5,112	23,050
Sex offenses (except forcible rape and prostitution)	2,284	2,409	2,499	2,544	2,781	13,198
Drug abuse violations	43,638	43,535	43,789	43,996	44,252	195,200
Gambling	338	315	325	381	443	2,179
Offenses against family and children	1,598	1,896	2,015	2,126	2,306	11,278
Driving under the influence	42,338	55,283	56,565	59,374	61,880	287,393
Liquor laws	53,737	18,605	13,992	12,060	10,593	37,506
Drunkenness	18,119	22,462	22,035	22,652	23,139	112,865
Disorderly conduct	27,616	29,281	27,388	26,370	26,168	106,010
Vagrancy	980	981	1,020	916	957	4,948
All other offenses (except traffic)	104,352	106,257	103,117	103,023	103,984	451,333
Suspicion	421	401	465	485	459	2,168
Curfew and loitering law violations	X	X	X	X	X	X
Runaways	X	X	X	X	X	X

SOURCE: U.S. Department of Justice, Federal Bureau of Investigation, *Crime in the United States, 1968* (Washington, DC: U.S. Government Printing Office, 1989), pp. 178, 179.

Note: This table presents data from all law enforcement agencies submitting complete reports for 12 months in 1988. Population figures are July 1, 1988 population estimates. Arrest data for 1988 were not available for Florida and Kentucky; therefore, these states were omitted by the source.
*9,970 agencies reporting; 1968 estimated population 188,928,000.

TABLE 2.3   *(continued)*

30 to 34	35 to 39	40 to 44	45 to 49	50 to 54	55 to 59	60 to 64	65 and older
1,379,390	881,397	515,881	298,220	181,896	119,888	76,647	78,369
13.6%	8.7%	5.1%	2.9%	1.8%	1.2%	0.8%	0.8%
2,084	1,500	908	539	297	223	151	230
4,255	2,660	1,562	856	449	308	178	188
13,294	6,433	2,746	1,091	433	223	118	105
47,070	30,122	17,990	10,229	6,124	3,748	2,282	2,418
31,102	16,782	7,341	3,166	1,535	832	364	350
1,128,645	84,499	46,752	26,393	16,707	12,335	8,995	12,595
11,744	6,224	2,844	1,295	581	339	152	157
1,275	924	531	351	214	142	101	77
66,703	40,715	23,206	12,715	7,303	4,502	2,729	2,941
14.5%	8.8%	5.0%	2.8%	1.6%	1.0%	0.6%	0.6%
172,766	108,429	57,468	31,205	19,037	13,648	9,612	13,179
10.4%	6.5%	3.5%	1.9%	1.1%	0.8%	0.6%	0.8%
239,469	149,144	803,674	43,920	26,340	18,150	12,341	16,120
11.3%	7.0%	3.8%	2.1%	1.2%	0.9%	0.6%	0.8%
104,602	64,389	36,874	20,589	11,359	6,745	4,059	4,392
12,137	6,805	3,227	1,608	730	373	185	178
47,149	32,971	19,702	9,810	5,172	2,768	1,501	1,778
1,695	1,124	689	418	175	99	47	33
13,253	7,811	3,862	1,957	988	625	341	289
19,389	10,843	5,671	2,852	1,543	924	560	690
20,693	12,989	7,859	4,640	2,887	1,891	1,167	1,208
14,104	6,300	2,810	1,401	764	474	352	338
11,096	8,266	5,732	3,417	2,259	1,701	1,296	1,483
135,683	74,284	33,635	14,223	6,444	3,252	1,558	1,191
2,170	2,037	1,952	1,857	1,496	1,243	939	1,025
10,034	6,854	3,973	1,956	919	489	248	258
219,147	151,054	102,410	66,419	42,879	29,048	18,817	16,160
23,708	15,806	10,269	6,747	4,571	3,171	2,046	1,941
99,192	75,800	51,944	36,000	26,176	19,634	13,065	11,643
74,093	44,947	26,254	15,261	9,225	5,770	3,934	4,110
4,488	3,765	2,394	1,648	927	678	415	377
325,636	205,171	115,443	63,263	36,904	22,775	13,742	15,110
1,652	1,037	527	234	138	78	34	45
X	X	X	X	X	X	X	X
X	X	X	X	X	X	X	X

[a]Because of rounding, percents may not add to total.
[b]Violent crimes are offenses of murder, forcible rape, robbery, and aggravated assault.
[c]Property crimes are offenses of burglary, larceny-theft, motor vehicle theft, and arson.
[d]Includes arson.

violations and loitering, the peak year for juveniles appears to be 15. Thereafter, declines in arrests are observed. Interestingly, liquor law violations involving juveniles show a progressively upward trend across years. The sheer numbers of arrests for liquor law violations increase dramatically between ages 10 and 18.

From time to time, the UCR reports arrest figures across decades. Table 2.4 shows a comparison of offenses charged by age group for the years 1979 and 1988.

General as well as specific arrest figures for different age groups for 1979 are contrasted with those of 1988 and percentage changes charted. Between 1979 and 1988, for example, arrests involving runaways decreased by 7.5 percent, while arrests for curfew and loitering law violations increased by 6.7 percent. However, arrests of juveniles for "suspicion" decreased during this same time interval by 41.9 percent. This downward change is probably due to the U.S. Supreme Court's decision finding local vagrancy and suspicion ordinances in various jurisdictions to be "unconstitutionally vague" and thus unenforceable.

Another interesting trend is that between 1979 and 1988, arrests of juveniles for drunkenness and driving under the influence of drugs or alcohol decreased by 54.7 and 36.4 percent respectively, although arrests of juveniles for liquor law violations increased by 3.1 percent. A general change in the legal drinking age in many jurisdictions, coupled with greater enforcement of traffic laws and rising insurance rates, no doubt prompted many juveniles to alter their drinking behavior but not necessarily to eliminate it.

Strengths of the UCR. One strength of the UCR with regard to crime in the United States is the sheer numbers of offenses reported. Few, if any, alternative sources of information about crime in the United States exhibit such voluminous reporting. Furthermore, regional and seasonal reports of criminal activity are provided. The UCR also reports the proportion of different types of crime that are "cleared by arrest." "Cleared by arrest" means that someone has been arrested and charged with a particular crime.

Another useful feature of the UCR is that the numbers of arrests and reported crimes can be compared across years. The UCR reports percentage increases or decreases in the amounts of different types of crimes for many different jurisdictions and over various time periods. While irregularities exist that are attributable to diverse factors, the information reported is usually regarded as "generally" indicative of national crime trends.

Weaknesses of the UCR. Certain limitations of the UCR are well documented (Gove et al., 1985; Green, 1985; Savitz, 1982; Sherman and Glick, 1984). Some of the more important weaknesses of these statistics are as follows:

1. *UCR figures do not provide an annual per capita measure of crime frequency.* Population increases are not taken into account directly, and thus, reported arrests across years may be suspect. To overcome this problem, researchers must calculate the annual general population increase and contrast this figure against reported numbers of arrests.

2. *Not all law enforcement agencies report crimes to the FBI, and those that do may fail to report crimes uniformly.* Because law enforcement agencies are not compelled to submit annual information to the FBI, some agencies fail to report their arrest activity. Also, crimes of the same name vary in definition among jurisdictions. Additionally, clerks in law enforcement agencies may misclassify certain crimes in their reports to the FBI (Green, 1985; Sherman and Glick, 1984).

3. *The UCR reports only arrests, not the actual amount of crime.* Based upon self-reported information from criminals and others, including **victimization** records from the NCS (National Crime Survey), many criminals escape detection and arrest for a large number of crimes they commit. The UCR provides a record only of those who happen to "get caught." And not all of those who get caught are subsequently convicted of those crimes. Charges may be dropped, prosecutors may fail to establish their cases against certain defendants, or suspects may eventually be released when their cases are not pursued beyond the initial arrest.

4. *When an arrest is reported in the UCR, often only the most serious aspect of the offense is recorded.* Thus, if a robbery suspect is apprehended, he may possess burglary tools, a concealed weapon, and stolen property. He may have caused physical injury to victims. All of these events are crimes, although only "robbery" will be recorded in the law enforcement agency's report to the FBI. Therefore, there is much basis for the belief that these official reports of crime are at best underestimates.

5. *Changes in arrest activity in the UCR may be attributable to fluctuations in police activity rather than to actual fluctuations in criminal activity.* It may be that an incumbent city official running for another term of office insists that police officers in his jurisdiction become more visible by effecting more arrests. Thus, police officers are instructed to "crack down" on criminals. One result is that many "suspicious" persons are arrested on weak evidence, and these are subsequently released. However, the politician may cite record numbers of arrests in his city as "proof" that police are combating crime more effectively. In reality, no actual change in the amount of crime has occurred.

6. *Although they only make up a fraction of national criminal activity, federal crimes are not reported in the UCR.* Thus, if the figures in the UCR are used for evaluating an agency's effectiveness, it would be impossible to assess various federal law enforcement agencies, including the FBI itself, and whether certain federal crimes are increasing or decreasing in frequency annually.

Despite these and other criticisms, the UCR provides valuable data for interested professionals. The fact that virtually all law enforcement agencies rely to some extent on these annual figures as valid indicators of criminal activity in the United States suggests their great utility. Supplementing this information are other, more detailed reports of selected offense activity. The

TABLE 2.4   Arrest comparison for 1979 and 1988 by Age Group*

Offense Charged	Total All Ages		
	1979	1988	Percent Change
Total	7,249,883	8,834,833	+21.9%
Murder and nonnegligent manslaughter	14,077	14,632	+3.9
Forcible rape	21,916	25,059	+14.3
Robbery	101,590	101,976	+0.4
Aggravated assault	192,660	270,981	+40.7
Burglary	348,084	288,364	−17.2
Larceny-theft	823,614	1,010,614	+22.7
Motor vehicle theft	113,556	136,424	+20.1
Arson	13,521	12,471	−7.8
Violent crime[a]	330,243	412,648	+25.0
Property crime[b]	1,298,775	1,447,873	+11.5
Total Crime Index[c]	1,629,018	1,860,521	+14.2
Other assaults	354,158	601,864	+69.9
Forgery and counterfeiting	53,524	63,122	+17.9
Fraud	187,525	235,507	+25.6
Embezzlement	6,576	10,329	+57.1
Stolen property; buying, receiving, possessing	83,002	110,356	+33.0
Vandalism	182,897	195,678	+7.0
Weapons; carrying, possessing, etc.	119,020	144,568	+21.5
Prostitution and commercialized vice	70,233	74,289	+5.8
Sex offenses (except forcible rape and prostitution)	47,927	69,231	+44.5
Drug abuse violations	394,632	749,468	+89.9
Gambling	41,888	16,579	−60.4
Offenses against family and children	39,379	42,530	+8.0
Driving under the influence	950,877	1,095,426	+15.2
Liquor laws	278,410	410,166	+47.3
Drunkenness	796,970	528,859	−33.6
Disorderly conduct	550,641	503,459	−8.6
Vagrancy	31,683	28,201	−11.0
All other offenses (except traffic)	1,272,154	1,940,863	+52.6
Suspicion (not included in totals)	9,679	4,427	−54.3
Curfew and loitering law violations	44,838	47,846	+6.7
Runaways	114,531	105,971	−7.5

SOURCE: U.S. Department of Justice, Federal Bureau of Investigation, *Crime in the United States, 1988* (Washington, DC: U.S. Government Printing Office, 1989), p. 172.

*6,808 agencies reporting; 1988 estimated population 160,451,000.
Note: This table presents data from all law enforcement agencies submitting complete reports for 12 months in 1979 and 1988. Population figures are July 1, 1988 population estimates. Arrest data for 1988 were not available for Florida and Kentucy; therefore, these states were omitted by the source.

Under 18 Years of Age			18 Years of Age and Older		
1979	*1988*	*Percent Change*	*1979*	*1988*	*Percent Change*
1,599,571	1,410,860	−11.8%	5,650,312	7,423,973	+31.4%
1,386	1,610	+16.2	12,691	13,002	+2.6
3,483	3,687	+5.9	18,433	21,372	+15.9
32,557	22,464	−31.0	69,033		+15.2
29,343	33,992	+15.8	163,317	236,989	+45.1
169,151	95,566	−43.5	178,933	192,798	+7.7
331,045	301,935	−8.8	492,569	708,679	+43.9
55,110	53,936	−2.1	58,446	82,488	+41.1
6,640	5,307	−20.1	6,881	7,164	+4.1
66,769	61,753	−7.5	263,474	350,895	+33.2
561,946	456,744	−18.7	736,829	991,129	+34.5
628,715	518,497	−17.5	1,000,303	1,342,024	+34.2
65,224	86,077	+32.0	288,934	515,787	+78.5
7,586	5,260	−30.7	45,938	57,862	+26.0
7,124	11,629	+63.2	180,401	223,878	+24.1
799	893	+11.8	5,777	9,436	+63.3
28,211	27,454	−2.7	54,791	82,902	+51.3
97,272	77,003	−20.8	85,625	118,675	+38.6
20,167	24,079	+19.4	98,853	120,489	+21.9
2,706	1,313	−51.5	67,527	72,976	+8.1
8,828	10,969	+24.3	39,099	58,262	+49.0
85,114	66,689	−21.6	309,518	682,779	+120.6
1,866	673	−63.9	40,022	15,906	−60.3
1,827	2,021	+10.6	37,552	40,509	+7.9
22,985	14,609	−36.4	927,892	1,080,817	+16.5
98,447	101,523	+3.1	179,963	308,643	+71.5
33,304	15,072	−54.7	763,666	513,787	−32.7
95,496	78,476	−17.8	455,145	424,983	−6.6
4,149	2,222	−46.4	27,534	25,979	−5.6
230,382	212,584	−7.7	1,041,772	1,728,279	+65.9
2,835	1,646	−41.9	6,844	2,781	−59.4
44,838	47,846	+6.7	X	X	X
114,531	105,971	−7.5	X	X	X

[a]Violent crimes are offenses of murder, forcible rape, robbery, and aggravated assault.
[b]Property crimes are offenses of burglary, larceny-theft, motor vehicle theft, and arson.
[c]Includes arson.

U.S. Department of Justice's Bureau of Justice Statistics publishes an incredible amount of information annually about different dimensions of crime and offender characteristics and behavior. This supplemental information, together with the data provided by the UCR, may be combined to furnish a more complete picture of crime in the United States. Several alternative data sources are discussed in the following section.

The National Juvenile Court Data Archive. One of the best compendiums of data specifically about juveniles and juvenile court adjudications is the **National Juvenile Court Data Archive** (National Center for Juvenile Justice, 1989). While the federal government has collected data pertaining to juveniles since 1926, the data were dependent upon the voluntary completion of statistical forms by juvenile courts in a limited number of U.S. jurisdictions. In 1975, however, the Office of Juvenile Justice and Delinquency Prevention (OJJDP) assumed responsibility for acquiring court dispositional records and publishing periodic reports of juvenile offenses and adjudicatory outcomes (National Center for Juvenile Justice, 1989:1–2).

By 1989, the National Juvenile Court Data Archive contained over 10 million automated case records of juveniles in various states. Numerous data sets are currently available to researchers and may be accessed for investigative purposes. These data sets are nonuniform, although they ordinarily contain information such as age at referral, gender, race, county of residence, offense(s) charged, date of referral, processing characteristics of the case (e.g., detention and manner of handling), and the case disposition.

The Sourcebook of Criminal Justice Statistics. Another compendium of offender characteristics of all ages is the **Sourcebook of Criminal Justice Statistics,** published annually by the Hindelang Criminal Justice Research Center and supported by grants from the U.S. Department of Justice (Jamieson and Flanagan, 1989). This is perhaps the most comprehensive source that we have discussed, since it accesses numerous government documents and reports annually to keep readers abreast of the latest crime figures. Among other things, it describes justice system employment and spending, jail and prison management and prisoner issues, judicial misconduct and complaints, correctional officer characteristics, crime victim characteristics and victimization patterns, delinquent behavior patterns and trends, and considerable survey information. Literally hundreds of tables are presented summarizing much of the information reported by various private and governmental agencies. Useful annotated information is provided to supplement the tabular material.

Statistics pertaining to juvenile offenders include number of juvenile admissions and discharges from public and private detention facilities, average length of stay of juveniles in these facilities, a profile of juvenile custody facilities, demographic information about juveniles detained for long terms, criminal history or prior records of juveniles, illegal drug and alcohol use among juveniles, waiver information, and offense patterns in relation to socioeconomic and demographic factors. Each annual sourcebook is somewhat different from those published in previous years, although much of the material in subsequent editions has been updated from previous years.

BOX 2.2

Juvenile Highlights

Is the nature of juvenile offenses changing? "Drive-by" shootings are becoming increasingly common-place, particularly in large cities where delinquent gangs are in a state of perpetual conflict. In January, 1988, an innocent victim of rival drug gangs was gunned down in a deadly crossfire in fashionable Westwood Village in South Central Los Angeles. Karen Toshima, a 27-year-old graphic artist, was shot down on a sidewalk outside a fancy Westwood restaurant, as rival juvenile gang members exchanged gunfire over drug distribution supremacy.

Incidents like this are not unusual, nor are they limited to rival gang wars. Ten days following the killing of Karen Toshima, a 67-year-old woman, Alma Lee Washington, was sitting peacefully in her wheelchair in the doorway of her rundown two-bedroom house in South Central Los Angeles. Youths drove by her home and opened fire with a .45 automatic pistol. Washington was struck in the right eye by one of the bullets and died instantly.

Efforts to combat such youth violence have been made by the Los Angeles Police Department and other law enforcement agencies. Special task forces have been created that are specifically designed to investigate gang activities and related shootings. But the preventive capabilities of Los Angeles police officers may not be adequate to the task. The Los Angeles police force consists of 7,350 officers to patrol a city of 3.3 million people. In contrast, a city of comparable size, Chicago, with 3 million people, has a police force of 12,500. A Los Angeles City Council move to hire an additional 150 police officers in the wake of such incidents as the drive-by shootings may represent only a token response to this violence, as well as an impotent one.

(Some factual information adapted from Margaret B. Carlson, "The Price of Life in Los Angeles," Time, February 22, 1988, p. 31.)

Referrals to Juvenile Courts. Arrest statistics are interesting, but they sometimes fail to disclose patterns pertaining to juveniles who are referred to juvenile courts for further processing. For instance, many police officers make **station house adjustments,** in which they exercise their discretionary authority, issue verbal warnings to juveniles they have taken into custody, and then release them to their parents or guardians. What about those juveniles who are arrested *and* referred to juvenile courts by police and others? Table 2.5 shows a profile of those referred to juvenile court, according to the types of offenses with which they have been charged.

Inspecting Table 2.5 shows that about 11 percent of those referred to juvenile court have been charged with violent crimes or crimes against persons. Interestingly, about 15 percent of all arrests by police officers of those under 18 are for violent crimes, as shown in Table 2.3. Some amount of

TABLE 2.5   Referrals to Juvenile Court According to Type of Offense.

Reasons for Referrals to Juvenile Courts	
11% Crimes against persons	
Criminal homicide	1%
Forcible rape	2
Robbery	17
Aggravated assault	20
Simple assault	59
	100%
46% Crimes against property	
Burglary	25%
Larceny	47
Motor vehicle theft	5
Arson	1
Vandalism and trespassing	19
Stolen property offenses	3
	100%
5% Drug offenses	100%
21% Offenses against public order	
Weapons offenses	6%
Sex offenses	6
Drunkenness and disorderly conduct	23
Contempt, probation, and parole violations	21
Other	44
	100%
17% Status offenses	
Running away	28%
Truancy and curfew violations	21
Ungovernability	28
Liquor violations	23
	100%
100% Total all offenses	

Note: percents may not add to 100 because of rounding.
SOURCE: *Delinquency in the United States 1983* (National Center for Juvenile Justice, July 1986).

attrition obviously occurs from the time juveniles are arrested and their eventual referral to the juvenile justice system. About 46 percent of all juvenile court referrals are for property crimes, although only about 32 percent of arrests of those under age 18 are for property crimes. Status offenses, technical violations of probation or parole programs, weapons and sex offenses, disorderly conduct and drunkenness, and other offenses against public order account for another 38 percent of those referred to juvenile courts. Drug offenses account for the remaining 5 percent of those referred.

What Is the Relationship Between Age and Crime? The FBI has conducted an examination of crime arrest rates over time as well as according to age. The *onset* of crime is the age at which one begins to commit offenses. Table 2.3 compiles information about those "under 10" years of age, but it does not give us more detailed information. Less than 1 percent of all arrests involve children under ten anyway. Virtually all of these children are placed within the jurisdiction of the juvenile justice system for processing. Most often, their "processing" involves treatment rather than punishment. Many of these youths are in need of supervision and may be placed in foster homes if they have no parents or if the parents or guardians are unfit. Figures 2.1 and 2.2 respectively show serious crime arrest rates as well as arrest trends by age group.

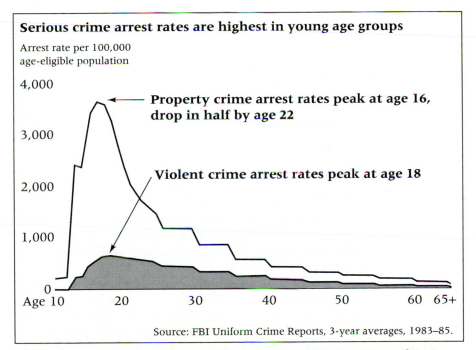

Serious crime arrest rates are highest in young age groups

Arrest rate per 100,000
age-eligible population

Property crime arrest rates peak at age 16, drop in half by age 22

Violent crime arrest rates peak at age 18

Source: FBI Uniform Crime Reports, 3-year averages, 1983–85.

Figure 2-1 Arrest Rates for Serious Crimes. (*Source:* U.S. Department of Justice, *Report to the Nation on Crime and Justice* [Washington, D.C.: U.S. Government Printing Office, 1988], p. 42)

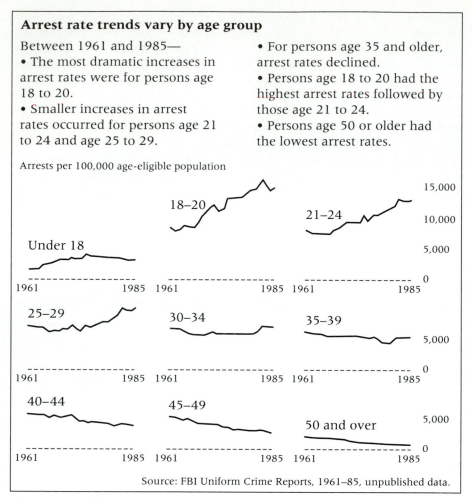

Figure 2-2   Trends in Arrest Rates by Age Group. (*Source:* U.S. Department of Justice, *Report to the Nation on Crime and Justice* [Washington, D.C.: U.S. Government Printing Office, 1988], p. 42)

For example, Figure 2.1 shows that property crime arrest rates tend to peak or level out at age 16, and that by age 22, many youths have desisted from or terminated their offending activity. In contrast, violent crime arrest rates increase at later ages and peak at age 18. From age 18 onward, the violent crime arrest rate decreases steadily. Figure 2.2 shows arrest trends between 1961 and 1985 according to age. During this 24-year interval, the arrest rate was greatest for those in the 18 to 20 age range. The lowest arrest rates, among those age 50 and over, declined during the 1961–1985 period.

How Do Men and Women Differ? Figure 2.3 shows arrest rates for males and females between 1971 and 1985. Overall, arrests of males have increased for all UCR index crimes by about 6 percent, compared with a 37 percent

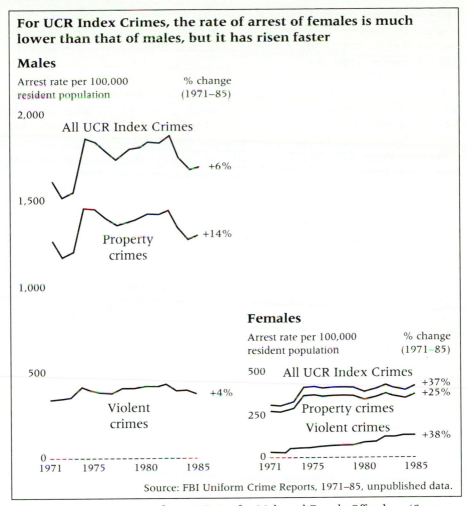

For UCR Index Crimes, the rate of arrest of females is much lower than that of males, but it has risen faster

Males

Arrest rate per 100,000 resident population   % change (1971–85)

All UCR Index Crimes   +6%

Property crimes   +14%

Violent crimes   +4%

Females

Arrest rate per 100,000 resident population   % change (1971–85)

All UCR Index Crimes   +37%

Property crimes   +25%

Violent crimes   +38%

Source: FBI Uniform Crime Reports, 1971–85, unpublished data.

Figure 2-3 Comparison of Arrest Rates for Male and Female Offenders. (*Source:* U.S. Department of Justice, *Report to the Nation on Crime and Justice* [Washington, D.C.: U.S. Government Printing Office, 1988], p. 46)

increase in arrests for females.

The differences are even more pronounced when divided into violent and property offense categories. Arrest rates of males for violent offenses between 1971 and 1985 increased by about 4 percent, but the increase among females was 38 percent. Female arrests for property offenses increased by about 25 percent during this same time interval, compared with a 14 percent increase in arrests of males. However, it should be noted that women account for only a small proportion of those arrested annually. For instance, only about 11 percent of all violent crime arrests involved females, while about 24 percent of all property crime arrests involved females. Presently, women make up less than 10 percent of the jail and prison inmate populations. Generally, men are more likely than women to be arrested for crimes such as murder, rape, robbery, or burglary. Women tend to be overrepresented in crime categories such as larceny-theft, fraud, embezzlement, and drug offenses (U.S. Department of Justice, 1988:46).

Race and Arrest Rates. A disproportionately large number of arrestees are black. About 12 percent of the general U.S. population is black. Of all persons arrested in 1988, about 33 percent were black. Of all of those under age 18 arrested in the same year, about 28 percent were black. Table 2.6 shows the distribution of arrests by type of offense and ethnic group for 1988.

Do these racial differences carry over into the juvenile justice system to the extent that similar characteristics are observed among those juveniles who are incarcerated in secure detention? Yes. In fact, the figures are even more dramatic. Table 2.7 provides a profile of juveniles who were in custody in public short-term or long-term detention facilities in 1989. For both short- and long-term detainees in all public juvenile incarcerative facilities, 60 percent were minority members, with about 42 percent of all of those incarcerated being black juveniles. Therefore, not only are greater proportions of black juveniles arrested compared with white juveniles, they are incarcerated at much greater rates as well.

Allegations of racism have been made against the criminal justice system. These arguments are well-documented elsewhere (Clayton, 1983; Kempf and Austin, 1986; Petersilia, 1983). It would seem that similar charges could be leveled against the juvenile justice system at various points. As we will see in Chapter 5, police discretion has a great influence on arrest trends. Other discretionary points in the juvenile justice system include intake, prosecutorial decision making, and judicial discretion in sentencing youthful offenders. Clearly, minorities are sanctioned disproportionately, and more severely, in each of these critical phases of system—juvenile interaction.

Self-Report Information. While official sources of crime and delinquency information are quite useful, a common criticism is that they tend to underestimate the amount of offense behavior that actually occurs in the United States. For many years, those interested in studying juvenile offense behaviors have made use of data derived from *self-reports.*

Self-reports *are surveys of youths (or adults) based upon disclosures they themselves make about the types of offenses they have committed and how frequently they have committed them* (Elliott *et al.,* 1987; Farrington, 1985; Giordano *et al.,* 1986; Griffith, 1983; Osgood *et al.,* 1988). High school students or other youths may be asked to complete a confidential questionnaire in which lists of offenses are provided (Fagan *et al.,* 1987; Jensen and Brownfield, 1987). Ordinarily, simple checklists are given to students and they are asked to identify those behaviors they have engaged in, not necessarily those for which they have been apprehended. Considered "unofficial" sources of information about delinquency and delinquency patterns, these self-disclosures are considered by many professionals to be more accurate than official sources. An example of such a checklist is shown in Figure 2.4 on page 66.

The "unofficial" aspect of such self-reporting is misleading, however, since the **National Youth Survey** (Elliott *et al.*, 1983; Menard, 1987) and the **Monitoring the Future Survey** (Osgood, 1987) are among several national surveys administered either annually or at other intervals through various organizations and agencies to large numbers of high school students. For instance, the Institute for Social Research at the University of Michigan regularly solicits information from over 3,000 high school students nationally (Osgood *et al.*, 1987). While these surveys are not supported fully by government grants or other public funding, their importance as sources should not be underestimated. Such information is regarded as highly credible by juvenile justice professionals, and this is indicated, in part, by the frequency with which such data are cited in the literature.

Self-report data about juvenile offenses suggests that a sizable gap exists between official reports of delinquent conduct and information disclosed through self-reports (Hartstone and Hansen, 1984; Wolfgang *et al.*, 1986). In essence, self-report disclosures by teenagers reveal far greater delinquency than is reported by the UCR (Elliott *et al.*, 1987; Osgood *et al.*, 1988). Self-reports of delinquency or status offense conduct have caused researchers to refer to these undetected offending behaviors as "hidden delinquency."

Not everyone believes that delinquency self-reports are necessarily more accurate than other sources of offense information, however. For example, Akers *et al.* (1983) have questioned the validity of self-report information relating to prohibited smoking behaviors among a sample of Muscatine, Iowa, children in grades 7−12. According to self-reports by over 4,300 students over a two-year period, smoking appeared to be prevalent among a sizable number of these youths. However, random biochemical measures of saliva specimens suggested a much lower incidence of smoking behavior. This indicates that many juveniles may be inclined to exaggerate their deviant conduct or to claim to have committed offenses when in fact they have not committed them.

For some authorities, at least, self-report information is of questionable validity, and it may actually be a better indicator of peer pressure to conform to certain deviant expectations (perhaps associated with "grown-up" behavior) than it is of the actual conduct of the juveniles involved. However, the question of validity can be raised about any data, official or otherwise. Wolfgang *et al.* (1986) wisely caution that *both* self-report data and official arrest information are needed, although we should exercise caution whenever we attempt to generalize from these sample sources to the general population.

All of these data sources have been used by researchers to try to assess whether there are changing offending patterns among juveniles over the years. There is much descriptive literature by professionals that attempts to characterize violent juvenile offenders and to conjecture about the many potential causative factors in juvenile violence. One concern of certain critics of DSO, for instance, is whether status offenders actually escalate to more

TABLE 2.6   Arrests in 1988 by Ethnic Background and Type of Offense*

| | Total Arrests | | | |
Offense Charged	Total	White	Black	American Indian or Alaskan Native
Total	7,869,070	5,137,436	2,583,330	79,663
Murder and nonnegligent manslaughter	12,356	4,567	7,610	64
Forcible rape	21,518	10,099	11,121	138
Robbery	98,535	33,877	63,564	406
Aggravated assault	238,178	127,545	106,859	1,858
Burglary	249,773	157,410	88,254	1,757
Larceny-theft	994,206	639,381	331,700	10,995
Motor vehicle theft	123,733	67,941	53,742	607
Arson	10,749	7,456	3,117	89
Violent crime[b]	370,587	176,088	189,154	2,466
Property crime[c]	1,378,461	872,188	476,813	13,448
Total Crime Index[d]	1,749,048	1,048,276	665,967	15,914
Other assaults	546,463	318,695	218,640	4,808
Forgery and counterfeiting	54,230	33,995	19,594	288
Fraud	140,589	87,810	51,248	474
Embezzlement	7,599	4,787	2,713	27
Stolen property; buying, receiving, possessing	99,563	53,495	44,919	514
Vandalism	181,886	129,837	48,908	1,541
Weapons; carrying, possessing, etc.	132,474	72,161	58,406	589
Prostitution and commercialized vice	75,156	42,983	31,024	376
Sex offenses (except forcible rape and prostitution)	59,221	43,313	14,802	618
Drug abuse violations	681,504	377,547	298,600	2,084
Gambling	15,020	6,301	7,825	21
Offenses against family and children	26,270	16,293	8,639	351
Driving under the influence	799,238	694,863	89,450	8,673
Liquor laws	380,916	330,442	39,647	8,618
Drunkenness	494,825	386,270	94,864	12,443
Disorderly conduct	509,352	310,447	190,735	5,538
Vagrancy	25,896	14,689	10,507	619
All other offenses (except traffic)	1,731,714	1,041,862	656,094	14,733
Suspicion	9,921	3,845	5,958	21
Curfew and loitering law violations	51,956	42,091	8,633	419
Runaways	96,229	77,434	16,157	994

*6,891 agencies reporting; 1988 estimated population 128,522,000.
[a]Because of rounding, percents may not add to total.
[b]Violent crimes include the offenses murder, forcible rape, robbery, and aggravated assault.
[c]Property crimes include the offense burglary, larcency-theft, motor vehicle theft, and arson.
[d]Includes arson

Asian or Pacific Islander	Percent[a]				
	Total	White	Black	American Indian or Alaskan Native	Asian or Pacific Islander
68,641	100.0%	65.3%	32.8%	1.0%	0.9%
115	100.0	37.0	61.6	0.5	0.9
160	100.0	46.9	51.7	0.6	0.7
688	100.0	34.4	64.5	0.4	0.7
1,916	100.0	53.6	44.9	0.8	0.8
2,352	100.0	63.0	35.3	0.7	0.9
12,130	100.0	64.3	33.4	1.1	1.2
1,443	100.0	54.9	43.4	0.5	1.2
87	100.0	69.4	29.0	0.8	0.8
2,879	100.0	47.5	51.0	0.7	0.8
16,012	100.0	63.3	34.6	1.0	1.2
18,891	100.0	59.9	38.1	0.9	1.1
4,320	100.0	58.3	40.0	0.9	0.8
353	100.0	62.7	36.1	0.5	0.7
1,057	100.0	62.5	36.5	0.3	0.8
72	100.0	63.0	35.7	0.4	0.9
635	100.0	53.7	45.1	0.5	0.6
1,600	100.0	71.4	26.9	0.8	0.9
1,318	100.0	54.5	44.1	0.4	1.0
773	100.0	57.2	41.3	0.5	1.0
488	100.0	73.1	25.0	1.0	0.8
3,273	100.0	55.4	43.8	0.3	0.5
873	100.0	42.0	52.1	0.1	5.8
987	100.0	62.0	32.9	1.3	3.8
6,252	100.0	86.9	11.2	1.1	0.8
2,209	100.0	86.7	10.4	2.3	0.6
1,248	100.0	78.1	19.2	2.5	0.3
2,632	100.0	60.9	37.4	1.1	0.5
81	100.0	56.7	40.6	2.4	0.3
19,025	100.0	60.2	37.9	0.9	1.1
97	100.0	38.8	60.1	0.2	1.0
813	100.0	81.0	16.6	0.8	1.6
1,644	100.0	80.5	16.8	1.0	1.7

TABLE 2.6 *(continued)*

Offense Charged	Arrests under 18			
	Total	White	Black	American Indian or Alaskan Native
Total	1,371,881	954,120	386,979	11,119
Murder and nonnegligent manslaughter	1,501	549	931	4
Forcible rape	3,267	1,414	1,819	10
Robbery	22,345	7,211	14,767	62
Aggravated assault	32,368	16,295	15,585	179
Burglary	85,246	60,224	23,139	641
Larceny-theft	308,328	217,190	82,057	3,432
Motor vehicle theft	51,096	28,269	21,638	263
Arson	4,964	3,962	892	43
Violent crime[b]	59,481	25,469	33,102	255
Property crime[b]	449,634	309,645	127,726	4,379
Total Crime Index[d]	509,115	335,114	160,828	4,634
Other assaults	83,476	47,933	33,815	499
Forgery and counterfeiting	4,996	4,055	866	30
Fraud	10,925	5,325	5,345	46
Embezzlement	799	554	232	4
Stolen property; buying, receiving, possessing	26,869	14,697	11,740	168
Vandalism	73,305	57,773	14,266	424
Weapons; carrying, possessing, etc.	23,805	13,624	9,757	77
Prostitution and commercialized vice	1,295	768	510	7
Sex offenses (except forcible rape and prostitution)	9,737	6,350	3,223	52
Drug abuse violations	66,166	35,209	30,301	264
Gambling	717	144	509	0
Offenses against family and children	1,821	1,352	433	7
Driving under the influence	11,862	11,153	472	160
Liquor laws	96,309	90,392	3,959	1,465
Drunkenness	15,065	13,682	1,049	280
Disorderly conduct	870,205	51,362	27,985	427
Vagrancy	1,985	1,529	422	18
All other offenses (except traffic)	203,416	142,030	56,222	1,138
Suspicion	1,828	1,549	255	6
Curfew and loitering law violations	51,956	42,091	8,633	419
Runaways	96,229	77,434	16,157	994

[a]Because of rounding, percents may not add to total.
[b]Violent crimes include the offenses murder, forcible rape, robbery, and aggravated assault.
[c]Property crimes include the offense burglary, larceny-theft, motor vehicle theft, and arson.
[d]Includes arson

| Asian or Pacific Islander | Percent[a] | | | | |
	Total	White	Black	American Indian or Alaskan Native	Asian or Pacific Islander
19,663	100.0%	69.5%	28.2%	0.8%	1.4%
17	100.0	36.6	62.0	0.3	1.1
24	100.0	43.3	55.7	0.3	0.7
305	100.0	32.3	66.1	0.3	1.4
309	100.0	50.3	48.1	0.6	1.0
1,242	100.0	70.6	27.1	0.8	1.5
5,649	100.0	70.4	26.6	1.1	1.8
926	100.0	55.3	42.3	0.5	1.8
67	100.0	79.8	18.0	0.9	1.3
655	100.0	42.8	55.7	0.4	1.1
7,884	100.0	68.9	28.4	1.0	1.8
8,539	100.0	65.8	31.6	0.9	1.7
1,229	100.0	57.4	40.5	0.6	1.5
45	100.0	81.2	17.3	0.6	0.9
209	100.0	48.7	48.9	0.4	1.9
9	100.0	69.3	29.0	0.5	1.1
264	100.0	54.7	43.7	0.6	1.0
842	100.0	78.8	19.5	0.6	1.1
347	100.0	57.2	41.0	0.3	1.5
10	100.0	59.3	39.4	0.5	0.8
112	100.0	65.2	33.1	0.5	1.2
392	100.0	53.2	45.8	0.4	0.6
64	100.0	20.1	71.0	X	0.9
29	100.0	74.2	23.8	0.4	1.6
77	100.0	94.0	4.0	1.3	0.6
493	100.0	93.9	4.1	1.5	0.5
54	100.0	90.8	7.0	1.9	0.4
431	100.0	64.0	34.9	0.5	0.5
16	100.0	77.0	21.3	0.9	0.8
4,026	100.0	69.8	27.6	0.6	2.0
18	100.0	84.7	13.9	0.3	1.0
813	100.0	81.0	16.6	0.8	1.6
1,644	100.0	80.5	16.8	1.0	1.7

TABLE 2.7　Juveniles in Custody by Minority Status and Type of Public Facility: 1989

			Minority			
	Nonminority[a]	Black[b]	Hispanic[c]	Other	Total (Minority)	Total Juveniles
Short-Term Facilities						
Institutional	7,199	8,417	3,057	473	11,947	19,146
Open	475	314	28	4	346	821
Total	7,674	8,731	3,085	477	12,293	19,967
Long-Term Facilities						
Institutional	9,502	11,417	4,151	634	16,202	25,704
Open	5,025	3,688	1,435	304	5,427	10,452
Total	14,527	15,105	5,586	938	21,629	36,156
All Facilities	22,201	23,836	8,671	1,415	33,922	56,123

[a]Includes whites not of Hispanic origin.
[b]Includes blacks not of Hispanic origin.
[c]Includes both blacks and whites of Hispanic origin.

Figure 2-4　A Hypothetical Checklist for Self-Report Disclosures of Delinquent or Criminal Conduct among High School Students. (Compiled by author.)

"How often during the past six months have you committed the following offenses?" Check whichever best applies to you.

Offense	Frequency				
	0 times	1 time	2 times	3 times	4 or more times
Smoked marijuana	_____	_____	_____	_____	_____
Stole something worth $50 or less	_____	_____	_____	_____	_____
Got drunk on beer or wine	_____	_____	_____	_____	_____
Got drunk on hard liquor	_____	_____	_____	_____	_____
Used crack or cocaine	_____	_____	_____	_____	_____

SOURCE:　Compiled by author.

serious types of offending behavior. Can trends be charted over the years that enable us to anticipate appropriate interventions for violence-prone juveniles or those likely to escalate to more serious offenses? Additionally, researchers are interested in whether significant differences exist between male and female juvenile offenders, apart from certain typical offense behaviors associated with each. Is female delinquency increasing? If so, what can be done about it? In the following sections, we will examine these topics and some of the literature relevant for each.

Violence and Nonviolence: Career Escalation?

What is the nature of violent crime among juveniles? Is there **career escalation**—that is, are juveniles likely to escalate to more serious offenses during their youthful years as they become more deeply involved in delinquent conduct? Are there certain kinds of juvenile offenders who are more or less susceptible to intervention programs and treatments as means of reducing or eliminating their propensity to engage in delinquent conduct? Certainly the media have helped to heighten our awareness of the presence of violent youth gangs in various cities. Startling information about extensive drug and alcohol use among juveniles is frequently reported in the media. Is there currently an unstoppable juvenile crime wave throughout the United States?

Trend data concerning the incidence of juvenile violence have been analyzed for the UCR. Strasburg (1984) describes some important juvenile offense trends over several decades which were derived from these sources. For instance, according to the UCR, a sharp upward curve in serious youth crime began during the late 1950s. Between 1960 and 1975, juvenile arrests grew by approximately 30 percent, more than twice the rate of arrests for adults. The largest juvenile arrest rates were for violent crimes rather than for property or nonviolent offenses.

Strasburg notes that in 1975, although juveniles comprised only 20 percent of the U.S. population, they accounted for 43 percent of all arrests for major UCR index offenses or index crimes (e.g., aggravated assault, forcible rape, robbery, burglary, vehicular theft, larceny, and homicide). One result of this rapid increase in juvenile arrests was that the public began to perceive that there was a juvenile "crime wave." During the 1970s, many interested persons and agencies produced various plans to combat rising delinquency. Many of the reforms that have either been suggested or implemented in juvenile courts or juvenile processing throughout the juvenile justice system are direct products of these actions.

However, Strasburg suggests that the dramatic shift in public policy that has strongly influenced the course of juvenile justice during the last few decades may have been premature. As Strasburg sees it, many of the institutional reforms that have been largely punitive may be overreactions and may be ill-advised, since the rate of juvenile offending behavior has either tapered off or declined appreciably since 1975. This observation has been independently confirmed in selected jurisdictions (Georgia Commission of Juvenile Justice, 1985).

Other researchers who have studied juvenile offense trends for the same period attribute much of the rising juvenile delinquency to high unemployment rates (Turner *et al.*, 1984). These investigators looked at data on U.S. unemployment among youths aged 16 to 19 and 20 to 23 for the years 1958–1979, and also at arrests for homicide and robbery for those age groups in those years. They found a strong association between the relative deprivation generated in part by high unemployment and the rate of violent crime. The high birth rate for the period 1947–1957 led to increasing numbers of youths competing for a limited number of jobs 16 to 19 years later, thus adversely affecting the unemployment rates in many jurisdictions. In part as a reaction to the frustration and deprivation brought about by unemployment, many youths turned to crimes of violence.

Hartstone and Hansen (1984) have found little evidence to support the idea that youths progress to more violent crimes during their teenage years. Random samples of 114 juvenile offenders who were arrested for violent crimes were investigated as part of a U.S. government-funded Violent Juvenile Offender Research and Development Program. These youths had an average of 10.5 delinquency petitions and 5.7 formal adjudications against them, as well as even higher levels of delinquency than official documents revealed, according to self-reported information. Essentially, the study showed that there was no evidence to indicate that they started out as nonviolent offenders and escalated to violent offenses. Lab (1984) reaches similar conclusions in his investigation of over 6,000 subjects from three different birth cohorts in 1942, 1949, and 1952. Most of the juveniles he examined tended to commit minor offenses, and no pattern of escalation was disclosed. For the most part, those juveniles who began a pattern of delinquent activity tended to continue the same type of activity over time rather than progress to more violent behaviors.

The actual proportion of juveniles who engage in violent behaviors is comparatively small. The Youth Policy and Law Center, Inc. (1984) investigated a sample of 265 cases in three Wisconsin counties in 1980 and found that only 6 percent could be classified as "chronic violent offenders" (i.e., arrested four or more times for violent offenses). Most of their violent behaviors were directed toward others of their age, typical of gang fighting. This general observation has been reported by others (Mathias *et al.*, 1984). A classic study assigning a large portion of chronic offending to a small core of juveniles is by Wolfgang *et al.* (1972).

Wolfgang's Chronic Six Percent. Perhaps the most influential study of chronicity of offending was a study by Wolfgang *et al.* (1972). This study examined a *birth cohort* of 9,945 boys born in Philadelphia in 1945. *A **birth cohort** is an aggregate of youths born during the same year and observed over time.* These boys were tracked until 1963, when they reached age 18. Wolfgang and his associates wished to determine (1) the age of onset of delinquency, (2) the progression or chronicity of delinquency, and (3) the age of cessation of delinquency. Basically, these researchers wanted to know *when* juveniles began their offending behavior, *what factors influenced them to continue their delinquent conduct,* and *when* they ended their delinquent behavior.

Wolfgang found that about a third of the boys had some type of police contact during those eighteen years. In view of what has already been said of ethnicity and its influence on arrests and incarcerations of juveniles, Wolfgang found ethnicity to be the most significant predictor of police contact in the sample studied. It was closely related to socioeconomic status, since about 84 percent of youths in the lower socioeconomic strata were minorities compared with about 31 percent of the white youths. One of the most interesting features of his study was that about 627 boys, or about 6 percent of the entire sample, had been arrested at least five times for different crimes. Further, this 6 percent accounted for about 52 percent of all offenses committed by the entire birth cohort. Thus, for at least a few of these offenders, there was great persistence in their offending behavior, and they were designated as **chronic recidivists.** Despite the sophistication of our measures of risk, dangerousness, and recidivism, however, we are still unable to identify in advance those juveniles who will chronically reoffend.

Gang Membership and Violence. Of particular interest to juvenile justice professionals is the increased incidence of gang behavior in recent years (Chicago Police Department, 1988; Maxon *et al.* 1986; Takata and Zevitz, 1987). The gang phenomenon seems to be spread throughout the United States rather than to be localized in major urban centers. Gangs are found in most jurisdictions and seem to organize along racial or ethnic lines, often for mutual protection against other gangs (Hagedorn, 1988). Of course, gang formation and membership would function to heighten the perception of community residents that their communities are being infested with lawless juveniles (Hagedorn, 1988; Spergel, 1986). Thus, there are not necessarily increasing numbers of juvenile delinquents running rampant in cities; instead, there may be more visible organizational activity among those juveniles already there.

Homicidal Juveniles. Juveniles who commit homicide are relatively rare. Of the 16,714 homicide arrests reported by the UCR in 1987, only 203 involved juveniles under age 15, and less than 10 percent of all homicide arrests involved persons under age 18 (Jamieson and Flanagan, 1989:490). The victims in juvenile homicides are predominantly strangers (49 percent) or casual acquaintances (33 percent). Only 17 percent of juvenile homicides tend to involve family members (Rowley *et al.,* 1987). Many juvenile homicides occurred during the commission of other crimes, such as burglary or robbery (Bjerregaard and Kratcoski, 1987). Most perpetrators tend to be males (Cornell *et al.,* 1987; Kriesman and Siden, 1982; Zimring, 1984). Interestingly, the victims of most female juveniles charged with homicides tended to be parents rather than strangers or acquaintances (Rowley *et al.,* 1987).

While there is no single profile that typifies all juvenile violent offenders, many of these youths have personal histories that include child abuse and/or parental neglect (Geller and Ford-Somma, 1984; Haizlip *et al.,* 1984;

Hartstone and Hansen, 1984; Kratcoski, 1985). Compared with boys, girls seemed to be nearly twice as likely to have been abused as children (Guarino, 1985). In over half of all cases, drugs and/or alcohol had been cited by youths as contributory to their violence (Hartstone and Hansen, 1984).

Female vs. Male Delinquency: Cataloging the Differences

Of the total number of juveniles held in either public or private facilities, annually, approximately 20 percent are female (Jamieson and Flanagan, 1988:595). In 1987, of the long-term detainees in secure juvenile facilities,

Compared with male juvenile offenders, who tend to commit more violent and aggressive acts, female juveniles commit proportionately more "passive offenses" (e.g., fraud, larceny-theft) and are incarcerated less frequently and for shorter time periods. Some evidence indicates that female delinquency is increasing at a faster rate than male delinquency. (© Lloyd Wolf)

females accounted for only about 7 percent of those confined (Beck *et al.,* 1988; Jamieson and Flanagan, 1988:598). These general figures seem applicable to previous years as well. Females are usually committed at a lower rate than males, and are returned to their communities at a greater rate after serving comparatively shorter detention terms (American Correctional Association, 1985; Massachusetts Department of Youth Services, 1984). While a more thorough examination of male and female juvenile differences in detention and corrections will be presented in Chapters 12 and 13, a preliminary profile of male–female offense differences is presented in Table 2.8.

TABLE 2.8   Types of Offenses and Reasons for Which Male and Female Juveniles Were Held in Public Juvenile Facilities: 1987 and 1989

	1987			1989		
	Total	*Male*	*Female*	*Total*	*Male*	*Female*
Total Juveniles	*53,503*	*46,272*	*7,231*	*56,123*	*49,443*	*6,680*
Delinquent offenses[a]	**50,269**	**44,757**	**5,512**	**53,037**	**47,843**	**5,194**
Offenses against persons	13,300	12,297	1,003	14,327	13,210	1,117
Violent—murder, forcible rape, robbery, and aggravated assault	7,943	7,438	505	8,566	7,976	590
Other—manslaughter, simple assault, sexual assault	5,357	4,859	498	5,761	5,234	527
Property offenses	23,431	21,272	2,159	22,780	20,849	1,931
Serious—burglary, arson, larceny-theft, and motor vehicle theft	15,746	14,595	1,151	15,181	14,112	1,069
Other—vandalism, forgery, counterfeiting, fraud, stolen property, unauthorized use of a motor vehicle	7,685	6,677	1,008	7,599	6,737	862
Alcohol/drug offenses	4,161	3,733	428	6,586	6,067	519
Public order offenses	2,380	1,864	516	2,788	2,406	382
Probation violations	4,200	3,183	1,017	4,920	3,942	978
Other delinquent offenses[b]	2,797	2,408	389	1,636	1,369	267
Nondelinquent reasons	**3,234**	**1,515**	**1,719**	**3,086**	**1,600**	**1,486**
Status offenses[c]	2,523	1,198	1,325	2,245	1,128	1,117
Abuse/neglect[d]	429	190	239	426	205	221
Others[d]	29	20	9	113	78	35
Voluntarily admitted	253	107	146	302	189	113

[a]Offenses that would be criminal if committed by adults
[b]Includes unknown and unspecified delinquent offenses.
[c]Offenses that would not be criminal for adults, such as running away, truancy, and incorrigibility.
[d]Also includes those held for emotional disturbance or mental retardation.
[e]Includes all other unspecified reasons for detention or commitment.

SOURCE: Sweet, 1991:4.

Generally, juvenile females in detention facilities are represented at a lower rate in violent offense categories than their male counterparts. Females are also represented at a lower rate than males in various property offense and drug categories, such as motor vehicle theft, fraud, and drug possession. However, females are detained more frequently for nondelinquent reasons, including status offenses. In 1989, for example, 22 percent of the incarcerated female juveniles were detained for nondelinquent offenses compared with only 3 percent of the male juveniles (Jamieson and Flanagan, 1988:505; Sweet, 1991:4).

Because female juvenile offenders are represented in such small numbers in national delinquency and status offense figures, and because relatively little reform has occurred with regard to females in juvenile courts and corrections, some experts have regarded these females as "the forgotten few" (Bergsmann, 1989:73). In almost every jurisdiction, the proportion of females turned over to youth services after initial arrest is less than 10 percent (California Department of the Youth Authority, 1985b; Wiebush et al., 1985).

Some evidence suggests that the paternalistic nature of the juvenile justice system, as well as the differential handling by police of juvenile female offenders, accounts in part for these low figures (Curran, 1984; Gelsthorpe, 1987). Historical observations by Gelsthorpe (1987) indicate that there are four main themes that guide responses to boys and girls in the juvenile justice system nationally. First, it seems that boys are more likely to offend at some point during their adolescence. Those few girls who offend during this period are often considered "abnormal" in some way (Bowker and Klein, 1983; Campbell, 1984). Second, much male offending is property-related, whereas it is assumed that female delinquency is predominantly sexual (Messerschmidt, 1987). Third, female delinquents seem to come from broken homes at a higher rate than their male counterparts. Therefore, their delinquency is often attributed to deficient family relationships (Campbell, 1984; Stewart and Zaenglein-Senger, 1984). Finally, female delinquency seems to be regarded by criminological theory as the result of mental instability and nonrational behavior, whereas male juvenile offenders are often regarded as rational and adventurous beings who are simply testing the bounds of their adolescence (Hagan et al., 1985). But Gelsthorpe (1987) concludes that much of this historical analysis of male and female juvenile differences is mythical and misconceived.

A similar analysis along political–legal lines has been made by Curran (1984). Curran examined the long-range impact of the women's movement in the United States during the period 1960–1980. A prevailing belief is that the women's movement brought about many changes in both the type and quantity of female offenses during this period, as well as in the way women were generally treated in both the criminal and juvenile justice systems. However, Curran disagrees. He suggests that certain political and legal changes in the United States during the 1960–1980 period furnish a better explanation for the way female juvenile offenders have been treated. Changes in the rate of female delinquency are likely attributable to these same factors.

The treatment of females was influenced by two major events which seemed to trigger a general shift from a liberal to a conservative approach to juvenile justice in many jurisdictions. First, state legislatures passed various laws designed to respond to public perceptions of rising violent crime among juveniles. Second, status offenses were removed from the jurisdiction of juvenile courts in many localities. High priority was given to "cracking down" on juvenile offenders by district attorneys in many cities. Regarding female juveniles, Curran has identified three major political–legal periods: (1) a "paternalistic" period (1960–1967), during which female delinquents were harshly treated by the courts "for their own good"; (2) a "due process" period (1968–1976), which reflected the impact of various legal decisions such as *In re Gault* (1967) (see Chapter 10 for a discussion of this case and the legal rights of juveniles generally); and (3) a "law and order" phase (1977–1980), during which the court adjusted to the new conservatism of the late 1970s (Curran, 1984). Therefore, changing rates in female juvenile offending are probably the result of changing policies in the treatment of female juveniles rather than representing an actual increase in the rate of female criminality.

Some investigators question the assumption that female juveniles have been treated differently from their male counterparts by the juvenile justice system in certain jurisdictions. Sampson (1985) reports no differences in the treatment of males and females who have had contact with the juvenile justice system in Seattle. But other researchers report extensive paternalistic treatment of female offenders by juvenile judges and others (Chesney-Lind, 1987a; Webb, 1984).

At least in some jurisdictions, female delinquency has increased proportionately faster than male delinquency (Lab and Doerner, 1987). Studies of female birth cohorts in 1942, 1949, and 1955 in Racine, Wisconsin, show that female offending rates rose faster than male offending rates across five general crime categories. But Lab and Doerner (1987) acknowledge that these changes might be a function of a change in the response of the juvenile justice system to young females over the years rather than of actual increases in female offending. It is generally accepted, however, that males commit more serious offenses than females in most jurisdictions (Barton and Figueira-McDonough, 1985).

Profiles of female delinquents have been few in number. Those that have been conducted parallel in some ways the historical descriptions noted by Gelsthorpe (Chesney-Lind, 1978; Sarri, 1983). For example, Bergsmann (1989:73) says that "young women in trouble with the law are typically 16 years old, live in urban ghettos, are high school dropouts . . . are victims of sexual abuse, come from single-parent families, have experienced foster care placement, lack adequate work skills . . . and are predominantly black or Hispanic." These same observations have been made by others (Bergsmann, 1988; Crawford, 1988; Sarri, 1988).

Evidence of the stereotyping of female juvenile offenders is extensive throughout the juvenile justice system (Bergsmann, 1989:74). Courts tend to view female juveniles as more "vulnerable" than males, and thus there is a tendency for many juvenile judges and others to treat them differently for even minor offense behaviors (Chesney-Lind, 1987; Webb, 1984). For example, in 1984, of all juveniles who appeared in juvenile courts, females represented 45 percent of all status offender cases, compared with only 19 percent of all delinquency cases. Of the 45 percent, 62 percent were runaways (Bergsmann, 1989:74). In many respects, present problems with female juvenile institutions and treatment programs are similar to adult female treatment program problems and patterns. The juvenile justice system has been traditionally geared to process male offenders in large numbers rather than female offenders. Thus, services and programs benefiting female juveniles have often been slighted compared with programs that accommodate male juvenile offenders. Additional information about these problems will be highlighted in Chapters 12 and 13.

Summary

Juveniles are persons who have not yet attained their eighteenth birthday, although in a limited number of jurisdictions, the maximum age of a juvenile is 15. Common law in many states places juvenile offender accountability at age 7. Delinquency refers to offenses that are committed by youths who have not reached the age of their majority and that would be considered crimes if committed by adults. However, many juveniles commit status offenses, or acts that would not be considered crimes if adults committed them. Status offenses include running away from home, violating curfew, violating liquor laws, and truancy. Deinstitutionalization of status offenses, DSO, is a popular juvenile justice reform.

Major sources of information about delinquency and status offenses are the *Uniform Crime Reports* (UCR), *The National Juvenile Court Data Archive*, self-reported information from juveniles themselves, and the annual *Sourcebook of Criminal Justice Statistics*. These sources reflect arrest information and reports from crime victims. Selected crimes reported in the UCR are known as index offenses. Felonies and misdemeanors are reported, as well as certain status offenses such as liquor law violations, running away from home, and curfew violations. These sources are regarded as official sources of information about delinquent conduct, although they have been extensively criticized.

Most delinquency is nonviolent, although there is a hard core of chronic, persistent, violent juvenile offenders. Most juvenile violent offenders are male. There is no juvenile crime wave, although there was an apparent increase in delinquency during the period 1960–1975. Certain male–female differences exist in delinquent conduct; much female delinquency is related to nonviolent offenses such as fraud and running away from home. Female delinquents seem to come from less stable, single-parent homes and are more deprived socioeconomically than many of their male counterparts. Provisions for female juveniles are lacking in many community-based public and private treatment programs. This is because the juvenile justice system has been geared primarily to service large numbers of male delinquents.

Key Terms

Birth cohort (68)
Career escalation (67)
Chronic offenders (37)
Chronic recidivists (69)
Curfew violator (37)
Decarceration (39)
Deinstitutionalization of status offenses (DSO) (39)
Dependent and neglected children (39)
Diversion programs (39)
Divestiture of jurisdiction (45)
Felony (45)
Incidence (45)
Index offenses (45)
Misdemeanor (45)
Monitoring the Future Survey (61)
National Juvenile Court Data Archive (54)
National Youth Survey (61)
Net-widening (40)
Part I and Part II offenses (45)
Relabeling (41)
Runaways (35)
Self-reports (60)
Station house adjustments (55)
Sourcebook of Criminal Justice Statistics (54)
Status offenses (35)
Truants (37)
Uniform Crime Reports (UCR) (43)
Victimization (51)

Questions for Review

1. How are juveniles generally defined in most jurisdictions? What seems to be the lowest age of majority for juvenile offenders in some states? Compare the federal definition of juveniles with the state conceptions you have identified.
2. What is delinquency? Is there a universally acceptable definition of delinquent conduct in the United States? What are several different interpretations of delinquent conduct among jurisdictions?
3. What are status offenders? Are status offenders also delinquents? Why or why not? What are some exceptions?

4. Are status offenders more likely to escalate to more serious offenses during their youthful years compared with delinquents? How do delinquents differ from status offenders relative to career escalation? What studies can you cite to support your views?
5. What is meant by DSO? What are some of the aims of DSO? Are these aims necessarily being realized in most jurisdictions today? Why or why not? Explain.
6. What is a chronic juvenile offender? Are most juvenile offenders chronic? Are most juvenile offenders violent? What

can be said about the nature of violent–nonviolent conduct exhibited by many juveniles arrested by police?

7. What is meant by divestiture of jurisdiction? What types of cases are usually targeted for divestiture? Why? How do judges and police in certain jurisdictions react to divestiture?

8. Is everyone in favor of DSO? Why do some experts believe that *parens patriae* should remain a dominant feature of juvenile courts? What events do you think triggered the juvenile justice reform toward greater DSO?

9. What are some of the positive and negative results of divestiture of jurisdiction? Specifically, how has divestiture affected rates of juvenile recidivism, net-widening, relabeling, and juvenile detention?

10. Describe the information generally presented about juveniles in the *Uniform Crime Reports* (UCR). What criticisms have been leveled at this information source? Are these criticisms valid? Why or why not? Explain.

11. Identify six of eight index offenses and define them. Are index offenses felonies or misdemeanors? Differentiate between felonies and misdemeanors.

12. What other sources exist to provide information about juvenile offending behavior? What information do these sources generally contain?

13. How do male and female juveniles differ in the types of offenses they generally commit?

14. What are self-reports? Are self-reports necessarily more valid than official sources of information about delinquency? Why or why not? Explain.

15. Describe the nature and extent of violent offense behaviors among juveniles.

16. What evidence exists that might suggest that females are treated differently than males by juvenile courts? What are some of the reasons traditionally given to explain the nature of female juvenile treatment? Are these reasons necessarily valid?

17. What differences seem to exist between male and female juvenile homicides?

Suggested Readings

ALBANESE, JAY S. (1985). *Dealing with Delinquency: An Investigation of Juvenile Justice.* Lanham, MD: University Press of America.

BAILEY, F. LEE, AND HENRY B. ROTHBLATT (1982). *Handling Juvenile Delinquency Cases.* Rochester, NY: Lawyer's Co-Operative Publishing Company.

BLACKMORE, JOHN, MARCI BROWN, AND BARRY KRISBERG (1988). *Juvenile Justice Reform: The Bellwether States.* Ann Arbor, MI: University of Michigan Press.

JANUS, MARK-DAVID, ET AL. (1987). *Adolescent Runaways: Causes and Consequences.* Lexington, MA: Lexington Books.

KRISBERG, BARRY (1988). *The Juvenile Court: Reclaiming the Vision.* San Francisco: National Council on Crime and Delinquency.

MILLER, FRANK W., ET AL. (1985). *The Juvenile Justice Process.* Mineola, NY: Foundation Press.

O'CONNOR, RODERICK, ET AL. (1984). *New Directions in Youth Services: Experiences with State-Level Coordination.* Washington, DC: U.S. Government Printing Office.

PALENSKI, JOSEPH E. (1984). *Kids Who Run Away.* Saratoga, CA: R & E Publishers.

ROSSUM, RALPH A., BENEDICT J. KOLLER, AND CHRISTOPHER MANFREDI (1987). *Juvenile Justice Reform: A Model for the States.* Claremont, CA: Rose Institute of State and Local Government and the American Legislative Exchange Council.

Some Theories of Delinquency

Introduction

Fifteen-year-old Deryl, an adopted child, had always been in trouble with the law, it seemed. When he was ten, he assaulted his adoptive stepmother with a kitchen knife. After receiving psychological counseling for several months, Deryl was declared "cured" by examining doctors. Two months later, he ran away from home. He lived for the next several weeks in farmers' barns in neighboring towns in southern Indiana, stealing food from kitchens and country stores, along with money, jewelry, and other items of value. Eventually apprehended, he was placed temporarily in a home for boys. Here, he received companionship from other boys, as well as guidance and assistance from those in charge of the facility. But because of juvenile overcrowding and the need to accommodate more serious youthful offenders, Deryl's experience was short-lived, and he was returned to the custody of his adoptive parents.

Six months later, he and a companion "rolled" a drunk in a back alley of the main street of their small community, stole an automobile, and drove to Chicago, where they bought food, gas, and entertainment with the stolen money and credit cards. Suspicious store clerks soon reported them to police, who apprehended them and returned them to Indiana authorities. When interviewed regarding Deryl and his unlawful behavior, a deputy sheriff who was familiar with his history told a reporter, "That Deryl . . . he's mean as a snake through and through . . . he's full of the devil . . . that's what makes him do all those terrible things, you know . . . you've gotta beat the devil out of him before he'll shape up. And even then I wouldn't trust him!"

For many interested professionals who study juvenile behavior generally and delinquency specifically, certain factors are believed to be important determinants of lawful as well as unlawful behavior. If these factors can be identified, isolated, and/or measured, we may eventually learn how to control them. This means that it may be possible to modify certain situational factors that influence juveniles to commit delinquent acts and other offenses. These behavioral modifications, manipulations, or controls exerted over factors believed to precipitate delinquent conduct may also indicate the means whereby such offending conduct or behaviors can be regulated or reduced, perhaps even eliminated.

This chapter will examine several popular *theories* of delinquent conduct. Ideally, **theories** *are integrated explanatory schemes that predict relationships between two or more phenomena. In the specific context of juvenile delinquency, they provide rational foundations to account for or explain juvenile behavior and help us to understand why juveniles are processed in different ways by the juvenile justice system.* Integral components of theories include **propositions** and **assumptions,** or different kinds of statements about the real world that vary in their tentativeness or uncertainty (Merton, 1957). Theories are also more or less plausible, meaning that some explanations for events are more plausible or believable than others. For example, the deputy sheriff in Deryl's case chose to use "the devil" as his explanation for Deryl's conduct. Criminal justice professionals, psychologists, criminologists, and other social scientists might prefer alternative, more easily testable explanations to account for the same behavior.

At the outset it is important to understand that *no single theory of delinquent conduct has been universally accepted by all criminologists or students of juvenile delinquency.* This is true, in part, because there are many different types of juvenile delinquency in need of explanation, and each theory is more or less effective at explaining certain types of delinquency when compared with other theories (Colvin and Pauly, 1983; Haas, 1988). Also, each theory has its own coterie of supporters as well as accompanying weaknesses and strengths when compared with other theories designed to explain or account for the same delinquent conduct. In fact, some of these theories contradict one another and compete for recognition and adoption.

If we become acquainted with the many different explanatory schemes that theorists have used over the years to account for delinquent behavior, we may acquire a better understanding of the different programs and treatment methods which have been devised by practitioners to modify delinquent conduct, reduce its incidence, or perhaps eliminate it (Mitchell and Williams,

1986). This is because different theories suggest specific strategies for coping with delinquents or promote certain solutions over others, and each delinquency prevention or intervention program is, in turn, influenced by these different proposed solutions (Baird *et al.*, 1986; Delorto and Cullen, 1985; Finckenauer and Kochis, 1984).

Changes within the juvenile justice system itself, particularly during the 1960s, 1970s, and 1980s, may also be explained or better understood by paying attention to theories that attempt to account for delinquent conduct or forecast its incidence. Although the precise association between delinquency theories and juvenile justice system reforms is unknown, available evidence suggests that juvenile justice is reactive and modifies, tailors, and adjusts itself according to recent research developments and findings (Dwyer and McNally, 1987).

Many delinquency intervention and prevention programs at local, state, and federal levels seem to have been established largely as the result of isolated research investigations that suggest causal, yet tenuous, relations between delinquency and assorted factors (e.g., alcohol and drug use, peer influence, achievement motivation and school success, family structure, personality and self-concept, work values, and institutional—primarily school and church—responsibilities) (Agnew, 1985a, 1985b; Arbuthnot *et al.*, 1987; Eskilson *et al.*, 1986; Greenwood, 1986c; Hawkins and Lishner, 1987; Sloane and Potvin, 1986; Windle and Barnes, 1988). Thus, emerging delinquency treatment and interventionist programs tend to reflect these factors and reinforce their importance by influencing and modifying juvenile justice policies at all levels, including offender handling and disposition at the time of detection, arrest, and initial processing, adjudicatory procedures by prosecutors and juvenile judges, and correctional alternatives.

This chapter consists of five parts. In the first four parts, we will examine in turn classical and biological theories, psychological theories, sociological theories, and extraneous factors as ways of explaining delinquent conduct from several perspectives or dimensions. A reading of this material will make it apparent that each theory does a better job of accounting for a particular kind of delinquent conduct than the other theories do. Also, some of these explanatory and predictive schemes are more popular than others, which means that they are more widely adopted by professionals and may significantly influence and enhance their research work. However, as we noted previously, it must be remembered that no theory of delinquent conduct has been accepted by all those who study delinquency. It must also be kept in mind that no theory yet devised can account for *all* types of delinquency. For instance, explanations for violence among juveniles may not apply with equal validity to property offenders and to the etiology of juvenile gangs, their emergence and persistence. A final section provides several criteria that may be used for evaluating the predictive and explanatory utility of each theory. While the presentation of delinquency theories in this chapter is not all-inclusive, it is nevertheless representative and will provide the reader with an ample array of explanations for juvenile delinquency.

Classical and Biological Theories

In this section, several classical and biological theories of criminality and delinquency will be examined. These include (1) *classical theory*, (2) *positivist theory or biological determinism*, (3) *sociobiology*, and (4) *the XYY theory*.

Classical Theories. While philosophers and others have speculated about the causes of crime for centuries, elaborate and widely recognized explanations for criminal conduct emerged primarily during the mid-1700s. These explanations are known as **classical theory.** Deeply rooted in Judeo-Christian principles, the **classical school** of criminology originated with a work by **Cesare Beccaria** (1738–1794), *On Crimes and Punishments* (1764). Later scholars who adopted perspectives about crime different from those of Beccaria labeled his views "classical," since they assumed the age-old conflict between good and evil as humanity's alternatives and provided a standard against which other views of crime could be evaluated.

The classical school assumes that people are rational beings who exercise free will in choosing between good actions and evil ones. At the other end of the continuum is **determinism,** the view that a specific factor, variable, or event determines one's actions or behaviors. Determinism rejects the notion of free will and free choice, relying instead on external factors that cause human beings to behave as they do. In the classical view, however, societal progress and perpetuation are paramount, and individuals, although they are free to choose their actions, must each sacrifice a degree of their freedom in order that all persons can pursue happiness and attain their goals. Evil actions are detrimental to societal progress and merit punishment. Because evil acts vary in their seriousness, the severity of punishments for those actions should be adjusted accordingly. Beccaria believed that punishment should be swift, certain, and "just," where the penalties are appropriately adjusted to fit particular offenses. The primary purposes of punishment are deterrence and "just deserts." Ideally, people will refrain from wrongdoing in order to avoid the pain of punishment. Further, whatever punishment is imposed is presumably equivalent in severity with the amount of social and physical damage originally inflicted by those found guilty of crimes. Fines and/or imprisonment respectively were acceptable penalties for those found guilty of property crimes or violent offenses.

It is fairly easy to trace the origins of different sentencing schemes in the United States today to Beccaria's classical thought. Most states have mandatory sentences for specific offenses, such as using a firearm during the commission of a felony. Also, most state statutes carry sentences of determinate lengths and/or fines that are roughly commensurate with the severity of the crime.

Less than two decades after Beccaria outlined his philosophy of crime and punishment, **Jeremy Bentham** (1748–1832), an English philosopher, advanced a similar scheme in his book *An Introduction to the Principles of Morals and Legislation* (1790). Bentham was known chiefly for his belief that **hedonism,** the pursuit of pleasure, was a primary motivator underlying social and personal action. To put it simply, humans seek to experience pleasure and avoid pain. In this pleasure–pain framework, Bentham formulated his views about the worth and intent of punishment. Like Beccaria, Bentham believed that punishment's objectives should be to deter crime and to impose sanctions sufficient to outweigh any pleasure criminals might derive from the crimes they commit. Therefore, many would-be offenders might desist from crime because the threat of punishment would more than offset the projected pleasure to be derived from criminal actions. In Bentham's scheme, persistent offenders would be subject to painful punishments adjusted according to the severity of their offenses.

Under the prevailing common law of that period, infants (juveniles) under the age of 7 were not ordinarily held accountable for their actions or subject to the same kinds of punishments prescribed for adults. However, older youths eventually were vested with responsibility for their own actions and were subject to punishments similar to those for adults. One contemporary view of juvenile delinquents is that *juveniles must accept responsibility for their actions. If they choose to ignore societal values and persist in violating the law, they must be held accountable for these offenses and punished accordingly.*

In reality, the classical school of criminology is not so much an explanation of why crime or delinquency exists as it is a statement about how various offenses should be punished in order to frustrate criminal conduct. However, some elements of explanation are contained in classical thought. Bentham, for instance, would probably speculate that persistent criminal offenders are gamblers, in a sense, since they regard the calculated risk of being caught and punished for crimes as secondary to the pleasurable benefits derived from committing crimes. The pleasure of crime outweighs the pain of punishment. Beccaria might argue that criminals are comprised of those who have failed to internalize societal values or respect for the common good.

This perspective has received attention from contemporary theorists such as Kohlberg (1981), who constructed a theory of moral development to account for both deviant and conforming behaviors. This theory is properly classified in a social learning context, and it will be discussed briefly in the section on psychological theories presented later. Although Kohlberg's theory of moral development has been both supported and rejected by adherents and critics, some experts believe that his views may have intuitive value in furnishing insight into more aberrant modes of criminality (Delorto and Cullen, 1985). Further, the theory may improve our understanding of a wide range of delinquent acts if integrated into a perspective that is sensitive to the ways in which varying social contexts shape individual inclinations (Delorto and Cullen, 1985).

Biological Theories. The notion of determinism mentioned earlier is strongly evident in biological theories of criminal and delinquent behavior. Generally, these theories seek to attribute criminal, delinquent, and deviant conduct to biological, biochemical, or genetic bases in a direct, causal relation. Juvenile delinquency is a selective phenomenon, according to this view, in that it does not occur spontaneously. In a sense, delinquents are those youths destined to be delinquent for reasons beyond their own control—the presence of certain internal factors—while nondelinquents are destined to be nondelinquent because of the presence of other internal factors. The idea that there are known predisposing factors that operate to prompt or elicit delinquent behavior conveniently shifts the responsibility for delinquent conduct from youths themselves to some internal or external source.

Although the attribution of criminality and delinquency to biological causes dates to prebiblical times, such determinism—called **biological determinism**—was given a degree of academic dignity in the work of an Italian physician and criminologist, **Cesare Lombroso** (1835–1909), during the 1860s. Considered by many professionals to be the father of criminology, Lombroso was profoundly influenced by Charles Darwin (1809–1882). Darwin's major work, *The Origin of Species,* was both revolutionary and evolutionary, arguing in part that human beings evolved from lower animal forms over many thousands of years. Natural selection and survival of the fittest were integral principles of Darwin's evolutionary theory. Lombroso was intrigued by these principles and applied them in his explanation of criminal conduct.

For Lombroso, criminals were products of heredity. Successive generations of human beings inherited from their ancestors not only physical features but also behavioral predispositions, such as propensities toward criminal conduct or antisocial activity. Since heredity is more or less binding on future generations, it made sense to Lombroso and many of his disciples that certain physical characteristics would also be inexorably related to criminal behavior. Therefore, physical appearance could help predict whether certain persons would be predisposed to criminality or other types of deviant behavior. This led Lombroso to conjecture extensively about criminal "types" and "born criminals." Height, weight, hair and eye color, physiognomic features such as jaw size, earlobe shape, finger length, and hand size, and assorted other anatomical characteristics were painstakingly measured and charted by Lombroso. Samples of both willing and unwilling volunteers were obtained for his analyses, including populations of Italian prisoners and soldiers. Eventually, Lombroso concluded that many of the physiological characteristics shared by criminals were indicative of stunted evolutionary growth. Indeed, Lombroso considered criminals to be throwbacks to earlier evolutionary stages. This view of criminals is **atavistic,** strongly suggestive of subhuman qualities.

Lombroso's views were known popularly as **positivism,** and became the basis for the **positivist school of criminology.** This school rejected the "free will" and choice doctrines espoused by Beccaria and other classical theorists. Rather, criminal conduct was attributed to biochemical and genetic factors peculiar to criminal types. Lombroso made refinements to his theory by concluding that certain physical features (e.g., sloping foreheads, compressed jaws, large earlobes, long, slender fingers, excessive facial and body hair) would tend to indicate the *type* of criminal behavior expected from those observed. Although Lombroso limited his theoretical and empirical work to

BOX 3.1

Juvenile Highlights

Can delinquents be identified strictly on the basis of their appearance? One of the most influential criminologists was Cesare Lombroso (1835–1909), an Italian physician. Because of his interest in criminal behavior and his background as a physician, he sought to define criminal behavior according to observable criteria, such as cranial structure and amount of body hair. In his early writings, he believed that persons were born to be either criminals or conformists. Thus, delinquents would be early biological versions of criminal adults.

Lombroso studied hundreds of Italian prison inmates. He observed that many had long, sloping foreheads, pointed ears, narrow or shifty eyes, receding chins, and overly long arms. He concluded that these physical features were somehow related to adult criminality. Possessing odd physical features could expose these persons to social rejection as children. Physical deformities or peculiar biological attributes might create social conditions that would give rise to delinquent conduct, and eventually, to criminal conduct. Labeling theorists have grasped the significance of the connection between social labeling and offending behaviors. Lombroso's notions about physique and criminal behavior have been discounted and replaced by more productive explanations, although these notions still have some currency among journalists and others who write about juvenile offenders. Often, journalists describe the physical features of juvenile murderers, inadvertently linking these features somehow with the offenses committed. Aside from the impact of social labeling, however, little if any connection exists between delinquent conduct and physique.

adult criminals, his strong focus on the heredity factor could easily be extended to juveniles.

In later years, Lombroso changed his opinion about the key role played by genetics in promoting criminal behavior. His beliefs changed, in part, as the result of extensive scientific studies of both juveniles and adults that disclosed little relation between physiological features and criminal behavior (Ferri, 1901; Goring, 1913). Also, the growth of other social sciences such as sociology and psychology led him to assign a more prominent role to social milieu as a determinant of criminal or delinquent conduct.

Despite the fact that specific biological features or characteristics could not be positively connected with specific types of criminal conduct, certain professionals in the early 1900s continued to regard biological determinism as a plausible explanation for criminality and delinquency. During the 1930s,

Hooton (1939) and Kretschmer (1936) established physical typologies of criminals that were given some credence in the academic community. In the 1940s, William H. Sheldon (1949) provided what later became a popular description of genetic types that supposedly manifested certain kinds of criminal characteristics. Sheldon defined three major categories of body types: **mesomorphs,** or strong, athletic individuals; **ectomorphs,** or thin, submissive people; and **endomorphs,** or fat persons. He assigned point evaluations to each person observed and attempted to describe behaviors most typical of them. Mesomorphs were believed to typify those who manifested criminal or delinquent behaviors. Unfortunately, little consistency existed in his descriptions of those sharing these bodily characteristics. Particularly disturbing was the fact that many nondelinquents and noncriminals were classified as mesomorphs. His work was soundly criticized by other professionals, who concluded that no relation between body type and criminality could be established positively (Sutherland, 1951).

Despite such criticism of Sheldon's scheme, some researchers continue to investigate the relationship between biology and criminal propensities and regard such a connection as plausible. For instance, research conducted by Sheldon Glueck and Eleanor Glueck in 1950 targeted 1,000 white male youths, 500 of whom were delinquent and 500 of whom were nondelinquent (Glueck and Glueck, 1950). Mesomorphic characteristics similar to those described by Sheldon were found among 60 percent of the delinquents studied, while only 30 percent of the nondelinquents shared these characteristics. While the Gluecks interpreted their findings conservatively and never said that delinquency is caused by mesomorphic characteristics, they nevertheless described delinquents generally as more agitated and aggressive than nondelinquents. More than four decades later, we can look back at the Gluecks' study and argue, particularly in view of the rise in the incidence of juvenile gangs in many of the nation's larger cities, that more muscular youths are probably more likely to be gang members than less muscular youths. Further, the fact that the Gluecks confined their analysis to white male juveniles means that they excluded from consideration several ethnic groups that have become increasingly conspicuous in American society and are associated with certain forms of delinquency. Additionally, the Gluecks have been criticized on both methodological and statistical grounds (Laub, 1987).

Sociobiology. In recent years, several criminologists have reaffirmed the significance of the biological contribution to criminality and delinquency (Jeffrey, 1979; Rowe and Osgood, 1984; Wilson and Herrnstein, 1985). Genetic researchers and biologists have evolved the discipline of **sociobiology,** or the study of the biological basis for social action (Wilson, 1975:16). While this new field is not necessarily biological determinism or positivism revisited, it nevertheless directs our attention toward the role of genetics in human behavior. At present, it is generally believed that a connection exists between genetics and behavior, but we are unable to elaborate this connection (Arbuthnot *et al.,* 1987; Trasler, 1987).

The XYY Theory. Closely associated in principle with the sociobiological explanation of criminality and delinquency is the **XYY theory.** This theory asserts that certain chromosomatic abnormalities may precipitate violence and/or criminal conduct. X chromosomes designate female characteristics and are regarded as passive, while Y chromosomes designate male characteristics and are regarded as aggressive. Normally, an XX chromosomatic combination produces a female, whereas an XY chromosomatic combination yields a male. Sometimes, an extra Y chromosome insinuates itself into the XY formula to produce an ''XYY'' type. The input from this additional ''aggressive'' chromosome is believed responsible, at least in some instances, for criminal behavior among those observed to possess it (Witkin, 1976). This chromosomatic combination exists in less than 5 percent of the population, however, and thus it lacks sufficient predictive utility when considered on its own merits (Witkin, 1976).

In addition to the identification of specific body types, physical features, and genetic patterns as crucial manifestations or causes of delinquency and criminal behavior, other biological and physical causes have been advanced in previous years. Feeblemindedness, mental illness, low intelligence, physical deformities including assorted stigmata, and glandular malfunction or imbalance have been variously described as concomitants of delinquency and criminality (Barnum, 1987; Gordon, 1986; Hirschi and Hindelang, 1977; Walsh *et al.*, 1987). Walsh (1987), for instance, studied 256 delinquents in Toledo, Ohio, and Boise, Idaho. He examined their I.Q. levels and the types of offenses they committed. Although he found that those delinquents with higher I.Q. levels tended not to engage in violent acts, he also found that those with lower I.Q. levels committed an inordinate amount of property crime—crime most likely to offer instant gratification to offenders. He argued accordingly that low I.Q. apparently predisposed delinquents to impulsive and spontaneous property crimes, while higher I.Q. disposed youths to commit crimes that required planning and offered deferred gratification. At present, however, most professionals are not prepared to acknowledge I.Q. as a valid indicator of delinquent propensities.

Other Biologically Related Explanations. Much research exists regarding the relationship of criminal and delinquent behavior to physical deformities and glandular malfunctions. While the idea that glandular malfunctions and physical defects are somehow causally related to various forms of deviant behavior is interesting, no consistent groundwork has been provided that empirically supports any of these notions. Regarding stigmata, for instance, Erving Goffman (1963) has observed that often, unusual behaviors are elicited from those possessing stigmata in reaction to others who regard such stigmata with repulsion. Thus, those with **stigmas** of one type or another, such as facial disfigurement, react to the reactions of others toward them, sometimes behaving as they believe others expect them to behave. It is not the stigma that causes deviant behavior, but rather, the reactions of stigmatized persons who respond to the reactions of others. No scientific continuity has been conclusively established between stigmata and criminality.

An integral feature of many community-based juvenile correctional programs is counseling designed to help juveniles acquire more positive self-concepts and self-assurance. Sometimes, disfigurements or physical inadequacies cause some of these youths to feel rejected by others or left out of group activities. Wilderness experiences and outdoors survival courses, discussed in Chapter 13, are designed, in part, to bolster confidence in the ability to set goals and accomplish them. If youths can cope with "roughing it" in the wilderness, by learning camping, cooking, and other pioneer crafts, they may come to believe that other problems can be overcome as well. While it is impossible to tell with certainty whether biological explanations of delinquent conduct have contributed to the establishment of such programs, it is clear that many individual and group activities involving youthful offenders are geared toward developing coping skills. And often, coping with one's own physical and/or psychological inadequacies is an essential part of growing out of the delinquent mode of conduct.

Psychological Theories

Theories that attribute criminal and delinquent behavior to personality maladjustment or to some unusual cognitive condition are categorically known as **psychological theories.** These theories focus upon the learning process—the process whereby humans acquire language, self-definitions, definitions of others, and assorted norms of behavior. Because the precise mechanisms involved in the learning process are elusive and cannot be inspected or investigated directly, psychological theories are inherently subjective, and their relative merits can be debated endlessly. In this section, two psychological explanations for delinquent conduct will be examined: (1) *psychoanalytic theory* and (2) *social learning theory.*

Psychoanalytic Theory. Some of the early pioneers of psychological theories of human behavior were Sigmund Freud, Karen Horney, and Carl Jung. These theorists conjectured about personality systems, how they are formed, and how personality and behavior are intertwined. Historically the most influential psychologist was Sigmund Freud (1856–1939). Freud was one of the few early theorists who presented a systematic scheme to explain personality emergence and development. Freud's investigations and writings eventually became widely known as **psychoanalytic theory.**

At the core of psychoanalytic theory, according to Freud, are three major personality components, known as the **id,** the **ego,** and the **superego.** The id is the uncontrolled "I want" component predominant in all newborn infants. The desire of the id is for immediate gratification. Thus, infants typically exhibit little or no concern for others as they seek to acquire things they like or desire. As infants mature to young children, the id is suppressed to a degree by the ego, the part of the personality that mediates interaction between the self and the outer world. One component of the ego is a recognition of others and a respect for their rights and interests. Eventually, a

BOX 3.2

Juvenile Highlights

Did you know that the arrest rate for male children aged 12 and under charged with rape increased 80 percent in the United States between 1976 and 1986? The rate of rape charges against 13- and 14-year-olds doubled in the United States during the same time period. Are these children mentally ill or are they fulfilling some biological predisposition toward sexual violence?

Many youth workers today blame easy access to illegal drugs for many of the ills that befall today's juvenile offenders. In 1983, for instance, the Washington State Division of Juvenile Rehabilitation appointed a task force to investigate substance abuse among youths in Washington detention facilities. It was found that over 80 percent of the incarcerated youthful offenders were drug-dependent or addicted to alcohol. However, underlying these addictions were assorted types of psychological problems and social maladjustments that seemed related in a causal fashion to the offenses committed.

Despite the fact that nearly half of those diagnosed by Washington authorities as having serious drug/alcohol dependencies denied such dependencies, it is believed that massive treatment programs should be implemented to assist these youths. In some jurisdictions, such as the State of Washington, peer-oriented treatment programs are perceived as the most effective and efficient method for breaking through client denial and beginning the recovery process. Yet the present trend in juvenile justice is to demand greater offender accountability and to de-emphasize treatment programs. Whether we are dealing with juvenile sex offenders or with drug/alcohol dependent youths, strategic treatments may be the best alternatives, despite the widespread reduction in their use in recent years.

(Some factual information adapted from David C. Brenna, "Substance Abuse among Juveniles: What Corrections Can Do," *Corrections Today* (1988) 50:208–211; and Hunter Hurst, "Turn of the Century: Rediscovering the Value of Juvenile Treatment," *Corrections Today* (1990) 52:48–50.)

---

higher stage of moral development is reached through the development of the superego, or conscience. When children begin to feel guilty when they have deprived others of something wrongfully, this is a manifestation of the superego in action, according to Freud. Another element in the personality is the **libido,** a basic drive for sexual stimulation and gratification which assumes great importance at the onset of puberty. The ego and superego function to keep the libido in check.

Deviant behavior in general, and criminal behavior and delinquency specifically, can be explained in psychoanalytic theory as the result of insufficient ego and superego development; in this personality pattern, the id dominates and seeks activities that will fulfill the urges or needs it stimulates. Parent–child relations are seen as primary in the normal development of the ego and superego. Therefore, if some children lack control over their impulses and desires, the blame is placed at the parents' feet for their failure to inculcate these important inhibitors into the youth's personality system.

Psychoanalytic theory stresses early childhood experiences as crucial in normal adult functioning. Traumatic experiences may prevent proper ego or superego development. Adults may develop neuroses or psychoses that may be traceable to bizarre childhood events. In a movie based on an actual case, *The Three Faces of Eve,* Joanne Woodward portrayed a housewife with multiple personalities. A psychiatrist portrayed by Lee J. Cobb sought to "psychoanalyze" the woman to discover which early childhood events may have been responsible for her current mental condition. Under hypnosis, the woman disclosed that when she was a young child attending a wake, or funeral, in a relative's home, she was forced by her parents to kiss the face of her aunt who had recently died and was lying in a coffin. Her revulsion and shock were sufficient to cause her to suppress this event deep within her subconscious mind. Certain coping mechanisms were triggered that apparently led to the formation of multiple personality systems.

While the case of "Eve" in the movie was to some extent related to adult deviant behavior and relied heavily on a psychoanalytic explanation, it did not deal directly with delinquency. However, psychoanalytic theory has been used either implicitly or explicitly in subsequent studies of juvenile sex offenders and others who commit crimes such as arson. A study of juvenile rapists, for instance, disclosed that compared with a matched sample of juvenile nonrapists, rapists tended to exhibit higher rates of social isolation, physical problems, and problems with sexual identification (Corder et al., 1986). In fact, it was concluded that it may be useful to view juvenile rape as a violent, impulsive act committed by youths with a low level of ego integration (Corder et al., 1986). Also, in a study of arson committed by juveniles, it was indicated that childhood firestarting behavior is a relatively common but serious psychiatric problem (Heath et al., 1988). Firestarting emerges from a confluence of factors, including learning contingencies that shape and mold normal childhood interest in fire, family and historical events that can lead to a conduct-disorder problem, and triggering factors that lead to specific instances of firestarting (Heath et al., 1988).

Many treatment programs have been established that operate to improve a youth's cognitive development. In Albany, New York, for example, the Juvenile Sex Offender Project (JSOP) was established by the St. Anne Institute to serve the needs of juvenile sex offenders ages 10 to 19 (Lombardo and DiGiorgio-Miller, 1988). Interestingly, each candidate for treatment is selected only after a detailed assessment procedure that examines psychosocial development, family processes, and past involvement with legal systems. Empathy for victims, an ego-related function, is stressed in the JSOP

(Lombardo and DiGiorgio-Miller, 1988). The psychoanalytic approach apparently continues to be widely used in treatment programs for errant adolescents. However, indications are that psychoanalytic theory is increasingly used in combination with other approaches that encourage systemic family therapy (Breunlin *et al.*, 1988).

Social Learning Theory. **Social learning theory** is somewhat different from psychoanalytic theory. It takes the view that traumatic early childhood experiences may be important determinants of subsequent adult personality characteristics, but the primary factors influencing whether one conforms to or deviates from societal rules are early experiences one has while interacting with others, such as parents and siblings. Adults in any institutional context (e.g., schools, churches, and homes) provide role models for children to follow. Homes that are beset with violence and conflict between spouses are poor training grounds for children. Children often learn to cope with their problems in ways that are labeled antisocial or hostile. The punishments parents impose on children for disobedience are seen as acceptable behaviors that children can direct toward their own peers.

Social learning theory implies that children learn to do what they see significant others do. Bandura (Bandura and Walters, 1959) has emphasized the importance of poor parental role models as a probable cause of poor adolescent adjustment and delinquent behavior. Also stressing the importance of the family in the early social development of children is Carlson (1986). Carlson believes that children who use violence to resolve disputes with other children probably have learned such behaviors in homes where violence is exhibited regularly by parents. Other experts also seem to share this view (LeFlore, 1988; Pope, 1988; Samenow, 1989; Stouthamer-Loeber and Loeber, 1988).

If delinquency is fostered through social learning, then it would seem that certain social learning intervention models might be useful for helping youths to learn different, more acceptable behaviors. In fact, provided that youths who exhibit learning or developmental disabilities in school can be identified accurately, teachers may modify their classroom curricula in ways that increase opportunities, skills, and rewards for these children (Hawkins and Lam, 1987). This view has received support from researchers in other parts of the world, including Canada (Stutt, 1986).

Several researchers have examined the relationship between **learning-disabled** children and delinquency (Fishbein and Thatcher, 1986). Learning-disabled children suffer a double disadvantage, in a sense, since their learning disabilities have probably contributed to poor school performance and poor social adjustment. Such learning disabilities may impair their judgment regarding peer associations, and they may have encounters with the law more frequently than other children. When they are evaluated at intake or later in juvenile court, their school records are "evidence" against them. Some persons may erroneously conclude that learning disabilities produce delinquent conduct, when, in fact, other factors are at work. Teachers may become impatient with learning-disabled children, particularly if their conditions have not been diagnosed in advance. A lack of rewards from teachers may have deep emotional impact for some learning-disabled children, thus creating a vicious cycle of failure for them.

More fruitful explanations of delinquent conduct have incorporated elements from several different theoretical schemes. For example, a 20-year longitudinal study of delinquency spanning the years 1954–1974 examined the predictive utility of both biological and psychosocial factors in early and middle childhood (Werner, 1987). A sample of 698 children was examined. Pediatricians and psychologists conducted extensive observations and applied batteries of aptitude tests. It was eventually determined that a child's low standard of living tended to increase the likelihood that he or she would be exposed to both biological and psychological risk factors. But it was only the joint effect of these factors, together with early familial instability, that precipitated serious delinquent patterns. Mother–child relations were generally more important in the early childhood years, while father-child relations became more important in the middle childhood years. Prominent in this research was the sociological dimension.

These psychological theories stress early moral and cognitive development as influential in relation to later behavior. Many delinquency prevention programs have been designed as interventions in the early years. Therefore, it is not surprising to see attempts by public agencies and professionals to intervene through early training or educational programs in schools. The California Office of Criminal Justice Planning, for example, designed a curriculum for children in grades K–4 to teach them how to reduce their vulnerability to certain crimes. They were taught about personal safety, how to recognize child abuse situations, how to protect personal property from others, and certain types of responsible behaviors, including respecting the rights of others (California Office of Criminal Justice Planning, 1984).

Davidson (1987) describes the thrusts of other delinquency prevention programs aimed at young schoolchildren. One such program is Elan One, a Maine program that emphasizes certain key elements, such as acquiring feelings of interpersonal competence, understanding the impact of peer pressure, learning respect for authority, and receiving cognitive therapy to reinforce one's values and suggest future behavioral options. This particular program stresses individual learning. Other programs, such as the Ounce of Prevention program in Illinois, attempt to involve the entire family in school-based interventions that help youths and their families learn more effective social skills (Zigler and Hall, 1987). Such familial support in the early years serves to reinforce values believed important by program planners.

Finally, the Perry Preschool project in Ypsilanti, Michigan was an attempt to identify certain children who exhibited a strong likelihood of dropping out of school (Berreuta-Clement *et al.*, 1987). These **children at risk** were targeted in their preschool years and placed in special education classes. Their special training was supplemented by weekly home visits. Compared with a birth cohort of youths not receiving such training, but also identified as high risks for failure, the experimental group of Perry Preschoolers experienced less than half the rate of arrests. Further, more of these youths stayed in school longer and tended to graduate, with some even obtaining graduate degrees. For some interventionists, then, exposure to special kinds of training in one's formative years does much to promote more socially and psychologically healthy school and home environments. The impact of psychological theories here is quite apparent.

Sociological Theories

It is worth noting that the theories advanced thus far have related deviant, criminal, and/or delinquent behaviors to factors almost exclusively within individuals. These notions have been described elsewhere as "inside" notions (e.g., the positivist view, glandular malfunction, XYY theory, sociobiology, low I.Q.) primarily because they identify internal factors as causally important for explaining deviation of any kind (Champion, 1990b). Although these "inside" notions have continued over the years to provide plausible explanations for why criminals and delinquents commit their offenses, rival explanations have been advanced that seek to shift certain causes of deviant conduct to factors "outside" of, or external to, the individual. Sociologists have encouraged strong consideration of social factors as the principal variables that may account for the emergence and persistence of delinquent conduct.

While a certain amount of ideological rivalry may exist among those favoring sociological, psychological, and biological variables as primary causes of delinquency, it is perhaps more realistic and profitable to regard these perspectives as mutually overlapping rather than as mutually exclusive. Thus, we might view social learning theory as predominantly a psychological theory with certain sociological elements. The biological factor may figure significantly in the delinquency equation, particularly when considering the matter of developmental disabilities of a physical nature in the social learning process. In any case, a pragmatic view will be adopted here, and we will regard any explanation as useful provided it is accompanied by a degree of predictive utility.

The Concentric Zone Hypothesis and Delinquency. During the early 1900s, large cities such as Chicago were undergoing rapid expansion as a result of the great influx of laborers from farms and rural regions to city centers to find work. Urbanization moved from the center of cities outward, and such expansion caused some of the older neighborhoods within the inner city to undergo dramatic transition. Sociologists at the University of Chicago and elsewhere studied the urban development of Chicago during the 1920s. Social scientists Ernest W. Burgess and Robert E. Park defined a series of concentric zones around Chicago, commencing with the core or "Loop" in downtown Chicago, and progressing outward away from the city center in a series of concentric rings. The ring or zone immediately adjacent to the central core was labeled by Burgess and Park as the "interstitial area" or "zone of transition." This was the immediate periphery of downtown Chicago and was characterized by slums and urban renewal projects. This area was also typified by high delinquency and crime. These researchers believed that other cities might exhibit similar growth patterns and concentric zones similar to those identified in the Chicago area. Thus, the **concentric zone hypothesis** of urban growth originated, accompanied by descriptions of different social and demographic characteristics of those inhabiting each zone.

Concurrent with Burgess's and Park's efforts was an investigation of delinquency patterns in Chicago conducted by Clifford Shaw and Henry McKay (1972). These researchers studied the characteristics of delinquent youths in the zone of transition and compared the backgrounds of these youths with other youths inhabiting more stable neighborhoods in the zones further removed from the inner core of downtown Chicago. They based their subsequent findings and explanations of probable causes of delinquency on the records of nearly 25,000 delinquent youths in Cook County, Illinois, between 1900 and the early 1930s. Essentially, Shaw and McKay found that over the 30-year period, delinquency within the interstitial zone was widespread and tended to grow in a fashion concomitant with the growth of slums and deteriorating neighborhoods. For many of these youths, both of their parents worked in factories for long hours. Large numbers of juveniles roamed these Chicago streets with little or no adult supervision. Family stability was lacking, and many youths turned to gang activities as a means of surviving, gaining recognition and status, and achieving certain material goals.

Compared with other zones, zones in transition were typically over-crowded, inhabited mainly by families of lower socioeconomic status. No zones were completely free of delinquency, but in other zones, families were more affluent and stable, and accordingly, the level of delinquency was lower than in interstitial areas. Shaw and McKay explained delinquency in these transitional areas as probably attributable to a breakdown in family unity and to pervasive social disorganization. Interstitial areas lacked recreational facilities, and schools and churches were rundown. As a result, youths played in the streets, with little or nothing to do to occupy their time other than to form gangs and commit delinquent acts. Because many of the same gangs that were formed at the turn of the century were still in existence in the early 1930s, Shaw and McKay believed that gang members perpetuated gang traditions and gang culture over time through **cultural transmission.**

One immediate effect of Shaw's and McKay's work was to divert students of delinquency away from biological explanations such as genetics and physical abnormalities (M. Gold, 1987). The long-range influence of the pioneering work of Shaw and McKay is evident in contemporary studies seeking to link neighborhood characteristics with delinquent conduct (Gardner, 1983; Heitgerd and Bursik, 1987; Simcha-Fagan and Schwartz, 1986). Generally, these studies have been supportive of Shaw's and McKay's work, although other factors closely associated with those residing in slum areas have also been causally linked with delinquency. One of these factors is socioeconomic status (SES).

Studies investigating the relationship between SES and delinquency have generally found more frequent and more violent types of juvenile misconduct among youths of lower SESs (Wolfgang and Ferracuti, 1967), whereas less frequent and less violent misconduct has been exhibited by youths from families in the upper SESs (Durham, 1988; LeFlore, 1988; Tolan, 1988a and 1988b; Tygart, 1988). Some of this research also suggests that juveniles who are identified with lower SESs seem likely to do less well in school than juveniles from higher SESs.

We might conjecture that students from families of lower SESs may reflect different values and achievement orientations than youths from families of higher SESs. This factor may figure significantly in the rate of juveniles' school successes or failures. School dropouts or underachievers may, in fact, turn toward other underachievers or dropouts for companionship, recognition, and prestige. Thus, a complex and vicious cycle is put into motion, with certain conditions and characteristics of lower SES leading to poor academic performance, growing antisocial behavior, and subsequent delinquent conduct. However, describing these conditions does not necessarily pinpoint the true causes of delinquent conduct in any predictive sense. After all, many lower SES youths adjust well to their academic work and refrain from delinquent activities. Conversely, many seemingly well-adjusted and academically successful youths from higher SESs may engage in certain forms of delinquent conduct.

The Subculture Theory of Delinquency. During the 1950s, sociologist Albert Cohen (1955) focused upon and described **subcultures of delinquency.** Delinquent subcultures exist, according to Cohen, within the greater societal culture. But these subcultures contain value systems and modes of achievement and gaining status and recognition that set them apart from the mainstream culture. Thus, if we are to understand why many juveniles behave as they do, we must pay attention to the patterns of their particular subculture.

The notion of a delinquent subculture is fairly easy to understand, especially in view of the earlier work of Shaw and McKay. Whereas middle- and upper-class children have lofty aspirations and educational goals and receive support for these aspirations from their parents and their predominantly middle-class teachers, lower-class youths are at a distinct disadvantage at the outset. They are born into families in which these aspirations and attainments may be alien and may in fact be rejected. Their primary familial role models have not attained these high aims themselves. At school, these youths are often isolated socially from upper- and middle-class juveniles, and therefore, social attachments are formed with others similar to themselves. Perhaps these youths dress differently from other students, wear their hair in a certain style, or use coded language when talking to peers in front of other students. They acquire a culture unto themselves, one that is largely unknown to other students. In a sense, much of this cultural isolation is self-imposed. But it functions to give them a sense of fulfillment, of reward, of self-esteem and recognition apart from other reward systems. If these students cannot achieve one or more of the various standards set by middle-class society, then they can create their own standards and prescribe the means to achieve those standards.

Cohen is quick to point out that delinquency is not a product of lower SES per se. Rather, children from lower SESs are at greater risk than others of being susceptible to the rewards and opportunities that a subculture of delinquency might offer in contrast with the middle-class reward structure of the dominant culture. Several experiments have subsequently been implemented with delinquents, in which these subcultures have been targeted and described, and in which the norms of these subcultures have been used as intervening mechanisms to modify delinquent behaviors toward nondelinquent modes of action. The Provo Experiment was influenced, to a degree, by the work of Cohen (Empey and Rabow, 1961). Samples of delinquent youths in Provo, Utah, were identified in the late 1950s and given an opportunity to participate in group therapy sessions at Pine Hills, a large home in Provo that had been converted to an experimental laboratory.

In cooperation with juvenile court judges and other authorities, Pine Hills investigators began their intervention strategies assuming that juvenile participants (1) had limited access to success goals, (2) performed many of their delinquent acts in groups rather than alone, and (3) committed their delinquent acts for nonutilitarian objectives rather than for money (Empey and Rabow, 1961). These investigators believed that since the delinquents had acquired their delinquent values and conduct through their subculture of delinquency, they could "unlearn" these values and learn new values by the same means. Thus, groups of delinquents participated extensively in therapy directed at changing their behaviors through group processes. The investigators believed that their intervention efforts were largely successful and that the subcultural approach to delinquency prevention and behavioral change was fruitful.

An interesting variation on the subcultural theme is the work of Wolfgang and Ferracuti (1967). It will be recalled that Wolfgang and other associates investigated large numbers of Philadelphia boys in a study of birth cohorts. In that study, he found that approximately 6 percent of all boys accounted for over 50 percent of all delinquent conduct from the entire cohort of over 9,000 boys (Wolfgang et al., 1972). These were chronic recidivists who were also violent offenders. Wolfgang has theorized that in many communities, there are subcultural norms of violence that attract youthful males. These males regard violence as a normal part of their environment, use violence, and respect the use of violence by others. On the basis of evidence amassed by Wolfgang and Ferracuti, it appeared that predominantly lower-class and less educated males formed a disproportionately large part of this subculture of violence. Where violence is accepted and respected, its use is considered normal and normative for the users. Remorse is an alien emotion to those who use violence and live with it constantly. Thus, it is socially ingrained as a subcultural value.

This theme would suggest that violence and aggression are learned through socialization with others. However, Ellis (1985) has questioned this generalization. He has conducted extensive investigations of apes and other animals, and his reports show that aggressive and violent behaviors are exhibited by these animals despite the fact that they do not experience the same type of socialization human beings do. However, animal studies, though important because of their intuitive value, are often criticized because of the completely different sets of assumptions that are applied to studies of animals and human beings.

The subcultural perspective toward delinquent conduct is indicative of a "strain" between the values of society and the values of a subgroup of delinquent youths. Therefore, some researchers have labeled the subcultural perspective a **strain theory.** Although many lower SES youths have adopted middle-class goals and aspirations, they may be unable to attain these goals because of their individual economic and cultural circumstances. This is a frustrating experience for many of these youths, and such frustration is manifested by the strain to achieve difficult goals or objectives. Although middle-class youths also experience strain in their attempts to achieve middle-class goals, it is particularly discouraging for many lower-class youths, since they sometimes do not receive the necessary support from their families. Another strain theory is Robert Merton's notion of **anomie.**

The Anomie Theory of Delinquency. Anomie is a term that was used by the early French social scientist Émile Durkheim. Durkheim investigated many social and psychological phenomena, including suicide and its causes. One precipitating factor leading to certain suicides, according to Durkheim, was anomie, or normlessness. What Durkheim intended to portray by the term was a condition wherein people's lives, their values, and various social rules were disrupted and they found it difficult to cope with their changed life conditions. Thus, they would experience anomie, a type of helplessness, perhaps hopelessness. Most persons are able to adapt to drastic changes in their lifestyles or patterns, but a few may opt for suicide since they lack the social and psychological means to cope with the strain of change.

Merton (1957) was intrigued by Durkheim's notion of anomie and how persons adapt to the strain of changing conditions. He devised a goals/means scheme as a way of describing different social actions that persons might use for making behavioral choices. Merton contended that a society generally prescribes certain approved cultural goals for its members to seek (e.g., new homes, jobs, automobiles). Furthermore, appropriate, legitimate or institutionalized means are prescribed for attaining these goals. But not everyone is equally endowed with the desire to achieve societal goals, nor is everyone necessarily committed to using the prescribed means to achieve these goals. Merton described five different **modes of adaptation** that people might exhibit. These modes included **conformity** (persons accept the goals of society and work toward their attainment using societally approved means),

innovation (persons accept the goals of society but use means to achieve goals other than those approved by society), **ritualism** (persons reject goals but work toward less lofty goals by institutionally approved means), *retreatism* (persons reject goals and reject the means to achieve goals—e.g., hermits, street people, and "bag ladies" typify those who retreat or escape from mainstream society and establish their own goals and the means to achieve them), and *rebellion* (persons seek to replace culturally approved goals and institutionalized means with new goals and means for others to follow).

Of these, the innovation mode characterizes juvenile delinquents, according to Merton. Juvenile delinquency is innovative in that youths accept culturally desirable goals, but reject the legitimate means to achieve those goals. Instead, they adopt illegitimate means such as theft, burglary, and violence. Many youths may crave new clothes, automobiles, and other expensive material items. Since they may lack the money to pay for these items, one alternative is to steal them. This is regarded by Merton as one innovative response arising from a condition of anomie and the strain it emits.

Many intermediate punishment programs today are designed to assist youths in devising new strategies to cope with everyday life rather than using crime or delinquent conduct to achieve their goals (McCarthy and McCarthy, 1984). VisionQuest, Homeward Bound, and various types of wilderness experiences incorporate adaptive experiences as integral features of these programs (Greenwood and Turner, 1987). Those youths with substantial energy are sometimes placed in camps or on ranches where they can act out some of their feelings and frustrations. These programs deliberately cater to youths who are innovative, but who lack a clear sense of direction. Some of these programs will be featured in Chapters 12 and 13.

Labeling Theory. One of the more "social" sociological approaches to delinquent conduct is **labeling theory.** Labeling theory's primary proponent is Edwin Lemert (1951, 1967a), although other sociologists have been credited with promoting this view (Becker, 1963; Kitsuse, 1962). Labeling theory stresses the definitions people have of delinquent acts rather than delinquency itself. Applied to delinquent conduct, Lemert was concerned with two primary questions. These were: (1) What is the process whereby youths become labeled as delinquent? and (2) What is the influence of such labeling upon these youths' future behavior? Lemert assumed that no act is inherently delinquent, that all persons at different points in time conform to or deviate from the law, that persons become delinquent through social labeling or definition, that being apprehended by police begins the labeling process, that youths defined as delinquent will acquire self-definitions as delinquents, and finally, that those defining themselves as delinquent will seek to establish associations with others also defined as delinquent.

Not every youth who violates the law, regardless of the seriousness of the offense, will become a hardcore delinquent. Some infractions are relatively minor offenses. For example, experimenting with alcohol and getting drunk or trying certain drugs, joyriding, and petty theft may be one-time events never to be repeated. However, "getting caught" enhances the likelihood that any particular youth will be brought into the juvenile justice system for processing and labeling. Youths who have adopted delinquent subcultures are often those who have attracted the attention of others, including the police, by engaging in wrongful acts or "causing trouble." Wearing the symbols of gang membership such as jackets emblazoned with gang names helps to solidify one's self-definition as being delinquent.

Lemert suggested that juvenile deviation may be *primary* or *secondary*. **Primary deviation** occurs when youths spontaneously violate the law by engaging in occasional pranks. Law enforcement authorities may conclude that these pranks are not particularly serious. However, if juveniles persist in repeating their deviant and delinquent conduct, they may exhibit secondary deviation. **Secondary deviation** occurs whenever the deviant conduct becomes a part of one's behavior pattern or lifestyle. Thus, delinquency is viewed as a social label applied by others to those youths who have relatively frequent contact with the juvenile justice system. The strength of such social labeling is such that juveniles themselves adopt such social labels and regard themselves as delinquent. This, too, is a vicious cycle of sorts, in that one phenomenon (social labeling by others of some youths as delinquent) reinforces the other (labeled youths acquiring self-definitions as delinquent and engaging in further delinquent conduct consistent with the delinquent label).

Some theorists believe that the first step toward becoming a hard-core delinquent is "getting caught." However, many first-offenders engage in nonserious behaviors, such as petty theft and vandalism, that may never be repeated.
(© Steve Starr/Picture Group Inc.)

Lemert's labeling perspective has probably been the most influential theory relative to policy decisions by juvenile courts to divert youths away from the formal trappings of court proceedings. The sentiment is that if we can keep youths away from the juvenile justice system, they will be less inclined to identify with it. Accordingly, they will be less likely to define themselves as delinquent and to engage in delinquent conduct. This theory is also more broadly applicable to adult first offenders. Criminal courts often use diversion as a means of keeping first offenders out of the system. This is done, in part, to give them another chance to conform to the law and avoid acquiring a criminal record. Diversion doesn't always work for either adults or juveniles, but at least we can better appreciate why the different justice systems employ it to deal with some adult and juvenile offenders in the early stages of their processing by the system.

One of the labeling theory's leading proponents was the late FBI director, J. Edgar Hoover. Hoover believed that many adult offenders have prior careers as juvenile delinquents. He believed that if authorities do not deal effectively with those who commit delinquent offenses, then these juvenile offenders will continue their criminal activities into adulthood. Although many adult offenders do not have previous delinquency histories, sufficient numbers of offenders with delinquency histories do exist to make Hoover's beliefs plausible. Therefore, Hoover devoted considerable time to delinquency prevention and treatment. He was an advocate of any treatment method for delinquent youths that would prevent them from acquiring the social label of delinquents. He supported **adolescent courts** for disposing of less serious juvenile offender cases. Adolescent courts were not really courts at all; juvenile judges might hold "court" in an offender's home or in the judge's home, and informal punishments might be imposed. These proceedings never became a matter of public record, and punishments were often constructive, such as cleaning up the grounds of public buildings or providing a degree of restitution to victims through manual labor.

Bonding Theory. **Bonding theory** or **social control theory** derives primarily from the work of Travis Hirschi (1969). This theory stresses processual aspects of youths becoming "bonded" or socially integrated into the norms of society. The greater the integration, or bonding, particularly with parents and schoolteachers, the less the likelihood that youths will engage in delinquent activity. Different dimensions of bonding include attachment (emotional linkages with those we respect and admire), commitment (enthusiasm or energy expended in a specific relationship), belief (moral definition of the rightness or wrongness of certain conduct), and involvement (intensity of attachment with those who engage in conventional conduct or espouse conventional values).

Hirschi investigated large numbers of high school students in order to test his bonding theory. The more academically successful students seemed to be bonded to conventional values and to significant others, such as teachers and school authorities, in contrast with the less successful students. Students who apparently lack strong commitment to school and to education generally are more prone to become delinquent than students with opposite dispositions. However, since Hirschi limited his research to students in high school settings, he has been criticized for not applying his bonding theory to juvenile samples in other, nonschool settings. Furthermore, Hirschi has failed to explain clearly the processual aspects of bonding. Also, because rejecting or accepting conventional values and significant others is a matter of degree, and because youths may have many attachments with both delinquent and nondelinquent juveniles, bonding theory has failed to predict accurately which youths will eventually become delinquent. This is regarded as a serious limitation.

Alternative Explanations

A myriad of other explanations for delinquent conduct have been advanced by various theorists. Those selected for more in-depth coverage earlier are by no means the best theories to account for delinquency. Their inclusion here is merely to describe some of the thinking about why juveniles may be attracted to delinquent conduct. Some of the other approaches that have been advocated include *containment theory, neutralization* or *drift theory, differential association theory,* and *differential reinforcement theory.*

Containment theory is closely associated with the work of sociologist Walter Reckless (1967). Reckless outlined a theoretical model consisting of "pushes" and "pulls" in relation to delinquency. By pushes he referred to internal personal factors, including hostility, anxiety, and discontent. By pulls he meant external social forces, including delinquent subcultures and significant others. The containment dimension of his theoretical scheme consisted of both outer and inner containments. Outer containments, according to Reckless, are social norms, folkways, mores, laws, and institutional arrangements that induce societal conformity. By inner containments, Reckless referred to individual or personal coping strategies to deal with stressful situations and conflict. These strategies may consist of a high tolerance for conflict or frustration, and considerable ego strength. Thus, Reckless combined both psychological and social elements in describing youths who have weak attachments to cultural norms, high anxiety levels, and low tolerance for personal stress. Youths with these characteristics are most inclined to delinquent conduct. A key factor in whether juveniles adopt delinquent behaviors is their level of self-esteem. Those with high levels of self-esteem seem most resistant to delinquent behaviors when they are exposed to such conduct while around their friends.

Neutralization or **drift theory** was originally outlined by David Matza (1964). Matza conjectured that most juveniles spend their early years on a behavioral continuum ranging between unlimited freedom and total control or restraint. These persons drift toward one end of the continuum or the other, depending upon their social and psychological circumstances. If youths have strong attachments with those who are delinquent, then they "drift" toward the unlimited freedom end of the continuum and perhaps engage in

Some programs for youths at risk involve self-improvement activities, such as working at part-time jobs after school, where youths may acquire greater personal and social responsibilities and positive self-concepts. (© Sara Putnam/The Picture Cube)

delinquent activities. However, Matza indicates that the behavioral issue is not a black and white one. Juveniles most likely to engage in delinquent conduct have associations with normative culture as well as the delinquent subculture. They may engage in delinquent conduct and regard their behavior as acceptable at the time they engage in it. Elaborate rationales for delinquent behavior may be invented (e.g., society is unfair, victims deserve to be victims, nobody is hurt by our particular acts), and thus, they effectively "neutralize" the normative constraints of society that impinge upon them. Therefore, at least some delinquency results from rationalizations created by youths that render delinquent acts acceptable under certain circumstances. Appropriate preventative therapy for such delinquents might be to undermine their rationales for delinquent behaviors through empathic means.

Differential association theory was first advanced by Edwin Sutherland (1939). In some respects, it is an outgrowth of the cultural transmission theory developed by Shaw and McKay in their investigations of juvenile offenders in Chicago. Sutherland described a socialization process (learning through contact with others) whereby juveniles would acquire delinquent behaviors manifested by others among their close associates. It would certainly be an oversimplification of Sutherland's views to say he claimed that associating with other delinquents would inevitably cause certain juveniles to adopt similar delinquent behaviors. His scheme was more complex and multifaceted than that. He suggested that several interpersonal dimensions characterize relations between law violators and others who behave similarly. Sutherland said that differential association consists of the following elements: frequency, priority, duration, and intensity. Thus, engaging in frequent associations and long-lasting interactions with others who are delinquent, giving them priority as significant others, and cultivating strong emotional attachments with them will contribute in a significant way to a youth's propensity to commit delinquent acts.

Explicit in Sutherland's scheme is the emphasis on attachments with others who are delinquent. Differential association theory shares this emphasis with containment theory and bonding. Sutherland sought to characterize relationships some juveniles have with delinquents as multidimensional; the association aspect was only one of several of these dimensions. Although Sutherland's work has been influential and has been widely quoted and utilized by criminologists, some experts have been critical of his theory on various grounds. He never fully articulated the true meaning of intensity and frequency, for instance. How "intense" must a relationship be between a delinquent and a nondelinquent before it makes a difference and causes the nondelinquent to adopt delinquent patterns of behavior? How frequently must nondelinquents be in the company of delinquents before such contact becomes crucial and alters nondelinquent behavior? These and other similar questions were never fully addressed by Sutherland. Nevertheless, differential association has influenced certain correctional policies and treatment programs for both juveniles and adults.

Much like labeling theory, differential association theory has encouraged minimizing contact between first offenders and hardcore criminal offenders. The use of prison is often the last resort in certain cases, since it is believed that more prolonged contact with other criminals will only serve to intensify any criminal propensities first offenders might exhibit. If they can be diverted to some nonincarcerative option, they may not become recidivists and commit new crimes. The same principle applies to delinquent first offenders, and it accounts for the widespread use of noncustodial sanctions that seek to minimize a juvenile's contact with the juvenile justice system.

In 1966, Robert Burgess and Ronald Akers attempted to revise Sutherland's differential association theory and derived what they termed **differential reinforcement theory.** Differential reinforcement theory actually combines elements from labeling theory and a psychological phenomenon known as conditioning. Conditioning functions in the social learning process as persons are rewarded for engaging in certain desirable behaviors and refraining from certain undesirable behaviors. Juveniles perceive when others respond negatively to their behaviors, and may thus be disposed to behave in ways that will maximize their rewards from others.

Also, in some respects, Burgess and Akers have incorporated certain aspects of the "looking-glass self" concept originally devised by the theorist Charles Horton Cooley. Cooley theorized that people learned ways of conforming by paying attention to the reactions of others in response to their behavior. Therefore, Cooley would argue that we imagine how others see us. We look for others' reactions to our behavior and interpret these reactions as either good or bad. If we define others' reactions as good, we will feel a degree of pride and will be likely to persist in the behaviors. But, as Cooley indicated, if we interpret their reactions to our behaviors as bad, we may experience mortification. Given this latter reaction, or at least our interpretation of it, we may change our behaviors to conform to what we think others want, and thereby elicit approval from them. While these ideas continue to evoke interest, they are difficult to conceptualize and investigate empirically. Akers and others have acknowledged such difficulties, although their work is insightful and underscores the value of a multidimensional view of delinquent conduct.

An Evaluation of Explanations of Delinquent Conduct

Assessing the importance or significance of theories of delinquency is difficult. First, almost all causes of delinquent conduct that have been espoused by experts during the past century continue to interest contemporary investigators. The most frequently discounted and consistently criticized views are the biological ones, although as we have seen, sociobiological and genetic explanations of delinquent conduct persist, and continue to raise unanswered questions about the role of heredity in the delinquency equation.

Psychological explanations seem more plausible than biological ones, although the precise relation between the psyche and biological factors remains unknown. If we focus upon psychological explanations of delinquency as important in fostering delinquent conduct, almost invariably we involve certain elements of the social world in such explanations. One's mental processes are influenced in various ways by one's social experiences. Self-definitions, important to psychologists and learning theorists, are conceived largely in social contexts, in the presence of and through contact with others. It is not surprising, therefore, that the most fruitful explanations for delinquency are those that seek to blend the best parts of different theories that assess different dimensions of youths, their physical characteristics and intellectual abilities, personalities, and social experiences. Intellectual isolationism, or complete reliance on biological, psychological, or sociological factors exclusively, may simplify theory construction, but in the final analysis, such isolationism is unproductive (Binder and Geis, 1984). Certainly, each field has importance and makes a contribution toward explaining why some youths exhibit delinquent conduct and others do not.

Applying a purely pragmatic approach in assessing the predictive and/or explanatory utility of each of these theories, we may examine contemporary interventionist efforts that seek to curb delinquency or prevent its resurgence. One way of determining which theories are most popular and/or influence policy and administrative decision-making relative to juveniles is to catalog the ways offenders are treated by the juvenile justice system after their apprehension by police or others.

A preliminary screening of juvenile offenders may result in some being diverted from the juvenile justice system. One manifest purpose of such diversionary action is to reduce the potentially adverse influence of labeling on these youths (Anderson and Schoen, 1985; Binder and Geis, 1984; Polk, 1984). A long-term objective of diversion is to minimize recidivism among divertees. While some experts contend that the intended effects of diversion, such as a reduction in the social stigmatization of status offenders, are presently unclear, inconsistent, and insufficiently documented (Anderson and Schoen, 1985), other professionals endorse diversion programs and regard them as effective in preventing further delinquent conduct among first offenders (DeAngelo, 1988; Frazier and Cochran, 1986; Regoli et al., 1985). In fact, the preponderance of evidence from a survey of available literature is that diversion, while not fully effective at preventing delinquent recidivism, nevertheless tends to reduce it substantially (Davidson et al., 1987; DeAngelo, 1988; Litton and Marye, 1983; Williams, 1984).

During the period 1983–1984, for example, the probation departments of Los Angeles and Contra Costa Counties, together with several community service agencies in southern California, conducted a **Youth at Risk program,** consisting of ten-day rural training courses for large samples of youths, ages 13 to 19 (MetaMetrics, Inc., 1984). These Youth at Risk programs included classes, outdoor recreational activities, and an emphasis on self-reliance and individual responsibility. Youths participating in the program were the subjects of a 15-month follow-up that sought to identify their recidivism rates. Compared with samples of delinquent youths not involved in this diversion program, the amount of recidivism among program participants was quite low. Program officials concluded that their program was a significant improvement over traditional processing methods by the juvenile justice systems in these jurisdictions. Diversionary programs in Denver, Colorado, and in various midwestern cities have yielded similar results (Davidson et al., 1987; Regoli et al., 1985).

These and similar diversionary studies have reported lower rates of recidivism among participating youths. Implicit in most of these studies has been the idea that minimizing formal involvement with the juvenile justice system has been favorable for reducing participants' self-definitions as delinquent and avoiding the delinquent label. Thus, labeling theory seems to have been prominent in the promotion of diversionary programs. Furthermore, many divertees have been exposed to experiences that enhance or improve their self-reliance and independence. Many have learned to think out their problems rather than act them out unproductively or antisocially. When we examine the contents of these programs closely, it is fairly easy to detect aspects of bonding theory, containment theory, and differential reinforcement theory at work in the delinquency prevention process.

Besides using diversion per se, with or without various programs, there are elements or overtones of other theoretical schemes in the particular treatments or experiences juveniles receive as they continue to be processed through the juvenile justice system. At the time of adjudication, for example, juvenile judges may or may not impose special conditions to accompany a sentence of probation. Special conditions may include obligating juveniles to make restitution to victims, to perform public services, to participate in group or individual therapy, or to undergo medical treatment in cases of drug addiction or alcohol abuse. Some investigators have suggested that those youths who receive probation accompanied by special conditions are less likely to recidivate compared with those who receive probation unconditionally (Nagoshi, 1986).

Learning to accept responsibility for one's actions, acquiring new coping skills to face crises and personal tragedy, improving one's educational attainments, and improving one's ego strength to resist the influence of one's delinquent peers are individually or collectively integral parts of various delinquency treatment programs, particularly where the psychological approach is strong. For example, a juvenile education program was implemented at the East Lansing (Kansas) Penitentiary in the late 1970s. Delinquent youths on probation and residing in three Kansas counties near the penitentiary were obligated to participate in the program, which stressed introducing the juveniles to the realities of prison life (Locke *et al.*, 1986) and ran from June to October, 1980. The program required them to make "field visits" to the prison, where inmates told them how bad prison was, but they were never confined.

In a follow-up investigation of their recidivism rates compared with a sample of other delinquents not exposed to the program, self-reported delinquency was considerably lower among program participants than among those who did not participate in the program. Researchers concluded that the experience of life in prison was to a degree therapeutic, and it appeared to change the perceived status of most participants. Such programs emphasize the "shock value" of exposure to prisons and prison life. Not everyone agrees that such exposures are effective in delinquency prevention, however.

Greenwood (1986b) has described programs in various jurisdictions that function as alternatives to state training schools. These programs include outdoor educational activities and wilderness challenges that encourage youths to learn useful skills and confront their fears. For those designated as "children at risk," preschool programs such as Headstart, parent training programs such as the Oregon Learning Center, selected school programs intended to increase the achievement of lower income children, and voluntary youth service programs such as California's Conservation Corps provide many participating youths with opportunities to avoid delinquent behavior patterns (Greenwood, 1986b).

Together with psychodrama, behavioral—cognitive techniques were used by the Clinic of the Wayne County, Michigan, Juvenile Court and were intended to reduce participants' acting-out and aggressive tendencies and to build their ego strength (Carpenter and Sandberg, 1985). The Jesness High

School Personality Questionnaire was administered to all adolescents participating in the program to chart before–after program changes. Researchers reported positive results, in which juveniles tended to exhibit higher ego strength, less introversive tendencies, and less antisocial behavior after program participation. Intervention techniques included:

1. *Behavioral contracting.* Behavioral contracting involves an agreement between the juvenile and the therapist—and possibly the parents—in which the youth agrees to behave or comply with the therapist's rules in exchange for favorable treatment or rewards. Successfully fulfilling the terms of the "contract" may mean that pending delinquency charges against a given juvenile will be dropped.
2. *Monetary reinforcement.* Financial rewards such as allowances may also be offered conditionally—e.g., for as long as one's good behavior continues.
3. *Alternative behavior rehearsal and psychodrama.* Psychodrama and alternative behavior rehearsals are both designed to force youths to "see" their own behaviors by getting them to act out different scenarios. Thus, a youth might pretend to be a principal who must deal with another unruly youth. The idea of such techniques is to increase youths' empathy for others, forcing them to deal first-hand with the kinds of problems which their own behavior leads to. Once youths realize the consequences of their behavior, they may consider changing it to a more acceptable form.

The aim of all these methods is to reduce the delinquent's acting-out tendencies (Carpenter and Sandberg, 1985).

Several psychologists have conducted an extensive review of group therapy literature as applied to the treatment of juvenile delinquents (Lavin *et al.*, 1984). They conclude that group therapy is particularly effective for more aggressive adolescents. They also report that much of the research surveyed is conducted in residential settings, such as group homes. In these less-traditional, nonthreatening circumstances, juveniles seem to be more amenable to behavioral change and improved conduct.

During the late 1970s, a program known as **"Getting It Together"** was established in a large-city juvenile court jurisdiction (Carpenter and Sugrue, 1984). The program emphasized a combination of affective (emotional) and social skills training designed to assist those with immature personalities and neurotic patterns of behavior. Over the next several years, many delinquent youths participated in this program. A majority reported improved self-esteem and socially mature behavior, better communication skills with authorities and parents, greater self-control, more positive values, and more adequate job skills. Ego strength levels for most participating youths improved, as did the quality of peer relationships, and there was a reduction in sexual problems. This program and similar enterprises (Berg, 1984; Lamson, 1983) have been guided to a great degree by social learning theory.

Program successes are often used as gauges of the successfulness of their theoretical underpinnings. Since no program is 100 percent effective in preventing delinquency, it follows that no theoretical scheme thus far devised is completely effective. Yet the wide variety of programs that are employed today to deal with different kinds of juvenile offenders indicates that most psychological and sociological approaches have some merit and contribute differentially to delinquency reduction. As we will see in subsequent chapters, policy decisions are made throughout the juvenile justice system and are often contingent upon the theoretical views adopted by politicians, law enforcement personnel, prosecutors and judges, and correctional officials at every stage of the justice process. For the present, we may appreciate most views because of their varying intuitive value, and selectively apply particular approaches to accommodate different types of juvenile offenders.

A bottom line concerning theories of delinquency generally is that their impact has been felt most strongly in the area of policy making rather than in behavioral change or modification. Virtually every theory is connected in some respect to various types of experimental programs in different jurisdictions. The intent of most programs has been to change behaviors of participants; however, high rates of recidivism characterize all delinquency prevention innovations, regardless of their intensity or ingenuity.

Policy decisions implemented at earlier points have long-range implications for present policies in correctional work. Probationers and parolees as well as inmates and divertees, adults and juveniles alike, are recipients or inheritors of previous policies put in place by theorists who have attempted to convert their theories into practical experiences and action. Current policy in juvenile justice favors the "get-tough" orientation, and there is increasing sponsorship of programs that heavily incorporate elements of accountability and individual responsibility. At an earlier period, projects emphasizing rehabilitation and reintegration were rewarded more heavily through private grants and various types of government funding. No particular prevention or intervention or supervision program works best. Numerous contrasting perspectives about how policy should be shaped continue to vie for recognition among professionals and politicians. The theories that have been described here are indicative of the many factors that have shaped our present policies and practices.

Summary

There are many different theories of delinquency. Theories are integrated explanatory schemes that predict relationships between two or more phenomena. Theories of delinquency may be grouped into biological, psychological, and sociological explanations. Biological theories strongly imply a causal relation between physical makeup and other genetic phenomena and delinquent behavior. Psychological theories employ psychoanalytic theory devised by Sigmund Freud and elaborated by others to explain delinquency. Social learning theory is similar to psychoanalytic theory, but it puts greater stress on imitation of significant others. Sociological theories stress social factors in delinquency. Concentric zone theory, for example, postulates that sociological factors such as urban growth patterns create living situations conducive to delinquent conduct.

A popular sociological view of delinquency is labeling theory. In this theory, those who engage in wrongdoing come to adopt self-definitions as delinquents, particularly if significant others and the police define them as delinquents. Having frequent contact with the juvenile justice system enhances such labeling. Labeling theorists often argue that delinquents are "acting out" the behaviors others expect from them. Closely related to labeling theory is bonding theory, in which juveniles are seen as developing either close or distant attachments to schools, teachers, and peers. Delinquency is regarded as a function of inadequate bonding or a weakening of social attachments. Other theories include containment theory, neutralization or drift theory, and differential association theory. Each of these views suggests the power or attraction of group processes in the onset of delinquent conduct.

Theories of delinquency are often evaluated according to how they influence public policy relating to juvenile conduct and its prevention or treatment. Diversionary programs that prevent further contact with the juvenile justice system are influenced largely by labeling theory, since it is believed that youths will become more deeply entrenched in juvenile misconduct to the extent that they are exposed to the formal system and to juvenile courts. Individual and group therapies, often a part of treatment programs for errant juveniles, seek to use ego development strategies coupled with various learning methods to improve self-definitions, reduce antisocial behaviors, and promote more healthy attitudes toward others. Programs that emphasize personal responsibility for one's actions or encourage youths to become more active in decision making seem to make a difference in reducing recidivism among program participants. No theory is universally accepted, however.

Key Terms

Adolescent courts (99)
Anomie (96)
Assumption (79)
Atavistic (83)
Cesare Beccaria (81)
Jeremy Bentham (81)
Biological determinism (83)
Bonding theory (99)
Children at risk (91)
Classical school (81)
Classical theory (81)
Concentric zone hypothesis (93)
Conformity (96)

Containment theory (100)
Cultural transmission (93)
Determinism (81)
Differential association theory (101)
Differential reinforcement theory (102)
Drift theory (100)
Ectomorph (85)
Ego (87)
Endomorph (85)
"Getting It Together" program (106)
Hedonism (81)

Questions for Review

1. What is a theory of delinquency? What are two important functions of theory? How do assumptions and propositions relate to theory?

2. Compare the views of Beccaria and Bentham and explain how each accounts for deviant conduct.

3. What is meant by determinism? Explain the difference between determinism and free will. What types of theories are associated with determinism? Explain.

4. How do contemporary sentencing patterns relate to the classical school?

5. How does the common law define accountability? At what age do children become responsible for their own actions under the common law?

6. How did the work of Charles Darwin influence various biological determinists? How would a biological determinist explain deviant conduct or criminal behavior?

7. Define the positivist school of criminology and briefly indicate how crime is explained by this school.

8. Describe three body types identified by Sheldon. To what extent might we say that a relationship exists between body type and delinquent conduct? Is there any empirical evidence that such a relationship exists?

9. What is sociobiology? In what respects would the XYY theory be related to sociobiology? Explain briefly.

10. How might stigmas contribute to deviant conduct or juvenile delinquency?

11. What are the major components of psychoanalytic theory? Describe the importance of the formative years in psychoanalytic theory. In what respect is one's childhood regarded as one's "formative years"?

12. How does social learning theory differ from psychoanalytic theory?

13. In the 1920s, Chicago sociologists investigated the concentric zone hypothesis. What is this hypothesis and how does it relate to crime? What areas of cities are most likely to have high delinquency rates?

14. How is cultural transmission related to the concentric zone hypothesis?

15. What seems to be the role of socioeconomic status in the complex picture of juvenile delinquency?

16. What is a delinquent subculture? How can we possibly use such information about a delinquent subculture to change delinquent behaviors in various communities?

17. Distinguish between strain theory and Merton's theory of anomie. What mode of adaptation is most likely to be invoked by juvenile delinquents? What other modes of adaptation are there?

18. Compare labeling theory with bonding theory. Define each and show how each may have influenced policies dealing with juvenile first offenders.

19. Define each briefly: (a) containment theory; (b) neutralization or drift theory; (c) differential association theory; and (d) differential reinforcement theory.

20. How are various theories of delinquent conduct evaluated?

Suggested Readings

DECKER, SCOTT H. (1984). *Juvenile Justice Policy: Analyzing Trends and Outcomes.* Beverly Hills, CA: Sage.

KAPLAN, HOWARD B. (1984). *Patterns of Juvenile Delinquency.* Beverly Hills, CA: Sage.

WALKER, SAMUEL (1989). *Sense and Nonsense About Crime: A Policy Guide* (2nd ed.). Pacific Grove, CA: Brooks/Cole.

WEISHEIT, RALPH A., and ROBERT G. CULBERTSON (1985). *Juvenile Delinquency: A Justice Perspective.* Prospect Heights, IL: Waveland Press.

WILSON, JAMES Q. (1981). *Thinking About Crime.* New York: Basic Books.

The Juvenile Justice System: Detection and Control

Part II includes three chapters that provide an overview of the juvenile justice system, juvenile interactions with law enforcement officers in different contexts, and the initial phases of a juvenile's entry into justice processing. Chapter 4 is especially important, since it describes the criminal justice system generally and shows how it interfaces with the juvenile justice system. There are comparatively few officers in most law enforcement agencies throughout the United States who focus exclusively on juveniles and their conduct. Most of the initial interactions juveniles have with the police occur in the course of a police officer's routine patrols or duties. Although police officers regard crimes committed by adults as taking priority over infractions contemplated or committed by juveniles, they must respond and react to suspicious circumstances involving youthful offenders.

Whenever a youth is stopped and questioned by police for whatever reason, officer discretion dictates whether further investigation is warranted and whether the youth should be temporarily detained. Evaluating youths on their appearance and on the circumstances under which they have been stopped and questioned, police officers may take them directly to juvenile bureaus or agencies for further processing and questioning. In many instances, however, it is not easy for police officers to determine whether youths are minors or adults. Thus, if the situation is especially suspicious or if the youths have been caught in the act of committing crimes or other infractions, they may be taken to jail temporarily, until officers can determine their ages and true identities. Temporary confinement of juveniles in jails is not only constitutional but is a common practice in most jurisdictions. These periods of preventive detention often last only a few hours.

Those offenders classified as juveniles may be transferred to juvenile authorities for alternative dispositions, or police officers at these jails may make in-house or in-station judgment calls and release these youths to the custody of parents or guardians. For alleged adult offenders and those youths who have committed especially serious crimes such as murder, forcible rape, armed robbery, aggravated assault, or grand larceny, suspects may be subject to prolonged detention in jails to await further processing within the criminal justice system.

The criminal justice system as described in Chapter 4 includes law enforcement, prosecutors and the courts, and corrections. The elements of criminal procedure to be covered include the booking process, initial appearance by defendants before magistrates, bail determination, preliminary examination, grand jury activity, arraignment, plea bargaining, jury selection, and trial proceedings. We will examine various defendant rights during trial proceedings, judicial responsibilities with regard to sentencing convicted offenders, and the roles of probation, incarcerative institutions, and parole.

Whether youthful offenders are processed by the criminal justice system or the juvenile justice system depends on which system has jurisdiction over them. If it is determined that the juvenile justice system has jurisdiction, then youths are funneled toward intake officers or juvenile probation officers, who screen them and make important decisions regarding their future processing within the system. A majority of youthful offenders are petty offenders and are considered nonserious. A frequently used option of intake officers is a verbal reprimand and release of these juveniles to the custody of their parents. In some instances, it may be necessary to send youths to community-based treatment centers for special help, particularly in cases where drug/alcohol dependencies or psychological problems are apparent. Sometimes these youths have been abused by family members, and the placement of some youths in foster homes or group homes may be the decision of the intake officer.

In the cases of especially serious, violent, or persistent nonviolent offenders, youths are eventually brought before juvenile judges to hear the charges against them and to have their cases adjudicated. Judges have considerable latitude in the types of punishments they may impose. These will be described, and they include nominal, conditional, and custodial sanctions. Of course, it is discretionary on the part of officials at every stage of these proceedings to divert youths from the juvenile justice system to an alternative resolution of their problems. Several of these options will be described briefly.

Chapter 5 discusses the roles and activities of police that bring them into initial contact with juveniles. Police officers exercise considerable discretionary powers, and they may decide to verbally warn youthful loiterers or bring them into custody temporarily for further investigation. Again, much of their discretion to act one way or another depends upon the totality of circumstances of their interactions with juveniles on the streets. In the last few decades, different classes of juvenile offenders have been created, including status offenders. Legislators in most states believe that these types of offenses should be dealt with more leniently than more serious offenses; thus, efforts have been made in most jurisdictions to deinstitutionalize status offenders through divestiture, and remove them from the adjudicatory powers of juvenile courts.

Divestiture, or the removal of certain classes of offenses from the jurisdiction of juvenile courts, has been received both positively and negatively by various components of the juvenile justice system. Proponents of divestiture believe that it is a way to protect youths from the adverse labeling effects that stem from appearances in juvenile courts, with their criminal trappings. Those diverted away from the juvenile justice system will presumably stand a better chance of avoiding future involvement with it than those exposed to it.

However, some police officers and judges believe that divestiture represents a direct attack on their discretionary integrity and authority. Accordingly, police officers in some jurisdictions have responded to divestiture by redefining certain acts as delinquent that would not previously have been considered delinquent. Thus, many youths are

brought into the "net" because police elect to label innocent youthful behaviors as criminal behaviors. Many cases sent to juvenile
judges involve trivial youthful infractions. Although judges retain
their original powers over these juveniles, they frequently do not
appreciate the heavier docket loads incurred in their courts largely
as the result of the actions of overzealous police officers.

At the same time that divestiture has gained in popularity in
many jurisdictions, a "get-tough" policy has evolved as a result of
an apparent escalation in juvenile offending behavior during the
1970s. One effect of this has been an increased use of transfers or
certifications to adult criminal courts for more serious juvenile offenders. These transfers to criminal courts will be examined briefly.
[A more thorough discussion of the transfer process will be presented in Chapter 7.]

Chapter 6 describes the important process of intake and screening.
Intake officers must exercise discretion and determine from interviews with youthful offenders and their parents whether juveniles
should be pushed further into the juvenile justice system or diverted
from it. They may decide to file petitions with the juvenile court to
have certain juveniles adjudicated as delinquent by juvenile judges.
However, there are several other options available to intake officers
at this stage that will be described. Additionally, several models for
dealing with juvenile offenders will be discussed, depending upon
the youths' age, gender, offense behavior, and prior records, if any.
Among the options that may be exercised by intake officers are diversion from the system or reassignment of guardianship to foster
homes or group homes, psychological counseling, and/or participation in an educational, vocational, or therapeutic program offered
through various community-based services.

CHAPTER 4

An Overview of the Juvenile Justice System

Introduction

This chapter provides a brief overview of both the criminal justice system and the juvenile justice system. Because the juvenile justice system interfaces in several important ways with the criminal justice system, and because a small proportion of the juveniles who are arrested by police will eventually fall within the jurisdiction of and be processed by the criminal justice system, it is important to understand the elements of *both* systems. The chapter begins with a general description of the criminal justice system and some of the preliminary procedures followed whenever youthful offenders are appre-hended.

Each year over one million juveniles are taken into police custody in the United States (Jamieson and Flanagan, 1988:516). Many of these youths are

Many youths who are arrested are held in local jails temporarily, where they will eventually be released in the custody of their parents following an investigation. (© Paul Conklin/Monkmeyer Press Photo Service)

taken initially to local jails where they are detained for brief periods. While approximately 90 percent of these juveniles are either referred to juvenile court jurisdiction or released to parents or guardians within hours after their arrests, the remainder are formally admitted to these jails or to other places of confinement to await further action (Jamieson and Flanagan, 1988:517, 606). Thus, approximately one million juveniles interface with the criminal justice system annually.

Preliminary classifications and dispositions of most offenders are routine and pose no problems for arresting officers and others. However, some of those taken into custody may require special handling and treatment. Arrestees may be mentally or physically ill, they may be under the influence of drugs or alcohol, or they may be dangerous either to themselves or to others. Discretionary actions by police officers in these cases are far from perfunctory. Therefore, the process of classifying juveniles and establishing the appropriate jurisdiction for them will be described.

Once it is determined that the juvenile justice system is where certain youthful offenders should be sent, these juveniles are brought to juvenile halls or other facilities where they will await further disposition by intake officers. Although specific procedures in the processing of juveniles vary among jurisdictions, the intake process normally involves several alternative actions that may or may not lead to a juvenile's further involvement with the juvenile justice system. Prosecutors in many jurisdictions decide whether to bring juveniles before juvenile courts for formal adjudicatory action by judges. The juvenile court is becoming increasingly adversarial as juveniles acquire constitutional rights more on a par with those enjoyed by adults in the criminal justice system. We will provide an overview of adjudicatory alternatives available to juvenile court judges and describe the array of punishments that may be imposed on those found delinquent or in need of special care. Finally, a brief overview of juvenile corrections will be presented.

The Criminal Justice System

The **criminal justice system** *is an interrelated set of agencies and organizations designed to control criminal behavior, to detect crime, and to apprehend, process, prosecute, punish, and rehabilitate criminal offenders.* Figure 4.1 provides a diagram of the working of the criminal and juvenile justice systems. As the diagram shows, cases that are judged to fall within the jurisdiction of the juvenile justice system are diverted to it. We will look at the way cases are processed through the different parts of the adult system, and then we will describe the case flow through the juvenile justice system.

The basic elements of the criminal justice system include **law enforcement agencies, prosecution and courts,** and **corrections,** although law-making bodies such as the **legislatures** of states and the federal government are sometimes included. (We might note that some experts prefer the term "process" to depict the way in which those accused of crimes move through the different parts of the system. There *is* a system, but it is a loosely integrated one. For instance, law enforcement officers seldom ask prosecutors and the courts if they have arrested too many criminals and if the system can handle them. In turn, prosecutors and the courts seldom ask prison wardens or jail superintendents whether there is enough space to accommodate all those convicted of crimes and sentenced to incarcerative terms.) Below are descriptions of the various criminal justice system components.

Legislatures. Criminal laws originate largely as the result of legislative actions in most *jurisdictions.* **Jurisdiction** refers to the power of courts to hear cases, although we generally define a jurisdiction in terms of various political subdivisions, including townships, cities, counties, states, or federal districts. Thus, when criminals cross state or county lines, they leave the state or local jurisdictions where violations of the law occurred. In certain circumstances,

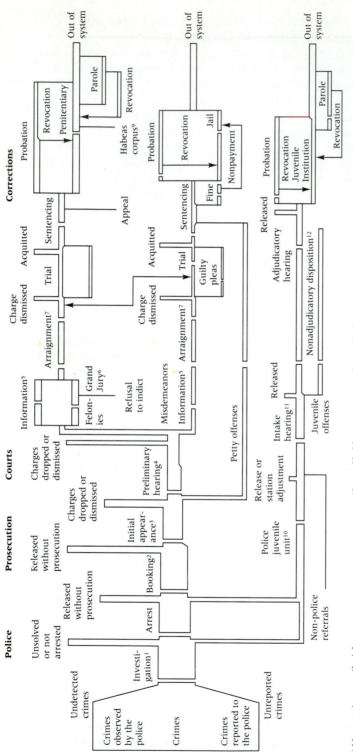

Figure 4-1 The Criminal Justice System. (*Source:* President's Commission on Law Enforcement and Administration of Justice, *The Challenge of Crime in a Free Society* [Washington, D.C.: U.S. Government Printing Office, 1967], pp. 8–9)

[1] May continue until trial.

[2] Administrative record of arrest. First step at which temporary release on bail may be available.

[3] Before magistrate, commissioner, or justice of the peace. Formal notice of charge, advice of rights. Bail set. Summary trials for petty offenses usually conducted here without further processing.

[4] Preliminary testing of evidence against defendant. Charge may be reduced. No separate preliminary hearing for misdemeanors in some systems.

[5] Charge filed by prosecutor on basis of information submitted by police or citizens. Alternative to grand jury indictment; often used in felonies, almost always in misdemeanors.

[6] Reviews whether government evidence sufficient to justify trial. Some states have no grand jury system; others seldom use it.

[7] Appearance for plea; defendant elects trial by judge or jury (if available); counsel for indigent usually appointed here in felonies. Often not at all on other cases.

[8] Charge may be reduced at any time prior to trial in return for plea of guilty or for other reasons.

[9] Challenge on constitutional grounds to legality of detention. May be sought at any point in process.

[10] Police often hold informal hearings, dismiss or adjust many cases without further processing.

[11] Probation officer decides desirability of further court action.

[12] Welfare agency, social services, counseling, medical care, etc., cases where adjudicatory handling not needed.

118

these jurisdictional boundaries may be crossed by pursuing authorities. At the federal level, any federal agency may enforce certain federal laws in any state, territory, or U.S. possession.

The Congress of the United States passes criminal laws that are enforceable by various federal agencies, including the **Federal Bureau of Investigation (FBI)**, the **Drug Enforcement Administration (DEA)**, and the **Criminal Investigation Division (CID)** of the Internal Revenue Service. State legislatures enact criminal laws that are enforced by state and local law enforcement officers. At the community level, city and county governments determine specific criminal laws, statutes, and ordinances that should be enforced, depending upon the circumstances in the locality. Some local ordinances are especially geared to regulate juvenile conduct. Such ordinances include curfews, truancy laws, and incorrigibility provisions, where parents or guardians cannot control the behaviors of their children.

Law Enforcement. There are over 20,000 law enforcement agencies in the United States (U.S. Department of Justice, 1988). These are distributed throughout the local, state, and federal governmental levels. Approximately 500,000 employees of these agencies are law enforcement officers (Jamieson and Flanagan, 1988). The most visible law enforcement officers are those in uniform, such as city police officers or sheriff's deputies. These are also the law enforcement officers who have the most direct contact with juveniles, because they patrol community streets. In some cities, special police forces are created to deal with certain kinds of juvenile offenders. In Honolulu, for example, the police department has established a Truancy Detail as a part of a larger Anti-Truancy Program (Ikeda *et al.*, 1985). Officers assigned to this detail seek out truants and either return them to school or take them into custody.

Many juveniles appear older than they really are. They may lie to police and give false names, addresses, and ages. Whenever juveniles are taken into custody by police officers, they may be taken to a local police station and questioned. Police discretion is very important, and circumstances often dictate which course of action police will follow. For example, juveniles loitering late at night near a store where a burglar alarm has been activated will probably arouse the suspicions of police officers. The police have a right to be suspicious of these juveniles and to investigate their presence in the area until they are satisfied that the youths are not involved in any crime.

Prosecution and Courts. When either adult or juvenile suspects are arrested or taken into custody by law enforcement officers, they are usually *booked* at a police station or sheriff's office. **Booking** *involves obtaining descriptive information about those arrested*, including their names, addresses, occupations (if any), next of kin, photographs, and fingerprints. Essentially, the booking process is a formality and provides an account or written record of the arrest or detention. Certain legal restrictions prevent law enforcement officials from fingerprinting and photographing juveniles, except under special circumstances and for limited purposes. These exceptions will be discussed in later chapters dealing with juvenile offender processing.

Figure 4.1 shows the stages of processing in the criminal justice system following the arrest and booking of adult suspects. Ordinarily, authorities transfer juvenile offenders to the juvenile justice system as soon as possible following their arrest or detention. Most adult offenders, however, must make an **initial appearance** before a magistrate or court official. Initial appearances of **defendants,** or those charged with crimes, are for the purpose of advising them of charges filed against them and determining whether they should be granted *bail.* **Bail** or a **bail bond** is a *surety in the form of money or property that may be posted by either a bonding company or others,* including defendants themselves, to obtain their temporary release from custody and to ensure their subsequent appearance at trial. But bail is often waived in cases involving petty offenses, and defendants are **released on their own recognizance** or **"ROR."**

After the initial appearance of defendants, prosecutors evaluate the sufficiency of evidence against alleged offenders (e.g., eyewitness reports, confessions, weapons, fingerprints), determine whether they have prior records, and weigh the seriousness of their alleged offenses. Frequently, interactions occur between prosecutors and defense counsels who represent defendants, and *plea bargains* are arranged. **Plea bargains** *are preconviction agreements between defendants and the state whereby defendants enter guilty pleas to certain criminal charges in exchange for some state benefit such as sentencing leniency* (McDonald, 1985). Probably over 90 percent of all criminal convictions are secured through plea bargaining in most U.S. jurisdictions at both the state and federal levels. In many instances, if the case against a defendant is weak, the prosecutor may elect to drop the charges and excuse the defendant from further processing.

Under a "worst case" scenario (for the defendant), defendants will eventually be arraigned. **Arraignment** *proceedings (1) list the charges against defendants, (2) solicit a plea of "guilty" or "not guilty" to the charges from the defendant, and (3) determine a trial date if a "not guilty" plea is entered.* Often, arraignments are preceded by **preliminary hearings** where *probable cause* is or is not established. **Probable cause** *is the reasonable suspicion that a crime has been committed and that the defendant probably committed it.* These hearings are not trial proceedings and do not determine a defendant's guilt or innocence. They only determine whether sufficient evidence exists against defendants to take the case to trial.

The preliminary hearing is an important stage because it is an opportunity for judges and others to hear **evidence** both for and against the defendant. Two types of evidence are **exculpatory** and **inculpatory,** meaning that the evidence may help to show the defendant's innocence (exculpatory) or guilt (inculpatory). A presiding magistrate concludes either that sufficient or insufficient evidence exists against the defendant to proceed further. Thus, criminal charges against defendants may be dropped or dismissed outright. Figure 4.2 shows this particular phase that is sandwiched between the initial appearance and arraignment.

Sometimes **grand juries** hear evidence or allegations against one or more suspects. Grand juries are comprised of 18 to 24 citizens from the community

BOX 4.1

Juvenile Highlights

Plea bargaining for juveniles? We know that about 90 percent of all guilty pleas in criminal courts are entered by defendants who have engaged in plea bargaining with prosecutors. Plea bargaining is a negotiated guilty plea, whereby defendants enter a plea in exchange for leniency in some form, from either prosecutors or judges. Ordinarily, plea bargaining is seen as primarily an adult enterprise. However, this may be changing.

It has been claimed that today, the juvenile justice system is a system of individualized and discretionary justice that is controlled by state agents who, at least theoretically, have the best interests of children in mind. The first point at which juvenile plea bargaining is most likely to occur is at intake. The leverage of intake probation officers is such that they may choose to file or not to file delinquency petitions against specific juvenile offenders. Thus, their decisions are important, particularly if we consider that many guidelines-based sentencing schemes adopted by various states require consideration of whether delinquency petitions have ever been filed in the past

against adults charged with crimes.

Critics of plea bargaining for adults argue that those entering guilty pleas relinquish their right to a trial, and to a full litigation of issues about their guilt or innocence. At least some defendants enter guilty pleas even when they are innocent of the crimes alleged. The guilty pleas are entered as a means of avoiding the possibility of harsher punishment, including incarceration, if they persist in taking their cases to court. Similar coercive aspects of plea bargaining are detected at the intake phase of processing juvenile offenders. In order to avoid the stigma of having delinquency petitions filed against them, some youths (and their parents) may consent to conditional diversionary actions, such as victim compensation, restitution, or community service. How much power should intake officers possess in plea bargaining? How should their power be monitored and by whom?

(Some factual information adapted from Joyce Dougherty, "Negotiating Justice in the Juvenile System: A Comparison of Adult Plea Bargaining and Juvenile Intake," *Federal Probation* (1988) 52:72–80.)

who hear evidence against defendants presented by prosecutors. They can indict defendants or decline to indict them. Grand juries frequently perform a function equivalent to that performed in preliminary hearings, because **indictments** *are simply charges against defendants that grand juries believe are supported by probable cause.* In sum, the common purpose of preliminary examinations or hearings and grand jury actions is to establish probable cause that a crime was committed and that the defendant probably committed it. The guilt or innocence of defendants is not an issue to be proved in either proceeding.

After a trial date is established following an arraignment, defendants may have either a *bench trial* or a *jury trial,* depending upon the seriousness of the crimes alleged. Trials are adversarial proceedings wherein a defendant's guilt or innocence is established. **Bench trials** are conducted by judges who determine the defendant's guilt or innocence. **Jury trials** involve evaluations of a defendant's guilt or innocence by several citizens. Jury trials vary in size among jurisdictions. In some states, for instance, juries may consist of six jurors. Traditionally, jury size in the majority of states and in federal district courts in criminal trials is twelve jurors. Jurors are selected by various methods from the community or jurisdiction where the trial occurs. Jury trials are designed to provide fundamental fairness in establishing whether charges against defendants are true. In most jurisdictions, jury voting must be unanimous, either for a defendant's guilt or for a defendant's innocence.

When defendants are convicted of a crime, they are punished by a sentence imposed by the judge. Sentences do not necessarily involve incarceration or detention. Judges consider factors such as whether the defendant took a leadership role in the crime and whether physical injuries were inflicted on victims during the crime's commission. Such circumstances are considered **aggravating circumstances,** and they may intensify the punishment convicted offenders receive. Other factors are considered, including whether offenders furnished helpful information to police that enabled them to apprehend others connected with the crime. An offender's youthfulness would be considered as well. Whether offenders were mentally ill when they committed their crimes would also be important. These factors are considered **mitigating circumstances,** and they often result in lessening the severity of punishment imposed by the judge.

The most frequently imposed sentence is *probation.* **Probation** *is a conditional nonincarcerative sentence in which the offender is under the management of probation department personnel or probation officers.* Probation is most often used for first offenders who have been convicted of minor crimes. However, evidence of its growing use in the United States annually for more serious crimes (e.g., felony probation) is well documented (Champion, 1988). Regardless of whether convicted offenders receive probation or a sentence involving incarceration for designated terms, offenders move to the final phase of the criminal justice process—corrections.

Corrections. **Corrections** *consists of all agencies and personnel who deal with convicted offenders after court proceedings.* As noted earlier, some convicted offenders may receive probation, or conditional sentences, in lieu of incarceration. The use of probation in the United States is widespread. In 1988 over two million offenders were on probation (Hester, 1988:2). Other offenders may be confined in jails or prisons, again depending upon the seriousness of their offenses, the jurisdiction where the conviction occurred, and the availability of jail or prison space. In 1988 nearly one million offenders were in jails or prisons in the United States (Hester, 1988).

Jails, Prisons, and Parole. **Jails are short-term facilities and are locally operated by city or county governments** (Mays and Thompson, 1991). Most jail functions include, but are not limited to, detaining those arrested for various offenses who are awaiting trial, maintaining witnesses in protective custody pending their testimony in court, providing confinement for short-term, petty offenders serving sentences of less than one year, and accommodating overflow from state or federal prisons in instances where chronic prison overcrowding exists (Mays and Thompson, 1991). **Prisons** *are long-term incarcerative facilities.* Most prisons have recreational yards, hospitals, work programs, and a host of other facilities to accommodate inmates who are confined for lengthy periods. Prisons are usually reserved for the most serious offenders.

In many jurisdictions, inmates of prisons and jails may be released before they have served their full sentences. This is usually accomplished through *parole.* **Parole** *is a conditional release from incarceration for a designated duration, usually the remainder of one's original sentence.* Thus, if offenders were sentenced to ten years' incarceration, they might be eligible for parole after serving four or five years. A **parole board** would consider their parole eligibility and grant them early release from prison. In parole situations, parolees are supervised by parole officers. In 1988, about 400,000 offenders were on parole in the United States (Hester, 1988).

Many other correctional options are available to judges besides probation or incarceration. Many types of *intermediate punishments* have been described by McCarthy (1987a). **Intermediate punishments** *are sanctions that fall somewhere between incarceration and probation on the continuum of criminal penalties* (McCarthy, 1987a:1). Intermediate punishments might include electronic monitoring, house arrest or home confinement, or community-based correctional alternatives such as halfway houses or intensive supervised probation or parole. Many of these options are available to juvenile as well as adult offenders. (Intermediate punishments will be discussed at length in Chapter 12.)

This brief overview has been intended simply to describe in a general way the criminal justice process outlined in Figure 4.1. We need to be somewhat familiar with the criminal justice process, since many juveniles enter it annually. The remainder of this chapter gives an overview of the juvenile justice system and describes how a juvenile's case might move through it. Subsequent chapters will provide more detailed coverage of each of these stages. This overview will begin at the point when youths have been arrested and taken to jail by law enforcement officers.

Arrest and Identification

It should be noted that being "taken into custody" and being "placed under arrest" are not equivalent expressions. When juveniles are taken into **custody,** they are not necessarily arrested, and they may not necessarily be arrested subsequently. "Taken into custody" means precisely what it says.

Officers take certain youths into custody in order to determine the best course of action in a particular situation. Youths who are taken into custody might include those suffering from child sexual abuse or physical abuse inflicted by parents or others, runaways, or missing children. Youths who wander the streets may also be apprehended by police and taken into custody if they are suspected of being truant. In fact, certain jurisdictions such as Newark, New Jersey, have truancy task forces as police units that conduct sweep operations, set up roadblocks, and search bus stops and other places teens might frequent in order to catch truants and return them to school (Skolnick and Bayley, 1986). Such activities have been reported as mildly successful in certain types of crime prevention.

When youths are arrested, it is usually in association with the commission of a crime. Charges will likely be placed against arrested youths once they have been classified and it is determined that the juvenile court has jurisdiction over them. Either police officers will file charges against juveniles, or other juvenile justice officers will file charges. However, the fact that an arrestee is under 18 years of age may be irrelevant in those jurisdictions with **automatic transfer laws.** These are laws that statutorily provide that if juveniles are age 16 or 17, and if certain violent offenses have been committed or alleged, such as murder, rape, or robbery, the juveniles are automatically subject to criminal court jurisdiction. New York, Illinois, and several other states have these automatic transfer provisions that compel officers to place certain juvenile arrestees in jail to be processed by the criminal justice system (Sagatun *et al.*, 1985).

direct-file

Other avenues by which juveniles enter the juvenile justice system include referrals from or complaints by parents, neighbors, victims, and others (social workers or probation officers, for example). Dependent or neglected children may be reported to the police initially. Following up on these complaints, police officers may take youths into custody until arrangements for their care can be made. Under the new Illinois juvenile detention law, apprehended youths or those taken into custody must eventually be transferred to a community-based program or to an approved juvenile detention home (Huskey, 1990:122). A further provision of the Illinois law is that children under the age of 10 may not be held in an adult jail. However, it is inevitable that some youths under the age of 10 will be held briefly in a jail, since there may be no immediately available facilities other than jails in which officers can hold youths briefly for questioning to determine their age and identity.

It is estimated that annually, 479,000 juveniles are locked up in adult jails in the United States (Dale, 1988:46). Only about 10 percent of these are actually being held for serious offenses. About 20 percent are status offenders. About 19,000 youths have been jailed on suspicion, even though they haven't committed offenses of any kind (Dale, 1988:46). States such as Illinois have recently passed laws to prevent police officers from holding juveniles in adult jails for periods of more than six hours (Huskey, 1990:122). For example, in 1988 in Illinois, more than 1,200 juveniles spent more than six hours in jails and lockups, while more than 100 were in jail for nearly three weeks

(Huskey, 1990:122). Most of these jailed youths were nonviolent offenders. Huskey (1990:122) notes that 700 of those jailed included status offenders, and about 1,000 were between the ages of 10 and 13.

Many juveniles are "clearly" juveniles. It is difficult to find youths age 13 or under who physically appear 18 or older. Yet Dale (1988) and others indicate that nearly 10 percent of all juveniles locked up in adult jails annually

Some juveniles who are held in adult jails or lockups may furnish police officers with false information about their ages and identities. In the absence of truthful information, it is sometimes difficult for arresting officers to determine whether their arrestees are juveniles or adults because of their youthful appearance. (© Andy Levin/Photo Researchers, Inc.)

are 13 years old or younger. For juveniles in the 14 to 17 age range, visual determination of juvenile or nonjuvenile status is increasingly difficult. Thus, at least some justification exists for police officers' taking many youthful offenders to jails for initial identification and questioning.

Despite the passage of new juvenile detention laws such as the one passed by the Illinois legislature, arrests and holdings of juveniles by police have not been curbed substantially. Furthermore, the six-hour limit on juvenile detentions seems severe in view of relatively recent juvenile jail suicide figures. Huskey (1990:122) reports incidents of suicide in Kentucky and Indiana involving youths who were in custody for only brief time periods. In an Indiana jail, for example, a 17-year-old girl hanged herself in a jail cell after being held for less than two hours on a charge of stealing a bottle of suntan lotion. She was awaiting the arrival of her parents. In a Kentucky jail, a 15-year-old boy was incarcerated for 30 minutes for refusing to go on a job interview. He was found dead in his cell a short while later, hanging from a bedsheet. Besides these and other jail suicides by juveniles, other tragic events experienced by youthful offenders in U.S. jails have included rape and aggravated assault. These and similar incidents have made it imperative that reliable classification schemes be in place in every jurisdiction to ensure that juveniles are properly placed initially whenever they are taken into custody.

Classification and Preliminary Disposition

When youths are taken into custody and are determined to require special care, to be needy or dependent, or to be otherwise unsupervised by adults or guardians, social welfare agencies or human service organizations may be identified as destinations for their removal from jails. Verification of a youth's identity and contacts with parents may result in verbal warnings by police and return of the youth to the parents. These actions are preliminary dispositions. Status offenders, including truants, runaways, and curfew violators, may be disposed of similarly. Figure 4.2 shows a more elaborate view of the juvenile justice system and provides details not shown in Figure 4.1.

Appropriate classifications of juveniles are crucial at all stages of juvenile justice processing. However, classification is particularly important when youths are first taken into custody. If it is true that less frequent contact with the juvenile justice system is better for juveniles in terms of decreasing their potential for reoffending, then it is logical to conclude that those who have least reason to be exposed to the system should be withheld from it. Truants, runaways, curfew violators—status offenders—are particularly vulnerable in this scenario's context. However, Baird (1984) observes that often, intuitive systems of classifying youths are used by juvenile professionals at various stages. He says that "juveniles differ considerably in terms of type of offense, likelihood of recommitting crimes, emotional needs, educational levels, vocational skills, honesty, and other factors. To deal effectively with this variety of people and problems requires an understanding of the individual as

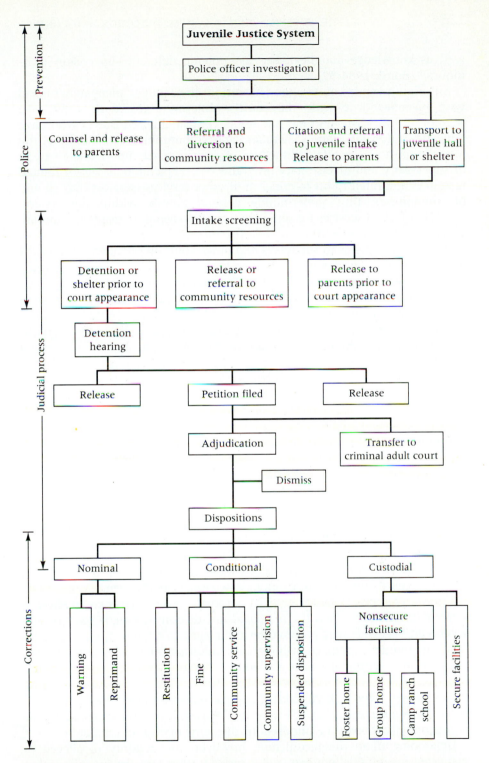

Figure 4-2 The Juvenile Justice System. (*Source:* The National Advisory Committee on Criminal Justice Standards and Goals, *Juvenile Justice and Delinquency Prevention* [Washington, D.C.: U.S. Government Printing Office, 1967], p. 9)

well as knowledge and flexibility in applying different supervision techniques'' (Baird, 1984:32).

But even juvenile courts often fail to train their judges adequately to deal with juveniles or execute the court's philosophy (Mixdorf, 1989:108). Mixdorf (1989:108) says that ''the initial contact children [have] who have gone beyond what schools, families, and communities can handle is the juvenile court and its related functions of probation, detention, and a variety of supervisory and diversionary programs. . . . Practitioners vie for limited resources and often resort to criticism of other services (services they should be supporting), thus undermining general morale within the system. . . .[The] lack of services for seriously troubled juveniles creates community crises.''

Responses of police to runaways and other youthful offenders are affected by their perceptions of youths, departmental structure and policy regarding juvenile operations, statutory constraints, and community characteristics and dispositional alternatives (Maxson *et al.*, 1988). Smaller and more geographically isolated communities may tend to have fewer sophisticated social services available compared with urban areas to accommodate those youths who have been apprehended by police ''on suspicion'' but who have not otherwise violated the law.

For the 10 percent of the youths taken into custody by law enforcement officers who are alleged to have committed serious crimes, their detention is expected. However, there are potential legal issues and problems arising from detaining youthful offenders in adult jails for any significant time (Dale, 1988:46). While a direct route to juvenile detention facilities is the desired course of action for apprehended youths where serious offenses are alleged, jurisdiction must first be established.

Establishing Jurisdiction

Jurisdiction is more than political boundaries or geographical landmarks outlining county lines and territories. As we have already seen, jurisdiction is the power of courts to decide cases. If automatic transfer laws are in effect in various jurisdictions, then the matter of jurisdiction is settled. Sixteen- and seventeen-year-olds who commit, or are alleged to have committed, crimes such as murder, rape, or robbery are automatically transferred to the jurisdiction of criminal courts for adults. These youths may contest such transfers of jurisdiction to criminal courts through **reverse waiver actions.** (See Chapter 7 for a discussion of reverse waivers.) Quite logically, one's potential punishment could be less severe in juvenile court compared with the punishment that could be imposed for the same offense in criminal court.

Depending upon the jurisdiction, however, the majority of alleged or suspected juvenile delinquents will ''track'' further into the juvenile justice system. Some status offenders, especially recidivists, will also be funneled further into the system. Youths whose offense is regarded as serious enough to warrant further action may or may not be released to parental custody. Some youths may be maintained in juvenile detention facilities temporarily to await further action. Other youths may be released in their parents' custody, but may be required to reappear later to face further action. These youths will eventually be subjected to an interview with an *intake officer*.

Intake

Intake varies in formality among jurisdictions. **Intake** *is a screening procedure conducted by a court officer or a probation officer, in which one or several courses of action are recommended* (see Figure 4.1). Some jurisdictions conduct intake hearings, where comments and opinions are solicited from "significant others" such as the police, parents, neighbors, and victims, if any. In other jurisdictions, intake proceedings are quite informal, usually consisting of a dialogue between the juvenile and the intake officer. These are important proceedings, regardless of their degree of formality. Intake is a major screening stage in the juvenile justice process, in which further action against juveniles may be contemplated or required.

Intake officers *are either court-appointed officials who hear complaints against juveniles and attempt early resolutions of them, or, more often, are juvenile probation officers who perform intake as a special assignment*. In many small jurisdictions, juvenile probation officers may perform diverse functions, including intake, enforcement of truancy statutes, and juvenile placements. While the intake process will be examined more thoroughly in Chapter 6, a brief overview of this step is as follows.

Intake officers consider youths' attitudes, demeanor, age, seriousness of offense, and a host of other factors. Has the juvenile had frequent prior contact with the juvenile justice system? If the offenses alleged are serious, what evidence exists against the offender? Should the offender be referred to certain community social service agencies, receive psychological counseling, receive vocational counseling and guidance, acquire educational or technical training and skills, be issued a verbal reprimand, be placed on some type of diversionary status, or be returned to parental custody? Interviews with parents and neighbors may be conducted as a part of an intake officer's information gathering.

Assisting intake officers are various guidelines and policies in certain jurisdictions. For instance, in Clark County Juvenile Court in Las Vegas, Nevada, dispositions of juveniles by intake officers are influenced by both legal and nonlegal variables, including the present offense, number of charges and prior petitions, the youth's attitude, grades in school, school status, gender, race, and social class (Shelden and Horvath, 1987). In some instances, a judge's punishment ideology has been cited by intake officers as an important consideration. However, an examination of 456 juvenile courts, 257 judges, and 480 probation officers throughout the United States showed that a judge's philosophy has little impact on the intake decision (Hassenfeld and Cheung, 1985).

In most jurisdictions, intake normally results in one of five actions, depending, in part, upon the discretion of intake officers: (1) dismissal of the case, with or without a verbal or written reprimand; (2) remanding of youths to the custody of their parents; (3) remanding of youths to the custody of their parents with provisions for or referrals to counseling or special services; (4) diversion of youths to an alternative dispute resolution program if one exists in the jurisdiction (see Chapter 6 for a discussion of such programs); or (5) referral of youths to the juvenile prosecutor for further action and possible filing of a delinquency petition.

Since few, if any, universally acceptable standards are currently in place in most jurisdictions defining the competencies that intake officers must possess to be "good" intake officers, they assume a tremendous responsibility, as screening agents, in the decisions they make about youths they confront. Budgetary constraints and an absence of licensing of such officers in most jurisdictions means that many untrained, but interested, juvenile justice professionals may attempt to diagnose a juvenile's problems at this early stage and provide appropriate treatments. If certain juveniles suffer from mental disorders, regardless of their etiology, how can their problems be diagnosed effectively at the time of intake? If intake officers believe that certain youths should have psychological counseling or diagnostic testing to determine whether they actually have psychological problems, which agencies should provide these services?

No agency currently has reliable national figures about how many youths suffer from one or more types of mental problems or disorders. One of the most controversial issues in juvenile corrections today is which agencies should be responsible for certain types of offender treatment (Hartstone, 1985:79). This presupposes that agencies exist to provide needed psychiatric services, if needed. In reality, relatively few jurisdictions have a broad spectrum of social and psychological services available for juveniles (Hartstone, 1985). Frequently children are sent to an agency for treatment, only to be rejected and sent to another agency. Thus, those in need of treatment may become "turnstile children," who fall between the cracks (Bederow and Reamer, 1981; Hartstone, 1985:79–80). Intake officers must walk a fine line between "doing what is best for the child" in the context of *parens patriae,* and pushing juveniles further into the system as a means of subjecting them to potential punishment in the context of a generalized societal expectation of "just deserts." This dilemma seems pervasive among many of those working with juveniles at all stages of offender processing (Hurst, 1990b:49).

Alternative Prosecutorial Actions

Cases that are referred to juvenile prosecutors for further action are usually, though not always, more serious cases. Exceptions include those youths who are chronic recidivists or technical program violators and nonviolent property

---

BOX 4.2

Juvenile Highlights

What should be the minimum age for waivers of juveniles to criminal court? In June, 1990, murder charges were filed against Richard Hubler, a 14-year-old Anaheim, California, youth who allegedly shot his 12-year-old sister in the head.

Anaheim police officers were called to the scene by worried neighbors who heard gunfire from a nearby house. Twelve-year-old Gema Marie Hubler was found by paramedics. She had been covered by a blanket, and her head had been wrapped in white bandages. She remained comatose for several days following surgery at the University of California, Irvine, Medical Center in Orange, but she eventually died.

Initially, police reported that Richard Hubler told them that three masked men had broken into their home and shot his sister. Numerous inconsistencies in his various statements to police, together with other circumstances and evidence they compiled, led them to conclude that Richard had murdered his sister. Police say that Richard told them he had been firing the murder weapon earlier in his back yard before his sister was shot. A detention hearing was scheduled in the Orange County juvenile court. Should this boy be tried as a juvenile or as an adult? What should be his punishment? What should be his treatment?

(Some factual information adapted from Jim Carlton, "Boy, 14, Charged with Murder of His Sister, 12," *Los Angeles Times*, June 19, 1990, p. A28.)

---

offenders (e.g., vandalism, petty theft). This is not to say that property offenses are not serious offenses. They are. But compared with aggravated assault, rape, murder, and armed robbery, property crimes and other similar nonviolent acts rank lower in seriousness.

Not unlike their criminal court counterparts, juvenile court prosecutors have broad discretionary powers. If they wish, they may drop prosecutions of cases against alleged offenders. Much depends upon the docket load or case activity of their own juvenile courts. Prosecutors further screen cases by diverting some of the most serious ones to criminal court through waiver, transfer, or certification (refer to Figure 4.2 and also see Chapter 7 for a more extensive discussion of waivers). **Prosecutorial waivers** are used for this purpose. Some cases are diverted out of the juvenile justice system for informal processing (Rothstein, 1985). (See Chapters 6 and 11 for a discussion of various forms of diversion.) Less serious cases that should remain within juvenile court jurisdiction are pursued, although prosecutors, like police officers, are aware that many juvenile judges seldom do much to seriously punish youths until the youths are five- or six-time offenders (*Criminal Justice Newsletter*, 1988:4).

Prosecutors either file *petitions* or act on the petitions filed by others (Laub and MacMurray, 1987). **Petitions** *are official documents filed in juvenile courts on the juvenile's behalf, specifying reasons for the youth's court appearance* (refer also to Figure 4.2). *These documents assert that juveniles fall within the categories of dependent or neglected, status offender, or delinquent, and the reasons for such assertions are usually provided* (Rogers and Mays, 1987:571). Filing a petition formally places the juvenile before the juvenile judge in many jurisdictions. But juveniles may come before juvenile judges in less formal ways.

In some jurisdictions, juveniles who are cited by highway patrol officers or other law enforcement personnel for driving while intoxicated (DWI) may be required to appear before a juvenile judge accompanied by a parent or legal guardian. For juveniles, the DWI standard in many jurisdictions is the mere presence of alcohol on the breath or in the bloodstream. The .08 or .10 percent standard for blood alcohol levels applicable to adults does not generally apply to juveniles accused of the same offense. A level of .001 percent alcohol for juveniles is sufficient to sustain an accusation of DWI. An officer may cite the juvenile, parents may be notified to pick up their children, and the juvenile may be required to appear in juvenile court later with a responsible adult. The judge has various options, including reprimands of parents as well as fines or other punishments for youths (e.g., loss of driving privileges or restitution to victims). Some research shows that about 50 percent of all cases initiated by police and others against juveniles result in judicial action by juvenile courts (McCarthy, 1987b).

Adjudicatory Proceedings

There is considerable variation in different jurisdictions in the way juvenile courts are conducted. Increasingly, juvenile courts are emulating criminal courts in many respects (Feeney, 1987; Krisberg, 1988; Springer, 1987). Most of the physical trappings are present, including the judge's bench, tables for the prosecution and defense, and a witness stand. In some jurisdictions such as Ocean County, New Jersey, however, these facilities are being redesigned to appear less courtlike and threatening (Kearney, 1989). Manuals are currently available that catalog various pleadings defense attorneys may enter in juvenile courtrooms, and there is growing interest in the rules of juvenile court procedure (Volenik, 1986). Further, there appears to be widespread interest in holding juveniles more accountable for their actions than was the case in past years (Feld, 1987c; Rossum *et al.*, 1987).

Besides the more formal atmosphere of juvenile courts, the procedure is becoming an increasingly adversarial one, in which prosecutors and defense attorneys do battle against and on behalf of juveniles charged with various offenses (Feld, 1988a). However, less than 50 percent of the juvenile offenders in most state jurisdictions have the assistance of counsel, although they are entitled to counsel (Feld, 1989). Both alleged status offenders and those charged with crimes are entitled to be represented by counsel in their court cases. However, an analysis of 17,195 cases in 1986 from various Minnesota juvenile courts shows that those youths who were represented by counsel tended to receive harsher penalties (e.g., twice as many confinements in secure detention and longer probationary sentences) compared with youths not represented by counsel (Feld, 1989). Essentially, the greater the formality imposed on these courts, the greater the punishment imposed on the juveniles by judges.

In some respects, these sentencing disparities are reminiscent of the disparities prevalent in criminal courts between defendants who plea bargain and forgo trials compared with those who insist on their right to a trial and are convicted anyway. Sentences are generally harsher for those convicted through trial proceedings than for those who enter guilty pleas in plea bargain agreements involving the same or similar types of charges (Champion, 1988, 1990b). In short, it doesn't always pay to insist on your full range of legal rights in courts, either criminal or juvenile.

In most jurisdictions, juvenile judges have almost absolute discretion in how their courts are conducted. Juvenile defendants alleged to have committed various crimes may or may not be granted a trial by jury if one is requested. Few states permit jury trials for juveniles in juvenile courts, according to legislative mandates. The doctrine of *parens patriae* is very much in evidence in juvenile courtrooms. After hearing the evidence presented by both sides in any juvenile proceeding, the judge decides or *adjudicates* the matter. An **adjudication** *is a judgment or action on the petition filed with the court by others*. If the petition alleges delinquency on the part of certain juveniles, the judge determines whether the juveniles are delinquent or not delinquent. If the petition alleges that the juveniles involved are dependent, neglected, or otherwise in need of care by agencies or others, the judge decides the matter. If the adjudicatory proceeding fails to support the facts alleged in the petition filed with the court, the case is dismissed and the youth is freed. If the adjudicatory proceeding supports the allegations, then the judge must sentence the juvenile or order a particular disposition.

Dispositions

At least twelve dispositions are available to juvenile judges if the facts alleged in petitions are upheld. These dispositions are generally grouped into (1) nominal, (2) conditional, and (3) custodial options. (Each of these dispositional options will be examined in greater detail in Chapter 9.) These dispositions are generally available, regardless of what is alleged in petitions. Thus, status offenders, those alleged to have committed delinquent acts or those in need of special treatment or care are subject to most, if not all, of these dispositions.

Nominal Dispositions. **Nominal dispositions** are the least punitive of the three major courses of action available to juvenile judges. These include either "verbal warnings" or "stern reprimands." The nature of such verbal

For many youths who are adjudicated as delinquent by the juvenile court, their punishment may be conditional rather than custodial. One conditional punishment sometimes imposed by these courts is to clean grafitti from public buses or to perform other community services. (© Rick Gerharter/Impact Visuals)

warnings or reprimands is exclusively a matter of judicial discretion. Release to the custody of parents or legal guardians completes the juvenile court action against the youth.

Conditional Dispositions. All **conditional dispositions** are probationary options. Youths are placed on probation and required to comply with certain conditions during the probationary period. Conditional options or dispositions usually provide for an act or acts on the part of juveniles to be fulfilled as "conditions" of the sentence imposed. These conditions might be placements in programs or community facilities where assorted treatments may be applied. If juveniles have been adjudicated as "delinquent" and if the delinquency involved damage to a victim's property or bodily harm, restitution to victims may be required in the form of payment for the property or payment of medical bills. Many jurisdictions provide for the performance of community services of various kinds by juveniles. They may be required to cut lawns in city parks, clean debris from local highways or public areas, or perform other services such as painting, maintenance work, or carpentry.

Youths may be required to take courses or therapy at various community service agencies. If they are alcohol- or drug-dependent, they may be required to take steps toward recovery from their dependencies. Another option available to judges is to sentence youths to custodial terms and suspend their sentences in favor of probation for a designated period such as six months or one year. In some jurisdictions, youths may be permitted to live at home and attend school, but they must wear electronic anklets or wristlets as a part of an **electronic monitoring program.** (Chapter 12 includes an extensive discussion of different types of electronic monitoring programs.) Such programs are designed to keep electronic tabs on offenders. Offenders wear devices that emit electronic signals that can be received at some central location, such as a juvenile probation department. Or youths may be tracked through special telephonic devices that require them to place their electronic wristlets into receptacles that enable the sender to verify the offender's presence at home. "Drive-bys" may also be conducted by juvenile probation officers, in which these officers drive by juveniles' homes with receivers and are able to determine whether the wearers of these wristlet or anklet electronic devices are on the premises. Electronic monitoring of both adult and juvenile offenders is becoming increasingly popular as an inexpensive method of managing probationers and others in many jurisdictions (Ball *et al.,* 1988; Charles, 1989a, 1989b, 1989c; McCarthy, 1987a).

Custodial Options. **Custodial options** are classified into **nonsecure custody** and **secure custody.** Nonsecure custody consists of placing certain juveniles into foster homes, group homes, or camp ranches or schools. These placements are often designed as temporary measures until more permanent arrangements can be made. Juveniles have freedom of movement, and they can generally participate in school and other youthful activities. If they are living in group homes or camp ranches, there are curfews to be observed. It is assumed that if they are in the care of others in foster homes or shelters, such curfews will be implicitly (if not explicitly) enforced.

The secure custodial option is considered by most juvenile judges as a last resort for the most serious juvenile offenders (*Criminal Justice Newsletter,* 1988:5−6; Krisberg *et al.,* 1986). Some of the reasons for this include overcrowding in secure juvenile facilities, a general reluctance among judges to incarcerate youths because of potential adverse labeling effects, and the potential effectiveness of certain intermediate punishments through community-service agencies. However, independent investigations show that often, excessive numbers of juveniles who are not among the worst offenders are placed in secure custody. In Oregon, for example, excessive numbers of runaways, youths with mental health problems, drug abusers, and child abuse victims have been institutionalized, primarily because of a lack of available community-based treatment programs (Bakal and Krisberg, 1987).

According to a fifty-state survey of juvenile judge sentencing dispositions issued by the National Conference of State Legislatures (1988), judges in some states may impose weekend confinement in secure facilities for some youths as a punishment. In eight states (Alaska, Arkansas, Illinois, Kansas,

Montana, New Mexico, Texas, and Vermont), courts commit adjudicated youths to the relevant youth corrections agencies, and those agencies decide what types of placements are appropriate (*Criminal Justice Newsletter*, 1988:5). Several states have moved to ensure that only the most serious juvenile offenders receive secure custody (*Criminal Justice Newsletter*, 1988:5).

Juvenile Corrections

The range of juvenile corrections is almost as broad as that existing for adult offenders convicted of crimes (Frost *et al.*, 1985). (Also see Chapter 13 for a more in-depth discussion of juvenile corrections.) Those juveniles adjudicated as delinquent may be placed on probation (Thomson and McAnany, 1984). Depending upon juvenile probation officer caseloads in various jurisdictions, this probation may be more or less intense, commensurate with intensive supervised probation for adults (Baird, 1987; Colley *et al.*, 1987). A youth's placement in different types of probationary programs is dependent upon how he or she is originally classified (Baird, 1984).

Probation, whether or not it is intensive, may be conditional and may involve restitution to victims and/or community services (Clarke and Craddock, 1987; Rubin, 1988). In 1987, there were 74,574 juveniles on probation in various state jurisdictions (American Correctional Association, 1988:xxx–xxxi). Juveniles may be placed in community-based residential programs or exposed to various therapies and treatments or to training (Maloney *et al.*, 1988; Rubin, 1988). A "balanced approach" to probation for juveniles in New Orleans combines protecting the community, equipping juveniles with competencies to live productively and responsibly in the community, and imposing accountability for their offenses (Maloney *et al.*, 1988). Also, there are many types of intermediate punishments, including several community-based interventions (Gottschalk *et al.*, 1987). Some of these interventions are group homes (Simone, 1984).

Confinement in state industrial schools is the juvenile equivalent of incarceration in a state prison for adults. This type of confinement is considered "hard time" for many juveniles. The California Youth Authority operates various facilities to house growing numbers of juvenile offenders in secure confinement. Lengths of commitment vary for offenders, depending upon the seriousness of their adjudication offenses (Wiederanders, 1983). In 1987, there were over 90,000 juveniles in public and private correctional facilities in the United States (Flanagan and Maguire, 1990:560). Three-fourths of those in secure detention are male (Flanagan and Maguire, 1990:563).

Finally, when juveniles have served a portion of their incarcerative sentences, they are paroled by a juvenile paroling authority to the supervision of an appropriate state or community agency. In 1987, there were 48,502 juveniles on parole in various state jurisdictions (American Correctional Association, 1988:xxx–xxxi). In Utah, for instance, a seven-member board, the Utah Youth Parole Authority, makes early-release decisions on large numbers of incarcerated youths monthly. Operated by the Utah Division of Youth Corrections, this board consists of three citizens and four staff members. In one 37-day period, the board conducted approximately 300 parole hearings (Norman, 1986). Although the board appears to be guided by certain eligibility criteria, institutional behavior while confined is considered quite important as an indicator of potential for future community reintegration (Norman, 1986).

Various jurisdictions have attempted to intensify the supervision youths receive while on parole. In New York, for instance, a pilot supervision program for juvenile parolees, PARJO, was implemented for 368 participants in 1983–1984 (New York State Division of Parole, Evaluation, and Planning, 1985). Juvenile parole officers were assigned relatively low caseloads and assisted parolees in finding jobs and needed services. The program was considered modestly successful at reducing recidivism among juvenile parolees and decreasing their unemployment rate. (Chapter 13 examines more extensively the use of parole for juveniles and the effectiveness of various parole programs.)

Summary

Approximately one million juveniles are arrested or taken into custody by police annually. The criminal justice system, an interrelated set of agencies and organizations designed to control criminal behavior, detect crime, and punish criminals, is a major receiver of juveniles initially after they are apprehended. The components of the criminal justice system include the legislature, law enforcement agencies, prosecution and the courts, and corrections. When juveniles are arrested, they are often brought to jails, where they are held while police officers investigate the circumstances leading to their apprehension. As with adults, after they have been apprehended, they are booked and are subject to an initial appearance before a magistrate.

The juvenile justice system parallels the criminal justice system in a number of respects. Police officers classify juveniles according to the offenses alleged, and preliminary dispositions of cases are made. At any point during processing, charges against juveniles may be dropped or dismissed. Youths may be returned to parental custody or placed in the care of community agencies or certain legal guardians. Those juveniles who move further into the juvenile justice system are screened through intake, a process of classification by a probation or court officer. Petitions are filed by various persons against juveniles, alleging either misconduct or specific needs in the case of dependent, neglected, and/or abused children. These petitions are presented in juvenile courts where the cases are adjudicated.

Nominal sanctions include verbal warnings or reprimands. Conditional sanctions include payment of fines or restitution to victims, community service, participation in drug- or alcohol-dependent programs, or in some educational training program or therapy treatment. Custodial sanctions include nonsecure and secure custody. Nonsecure custody may be placement in a foster or group home, or in a camp ranch. Secure custody in state industrial schools is similar to prison incarceration for adults. These facilities are typically designed for the more serious offenders, although many nonserious offenders are incarcerated because of a lack of appropriate community-based treatment programs in some jurisdictions.

Key Terms

Adjudication (133)

Aggravating circumstances (122)

Arraignment (120)

Automatic transfer laws (124)

Bail (120)

Bail bond (120)

Bench trial (122)

Booking (119)

Conditional dispositions (134)

Corrections (122)

Criminal Investigation Division
  (CID) (119)

Criminal justice system (117)

Custodial options (134)

Custody (134)

Defendant (120)

Drug Enforcement Administration
  (DEA) (119)

Electronic monitoring program
  (134)

Evidence (120)

Exculpatory evidence (120)

Federal Bureau of Investigation
  (FBI) (119)

Grand jury (120)

Hearing (129)

Inculpatory evidence (120)

Indictment (121)

Initial appearance (120)

Intake (129)

Intake officer (129)

Intermediate punishment (123)

Jail (123)

Jurisdiction (117)

Jury trial (122)

Law enforcement agencies (117)

Legislature (117)

Mitigating circumstances (122)

Nominal dispositions (133)

Nonsecure custody (135)

Parole (123)

Parole board (123)

Petition (132)

Plea bargains (120)

Preliminary hearing (120)

Prison (123)

Probable cause (120)

Probation (122)

Prosecution and courts (117)

Prosecutorial waiver (131)

Released on own recognizance
  (ROR) (120)

Reverse waiver action (128)

Secure custody (134)

Questions for Review

1. What is the criminal justice system? Why is it important to understand the criminal justice system as a means of better understanding the juvenile justice system?

2. What are the components of the criminal justice system? Briefly describe each.

3. What is meant by jurisdiction? How do police officers and others determine which courts have jurisdiction over certain juveniles?

4. What are several ways in which juveniles may be brought into the juvenile justice system? Are delinquents the only ones who enter the juvenile justice system? Why or why not?

5. Distinguish between booking and initial appearance. What is bail? What is the function of bail? Is everyone entitled to bail? Under what circumstances are defendants not entitled to bail? What is meant by ROR?

6. What is meant by plea bargaining? Why is it used in state and federal courts?

7. What is an arraignment? What are its functions?

8. What is a preliminary hearing? What are some alternatives to preliminary hearings in various jurisdictions?

9. Under what circumstances are persons entitled to trials? Distinguish between bench and jury trials. Is everyone entitled to a jury trial? Why or why not? What factors determine whether one may receive a jury trial if requested?

10. Distinguish between aggravating and mitigating circumstances. How do these circumstances respectively affect or influence sentencing of offenders?

11. Distinguish between probation and parole. What is meant by corrections? What kinds of probation programs are there? What are intermediate punishments?

12. What is a waiver, certification, or transfer? What is an automatic transfer and under what conditions might such a transfer be used? Relate transfers to jurisdiction.

13. Are jail officials entitled to hold juveniles for brief periods? Under what conditions?

14. What is intake? Who performs the role of intake officer? Are there ordinarily any special requirements or prerequisites for becoming an intake officer?

15. What is a petition? Who can file a petition? What is the result of filing a petition with the juvenile court? Do all petitions pertain to juvenile delinquents? Why or why not?

16. What is an adjudication? What are three major sentencing options available to juvenile judges?

17. What is meant by electronic monitoring? What are its primary functions?

18. Identify two types of custodial alternatives and describe them briefly.

19. Can juveniles be paroled from juvenile correctional institutions? Describe probation and parole programs for juveniles.

Suggested Readings

AMERICAN BAR ASSOCIATION (1986). *Criminal and Juvenile Justice Policies: A Road Map for State Legislators and Policymakers.* Washington, DC: American Bar Association.

GUERNSEY, CARL E. (1985). *Handbook for Juvenile Court Judges.* Reno, NV: National Council of Juvenile and Family Court Judges.

MILLER, FRANK W. ET AL. (1985). *The Juvenile Justice Process.* Mineola, NY: Foundation Press.

ROSSUM, RALPH A., BENEDICT J. KOLLER, AND CHRISTOPHER MANFREDI (1987). *Juvenile Justice Reform: A Model for the States.* Claremont, CA: Rose Institute of State and Local Government and the American Legislative Exchange Council. Prepared for the U.S. Office of Juvenile Justice and Delinquency Prevention.

SINGER, SIMON I. (1985). *Relocating Juvenile Crime: The Shift from Juvenile to Criminal Justice.* Albany, NY: Nelson A. Rockefeller Institute of Government, State University of New York.

Juveniles and the Police

Two police officers are cruising a back alley of a high-crime neighborhood at 3:00 A. M. on a Sunday morning. As they pass a house, one of the officers notices the rear door standing wide open. She advises her partner to stop the car so they can investigate. As they approach the rear of house with their flashlights, a loud crash is heard coming from the front of the house. The officers proceed around toward the front and see two people running up the street away from the house. One officer chases them up the street, shouting for them to halt, while the other officer returns to the cruiser to head them off. Two blocks from the scene the chase ends. The officer chasing the suspects on foot corners them in a blind alley. The other officer joins the partner. Two youths, one black and one white, show the officers identification cards, and one of the cards appears to be altered. The cards indicate that the youths are 20 and 22 respectively, although they both appear to be only 16 or 17. A "pat-down" of the youths produces a bottle opener and a small pocket knife. Each youth is carrying several $20 bills and pocket change. The police officers return the youths to the home from which they fled. It turns out to be an unoccupied dwelling. The boys claim they were using the house to "crash" after a late party a few blocks down the street, that they were on their way home and stopped there to keep warm, that the doors were open when they approached the house, and that other youths in the neighborhood used the house frequently for the same purpose. They heard sounds from the back of the house (the police arriving), became frightened, and fled. What should the police officers do?

A youth is looking at clothes in a well-known and exclusive department store. The sales clerk, a 65-year-old man, smells what seems to be alcohol on the young man's breath but says nothing. The youth selects fourteen dress shirts, five sport jackets, and twenty pairs of pants and produces an American Express Gold Card to pay for his purchases. The total purchase comes to $1,792.20. The clerk calls American Express to verify the purchase, and verification is received. The sales clerk asks the youth to produce a driver's license and one other credit card. The youth pulls out another credit card but claims to have left his driver's license at home. The name on the other credit card, a VISA card, reads "JAMES E. BAKER." The American Express Gold Card says "ALEXANDER BAKER ANDERSON." When questioned about the name discrepancy, the youth says "Alex Anderson is my stepfather. I'm Jim Baker, his stepson. He loaned me his card to buy some school clothes for next semester. I'm a senior at Yale University." The youth then produces a current Yale University student activities card that reads "JAMES ELWIN BAKER." The sales clerk asks the youth to wait and notifies police, believing that the American Express card is probably stolen. A police officer arrives at the store a few minutes later. By this time, the youth is belligerent and is demanding the return of his credit cards and Yale ID. The officer smells what seems to be alcohol on the youth's breath, and he asks him if he has been drinking. "No, I'm a diabetic. Call my stepfather if you don't believe me," the youth says. He gives the officer a telephone number, the number is dialed, and no one answers. The officer listens to the clerk's story, and then hears the complaints from the youth. The youth looks 15 or 16 years of age and has no other identification beyond the two credit cards and the student ID. What should the police officer do?

Two young girls are walking toward the on-ramp of a major interstate highway on a Wednesday afternoon in early spring. They are carrying backpacks. One girl appears to be about 12 or 13, and the other looks about 8 or 9. An off-duty highway patrolman in a marked cruiser sees the girls attempt to thumb rides from passing motorists. He drives over to the girls, gets out of his car, and approaches them. Showing them his badge, he asks the girls for some identification. They have no identification, but they both claim that they live in a small community, Birchfield, just a few miles away and are just trying to hitch a ride "back home." They also claim to be sisters, giving their names as "Susan Smiley" and "Rae Ann Smiley." They claim that they have been "on a long hike" since early that morning and are getting tired of walking. The older girl has $6 in her small purse, a breakfast receipt from the McDonald's in Birchfield, and some photographs of others. The officer asks the girls to get into the back of his cruiser and he drives across the interstate highway to a filling station. The girls claim their father is "Peter Smiley," and the officer finds a listing in the Birchfield telephone directory for a "Peter

Smiley, Route 3, Birchfield." He dials the number and no one answers. Next, he calls the Birchfield Police Department and asks the dispatcher if any girls have been reported as missing recently. The dispatcher says that no one has been reported missing. What should the officer do?

Introduction

All of the encounters described above may be just as they are represented to investigating police officers. The two youths in the unoccupied home *may have been* at a party, may have been walking back to their homes, and may have decided to "crash" for a while in the vacant house. The youth buying clothes in the exclusive department store *may have been* using his stepfather's credit card with permission. The two girls hitching rides on the highway *may have been* on a hike and may have been heading home. How are these police officers to decide the best course of action to follow? In each case, should the officers involved take the youths to where they say their homes are and check with their parents or guardians about their respective claims? What about the unanswered telephones? Are the police officers dealing respectively with burglars, a credit card thief, or runaways?

There are no textbook answers to these questions. Each scenario is different and presents police officers with different problems. Much of their decision making will depend on the demeanor of the youths involved. Much will depend on the "totality of circumstances" presented by each situation. Probably every police officer in every city or county law enforcement agency in the United States who has ever engaged in neighborhood patrol work has encountered at least one of these situations. In most of these encounters, there are no clear-cut guidelines to follow. Police must exercise their discretion. A failure to act correctly in these situations could have serious consequences.

This chapter examines police discretion as it pertains to wide varieties of juvenile conduct. How should police officers react to youths under different circumstances? When is formal action necessary or strongly suggested? What statutory provisions exist for handling certain types of encounters with juveniles? Under what circumstances should juveniles be arrested and taken into custody to local jails or lockups? These and similar questions will be examined.

Since there have been several significant changes in state and federal laws during the last few decades concerning how juvenile offenders are defined and should be processed, police procedures involving juveniles have been modified greatly. Certain classes of juvenile offenders have been reclassified by law. Most notably, a clear distinction now exists between status offenders and delinquent offenders in every jurisdiction. However, police officers are those who interface most often with juveniles on the streets. Because many of these encounters between police officers and juveniles are diffuse and it is unclear whether any criminal laws have been violated, police officers must use their discretion when interpreting each situation and the events observed. What is the nature of police response to changing procedures about how certain types of juveniles should be processed? Do police officers generally follow procedure and make the distinctions between juveniles that the law requires? The implications of deinstitutionalizing status offenders (DSO) for influencing police discretion and conduct will be examined.

Police Discretion: Use and Abuse

Few will contest the idea that police officers make up the "front line" or "first line of defense" in the prevention and/or control of street crime, although the effectiveness of this line in crime control continues to be questioned (Conrad, 1987; Walker, 1984). Police officers are vested with considerable *discretionary powers*, depending on the circumstances, ranging from verbal warnings in confrontations with the public to the application of deadly force (Conner, 1986; Scharf and Binder, 1983; *Tennessee* v. *Garner*, 1985). **Police discretion** *is the range of behavioral choices police officers have within the limits of their power* (Davis, 1969). Beyond the formal training police officers receive from law enforcement agency training academies, police discretion is influenced by many other factors, among them the situation (Brown, 1984; Williams *et al.*, 1983), and the race, ethnicity, gender, socioeconomic status, and age of those confronted (Willis and Wells, 1988). Many of those individuals stopped by police, questioned, and subsequently arrested and detained in jails or other lockup facilities, even for short periods, are juveniles.

The Diffuseness of Police Officer Roles. The public tends to define the police role diffusely; police are expected to be able to handle a wide variety of human problems (Bittner, 1985; Whitaker *et al.*, 1985). The nature of this "expected" police intervention is that the police will intervene in various situations and ensure that matters do not get worse (Bennett and Baxter, 1985; Bittner, 1985). Thus, police training in various jurisdictions is geared to reflect this broad public expectation of the police role. One training manual for police officers includes at least 476 field situations, including how to deal with domestic disturbances, traffic violations, narcotics, civil disorders, vice, drunkenness, federal offenses, and juveniles (Kenney and More, 1986).

Much of this **situationally based police discretion** in confronting crime in the streets and the public is covert. Most of what transpires in the interaction between police officers and suspects is known only to these actors. Thus, it is often difficult to enforce consistently high standards of accountability for police to observe in their diverse public encounters (Butler, 1985; Klockars, 1985). In short, police officers must make on-the-spot decisions about whether to move beyond simple verbal warnings or reprimands to more formal actions against those stopped and questioned "on suspicion." Considering the circumstances or situation, law enforcement officers may be more or less aggressive.

Contributing to the diffuseness of police officer roles in communities is a relatively recent phenomenon known as *community policing*. **Community policing** *is a major policing reform that broadens the police mission from a narrow*

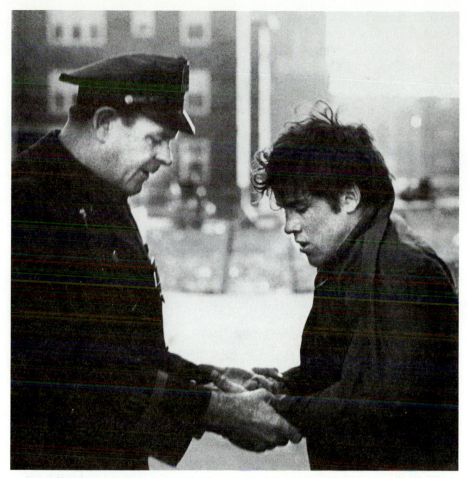

Police officer encounters with juveniles almost always involve situationally based discretion. In such encounters, officers may issue youths verbal warnings or take them into custody. Often, nonlegal factors, such as a youth's appearance and demeanor, time of the day or night, and the particular neighborhood, may determine a police officer's subsequent action. (© Patricia Holland Gross/Stock Boston)

2ND EXAM

focus on crime to a mandate that encourages the police to explore creative solutions for a host of community concerns, including crime, fear of crime, disorder, and neighborhood decay. It rests on the belief that only by working together will people and the police be able to improve the quality of life in the community, with the police not only as enforcers, but also as advisors, facilitators, and supporters of new community-based police-supervised initiatives (Trojanowicz and Bucqueroux, 1990:3).

One immediate effect of community policing in many neighborhoods is to place greater discretionary power in the hands of police officers, whether they are on foot or in cruisers. An implicit consequence of community policing is to create better relations between the police department and the community, to enable community residents to place greater trust in the police rather than to fear them. In communities where such power shifts occur through planning, police officers may be expected by higher-ups to take a greater interest in youths, even where petty infractions are involved (Trojanowicz and Bucqueroux, 1990:238–239). Police officers may be *punished* for failing to take minor infractions seriously and for not intervening when necessary. Thus, they may be placed in a dilemma about whether to get involved in the activities of minor offenders.

For many police officers, stopping and detaining juveniles is not a particularly popular activity (Mixdorf, 1989:106). One reason is that the courts, both juvenile and criminal, are inclined to do little or nothing to juvenile first offenders or minor offenders (*Criminal Justice Newsletter*, 1988:4). Most juvenile courts wait until youths are five- or six-time offenders before they consider them "chronic offenders" (National Center for Juvenile Justice, 1988). Howard Snyder, Director of Systems Research at the National Center for Juvenile Justice, says that "second appearance(s) [by juveniles] serves as a good bellwether that [they are] coming back. . . . Most of the offenses committed by younger juveniles are relatively minor. . . . There aren't many 13- and 14-year olds committing armed robbery" (*Criminal Justice Newsletter*, 1988:4). Additionally, Mixdorf (1989:106) says that "In law enforcement . . . police officers now spend less time with juveniles, and many have discontinued preventive activities to focus resources on major crimes that have been committed by adults." Besides the fact that the courts are lenient with minor first offenders, some paperwork is involved whenever juveniles are taken into custody. Many police officers are reluctant to involve themselves in trivial juvenile affairs that may take more time to process than cases involving adult criminals.

Nevertheless, police officers in every jurisdiction inevitably encounter large numbers of juveniles in their community patrols and on their "beats." Because of the informal nature of many of these police officer–juvenile encounters, the UCR and other official sources of arrest information fail to disclose the true extent of juvenile contacts with the law. According to official sources, however, there were in excess of 1.4 million arrests of youths under age 18 in the United States in 1988 (U.S. Department of Justice, 1988:172). Furthermore, self-reports from juveniles in elementary schools and high schools suggest considerably greater delinquent activity, as well as contacts with police that do not necessarily result in arrests or being taken into custody (Flanagan and Maguire, 1990:322–364).

Juvenile Units in Police Departments. For many years, police departments throughout the nation, particularly larger municipal police departments with 200 or more officers, have had specialized juvenile units as a part of their organizational structure to deal with juvenile offenders. Even relatively small departments in remote areas usually have at least one officer who deals exclusively with juvenile affairs. Despite this specialization, however, *every* police officer who encounters juveniles while policing becomes a juvenile officer temporarily (Rogers and Mays, 1987:314).

BOX 5.1

Juvenile Highlights

Do public statistics show the true extent of delinquency in the United States? What do we know about drug use and alcohol consumption among teenagers? Self-reports of this behavior are illuminating. Boston College reported in 1990 that the number of students hospitalized for alcohol-related problems had doubled since 1989. Many of the youths who were hospitalized had blood alcohol levels of .30 or higher, and some youths were on the brink of death from alcohol poisoning.

A researcher affiliated with the Harvard School of Public Health, Dr. Henry Wechsler, reports from his survey of 1,600 freshmen at 14 Massachusetts colleges that among youths who drink, about 92 percent of the males consume at least five drinks in a row, while 82 percent of the females have similar rates of consumption. A majority of these youths are below the minimum drinking age of 21 in the state.

Some experts believe that the minimum drinking age should be lowered to 18, and they speculate that the prohibition against drinking before age 21 prompts many college students who are experiencing new-found freedoms away from home to overuse and abuse alcoholic beverages. One difficulty in obtaining accurate information about the extent of drug or alcohol use among college students is the reluctance of various campuses to be portrayed negatively in the public view. Campuses want to attract students, not repel them. Many parents might be reluctant to permit their children to enroll at certain schools if the alcohol consumption rates of these schools were known. Self-reports of college students suggest that alcohol abuse is widespread, and no campus is immune from such problems.

(Some factual information adapted from Debra Rosenberg, "Bad Times at Hangover U.," *Newsweek*, November 19, 1990, p. 81.)

The activities of juvenile units or "youth squads" are largely directed toward delinquency prevention (McKeachern and Bauzer, 1967). These units tend to be **reactive**, in that they respond to public requests for intervention and assistance whenever offenses committed by juveniles are reported. That is, these officers react to calls from others about crimes that have already been committed or are in progress. Gang fights or break-ins involving youths would activate these juvenile units. In contrast, police officers who patrol city streets are most often **proactive**, in that they are involved in contacts with juveniles who may or may not be offenders and/or law violators. These officers are almost constantly on the lookout for suspicious activities. They monitor the streets and investigate potentially troublesome situations as they present themselves.

BOX 5.2

Juvenile Highlights

Can you tell the ethnicity or gang membership of juveniles by the color or style of their clothes? Police officers who specialize in juvenile gang matters will tell you that juveniles' clothing is definitely symbolic of membership in a particular gang. Gang regalia and other distinguishing materials can be particular colors worn by gang members in particular neighborhoods. To wear an "enemy" color on specific streets is to invite a violent attack by rival gangs. The Los Angeles juvenile gang known as the "Crips" has been in a lengthy feud with a rival gang, the "Bloods." The Crips gang has adopted a particular brand of British sneaker, British Knights, because the symbolic "B.K." on the shoes may also be interpreted as "Blood Killers." Wearing B.K. shoes in the wrong neighborhood may result in serious bodily injury or death to the wearer.

Los Angeles County has over 500 juvenile gangs, of which the best-known and most violent are the Bloods and the Crips. Between them they are believed to control a 43-square-mile area of South Central Los Angeles. Gang members are inducted as members after they have gone on certain "missions." One mission for "Little Ducc," a 12-year-old Crips gang member, was a drive-by shooting.

These and other gangs are reflective of the extensive cultural diversity of the Los Angeles area, including large concentrations of Samoans, Vietnamese, Laotians, Chinese, Japanese, blacks, Afghanistanis, and Cambodians. These different cultures wear certain types of clothing to set them apart from rival gangs and to enhance their territoriality and turf dominance.

(Factual information adapted from *Time*, June 18, 1990, pp. 50–52.)

Youth Gangs and Minority Status. The increased visibility of delinquent gangs organized along ethnic and racial lines in many cities, and the violence such gangs manifest, have caused police departments to establish task forces of special police officers who do nothing but monitor and investigate gang activities (Chicago Police Department, 1988; Hagedorn, 1988; Takata and Zevitz, 1987). Some professionals have classified these gangs as *scavenger gangs* and *corporate gangs* (Taylor, 1986). **Scavenger gangs** *form primarily as a means of socializing and for mutual protection*, while **corporate gangs** *emulate organized crime* (Taylor, 1986). While both types of gangs pose dangers to the public, corporate gangs are more profit-motivated and rely on illicit activities such as drug trafficking to further their profit interests. Corporate gangs use excessive violence, including murder, to carry out their goals. Often, innocent bystanders are gunned down in the course of fighting between rival gangs (Taylor, 1986).

Police officers who observe juveniles in pairs or larger groupings, particularly in areas known to be gang-dominated, may assume that these youths are gang members, and this observation may heighten police interest in and activity against them. This heightened interest and activity may take the form of more frequent stopping and questioning of certain juveniles on the basis of their appearance, where they are seen, and whether they are minority youths.

While some investigators question the suggestion that police officers tend to discriminate against certain youths or single them out for stopping and questioning on the basis of racial or ethnic factors (Griswold, 1978; Wilbanks, 1987), other researchers have found patterns of police behavior that appear discriminatory on racial or ethnic grounds (Huizinga and Elliott, 1987; Thornberry, 1979). At least in some jurisdictions, stops, arrest rates, and detentions of minority youths are at least three times as high as those for white youths (Black and Reiss, 1976; Huizinga and Elliott, 1987; Sampson, 1986).

However, much police officer activity is centered in high-crime areas, which also tend to be areas inhabited by large numbers of persons of lower socioeconomic status (SES). And those areas with larger numbers of persons in the lower socioeconomic strata are also those that contain larger concentrations of minorities (Sampson, 1986). Thus, some selectivity regulates where police officers will concentrate their patrol efforts as well as those youths they target for questioning and those they choose to ignore. Experts believe that this opens the door to allegations of police officer harassment against certain classes of juvenile offenders on the basis of subjectively determined stereotypical features such as a youth's appearance (Yablonsky and Haskell, 1988:38).

Juvenile Response to Police Officer Contacts. Interestingly, how youths behave toward police officers when they are stopped and questioned seems to have an important effect on what the officers will eventually do. Early research about the appearance and demeanor of youths stopped by police officers and their subsequent actions indicates that youths who were poorly dressed and/or behaved defiantly and belligerently toward police were more likely to be harassed, and possibly arrested (Piliavin and Briar, 1964; Tomson and Fielder, 1975). Subsequent research is consistent with these early findings and suggests that cooperative, neatly dressed youths stand a better chance of avoiding being stopped, questioned, or arrested by police (Morash, 1984).

In fact, some police officers insist that a youth's demeanor when responding to police questioning on the street is crucial to whether the youth will be taken into custody, even if only temporarily. If youths do not display the proper amount of deference toward police officers when they are stopped and questioned, they stand a good chance of being taken to the police station for further questioning (Smith and Visher, 1981). Interestingly, youths may also arouse the suspicions of police officers when they are too polite. There is an elusive "range of politeness" that minimizes a youth's chances of being taken into custody. If a youth is too polite or is not polite enough, police officers will be sufficiently motivated to act. According to experts, police officer discretionary abuse occurs when "juveniles are detained when there is little or no evidence that detention is necessary or desirable to meet the generally accepted goals of detention" (Roberts, 1989:150).

Despite statutory safeguards about holding youths in adult jails for long periods and the division of labor relating to youthful offender processing in any jurisdiction, police officers are free to do pretty much whatever they want relative to juveniles they question who are acting either suspiciously or belligerently. If any pretext exists for assuming that certain youths have been or are engaging in delinquent acts, they are subject to temporary detention by police officers. In many instances, these detention decisions by police are purely arbitrary (Frazier and Bishop, 1985).

The following is a listing of discretionary actions that may be taken by police officers when they encounter youths on the street:

1. *Police officers may ignore the behaviors of youths they observe in the absence of citizen complaints.* The most frequent types of encounters police officers have with juveniles do not stem from complaints filed by others. Rather, police officers observe youths under a wide variety of circumstances. The situation and circumstances are important, since youths walking down a street in pairs during daylight hours would not attract the same kind of attention as would pairs of youths walking the same street late at night. Much depends on what the officers regard as menacing behavior. If youths are on skateboards on the sidewalks of the main street of a local community, they may or may not be posing risks to other pedestrians. If youths are playing ball on a vacant lot near other homes in a neighborhood, they may or may not be disturbing others. Police action in each of these instances is probably unwarranted.

2. *Police officers may act passively on someone's complaint about juvenile behaviors.* If a store owner complains that youths are jeopardizing the safety of store customers by riding their skateboards down the street in front of the store, police officers may respond by directing the youths to other streets for their skateboarding. If neighbors complain that youths are making too much noise playing in a nearby vacant lot, police officers may appear and advise youths to play elsewhere.

The intent of police officers in these situations is twofold. First, they want citizens to know they are there doing something. Second, they want citizens to know that action has been taken and the problem no longer exists. Police officers continue to view the behaviors they observe as not especially serious. In these instances, police warnings are ordinarily sufficient to satisfy complainants. Since complaints were registered, dispositions of those complaints are usually logged officially. Police officers may or may not choose to name those youths warned. Rather, they may file a generalized report briefly describing the action taken.

3. *Police officers may take youths into custody and release them to parents or guardians without incident.* Those youths who may be acting suspiciously or who are in places where their presence might indicate an intent to do something unlawful (for example, the youths who were in the uninhabited house to "crash" after their party) are likely to be taken into custody for more extensive questioning. In many instances, these **station adjustments** may result in their release to parents with warnings from police about refraining from suspicious conduct in the future (Krisberg and Austin, 1978). While these actions are official in the sense that police officers actually took youths into custody for a brief period and made records of these temporary detentions, they do not result in official action or intervention by intake officers or juvenile courts.

4. *Police officers may take youths into custody and refer them officially to community service agencies for assistance or treatment.* Sometimes youths appear to police to be under the influence of drugs or alcohol when they are stopped and questioned. Other youths may not have parents or guardians who are responsible for their conduct. They may be classified by police as runaways. In these cases, police officers will arrange for various community services to take custody of these juveniles for treatment or assistance. These youths will be under agency care until arrangements can be made for their placement with relatives or in foster homes. Those youths with chemical dependencies may undergo medical treatment and therapy. In either case, juvenile courts are avoided.

5. *Police officers may take youths into custody, file specific charges against them, and refer them to juvenile intake where they may or may not be detained.* Only a small percentage of all juveniles detained by police will subsequently be charged with offenses. Conservatively, probably less than 10 percent of all juveniles who have contact with police officers annually engage in serious violence or property offenses (Hawaii Crime Commission, 1985; Lab, 1984; Mathias *et al.*, 1984; Youth Policy and Law Center, Inc., 1984). Many youths are taken into custody for minor infractions, and their referrals to juvenile intake may or may not result in short- or long-term confinement. The discretion shifts from police officers to intake officers as to whether to process certain juveniles further into the juvenile justice system. Figure 5.1 shows a petition that may be filed by an officer or concerned citizen to have a juvenile's case considered by a juvenile judge.

Those juveniles who are deemed dangerous, violent, or persistent-nonviolent will most often be subject to pretrial detention until adjudication by a juvenile court. Police officers may respond to citizen complaints or may actually observe juveniles engaging in illegal conduct. The likelihood of their

AFFIDAVIT AND APPLICATION FOR FILING OF JUVENILE COURT PETITION
(Welfare and Institutions Code Section 653)

I,_____
    Officer's/Citizen's Name

_____ hereby state that
Officer's Agency & Duty station or Citizen's Address

_____ a minor, DOB _____

    ____is within San Diego County   ____resides within San Diego County
    ____was within San Diego County   ____committed an offense described within
                                 sections 601/602 within San Diego County

and that said minor comes within the provisions of sections 601/602 of the Welfare and
Institutions Code of the State of California as evidenced by the case reports
dated_____and consisting of ___ pages, which are attached hereto and incorporated
by reference herein. On the basis of this information, the undersigned requests that a
Juvenile Court Petition be filed on the above named minor for the offense(s) of

_____
    (State the name of the offense and the appropriate statutory authority)

I declare under penalty of perjury that the facts set forth in this affidavit and its
attachments are true and correct to the best of my knowledge.

Dated:_____ Signed:_____

Companions referred_____

Companions not referred_____

                    REPORT OF ACTION AND ENDORSEMENT
The following action was taken on this application: _____
                                      (JDA No. or Misd. No.)
____Petition requested under section(s)_____
____D.A. Reject
____Referred to Traffic Court

____Referral Recorded and Handled Informally**
____Active Delinquent Ward (602 W&I)/Offense reported to Juvenile Court**
____6 Months Probation Supervision (654 W&I)**

    **REASON(S):
    ____Active to another jurisdiction   ____Family moving
    ____Active Dependent Ward (300 W&I)   ____Referred to Community Agency
    ____Minor Offense   ____PC 26 problem
    ____No prior referral   ____Administrative exception
    ____No prior arrests (2 yr. period)   ____Minor cannot be located
    ____Transient   ____Parents handling appropriately
    ____Restitution paid/property recovered ____Low maturity/intellectual level

Other reasons/Additional Information (if any):_____
_____
_____
_____

_____   _____   _____
  (Date)   (Please Print) (Deputy Probation Officer)   (Phone No.)
Prob. 419 (8-87)   Dist: White-Ref.Agency   Canary-Prob.Clerk   Pink- Prob.File

Figure 5-1 Affidavit and Application for Filing of Juvenile Court Petition.

taking these youths into custody for such wrongdoing, alleged or observed, is
increased accordingly.

    6. *Police officers may take youths into custody, file criminal charges against them,
and hold them in jails for brief periods pending their initial appearance, a
preliminary hearing, and a subsequent trial.* As we will see in Chapter 7, some
juveniles may be classified as adults for the purpose of transferring them to

criminal courts, where they may receive harsher punishments. Jurisdictions such as Illinois, Washington, D.C., New York, and California are a few of many places where automatic transfer laws exist and where some juveniles are automatically placed within the power of criminal courts rather than juvenile courts. In these jurisdictions, police officers *must* act in accordance with certain statutory provisions when handling certain juvenile offenders. They have no choice in the matter.

In sum, police discretion is exercised to the greatest extent during the normal course of police patrols or "beats." Those youths who stand the best chance of being targeted for special police attention include minorities who are acting suspiciously and live in high-crime neighborhoods known as gang territories. Also increasing the likelihood of being taken into custody is the demeanor or behaviors exhibited by youths, whether they are overly polite or overly impolite to police officers. Short of any illicit conduct actually observed by or reported to police officers, a youth's appearance and behavior are key considerations in whether the youth will be questioned and/or detained temporarily by police. However, comparatively few youths are actually arrested in relation to the actual number of police officer–juvenile encounters on city streets.

Arrests of Juveniles

As we have seen, police officers need little, if any, provocation to bring juveniles into custody. Arrests of juveniles are more serious than acts of bringing them into custody. Since any juvenile may be taken into custody for suspicious behavior or on any other pretext, all types of juveniles may be detained at police headquarters or at a sheriff's station, department, or jail temporarily. Suspected runaways, truants, or curfew violators may be taken into custody for their own welfare or protection, not necessarily for the purpose of facing subsequent charges. It is standard policy in most jurisdictions, considering the sophistication of available social services, for police officers and jailers to turn over juveniles to the appropriate agencies as soon as possible after they have been apprehended or taken into custody.

Before police officers turn juveniles over to intake officials or juvenile probation officers for further processing, they ordinarily complete an arrest report, noting the youth's name; address; parent's or guardian's name and address; offenses alleged; circumstances; whether other juveniles were involved and apprehended; the juvenile's prior record, if any; height; weight; age; and other classificatory information. Figure 5.2 is a booking form used by the San Diego (California) Police Department.

Juvenile–Adult Distinctions. According to the National Advisory Committee on Criminal Justice Standards and Goals (1976), juveniles must be separated from adults and treated as juveniles as soon as possible following their apprehension (unless, of course, statutory provisions exist in the

SAN DIEGO REGIONAL
ARREST/JUVENILE CONTACT REPORT

REPORT								
☐ ARREST REPORT							AGENCY NUMBER	
☐ JUVENILE CONTACT	WARRANT ☐ LOCAL ☐ OUT	AGENCY		ARJIS ASSISTED? ☐Y ☐N	PAGE 1 OF		SDSO BOOKING NUMBER	
☐ NOTIFY WARRANT	ARREST DATE / /	TIME	BEAT/DISTRICT	RELATED REPORTS (TYPE, NUMBER)			CITATION NUMBER	

ARRESTEE – CRIME

CHARGE(S) — ADDN'L. CHGS. ☐ — ADULT RELEASES OR ☐ 849PC B1☐ B2☐

PERSON ARRESTED (L,F,M) — NICKNAME

B = BLACK H = HISPANIC O = OTHER ORIENTAL X = UNKNOWN/ALL OTHER
C = CHINESE I = AM. INDIAN P = PACIFIC ISLANDER
F = FILIPINO J = JAPANESE W = WHITE

RACE	SEX	AGE	D.O.B. / /	P.O.B.	HT.	WT.	BUILD	HAIR	EYES

ALIAS/MAIDEN NAME (L,F,M) — ARRESTEE'S ADDRESS — CITY — HOME PHONE

MILITARY YES ☐ | OCCUPATION/RATE | EMPLOYER/SCHOOL | ADDRESS | CITY | BUS. PHONE

EMERGENCY CONTACT/NEXT OF KIN (L,F,M) | ADDRESS | CITY | HOME PHONE

IS SUBJECT A SUSPECTED USER OF NARCOTICS/DRUGS? YES ☐ | INTERPRETER REQUIRED? YES ☐ | LANGUAGE | SUSPECT'S RELATION TO VICTIM(S): | RELATIVE ☐ | ACQUAINTANCE ☐ | STRANGER ☐

LOCATION OF ARREST | CITY | LOCATION OF OFFENSE | CITY | OFFENSE DATE / / | OFFENSE TIME

CITIZEN ARREST? YES ☐ | ARRESTING OFFICER | I.D. | ADMONISHED BY | DO YOU UNDERSTAND EACH OF THESE RIGHTS THAT I HAVE EXPLAINED TO YOU?

HAVING IN MIND AND UNDERSTANDING YOUR RIGHTS AS I HAVE TOLD YOU, ARE YOU WILLING TO TALK WITH US? — STATEMENT YES ☐

ARRESTEE DESCRIPTION

HAIR LENGTH/TYPE	HAIR STYLE	FACIAL HAIR	COMPLEXION	SPEECH	VOICE	IDENTIFICATION NUMBERS
1 BALD 2 COLLAR 3 LONG 4 NECK 5 SHORT 6 SHOULDER 1 COARSE 2 FINE 3 THICK 4 THINNING 5 WIRY 6 OTHER:	1 AFRO/NAT. 2 BRAIDED 3 BUSHY 4 GREASY 5 MILITARY 6 PONYTAIL 7 PROCESSED 8 STRAIGHT 9 WAVY/CURLY 10 WIG 11 OTHER:	1 CLEAN SHAVE 2 FULL BEARD 3 FU MANCHU 4 GOATEE 5 LOWER LIP 6 MUSTACHE 7 NONE/FUZZ 8 SIDEBURNS 9 UNSHAVEN 10 VAN DYKE 11 OTHER:	1 ACNE 2 DARK 3 FRECKLED 4 LIGHT 5 MEDIUM 6 PALE 7 POCKED 8 RUDDY 9 SALLOW 10 TANNED 11 OTHER:	1 ACCENT 2 LISPS 3 MUMBLES 4 OFFENSIVE 5 QUIET 6 RAPID 7 SLOW 8 STUTTERS 9 TALKATIVE 10 OTHER:	1 DISGUISED 2 HIGH PITCH 3 LOUD 4 LOW PITCH 5 MEDIUM 6 MONOTONE 7 NASAL 8 PLEASANT 9 RASPY 10 SOFT 11 OTHER:	DRIVER'S LICENSE NO.　STATE SOCIAL SECURITY NO. FBI NO. CII NO. OTHER I.D.　TYPE
☐ ☐	☐	☐ ☐ ☐	☐ ☐ ☐	☐ ☐ ☐	☐ ☐ ☐	UNDOCUMENTED PERSON　YES ☐

FURTHER SUSPECT DESCRIPTION (I.E., GLASSES, TATTOOS, TEETH, BIRTHMARKS, JEWELRY, SCARS, MANNERISMS, ETC.)

CLOTHING DESCRIPTION

SUSPECT VEHICLE:	YEAR	MAKE	MODEL	COLOR/COLOR	BODY TYPE	LICENSE NO.	STATE

ADDITIONAL VEHICLE IDENTIFIERS (CHROME, DAMAGE, ETC.) | VIN NUMBER | DISPOSITION OF VEHICLE

REGISTERED OWNER (L,F,M) | ADDRESS | CITY

EVID.

PROPERTY TAG NOS. | DISPOSITION OF EVIDENCE

COMPAN'S.

#1 NAME (L,F,M)	ADDRESS	CITY	PHONE	RACE	SEX	AGE	D.O.B. / /	ARRESTED YES ☐	ADDN'L. COMPANIONS LISTED YES ☐
#2 NAME (L,F,M)	ADDRESS	CITY	PHONE	RACE	SEX	AGE	D.O.B. / /	ARRESTED YES ☐	

VIC./WIT.

V W RP D C | NAME (L,F,M) | RES. ADDRESS | CITY | HOME PHONE

BUS. ADDRESS | CITY | BUS. PHONE | RACE | SEX | D.O.B. / / | ADDN'L. VIC./WIT. YES ☐

REPORTING OFFICER	I.D.	DIVISION	REPORT DATE / /	TIME	REPORT APPROVED	I.D.	BOOKING APPROVED

ARJIS-8 (Rev. 1-87)

Figure 5-2　San Diego Regional Arrest/Juvenile Contact Report.

jurisdiction for automatic transfer of juveniles to the criminal justice system). If juveniles are brought into custody and charged with offenses that might be either felonies or misdemeanors if committed by adults, they may or may not be clearly distinguishable as juveniles. It would be difficult to conclude that an eight-, nine-, or ten-year-old could pass for 18 or older. But in the case of older youths who are taken into custody, their appearance may be deceptive, and if they deliberately wish to conceal information about their identity or age

PAGE		AGENCY NUMBER	
2 OF			

JUVENILE ONLY

FATHER/STEPFATHER'S NAME (L,F,M)	ADDRESS	CITY	HOME PHONE	BUS. PHONE
MOTHER/STEPMOTHER'S NAME (L,F,M)	ADDRESS	CITY	HOME PHONE	BUS. PHONE

SCHOOL	GRADE	PARENTS NOTIFIED BY: WHOM AND HOW	DATE / /	TIME

LIVES WITH | | | RELEASE DATE / / | TIME

FIELD DISP.: [1] - JUVENILE HALL [2] - OTHER POLICE AGENCY: _____ AGENCY [3] - OTHER: _____ NAME/RELATIONSHIP OR ORGANIZATION

ATTITUDE OF JUVENILE AND PARENTS/GUARDIAN

DET. DISPO.: [1] - REFER COURT/PROB [2] - DEPT. DIVERSION [3] - COUNSEL/INFORMAL [4] - OTHER _____

NARRATIVE

ADDITIONAL CHARGES:

NARRATIVE:

CONTINUED ☐

CITIZEN ARREST

I have arrested _____

☐ For a public offense committed or attempted in my presence.

☐ When the person arrested has committed a felony, although not in my presence.

☐ When a felony has been in fact committed, and I have reasonable cause for believing the person arrested to have committed it.

I know that pursuant to Section 849 of the Penal Code of the State of California, it is necessary for me to sign a complaint stating the charge against the prisoner, which complaint must be made before a magistrate, and I agree to sign said complaint and appear in said matter without delay.

Date: _____   Signed: _____

ARRESTING CITIZEN (L,F,M) PRINT	RES. ADDRESS	CITY	HOME PHONE
BUS. ADDRESS	CITY	BUS. PHONE	RACE	SEX	D.O.B. / /

ADULT - MISD. ONLY

Check each reason for not releasing the subject with a written notice to appear.   **(ADULTS ONLY)**

☐ 1. The person arrested was so intoxicated that he could have been a danger to himself or to others.

☐ 2. The person arrested required medical examination or medical care or was otherwise unable to care for his own safety.

☐ 3. The person was arrested for one or more of the offenses listed in section 40302 of the vehicle code.

☐ 4. There were one or more outstanding warrants for the person.

☐ 5. The person could not provide satisfactory evidence of personal identification.

☐ 6. The prosecution of the offense(s) for which the person was arrested or the prosecution of any other offense(s) would be jeopardized by immediate release of person arrested.

☐ 7. There was a reasonable likelihood that the offense(s) would continue or resume, or that the safety of persons or property would be imminently endangered by release of the person arrested.

☐ 8. The person arrested demanded to be taken before a magistrate or refused to sign the notice to appear.

☐ 9. Any other reason: _____

from officers, it is relatively easy for them to do so. This is a common occurrence, since many juveniles are afraid that police will notify their parents. The fear of parental notification may sometimes be more compelling than the fear of police officers and of possible confinement in a jail.

Because juveniles generally have less understanding of the law than adults, especially those adults who make careers out of crime, they may believe that they will fare better if officers believe that they are adults and not juvenile

BOX 5.3

Juvenile Highlights

Are juveniles who are suspected of crimes guilty until proven innocent? In Los Angeles, it appears that an overzealous police department has brought upon itself a $5.2 million civil rights suit alleging violations of the constitutional rights of suspected gang members.

In February 1990, 18-year-old Xavier Gonzales and 25 other youths were playing in a Pacific Palisades, California, park. Police officers converged on the park and made all the youths lie face down in the dirt. Each youth was allegedly asked by police whether he was a gang member. A "no" response was answered by slamming the youth's face violently into the ground. Gonzales himself was tripped and shoved by police, and he alleges that they called him a "beaner" (a derogatory name for Hispanics) repeatedly. All youths were subsequently taken to a nearby Los Angeles County Jail facility, where they were held in preventive detention for an indeterminate period.

The American Civil Liberties Union labels such police actions as discriminatory and racist, since many youths targeted for excessive force by police officers appear to be Hispanic or black. Their age and color make them suspect, according to ACLU authorities. The LAPD, however, contends that it is law enforcement officers who are the real victims of increasing youth violence. Police say that an increasing lack of respect for authority and attacks on police officers by youths with automatic weapons and assault rifles intensify problems between police and the community. Currently, papers such as *L.A. Youth* distributed to students at Los Angeles city schools include special clip-and-save coupons that explain juveniles' rights whenever they encounter police on the streets.

(Some factual information adapted from Sylvester Monroe, "Complaints About a Crackdown," *Time,* July 16, 1990, pp. 20–25.)

offenders. Perhaps there is a chance they might be released after spending a few hours or even a day or two in jail. However, if they are identified positively as juveniles, then parents will invariably be notified of their arrest. But these youths often underestimate the resources police have at their disposal to verify information they receive from those they book. With proper identification, adults are ordinarily entitled to make bail and obtain early temporary release from jail. If fake IDs are used by juveniles, however, this phony information is easily detected and arouses police suspicions and interest in these youths. They will likely be held as long as it takes to establish their true identities and ages. Furnishing police officers with false information is a certain way to be held for an indefinite period.

The Ambiguity of Juvenile Arrests. Little uniformity exists among jurisdictions about how an "arrest" is defined. There is even greater ambiguity about what constitutes a juvenile arrest. Technically, *an* **arrest** *is the legal detainment of a person to answer for criminal charges or (infrequently at present) civil demands* (Rush, 1990:16).

Early research by Klein *et al.* (1975) focused on the juvenile arrest procedures followed by 49 suburban and urban police departments in a large metropolitan county. Over 250 police chiefs and juvenile officers and their supervisors were surveyed, some of whom participated in follow-up, in-depth interviews about juvenile arrests and processing. Among police chiefs, fewer than 50 percent agreed that booking juvenile suspects was the equivalent of arresting them. Further, respondents variously believed that arrests involved simple police contact with juveniles and "cautioning" behavior. Others believed that "taking youths into custody" and releasing them to parents constituted an arrest. Less than half of those surveyed appeared thoroughly familiar with juvenile rights under the law, and with the different restrictions applicable to their processing by police officers.

Fingerprinting, Photographing, and Booking Juveniles. The Juvenile Justice and Delinquency Prevention Act of 1974, its subsequent revisions, and the recommendations of the National Advisory Committee on Criminal Justice Standards and Goals (1976) have led to some important modifications in the procedures used to process juveniles through the system and in the disposition of all records relating to such processing. Under the provisions of the 1974 act, for instance, status offenders should not be treated the same as delinquent offenders—i.e., they should be separated from them through deinstitutionalization or DSO. Nor should status offenders be taken to jails for temporary detention; rather, they should be taken to juvenile agencies to undergo less formal dispositions. No doubt one intent of such legislative recommendations and committee decision making was to minimize the adverse impact and labeling influence that jailing or partial criminal processing might have on status offenders.

While DSO is fairly common in most jurisdictions, police officer discretion causes a fairly large proportion of status offenders to be handled initially as delinquent offenders anyway. Thus, large numbers of status offenders continue to be jailed, even if only for a few hours.

Since most juveniles fall legally within the jurisdiction of juvenile courts, which are extensions of civil authority, statutory prohibitions obligate police officers and jail officials to depart from certain procedural steps normally followed when processing adult offenders. For example, it is commonplace for officers to photograph and fingerprint adult offenders. This is an integral part of the booking procedure. Juveniles, however, may not be photographed or fingerprinted by police officers as "common procedure." Rather, photographs and fingerprints of juveniles may be taken only after a showing by police officers that their use is either to establish identity or for some investigative purpose (e.g., theft of property where fingerprints of the possible thieves have been obtained).

Furthermore, if photographs and fingerprints are taken, they must be destroyed as soon as possible following their use by police. If such records exist in police department files after juveniles have reached the age of their majority, they may have their records *expunged*, or obliterated, through *expungement orders*. **Expungement orders** *are usually issued from judges to police departments and juvenile agencies to destroy any file material relating to a juvenile's offense history*. Policies relating to records expungement vary among jurisdictions (Dunn, 1986). Expungement of juvenile records, sometimes known as a **sealing of records,** is a means of preserving and insuring confidentiality of information that might otherwise prove harmful to adults if disclosed to third parties such as employers. Sealing of records is intended as a rehabilitative device, although not all juvenile justice experts believe that sealing records and enforcing confidentiality about a juvenile's past through expungement is always beneficial to the general public (Dunn, 1986).

Status Offenders and Juvenile Delinquents

One of the more controversial issues in juvenile justice is how status offenders should be classified and managed. The fact that status offenders are labeled as such contributes significantly to this controversy. Such a label implies that all status offenders are somehow alike and should be treated similarly in all jurisdictions. But this implication is about as valid as assuming that all juvenile delinquents are alike and should be treated similarly. If we think about the etiology of runaway behavior compared with the etiologies of curfew violation, truancy, incorrigibility, liquor law violation, and sex offenses, it is likely that different sets of explanatory factors account for each type of deviant conduct. Accordingly, different treatments, remedies, or solutions are required for dealing effectively with each.

Shelden *et al.* (1989) and others concur. As was seen in the discussion of status offenders in Chapter 2, those juveniles classified as runaways and incorrigibles in some jurisdictions were less likely to commit more serious offenses later in their teens compared with truants, curfew violators, and liquor law violators (Shelden *et al.*, 1989). But for some experts, even runaways do not comprise a homogeneous category of status offenders, and distinctions should be made between different kinds of runaway behavior (Kufeldt and Perry, 1989; Speck *et al.*, 1988).

In 1974, the Juvenile Justice and Delinquency Prevention Act acknowledged some major differences between status offenders and delinquents by recommending that status offenders should not be institutionalized as though they had committed crimes. Rather, they should be diverted away from the trappings of juvenile courts that seemingly "criminalize" their behaviors. The long-range implication of such differential treatment is that status offenders will not be inclined to escalate to more serious types of offenses compared with those more serious delinquent offenders who are exposed to the "criminogenic" environment of the juvenile courtroom (Rankin and Wells, 1985).

As a category, status offenders exhibit less recidivism compared with those referred to juvenile court for delinquent acts (Snyder, 1988:22). Further, the earlier juveniles are referred to juvenile court, for whatever reason, the more likely they will be to reoffend and reappear in juvenile court (Snyder, 1988:33–34). Therefore, diversionary procedures employed by police officers at their discretion when confronting extremely youthful offenders or those who are not doing anything particularly unlawful would seem to be justified on the basis of existing research evidence.

But deinstitutionalizing status offenders is seen by some critics as tantamount to relinquishing juvenile court control over them, and not all experts favor this particular maneuver. A strong undercurrent of *parens patriae* persists, especially with regard to status offenders who need supervision and guidance from caring adults. Retaining control over status offenders is one means whereby the juvenile court can compel them to receive needed assistance and/or appropriate treatment. But disagreement exists about the most effective forms of intervention to be provided status offenders (Clarke *et al.*, 1985).

Divestiture and Its Implications: Net-Widening

Under **divestiture** provisions such as those enacted by the Washington State legislature, status offenders were simply removed from the jurisdiction of juvenile courts. Various community agencies and social service organizations would assume responsibility for insuring that status offenders received proper assistance and treatment (Colley and Culbertson, 1988). Referrals to juvenile court, detention, and the imposition of formal sanctions are no longer justified on the basis that one is a status offender (Schneider, 1984a).

But because of police discretion, curfew violation, runaway behavior, and truancy can easily be reinterpreted or relabeled as "attempted burglary" or "attempted larceny." "Hanging out" or common loitering may be defined by police as behaviors associated with "casing" homes, businesses, and automobiles as future targets for burglary and theft—and these acts are sufficiently serious and provocative to bring more juveniles into the juvenile justice system, thereby "widening the net." As we noted in Chapter 2, widening the net occurs whenever juveniles are brought into the juvenile justice system who would have been dealt with differently by police prior to divestiture. Before divestiture, many status offenders would have received "wrist-slaps" and verbal warnings by police instead of being taken into custody.

At least in the cities of Yakima and Seattle, Washington, police officers were not particularly receptive to the idea that their discretion in certain juvenile matters was abolished by legislative mandate in the late 1970s. In

Innocent loitering on the streets by two or more youths may arouse police officer suspicions, particularly in high-crime or gang-dominated neighborhoods.
(© Martha Tabor/Impact Visuals)

effect, the police officers in these cities created a fictitious wave of juvenile delinquency in the post-divestiture period, in which the rate of delinquency appeared to "double" overnight. Such an artificial "wave" was easily accomplished, since these "front-line" officers merely defined juvenile behaviors in a different way than they had before. A similar phenomenon occurred in Connecticut at approximately the same time (Logan and Rausch, 1985). The primary implication of these actions by police seems to be that they perceived divestiture as a criticism of their integrity and judgment in dealing with juvenile matters, rather than as a positive move to help youths avoid the "delinquency" label (Schneider, 1984a).

Opposition to divestiture has come from other quarters, too. Some experts oppose removing status offenders from the jurisdiction of juvenile courts because the courts are perceived as helpful in shielding children from their most self-destructive urges (Kearon, 1989). Many runaways and truants may have mental health needs that can be met only through mandatory participation in a mental health therapy program. Court intervention may be necessary to ensure that juveniles take advantage of these services (Shaffer and Caton, 1984). Informal disposition of a status offense case may not have the legal force of a juvenile court order; rather, participation in an assistance program may be either voluntary or "strongly recommended." At the same time, agency response in accommodating youths with various problems seems selective and discriminatory. Often, those youths most in need of agency services are turned away as "unqualified" (U.S. General Accounting Office, 1983). Thus, status offender referrals to certain agencies may be unproductive, particularly if the status offenders are psychotic, violent, or drug- or alcohol-dependent (U.S. General Accounting Office, 1983).

Divestiture also assumes that agencies exist "out there" to meet status offender needs. But many communities lack the wide array of needed services to accommodate all types of status offenders (Baker and Naidich, 1986). No single community-based agency or organization is equipped to be all things to all status offenders (Baker and Naidich, 1986; Ritter, 1987). Underscoring the inadequacies of existing social services designed to meet the needs of status offenders is a study of 210 U.S. youth service agencies by Bucy (1985). Bucy found that during 1983 and 1984, these agencies collectively provided at least one night of shelter to 50,354 youths. They also provided services to 101,568 nonsheltered youths and to 171,931 hotline callers and contacts. But 6,732 youths were turned away because of a lack of available bed space. More important, 3,518 youths were not accommodated because these agencies were not considered appropriate for their particular needs.

Bucy surveyed the range of services provided by these centers. These services included shelter care, individual counseling, outreach, education, preemployment training, employment, transportation, mental health services, foster care, family counseling, drug and alcohol counseling, juvenile court-related diversion services, independent living arrangements, recreation, community hotline services, group counseling, legal services, missing children assistance, and aftercare. However, Bucy noted that these agencies had critical problems in the areas of numbers and quality of staff. There was a need for better salaries and benefits, more staff, more staff training, capital improvements for shelters, mental health services, foster care, and long-term placement. Most of these needs are influenced by budgetary considerations and are logically within the purview of state legislatures to provide.

A crossroads is rapidly being approached wherein *parens patriae* interests are increasingly in conflict with the "due process" interests that are coming to characterize juvenile court procedures and the juvenile justice system generally. Status offenders are caught in the middle of this conflict. Reducing admissions of status offenders to various detention centers and treatment facilities is seen by some experts as a reversal of the "hardening effect" of custodial confinement on these youths (U.S. Senate Judiciary Committee, 1984). But removing such youths from detention centers and other places where they could receive mandatory treatment may deprive them of the help they may need to learn to control their self-destructive urges (Kearon, 1989).

Some analysts see little difference in the treatment of status offenders under institutionalization and deinstitutionalization formulas. For example, Illinois enacted a Minor Requiring Authoritative Intervention (MRAI) status offender

Field trips to local correctional facilities are sometimes used as intervention mechanisms to prevent delinquency. Guest speakers may inform youths about the risks of using drugs and certain techniques for avoiding illegal activities. (© F. M. Kearney/ Impact Visuals)

statute in 1983 (Colley and Culbertson, 1988). The essence of this legislation was to substantially limit the jurisdiction of juvenile courts over the broad class of status offenders and to promote mandatory community-based services for such youths instead of traditional incarceration in state facilities. An examination of case records in selected Illinois jurisdictions from April 1980 to February 1985 revealed little difference in confinement rates and dispositions of youths before and after the MRAI legislation. Colley and Culbertson (1988) believe that much of the lack of change in these dispositional arrangements is attributable to judicial resistance to these legislative reforms. Further, judges increasingly used criminal contempt citations and convictions for formerly noncriminal behaviors. Thus, status offenders who were ordered to receive specific treatments and disobeyed these orders quickly became "criminals" in the sense that they had violated legitimate court-ordered therapies.

Currently, legislative committees and interested agencies in many states are considering options and exploring various dispositional alternatives for dealing with status offenders. Among other committee priorities, there is a clear mandate to clarify the nature of social intervention in the lives of status offenders and the programs they are required to complete as "cures" for their deviant behaviors. Further, the training of staff for various community-based agencies who cater to status offenders is in need of improvement. The training of volunteers who work in these agencies also needs to be improved. Finally, the specific objectives of community-based intervention need to be clarified and articulated into meaningful strategies for action (Shane, 1989; Twain and Maiello, 1988).

Redefining Delinquency

It has been suggested that within the framework and spirit of community policing, police officers might consider taking a more proactive role as interventionists in the lives of juvenile offenders encountered on the street. For instance, Trojanowicz and Bucqueroux (1990:238) say that "young people do not launch long-term criminal careers with a daring bank robbery, an elaborate kidnapping scheme, or a million-dollar dope deal. Yet the traditional police delivery system does not want officers 'wasting' much time tracking down the kid who may have thrown rocks through a few windows at school. Narcotics officers on their way to bust Mr. Big at the dope house cruise right by those fleet-footed 10-year-old lookouts. And a call about a botched attempt by a youngster to hotwire a car would not be much of a priority, especially where far more serious crimes occur every day." These professionals indicate that officers should be encouraged to intervene and to take these petty offenses and juvenile infractions more seriously. It is possible for police officers to identify those youngsters most at risk in particular neighborhoods and perhaps to do something to help them avoid future lives of crime.

However, it is clear that the nature of systems is such that the actions of particular parts of the system may not function properly or be permitted to function properly in relation to other parts. It would be difficult, for instance, for Trojanowicz and Bucqueroux to sell their ideas to the police departments in Yakima or Seattle, Washington, at least to the officers on duty there in the late 1970s and early 1980s. Whether or not these officers were justified in doing so, they took it upon themselves to intervene significantly in the lives of status offenders after divestiture was enacted. However, the nature of their intervention was contrary to the spirit of intervention explicitly outlined by Trojanowicz and Bucqueroux in their description of police actions under community policing policies. More status offenders and petty offenders on the streets of Yakima and Seattle were herded more vigorously into jails and juvenile courtrooms after divestiture than before. This is a far cry from officers' taking it upon themselves to act as interventionists and doing something creative for these youngsters at risk as an alternative to detaining them.

If significant adjustments are to be made within any system, some degree of homeostasis and equilibrium are necessary to enable the parts of the system to adjust in ways that permit the entire system to benefit from change. But it is quite difficult to tell judges and police officers to give up their discretionary powers over status offenders and expect them to do so willingly. Schneider (1984a), Colley and Culbertson (1988), Schwartz (1989), and Rankin and

Wells (1985) provide ample evidence that old habits are hard to break and that power is not easily relinquished by those who possess it.

Snyder (1988:2–3) has succinctly summarized some of the major findings of delinquency researchers who have conducted extensive investigations of large samples of juveniles who have engaged in law-violating behavior. Snyder argues that a goal of delinquency research should be to establish a base of valid information that will permit legislators, court personnel, social planners, and policy makers to understand the various problems they face with juveniles and what can be done to minimize these problems (Snyder, 1988:2). Below are some of the major study findings from the research Snyder has surveyed:

- Over 90 percent of males and 75 percent of females are involved in at least one incident during their juvenile years for which they could be arrested (Shannon, 1982)
- About one third of juvenile males are involved with the police to the extent that the incident is recorded in their official records (Tracy *et al.*, 1985; Wolfgang *et al.*, 1972)
- About half of all juveniles with a police record have only one police contact, while the other half recidivate (Tracy *et al.*, 1985; Wolfgang *et al.*, 1972)
- A small percentage of juveniles are responsible for the vast majority of serious offenses committed by juveniles (Tracy *et al.*, 1985; Shannon, 1982; Hamparian *et al.*, 1978; Wolfgang *et al.*, 1972)
- There is some evidence to support the belief that the earlier the age of onset of delinquency careers, the longer and more serious the careers will be (Tracy *et al.*, 1985; Shannon, 1982; Hamparian *et al.*, 1978; Wolfgang *et al.*, 1972)
- There is little evidence to support the belief that the offenses committed during a juvenile's career systematically progress from less to more serious (Shannon, 1982; Hamparian *et al.*, 1978; Wolfgang *et al.*, 1972)
- Less than 2 percent of juveniles come to the attention of the police for a violent offense (Hamparian *et al.*, 1978; Wolfgang *et al.*, 1972)
- Chronically violent juvenile offenders are rare (Hamparian *et al.*, 1978)
- Juvenile delinquents do not specialize, but drift from one kind of offense to another (Klein, 1984; Hamparian *et al.*, 1978; Wolfgang *et al.*, 1972)
- There is evidence both to support and to refute the belief that the commission of a status offense is predictive of a future delinquency career (Farrington, 1986; Kobrin *et al.*, 1980; Clarke, 1975)

Although several of these studies are dated and inconclusive, they nevertheless suggest trends and characteristics that have been supported by more recent research. One major area for improvement would be to clarify for police officers those juveniles who should be taken into custody initially. Currently, these criteria are generally so broad and so unclear that officials are left with almost entirely unguided discretion (Roberts, 1989:151). Consequently, virtually any observed juvenile behavior may be interpreted to justify apprehension and detention.

It has been recommended by experts that police departments should have separate units to interface with juveniles and manage them, but the reality is that many smaller police departments and sheriff's offices do not have the staff or facilities to accommodate such specialties. These luxuries are usually enjoyed only by larger departments. Smaller departments must be content with individual officers who assume responsibilities for managing juvenile offenders and performing related tasks. The majority of initial contacts with juveniles who engage in unacceptable behaviors continue to be made by uniformed police officers while on patrol (Kratcoski and Kratcoski, 1986:220).

Police officers will continue to exhibit interest in those juveniles who violate criminal laws. Offense seriousness and the **totality of circumstances** will usually dictate their reactions in street encounters with these youths. But most juveniles who are the subjects of police-initiated contacts have committed no crimes. They may be status offenders or those reported to police as **children in need of supervision (CHINS).** *CHINS include children who are being or have been abused by others in their families, children who are unsupervised by parents or responsible guardians, or children otherwise in need of some type of care or assistance.* The wise use of discretion by police officers is especially crucial in dealing with status offenders. Fine lines may be drawn by academicians and others to distinguish between offender arrests and temporary detentions resulting from being taken into custody, but the bottom line is usually that a record of the contact is entered in a juvenile file (Kratcoski and Kratcoski, 1986:223−224). The price of such discretionary measures may not be realized fully until one's adult years.

Positive Interventions by Police Officers

Police officers have done much to provoke negative images and stereotypes of themselves among teenagers on the streets. Juveniles believe they are often stopped simply because they are walking on the street. They cannot or do not want to understand the point of view of police officers, who may see the potential for gang violence or crime resulting from youths' congregating on corners at night. Police officers acquire a professional defensiveness, assuming that their authority will be challenged. In certain cities, this defensiveness is justified, since police cruisers have sometimes been targets of random shootings from alleyways or rooftops.

One strategy that has been mentioned is community policing, in which police officers attempt to become acquainted with the neighbors they wish to protect. These efforts are sometimes dubbed "back to the people" methods. One way community policing has been varied in different jurisdictions is by changing police officer patrol styles. Foot patrols have been used in Flint, Michigan, and golf cart patrols have been tried in Tampa, Florida. In each case, officers walk beats or ride golf carts, thus helping to counter the image of riding dispassionately in a cruiser through the community. Some critics say that these patrol variations have not reduced crime particularly, but they admit that they have some public relations value. Perhaps this should be at least one police officer objective—to improve the officer's public relations image in the neighborhood.

In accordance with the psychological theories described in Chapter 3, many experts believe that intervention programs designed to prevent delinquency should be implemented in early childhood. One convenient and systematic way of introducing intervention programs is through the public schools. Schools are logical targets of intervention programs for various reasons. Large numbers of youths assemble there regularly, and a considerable amount of illicit activity, including drug use and abuse and gang violence, may take place there. Many students walk to school, and thus become likely targets for various types of exploiters, including child sexual abusers, youth gangs, and street people.

D.A.R.E. In an effort to combat illicit drug use among elementary school children, the Los Angeles Police Department implemented an intervention program known as *Drug Abuse Resistance Education,* or D.A.R.E. D.A.R.E. utilizes officers familiar with drugs and drug laws who visit schools in their precincts and talk to youths about how to say no to drugs. Children are taught how to recognize different types of illegal drugs and their adverse effects.

Project Heavy. Another program located in Los Angeles County is *Project Heavy.* This project involves a peer- as well as a group-counseling program for children and youths ages 8 to 18, and youth leaders are targeted for change so that they can set good examples for others (Keith, 1989:117).

Hire a Gang Leader. In El Monte, California, a delinquency prevention program was pioneered in 1975, sponsored by members of the local police department. Groups of ten to fifteen gang leaders met with police officers and designed a program to provide job opportunities for gang members who were unemployed. This cooperative effort was successful in several respects. First, it taught gang members that police officers are not always their enemies. Second, it gave them a new view of the police officer as an "enabler" and "facilitator," since there were numerous successful job placements. Police officers benefited as well, because delinquency rates in the El Monte area dropped in those areas where gangs participated in the program (Amandes, 1979).

Dickerson's Rangers. An antidrug program in the San Fernando Valley of southern California is called *Dickerson's Rangers.* This program targets children ages 7 through 13, and it operates in various city parks and recreational centers. Children meet weekly and discuss drug abuse in their schools and communities. Police officers advise them on how to resist overtures made by drug dealers or their peers who might use drugs. Field trips are also sponsored, in which the children hear speakers whose specialties include drug abuse and prevention of illicit drug use.

Campus Pride. In various school districts throughout the United States, *Campus Pride* programs have been initiated. These programs seek to remove gang graffiti from school grounds. Police officers can assist school leaders in identifying gang slogans and symbols, and often, gang members themselves may be ordered by juvenile courts to remove this graffiti. Otherwise, the students act in concert to keep their schools clean of gang graffiti and of possible violence. Gangs often define certain areas, including schools, as their "turf" or territory. However, the students, acting together, can force gang members out of their turf and into another one.

Alateen. Children may be alcoholics. *Alateen* is the teen counterpart to Alcoholics Anonymous. Police officers can function in an instructive capacity to alert children to the signs of alcoholism among themselves and their friends. They can be of assistance in directing children to others who can offer help.

TOPS. In the early 1980s in Rochester, New York, police officers decided to use teens themselves to "police" other teens (Lipson, 1982). In a privately funded program known as TOPS (Teens on Patrol), police officers selected about 125 youths to maintain security and patrol city parks and recreational areas. Interestingly, these teens did a reasonably good job at deterring others from committing delinquent acts in the parks and causing trouble for park patrons. Ultimately, some of the TOPS became police officers and were hired by the Rochester Police Department.

These are only a few of the many programs operating throughout the United States to involve police in proactive and positive roles in which they take an active interest in preventing delinquent conduct through interacting closely with youths. These programs will not make juvenile offenders desist from delinquent conduct, but they will make many of them aware of a positive side of police officers. Further, they will have the effect of helping police officers better understand juveniles and their motives.

Summary

Police officers are the primary means whereby juveniles are brought into the juvenile justice system. Police exercise much discretion in this area, acting within a range of behavioral choices and within the limits of their power. Police officers perform diffuse roles, and much is expected of them from the public. They are expected to resolve disputes and to investigate any citizen complaints. These complaints may sometimes involve juveniles who may or may not be violating criminal laws. Officers who encounter youths must define their behaviors, largely on the basis of situational factors. Such situationally based discretion is believed by some experts to be discriminatory and unfair. What influences a police officer's discretion to take youths into custody is their appearance and demeanor. Youths who are of minority status, in the lower socioeconomic statuses, who dress poorly, or who do not show police officers the proper amount of deference stand a better chance of being taken into custody than those with opposite characteristics.

Juveniles may be fingerprinted and photographed only if such measures are taken to determine their identity, age, and relation to any ongoing criminal investigation. Their photographs and fingerprints are usually destroyed soon after their identity has been established or the investigation has been completed by police. Juveniles brought to jails or comparable facilities are usually booked, and records are maintained of these incidents until juveniles reach the age of their majority. At such time, juveniles may have their records as juveniles expunged and/or sealed as a means of constitutionally protecting their privacy and other rights.

The question of whether juvenile courts should retain control over certain types of juvenile offenders continues to be debated. Little agreement exists about whether the *parens patriae* doctrine should be abandoned in favor of the due process doctrine, wherein juveniles are vested with increasing numbers of rights commensurate with those of adults.

Police officers are encouraged by some experts to become more actively involved in preventing delinquency through creative solutions to juvenile problems. Police officers may take a more proactive role as interventionists for the purpose of identifying and helping children at risk. Various programs exist in which police officers become involved with youth in delinquency prevention programs and show youths more favorable dimensions of police work.

Key Terms

Arrest (157)
Children in need of supervision
  (CHINS) (165)
Community policing (144)
Corporate gangs (148)
D.A.R.E. (Drug Abuse Resistance
  Education) (166)
Divestiture (159)
Expungement orders (158)
Police discretion (144)

Proactive (147)
Project Heavy (166)
Reactive (147)
Scavenger gangs (148)
Sealing of records (158)
Situationally based police discretion
  (144)
Station adjustment (151)
Totality of circumstances (165)

Questions for Review

1. What is meant by police discretion? In what ways may police officers abuse their discretion in handling encounters with juveniles?

2. What is meant by discretionary power generally? In what way is the police officer role diffuse?

3. What is situationally based discretion? How is the "totality of

circumstances" relevant to influencing police discretion? What are some of the extralegal or nonlegal factors that cause police officers to take youths into custody who have not otherwise violated the law?

4. What is community policing? How does community policing influence police officer discretion? What role should police officers play in relation to juveniles, within a community policing framework?

5. Differentiate between proactive and reactive police work. In what sense is every police officer a juvenile officer?

6. Distinguish between corporate and scavenger delinquent gangs. What are their respective objectives and ambitions?

7. Why are police officers interested in gang activities?

8. What are six discretionary options police may exercise in their encounters with juveniles?

9. What is a station adjustment? Relate station adjustments to labeling of juveniles as delinquent.

10. Under what circumstances are police justified in taking youths into custody for further investigation? What factors may influence their decision to take youths into custody?

11. Differentiate between being "taken into custody" and being arrested.

12. What are some general limitations and prohibitions about photographing and fingerprinting juveniles in jails or lockups?

13. What is meant by expungement or record-sealing? Why is it important for adults with records of juvenile offenses?

14. What was the Juvenile Justice and Delinquency Prevention Act of 1974? What were its provisions with regard to status offenders and juvenile delinquents?

15. What is meant by divestiture as applied to juveniles? In what ways can police officers and judges resist divestiture? Give examples of ways in which police officers and judges might resist divestiture.

16. What is the nature of the conflict between the *parens patriae* doctrine and due process?

17. What is meant by CHINS? Can police officers remove juveniles from their homes and take them into custody? What might be some circumstances that would cause such police officer action?

Suggested Readings

August, Robin (1981). *A Study of Juveniles Transferred for Prosecution to the Adult System*. Miami, FL: Office of the Dade-Miami Criminal Justice Council.

Krisberg, Barry (1988). *The Juvenile Court: Reclaiming the Vision*. San Francisco: National Council on Crime and Delinquency.

Metchik, F. (1987). *Recommending Juvenile Offenders for Pretrial Release*. New York: New York City Criminal Justice Agency.

REED, DAVID (1983). *Needed: Serious Solutions for Serious Juvenile Crime*. Chicago: Chicago Law Enforcement Study Group.

SCHACK, ELIZABETH T., AND HERMINE NESSEN (1987). *The Experiment That Failed: The New York Juvenile Offender Law—A Study Report*. New York: Citizen's Committee for Children of New York, Inc.

SPRINGER, CHARLES E. (1987). *Justice for Juveniles*. Rockville, MD: U.S. National Institute for Juvenile Justice and Delinquency Prevention.

CHAPTER 6

Intake and Preadjudicatory Processing

Introduction

On more than one occasion, I have observed intake probation officers in action, making on-the-spot decisions about youths apprehended for various infractions. One memorable scene involved an 11-year-old youth who was taken into custody by police officers for stealing a neighboring youth's bicycle. The boy had attempted to disguise the bicycle's identity by painting it a different color. Taking two cans of white spray paint from his father's garage, he sprayed the red bicycle parts white. Later, he claimed to have "found" the bicycle in a large field. However, his neighbor spotted the pilfered bicycle immediately, despite its new color, and called the police.

The intake officer notified the boy's parents, who attended the hearing. Both parents worked during daytime hours. The mother worked in a woolen mill, and the father was an automobile mechanic at a local car dealership. Both parents sat in the room near their son, who was dressed in jeans and a plaid shirt. The jeans had holes in both knees, but it was apparent that this clothing was the best his parents could afford. Fidgeting nervously, the boy responded quietly to each of the intake officer's questions.

"Did you take the other boy's bicycle?" he was asked.

"Yes," he replied.

"Do you know it's wrong to steal from someone else?"

"Yes."

"Have you ever been in trouble with the law before?"

"No."

"Then why did you take the bicycle?"

"Because I didn't have one."

No arrogance was exhibited by the boy, no defiance, no resentment of or disrespect for authority, and certainly no levity about the situation. The youth was providing an honest answer to a direct question. The parents could not afford to buy their son a bicycle. He saw the neighbor's bicycle and took it, knowing it was wrong to do so. How should the intake officer judge this situation? Should he pass the problem along to the prosecutor and juvenile judge for further disposition? Should he compel the boy to pay for the bicycle when he is clearly unable to do so? Should he require the youth to attend group or individual counseling? What damages should the parents incur as a result of their son's wrongdoing? These and other questions must often be decided by an intake officer and not necessarily by a juvenile judge later in the juvenile justice process.

This chapter is about the intake process. Scenes like the one described above are repeated daily, probably in every jurisdiction in the United States. Intake officers encounter virtually every sort of juvenile offender imaginable. They must assess the circumstances and make fairly rapid decisions about whether to advance certain youths further into the juvenile justice system. The "circumstances" are not limited to the allegations or infractions. Rather, they encompass numerous dimensions, including age of offender, gender, ethnicity or race, type and seriousness of offenses alleged, school record, parental behavior, and prior record, if any. Did the juvenile act alone or in concert with others? Were victims harmed in any way?

Because of the differential training juvenile probation officers receive and the differing orientations they manifest, their behaviors as intake officers may be better understood by paying attention to certain models that are commonly used in dealing with juvenile offenders. Several popular treatment models and orientations will be described and discussed. Many youths appearing before intake officers are first offenders. Because of the continuing belief by many experts that one major function of juvenile justice is to rehabilitate and redirect deviant behaviors toward more legitimate and proper conduct, intake officers give serious consideration to diversion as a nonpunitive option. Several forms of diversion will be described, although a more thorough discussion of diversion and diversion programs will be presented in Chapter 11.

Intake also functions as one of the first screening mechanisms for drawing the most serious offenders further into the system and diverting the least serious offenders away from it. A major consideration in the diversion decision, therefore, is whether responsible guardianship exists for managing youthful offenders. The importance of this consideration will be discussed, and various juvenile offender implications will be assessed.

What Is Intake?

Beyond the discretionary initiatives available to police officers and others who interface with juveniles who may be violating the law, **intake** *or an intake screening is the second major step in the juvenile justice process. It is a more or less informally conducted screening procedure whereby intake probation officers or other juvenile court functionaries decide whether detained juveniles should be (1) unconditionally released from the juvenile justice system, (2) released to parents or guardians subject to a subsequent juvenile court appearance, (3) released or referred to one or more community-based services or resources, (4) placed in secure detention subject to a subsequent juvenile court appearance, or (5) waived or transferred to the jurisdiction of criminal courts.* → Look at waiver possibilities

The Discretionary Powers of Intake Probation Officers. The pivotal role played by **intake probation officers** should not be underestimated. While police officers are often guided by regulations that require specific actions, such as taking juveniles into custody when certain events are observed or reported, the guidelines governing intake actions and decision making are less clear-cut. In most jurisdictions, intake proceedings are not open to the public, involve few participants, and do not presume the existence of the full range of a juvenile's constitutional rights. This is not meant to imply that juveniles may not exercise one or more of their constitutional rights during an intake hearing or proceeding but, rather, that the informal nature of many intake proceedings is such that constitutional rights are not usually a primary issue. The substance of these proceedings consists of information compiled by intake officers during their interviews with juvenile arrestees. Many jurisdictions have standard forms to be completed by probation officers during these interviews. One of these forms is illustrated in Figure 6.1.

The U.S. Supreme Court has consistently rejected attempts by various interests to extend the full range of due process guarantees to intake proceedings, largely because of their informal nature (Binder, 1982;17–20). Thus, there are numerous interjurisdictional variations concerning the intake process and the extent to which constitutional rights are safeguarded or protected (Dougherty, 1988:77). Generally, these proceedings are conducted in a relaxed manner, without court reporters and other personnel who are normally equated with formal court decorum. A casually dressed, folksy juvenile probation officer sits at a desk with the juvenile who is accused of

Arrested teenagers will subsequently be screened by intake probation officers according to the seriousness of the offense alleged. (© Bill Powers/Frost Publishing Group, Ltd.)

some infraction or crime, or who is alleged to be in need of some special supervision or care. One or both parents may be present, although it is not unusual for parents or guardians to be absent from such proceedings. Victims may or may not attend, again depending upon the jurisdiction.

Intake Proceedings

Intake Compared with Plea Bargaining. An intriguing parallel has been drawn by Dougherty (1988) between the juvenile intake hearing and criminal **plea bargaining.** In plea bargaining, prosecutors and defense attorneys try to

SOCIAL HISTORY REPORT

Routing Information   Case Identification

TO: _____   CASE NAME: _____

FROM: _____ DATE: _____   SERIAL: _____ STATUS: _____

AREA: _____ OFFICE: _____   BIRTH DATE: _____ SEX: _____ RACE: _____

REPORT REQUESTED BY: _____   JPC ASSIGNED CASE: _____

1. IDENTIFYING DATA

    a. Youth's Birthplace: _____
    b. Youth's Birth Status: _____
    c. Other Names Used: _____
    d. Youth's Address at Time of Commitment: _____
    e. With Whom Living at Time of Commitment: _____
    f. Family's Relationship to Youth: _____
    g. Legal Guardian: _____
    h. Social Security Number: Youth: _____ Father: _____ Mother: _____

2. PERSONS AND AGENCIES INTERVIEWED

3. AGENCIES THAT HAVE WORKED WITH YOUTH AND FAMILY

4. DELINQUENCY HISTORY (Use only as supplemental to court report. Identify any particular chronic and/or peculiar problems.)

5. DEVELOPMENTAL HISTORY
    a. Early History (Use only when obvious value in detailing youth's problems.)
    b. Medical History (Detail only if pertinent.)
    c. Description of Youth (Use as parents perceive youth, attitudes, and behavior patterns.)

6. FAMILY HISTORY—Revised
    a. Marital History and Youth's Previous Living Situations
    b. Father
    c. Mother
    d. Siblings
    e. Family Income
    f. Parents' Perception of Problem
    g. Impression of Family Functioning
        (1) How parents relate to youth
        (2) Parents' concept of discipline
        (3) Evaluation of parent role (how they should/do perform as parents).
        (4) JPC's impression of performance and evaluation (identify strengths and weaknesses).
        (5) Family's financial resources, including benefits, veterans, social security, welfare, etc., medical/hospital insurance. (Note: Income is reported elsewhere—Pre-Admission History).

7. COMMUNITY INFORMATION
    a. Placement possibilities, including own home. (Note attitudes, family structural compatibility, and other placement considerations.)
    b. Community attitudes toward placement
        (1) Neighbors
        (2) School Officials
    c. Community support services available.

8. SCHOOL AND VOCATIONAL HISTORY
    a. School Performance
        (1) Last school attended and grade completed
        (2) Level of scholastic performance
        (3) Attendance and general conduct
    b. Vocational History
        (1) Part-time or full-time jobs held
        (2) Performance evaluation

9. IMPRESSIONS AND RECOMMENDATIONS
    a. Overall evaluation by JPC
    b. Family's willingness to become involved and cooperate
    c. Problem list (JPC's perception of specific problems)
    d. Strengths and assets of family and youth which can be used in dealing with problems

Figure 6-1 Social History Report. (*Source:* Thomas G. Pinnock, *Necessary Information for Diagnosis* [Olympia, WA: Bureau of Juvenile Rehabilitation, Department of Social and Health Sciences, 1976], p. 11)

negotiate a guilty plea and a punishment that are acceptable to both parties. Ordinarily, plea bargaining occurs before any formal disposition or trial. Thus, the accused waives certain constitutional rights, including the right to a trial by jury, the right to confront and cross-examine witnesses, and the right against self-incrimination. A plea bargain is an admission of guilt to one or more criminal charges, and it is anticipated by those entering guilty pleas that leniency will be extended to them in exchange for their guilty pleas (Alschuler, 1979; McDonald, 1985; Stitt and Siegel, 1986). The theory is that the accused will save the state considerable time and expense that would otherwise be allocated to trials, as well as the important prosecutorial burden of proving the defendant's guilt beyond a reasonable doubt. Although some jurisdictions prohibit plea bargaining (e.g., Alaska and selected counties throughout the United States), the U.S. Supreme Court has ruled that plea bargaining is constitutional in any jurisdiction that wishes to use it (Brady v. United States, 1970).

In many cases, this is a reasonable exchange. The state often has overwhelming evidence, direct and/or circumstantial, that will persuade juries of a defendant's culpability. By entering a guilty plea to less serious charges, defendants are spared the harsh sentences judges might be obligated to impose if juries were to return guilty verdicts against them. Sentencing severity comparisons have been made by numerous researchers, weighing those sentences meted out by judges as the result of plea bargain agreements and those sentences imposed as the result of jury deliberations. Crime for crime, other factors being reasonably equal, convicted offenders who plea bargain fare much better and receive more lenient treatment than those who undergo jury trials (Champion, 1988; Nardulli, 1978; Tiffany et al., 1975).

Plea bargaining is applauded by those who believe that it accelerates the criminal justice process. Over 90 percent of all criminal convictions are obtained by prosecutors through plea bargaining (Alschuler, 1979; Champion, 1989). The state saves time and money, and is spared the burden of making cases against defendants. However, opponents of plea bargaining view the procedure as disenfranchising citizens of their rights to jury trials and other constitutional guarantees.

Furthermore, an unknown number of innocent defendants are coerced into plea bargain agreements, simply because it is likely that they would be convicted of one or more crimes anyway if a jury trial were conducted. These persons have no alibis, few if any resources to pay for quality defense counsel, and may appear guilty to juries on the basis of circumstances. Coercion by prosecutors is expressly prohibited as a means of soliciting guilty pleas from defendants, but it is permissible to threaten defendants with other charges that are otherwise justified by the evidence if they entertain any doubts about entering guilty pleas (Bordenkircher v. Hayes, 1978).

During intake hearings, intake probation officers have virtually unlimited discretion regarding a youth's chances in the system. Apart from certain state-mandated hearings that must precede formal adjudicatory proceedings by juvenile judges, no constitutional provisions require states to conduct such hearings (Wadlington et al., 1983). Intake officers seldom hear legal arguments or evaluate the evidence for or against youths sitting before them. Intake hearings usually result in **adjustments,** in which intake officers "adjust" the matter informally to everyone's satisfaction. Dougherty (1988:78) notes that while intake officers may advise juveniles and their parents that they *may* have attorneys present during such proceedings, they usually indicate that the presence of attorneys may "jeopardize" the "informal" nature of the proceedings and any possible "informal" resolution of the case that might be made. Thus, parents and youths are tacitly discouraged from having legal counsel to assist them at this critical screening stage (Guggenheim, 1985b).

In a very real sense, intake officers are in the behavioral prediction business. They must make important predictions about what they believe will be the future conduct of each juvenile, depending upon their decision. In some jurisdictions, personality tests are administered to certain youths in order to determine their degree of social or psychological adjustment or aptitude. Those determined to be dangerous, either to themselves or to others, may be detained at youth centers or other juvenile custodial facilities, until a detention hearing is conducted. Youths who are runaways and happen to be some distance from their originating jurisdiction may also be held, not necessarily because they are considered dangerous but, rather, because they are likely to flee the present jurisdiction if released. Jurisdictions vary in the degree to which personality and aptitude assessment devices are used during intake as a means of facilitating decision making.

The essence of these procedures is that intake officers perform early judiciary functions and decide cases based, in part, on their reactions to events or circumstances and to the factual information gathered by investigating officers or complainants. If they decide to dismiss a complaint against a juvenile, the matter is ended. If they decide to refer juveniles to community-based services or agencies where they can receive needed treatment in cases such as alcohol or drug dependency, that is their option. They may decide that certain juveniles should be detained in secure facilities to await a subsequent adjudication of the case by a juvenile judge. Any action they take, other than outright dismissal of charges, that requires juveniles to fulfill certain conditions (e.g., attend special classes or receive therapy from some community agency or mental health facility) is based on their presumption that the juvenile is guilty of the acts alleged by complainants. If parents or guardians or the juveniles themselves insist that the intervention of an attorney is necessary during such informal proceedings, this effectively eliminates the informality and places certain constraints on intake officers. The coercive nature of their position is such that they may compel youths to receive therapy, make restitution, or comply with any number of other conditions to avoid further involvement in the juvenile justice process. It is relatively easy to file petitions against juveniles and compel them to face juvenile court judges.

Dougherty (1988:78) sums up the intake scenario and its relation to plea bargaining as follows: "The fact is that both adult plea bargaining and juvenile intake function to negotiate discretionary justice. They both create formal settings, where individuals who are, for all intents and purposes, presumed to be guilty . . . are 'convinced' to agree 'voluntarily' to the officials' resolution of their cases or face the potential harsher consequences of formal processing. Individual rights are at best ignored, or at worst denied. One might argue that the only true beneficiaries of these negotiations are the judges who are relieved of the burden of having to preside over the majority of cases that enter the adult and juvenile justice systems."

Parens Patriae *Perpetuated.* Some evidence suggests that intake probation officers in many jurisdictions are perpetuating the *parens patriae* philosophy that has been systematically undercut by several important U.S. Supreme Court decisions during the 1960s, 1970s, and 1980s. For example, a study of intake probation officers in a southwestern United States metropolitan jurisdiction revealed that probation officers believed that they were the primary source of their juvenile clients' understanding of their legal rights, although these same probation officers did not themselves appear to have a sound grasp or understanding of these same juvenile rights (Lawrence, 1984). In this jurisdiction, juveniles believed that they clearly understood their legal rights. However, interview data from them suggested that in general, they tended to have a very poor understanding of their rights. Emerging from this study was a general recommendation that probation officers who perform the intake function should receive more training and preparation for this important role (Lawrence, 1984).

An examination of 373 intake dispositions in a midwestern juvenile probation office disclosed that most dispositions tended to be influenced by extralegal factors, such as family, school, and employment (Sellers, 1987). The preoccupation of intake probation officers in this jurisdiction with social adjustment factors rather than legalistic ones reflected a strong paternalistic orientation in dispositional decision making. Many of these officers disposed of cases according to what they perceived to be the best interests of the children involved, rather than give primary consideration to the sufficiency of evidence against those accused of infractions, witness credibility, and other legal criteria.

Intake probation officers do not deal exclusively with cases that require fine judgment calls and discretionary hair-splitting. Many youths appearing before intake officers are hard-core offenders and recidivists who have been there before. Also, evidentiary information presented by arresting officers is overwhelming in many cases, and a large proportion of these cases tends to be rather serious. Intake officers will send many of these more serious offenders to juvenile court and/or arrange for a detention hearing so that they may be confined for their own safety as well as for the safety of others. Increasingly, serious juvenile offenders will be referred to juvenile prosecutors with recommendations that they be transferred to the jurisdiction of criminal courts. The theory behind this is that juveniles who are transferred to criminal courts will be subject to the more severe punishments normally meted out to adult offenders. However, it is questionable at present whether those who are transferred to criminal courts actually receive punishments that are more severe than they would receive if their cases were adjudicated in juvenile courts (Champion and Mays, 1991). There are several explanations for this phenomenon that will be covered in a later chapter. (Chapter 7 will examine the transfer process in greater detail.)

Intake, then, is a screening mechanism designed to separate the more serious cases from the less serious ones as juveniles are processed by the system. Intake officers perform classificatory functions, in which they attempt informally to classify large numbers of juveniles according to abstract criteria. Clearly, intake is not an infallible process. Much depends upon the experience and training of the individual intake probation officer, the caseload of juvenile courts, and the nature of cases subject to intake decision making.

The discretionary powers of intake probation officers are in some ways equivalent to those of prosecutors in criminal courts. Intake officers may direct cases further into the system, they may defer certain cases pending some fulfillment of conditions, or they may abandon cases altogether and dismiss them from further processing. As Dougherty (1988) and others have noted, however, the intake probation officer position may lend itself to some degree of abuse, largely because of its coercive aspects. Regardless of the manipulative propensities of certain intake probation officers, however, a majority tend to exercise judgments that, for better or worse, are designed to provide long-term benefits for both the juveniles affected and the communities these officers are sworn to serve. Many of these intake officers pattern their decision making behaviors after several well-known treatment models that continue to characterize juvenile offender management within the juvenile justice system at various critical stages.

Models for Dealing with Juvenile Offenders

Six models for dealing with juvenile offenders are described here. These are not the only models that are used by intake probation officers in their decision making, and many intake probation officers would characterize their particular decision-making activities as unique and not conforming to any specific model. However, these models will serve as a guide to the different types of decisions that are made on behalf of or against specific juvenile offenders. Because each model includes aims or objectives that are related to a degree to the aims or objectives of other models, there is sometimes confusion about model identities. For example, professionals may use a particular model label to refer to orientations that are more properly included in the context of other models.

Additionally, some recently developed interventionist activities have combined the favorable features of one model with those of others. These hybrid models are difficult to categorize, although they are believed to be helpful in diverting youths to more productive and nondelinquent activities. One way of overcoming this confusion is to highlight those features of models that most directly reflect the models' aims. The models to be discussed include

(1) *the rehabilitation model,* (2) *the treatment or medical model,* (3) *the noninterventionist model,* (4) *the due process model,* (5) *the ''just deserts''/justice model,* and (6) *the crime control model.*

The Rehabilitation Model. Perhaps the most influential model that has functioned in the handling of first offender juveniles is the **rehabilitation model.** *This model assumes that delinquency or delinquent conduct is the result of poor friendship or peer choices, poor social adjustment, the wrong educational priorities, and/or a general failure to envision realistic life goals and internalize appropriate moral values.* In corrections, the rehabilitation model is associated with programs that change offender attitudes, personalities, or character. These programs may be therapeutic, educational, or vocational. At the intake stage, however, there is little, if any, reliance on existing community-based programs or services that cater to juvenile needs. Intake probation officers who use the rehabilitation model in their decision-making activities will often attempt to impart values and personal goals to juveniles through a type of informal teaching.

At the beginning of this chapter, we described a youth who stole a bicycle belonging to another youth. The intake officer assigned to this case may have asked the juvenile, "Would you want someone to take something that belonged to you? . . . How would you feel if your property were taken? . . . What are some ways you could earn money to buy a bicycle for yourself rather than steal one? . . . Maybe your parents can help you think of things to do to earn extra money to buy things you want." The intake officer doesn't particularly want to involve the youth further in the system. Perhaps the officer's intent is to give certain youths a stern warning and then release them to the supervisory responsibility of their parents. But lessons should be learned, and the exercise of intake should be a learning experience, according to this rehabilitative philosophy.

While theft is a serious offense, it is considerably less serious than aggravated assault, rape, armed robbery, or homicide. Intake probation officers rely heavily upon their personal experience and judgment in determining the best course of action to follow. The fact that the youth who stole the bicycle is 11 years old and has committed no previous theft offense provides an ideal situation in which the intake officer can exercise strategic discretion and temper the decisions with a degree of leniency. But in the context of *parens patriae* and the rehabilitative framework guiding some of these officers, leniency does not mean tokenism or ineffective wrist-slapping. "Doing nothing" may send the wrong message to youths who have violated the law. The same may be said of police officers who encounter youths on the street and engage in **police cautioning** or station adjustments as alternative means of warning juveniles to refrain from future misconduct (Wilkinson and Evans, 1990). It is believed that the informal intake hearing itself is sufficiently traumatic for most youths so that they will not be eager to reoffend subsequently. Advice, cautioning, and warnings given under such circumstances are likely to be remembered.

The Treatment or Medical Model. The **treatment or medical model** *assumes that delinquent conduct is like a disease, the causes of which can be isolated* *and attacked. Cures may be effected by administering appropriate remedies*. The treatment model is very similar to the rehabilitation model. Indeed, some experts consider the treatment or medical model to be a subcategory of the rehabilitation model (Bartollas, 1990:546). The aim of the treatment model is to set forth for offending juveniles conditional punishments that are closely related to treatment. Intake officers have the authority to refer certain youths to selected community-based agencies and services where they may receive the proper treatment. This treatment approach assumes that these intake officers have correctly diagnosed the "illness" and know best how to cure it. Of course, compliance with program requirements that are nonobligatory for juveniles is enhanced merely by the possibility that the intake officer may later file a delinquency petition with the juvenile court against uncooperative youths. This possibility is not lost on participating juveniles.

In San Diego County, California, for instance, an **Interagency Agreement Plan** was instituted in December, 1982, for the purpose of reducing delinquency through consistent, early intervention and graduated sanctions, and holding youths accountable for their acts (Pennell *et al.*, 1990). Specific guidelines were used by police and intake probation officers for determining the best disposition of any particular case following a juvenile's arrest. First-time, nonserious offenders were to be handled informally, with an emphasis upon diversion to and participation in various community-based services, and restitution for the purpose of establishing a youth's accountability. Recidivist youths would receive more in-depth counseling and referrals to formal probation, and eventually, formal petitions would be filed against them (Pennell *et al.*, 1990). The plan followed by San Diego intake probation officers appeared to have a favorable effect in reducing juvenile recidivism rates, when a pre- and post-test design was used over one- and two-year experimental periods.

One problem with the treatment model generally is that great variations exist among community agencies regarding the availability of certain services as remedies for particular kinds of juvenile problems (Kamerman and Kahn, 1990). Also, the intake officer may diagnose an "illness" incorrectly and prescribe inappropriate therapy. Certain types of deep-seated personality maladjustments cannot be detected through superficial informal intake proceedings. Simply participating in some community-based service or treatment program may be insufficient to relieve particular juveniles of the original or "core" causes of their delinquent behaviors. Nevertheless, intake screenings may lead to community-based agency referrals that eventually may or may not be productive. In most jurisdictions, these are conditional sanctions that may be administered by intake probation officers without judicial approval or intervention.

The Noninterventionist Model. As the name implies, *the* **noninterventionist model** *means the absence of any direct intervention with certain juveniles who have been taken into custody*. The noninterventionist model is best understood when considered in the context of labeling theory (Lemert, 1967a). As we saw in Chapter 3, labeling theory stresses that direct and frequent contact with the juvenile justice system will cause those having

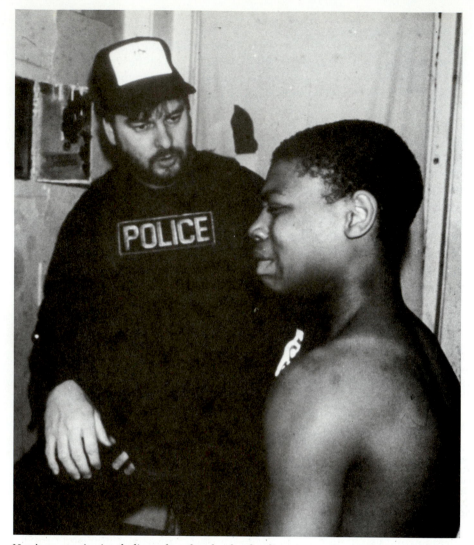

Noninterventionists believe that the shock of police contact is a sufficient deterrent for some teenagers who offend. Therefore, further involvement with the juvenile justice system may be harmful for them and commence the labeling process. (© John Chiasson/Gamma Liasion)

contact with it to eventually define themselves as delinquent. This definition will prompt self-definers to commit additional delinquent acts, since such behaviors are "expected" of those defined or stigmatized as such by others. Labeling theory advocates the removal of nonserious juveniles and status offenders from the juvenile justice system, or at least from the criminalizing influence and trappings of the juvenile courtroom.

The noninterventionist model is strategically applied to only those juveniles who the intake officer believes are unlikely to reoffend if given a second chance, or who are clearly status offenders without qualification (e.g., drug-

or alcohol-dependent, chronic or persistent offenders) (Downs and Robertson, 1990). An intake probation officer who elects to act in a noninterventionist fashion with certain types of offenders may simply function as a possible resource person for juveniles and their parents. In cases involving runaways, truants, or curfew violators, it becomes a judgment call whether to refer youths and/or their parents to certain community services or counseling. The noninterventionist model would encourage that no action be taken by intake probation officers in nonserious or status offender cases, except under the most compelling circumstances. Since not all runaways are alike, some runaways may be more in need of intervention than others (Miller *et al.*, 1990). Again, the aim of nonintervention is to help youths avoid the stigma and unfavorable labeling that might result from deeper involvement with the juvenile justice system (Downs and Robertson, 1990). Even minor referrals by intake officers might prompt adverse reactions from offenders, who might react by committing future offenses as a way of "getting even" with the system.

The noninterventionist model is popular today, particularly because it fits in well with the deinstitutionalization of status offenses (DSO) movement that has occurred in most, if not all, jurisdictions. DSO was designed to divest juvenile courts of their jurisdiction over status offenders. The primary intent of DSO was to minimize the potentially adverse influence of labeling that might occur should juveniles have to appear before juvenile judges and have their cases adjudicated in a courtroom. Another intended byproduct of DSO was to reduce the caseload for many juvenile judges by transferring their jurisdiction over status offenders to community agencies and services. The noninterventionist strategy is significant here because it advocates "doing nothing" about certain juvenile dispositions. Siegel and Senna (1988:349) highlight the works of Lemert (1967a) and Schur (1973) as relevant for the noninterventionist perspective. These authors have promoted **judicious nonintervention** and **radical nonintervention** as terms that might be applied to noninterventionist "do nothing" policy.

While it may appear to some observers that the noninterventionist philosophy is the equivalent of a nonstrategy and is pointless, noninterventionism does *not* rule out certain types of helpful therapies and useful interventions. Even within a noninterventionist framework, intake probation officers may refer juveniles and/or their parents or guardians to certain community resources for assistance. The importance of noninterventionism is that it prevents juveniles from needless exposure to the criminalizing influences of involvement with the police, the courts, and detention. Again referring to the story at the beginning of this chapter, the boy who stole the other boy's bicycle could have been diverted to **alternative dispute resolution,** in which the matter could be resolved between the two families involved, informally and without legal fanfare (Fine, 1984; Hughes and Schneider, 1989; National College of Juvenile and Family Law, 1989).

The Due Process Model. The notion of *due process* is an integral feature of the criminal justice system. **Due process** *is the basic constitutional right to a fair trial, to have an opportunity to be heard, to be made aware of matters that are* pending, to a presumption of innocence until guilt is established beyond a reasonable doubt, to make an informed choice whether to acquiesce to or contest a charge, and to provide the reasons for such a choice before a judicial official (Champion, 1990b:75). An important aspect of due process is that police officers must have probable cause to justify their arrests of suspected criminals. Therefore, constitutional rights are given considerable weight in comparison with any incriminating evidence obtained by police or others.

Intake officers who rely heavily upon the **due process model** in their dealings with juveniles are concerned that the juveniles' rights be fully protected at every stage of processing. Therefore, these officers would pay particular attention to how evidence was gathered by police and whether police officers advised the juvenile of the right to counsel at the time of the arrest and/or subsequent interrogation. The higher priority given to due process in recent years is considered by some researchers to be a significant juvenile justice reform (Blackmore et al., 1988).

An intake officer's emphasis on due process requirements in juvenile offender processing stems, in part, from several important U.S. Supreme Court decisions during the 1960s and 1970s (see Chapter 10), although professional associations and other interests have strongly advocated a concern for greater protection of juvenile rights in recent years (Green, 1984; Shaffner, 1985). In 1984, for instance, the Juvenile Justice Standards Project of the American Bar Association recommended that the rights of all minors be safeguarded by having legislatively created and narrowly defined doctrines dealing with specific problem areas, such as a juvenile's waiver of the right to counsel prior to interrogation by police, searches of juveniles and their premises and seizures of their property, and the rights of juveniles against self-incrimination (Gonzales, 1982; Green, 1984). In this regard, some states have enacted statutes that render inadmissible any evidence police may have obtained as the result of a juvenile's waiver of one or more constitutional rights, without parental guidance or consent (Shaffner, 1985). Thus, an intake officer's actions in certain states would be intended to comply with statutory requirements of juvenile case processing.

Because of the interest certain intake probation officers might take in the right to due process, some intake hearings may be more formally conducted than others (Sellers, 1987; Shelden and Horvath, 1987). Legal variables, such as nature of offense, numbers of charges, and prior petitions, would be given greater weight in the context of due process. Shelden and Horvath (1987) have noted that legal variables such as these have accounted for or explained as much as 40 percent of the variance in intake processing in the jurisdictions they have investigated. Thus, intake guidelines in these jurisdictions promote legal factors and downplay the significance of nonlegal elements. However, many case dispositions seem to be affected by nonlegal variables as well, including the youth's attitude, grades in school, and school status. Gender, race, and social class are only moderately related to case dispositions (Shelden and Horvath, 1987).

The "Just Deserts"/Justice Model. It is apparent that the juvenile justice system has strong rehabilitative underpinnings, and the emphasis in past

---

BOX 6.1

Juvenile Highlights

Should juveniles be punished before being adjudicated for delinquent conduct? In Colorado, a program known as SHAPE-UP (Showing How Experience Undermines People) is used in various jurisdictions as a juvenile diversion program through a cooperative effort of the Colorado District Attorney's Council and the Colorado Department of Corrections. Aimed at "delinquency-prone" males aged 13 to 18, the program is designed to make them fully aware of the meaning of incarceration through a prison visit.

This program consists of a two-day visit to the Colorado Territorial Correctional Facility at Canon City. This is an old medium-security facility, constructed in 1870, and it houses about 700 inmates. On the first day, youths are brought to the facility and each one is paired with an inmate who discusses his incarcerative experiences. Matching of inmates with youths is done on the basis of similar offending patterns. This informal "counseling" involves exploring some of the root causes of offending, including the influence of peer pressure, family, self-image problems, and drug and alcohol abuse.

The second-day visit, conducted one week later, is for the purpose of reinforcement of the earlier initial exposure to prison life. Youths are accompanied by parents or guardians who tour the facility. Again, limited inmate counseling occurs. Viewed chiefly as a deterrent to delinquent conduct, the SHAPE-UP program has been modestly successful, despite limited state funding. Delinquency is viewed as a long-term problem, and unraveling its causes takes time. Effective treatment takes even longer. Nevertheless, almost all youthful participants consent to involvement in the program prior to any formal adjudication of their alleged delinquent conduct. In some respects, this is a form of conditional punishment, although juveniles who participate do not advance further into the juvenile justice system.

(Some factual information adapted from Bill Mitchell and Gene Shiller, "Colorado's Shape-Up Program Gives Youths a Taste of the Inside," *Corrections Today* (1988) 50:76, 88, 110.)

---

years has been upon serving the best interests of offending youths and the delivery of individualized services to them on the basis of their needs (Steinhart, 1988). *Parens patriae* explains much of the origin of this emphasis in the United States. However, the changing nature of juvenile offending during the last several decades and a gradual transformation of public sentiment in the direction of more punitive measures have prompted certain juvenile justice reforms aimed at holding youths increasingly accountable for their actions and punishing them accordingly (Challeen, 1986; Watkins, 1987). Two proposed acts—the Model Delinquency Act and the Model Disobedient Children's Act—have been spawned through the federally funded Juvenile Justice Reform Project (Rossum *et al.*, 1987). These acts stress the importance of juvenile accountability to victims and society, as well as the responsibility of the system to punish these juveniles accordingly.

The **"just deserts" model** *is punishment-centered and seemingly revenge-oriented; the state's interest seen as ensuring that juveniles are punished in proportion to the seriousness of the offenses they have committed. Further, those who commit identical offenses should be punished identically.* This introduces the element of fairness into the punishment prescribed (Fogel, 1984; Fogel and Hudson, 1981; Schneider and Schram, 1986). This "get tough" approach to disposing of juvenile cases has both proponents and opponents and is clearly controversial (Conrad, 1983; Feld, 1987; Treanor and Volenik, 1987). It is significant that such an approach represents a major shift of emphasis away from juvenile offenders and their individualized needs and toward emphasis on the nature and seriousness of their actions. "Just deserts" as an orientation has frequently been combined with the **justice model** of orientation. *The justice orientation is the idea that punishments should be gauged to fit the seriousness of offenses committed.* Therefore, juveniles who commit more serious acts should receive harsher punishments, treatments, or sentences than those who commit less serious offenses. Besides promoting the idea of punishment in proportion to offending behavior, the justice model includes certain victim considerations, such as provisions for restitution or victim compensation by offending juveniles.

Intake probation officers who use the "just deserts"/justice philosophy in their dealings with juveniles at the intake stage are concerned with ensuring that the intake disposition be calculated to deliver "just" punishments. Punishment in this sense is regarded as a fair and equitable way of disposing of cases before they reach the juvenile court adjudication stage. Intake officers may suggest **consent decrees,** or *formal agreements that involve children, their parents, and the juvenile court, in which youths are placed under the court's supervision without an official finding of delinquency, with judicial approval* (Rogers and Mays, 1987:565). Consent decrees often contain provisions for victim restitution and compensation by the juvenile or obligatory participation in some treatment program. These decrees may be entered into prior to any court appearance by juveniles. Intake probation officers may initiate these actions, again with court approval, provided all parties agree to their provisions and conditions.

While the major thrust of this orientation is punitive, it has certain instructional and rehabilitative properties that embrace other views or orientations. Youths may be made to appreciate the harm they have caused others, at least financially, through some form of restitution or compensation (Seljan, 1983). Through their work and involvement in one or more assistance or treatment programs, they may acquire new values, outlooks, and self-concepts. But one important criticism of this approach is that intake officers who use it must make discretionary judgments and recommendations that involve punishments that may or may not be deserved. If certain juveniles had their cases adjudicated in a formal juvenile court proceeding, they might be more capably represented by attorneys who could introduce exculpatory evidence in their behalf. Juvenile judges might be persuaded in these instances that the juvenile's guilt has not been sufficiently established to warrant the imposition of punishment. But, as with plea bargaining, some juveniles and their parents may believe that informally administered conditions as punishments offer relief from a formal court appearance, whether or not they are warranted by evidence and other circumstances.

The Crime Control Model. Perhaps the harshest of the intake orientations, *the* **crime control model** *asserts that one of the best ways of controlling juvenile delinquency is to incapacitate juvenile offenders, either through some secure detention or through an intensive supervision program operated by a community-based agency or organization.* Consent decrees might include provisions for the electronic monitoring of certain juvenile offenders in selected jurisdictions. These juveniles might be required to wear plastic bracelets or anklets that emit electronic signals and notify juvenile probation officers of an offender's whereabouts (see Chapter 12 for an in-depth discussion of electronic monitoring systems applied to juvenile offenders.) Or juvenile offenders might be incarcerated in detention facilities for short- or long-term periods, depending upon the seriousness of the offense.

The crime control perspective would influence intake officers to move certain chronic, persistent, and/or dangerous juvenile offenders further into the juvenile justice system. If they believe certain juveniles pose serious risks to others or are dangerous, these intake officers might decide that these juveniles should be held in secure detention pending a subsequent detention hearing. If juveniles who are chronic or persistent offenders are incapacitated, they cannot reoffend. Treatment and rehabilitation are subordinate to simple control and incapacitation. Intake officers who favor the crime control view have few illusions that the system can change certain juvenile offenders (Gelber, 1988). Rather, they believe that the best course of action is secure detention for lengthy periods, considering the availability of space in existing juvenile detention facilities. In this way, offenders are directly prevented from reoffending, since they are totally incapacitated. The cost-effectiveness of such incarceration of the most chronic and persistent juvenile offenders in relation to the monies lost resulting from thefts, burglaries, robberies, and other property crimes is difficult to calculate. Incarceration itself is costly, and immense overcrowding in existing juvenile detention facilities already plagues most jurisdictions.

Experts in various jurisdictions acknowledge that often, traditional treatment and rehabilitation strategies do not work or are not particularly effective with certain hard-core, violent, or chronic offenders (Minnesota Criminal Justice Statistical Analysis Center, 1989). However, if courts and other actors in the juvenile justice system, including intake officers, move toward more punitive measures against even the smaller numbers of these more dangerous offenders, including widespread incarceration, we can expect to see a substantial increase in the need for additional facilities (Minnesota Criminal Justice Analysis Center, 1989).

While many intake probation officers might not admit to being influenced by one particular orientation or another, it would be relatively easy to classify them by their overall orientation toward juveniles after observations of some duration. Also, much seems to depend upon the different roles officers are assigned in the juvenile justice system. A survey of 772 juvenile justice officials in Florida showed, for instance, that different degrees of commitment to either a rehabilitation philosophy or a "just deserts" perspective were influenced by an officer's assignment to either low-risk or hardcore offenders (Farnworth *et al.,* 1988). However, the educational backgrounds and professional identifications of these officers appeared to modify these seemingly opposing commitments somewhat.

Even in those jurisdictions where intake officer behaviors are more or less prescribed, there is not always a perfect pattern of consistency among officers in their management of intake screenings. For example, in San Diego County, California, where an Interagency Agreement plan was implemented as described above to handle informally all nonserious, first-offender juveniles in a standardized way (see earlier treatment model discussion), not all intake probation officers complied and followed consistent sets of program guidelines, even though there was a general agency commitment to do so. Individualized styles for juvenile offender dispositions and decision making were observed by investigators (Pennell *et al.,* 1990).

But at least we can understand why intake officers in most jurisdictions do not always resolve common juvenile offender problems in the same ways. The preceding discussion should have enabled us to appreciate the complexities of intake screening and decision-making behaviors. We can now examine the various legal and extralegal criteria that operate to influence decisions made by these intake officers.

Legal Factors: Offense Seriousness, Type of Crime Committed, Evidence, and Prior Record

A distinction must be made between *legal factors* and *extralegal factors* that relate to decision making at the intake stage, as well as at other points in the juvenile justice process. **Legal factors** *relate to purely factual elements of the offenses alleged, such as crime seriousness, type of crime committed, inculpatory (incriminating) or exculpatory (exonerating) evidence, and the existence or absence of prior juvenile records or delinquency adjudications.* **Extralegal factors** *include, but are not limited to, juvenile offender attitudes, school grades and standing,* *gender, race or ethnicity, socioeconomic status, and age* (Note: age also functions as a legal factor in certain types of offenses).

Both legal and extralegal factors are important in influencing an intake probation officer's screening decision during an intake hearing. While purely legal factors probably should be used exclusively in deciding whether to pursue any case, it is a fact that extralegal factors impact upon this decision, adversely for some offenders and favorably for others. Thus, it is questionable whether juveniles can receive equitable treatment from those intake officers who stress certain extralegal factors such as gender or race in their decision making. Each of these sets of factors will be examined here.

Offense Seriousness. Offense or crime seriousness pertains to whether bodily harm was inflicted or death resulted from the youth's act. Those offenses considered "serious" include forcible rape, aggravated assault, robbery, and homicide. These are crimes against persons or violent crimes. By degree, they are more serious than the conglomerate of property offenses, which include vehicular theft, larceny, and burglary. In recent years, drug use has escalated among youths and adults in the United States and is considered one of the most serious of the nation's crime problems. One general deterrent

Law enforcement officers and others are interested in fostering delinquency prevention through various educational programs, including visits to schools. Students can learn respect for the property of others and some of the consequences they might face for violating the law. (© Gary Wagner/Impact Visuals)

in every jurisdiction has been the imposition of stiff sentences and fines on those who sell drugs to others, and lesser punishments imposed on those who possess drugs for personal use. All large cities in the United States today have numerous youth gangs, many of which are involved rather heavily in drug trafficking (Fagan, 1988; Waldorf *et al.*, 1990). One result of such widespread drug trafficking among youths is the provision in most juvenile courts for more stringent penalties for drug sales and possession. Thus, crimes don't always have to be violent in order to be considered serious.

It should be noted that given the vast number of juvenile justice reforms that have occurred in recent years, much ambiguity persists among the various actors in the juvenile justice system about how best to evaluate crime seriousness (Mahoney, 1989). For example, a survey of 32 prosecutors and six law clerks in a Union County, New Jersey, county prosecutor's office was conducted to determine how these professionals rated the seriousness of selected crimes when committed by offenders of different ages (Harris, 1988). Five hundred robbery and aggravated assault cases involving male offenders were selected from both juvenile and criminal court records and rated by these prosecutors and clerks according to their seriousness. Overall, the same robbery and aggravated assault behaviors considered serious when committed by juveniles were considered substantially less serious when committed by adults. Not only does this finding suggest that more effort should be made to give crime seriousness a more precise definition; it also suggests why there are constant allegations of lenient treatment of serious juvenile offenders made by diverse critics of the juvenile justice system.

Type of Crime Committed. Another key factor in screening cases for possible subsequent processing by the juvenile justice system is the type of crime or offense committed. Was the offense property-related or violent? Was the act either a felony or a misdemeanor? Were there victims with apparent injuries? Did the youths act alone or did they act in concert with others, and what was the nature of their role in the offense? Were they initiators or leaders, and did they encourage or incite others to offend?

Intake officers are more likely to refer cases to juvenile prosecutors when juveniles are older (i.e., 16 years of age and over), and when the offenses alleged are especially serious, than when juveniles are younger and are first offenders. An interesting study by McCarthy (1989) of numerous intake decisions suggests that at least in some jurisdictions, an overwhelming majority of juvenile cases are disposed of informally during intake. McCarthy studied data pertaining to 76,150 delinquent acts committed by 17,773 juveniles born between 1962 and 1965 in Maricopa County (Phoenix, Arizona). Gathered from juvenile court files, these data showed that the vast majority of cases of first offenders under age 16, 89 percent, were handled informally at the intake level, without the formal filing of delinquency petitions. Juveniles committing violent offenses such as robbery and aggravated assault and the property crime of burglary were more likely to be detained compared with other youthful offenders. Of particular interest is the fact that detainees and those who progressed further into the juvenile justice system had much higher recidivism rates compared with nondetainees. However, about half of all offenders became repeat offenders, with approximately 25 percent of these juveniles reoffending at least three or more times.

One mild implication of these findings for juvenile justice policy is that generally, leniency with many offenders, particularly first offenders, is accompanied by less recidivism. However, this conclusion may be premature and misleading. McCarthy also noted that greater intrusion into the juvenile justice system characterizes more serious offenders, probably meaning more chronic, persistent, dangerous, or habitual offenders—precisely the category of youthful offenders who are more likely to reoffend anyway. Perhaps the term **strategic leniency** would be appropriate here. When studying a sample of 93 Hawaiian juvenile delinquents, Nagoshi (1986) found, for example, that those who received special conditions of probation as punishments (e.g., restitution, community service) recidivated at a lower rate than those youths who were placed on probation without special conditions. The implication here is that at least some punishment, properly administered, appears to have therapeutic value for many juvenile offenders compared with no punishment.

Again, for particular juvenile offender categories in selected jurisdictions, intake officers may be obligated to move certain types of offenders deeper into the juvenile justice system. An example of an absence of intake probation officer discretion in the disposition of certain juvenile cases is the State of Washington. In 1978, the Washington legislature drastically overhauled its juvenile justice system (Schneider and Schram, 1986). One result of these changes in juvenile code legislation was to remove completely from intake officers the power to adjust cases informally at intake. Sentencing guidelines and other criteria evolved to dictate the direction of intake officer discretion in many juvenile cases. The legislature's concern was for "just deserts," for fairness, uniformity, and proportionality in the processing of juvenile offenders at all stages throughout the system. Status offenders were removed from the jurisdiction of juvenile courts. However, considerable relabeling of offenders by police officers and others occurred, and the result was that the intent of these behavioral guidelines was circumvented at various stages. Changes in system processing of different types of youthful offenders have made it difficult for Washington officials to measure the impact of their juvenile reforms on recidivism rates among youthful offenders.

Evidence. While offense seriousness and type of crime are considered quite influential at intake hearings, some attention is also given by intake officers to the evidence police officers and others have acquired to show offender guilt. Direct evidence, such as eyewitness accounts of the youth's behavior, tangible objects such as weapons, and the totality of circumstances, give the intake officer a reasonably good idea of where the case would end eventually if it reached the adjudicatory stage in a juvenile court.

Also, intake officers can consider exculpatory evidence, materials, and testimony that provide alibis for juveniles or mitigate the seriousness of their offenses. Evidentiary factors are important in establishing guilt or innocence,

BOX 6.2

Juvenile Highlights

Can a juvenile's dangerousness and risk to others be effectively predicted? Classification is used at various strategic points throughout the juvenile justice process, particularly at intake, to diagnose a juvenile offender's needs and make the best choices possible. Unfortunately, mostly subjective criteria have been applied for such decision making, with little attempt to follow up on the individual's actual behaviors in juvenile institutions or while under the care of community-based correctional services.

The major challenges facing those who are interested in devising effective predictive devices are to determine which predictor variables are most salient in forecasting disruptive behaviors, and to establish a statistically valid basis for analyzing such classification data. The problem with the use of unreliable predictor variables and unstable dangerousness scales is that some youths will be overpenalized or un-

derpenalized because of false predictions made about them. Those who commit delinquent acts after being classified as nondangerous or unlikely to reoffend are considered "false negatives," while those who are judged dangerous but who never reoffend are "false positives." The intent of good prediction measures is to minimize both false negatives and false positives.

Sound outcome measures need to be defined and used. Such measures might include records of disciplinary actions taken, institutional moves, security changes, program participation, and conforming behaviors. One of correction's greatest challenges is the development of effective and valid classification systems to ensure the full protection of a juvenile's rights.

(Factual information adapted from Nola M. Joyce, "Classification Research: Facing the Challenge," *Corrections Today* (1985) 47:78–86.)

but when police officers refer juveniles to intake, it is usually an indication that the officers were persuaded by the evidence that such action was warranted. It is extraordinary for officers to pursue juvenile cases to the intake stage purely on the basis of whim, although some officers may do so as a means of punishing certain juvenile offenders with poor attitudes.

Most intake officers screen the least serious cases quickly at intake or provide dispositions for juveniles other than formal ones. For instance, McCarthy (1987b) investigated the attrition rate of 620 juvenile cases in a metropolitan court in the United States during 1982. She found that charges were dropped against 23 percent of these juveniles at intake, that 12 percent received informal adjustments of their cases by intake officers, and that an additional 15 percent were granted consent decrees. About 50 percent of all youths were referred to prosecutors for judicial handling. These seem to be normal case attrition figures, in accord with investigations conducted by others of this process in other jurisdictions.

Another consideration made by the intake officer is what will likely happen to youths once they are brought before juvenile judges, regardless of the amount of inculpatory evidence. In many jurisdictions, even violent juvenile offenders typically receive probation as a punishment (McCarthy, 1989). But for many intake officers, a juvenile judge's punishment ideology has little or no bearing on their initial intake decisions (Hassenfeld and Cheung, 1985). Nevertheless, since leniency will likely be extended once an adjudicatory proceeding has been conducted, many intake officers may believe that they can reduce judicial caseloads by taking the initiative of exercising leniency themselves.

Prior Record. For intake officers in the State of Washington and other jurisdictions where guidelines are followed relating to intake dispositions, prior records of delinquency adjudications are factored into their decisions. In other jurisdictions, prior records strongly suggest that prior treatments and/or punishments were apparently ineffective at curbing offender recidivism. It would be logical to expect that intake probation officers would deal more harshly with those having prior records of delinquency adjudications. In fact, some research has demonstrated that greater numbers of prior offenses tend to result in a youth's further involvement in the juvenile justice process beyond intake (Grisso *et al.*, 1988).

No doubt a prior record of juvenile offenses would suggest persistence and chronicity, perhaps a rejection of and resistance to prior attempts at intervention and treatment. And in some of these cases, harsher punishments and dispositions have been observed (Greenwood, 1986a). However, this is not a blanket generalization designed to cover all offense categories. Some offense categories have priority over others for many intake officers.

Also, the previous disposition of a particular juvenile's case seems to be a good predictor of subsequent case dispositions for that same offender. For example, a study of the influence of prior records and prior adjudications on instant offense dispositions has shown that dispositions for prior offenses have a significant impact on current dispositions for those same offenses, regardless of the type or seriousness of the offense (Thornberry and Christenson, 1984). Thus, if a juvenile has formerly been adjudicated delinquent on a burglary charge and probation for six months was imposed as the punishment, a new burglary charge against that same juvenile will likely result in the same punishment. Only offense seriousness has a greater impact on the punishment meted out to repeat offenders than prior dispositions.

While we will examine transfers or waivers more extensively in Chapter 7, it is important to note here that often, repeat offender appearances before the same juvenile judge, regardless of the violent or nonviolent nature of the offense, may result in transfer of jurisdiction over that offender to criminal courts. This is the judge's way of getting rid of particularly bothersome juveniles who are neither dangerous nor serious offenders (Champion and Mays, 1991).

Extralegal Factors: Age, Gender, Race and Ethnicity, and Socioeconomic Status of Juvenile Offenders

Most intake probation officers have vested interests in the decisions they make during screening hearings. They want to be equitable, but at the same time, they want to tailor their decisions to suit each individual case. This means that they must balance their interests and objectives to achieve multiple goals. Furthermore, in recent years, greater pressure has been put on all juvenile justice officers to implement those policies and procedures that will increase offender accountability at all stages of processing (Harris and Graff, 1988).

A balanced approach has been suggested by Maloney *et al.*, (1988). They envision three major goals of probation officers serving in various capacities in relation to their clients. These goals include (1) protecting the community, (2) imposing accountability for offenses, and (3) equipping juvenile offenders with competencies to live productively and responsibly in the community. Ideally, each of these goals is of equal importance. These researchers say that such balanced objectives have been used by probation officers in Deschutes County, Oregon; in Austin, Texas; and on the Menominee Indian Reservation in Wisconsin. Individuality in decision making, where all three goals can be assessed for each juvenile offender, is sought. However, in other jurisdictions, these three goals may have variable importance to probation officers performing intake functions. Depending upon their orientation, some intake officers may emphasize their community protection function, while others may emphasize juvenile offender accountability. Those officers with rehabilitative interests would tend to promote educational programs that would enable youths to operate productively in their communities.

In the context of attempting to achieve these three objectives and balance them, several extralegal characteristics of juvenile offenders have emerged to influence adversely the equality of treatment these youths may receive from probation officers at intake: (1) age, (2) gender, (3) race/ethnicity, and (4) socioeconomic status.

Age. As we have seen, age is both a legal and an extralegal factor in the juvenile justice system. Age is legally relevant in decisions regarding waivers to criminal court jurisdiction. Waivers of juveniles under the age of 16 to criminal courts are relatively rare, for example (Nimick *et al.*, 1986). Also, age has extralegal relevance. At least in some jurisdictions, such as Maricopa County (Phoenix), Arizona, intake officers seem to manage and informally dispose of large numbers of cases against youths under age 16 (McCarthy, 1989). Older youths are perhaps assumed to be more responsible for their actions than younger ones, and they are often treated accordingly. Also, older youths are more likely to have prior records as juvenile offenders, to be resistant to or unwilling to accept intervention, and to manifest adultlike self-reliance (Grisso *et al.*, 1988). Further, arrest data show that the peak ages of criminality lie between the sixteenth and twentieth birthdays (Greenwood, 1986c). Perhaps some intake officers believe that more aggressiveness in their decision making should be directed against older juveniles than against the younger ones.

Greenwood (1986c) has assessed the value of various predictors of delinquent conduct in various jurisdictions. While he is pessimistic about the ability of various devices to forecast delinquent behavior adequately for adolescents of any age, he suggests that chronic offenders are best identified on the basis of the juvenile records they acquire after their sixteenth birthday rather than before it. He indicates, for example, that a delinquent 13-year-old may become a model student within a year, without intervention. Further, he believes that there are certain risks generated by early interventions imposed on youths, and that we may risk producing adverse effects with some youths who would have voluntarily desisted from delinquent behavior eventually. Intake officers, therefore, might be inclined to handle cases involving younger offenders more informally, without the use of specific interventions, since they might feel that misplaced treatment would be counterproductive in facilitating social and psychological adjustment. Snyder (1988:19) suggests, however, that although some research shows that younger offenders who have contact with the juvenile justice system are more active and recidivate more than youths who have contact with the system in their later teen years, the differences in recidivism rates are not that prominent. He concludes that "therefore, early age of onset youth were not more active, they simply had more time to accrue a larger number of court referrals" Snyder (1988:19).

In any event, for many intake probation officers, the age dimension appears to function in much the same fashion in influencing their intake decision making as it does when prosecutors assess the relative seriousness of identical offenses committed by youths and adult offenders (Harris, 1988). For an assortment of nonrational reasons, armed robbery is not as serious for some prosecutors when committed by a 12-year-old as it is when it is committed by a 21-year-old. Applied to intake decision making, probation officers may regard certain serious offenses as "less serious" when committed by those 13 and under, while 14-year-olds and older youths may have those same offenses judged as "more serious." There are no precise age divisions that separate younger from older youthful offenders when age is an extralegal consideration. Unquestionably, however, there are general differences in leniency or harshness of treatment received by youths across broad age categories.

Gender. Allegations that female delinquency patterns have changed dramatically since the early 1970s are rather consistently disputed (Berger,

1989). Generally, traditional patterns of female delinquency have persisted over the years. Because there are so few female juvenile offenders compared with their male counterparts, the influence of gender on intake decision making and at other stages of the juvenile justice process has not been investigated extensively. Juvenile females make up approximately 10 percent or less of the juvenile detention population in the United States annually (American Correctional Association, 1990). Females are only slightly more represented proportionately among those on probation or involved in assorted public and private aftercare services.

Differential treatment of males and females in both the juvenile and criminal justice systems is well documented and has been discussed at some length in an earlier chapter (see Chapter 2). However, some of the traditional reasons given for such differential treatment, especially with regard to female juveniles and their delinquency patterns, appear to be largely mythical and misconceived (Curran, 1984; Gelsthorpe, 1987). Contemporary assessments of the impact of gender on intake decision making show that it is only moderately related to dispositions, consistent with intake guidelines in selected jurisdictions such as Las Vegas, Nevada (Shelden and Horvath, 1987). Investigations of other jurisdictions such as Massachusetts, as well as analyses of national figures, show generally that female juveniles seem to be detained less often than male juveniles, and/or they are returned to the community at a greater rate than males, and/or they are committed to detention at a much lower rate than males (Frazier and Bishop, 1985; Massachusetts Department of Youth Services, 1984; McCarthy, 1985).

Within the "just deserts," justice, or crime control frameworks, attention of interested actors in the juvenile justice system is focused upon the act more than upon the juveniles committing the act or their physical or social characteristics. Thus, gender differences leading to differential treatment of offenders who behave similarly would not be acceptable. However, the differential treatment of male and female juveniles in the United States and other countries persists (Chesney-Lind, 1987a; Hagan *et al.*, 1985; Webb, 1984).

A strong contributing factor is the paternalistic view of juvenile judges and others in the juvenile justice system that has persisted over time in the aftermath and influence of *parens patriae*. Differences between the arrest rates of female and male juveniles and the proportion of females to males who are subsequently adjudicated as delinquent suggests that the case attrition rate for females is significantly higher at intake than it is for male juveniles. Specific studies of intake decision making have disclosed, however, that gender exerts only an indirect impact on such decision making by officers (McCarthy and Smith, 1986). Paradoxically, female juveniles with prior referrals to juvenile court seem to be treated more harshly than male offenders with prior referrals, especially in the case of several index violent offenses. Based upon his analysis of the court careers of 69,504 juvenile offenders in Arizona and Utah, Snyder (1988) calculated probabilities of being referred to juvenile court for an index violent offense, where both male and female juveniles had similar numbers of prior court referrals. He found that males with eight prior referrals were more than three times as likely to be referred to juvenile court for an index violent offense as males with only one previous referral, and more than twice as likely as males with two prior referrals. However, females with eight prior referrals were six times as likely to be referred to juvenile court for an index violent offense compared with females who had only one prior referral, and three times as likely to be referred compared with females with two prior referrals Snyder (1988:44–45). There were negligible differences between male and female juvenile offenders relating to referrals for property crimes.

It would seem that first-offender females are more likely to experience favorable differential treatment from the juvenile justice system compared with those females with records of prior referrals. In Snyder's study, the great differential referral rate between male and female juveniles may have been the result of a backlash phenomenon, whereby females were being unduly penalized later for the greater leniency extended toward them earlier by juvenile justice authorities. However, this is only speculation.

Race and Ethnicity. Considerably more important as predictors of decision-making behavior by intake officers and dispositions at subsequent stages of the juvenile justice process are the factors of race and ethnicity. One investigation of the impact of race upon dispositional decision making at intake was conducted by Bell and Lang (1985). These researchers found that the relationship between race and decision making was apparently indirect. Similarly, Shelden and Horvath (1987) found no direct influence of race on the nature of intake processing in 436 cases they analyzed for a Nevada county. Finally, McCarthy (1985) studied 649 juvenile delinquents who had been referred to family courts in 1982. Her preliminary impression was that at least at the adjudicatory stage, juvenile judges did not seem to be influenced by racial or gender factors.

However, a subsequent analysis of the same data by McCarthy and Smith (1986) disclosed that some racial discrimination in handling existed, although it was unevenly distributed throughout various stages of the system. For example, these researchers discovered that at intake hearings, the racial factor did not appear significant in dispositions or adjustments made by intake officers. However, juvenile court adjudications and detention decisions seemed influenced by racial factors. Specifically, greater proportions of blacks than whites were adjudicated delinquent and sentenced to detention. While this is not absolute proof of discrimination, it nevertheless implies that minority juveniles, particularly blacks, were disadvantaged by their race in judicial decision making. McCarthy and Smith (1986) suggest that a better understanding of the impact of race and other factors on decision making at various stages of the juvenile justice process can be gained by considering several different stages of this process rather than focusing in on one single stage such as intake or adjudicatory hearings.

In a case study of a random sample of 228 cases involving juveniles referred by police officers and others to the juvenile probation intake and detention screening process in Travis County, Texas, it was determined that most juvenile referrals were between the ages of 13 and 15, and were disproportionately black (Arrigona and Fabelo, 1987). Although fewer than 50 percent of these had subsequent referrals within a six-month period following their initial referrals, about 60 percent of all first-referrals were diverted informally by intake officers. Thus, disproportionate racial representations at the front-end of intake help to explain subsequent racially disproportionate managements and dispositions of cases through the intake, detention hearing, and adjudicatory stages (Arrigona and Fabelo, 1987).

When we consider the detention rate of black juveniles in relation to whites, there are much sharper distinctions and treatment differentials suggesting widespread discrimination exists. For instance, the Humphrey Institute of Public Affairs (1986) found that during the period 1979–1982, blacks and other minorities were incarcerated in secure detention facilities three to four times more frequently than white offenders. More recent research that profiles secure juvenile detention facilities in Wisconsin shows that black juvenile offenders make up nearly one half of the incarcerated population, although blacks comprise only about 12 percent of the entire United States population (Grohmann and Barritt, 1987). However, if McCarthy's and Smith's (1986) observation is accurate—that we can better understand the impact of race by considering all stages of the juvenile justice process—then certainly our attention should be drawn backward in the system to the originating actors: the law enforcement officers who took the youths into custody initially.

A majority of police officers patrol the streets and are responsive to street crime. Street crime generally is overrepresented among those in the lower socioeconomic strata, including minority youths. However, as screening agents, intake probation officers may influence the influx of cases further into the system through informal adjustments. These adjustments depend, in part, on an officer's perception of family stability and the overall environment of the juvenile. Socioeconomically disadvantaged and minority youths are particularly vulnerable here. For instance, Farnworth (1984) argues that economic dimensions of the lives of black families are more relevant as explanations for delinquency among black youths than black familial instability. However, a similar analysis and conclusion may be made about white youths who are socioeconomically disadvantaged and engage in delinquent conduct. Race and ethnicity appear prominent as predictor variables in arrest and detention discretion, but at present, our accumulated evidence has failed to delineate the precise nature of the race–arrest–detention relationship.

One additional consideration is whether juveniles are gang members. Youth gangs often form along racial and ethnic lines. Furthermore, the presence of gangs in neighborhoods makes them more visible to police officers (Moore, 1985). In many jurisdictions, such as Milwaukee, Wisconsin, juvenile gang members and their activities have been targeted for special handling and procedures by subdivisions within police departments (Hage-dorn, 1988). However, responses to gang members and their activities by police are not always appropriate or productive. In some cases, police departments have exaggerated the importance and influence of specific gangs, and have equated their organization and operations with those of organized crime. This approach is destructive, and it obscures legitimate attempts by others to reinforce and emphasize conventional behaviors and social linkages available to youths who happen to identify with these gangs (Hagedorn, 1988).

One solution to combat gang recruitment and involvement in the southern California area is the **Graffiti Removal Community Service Program** (Agopian, 1989). Juveniles who are apprehended and found to be affiliated with gangs are assigned to a community service program as a condition of their probation. They must perform an average of 140 hours of community service, which consists of removing graffiti from buildings and other structures in their communities, together with other probationary conditions. According to Agopian, the removal of gang graffiti benefits the community as well as gang members, who hopefully learn that law-abiding behavior and respect for property are expected of them. Agopian reports that during the first two years the program operated, nearly 90 percent of all participating youths completed this requirement of their probation. Further, rearrests of these youths during the two-year period were minimal. However, these youths, once released from their probation programs, are placed back in their original environments and are subject to the same social pressures and economic conditions that brought them to the attention of police officers initially.

Socioeconomic Status (SES). Closely related to racial and ethnic factors as extralegal considerations in intake decision making is the **socioeconomic status (SES)** of juvenile offenders. The Humphrey Institute of Public Affairs (1986) has found that generally, the poor as well as racial and ethnic minorities are disenfranchised by the juvenile justice system at various stages.

One immediate explanation for this alleged disenfranchisement is the more limited access to economic resources among the poor and minorities. More restricted economic resources reduce the quality of legal defenses that may be accessed by the socioeconomically disadvantaged. Greater reliance on public defenders is observed among the poor compared with those who are financially advantaged. A greater proportion of the socioeconomically disadvantaged tend to acquiesce and quietly accept systemic sanctions that accompany charges of wrongdoing rather than acquire counsel and contest the charges formally in court. However, Feld (1988c, 1989) observes that the presence of defense attorneys in juvenile proceedings aggravates rather than mitigates the harshness of dispositions and subsequent sentences imposed by judges. In any event, if we can elevate these generalizations to general principles that apply to the majority of cases involving socioeconomically disadvantaged youths and adults who are charged with crimes, then SES becomes a powerful consideration in decision making at all stages of the juvenile justice system. However, not all investigators believe that the relation between SES and delinquency is necessarily strong or negative (Tittle and Meier, 1990).

A direct indicator of one's SES is **appearance,** although appearance is not always a totally reliable criterion. A national sample of 1,886 high school students was examined by interviewers and given self-administered questionnaires (Agnew, 1984). Interviewers were asked to make predictions about whether those interviewed "appeared" to be delinquents or nondelinquents. Also, youths acknowledged their involvement or noninvolvement in delinquent activities through individual self-reports on their questionnaires. One hypothesis tested in this study was that "unattractive people will be more delinquent than attractive people." Attractiveness and unattractiveness evaluations were made on the basis of interviewer judgments of appearance, demeanor, and general attire. Agnew (1984) found support for this hypothesis. At least some evaluators can make reasonably accurate judgments about youths strictly on the basis of their personal appearance, according to these findings. If interviewers can make such judgments, so can intake probation officers during intake hearings. Also, probation officers are further assisted by the personal appearances of parents or guardians and other personal information acquired during the intake interview and screening process.

Although SES is believed to be an important consideration in virtually all stages of juvenile justice processing, there are inter- and intraregional inconsistencies reported. In Colorado, for example, studies of youths in Denver, Pueblo, Grand Junction, and the Thirteenth Judicial District were conducted (Hartstone *et al.*, 1986). The official juvenile records of nearly 700 youths were examined in these jurisdictions. Minority and lower SES youths tended to receive more severe sanctions at various decision points in the Denver jurisdiction, while harsher decisions were meted out to white and middle- and upper-SES youths in the Pueblo and Thirteenth Judicial District jurisdictions. The Grand Junction jurisdiction had mixed degrees of harshness in the handling of minorities and other youths.

It is difficult to list all of the criteria that intake officers use in the screening process to prevent certain youthful offenders from being involved more deeply in the system. How does one describe accurately a youth's demeanor and attitude when the youth is arrested by the police or interviewed during intake? How do we translate impressions of youths and their parents or guardians during interviews, and the significance given to answers to specific questions, into decision-making actions? Feelings cannot be calibrated to the extent that we can measure them on a scale and determine their influence on whether petitions are filed or not filed. Yet, intake officers manifest complex decision-making styles. For some officers, their decisions may be perfunctory, particularly if they are involved in the processing of numerous youths daily. In less densely populated jurisdictions where lower caseloads are likely to be assigned, more individualized decision making can be applied, and the philosophical models discussed earlier in this chapter have increased significance. It is evident that both legal and extralegal criteria are always operative, to varying degrees, as these intake officers perform their difficult tasks.

Preliminary Decision Making: Diversion and Other Options

A long-range interest of most, if not all, intake probation officers is minimizing **recidivism** among those diverted from the system at the time of an intake hearing. Recidivism is also a commonly used measure of program effectiveness in both adult and juvenile offender treatment and sanctioning schemes (Maltz, 1984). Intake officer interest in the type of offense committed is triggered not only by the seriousness of the act itself and what should be done about it, but by evidence from various jurisdictions which suggests that recidivism rates vary substantially for different types of juvenile offenders. For example, studies of violent and nonviolent and chronic and nonchronic juvenile recidivists in Philadelphia suggest that greater proportions of chronic offenders repeat violent offenses than nonchronic offenders (Piper, 1985). However, chronic offenders also commit subsequent nonviolent acts as well as violent ones. In this particular study, the selective incapacitation and incarceration of chronic violent juveniles was a policy recommendation as a means of reducing both violent and nonviolent juvenile crime.

Closely associated with recidivism among chronic violent offenders in certain jurisdictions are predictor variables such as whether the delinquent has delinquent siblings and/or significant others as associates, whether the delinquent has school problems, and whether the acts committed were misdemeanors or felonies (Grenier and Roundtree, 1987). It is arguable whether juveniles escalate to more serious offenses over their careers as delinquents (Hartstone and Hansen, 1984). The evidence seems to suggest that generally, career escalation does not occur with the frequency that some experts have implied in recent years (review Chapter 2 for a discussion of career escalation among juvenile offenders).

Interagency agreements, experimental diversion policies in various jurisdictions such as San Diego County, California, which divert and process nonserious and first offenders informally, seem to be modestly successful at reducing recidivism (Pennell *et al.*, 1990). For more serious offenders designated as chronic, violent, aggressive, or persistent, various types of mandatory group therapy have been regarded as successful interventions in past years (Agee and McWilliams, 1984; Goldberg, 1984). However, there is strong sentiment and agreement among professionals that a combination of behavioral strategies or approaches is necessary to treat most aggressive teenagers effectively (Varley, 1984).

In some jurisdictions such as Hawaii, chronic violent or serious offenders and other aggressive youths have been targeted for "priority processing" at intake and other stages (Hawaii Crime Commission, 1985). Harsher measures, including rapid identification of youths, expedited hearings, close monitoring of their cases, and their segregation from other, less serious offenders, have been employed by different Hawaiian juvenile justice units as a means of crime control. Continuous counseling, placement in long-term secure detention facilities, extended court jurisdiction, and the revelation of these youths' identities to the public seem effective at curbing recidivism among these hard-core offenders (Hawaii Crime Commission, 1985). Of course, there are certain constitutional issues that must be resolved concerning identities of juvenile offenders and the publication of information about them made available to others (Sagatun and Edwards, 1988; Schlesinger *et al.*, 1990) (see Chapter 10 for an in-depth discussion of juvenile rights).

Also, many jurisdictions are hard-pressed to provide adequate treatment facilities and interventions that contain the ingredients for effectiveness (Hamparian, 1987). Hamparian (1987) suggests that such programs might have security without a jail-like atmosphere, close coordination and cooperation between the community and the criminal justice system, paraprofessional staffs, and provisions for remedial education and job training for these youths. But existing limited budgets and other priorities in many jurisdictions prevent the development of such sophisticated interventions (Rapoport, 1987). Yet other experts believe that interventions should be aimed at modifying the social and psychological environment that fostered such violence and chronicity originally (Kupfersmid and Monkman, 1987).

Intake officers are also influenced by existing services and programs, especially in their decisions about violent offenders. In Tucson, Arizona, for example, a **Stop Assaultive Children (SAC) Program** was created in the late 1980s and designed especially for those youths who committed family violence (Zaslaw, 1989). In this SAC program, the child is usually detained or locked up in a juvenile detention center for one day, and release from detention is contingent upon the youth's attendance at school, abiding by a curfew, refraining from committing future delinquent acts or violence, and an agreement by the youth to be interviewed by the intake probation officer. Children in the SAC program are ordered to reappear within two weeks, at which time their prosecution is deferred for three months, provided that they are accepted into SAC. All of the SAC participants must sign a contract acknowledging responsibility for their acts, agreeing further to participate in counseling and/or volunteer work, or to make a donation to a domestic violence service or agency. If the contract is unfulfilled for any reason, the juvenile is subsequently prosecuted.

Parents are also obligated to sign the contract and to enforce its conditions. The result of the successful completion of the SAC program is a dismissal of all charges against the juvenile (Zaslaw, 1989). Zaslaw (1989) reports that the SAC program has had a recidivism rate of only 9.6 percent compared with a recidivism rate of 48.7 percent among a control group of assaultive delinquent nonprogram participants in the same jurisdiction. But while Tucson may be able to operate such programs successfully, other jurisdictions may not be as fortunate, or intake officers elsewhere may believe their own plans for intervention are more effective. (Various types of diversion programs are discussed in Chapter 11.)

Of course, for persistent offenders and otherwise hard-core violent recidivists, even for some violent first-offenders, the strategy employed at intake may be a waiver of jurisdiction to criminal courts (Rudman *et al.*, 1986). Some jurisdictions, such as New York, Washington, and Illinois, have automatic transfer laws that compel juvenile authorities to send certain types of juvenile offenders in a particular age range (normally 16 or 17 years of age) directly to criminal court to be processed as adults (see Chapter 7 for a discussion of waivers or transfers). The manifest intent of such waivers to criminal court is for harsher punishments to be imposed on these youthful offenders beyond those that can ordinarily be administered within the power of juvenile court judges (Champion and Mays, 1991).

Assessment of Guardianship

While most cases that reach the intake stage of the juvenile justice process involve some type of juvenile offending, criminal or otherwise, intake probation officers are often confronted with cases that require assessments of a youth's parents or guardians and the general sociocultural environment. Ordinarily, **children in need of supervision (CHINS),** including unruly or incorrigible youths, dependent and/or neglected youths, and abused children, are diverted by police officers to the appropriate community agencies for special services and placement. Departments of Health and Human Services, social welfare agencies, and family crisis or intervention centers are frequently contacted and receive youths for further processing. However, if some youths in need of supervision are eventually subject to intake screenings, probation officers must evaluate the nature of the needs and the seriousness of the situation before a disposition of the case is made. Beyond the broad classification of CHINS, many youths may have chemical dependencies that precipitated their delinquent conduct and require medical attention rather than punishment.

Examples of such youths include youthful male and female prostitutes who originally may have been runaways and/or incorrigible, alcohol- or drug-dependent youths who have turned to burglary and petty theft to support their dependencies, psychologically disturbed or mentally retarded juveniles, and sexually exploited children. If the facts disclosed at intake enable probation officers to make the strong presumption that certain youths should be diverted to human services shelters or community welfare agencies for treatment or temporary management, then this conditional disposition can be made of the case. This decision is often predicated on the belief that a strong connection exists between the child's delinquency and physical, psychological, or sexual abuse received from adults or significant others (Sandberg, 1989). However, evidence has also been presented showing lack of a causal relation between child maltreatment seriousness and juvenile delinquency (Doerner, 1987).

It has also been found that parents who either maltreat their children or engage in substance abuse themselves often suffer multidimensional problems and may be disproportionately disposed to personality disorders, depression, criminality, and difficulty in relating to peers and spouses (Famularo *et al.*, 1988). While testing for substance abuse among parents of those youths brought before juvenile courts is only a recommendation at this stage and not a requirement of any particular jurisdiction, it may be that such drug testing in the future could provide intake officers with mitigating factors that would modify their decision making and dispositions of certain juvenile cases.

Summary

This chapter has examined a crucial phase of the juvenile justice process—intake hearings. Intake proceedings are generally informal, and although juveniles interviewed during intake may have counsel present, the usual rules and constitutional provisions that govern juvenile court proceedings and matters of an evidentiary nature are not normally observed. In fact, the presence of defense counsel may prejudice cases adversely against juveniles. In some respects, intake for juveniles is similar to plea bargaining for adults.

Intake functions also to screen the less serious offenders from those considered chronic, persistent, dangerous, or serious. Various models that have been used by intake officers in their decision making include the rehabilitation model, the treatment or medical model, the noninterventionist model, the due process model, the "just deserts" or justice model, and the crime control model. Each of these models embraces philosophical views that influence decision-making efforts during intake.

Also functioning as considerations in disposing of cases at intake are both legal and extralegal factors. Legal factors pertain to strictly factual information about crimes or offenses alleged. These include crime seriousness, type of offense, prior record, if any, age of offender, and the existence of either exculpatory or inculpatory evidence. Extralegal factors pertain to the characteristics of juveniles themselves that are extraneous to the formal intake decision, but nevertheless are believed to have significant impacts on it. These include age, race, ethnicity, gender, and socioeconomic status. Age plays a dual role as a legal and an extralegal factor, especially as it is relevant for waiver decisions. As an extralegal factor, it may influence the harshness or leniency of dispositions made by intake officers.

Intake officers are encouraged to adopt a balanced approach that includes the goals of protecting society, making youths accountable for their actions, and providing juveniles with worthwhile activities and skills that will assist them in becoming more productive citizens of their communities. Although most youths reaching the intake stage have been accused of one type of offense or another, some youths are in need of supervision by various community-based agencies and organizations. An intake officer's training and educational background are helpful in judging the familial and other social and psychological circumstances of youths if they are to be released to parental custody. The quality of existing community services also influences their release and diversion decisions.

Key Terms

Adjustments (177)
Alternative dispute resolution (183)
Appearance (200)
Children in need of supervision (CHINS) (203)
Consent decree (186)
Crime control model (187)
Due process (183)
Due process model (184)
Extralegal factors (188)
Graffiti Removal Community Service Program (199)
Intake (173)
Intake probation officer (173)
Interagency Agreement Plan (181)

Judicious nonintervention (183)
"Just deserts" model (186)
Justice model (186)
Legal factors (188)
Noninterventionist model (181)
Plea bargaining (174)
Police cautioning (180)
Radical nonintervention (183)
Recidivism (201)
Rehabilitation model (180)
Socioeconomic status (SES) (199)
Stop Assaultive Children (SAC) Program (202)
Strategic leniency (191)
Treatment or medical model (180)

Questions for Review

1. What is meant by intake? What are its functions? Why is intake considered more or less informal? Explain.
2. Compare and contrast the intake process in the juvenile justice system with plea bargaining in the criminal justice system. Show the similarities and differences of each. What are the implications of intake for affected juveniles?
3. How might an intake hearing be considered manipulative?
4. What are six philosophical models that may guide intake probation officers in their dispo-

sitions of juvenile cases? Do all officers subscribe to one model or another? Why or why not? What factors seem to influence an officer's views about intake decision making?
5. In what respect would the presence of a defense attorney during an intake hearing adversely affect the hearing outcome? Explain.
6. Do intake hearings require that all constitutional safeguards be observed, including the same evidentiary standards that would apply in juvenile courts? Discuss your answer briefly.

7. Of the various philosophies or models used by intake officers in their decision making, which do you prefer and why?

8. Which philosophy or model seems to fit the present "get tough" movement that seems to be pervasive in both the criminal and juvenile justice systems? Write a short paragraph outlining your argument.

9. What are legal factors that are normally considered in an intake hearing? Describe each of the factors you list and cite some research to show the relevance of each for intake decision making.

10. What do you believe is meant by the term *judicious nonintervention?*

11. Differentiate between inculpatory and exculpatory factors. Why are they important and how might they influence an intake decision favorably or unfavorably?

12. Identify four major extralegal factors that may have an impact on an intake hearing. Are these factors easy to list? Can we show direct connections between these factors and intake decision making? Why or why not?

13. Some researchers say that we can better understand the influence of extralegal factors as they impact on the juvenile justice system by considering several different stages of the system simultaneously. Why?

14. How is an offender's appearance related to intake decision making? Cite some research pertaining to the influence of the attractiveness or unattractiveness of youths on whether they are treated harshly or leniently.

15. What is the justification for making assessments of parents or guardians during the intake process?

16. Do intake officers deal exclusively with criminal or status offenders? What are some exceptional cases?

17. What are CHINS? Briefly relate parenting behavior and delinquency, based upon the research presented in this chapter.

Suggested Readings

ARMSTRONG, TROY (ED.) (1990). *Intensive Interventions with High-risk Youths: Promising Approaches in Juvenile Probation and Parole.* Monsey, NY: Criminal Justice Press.

SHEPHERD, J. R., AND D. M. ROTHENBERGER (1980). *Police–Juvenile Diversion: An Alternative to Prosecution* (2nd ed.). Ann Arbor, MI: Michigan Department of State Police.

SIMONSEN, CLIFFORD E. (1991). *Juvenile Justice in America* (3rd ed.). New York: Macmillan.

STURZ, ELIZABETH LYTTLETON (1983). *Widening Circles.* New York: Harper & Row.

The Juvenile Justice System: Prosecution, Courts, and Juvenile Rights

Part III includes four chapters that continue to explore the range of options available to juvenile justice authorities as juveniles are processed further by the juvenile justice system. Chapter 7 examines the classificatory schemes used to differentiate more serious offenders from less serious ones. Beyond the simple distinction between status offender and delinquent offender, there are more detailed analyses to be made. Some juveniles require extensive psychological counseling and other forms of therapy. Others require medication and intensive participation in withdrawal programs if addicted to drugs, alcohol, or other substances. A small proportion of juveniles, because of the seriousness of their offenses, are transferred to criminal courts, where they can be processed as though they were adults. In the eyes of these courts, the youths transferred from the juvenile justice system *are* adults for all practical purposes, and they are subject to the full range of adult punishments, including the death penalty.

Waiver or transfer processes vary among states and jurisdictions, and therefore, different types of waiver schemes will be examined. There are serious implications for juveniles who may be transferred to criminal courts or certified as adults for criminal prosecution. These transfers may be contested through waiver hearings. Some states have legislatively mandated automatic transfer provisions whereby youths of a certain age, usually 16 or 17, are transferred automatically to the jurisdiction of criminal courts if they have allegedly committed especially serious crimes. These crimes are usually cataloged and are fairly uniform among states having automatic transfer statutes.

Youths may challenge such automatic transfers through a reverse waiver action, although their chances of success in challenging such transfers are remote. Negotiations between defense and prosecuting attorneys are crucial at this stage, and some amount of juvenile plea bargaining occurs. Because transfers bestow the full range of adult rights and constitutional guarantees on juveniles, and because this full range of rights is not available to them in juvenile proceedings, there are advantages and disadvantages to be weighed in deciding whether to contest such waiver actions.

Chapter 8 focuses on the role of prosecutors in juvenile courts. A brief review of the history and theory of juvenile courts is presented, together with an ideal view of the roles of the respective actors in juvenile courtrooms. There continues to be a strong discord between competing philosophies about how best juveniles should be managed. The *parens patriae* doctrine of past years is in increasing conflict with "get tough" proponents who believe that juveniles should be held accountable for their actions in similar ways to adults. Defense attorneys are advocates for juvenile offenders, and they attempt to persuade judges and juries (in those jurisdictions where juries for juveniles are permitted) that leniency should be extended to their youthful clients. Practical matters such as the dangerousness of certain juvenile offenders and their propensity for future violence are considered by the court at the time of adjudication. Juvenile courts are becoming increasingly like criminal courts in their operations, and a unified court system has been proposed that would obscure any significant differences in the ways juveniles and adults are processed. The controversy surrounding such unification proposals will be explored.

Chapter 9 examines the judicial role in the juvenile justice system. Juvenile judges must balance their personal interests with those of the community at large. Considerable controversy exists about the amount of discretion currently exercised by these juvenile judges. Consideration is given to whether youthful offenders are first offenders or recidivists, and whether their offenses are violent or nonviolent. Are there any especially aggravating or mitigating circumstances that must be considered by judges if they find that juveniles are delinquent as charged? A wide array of punishments may be meted out, ranging from most lenient to most strict. Most-lenient punishments include nominal warnings, admonitions, and restrictions accompanying conditional release to parents. Some youths may be placed in community-based treatment programs and may be obligated to perform restitution, pay fines, or engage in community service to offset the financial damage their actions have caused victims. The most stringent punishment includes secure confinement in long-term detention facilities such as state industrial schools. Often, these industrial schools are the equivalent of medium-security prisons or penitentiaries for adults. The implications of judicial decision making for juvenile well-being and future progress are examined.

Chapter 10 is a general discussion of the legal rights of juveniles. Several important landmark cases involving juveniles are examined in detail, with attention given to their implications for more extensive juvenile rights. Because the juvenile court was dominated by the *parens patriae* doctrine for so many decades, it wasn't until the 1960s that major changes began to occur in the ways juveniles were treated legally. Until the mid-1960s, the destiny of juveniles rested in the hands of prosecutors and judges who made decisions which they believed to be in the child's interests. Constitutional rights were not seriously considered as pertinent to juvenile case-processing. However, major cases were decided by the U.S. Supreme Court in ways that caused significant modifications in the rules of juvenile court procedure.

Rights of juveniles to be represented by counsel, to have the Miranda warning read to them when arrested, to cross-examine witnesses against them, to avoid self-incrimination, and to avoid double jeopardy have been extended to juveniles only in recent decades. Previously, these rights existed only for adults charged with crimes. Other cases pertaining to the preventive detention of juveniles and the conditions under which their personal possessions may be searched on school premises and elsewhere will be described. Again, the future points to an increasing criminalization of juvenile courts and procedure, a prospect that has both opponents and proponents. Different sides of this controversy will be examined.

CHAPTER 7

Classification and Preliminary Decision Making: Waivers and Other Alternatives

Twenty-two-year-old Brian Watkins from Provo, Utah, went to New York City with his family during the Labor Day weekend, 1990. He watched the New York Mets beat the San Francisco Giants 4–3 at Shea Stadium, and the following afternoon, he attended the U.S. Open tennis tournament. In the evening, after changing clothes in their hotel room, the family headed for Greenwich Village to eat dinner at a well-known Moroccan restaurant. In less than an hour, Brian Watkins would be killed by muggers in a New York subway station when a youth gang member plunged a knife deep into his chest. The muggers, members of Fuck That Shit (FTS), one of hundreds of gangs that roam New York City streets, wanted fast money so they could attend a big disco party at Roseland Dance City, a local disco. After taking $203 from Brian's father by cutting his wallet from his pocket with razor blades, they turned on his mother. Brian, weaponless, died trying to protect her. Using the blood money to gain admission to Roseland, several gang members enjoyed music and drinks for the rest of the evening. Eight teenagers out of the 10 who attacked the Watkins were arrested the following day. Showing no remorse in video-taped confessions, 7 of the FTS gang members ratted on their buddy, 18-year-old Rocstar, the alleged stabber, who always carried a "butterfly" knife (a double-edged device with four-inch blades). For the Watkins, it was the beginning of terrifying memories of a tragedy and a silent trip back to Provo with the coffin of their son. For Rocstar and his pals, it was just another day in the city after a wild disco concert.

On May 1, 1989, a 17-year-old mildly retarded girl was allegedly raped, brutally beaten, and sodomized by 5 Glen Ridge High School (New Jersey) sports stars, while 8 friends observed and cheered. The girl, forced to perform various sex acts, was raped with various objects, including a miniature baseball bat and a broom handle. One onlooker was the 18-year-old son of a Glen Ridge police lieutenant who was later assigned the case for investigation. The girl reported the attack to teachers on March 4. Police were notified 3 weeks later. Arrests of the participants were belatedly made in late May after television news programs highlighted the incident and raised incriminating questions, and jurisdiction for the case passed from the police lieutenant to Essex County authorities. Twins Kyle and Kevin Scherzer and their classmate Peter Quigley, all 18, were taken into custody in late May 1989 and charged with aggravated sexual assault. Two other arrested youths remained unnamed because they were underage and considered juveniles.

In April 1989, at least 6 teenagers assaulted a 29-year-old female jogger in New York's Central Park. **"Wilding,"** they called it—vicious, brutal, random assaults. After tearing her clothes from her body, raping her repeatedly, and beating her with bricks and pipes, her attackers left her for dead. The blows were so severe that one eyeball exploded rearward through the back of her eye socket. Portions of her brain's surface were flattened out by the pipes and bricks, according to a testifying physician who treated her. Miraculously, she survived. In August 1990, 3 of the 6 attackers were tried and convicted of rape and aggravated assault. A subsequent trial awaited the other 3 attackers. Although an attempted murder was brought against these youths by prosecutors, jurors demurred. One juror declared that youths that age could not know how many blows it takes to kill someone. As one member of the Guardian Angels (an organized group which patrols streets and subways in at attempt to minimize crime) summed it up, when jeered by supporters of the convicted youths, "They got a fair trial, which is more than they gave the jogger" (*Newsweek*, August 27, 1990:39).

Introduction

The incidents just described are only a few of the hundreds of thousands of arrests in the United States annually of youths aged 18 or younger. In 1988, youths aged 18 and under accounted for more than 2,500 arrests for murder and nonnegligent manslaughter, over 5,300 arrests for forcible rape, over 31,000 arrests for robbery, and more than 50,000 arrests for aggravated assault (Flanagan and Maguire, 1990:426). What responses to these offenses should be made by the juvenile justice system? What are the limits of sanctions to be imposed by juvenile courts? Should some youths be held more accountable than others, in view of the crimes they commit? Are some youths more deserving of criminal punishment than others? Where should the line be drawn about who should receive criminal penalties and who should not receive them?

This chapter examines *waiver* decision making. **Waivers, also known** in some jurisdictions as **transfers** and **certifications,** are *transferrals or shifts of jurisdiction over certain types of cases from juvenile courts to criminal courts*. These terms will be used throughout this and other chapters interchangeably. Youths who are subjected to waivers are not tried as juveniles in juvenile courts. Rather, they are redefined and classified as adults and eventually tried in criminal courts. Only a small proportion of juveniles are subject to criminal court transfer annually. Preliminary determinations are made of crime seriousness, the youth's characteristics, such as age and other factors associated with the type of crime committed, and the amount or degree of victim injuries inflicted. This process will be described.

Several types of waivers may be exercised by either judges or juvenile prosecutors, depending upon the jurisdiction. In some jurisdictions, provisions exist for the automatic transfer of certain juvenile offenders to criminal court. These variations in waiver procedures will be outlined and discussed. Because of the potentially serious nature of penalties that criminal courts may impose if youths are eventually found guilty through bench or jury trials or plea bargaining, several implications of waivers for affected juveniles will be examined. Waivers may be contested, and these procedures are known as **waiver hearings.** In those jurisdictions with statutory automatic transfer provisions, juveniles are entitled to reverse waiver hearings. Both options have strengths and weaknesses, benefits and disadvantages, for youths charged with crimes. These will be described. Because waivers of juveniles to criminal court may be made at several junctures in the juvenile justice process (e.g., automatically by statute, before or after intake, at the prosecution stage, or at adjudication in juvenile court), it is important to discuss this event now rather than in a later chapter. Subsequently, we will see how waivers function as options for various actors in the juvenile justice system, and we will be able to understand their significance as well as their various implications for affected juveniles.

An integral feature of the juvenile justice process is the adversarial relation between defense counsel and prosecutors. Both of these roles will be examined as they relate to waiver decisions. Finally, a "get tough" movement has been observed over the last few decades, within both the criminal and juvenile justice systems. For criminals, "get tough" means stiffer sentences and heavier fines, fewer loopholes that may be used to elude convictions for crimes, and less prosecutorial and judicial discretion relating to minimizing charges filed and penalties assessed. For juveniles, "get tough" means moving away from the traditional rehabilitative orientation that characterized early juvenile court processes and decision making and toward more punitive sanctions, greater use of detention, especially for more serious youthful offenders, obligating more youths to be held accountable for their actions, and more liberal use of waivers to criminal courts for the most serious offenders. Waivers represent a "hard line" against selected juvenile offenders. However, some experts are not enthusiastic about adopting such a hard line, and they believe that alternative nonincarcerative interventions should be experimented with and utilized before a hard line against juveniles becomes widely adopted as policy (Conrad, 1983). Contemporary waiver patterns among the states will be illustrated and waiver trends described.

Seriousness of the Offense, Offender Characteristics, and Waiver Decision Making

Among criminal justice professionals and those who study crime and delinquency, it is generally conceded that juvenile violence in the United States escalated dramatically during the 1960s and 1970s—especially the incidence of juvenile homicides (Kriesman and Siden, 1982; Mathias *et al.,* 1984; Strasburg, 1984). Reports differ about whether this trend has continued, however (Osgood *et al.,* 1987). One explanation for greater juvenile violence has been the widespread availability of firearms to youths. In some areas such as New York, Los Angeles, and Chicago, gang warfare has escalated to the point where more dominant gangs tend to possess more sophisticated weaponry than the rest of the gangs. Thus, city streets or "turfs" have become major combat zones for rival groups of youths seeking territorial control.

In an effort to stem the rising tide of juvenile violence that typified much of the 1970s, various programs and policies were implemented legislatively that were intended as "get tough" measures. Juvenile courts were seen as too lenient in their dealings with youthful offenders. Rehabilitation of youths and various experimental treatment programs and helping strategies did not seem be working (Walker, 1989). Public sentiment seemed to favor more punitive measures and tactics that would incapacitate the more serious or violent offenders.

Offense Seriousness. One of the first measures designed to separate juveniles into different offending categories was the widespread deinstitutionalization of status offenders or DSO (see Chapter 2 for a more complete discussion of the phenomenon). Also known as divestiture, this major juvenile justice reform was calculated to remove less serious and noncriminal offenders from the jurisdiction of juvenile courts in most jurisdictions. Presumably and ideally, after DSO, only those juveniles who were charged with felonies and/or misdemeanors would be brought into the juvenile justice process and formally adjudicated in juvenile courts. These courts would also retain managerial control (in the *parens patriae* sense) over children in need of supervision, abused children, or neglected children. In reality, we have seen

Metal detectors on school grounds? The advent of large-scale gang warfare among juveniles and the increasingly sophisticated weaponry used to control their turfs compels school officials in various jurisdictions to take extraordinary precautionary measures to prevent violence on elementary and high school campuses. (© Tom McKillerick/Impact Visuals)

that events have not turned out as legislators had originally anticipated, and that considerable improvement remains to be made in juvenile justice operations and functions. Many status offenders continue to filter into the juvenile justice system in various jurisdictions. Many of these offenders are the victims of net-widening by police officers, who have sometimes taken it upon themselves to redefine previously noncriminal behaviors as criminal ones.

When DSO originated on a large scale throughout the United States during the late 1970s, several jurisdictions, including West Virginia, made policy decisions that would affect the ways in which both nonserious and serious offenders would henceforth be treated by juvenile justice systems. In West Virginia, the Supreme Court of Appeals ruled in 1977 that an adjudicated delinquent was constitutionally entitled to receive the *least restrictive alternative treatment consistent with his or her rehabilitative needs* (emphasis mine) (*State ex rel. Harris* v. *Calendine* 1977) (Mones, 1984). While this decision didn't rule out incarcerating more serious or violent juveniles, it encouraged juvenile judges to consider seriously various alternatives to incarceration as punishments for youthful offenders. Relating to DSO, the Court also prohibited the commingling of adjudicated status offenders and adjudicated criminal (juvenile) offenders in secure, prisonlike facilities (Mones, 1984). Again, the Court didn't necessarily rule out the secure detention, long-term or otherwise, of status offenders as a possible sanction by juvenile judges, although it encouraged judges to first attempt to apply nonincarcerative sanctions before imposing incarcerative penalties.

These mixed messages sent by the West Virginia Supreme Court of Appeals did little, if anything, to restrict the discretionary powers of juvenile court judges. The Court's emphasis on rehabilitation and alternative treatments to be considered by juvenile judges reinforced its traditional concept of juvenile courts as rehabilitative rather than punitive sanctioning bodies. However, the ruling led to a drastic overhaul of the West Virginia juvenile code as well as to a substantial drop in the incarcerated juvenile offender population in state-operated correctional facilities.

In other jurisdictions, DSO has reduced the volume of juvenile court cases over the years, but it has not prevented juvenile courts from continuing to adjudicate rather large numbers of status offenders annually. A study of juvenile courts in thirteen states between the years 1984 and 1985 shows systematic increases in the absolute numbers of status offenders adjudicated across all status offense categories (Snyder *et al.*, 1985:75). Table 7.1 illustrates the numbers of status offense cases adjudicated in these courts by offense and race. In these jurisdictions, status offender adjudications increased between 1984 and 1985 from 69,707 to 76,930, a 10.4 percent increase. While runaways accounted for the largest percent increase between the two time periods, liquor law violations contained the largest numbers of offenders for both years.

Assuming that in the majority of jurisdictions, juvenile courts have effectively weeded out the bulk of the nonserious, noncriminal cases, the remainder should theoretically comprise mostly criminal offenses. Acknowledging that this assumption is debatable (McCarthy, 1987b; Sametz, 1984), we might expect our juvenile courts to have become increasingly criminalized in several respects, including growing parallels between juvenile and criminal court procedures (Feld, 1987a, 1987b; Harris and Graff, 1988; Volenik, 1986; Watkins, 1987). Judges must now reconceptualize what is meant by offense seriousness and make new distinctions among youths, since the current aggregate of juvenile offenders is categorically more serious than previous aggregates. But juvenile courts still retain certain *parens patriae* elements and lack certain due process features that typify the full range of constitutional rights available to adults in criminal courts. For especially violent, chronic offenders, waivers may accomplish what juvenile judges and their powers are unable to accomplish.

Several reasons are cited to justify the use of waivers. One is that the most serious juvenile offenders will be transferred to the jurisdiction of criminal courts, where the harshest punishments, including capital punishment, may be imposed as sanctions. Since juvenile courts lack the jurisdiction and decision-making power to impose anything harsher than detention sentences

TABLE 7.1   Delinquency Cases Waived to Adult Criminal Court in 10 States (By Offense, and Sex and Age of Juvenile, 1985[a])

		Delinquency Cases Waived to Criminal Court				
		Sex		Age		
	Total	Male	Female	15 Years or Younger	16 Years	17 Years or Older
All Offenses	1,917	1,855	62	92	438	1,385
Percent	100%	100%	100%	100%	100%	100%
Index Violent Offenses						
Murder	5	5	5	5	5	5
Forcible rape	4	4	0	7	3	4
Robbery	17	17	13	26	20	15
Aggravated assault	9	9	11	8	11	9
Index Property Offenses						
Burglary	19	19	3	13	16	20
Larceny-theft	12	12	11	13	9	12
Motor vehicle theft	6	6	3	4	6	6
Arson	(b)	(b)	(b)	1	(b)	(b)
Nonindex Delinquency Offenses						
Simple assault	3	3	2	8	2	3
Drug law violations	7	7	6	2	8	7
Other nonindex	19	18	45	13	20	19

Note: See Note, Table 5.71, Snyder, 1985. States included in this table are Alabama, Arizona, California, Hawaii, Maryland, Mississippi, Ohio, Pennsylvania, Utah, and Virginia. These states represent 26.4 percent of the U.S. youth population at risk. For methodology, definitions of terms, and offenses within categories, see Appendix 15 of source.
[a]Detail may not add to totals due to rounding or interpolation techniques.
[b]Less than 0.5 percent
SOURCE: Howard N. Snyder et al., *Juvenile Court Statistics 1985*, U.S. Department of Justice. Office of Juvenile Justice and Delinquency Prevention (Washington, DC: U.S. Department of Justice, 1989), p. 53.

of limited duration in secure juvenile facilities, it would seem that the waiver would be an ideal way to accomplish certain punitive aims beyond the range of juvenile court sanctions. A second reason is that those to be transferred are not believed to be amenable to the available treatment programs within the juvenile justice system. Procedurally, at least, all requisite mechanisms are currently in place in all jurisdictions in the United States so that transfers of serious juvenile offenders to criminal courts may occur smoothly. Thus, this particular dimension of the "get tough" movement and the reforms it has spawned in juvenile proceedings has seemingly been satisfied.

Indeed, some investigators have reported precisely this outcome. For instance, Rudman *et al.* (1986) has studied 177 violent youthful offenders considered for transfer in four urban courts, including Boston, Memphis, Newark, and Phoenix during the early 1980s. While he has noted that the procedures for effecting transfers in these jurisdictions vary, and that there are differences in the criteria upon which transfers are based as well as in the rules followed in these juvenile courts, a majority of these youths were transferred to criminal courts. Those transferred who were subsequently convicted received sentences that were comparatively harsher in nature and length than might have been received had the cases been adjudicated in juvenile courts. Of those youths who were considered for transfer but remained in juvenile courts to have their cases adjudicated, those who were adjudicated delinquent tended to receive maximum incarcerative sentences and the least desirable placements (e.g., maximum-security juvenile facilities).

Rudman *et al.* also observed that alternatives to incarceration, such as intensive supervised probation, community service, home confinement/ electronic monitoring, victim restitution and compensation, and fines, were rarely imposed. These researchers acknowledged that while little empirical evidence is available about the transfer process, the transfer of violent youths from juvenile to criminal court is widespread. (A similar study of waivers of nearly 250 juveniles to criminal courts in New Jersey during the period 1983–1984 yielded essentially the same results (New Jersey Division of Criminal Justice, 1985.)

Both of Rudman *et al.*'s statements are true. There is widespread use of transfers of violent youths from juvenile to criminal courts. There is little empirical evidence available about the transfer process. However, these statements may be unintentionally misleading. First, while it is true that there is widespread use of transfers of violent youths from juvenile to criminal courts, there is also widespread use of transfers of nonviolent youths, persistent or chronic petty or property offenders, and even status offenders who have violated court orders (Champion and Mays, 1991). In fact, by the end of 1987, the proportion of violent offenders in long-term, state-operated, juvenile detention facilities was only 39.3 percent, while property offenders, drug offenders, and public order offenders made up most of the remainder. Further, these long-term facilities housed a fairly large number of status offenders, who accounted for about 2.2 percent of the 78,000 youths confined in state-operated secure institutions (U.S. Department of Justice, 1988:3; American Correctional Association, 1989:xxviii–xxix).

Second, while there has been little empirical study in the past of the transfer process and of the characteristics and subsequent dispositions of those transferred, a rich body of information has evolved recently, as larger numbers of researchers have investigated this topic in different jurisdictions. While these research reports are somewhat inconsistent and at times even contradictory, they reveal an emerging pattern of transfers nationwide that is disturbing and suggestive of the idea that transfers are being used in most jurisdictions increasingly in ways that were not originally intended.

For example, Rubin (1985) and others indicate that in many jurisdictions, transfers are being used for cosmetic purposes, to create the illusion that juvenile courts are developing and implementing tougher policies against the hard-core, violent youthful offender. Thus, because transfers are being used more frequently by judges in juvenile court *X*, these judges must be doing a good job at "getting tough" and "fighting crime." In reality, many juvenile judges are using transfers simply to rid their courts of petty offenders and nonviolent youths who reappear before them with irritating frequency. In short, they are "passing the buck" to criminal court judges to decide what to do with these troublesome, but nonviolent, youths. Later in this chapter, we will see that a rather large proportion of those transferred in most jurisdictions either have their cases dropped, have the charges against them lessened, or have probationary sentences imposed largely through plea bargaining.

Offender Characteristics. Those offenders designated for transfer or waiver by various participants in the juvenile justice process may exhibit certain standard characteristics. *Age*, *type of offense alleged*, and *prior record* (prior involvement with the juvenile justice system—either previous referrals to juvenile court, intake processings and dispositions, or adjudications of delinquency or nondelinquency) are the standard characteristics. Table 7.2 shows the youngest age at which juveniles may be transferred or waived to criminal courts in most U.S. jurisdictions. Beyond these factors, little appears to be standard about the characteristics of those selected for waivers.

For example, Grisso *et al.* (1988) indicate that several extralegal factors function to enhance the likelihood that a juvenile will be waived to criminal court. These researchers gathered data from fifty state juvenile codes. Using content analysis, they searched court records and read decisions involving transferred juveniles, appeals of these transfers to appellate courts, and various law review articles pertaining to transfers. They supplemented their

TABLE 7.2   Youngest Age at Which Juvenile May Be Transferred to Criminal Court by Judicial Waiver

Age	States
No specific age	Alaska, Arizona, Arkansas, Delaware, Florida, Indiana, Kentucky, Maine, Maryland, New Hampshire, New Jersey, Oklahoma, South Dakota, West Virginia, Wyoming, Federal districts
10	Vermont
12	Montana
13	Georgia, Illinois, Mississippi
14	Alabama, Colorado, Connecticut, Idaho, Iowa, Massachusetts, Minnesota, Missouri, North Carolina, North Dakota, Pennsylvania, South Carolina, Tennessee, Utah
15	District of Columbia, Louisiana, Michigan, New Mexico, Ohio, Oregon, Texas, Virginia
16	California, Hawaii, Kansas, Nevada, Rhode Island, Washington, Wisconsin

Note: Many judicial waiver statutes also specify offenses that are waivable. This chart lists the states by the youngest age for which judicial waiver may be sought without regard to offense.
SOURCE: Linda A. Szymanski, "Waiver/transfer/certification of juveniles to criminal court: Age restrictions: Crime restrictions" (Pittsburgh, PA: National Center for Juvenile Justice), February 1987.

analysis with interviews with 85 court personnel and a survey of 1,423 representatives from 127 courts in 34 states. They concluded several things about the juveniles who were subjects of transfers. First, an obvious legal factor (see Chapter 6) emerged as significant. Those with extensive prior records or involvement with the juvenile justice system were more frequently detained and subjected to transfer.

Second, many of these youths exhibited "emotional disturbances" of various kinds. This emotional disturbance seemed to promote self-destructive behavior and poor school adjustment. These youths were highly unlikely to accept interventions suggested originally by juvenile courts and intake officers. Thus, *unwillingness to accept intervention* became an important extralegal factor that adversely influenced the transfer decision. Third, the researchers found that those transferred tended to lack self-discipline and failed to comply with rules in various social and legal settings. Therefore, a youth's *degree of behavioral compliance* with institutional rules became another extralegal factor impinging upon the waiver decision.

Some of the characteristics of transferred youths have been profiled by Snyder *et al.* (1989) in a study of 1,917 cases waived to criminal court in ten states in 1985. These are shown in Table 7.3. First, over 90 percent of those transferred were male. Approximately 25 percent were age 16 or younger. Not surprisingly, 35 percent of those transferred were charged with violent offenses, compared with 65 percent who were charged with property and non-index delinquency offenses. These results, at least for the jurisdictions investigated, suggest that not always are the most serious cases selected for transfer. We might assume here that chronicity may have been an important factor, especially in cases where property and non-index delinquency offenders had extensive prior records. An earlier study by August (1981) showed a similar offender profile for 230 juveniles who were transferred to criminal courts in Dade County, Florida. August concluded that many of the transferred youths had extensive delinquent histories and were frankly difficult to treat under Florida's Youthful Offender Program. In all likelihood, Snyder *et al.*'s sample had similar background characteristics.

Snyder *et al.*'s (1989) and August's (1981) work is consistent with the research of others. Data relating to 2,335 transfer cases were examined from the automated court records of 552 juvenile courts in Arizona, California, Hawaii, Iowa, Kansas, Mississippi, Pennsylvania, Tennessee, and Virginia for 1982 (Nimick *et al.*, 1986). These cases represented approximately 2 percent of all juvenile cases heard by these courts during that year. Only about a third of the transferred youths had been charged with violent index offenses, while most of the waived cases related to property offenses, primarily burglary. These investigators have shown that those transferred tended to have lengthy prior juvenile court records and were seldom less than 16 years of age.

Waiver Decision Making. Bortner (1986) observes that since 1979, the rate of transfers in various U.S. jurisdictions has more than tripled. He says, however, that there is little evidence to show that those transferred have been particularly dangerous or intractable, or that public safety has been enhanced

TABLE 7.3   Delinquency Cases Waived to Adult Criminal Court in 10 States (By Offense, and Sex and Age of Juvenile, 1985[a])

| | | Sex | | Age | | |
	Total	Male	Female	15 years or Younger	16 Years	17 Years or Older
All Offenses	1,917	1,855	62	92	438	1,385
Percent	100%	100%	100%	100%	100%	100%
Index Violent Offenses						
Murder	5	5	5	5	5	5
Forcible rape	4	4	0	7	3	4
Robbery	17	17	13	26	20	15
Aggravated assault	9	9	11	8	11	9
Index Property Offenses						
Burglary	19	19	3	13	16	20
Larceny-theft	12	12	11	13	9	12
Motor vehicle theft	6	6	3	4	6	6
Arson	(b)	(b)	(b)	1	(b)	(b)
Nonindex Delinquency Offenses						
Simple assault	3	3	2	8	2	3
Drug law violations	7	7	6	2	8	7
Other nonindex	19	18	45	13	20	19

Note: See Note, Table 5.71, Snyder, 1985. States included in this table are Alabama, Arizona, California, Hawaii, Maryland, Mississippi, Ohio, Pennsylvania, Utah, and Virginia. These states represent 26.4 percent of the U.S. youth population at risk. For methodology, definitions of terms, and offenses within categories, see Appendix 15 of source.
[a]Detail may not add to totals due to rounding or interpolation techniques.
[b]Less than 0.5 percent

SOURCE: Howard N. Snyder et al., *Juvenile Court Statistics 1985*, U.S. Department of Justice. Office of Juvenile Justice and Delinquency Prevention (Washington, DC: U.S. Department of Justice, 1989), p. 53.

significantly as the result of these numerous waivers. Like Rubin (1985), Bortner suggests that organizational and political factors are at work to influence the upward trend in the use of transfers. Those politicians who wish to present a "get tough" facade to the public perhaps believe that citing waiver statistics and showing their increased use is an effective political response to the rise in serious youth crime. However, statistical information has not supported the idea that serious crime among juveniles is increasing dramatically or even increasing beyond the absolute increases that would be expected in view of normal U.S. population growth. Further, considerable evidence exists independent of Bortner's research to support his generalizations and arguments about the politicalization of waiver decision making. (Jurisdictions such as Minnesota have reported slight increases in the rate of violent juvenile crime in recent years, despite a decline in the absolute numbers of juveniles in the state. However, Minnesota officials indicate that only 2 percent of all violent crime arrests in the state involve juveniles (Minnesota Criminal Justice Statistical Analysis Center, 1989.)

As will be seen in the following section, there are several types of waivers that can be used to negotiate transfers of jurisdiction from juvenile to criminal courts. One of these is the **automatic transfer** or **automatic waiver** which several jurisdictions currently employ. This means that if youthful offenders are within a particular age range, usually ages 16 or 17, and are charged with specific types of offenses (usually murder, robbery, rape, aggravated assault, and other violent crimes), they will be transferred automatically to criminal courts. They may challenge this transfer to criminal court through a **reverse waiver hearing.** This will be discussed in greater detail later in the chapter. The point is that these types of waivers, also known as legislative waivers because they were mandated by legislative bodies in various states and carry the weight of statutory authority, involve no discretionary action among prosecutors or judges. For other types of waivers, the decision-making process is largely discretionary.

[handwritten margin note: transferred by district attorney.]

Because of the discretionary nature of the waiver process, large numbers of the "wrong" types of juveniles are transferred to criminal courts. The "wrong" types of juveniles are "wrong" because they are not those intended by juvenile court reformers to be the primary targets of transfers. Again, the primary targets of waivers are *intended* to be the most serious, violent, and dangerous juveniles, who are most likely to deserve the sanctions criminal courts may impose. But there is a vast difference between those juveniles who are actually transferred annually and those who are the intended subjects of waiver actions. Furthermore, waived cases take considerably longer to process than other cases. Rudman *et al.* (1986) indicates that case processing time of waived juveniles is about 2.5 to 3 times as long as the processing time required by other cases.

Types of Waivers

There are four types of waiver actions. These include (1) *prosecutorial waivers,* (2) *judicial/discretionary waivers,* (3) *demand waivers,* and (4) *legislative or automatic waivers.*

Prosecutorial Waivers. When offenders are screened at intake and referred to the juvenile court for possible prosecution, prosecutors in various jurisdictions will conduct further screenings of these youths. They will determine which cases merit further action and formal adjudication by judges. Not all cases sent to prosecutors by intake probation officers automatically result in subsequent formal juvenile court action. There may be a **nolo prosequi**—that is, prosecutors may decline to prosecute certain cases, particularly if there are problems with witnesses who are either missing or who refuse to testify, if there are evidentiary issues, or if juvenile court dockets are overloaded. A relatively small proportion of cases may merit waivers to criminal courts.

Generally, prosecutors have considerable discretion in both criminal and juvenile courts. As we have already learned, they may decline to prosecute certain cases or vigorously pursue others, at their discretion. Juvenile court prosecutors in twelve states currently possess **concurrent jurisdiction** or *the power to file charges against juveniles in either criminal courts or juvenile courts.* Essentially, some prosecutors may bypass juvenile courts altogether and file charges against youths with the criminal court. The charges may be very serious ones or extremely minor offenses. Thus, prosecutors may charge youths with traffic violations and file these charges in either juvenile or criminal court. In Florida, one of the states where prosecutors possess concurrent jurisdiction, prosecutors may file extremely serious charges (e.g., murder, rape, aggravated assault, robbery) against youths in criminal courts and present cases to grand juries for indictment action, or they may decide to file the same cases with the juvenile court.

Despite these prosecutorial options, all juveniles, as defined by their particular jurisdictions, are constitutionally entitled to a waiver hearing as one of their due process rights extended by the early landmark case **Kent** v. **United States** (1966). (See Chapter 10, "The Legal Rights of Juveniles," for a detailed presentation of juvenile rights.) Such hearings are particularly important if the juvenile wishes to contest the **prosecutorial waiver** and remain within the jurisdiction of the juvenile court. If charges against certain juveniles have been filed with the criminal court, juveniles may contest this action through a *reverse waiver hearing.* Waiver and reverse waiver hearings will be discussed in a later section of this chapter.

Judicial/Discretionary Waivers. The largest numbers of waivers from juvenile to criminal court annually come about as the result of direct judicial action. Juvenile judges in most jurisdictions may take independent action and waive certain juveniles to criminal court jurisdiction. **Judicial waivers** are also known as **discretionary waivers,** since judges exercise their discretion when transferring jurisdiction over these juveniles to criminal court judges.

Feld (1987b) and others have criticized judicial waivers largely because of their highly subjective qualities. Two different youths charged with identical offenses may appear at different times before the same judge. On the basis of impressions formed about the youths, the judge may decide to transfer one youth to criminal court and to adjudicate the other youth in juvenile court. Obviously, the intrusion of extralegal factors into this important action generates a certain degree of unfairness and inequality. A youth's appearance and attitude emerge as significant factors that will either make or break the offender in the eyes of the judge. These socioeconomic and behavioral criteria often overshadow the seriousness or pettiness of offenses alleged. In the context of this particular type of transfer, it is easy to see how some persistent, nonviolent offenders may suffer waiver to criminal court. This is an easy way for the judge to get rid of them.

New Ohio Law — for serious charges — min. amt. of time served has been increased →1–3 yrs. age is lowered from age 15 →14 yrs. old

Although judges have this discretionary power in most jurisdictions, youths are still entitled to a hearing at which they can protest the waiver action. While it is true that the criminal court poses risks to juveniles in terms of potentially harsher penalties, it is also true that being tried as an adult entitles youths to all adult constitutional safeguards, including the right to a trial by jury. In a later section of this chapter, we will examine closely this and other options that may be of benefit to certain juveniles. Thus, some juveniles may choose not to fight the waiver action, feeling they may be treated more leniently and/or fairly by criminal courts. (See Chapter 10 for a detailed discussion of juvenile rights.)

Demand Waivers. Under certain conditions and in selected jurisdictions, juveniles may submit motions for **demand waiver** actions. Demand waiver actions are demands by juveniles to have their cases transferred from juvenile courts to criminal courts. Why would they want to do this? Most U.S. jurisdictions do not provide jury trials for juveniles in juvenile courts as a matter of right (**McKeiver** v. **Pennsylvania,** 1971). However, about a fifth of the states have legislatively provided for jury trials for juveniles at their request and depending upon the nature of the charges against them. In the remainder of the states, jury trials for juveniles are granted only at the discretion of the juvenile judge. Most juvenile judges are not inclined to grant jury trials to juveniles. Thus, if juveniles are (1) in a jurisdiction where they are not entitled to a jury trial even if they request one from the juvenile judge, (2) face serious charges, and (3) believe that their cases would receive greater impartiality from a jury in a criminal courtroom, they may seek a demand waiver in order to have their cases transferred to criminal court. Florida permits demand waivers as one of several waiver options (Carter, 1984).

Legislative or Automatic Waivers. **Legislative waivers** or **automatic transfers** *are statutorily prescribed actions that provide for a specified list of crimes to be excluded from the jurisdiction of juvenile courts, where offending juveniles are within a specified age range, and where the resulting action gives criminal courts immediate jurisdiction over these juveniles.* By the mid-1980s, 36 states excluded certain types of offenses from juvenile court jurisdiction. These excluded offenses could be either very minor or very serious, ranging from traffic or fishing violations to rape or murder (U.S. Department of Justice, 1988:79). Also, many state jurisdictions have made provisions for automatic transfers of juveniles to criminal court. Among those states with automatic transfer provisions are Washington, New York, and Illinois (Sagatun *et al.,* 1985).

Illinois's legislative waiver provisions were enacted in 1982 (Reed, 1983). While each state with automatic transfer provisions lists similar offenses as subjects of these waiver actions, some lists of offenses are longer than others. Usually, very serious crimes are listed, such as murder, rape, aggravated assault, and robbery. Certain types of theft, possessing cocaine, heroin or other illicit substances for resale, and burglary may also be included. The typical age range for those subject to automatic transfers is 16 to 17 years of age. Thus, if a 16-year-old youth has been charged with murder or rape and is in a state with an automatic transfer provision, the youth will automatically be transferred to the jurisdiction of criminal court. Again, such actions may be contested. In these instances, the contestations are conducted through reverse waiver hearings.

Although the jurisdiction of juvenile courts is limited, it should not be underestimated. We cannot conclude that all cases involving juveniles that are processed by juvenile courts always have more favorable outcomes than all juvenile cases heard in criminal courts as the result of transfers. Also, we cannot say that criminal court processing of offenses is generally better than juvenile court processing, in any absolute sense. There are advantages and disadvantages associated with both processes, and we must consider each accordingly in order to grasp the full range of implications for affected juveniles.

Waiver and Reverse Waiver Hearings

Waiver hearings are normally conducted before the juvenile judge. These hearings are to some extent evidentiary, since a case must be made for why criminal courts should have jurisdiction in any specific instance. Usually, juveniles with lengthy prior records, several previous referrals, and/or one or more previous adjudications as delinquent are more susceptible to being transferred. While the offenses alleged are most often crimes, it is not always the case that the crimes are the most serious ones. Depending upon the jurisdiction, the seriousness of crimes associated with transferred cases varies. As has been shown by previous research, large numbers of cases involving property crimes are transferred to criminal courts for processing. In some instances, chronic, persistent, or habitual status offenders have been transferred, particularly if they have violated specific court orders to attend school, participate in therapeutic programs, perform community service work, make restitution, or engage in some other constructive enterprise.

If waivers are to be fully effective, then only those most serious offenders should be targeted for transfer. Transferring less serious and petty offenders accomplishes little in the way of enhanced punishments for these offenders. Criminal courts often regard transfers of such cases as nuisances, and it is not uncommon to see the widespread use of probation or diversion here. Criminal court prosecutors may decline to prosecute many of these cases before they reach the trial stage. In a significant number of other cases, plea bargaining agreements are concluded that result in substantially more lenient penalties than if those cases went to trial and defendants were convicted. (Osbun and Rode, 1984; Schack and Nessen, 1984).

Reverse waiver hearings in those jurisdictions with automatic transfer provisions are also conducted in the presence of judges. For both waiver and reverse waiver hearings, defense counsel and the prosecution attempt to make a case for their desired action. In many respects, these hearings are the equivalent of preliminary hearings or preliminary examinations conducted

BOX 7.1

Juvenile Highlights

Can electronic monitoring prevent or deter delinquency? The use of electronic monitoring in probation supervision is increasing nationally. Originally described in 1964 by Ralph Schwitzgebel as a means of keeping track of the whereabouts of mental patients and low-risk probationers, electronic monitoring is currently used in connection with home confinement programs to verify a client's location.

The use of electronic monitoring in the supervision of juvenile offenders is increasing in many U.S. jurisdictions. Although research in this area is still somewhat limited, recent studies suggest that adjudicated juvenile burglars who are electronically monitored appear to be incapacitated from committing further burglaries, at least for the duration of their electronic monitoring programs.

Electronic monitoring for juvenile offenders is supplemented with telephone checks by juvenile personnel who conduct independent verifications of the subject's whereabouts and behaviors. Individual contact through personal visits helps to ensure program accuracy when such electronic devices are used. Juvenile offenders must wear electronic wristlets or anklets that emit electronic signals that may be received in a central location, such as a police station or juvenile probation facility. Both public and private juvenile enterprises currently use electronic monitoring to a limited degree. Although long-range projections for the use of electronic monitoring are that even violent offenders can be managed or supervised, currently most violent offenders are screened from such electronic monitoring programs.

The wristlets and anklets worn by juveniles are of a type used by hospitals to keep track of temporary patients. They are not tamper-proof, but tampering with such devices is easily detected. The penalty is severe, usually confinement in a secure juvenile facility. In some jurisdictions, such as Knoxville, Tennessee, electronic monitoring is used as the last resort before secure confinement in long-term detention facilities.

(Some factual information adapted from Michael T. Charles, "The Development of a Juvenile Electronic Monitoring Program," Federal Probation (1989) 53:3–12.)

within the criminal justice framework. The main function of these examinations or hearings is to establish probable cause that one or more crimes were committed, and that the accused probably committed those crimes. Some evidence and testimony are permitted, and arguments from both sides are heard. Once all arguments have been presented and each side has had a chance to rebut the opponents' arguments, judges decide the matter.

Implications of Waiver Hearings for Juveniles

Those juveniles who contest or fight their transfers to criminal courts or attempt to obtain a reverse waiver are those who wish to remain within the juvenile justice system, be treated as juveniles, and be adjudicated by juvenile judges. But not all juveniles who are the subject of transfer are eager to contest the transfer. There are several important implications for youths, depending upon the nature of their offenses, their prior records, and the potential penalties the respective courts may impose. Under the right circumstances, having one's case transferred to criminal court may offer juvenile defendants considerable advantages not normally enjoyed if their cases were to remain in juvenile court. In the following discussion, some of the major advantages and disadvantages of being transferred will be examined.

Benefits of Juvenile Court Adjudication. Among the benefits of having one's case heard in juvenile court are the following:

1. Juvenile court proceedings are civil, not criminal; thus, juveniles do not acquire criminal records.
2. Juveniles are less likely to receive sentences of detention.
3. Compared with criminal court judges, juvenile court judges have considerably more discretion in influencing a youth's life chances prior to or at the time of adjudication.
4. Juvenile courts are traditionally more lenient than criminal courts.
5. There is considerably more public sympathy extended to those who are processed in the juvenile justice system, despite the general public clamor for a "get tough" policy.
6. Compared with criminal courts, juvenile courts do not have as elaborate an information-exchange apparatus to determine whether certain juveniles have been adjudicated delinquent by juvenile courts in other jurisdictions.
7. Life imprisonment and the death penalty lie beyond the jurisdiction of juvenile judges, and they cannot impose these harsh sentences.

Since juvenile courts are civil bodies, records of juvenile adjudications are suppressed, expunged, or otherwise deleted when these adjudicated juveniles reach adulthood (Michigan Law Review, 1983; Dunn, 1986). Also, juvenile judges often act compassionately by sentencing youthful offenders to probation, or by issuing verbal warnings or reprimands, or by imposing nonincarcerative, non-fine alternatives as sanctions (Conrad, 1983; Challeen, 1986).

As noted in item 4 of the preceding list, juvenile courts are traditionally known for their lenient treatment of juveniles (Rubin, 1988). This seems to be more a function of the influence of priorities in dealing with juvenile offenders than of some immovable policy. For example, a national conference of juvenile justice experts in New Orleans, Louisiana, recommended that juvenile courts should emphasize three general goals in their adjudication decisions: (a) protection of the community; (b) imposing accountability; and (c) helping juveniles and equipping them to live productively and responsibly in the community (Maloney *et al.*, 1988). This "balanced approach" is largely constructive, in that it heavily emphasizes those skills that lead to the rehabilitation of youthful offenders. And in the minds of many citizens, rehabilitation is equated with leniency. Increasingly used, however, are residential placement facilities in various jurisdictions, where the rate of recidivism among juveniles is relatively low compared with those offenders with more extensive histories of delinquent conduct (Goodstein and Southeimer, 1987).

Another advantage of juvenile court processing is that sympathy for youths who commit offenses is easier to extend in sentencing. Many juveniles get into trouble because of sociocultural circumstances. Individualized treatment may be necessary, perhaps administered through appropriate community-based facilities, in order to promote greater respect for the law as well as to provide needed services (Blackmore *et al.*, 1988; Krisberg, 1988; American Correctional Association, 1985; Teschner and Wolter, 1984). Mandatory diversion policies have received some public support in various jurisdictions, especially where less serious youthful offenders are involved and they are charged with nonviolent, petty crimes (McDermott *et al.*, 1985). Many of these juveniles may not require intensive supervised probation or incarceration but, rather, may require responsible supervision to guide and assist them in various services and treatment-oriented agencies (McDermott *et al.*, 1985).

Juvenile courts do not ordinarily exchange information with other juvenile courts in a massive national communication network. Local control over youthful offenders accomplishes only this limited objective—local control. Thus, juveniles might migrate to other jurisdictions and offend repeatedly, and getting caught in those alternative jurisdictions would not be treated as recidivism in the original jurisdiction. For juveniles who commit numerous offenses in a broad range of contiguous jurisdictions, the probability that their acts in one jurisdiction will come to the attention of juvenile officials in another jurisdiction is often remote.

Furthermore, juveniles in certain jurisdictions may reappear before the same juvenile judge frequently. Multiple adjudications for serious offenses do not automatically mean that these youths will be placed in juvenile detention or transferred to criminal court (August, 1981). Even those who reappear before the same juvenile judge may be adjudicated repeatedly without significant effect. In one investigation, it was found that a sample of serious juvenile offenders had been adjudicated in the same jurisdiction an average of ten times (Hartstone and Hansen, 1984). Thus, juvenile judges may give juveniles the "benefit of the doubt" and impose nondetention alternatives. Nondetention alternatives as sentences are influenced significantly by the large degree of overcrowding in secure juvenile facilities. Thus, the "leniency" displayed by juvenile judges may really be a result of necessity rather than of some personal belief that incarceration should be avoided.

Finally, it is beyond the jurisdiction of juvenile judges to impose life imprisonment or the death penalty, despite the potential for jury trials in some juvenile court jurisdictions (Streib, 1987; Thomas and Hutcheson, 1986). Thus, if offenders come before a juvenile judge for processing and have committed especially serious violent or capital offenses, the juvenile judge's options are limited. Incarceration in a juvenile facility, possibly for a prolonged period, is the most powerful sanction available to these judges. However, if waiver actions are successful, they can pave the way for the possible application of severer punishments in criminal courts (Streib, 1983). (The death penalty applied to juvenile offenders will be examined later in this chapter and at greater length in Chapter 10.)

Unfavorable Implications of Juvenile Court Adjudication. Despite their many advantages, juvenile courts also have some disadvantages for youthful offenders. Some of their major limitations are the following:

1. Juvenile courts have the power to administer lengthy sentences of detention, not only for serious and dangerous offenders, but for status offenders as well.
2. In most states, juvenile courts are not required to provide juveniles with a trial by jury.
3. Because of their wide discretion in handling juveniles, judges may underpenalize a large number of those appearing before them on various charges.
4. Juveniles do not enjoy the same range of constitutional rights as adults in criminal courts.

On the negative side, juvenile judges may impose as punishment short-term or long-term detention in secure juvenile facilities, regardless of the pettiness of the offense. The case of **In re Gault** (1967) involved a 15-year-old, Gerald Gault, who was sentenced to nearly six years in the Arizona State Industrial School for making an obscene telephone call to a female neighbor (see Chapter 10 for an expanded discussion of juvenile rights.) This sentence was arbitrarily imposed on Gault by the presiding juvenile judge. For committing the same offense, an adult would have been fined $50 and might have served up to 30 days in a local jail. In Gault's case, the sentence was excessive and there were constitutional irregularities. This unusual incarcerative sentence was subsequently overturned by the U.S. Supreme Court on several important constitutional grounds. However, juvenile judges continue to have broad discretionary powers and may impose similar sentences, provided that the constitutional guarantees assured by the *Gault* decision are present.

Another disadvantage of juvenile courts is that granting any juvenile a jury trial is mostly at the discretion of prosecutors and juvenile judges. If the judge approves, the juvenile may receive a jury trial in selected jurisdictions if a jury trial is requested. This is true of juvenile courts in 38 states. In the remaining states, juveniles may request and receive trials under certain circumstances. In other words, the state legislatures of at least 12 states have made it possible for juveniles to receive jury trials upon request, although the circumstances for such jury trial requests parallel closely the jury trial requests of defendants in criminal courts. Again, we must remember the civil–criminal distinction that adheres to juvenile and criminal court proceedings. Jury trials in juvenile courts retain the civil connotation, in that juveniles do not acquire criminal records. In contrast, jury trials in adult criminal courts result, upon the defendant's conviction, in the acquisition of a criminal record.

A third limitation of juvenile proceedings is that the wide discretion enjoyed by most juvenile judges is often abused (Osbun and Rode, 1984). This abuse is largely in the form of excessive leniency, and it doesn't occur exclusively at the adjudicatory stage of juvenile processing. Earlier, during intake, many cases are resolved, diverted, or dismissed without a formal petition being filed for a subsequent adjudication. One investigator, Belinda McCarthy, has reported that in Maricopa County, Arizona, near Phoenix, 17,773 juvenile delinquents who were born between 1962 and 1965 were tracked and determined to have committed over 76,000 delinquent acts (McCarthy, 1989). Nearly 90 percent of these juveniles who were referred to juvenile court had their cases informally adjusted or dismissed at the intake stage. Furthermore, although more serious violent crime cases were more likely to result in detention than other offenses, the most frequent disposition was probation. And a majority of those who had committed robbery, aggravated assault, and burglary recidivated within two years of their original adjudications for these offenses (McCarthy, 1989). Because of this leniency and wide discretion, real or imagined, many juvenile courts have drawn criticism over the years from the public and professionals alike. A common criticism is that juvenile courts neglect the accountability issue through the excessive use of probation or diversion (Harris and Graff, 1988).

Another major criticism of these courts is that juveniles do not enjoy the full range of constitutional rights that apply to their adult counterparts in criminal courts (Mones, 1984; Rubin, 1985; Thomas and Bilchik, 1985). In many jurisdictions, transcripts of proceedings are not made or retained for juveniles where serious charges are alleged, unless special arrangements are made beforehand. Thus, when juveniles in these jurisdictions appeal their adjudications to higher courts, they may or may not have the written record to rely on in their attempt to override the juvenile judge's sentence. (See Chapter 10 for a more extensive discussion of juvenile rights.)

Defense and Prosecutorial Considerations Relating to Waivers

Juvenile Trial Options: Interstate Variations. As we have seen, juveniles are infrequently given a jury trial if their cases are adjudicated by juvenile courts. As of 1988, twelve states legislatively mandated jury trials for juveniles if they made such requests during their adjudicatory hearings and the charges carried possible incarcerative penalties. Also in 1988 in twenty-three other states, juveniles were denied the right to a jury trial. In the remaining states, with the exception of South Dakota, no mention was made of whether juveniles were entitled to jury trials. It is presumed that in these jurisdictions, at least, the sole authority in granting jury trial privileges is the juvenile judge. In South Dakota, a court order is required in order for a jury trial to be conducted in juvenile court (Jamieson and Flanagan, 1988:156–157). Table 7.4 shows different jury trial provisions in juvenile courts by state.

Implications of Criminal Court Processing. When juveniles are transferred, waived, or certified to criminal court, then all rules and constitutional guarantees that apply to adults apply to them as well. We have already examined the advantages of permitting or petitioning the juvenile court to retain jurisdiction in certain cases.

An absence of a criminal record, limited punishments, extensive leniency, and a greater variety of discretionary options on the part of juvenile judges make juvenile courts an attractive adjudicatory medium if the juvenile has a choice. Even if the crimes alleged are serious, leniency may assume the form

TABLE 7.4   Interstate Variation in Jury Trials for Juveniles, 1988

Provision	States
Jury trial granted upon request by juvenile	Alaska, California, Kansas, Massachusetts, Michigan, Minnesota, New Mexico, Oklahoma,Texas, West Virginia, Wisconsin, Wyoming
Juvenile denied right to trial by jury	Alabama, Florida, Georgia, Hawaii, Indiana, Iowa, Louisiana, Maine, Maryland, Mississippi, Nebraska, Nevada, New Jersey, North Carolina, North Dakota, Ohio, Oregon, Pennsylvania, South Carolina, Tennessee, Utah, Vermont, Washington
No mention	Alaska, Arizona, California, Connecticut, Colorado, Idaho, Illinois, Missouri, New Hampshire, New Mexico, New York, Virginia
By court order	South Dakota

SOURCE: Katherine M. Jamieson and Timothy J. Flanagan (eds.), *Source of Criminal Justice Statistics—1988* (Washington, DC: U.S. Department of Justice), pp. 156–157.

of a dismissal of charges, charge reductions, warnings, and other nonadjudicatory penalties.

The primary implications for juveniles of being processed through the criminal justice system are several, and they are quite important. First, depending upon the seriousness of the offenses alleged, a jury trial may be a matter of right. Second, a period of lengthy incarceration in a minimum, medium, or maximum security facility with adults becomes a real possibility. Third, criminal courts in a majority of state jurisdictions may impose the death penalty in capital cases. This is regarded as the ultimate punishment and is hotly debated as a formal criminal sanction (Smith, 1986; Hochstedler, 1986; Scoville, 1987; Smykla, 1987; Doerner, 1988). (For an excellent, readable summary of major arguments for and against the death penalty, see van den Haag and Conrad, 1983.) An especially sensitive subject with most citizens is whether juveniles should receive the death penalty if convicted of capital crimes. In recent years, the U.S. Supreme Court has addressed this issue specifically. The issue of imposing the death penalty on juveniles will be discussed more extensively in Chapter 10. (For an in-depth treatment of this subject see Streib, 1987.)

Jury Trials as a Matter of Right for Serious Crimes. A primary benefit of a transfer to criminal court is the absolute right to a jury trial. This is conditional, however, and depends upon the minimum incarcerative period associated with one or more criminal charges filed against defendants. In twelve states, juveniles have a jury trial right granted through legislative action (Mahoney, 1985). However, when juveniles reach criminal courts, certain constitutional provisions apply to them as well as to adults. First, anyone charged with a crime where the possible sentence is six months' incarceration or more, with exceptions, is entitled to a jury trial if one is requested (**Baldwin** v. **New York,** 1970). Therefore, jury trials are not discretionary matters for judges to decide. Any defendant who *may be* subject to six months or more in jail or prison on the basis of the prescribed statutory punishment associated with the criminal offenses alleged may request and receive a jury trial from any U.S. judge, in either state or federal courts.

Juveniles who are charged with particularly serious crimes, even if aggravating circumstances are apparent, stand a good chance of receiving favorable treatment from juries. Aggravating circumstances include a victim's death or the infliction of serious bodily injuries, commission of an offense while on bail for another offense or on probation or parole, use of extreme cruelty in the commission of the crime, use of a dangerous weapon in the commission of a crime, a prior record, and leadership in the commission of offenses alleged. However, mitigating circumstances, those factors that tend to lessen the severity of sentencing, include duress or extreme provocation, mental incapacitation, motivation to provide necessities, youthfulness or old age, and no previous criminal record (Just, 1985).

What criteria persuade juries to decide cases in particular ways? No one knows. While some evidence exists to show the influence of race and gender on jury decision making, it is inconsistent and inconclusive (Spohn *et al.,*

1985; Kempf and Austin, 1986; Petersilia, 1983; Clayton, 1983; LaFree, 1985; Humphrey and Fogarty, 1987). Impressions gleaned from various surveys of U.S. citizens suggest that extreme youth or age might function favorably to reduce sentencing severity in jury trials. For example, a 1986 survey of 917 Georgia residents disclosed that while three fourths favored the death penalty, over two thirds favored replacing the death penalty with life imprisonment as the *maximum punishment* for youthful offenders (Thomas and Hutcheson, 1986). Such comparative leniency on the part of state residents might be indicative of how juries comprised of such residents might view youthful defendants in capital crimes as well as in those lesser crimes associated with less serious punishments. Thus, youthfulness itself is an inherent mitigating factor in almost every criminal courtroom.

Among the several aggravating and mitigating circumstances listed earlier, having a prior record or not having one becomes an important consideration. Youths who are transferred to criminal courts sometimes do not have previous criminal records. This doesn't mean that they haven't committed earlier crimes but, rather, that their records are juvenile court records. As such, technically, they do not bring "prior criminal records" into the adult courtroom. This is a favorable factor for juveniles to consider when deciding whether to challenge transfers or have their automatic waivers reversed. An absence of a prior criminal record, together with youthfulness, might be persuasive enough for juries to acquit certain defendants or find them guilty of lesser offenses. Again, we cannot be certain about the precise influence of a defendant's age on jury decision making (Hastie *et al.*, 1983; Hans and Vidmar, 1986).

Another important factor relative to access to a jury trial is that prosecutors often try to avoid them, opting for a simple plea bargain agreement instead (McDonald, 1985).

Jury trials are costly, and the results of jury deliberations are unpredictable. If prosecutors can obtain guilty pleas from transferred juveniles, they help the state and themselves, both in terms of the costs of prosecution and the avoidance of jury unpredictability in youthful offender cases. Also, plea bargaining in transferred juvenile cases often results in convictions on lesser charges, specifically charges that would not have prompted the transfer or waiver from juvenile courts initially (Reed, 1983). However, this is a bit ironic, since it suggests that the criminal justice system is inadvertently subverting the primary purpose of juvenile transfers through allowing plea bargaining arrangements that are otherwise commonplace for adult criminals.

Furthermore, when prosecutors decide to file charges, the charges should be serious ones, and sufficient evidence should exist to increase the chances of a successful prosecution. But transferred juveniles are not necessarily the most serious youthful offenders, and the standard of evidence in juvenile courts is sometimes not as rigorous as it is in criminal courts. Thus, many transferred cases fall apart at the outset and are dismissed by the prosecutors themselves (Schack and Nessen, 1984). A 1983 study of 6,951 transferred juveniles in New York showed that 68.6 percent of the juveniles had their cases dismissed, were not prosecuted, and had left the court system before the end of the justice process (Schack and Nessen, 1984). Furthermore, the same study showed that only 4.2 percent of all juveniles arrested eventually received incarcerative sentences longer than what they would have received had they elected to have their cases adjudicated in juvenile courts (Schack and Nessen, 1984).

Closely associated with prosecutorial reluctance to prosecute many of these transferred juveniles is the fact that a majority of those transferred are charged with property crimes (August, 1981; Gillespie and Norman, 1984; Champion, 1989b). While these cases may stand out from other cases coming before juvenile judges, prosecutors and criminal court judges might regard them as insignificant. Thus, juveniles enter the adult system from juvenile courts, where their offenses tend to set them apart from most other juvenile offenders. But alongside adults in criminal courts, they become one of many property offenders who face criminal processing. Their youth works in their behalf to improve their chances of having their cases dismissed or of being acquitted by juries. Most prosecutors wish to reserve jury trials for only the most serious offenders. Therefore, their general inclination is to treat youthful property offenders with greater leniency, unless they elect to drop the case outright.

Incarceration. Arguing that it is cheaper to build more prisons than it is to tolerate a growing crime rate, van den Haag (1986) advocates blanket punishment of juveniles in criminal courts, where those juveniles have committed crimes. Van den Haag advocates the abolition of parole. However, many experts believe that the detention of juveniles is overused (Margolis, 1988; Rosner, 1988). Further, juveniles who are incarcerated in prisons together with adults are more frequently victimized by other prisoners than juveniles who are remanded to secure juvenile facilities (Forst *et al.*, 1989). Additionally, institutional life is often difficult for juveniles to accept. A study of 146 juveniles incarcerated in adult facilities by the Texas Department of Corrections disclosed that juvenile inmates were twice as likely as adult inmates to be problem inmates, resulting in their failure to work or earn good-time credit (McShane and Williams, 1989).

There is strong public sentiment for keeping most juveniles away from adult prisons and jails, because such facilities are not well equipped to meet juvenile offender needs, and also because a greater range of community-based services exists for juveniles diverted or placed on probation in their respective communities (Griffiths, 1988). An offsetting argument is made for preserving incarceration as a punishment, in part because of the deterrent effect of fear of apprehension and punishment among juveniles, who may thus tend to suppress their propensity to engage in juvenile crime (Fraser and Norman, 1988). This particular view lacks empirical support, however.

The number of incarcerated offenders under age 18 in state and federal prisons is relatively small, accounting for about 0.5 percent of all inmates nationally in 1987 (Innes, 1988). In fact, this figure represents a decrease of juvenile inmates from a figure of 0.9 percent in 1979 (Innes, 1988). At the

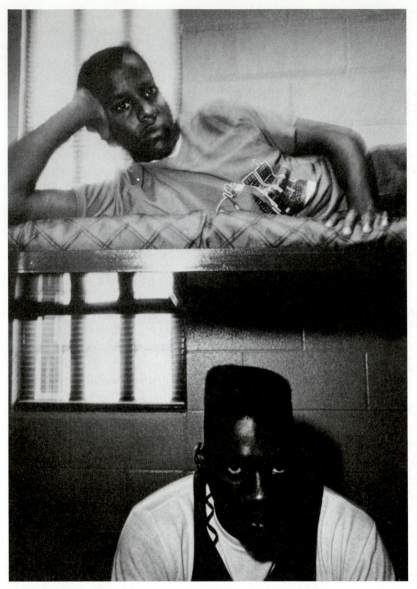

Several states have automatic transfer laws whereby more serious youthful offenders are transferred to the jurisdiction of criminal courts. Subsequently, some of
these offenders may be incarcerated for long terms in adult prison facilities.
(© Nubar Alexanian/Woodfin Camp & Associates)

same time, there has been a gradual increase in the numbers of juveniles
detained for short- or long-term periods in secure juvenile facilities (Reuterman and Hughes, 1984). Thus, the place, rather than the rate, of juvenile
incarcerations is changing perceptibly. Regardless of how few youths are

imprisoned in adult facilities, however, the fact of such incarcerations is troubling to more than a few citizens (Carter, 1984). Among the arguments against juvenile incarceration is that misbehavior and crime in youth are transient, and that with proper guidance, most youths mature out of criminality in a relatively short time (Rutherford, 1986).

For many of those juveniles who reach criminal courts, the possibility of incarceration is real. Many states currently employ presumptive or determinate sentencing guidelines that establish standard punishments for all criminal offenses (Goodstein and Hepburn, 1985). While judges in those jurisdictions have some latitude in varying the amount of incarceration, some incarceration must be imposed, especially for those convicted of serious crimes. Of course, age is a mitigating factor for convicted juveniles. Judges may tend to select the low end of the punishment range rather than the high end when sentencing convicted youths. With some exceptions, the average length of incarceration for juveniles convicted in adult courts is relatively short compared with their adult counterparts convicted of similar offenses (August, 1981; Singer, 1985; Reed, 1983). Furthermore, the average length of incarceration is no longer or greater than what these affected juveniles would have received if they had been adjudicated and sentenced to a secure juvenile facility by a juvenile judge (Schack and Nessen, 1984). These grounds alone are sufficient to challenge the "get tough" policy of contemporary juvenile courts and the value of certifications or waivers to criminal courts.

The Potential for Capital Punishment. The most important implication for juveniles transferred to criminal courts is the potential imposition of the **death penalty** upon their conviction for a capital crime. About two thirds of the states use **capital punishment** for prescribed offenses that are especially aggravated. The methods of execution in those states that authorize the death penalty include lethal injection, electrocution, lethal gas, hanging, and firing squad (U.S. Department of Justice, 1988:5).

At the beginning of 1988, there were 1,984 prisoners under sentence of death in U.S. prisons. Ninety-nine percent of these were males. Less than 0.5 percent of these were under age 20 (U.S. Department of Justice, 1988:6−7). The administration of the death penalty as a criminal sanction is not unique to the United States. In fact, a study of 128 nations has disclosed that 87 percent currently authorize the death penalty as a form of punishment, an increase from 78 percent in 1979 and 85 percent in 1985 (Weichman and Kendall, 1987). Males are almost always the exclusive recipients of the death penalty. Few females, especially female juveniles, are ever executed. The earliest documented case of the execution of a female juvenile in this country was in 1767 (Streib and Sametz, 1989). In 1989 only one female juvenile was on death row in the United States. In all likelihood, she will never be executed (Streib and Sametz, 1989).

While the death penalty has long been accepted as a constitutional means to "redress grossly unacceptable antisocial behavior" (Smith, 1986), it was temporarily suspended (but not prohibited) in 1972 as the result of the

CASE ⟶

BOX 7.2

Juvenile Highlights

Should deadly force be used to stop juveniles in the act of committing violent crimes? Sometimes, there is no alternative. A 14-year-old youth was shot to death one evening as he attempted the armed robbery of a pizza store in Bixby Knolls, a suburb of Long Beach, California.

Marquise Williams, 14, wore a mask and brandished a gun as he entered the Pizza Man restaurant on Long Beach Boulevard at 8:40 P.M. on a busy Friday night after Christmas, 1990. The owner of the store, Cathy Hsia, 48, was petrified with fear when Williams entered and yelled at four people inside to lie on the floor. "I want money, money," he shouted, and he waved his gun in the air. One of Hsia's friends attempted to open the cash register but was too slow for Williams. Williams hit the man in the head with the gun butt. The friend grasped Williams' gun and it discharged four times. Hsia sought a hidden pistol from behind the counter and fired it at the masked robber. Williams ran out of the store, staggered down an alley, and collapsed. He died less than an hour later at Long Beach Memorial Medical Center. His mother, interviewed later, claimed that the lack of public parks for recreational opportunities in the city drove him to the streets.

"I fired a couple of times. I was panicked. I never shot anyone before," said Hsia. She said there was no way to tell Williams' age because of the mask he wore. Who should be blamed for Williams' actions? Society? The City of Long Beach? The Commissioner of Public Parks? Mrs. Williams, the boy's mother? Or Marquise Williams himself?

(Some factual information adapted from Neil Strassman, "Boy, 14, Slain Trying to Rob Pizza Parlor," *Press-Telegram*, December 30, 1990, A1, A10.)

Furman v. **Georgia** decision. This decision by the U.S. Supreme Court criticized the racially discriminatory and arbitrary nature of the death penalty as it was currently being applied in Georgia. For example, many blacks in Georgia were being executed for crimes of rape and robbery, whereas white defendants convicted of similar offenses received incarcerative terms rather than death. No provisions existed for Georgia juries to consider aggravating and mitigating circumstances associated with these capital offenses. Subsequently, Georgia statutes were changed to comply with the U.S. Supreme Court decision in the case of **Gregg** v. **Georgia** (1976). A major change in Georgia criminal procedure was the establishment of the **bifurcated trial.** A bifurcated trial is a two-stage proceeding, with guilt being decided first in the trial phase, and the punishment being decided in the second phase. Currently, the two-phase nature of jury deliberations permits jurors to consider any especially aggravating or mitigating circumstances before deciding whether to impose the death penalty.

An alternative to the death penalty applied to juveniles is the **life-without-parole** option. In 1987, 29 states had life-without-parole provisions for capital offenses, including aggravated homicide, as well as for habitual or career offenders (Cheatwood, 1988). No other penalty in our history has generated the amount of controversy that accompanies capital punishment (Shelleff, 1987; Zimring and Hawkins, 1986; Rogers and Wettstein, 1987; Friedlander, 1987; Lester, 1987; Acker, 1987; Smith, 1987; van den Haag and Conrad, 1983).

Persons who favor the death penalty often believe that (1) it functions as a deterrent to those contemplating committing capital crimes; (2) it is "just" punishment within the context of the philosophy prevailing in our criminal justice system; (3) it is appropriate punishment in the retributive sense; (4) it is incapacitating in that it eliminates the offender; and (5) it is economical, especially when contrasted with lengthy incarceration. Persons who oppose the death penalty say that (1) it does not function as an effective deterrent to capital crimes; (2) it is barbaric, unbecoming, and uncivilized—a "cruel and unusual punishment"; (3) it is discriminatory on racial, gender, and socioeconomic grounds; (4) there are more humane alternatives such as life without parole, and (5) when the state takes a life, it may appear that homicide is acceptable. In fact, U.S. Supreme Court Justice Thurgood Marshall and former U.S. Supreme Court Justice William J. Brennan regularly entered into the record their categorical opposition to the death penalty, administered for whatever reason and under any circumstances, whenever appeals of death sentences reached the U.S. Supreme Court (Brennan, 1986; Burris, 1987). Since the pros and cons associated with the imposition of capital punishment are for the most part closely intertwined, they will now be examined.

Regarding the question of deterrence, Forst (1983) observes that some support exists for the death penalty as both a specific and general deterrent to homicide. However, he also suggests that the data are inconclusive, regardless of the argument one adopts, either for or against the use of the death penalty as a deterrent. Most research correlating the death penalty with deterrence or reduction in the homicide rate has revealed that the death penalty is ineffective in this regard (Bailey, 1983, 1984; Decker and Kohfeld, 1984, 1987; Rogers and Wettstein, 1987).

Depending on those surveyed, the death penalty serves the ends of justice and should be imposed retributively. Families and loved ones of murder victims, with some exceptions, are likely to favor the death penalty, in contrast to the opinions of families and loved ones of the condemned (Warr and Stafford, 1984; Smith, 1986; Smykla, 1987; Radelet, 1989; Wallace, 1989). Friedlander (1987) says that during the past half century, no executions of so-called innocent persons have occurred. He suggests that the average stay of condemned prisoners on death row awaiting execution, averaging six years, is more of a "cruel and unusual punishment" than the executions themselves. In recent years, there have been attempts to make the death penalty more acceptable to the American public. Lethal injection as a form of capital punishment is supposedly the least painful to those executed and should therefore be more acceptable to society as a humane way of administering death to the condemned (Draper, 1985).

An economic view is taken by some experts in determining whether the death penalty should be used. Is capital punishment cost-effective relative to long-term incarceration? While it is clear that each execution makes additional precious prison space available, the morality of executing offenders for this purpose remains questionable (Bedau, 1982). Other researchers contend that the elimination of capital offenders increases respect for the law. However, elimination is a defensible rationale only if the death penalty is applied frequently and consistently, which it isn't (Fattah, 1985). Fattah (1985) argues that incarceration fulfills the elimination function through incapacitation. He finds it difficult to justify how official killings by the state can promote respect for human life. What about convicted murderers who kill while in prison serving life terms (Vollmann, 1987)? Again, there are no easy answers to the dilemma of what to do about "lifers" who kill other prisoners. New York State has provided for a mandatory death penalty in such cases, provided that a bifurcated proceeding occurs before the death sentence is passed. But even the mandatory death penalty for convicted murderers who kill while in prison is regarded in some sectors as arbitrary and discriminatory (Galbo, 1985).

The search for alternatives to the death penalty, especially applied to juvenile offenders, narrows very quickly to life-with-parole arguments and proponents. In 1987, 29 states had life-without-parole provisions (Cheatwood, 1988). One fear is that authorities with the power to pardon will commute many of these life sentences to a relatively short term of years, and that many convicted youthful murderers will wind up on the streets again, possibly to kill again (Cheatwood, 1988). Perhaps the most drastic life-without-parole solution has been described by Snellenburg (1986). Snellenburg has suggested that convicted murderers should receive solitary confinement for life as an alternative to the death penalty. But even those who support life-without-parole solutions consider this alternative to be "cruel and unusual" punishment (Galbo, 1985; Radelet, 1989).

Waiver Patterns and Trends

Increasing the frequency with which juveniles are waived to criminal courts means that transferred juveniles will be exposed to a broader range of punishments than could be imposed by juvenile courts. While the death penalty is the ultimate punishment for capital offenses in a majority of states in criminal courts, juvenile courts do not have this jurisdiction. Once juveniles have been transferred, it does not mean that they will automatically be prosecuted. Further, it does not mean that more severe punishments *will* be imposed, although this motive is the intended objective of such transfers. Little is known about what happens to juveniles once they have been transferred to adult courts. Studies by August (1981) and others (Sagatun *et al.*, 1985; Reed, 1983; Schack and Nessen, 1984) consistently reflect a high degree of leniency in dealing with those transferred. If charges are not dismissed or reduced, then the penalties are not as severe, compared with those for adult offenders, crime for crime.

A relatively recent study of the ultimate dispositions of transfers of juveniles in selected counties in four southern states for the years 1980–1988 appears to coincide with the general findings of others (Champion, 1989a). Out of 3,424 transfer hearings during this nine-year period, 2,818 (82 percent) resulted in successful waivers. Proportionately, there were increasing numbers of successful waiver hearings during the period 1980–1988. However, the proportion of property offenses as subjects of these successful waiver hearings increased over the years from 19 percent to about 50 percent. During the same period, violent crimes accounted for a decreasing proportion of these successful waiver hearings, from 80 percent in 1980 down to 41 percent in 1988. The actual numbers of cases involving violent crimes increased during the same time interval, although proportionate decreases were observed. Tables 7.5, 7.6, and 7.7 show respectively the yearly waiver trends, the proportionate annual distribution of transfer offenses, and final annual dispositions.

These findings suggest that at least in these jurisdictions, juveniles are not receiving harsher penalties, on the average, when transferred to criminal courts for a broad range of offenses. As Rubin (1985,26) suggests, these waivers appear to be cosmetic, primarily public-placating "escape valves" used to rid juvenile courts of chronic recidivists, largely property offenders.

TABLE 7.5   Aggregate Numbers of Waiver Hearings and Transfers to Adult Courts in Virginia, Tennessee, Mississippi, and Georgia, 1980–1988

Year	Number of Hearings	Waivers	Percentage
1980	228	163	71.5
1981	249	179	71.9
1982	301	226	75.1
1983	356	294	82.6
1984	451	385	85.3
1985	416	337	81.0
1986	485	419	86.1
1987	472	413	87.6
1988	466	402	86.2
Totals	3,424	2,818	82.3

1980–1988 increase: 238 cases (104.3%)

SOURCE: Dean J. Champion, "Juvenile Transfers: Some Implications." Unpublished paper presented at the American Society of Criminology Meetings, Baltimore, MD (November 1990).

TABLE 7.6   Offense Categories for Successful Waiver Hearings, 1980–1988

	Year (percent rounded to nearest whole number)								
Offenses	1980	1981	1982	1983	1984	1985	1986	1987	1988
Homicide	42	39	38	36	35	34	35	32	31
Vehicular theft	6	7	7	8	9	11	15	16	17
Arson	NA	NA	NA	2	3	4	4	3	5
Aggravated assault	4	5	5	2	2	2	2	5	4
Burglary	4	7	8	16	17	16	14	16	17
Larceny	9	12	14	16	17	20	15	15	16
Robbery	20	17	13	11	8	7	6	5	8
Rape	14	12	11	8	7	4	4	3	3
Other	1	1	4	1	2	2	5	5	3
Total percent	100	100	100	100	100	100	100	100	100
Number	163	179	226	294	385	337	419	413	402

Grand total = 2,818 waivers

SOURCE: Dean J. Champion, "Juvenile Transfers: Some Implications." Unpublished paper presented at the American Society of Criminology Meetings, Baltimore, MD (November 1990).

TABLE 7.7   Criminal Court Dispositions of 2,818 Waivers, 1980–1988 (percentages rounded)

Year	Dismissed, Acquitted	Probation	Jail	Prison	Other[a]
1980	62 (38%)	66 (40%)	11 (7%)	8 (5%)	16 (10%)
1981	65 (36%)	82 (46%)	17 (9%)	7 (4%)	8 (4%)
1982	74 (33%)	107 (47%)	18 (8%)	14 (6%)	13 (6%)
1983	79 (27%)	156 (53%)	28 (9%)	14 (5%)	17 (6%)
1984	92 (24%)	221 (57%)	19 (5%)	17 (4%)	36 (10%)
1985	84 (25%)	195 (58%)	20 (6%)	17 (5%)	21 (6%)
1986	101 (24%)	234 (56%)	25 (6%)	17 (4%)	42 (10%)
1987	87 (21%)	248 (60%)	25 (6%)	21 (5%)	32 (8%)
1988	88 (22%)	249 (62%)	16 (4%)	20 (5%)	29 (7%)
Total	732 (26%)	1,558 (55%)	179 (6%)	135 (5%)	214 (8%)

Grand total = 2,818 (100%)

aSplit sentences, home incarceration, electronic monitoring, community-based supervision, etc.
SOURCE: Dean J. Champion, "Juvenile Transfers: Some Implications." Unpublished paper presented at the American Society of Criminology Meetings, Baltimore, MD (November 1990).

Automatic transfer laws in various states such as Florida, Illinois, and New York seem to be having the desired effect, however, although an inconsistent pattern has developed.

It has been reported in one jurisdiction that of 1,817 successful waivers that took place place by the end of 1983, 33 percent resulted in incarcerative terms no longer than would have been levied in family or juvenile courts had transfers not been initiated (Schack and Nessen, 1984). A study by Reed (1983) of 346 transfers in the period 1975–1981 also showed that while most of those transfers involved serious crimes (e.g., murder, rape, robbery), 66 percent were either dropped, led to acquittals, or were plea bargained to lesser charges. Singer's (1985) investigation of transfers in New York State also discloses greater use of probation and shorter incarcerative sentences for those juveniles transferred to criminal court. Thus, these so-called "tough new laws" are not as tough as they at first appear.

In view of the types of cases that eventually reach criminal courts for disposition and how those cases are ultimately concluded, it would seem that juvenile court prosecutors and judges should be highly selective in the cases they designate for waiver. Ideally, cases selected for waiver or transfer would be only the most serious cases, in which the charges against juveniles consist of violent crimes such as homicide, rape, robbery, and aggravated assault. Indeed, in at least a few jurisdictions, it seems to work this way. A 1984 New Jersey survey of juvenile cases prosecutorially waived to adult courts, for instance, showed that prosecutors' motions for waiver generally involved violent crimes (New Jersey Division of Criminal Justice, 1985). Of those cases waived, the majority resulted in guilty pleas through plea bargaining. Of those cases that went to trial, over 70 percent resulted in guilty verdicts, with 95 percent of these involving incarcerative terms (New Jersey Division of Criminal Justice, 1985).

In states with automatic transfer laws, such as New York and Illinois, comparatively larger numbers of serious offenders are waived to criminal courts contrasted with those states without automatic transfer provisions (August, 1981; Sagatun et al., 1985). Reed (1983) has shown, for example, that of the offenses charged against transferred juveniles in Illinois between 1978 and 1981, 49 percent were for murder, 22 percent for robbery, and 14 percent for rape.

But abundant evidence exists to show that in many jurisdictions, particularly those without automatic transfer provisions, transferred juveniles consist primarily of property offenders or those charged with nonviolent, petty crimes (Bishop et al., 1989; Nimick et al., 1986; Bortner, 1986). In a 1982 study of 2,335 prosecutorial and judicial waivers in 552 courts in Arizona, California, Hawaii, Iowa, Kansas, Mississippi, Pennsylvania, Tennessee, and Virginia, only a third of those youths transferred to criminal courts were charged with an index violent offense (Nimick et al., 1986). Most waived cases involved index property offenses, particularly burglary. Also in these jurisdictions, transfers accounted for only 2 percent of all petitioned cases. Gillespie and Norman (1984) and Bortner (1986) have reached similar conclusions. In their investigation of Utah certifications during the years 1967–1980, Gillespie and Norman (1984) found that over 60 percent of those certified to adult courts were property offenders. Bortner (1986) conducted a four-year study of waiver trends in a large western U.S. metropolitan county. He found little or no support for the idea that transferred juveniles were singularly dangerous or violent offenders. Furthermore, Bortner noted that between

1979 and 1982, the rate of transfers had tripled, although the rate of major felonious index crimes remained fairly stable.

An examination of 583 prosecutorial waivers of 16- and 17-year-old juveniles in Florida for the period 1981–1984 revealed findings similar to those of Gillespie and Norman (1984) and Bortner (1986). Bishop *et al.* (1989) found that most transferred juveniles were property and low-risk offenders, and not the kinds of dangerous, repeat offenders for whom waivers are arguably justified. They have explained this phenomenon by attacking the prosecutorial waiver. This type of waiver, they say, allows prosecutors too much latitude in determining whether to initiate proceedings in juvenile or criminal courts. Since few, if any, statutory guidelines exist (in the jurisdictions they studied) to govern which cases are selected for transfer, prosecutorial decision making in this regard has been largely subjective.

The study by Bishop *et al.* is particularly insightful since it enables us to understand why proportionately larger numbers of property offenders are selected for transfer. In many jurisdictions, there are no guidelines for prosecutors or judges to follow when deciding whether to transfer juveniles to criminal courts. Of course, the automatic transfer provision in selected states is quite clear about who qualifies for waiver. If youths are 16 or 17 years of age, and if they have been charged with homicide, rape, or armed robbery (New York and Illinois), they will automatically be transferred to adult court for processing. They may fight the waiver and have their attorney move to have it reversed, but the provisions for who should be transferred remain clear-cut.

But transfers of juveniles in most jurisdictions are initiated and decided by prosecutors and judges. Obviously, this is a highly subjective process. Troublesome teenagers, not necessarily serious offenders, may be targeted for transfer by prosecutors and judges who have grown weary of seeing them in their courtrooms. These include habitual or persistent petty offenders who commit burglary or larceny, or who deal in illicit drugs. They may also include habitual truants and runaways who have violated court orders to participate in treatment programs, attend school, observe curfew, and other conditions imposed at the time of their original adjudications. Rubin (1985), who has been a juvenile judge himself, concurs with this view. His own research discloses a similar pattern relating to the nonseriousness of large numbers of those transferred to criminal courts.

Apart from drafting automatic waiver statutes, attempts to rationalize the transfer process have been undertaken in several states. In 1980 Minnesota sought to codify transfer procedures to be followed by prosecutors and judges. The state relied heavily on criteria such as age, alleged offense, and prior record (Osbun and Rode, 1984). Minnesota's attempt at juvenile court reform was designed to identify those juveniles considered unfit for retention in juvenile court. But Osbun and Rode (1984) found these "accurate and reliable predictive criteria" to be elusive, they concluded that Minnesota's "objective criteria" were inadequate for making acceptable transfer decisions.

All too frequently, the waiver is used merely as a convenient tool for shifting jurisdiction over certain juveniles to adult courts. Cosmetically, it appears as though juvenile courts are "getting tough" with juveniles by remanding them to criminal court. The increased use of waivers by prosecutors and judges in recent years is indicative of their response to public outcry over perceived rampant, increasing juvenile violence in various communities. Whether the amount of violence among juveniles is actually increasing is academic and irrelevant. The fact is that the public perceives it to be increasing, and therefore, it must be increasing. Something must be done about it, and the waiver is a tangible manifestation of action taken by juvenile courts to attack crime committed by juveniles.

Numbers of transfers in any jurisdiction are easily measured and counted, and transfer "trends" may be plotted as evidence of their increased use by prosecutors and judges. But as we have seen repeatedly, many juveniles entering criminal courts through the method of waiver become anonymous cases like so many others. Criminal court prosecutors must decide whether to prosecute or drop certain cases. In short, all options presented in an earlier section of this chapter are now available to transferred juveniles, including declined prosecution, diversion, plea bargaining, and strategic leniency from compassionate criminal court judges in the form of probation or one of several intermediate punishments, or short incarcerative terms in local jails or prisons.

Summary

Public perceptions of the supposed increase in juvenile violence throughout most U.S. jurisdictions have caused the "get tough" movement to permeate the juvenile justice system. Several types of waivers or transfers are used, depending on the jurisdiction. The most popular waiver, the judicial or discretionary waiver, is a decision made unilaterally by a juvenile judge that a specific juvenile's case will be heard in criminal court rather than in juvenile court. Prosecutorial waivers are also used, whereby prosecutors may move to transfer certain juveniles from their courts to criminal courts. In many jurisdictions, legislative provisions exist for the automatic transfer of particularly serious cases to criminal court jurisdiction. Illinois and New York are among several states having such automatic transfer provisions. Offenses subject to these automatic transfers include, but are not limited to, murder, rape, and robbery. Also, those transferred under such automatic transfer statutes must be either 16 or 17 years of age.

The characteristics of those transferred vary widely among jurisdictions. However, most transferred youths have prior records of delinquency, prior adjudications, or some other type of involvement with the juvenile justice system. Many are 16 years of age or older, and the offenses alleged are particularly serious. All juveniles are entitled to a hearing, either before their cases are waived or after they have been waived under automatic transfers.

These are known as waiver hearings and reverse waiver hearings. Juveniles who are able to keep their cases within juvenile court jurisdiction generally enjoy a greater degree of leniency than they would find in criminal courts. Juveniles who are transferred to criminal courts are entitled to jury trials as a matter of right if their offenses carry incarcerative penalties of six months or more. But in criminal courts, the death penalty may be applied in capital cases.

Waiver patterns and trends are sketchy, since few researchers have studied this phenomenon during the past few decades. An analysis of findings from existing studies suggests inconsistent patterns. However, it is apparent from much research that less serious juvenile offenders, rather than more serious ones, are often transferred to criminal courts. Subjective factors, such as chronicity or frequency of appearances before juvenile judges, or rebellious attitudes, often influence judges to transfer such cases out of their jurisdiction, simply to get rid of them. This is not the intended purpose of transfers, which is to provide for harsher penalties to be imposed on the most serious and dangerous juvenile offenders. Some jurisdictions report that this objective is being achieved, although many other jurisdictions report the waivers of large numbers of property and petty offenders. Automatic transfer laws have been enacted to minimize the subjectivity inherent in judicial discretion, but their implementation has been uneven and questionably effective.

Key Terms

Automatic transfers or waivers (222)
Baldwin v. New York (1970) (231)
Bifurcated trial (236)
Capital punishment (235)
Certifications (212)
Concurrent jurisdiction (222)
Death penalty (235)
Demand waivers (223)
Furman v. Georgia (236)
In re Gault (1967) (228)
Gregg v. Georgia (236)

Judicial/discretionary waivers (222)
Kent v. United States (1966) (222)
Legislative (automatic) waivers (223)
Life-without-parole (237)
McKeiver v. Pennsylvania (1971) (223)
Prosecutorial waivers (222)
Reverse waiver hearing (221)
Transfers (212)
Waiver hearings (224)
Waivers (212)
Wilding (211)

Questions for Review

1. What is a waiver? What are other terms that may be used interchangeably with this word? What is the purpose of a waiver?

2. What is a waiver hearing? Are all youths who are designated for waivers entitled to a hearing? What landmark case can you discuss briefly that pertains to waivers?

3. Are youths in some jurisdictions entitled, as a matter of right, to the least restrictive alternative

treatments whenever they are adjudicated as delinquent? Where?

4. What is the nature of the mixed message sent to juvenile courts in West Virginia by its Supreme Court of Appeals?

5. What are the general characteristics of those youths who are transferred to criminal courts? What legal and extralegal factors can you cite that might typify them and set them apart from other juvenile offenders?

6. Write a short essay contrasting the intended or ideal consequences and the real consequences of transfers in many jurisdictions.

7. Distinguish between four different kinds of waivers. In each case, describe the waiver action and who initiates it.

8. How does judicial discretion influence waiver actions? What appears to be the degree of subjectivity that is inherent in such waiver decisions by judges? What evidence is there that might support charges of bias in judicial discretion in certain judicial waiver actions?

9. What is a reverse waiver hearing and what are its purposes?

10. What is meant by concurrent jurisdiction, as it is currently applied to waiver decision making?

11. Under what circumstances might youths wish to have their cases heard in criminal courts rather than juvenile courts? What type of waiver action might they use to accomplish this?

12. Briefly compare and contrast the positive and negative aspects for juveniles of having their cases adjudicated in juvenile courts.

13. Outline the favorable consequences possibly accruing to juveniles when their cases are heard in criminal courts rather than in juvenile courts.

14. Discuss the major limitations or adverse implications for juveniles of having their cases tried in criminal courts.

15. Under what circumstances are youths entitled to a jury trial in juvenile courts, as a matter of right? What is criminal court policy relating to jury trials for criminals? What U.S. Supreme Court case is relevant here, and what did it prescribe?

16. Summarize some of the major arguments both for and against the death penalty. What alternatives have been proposed for capital juvenile offenders?

17. Recent research has disclosed several patterns and trends relating to those who are transferred. Briefly review some of these trends and discuss their implications for "getting tough" with more serious juvenile offenders.

Suggested Readings

BAIRD, S. CHRISTOPHER (1984). *Classification of Juveniles in Corrections: A Model Systems Approach.* Washington, DC: Arthur D. Little.

BORTNER, M. A. (1982). *Inside a Juvenile Court: The Tarnished Ideal of Individualized Justice.* New York: New York University Press.

CHAMPION, DEAN J., and G. LARRY MAYS (EDS.) (1991). *Transferring Juveniles to Criminal Courts: Implications for Criminal Justice.* New York: Praeger.

HAMPARIAN, DONNA M., ET AL. (1982). *Major Issues in Juvenile Justice Information and Training: Youth in Adult Courts: Between Two Worlds.* Columbus, OH: Academy for Contemporary Problems.

MILLER, F. W. (1985). *The Juvenile Justice Process.* Mineola, NY: Foundation Press.

NEW JERSEY DIVISION OF CRIMINAL JUSTICE (1985). *Juvenile Waivers to Adult Court: A Report to the New Jersey State Legislature.* Trenton, NJ: New Jersey Division of Criminal Justice.

WADLINGTON, W. (1983). *Children in the Legal System.* Mineola, NY: Foundation Press.

CHAPTER 8

The Juvenile Court: Prosecutorial Decision Making

Introduction

As juvenile courts become increasingly adversarial, pitting defense attorneys and prosecutors against one another, they grow more and more like criminal courts. Juvenile courts continue to retain many of their historical antecedents, however. Much of what prosecutors and judges do is influenced by these antecedents, although contemporary reforms have included the setting of new and contrasting priorities. Chapter 7 explored the major procedural shift from juvenile to criminal courts where more serious offenders are involved and where violent and capital crimes are alleged. This chapter continues to examine the roles of prosecutors and defense attorneys and how these roles have taken on a new significance in recent decades.

The first section will review briefly some of the highlights of the historical evolution of the juvenile court and its original conception. The influence of tradition, of *parens patriae,* on juvenile justice procedures remains strong. However, in the wake of numerous juvenile justice reforms, both prosecutors and defense attorneys alike are having to adjust their thinking about the treatment of juveniles. New juvenile laws are being enacted in most jurisdictions, and assorted legal bodies, such as the American Bar Association and the American Law Institute, are undertaking the complicated tasks of formulating revised juvenile model procedural and penal codes.

The prosecutorial role is taking on greater significance commensurate with the more limited role and jurisdiction of juvenile judges. As is the case in the criminal justice system in response to "get tough" criminal justice reforms, many of the juvenile reforms that have occurred in recent decades have shifted much of the discretionary power backward in the juvenile justice system, toward prosecutors, intake probation officers, and law enforcement officers. The deinstitutionalization of status offenders has removed from most juvenile judges a substantial number of juveniles who may have appeared before them previously for lesser offenses and infractions. Prosecutors are confronted with more serious youthful offenders currently, and their tasks are made more complex because of the increased prominence given to defense attorneys in juvenile court proceedings by the U.S. Supreme Court. The nature of these changing roles will be explored here.

Defense attorneys are increasingly important as negotiators in juvenile proceedings, elevating the formality of these proceedings to new levels. Some feel that such formality in the handling of juvenile offenders is undesirable, although juveniles have been extended increasing numbers of constitutional guarantees by the U.S. Supreme Court. One important function performed by defense counsels involves subjecting the juvenile justice system to frequent constitutional tests. It is largely through the appellate process that juveniles are able to acquire new rights and responsibilities. Both this and the following chapter lay the foundation for Chapter 10, which examines juvenile rights in detail. The extensiveness of appeals of juvenile cases and the rate of success of such appeals lead many experts to wonder whether we are heading toward a unified court system. While the concept of a unified court system refers to several innovative changes in general court reorganization, applied here it means greater centralization and unification of criminal and juvenile courts. This proposed reform will be described and examined. Some of the more important implications of court unification for juveniles will also be described.

The Juvenile Court: A Historical Framework

Juvenile courts are primarily an American creation. As was seen in Chapter 1, the first juvenile court was established in Illinois in 1899 under the **Illinois Juvenile Court Act.** That does not mean that other states were unconcerned about juveniles at the time, or that other events had not occurred relating to youths, their conduct, and their welfare. In fact, numerous agencies and organizations had been established earlier in other jurisdictions, particularly during the latter half of the 1800s.

Reformatories. For example, the first public reformatory, the **New York House of Refuge,** was established in New York City in 1825 by the **Society for the Prevention of Pauperism** (Cahalan, 1986:101). This house of refuge had several goals with regard to juveniles, including providing food, clothing, and lodging for all poor, abused, or orphaned youths. However, the Society for the Prevention of Pauperism was comprised, in part, of many benefactors, philanthropists, and religionists, and these individuals sought to instill within the youths they served a commitment to hard work, strict discipline, and intensive study. These houses were established in various parts of New York and staffed largely by volunteers who knew little or nothing about individual counseling, group therapy techniques, or other useful interventions that might assist youths in surviving city hazards. Because the organization of these houses was decentralized, there were few, if any, external controls that could regulate the quality of care provided. Even today, historians are hard-pressed to decide whether these houses had any impact on the rate of delinquency in the areas where they were established or if they functioned positively to reduce delinquency among the youths they served (Cahalan, 1986; Rogers and Mays, 1987:426).

Other efforts were made in New York several years later to establish placement services for parentless youth. **Charles Loring Brace** created the **New York Children's Aid Society** in 1853. This organization was of assistance in finding foster homes for displaced youths, orphaned youths, runaways, and others. It was especially effective following the Civil War, when large numbers of orphaned youths roamed city streets without any sort of parental supervision.

Child Savers. While these organizations operated to service misplaced youths, there were numerous random efforts in many jurisdictions to perform similar tasks. These efforts led to the creation of various juvenile programs that were more or less interested in "saving children." **Child savers** referred to no one in particular, because anyone who wished to be of assistance in helping children and intervening in their lives for constructive purposes could be defined as a child saver. The precise nature of child saving was not defined at the time, although houses of refuge and children's aid groups and societies could be included within this appellation.

During the mid-1800s, a variety of troublesome juvenile behaviors were identified by different interests and targeted for differential treatment. A certain amount of specialization led to many of the distinctive terms we use today to describe different kinds of status offenders and delinquents. Generally, child savers appeared to have humanitarian interests and seemed interested in helping youths avoid crime and pursue more normal lives. Unfortunately, the influence of charitable and private foundations and religious sponsorship created a coercive atmosphere in which children often received punishment as therapy. The reform school atmosphere of the New York houses of refuge increasingly characterized many of the organizations and homes that purportedly catered to juvenile needs. Youths were compelled to learn crafts and other skills that might be of use in adulthood. This work was most often compulsory, in exchange for food and lodging provided by the child savers.

Community-based Private Agencies. There were exceptions. **Jane Addams** was instrumental in creating Hull House in Chicago in 1889. Hull House was a settlement home used largely by children from immigrant families in the Chicago area. In those days, adults worked long hours, and many youths were otherwise unsupervised and wandered about their neighborhoods looking for something to do. Using money from various charities and philanthropists, Addams supplied children with creative activities to alleviate their boredom and idleness. She integrated these activities with moral, ethical, and religious teachings. In her own way, she was hoping to deter these youths from lives of crime with her constructive activities and teaching. Thus, her approach was consistent with the philosophy of **Cesare Beccaria,** the father of classical criminology. Beccaria wrote in 1764 that the purpose of punishment was deterrence, and that punishment should be measured according to the seriousness of the criminal acts committed.

Truancy Statutes. Truants were "invented" by Massachusetts in 1852, where the first compulsory school attendance statutes were passed. Many other states soon followed suit, until all jurisdictions had compulsory school attendance provisions by 1918. Colorado has been singled out by some historians as having drafted the first juvenile court provisions, although in reality, the Colorado legislature passed its Compulsory School Act in 1899, the same year a juvenile court was established in Illinois. The Colorado action was aimed at preventing truancy, specifically mentioning those youths who were habitually absent from school, wandered about the streets during school hours, and had no obvious business or occupation. Colorado legislators labeled such youths "juvenile disorderly persons," but this action was not the juvenile court equivalent of what the Illinois legislature accomplished.

Original Interpretations of Juveniles and Juvenile Delinquency

We can gain some insight about how juveniles were originally viewed by examining the provisions of Illinois's Juvenile Court Act. The full title of the act is revealing. On July 1, 1899, the Illinois legislature passed the **Act to Regulate Treatment and Control of Dependent, Neglected, and Delinquent Children.** According to the act, it was applicable only to

> . . . children under the age of sixteen (16) years not now or hereafter inmates of a State institution, or any training school for boys or industrial school for girls or some institution incorporated under the laws of this State, except as provided[in other sections] . . . For purposes of this act the words *dependent child* and *neglected child* shall mean any child who for any reason is destitute or homeless or abandoned; or dependent upon the public for support; or has not proper parental care or guardianship; or who habitually begs or receives alms, or who is found living in any house of ill fame or with any vicious or disreputable person; or whose home, by reason of neglect, cruelty or depravity on the part of its parents, guardian or other person in whose care it may be, is an unfit place for such a child; and any child under the age of eight (8) years who is found peddling or selling any article or singing or playing any musical instrument upon the streets or giving any public entertainment. The words

Early juvenile court proceedings were conducted in the context of the *parens patriae* doctrine, where the welfare of children was considered paramount. These proceedings were informal and youths were prohibited from making statements on their own behalf or challenging the decisions of juvenile judges. (Courtesy of the Library of Congress)

> *delinquent child* shall include any child under the age of 16 years who violates any law of this State or any city or village ordinance. The word *child* or *children* may mean one or more children, and the word *parent* or *parents* may be held to mean one or both parents, when consistent with the intent of this act. The word *association* shall include any corporation which includes in its purposes the care or disposition of children coming within the meaning of this act.

Even more instructive is what happens when such children are found. What are the limits of court sanctions? Illinois law authorized juvenile judges to take the following actions in their dealings with dependent and neglected children:

> When any child under the age of sixteen (16) years shall be found to be dependent or neglected within the meaning of this act, the court may make an order committing the child to the care of some suitable State institution, or to the care of some reputable citizen of good moral character, or to the care of some training school or an industrial school, as provided by law, or to the care of some association willing to receive it embracing in its objects the purpose of caring or obtaining homes for dependent or neglected children, which association shall have been accredited as hereinafter provided . . .

For juvenile delinquents, similar provisions were made. Judges were authorized to continue the hearing for any specific delinquent child "from time to time" and "may commit the child to the care and guardianship of a probation officer." The child might be permitted to remain in *its* own home, subject to the visitation of the probation officer. [Emphasis mine.] Judges were also authorized to commit children to state training or industrial schools until such time as they reached the age of their majority or adulthood.

Juveniles as Chattel. The curious word choice, "it," used here in reference to children, is indicative of how youths were viewed in those days. In early English times, children were considered chattel, lumped together with the cows, pigs, horses, and other farm property one might lawfully possess. The act itself was sufficiently ambiguous to allow judges and others considerable latitude or discretion in interpreting juvenile behaviors. For example, what is meant by "proper" parental care or guardianship? Who decides what is to be considered "habitual begging?" Would occasional begging be acceptable? Would a child be subject to arrest and juvenile court sanctions for walking city streets playing a flute or other musical device? Who decides what homes and establishments are "unfit"? What are the criteria that describe a home's fitness? Juvenile judges know the answers to these questions in much the same way that courts generally have viewed and defined obscenity: they know it when they see it.

These statements are not intended to belittle the Illinois legislature and the intentions of the act "it" passed. Rather, they are intended to characterize the traditionalism that juvenile court judges have manifested over the years, and the spirit of *parens patriae* that has dominated judicial decision making and adjudicatory outcomes. Taking dependent and neglected or abandoned children and placing them in training or industrial schools is the functional equivalent of adult incarceration in a prison or jail. By a stroke of the pen, the Illinois legislature gave juvenile court judges absolute control over the lives of all children under age 16 in the state of Illinois.

The Lack of Juvenile Court Uniformity. Currently, little uniformity exists among jurisdictions regarding juvenile court organization and operation. Even within state jurisdictions, great variations exist among counties and cities relating to the way juvenile offenders are processed. Historically, family or domestic courts have retained jurisdiction over most, if not all, juvenile matters. Table 8.1 shows the different types of courts that handle juvenile matters in the United States. It is apparent that not all jurisdictions have juvenile courts per se. Rather, some jurisdictions have courts that adjudicate juvenile offenders as well as decide other matters. Thus, while it is true that all jurisdictions presently have juvenile courts, these courts are not always called juvenile courts.

The Shift from Gemeinschaft *to* Gesellschaft *and a Gradual Reconceptualization of Juveniles.* How were juveniles processed, adjudicated, and punished before the establishment of these specialized courts? How were dependent and neglected children treated? Social scientists would probably describe village and community life in the 1700s and 1800s by referring to the dominant social and cultural values that existed then. The term *gemeinschaft* might be used here to describe the lifestyle one might find in such settings. It is a term used to characterize social relations that are highly dependent on informal verbal agreements and understandings. Ferdinand Tonnies, a social theorist, used *gemeinschaft* to convey the richness of tradition that would typify small communities where everyone knew everyone else. In these settings, formal punishments, such as incarceration in prisons or jails, was seldom used. More effective than incarceration were punishments that heightened public humiliation through stocks and pillories and other corporeal measures. Sufficient social pressure was exerted so that most complied with the law. Thus, in *gemeinschaft* communities, people would fear social stigma, ostracism, and scorn more than the loss of freedom through incarceration.

In these communities, children would remain children through adolescence, eventually becoming adults as they began to perform trades or crafts and earned independent livings apart from their families. Children performed apprenticeships over lengthy periods under the tutorship of master craftsmen and others. Many of the terms we currently use to describe delinquent acts and status offenses were nonexistent then.

As the nation grew, urbanization and the increasing population density of large cities changed social relationships gradually but extensively. Tonnies described the nature of this gradual shift in social relationships as a change from a *gemeinschaft* type of social network to a *gesellschaft* type of society. In the context of *gesellschaft*, social relationships are more formal, contractual, and impersonal. There is greater reliance on codified compilations of appropriate and lawful conduct as a means of regulating social relations.

With the coming of urbanization, the position of children in society changed. During the period of Reconstruction following the Civil War, there were no child labor laws, and children were increasingly exploited by industry and business. Children were thrust into employment in their early years, and they were paid meager wages in "sweatshops"—manufacturing companies where long hours were required and people worked at repetitive jobs. By the end of the nineteenth century, in part because of these widespread nonunionized and unregulated sweatshop operations and compulsory school attendance for youths in their early years, loitering youths became increasingly visible and drew the attention of the general public as well as of law enforcement officials.

Specialized Juvenile Courts. It became more convenient to establish special courts to adjudicate juvenile matters. The technical language describing inappropriate youthful conduct or misbehaviors was greatly expanded and refined. The courts were also vested with the authority to appoint probation officers and others deemed suitable to manage juvenile offenders and enforce new juvenile codes that most cities created. Today, most larger police departments have specialized juvenile sections or divisions, where only juvenile law violations or suspicious activities are investigated. In retrospect, Platt (1969) believes that the original child savers had much to do with inventing delinquency and its numerous specialized subcategories as we now

TABLE 8.1   Organization of American Juvenile Courts

Court System	State(s)
Family and domestic relations court	Delaware, Hawaii, New York, Rhode Island, South Carolina
Juvenile and domestic relations court	New Jersey, Virgin Islands, Virginia
Independent juvenile court	Utah, Wyoming
Court of common pleas	Ohio, Pennsylvania
Juvenile division of probate court	Michigan
Circuit and district courts, concurrently	Alabama
Circuit and magistrate's courts, concurrently (the latter having limited jurisdiction and no authority to confine)	West Virginia
Independent juvenile court or superior court judge sitting as juvenile court judge	Georgia
County court	Arkansas
Trial division of high court	American Samoa
Juvenile division of district court plus juvenile court for specific counties (only Denver County in Colorado)	Colorado and Massachusetts
Each county chooses which court is juvenile court	Texas
Independent juvenile and county courts	Nebraska, Tennessee
Judges are assigned juvenile jurisdiction, plus there are separate provisions for specific counties	Wisconsin
Special juvenile courts or family courts in specific parishes: where these have not been established, district courts have jurisdiction in parishes within their districts and parish courts plus city courts have concurrent jurisdiction with district courts only within their constitutionally established jurisdictional boundaries	Louisiana
District court is juvenile court in specific counties; in counties of not more than 200,000 (and in St. Louis County), the probate court handles juvenile matters	Minnesota
Youth court division of the family court or the county court of the chancery court or certain municipal courts	Mississippi
Trial division of the high court or the district or community courts	Trust Territories
Juvenile cases are heard in district court by a judge or judges who volunteer to specialize in juvenile cases. Where no judge volunteers to specialize, the chief district court judge assigns individual judges to serve in juvenile court on a rotating basis.	North Carolina

SOURCE: U.S. Department of Justice, *A Comparative Analysis of Juvenile Codes* (Washington, DC: U.S. Government Printing Office, 1980), p. 7.

know them. At least they contributed to the formality of the present juvenile justice system by defining a range of impermissible juvenile behaviors that would require an operational legal apparatus to address. Once officialdom was properly armed with the right conceptual tools, it was a relatively easy step to enforce a fairly rigid set of juvenile behavioral standards and regulate most aspects of juveniles' conduct. Sutton (1985) sees the increasing bureaucratization of juvenile courts today both as a national trend and as an institutional compromise between law and social welfare.

As juvenile court systems proliferated, it was quite apparent that their proceedings were decidedly different from those of criminal courts. Largely one-sided affairs, these proceedings typically involved the juvenile charged with some offense, a petitioner claiming the juvenile should be declared delinquent, or dependent, or neglected, and a judge who would weigh the evidence and decide matters. Juveniles themselves were not given the opportunity to solicit witnesses or give testimony. Defense attorneys were largely unknown in juvenile courtrooms, since there were no issues to defend.

The Closed and Arbitrary Nature of Juvenile Court Proceedings. The proceedings were closed to the general public, ostensibly to protect the identities of the youths accused. While these proceedings were conducted behind closed doors for this manifest purpose, a latent function of the secrecy of juvenile courts was to obscure from view the high-handed and discriminatory decision making that characterized many juvenile judges. In short, they didn't want the general public to know about the great subjectivity and arbitrary nature of their decisions. On the basis of allegations alone, together with uncorroborated statements and pronouncements from probation officers and others, juvenile judges were free to declare any particular juvenile either delinquent or nondelinquent. The penalties that could be imposed were wide-ranging, from verbal reprimands and warnings to full-fledged incarceration in a secure juvenile facility. Virtually everything depended upon the opinions and views of presiding juvenile judges. And their decisions could never be appealed to higher courts.

For two thirds of the twentieth century, juveniles had no real legal standing in American courts. Their constitutional rights were not at issue, since they did not enjoy any constitutional protections in the courtroom. No rules of evidence existed to govern the quality of evidence admitted or to challenge the reliability or integrity of testifying witnesses. Juveniles were not entitled to jury trials, unless juvenile court judges permitted them. And comparatively few juvenile court judges ever approved jury trials for juveniles. Because the proceedings were exclusively civil, the rules of criminal procedure normally governing criminal courts did not apply. Juveniles did not acquire criminal records. Rather, they acquired civil adjudications of delinquency. Yet the detention dimension of the juvenile justice system has almost always paralleled that of the criminal justice system. Industrial or training schools, reform schools, and other types of secure detention for juveniles have generally been nothing more than juvenile prisons. Thus, for many adjudicated juvenile offenders sentenced to one of these industrial schools, these sentences were the equivalent of imprisonment.

It is remarkable that such unbridled discretion among juvenile judges continued for so many decades during this century. One explanation might be mass complacency or apathy among the general public about juvenile affairs. Juvenile matters were relatively unimportant and trivial. Another explanation might be a prevailing belief in the myth that juvenile courts know what is best for adjudicated offenders and usually prescribe appropriate punishments, whatever they may be. Juvenile judges and others often viewed juveniles as victims of their environment and peer associations. It might be easier to explain why new environments are required, including detention in the name of training, education, and rehabilitation, if the adverse effects of former environments could be illustrated (McDermott and Laub, 1987). However, in 1967, the U.S. Supreme Court decided the case of *In re Gault*, and it introduced for the first time the notion of juvenile judge accountability to others.

While the case of *Gault* is discussed at length in Chapter 10, it is briefly mentioned here because of its profound consequences for juvenile justice generally and juvenile court judges specifically. In a nutshell, Gerald Gault was a 15-year-old Arizona youth who allegedly made an obscene telephone call to an adult female neighbor. The woman called police, suggested that the youth, Gault, was the guilty party, and Gault was summarily taken into custody and detained for nearly two days. The woman was never brought to court as a witness, and the only evidence she provided was her initial verbal accusation made to police on the day of Gault's arrest. Gault himself allegedly admitted that he dialed the woman's number, but he claimed that a boyfriend of his actually spoke to the woman and made the remarks she found offensive. Partly because Gault had been involved in an earlier petty offense and had a "record," the judge, together with the probation officer, decided that Gault was dangerous enough to commit to the Arizona State Industrial School, Arizona's main juvenile penitentiary, until he reached 21 years of age or until juvenile corrections authorities decided he was rehabilitated and could be safely released. According to Arizona law, the sentence was unappealable. An adult convicted of the same offense might have been fined $50 and/or sentenced to a 30-day jail term. Gault received six years in a juvenile prison, complete with correctional officers with firearms and barbed wire.

It is a sad commentary on juvenile courts and the justice dispensed by many of these judges prior to the *Gault* decision that numerous similar adjudications had been made against other juveniles in other jurisdictions. Appropriately, the U.S. Supreme Court referred to the court of the judge who originally sentenced Gault as a "kangaroo court." Gault's sentence was reversed and several important constitutional rights were conferred upon all juveniles as a result. Specifically, all of Gault's due process rights had been denied. He had been denied counsel, had not been protected against self-incrimination, had not been permitted to cross-examine his accuser, and had not been provided

Reform schools in the early 1900s rarely reformed youths. Such institutions made juveniles perform various manual tasks, such as making shoes or other products. (Courtesy of Culver Pictures, Inc.)

with specific notice of the charges against him. Now all juveniles enjoy these rights in every U.S. juvenile court.

The Increasing Bureaucratization and Criminalization of Juvenile Justice. For better or worse, the wheels were set in motion for major juvenile court reforms. After *Gault* and several other important Supreme Court decisions affecting juveniles directly, the nature of juvenile courts underwent a gradual transformation. But the transformation was anything but smooth. Even the U.S. Supreme Court continued to view juvenile courts as basically rehabilitative and treatment-centered apparatuses, thus reinforcing the traditional *parens patriae* doctrine within the context of various constitutional restraints. Nevertheless, annual changes in juvenile court procedures and the juvenile justice system generally suggested that it was becoming increasingly criminalized (Feld, 1984). Feld (1984) observes that in Minnesota and other jurisdictions, the development of new Rules of Procedure for Juvenile Court and the current administrative assumptions and operations of these courts, with limited exceptions, often render them indistinguishable from criminal courts and the procedures these courts follow.

In general, juvenile courts are now viewed as **due process courts** rather than **traditional courts** (Ito, 1984). Due process juvenile courts are characterized by more formal case dispositions, a greater rate of intake dismissals, and greater importance attached to offense characteristics and seriousness. Traditional juvenile courts are characterized as less formal, with greater use made of detention. Both defense and prosecuting attorneys play more important roles in due process juvenile courts compared with traditional ones (Ito, 1984).

Currently, there continues to be widespread debate about the nature of and functions to be performed by juvenile courts (Blackmore *et al.*, 1988; Feld, 1988b; Harris and Graff, 1988; Krisberg, 1988). Should they be principally rehabilitative and treatment-oriented, or should they be punishment-centered, "just-deserts" courts where juvenile offenders should get whatever they deserve? Feld (1988a) notes that today, juveniles suffer the "worst of both worlds," in that they are subjected to harsh punishments in juvenile courts but lack the full range of constitutional guarantees extended to adults in criminal courts. Feld favors the abolition of juvenile courts and the establishment of full procedural parity as in criminal courts, believing that this will end our fruitless attempts to bring all due process safeguards into the juvenile courtroom. Other experts report public attitudes and sentiments favoring a continuation of juvenile courts in their present form, with an emphasis on rehabilitation (Steinhart, 1988). However, an emerging sentiment is that all youths should be vested with a greater degree of responsibility and accountability to others. This has been one of the intended aims of juvenile justice reform in the State of Washington and other jurisdictions, where *both* rehabilitation and punishment may be combined to heighten offender accountability (Challeen, 1986; Schneider and Schram, 1986; Springer, 1987).

One important result of the U.S. Supreme Court decision in *Gault* giving youths the right to be represented by counsel in juvenile court was the immediate transformation of juvenile proceedings from unilateral hearings into *adversarial* ones, with much higher levels of procedural formality (Feld, 1987c). In the **adversarial system**, which has long been a feature of American courts for adults, plaintiffs and defendants litigate cases civilly for damages, and prosecutors and defense attorneys respectively attempt to convince judges or juries of the guilt or innocence of criminal defendants and seek either their conviction or their exoneration. This higher level of procedural formality associated with due process in juvenile justice has encouraged the development of new proposed juvenile codes that only serve to further bureaucratize an already bureaucratized system (Ito, 1984).

The Rose Institute and the American Legislative Exchange Council have proposed a new model juvenile code. However, experts have criticized this model code as weakening current protections extended to dependent children, eliminating judicial discretion in disposition, requiring pretrial detention of juveniles accused of serious crimes, and permitting the detention of status offenders who violate court orders (Orlando *et al.*, 1987). The developers of such codes claim that their proposals will instill within juveniles a greater degree of accountability for their actions (Rossum *et al.*, 1987).

Public Defenders for Juveniles. Greater procedural formality in the juvenile justice system has been observed relating to the appointment of public defenders for juvenile indigents. More than a few juvenile court jurisdictions, including Los Angeles County and Alameda County, California, now provide public defenders for juveniles and their families who cannot afford to appoint private counsel, especially in more serious cases where incarceration in secure detention facilities is a strong possibility (Feeney, 1987; Hancock et al., 1985). Formerly, defense counsels for juveniles often were the juvenile's probation officer or a social caseworker with a vested interest in the case. It is not entirely clear how these officers and workers were able to separate their law enforcement and defense functions to avoid allegations of conflicts of interest. But little interest in the quality of defense of juvenile cases was exhibited by the public in previous years anyway. While some experts believe that juveniles are now insulated to some extent from the whims of juvenile court prosecutors and judges, others suspect that defense attorneys have in some instances made it more difficult for juveniles to receive fair treatment.

During the intake process discussed in Chapter 6, it was found that the presence of attorneys, who represented juveniles' interests and attempted to protect them so that their full range of constitutional rights were observed at each stage of the juvenile justice process, actually detracted from the informal nature of intake. Intake officers would change such proceedings into formal ones, and recommendations for subsequent dispositions might be harsher than if attorneys had not been present. In fact, intake officers have openly discouraged juveniles and their parents from availing themselves of an attorney's services at this stage, since the attorney's presence hampers informal adjustments of cases and limits a youth's compliance with informal probationary conditions. In some cases, intake officers consider themselves the primary source of a youth's understanding of legal rights, although a recommendation that these officers receive more training and preparation in law and juvenile rights suggests that their own understanding of the law merits improvement (Lawrence, 1984). If it is true that some intake officers are frightened or inhibited by the presence of attorneys for juvenile offenders to the extent that they find it difficult to make informal adjustments in particular cases, one wonders whether certain allegations of discrimination and juvenile rights violations by these and other juvenile justice system actors are true.

It *is* true, however, that juvenile court proceedings have become increasingly formalized. Further, public access to these proceedings in most jurisdictions is increasing. The presence of defense counsel, an adversarial scenario, a trial-like atmosphere where witnesses testify for and against juvenile "defendants," and adherence to Rules of Procedure for Juvenile Courts are clear indicators of greater formalization, bureaucratization, and criminalization, as Feld (1987b) and others have suggested. We are but a few rights away from full-fledged criminal proceedings in many juvenile court jurisdictions.

The Changing Prosecutorial Role in Juvenile Matters

Juvenile court prosecutors have been forced to change and adapt to these new procedures as well. As juveniles acquire more legal rights, prosecutors must be increasingly cognizant of these rights and constitutional safeguards and must ensure that they are not violated. Rights violations, particularly those involving constitutional issues, can and will be challenged in the event of unfavorable juvenile court adjudications and/or sentences.

While a more extended discussion of juvenile rights will be presented in Chapter 10, it may be indicated here, for example, that the standard of proof in juvenile proceedings, as well as the rules for introduction of evidence against youths, are currently different compared with pre-*Gault* times. Defense counsel may now challenge the quality of evidence against youths and the way it was obtained, the accuracy of confessions or other incriminating utterances made by youths while in custody and under interrogation, the veracity of witnesses, and whether juveniles understand the rights they are asked to waive by law enforcement officers and others.

Regarding the standard of proof, it was traditionally the case that the **standard of proof** in determining delinquency and that was followed in juvenile courts (which were and still remain civil proceedings) was the **preponderance of the evidence** standard. In criminal proceedings, the standard of proof followed in determining a defendant's guilt is **beyond a reasonable doubt.** A juvenile case discussed elsewhere (see Chapter 10), *In re Winship* (1970), resulted in the U.S. Supreme Court declaring that, particularly where juveniles were in jeopardy of losing their freedom through placement in secure detention for any period of time, they were entitled to the same standard of proof currently extended to adults in criminal proceedings—beyond a reasonable doubt. Although some jurisdictions retain the preponderance of evidence standard for certain juvenile proceedings, these jurisdictions are obligated to use the criminal standard of proof, beyond a reasonable doubt, whenever an adjudication of delinquency can result in confinement or a substantial loss of privileges.

Juveniles have benefited in at least one respect as a result of these new rights and standards of proof. These changed conditions have forced law enforcement officers, prosecutors, and judges to be more careful and discriminating when charging juveniles with certain offenses. However, changing the technical ground rules for proceeding against juveniles has not necessarily resulted in substantial changes in police officer discretion, prosecutorial discretion, or judicial discretion. Juveniles remain second-class citizens, in a sense, since they continue to be subject to street-level justice by police officers.

Prosecutors appear similarly unaffected by these juvenile justice changes. Studies of greater prosecutorial presence in juvenile courts suggest that their overall effect on juvenile adjudicatory proceedings has been minimal (Laub and MacMurray, 1987). Greater formality in the juvenile court proceedings of Middlesex County, Maryland, has brought little change in the use and behaviors of **police prosecutors,** despite a substantially greater presence of assistant district attorneys in juvenile courts. Laub and MacMurray (1987) indicate that one explanation for this is the continued emphasis of the court on the youth's rehabilitation. Further, the organizational structure of these courts has remained unchanged.

It has long been a traditional feature of the juvenile justice system in many jurisdictions for police officers to function in prosecutorial capacities in juvenile court proceedings. Thus, they might arrest juveniles and retain the responsibility for their ultimate prosecution in juvenile courts. Interestingly, this would place police officers in the position of having to justify the probable cause leading to a juvenile's arrest at intake, to present the case against the juvenile in court, and to testify against the juvenile as a witness for the prosecution. The conflicts of interest inherent in this scenario are untenable in any criminal court today. Despite this conflict of interest situation, police prosecutors are still permitted in various jurisdictions.

The Laub-MacMurray study seems to typify much of what has happened in juvenile courts in recent years. Despite the increased bureaucratization of these courts, they seem to exhibit much of the traditionalism of the pre-*Gault* years. This means that little change has occurred in the nature of juvenile adjudications. Juvenile judges, with the exception of those few jurisdictions that provide jury trials for serious juvenile cases, continue to make adjudicatory decisions as before. Regardless of new evidentiary standards and proof of guilt requirements, these judges continue to exercise their individual discretion and decide whether guilt or delinquency has been established "beyond a reasonable doubt." How are we ever to know whether these judges are continuing to use old proof standards (i.e., preponderance of the evidence) and merely saying that they are following new ones (i.e., beyond a reasonable doubt)?

Enhancing the accountability of juvenile courts is greater public access to them under the provisions of the First Amendment. The *Michigan Law Review* (1983) has argued editorially that such access would fulfill the First Amendment's structural role of ensuring the free flow of information necessary to effective self-government and of checking the abuse of official power. Acknowledging that the state's interest in preserving the privacy of juvenile courts is designed to protect the identity of juvenile offenders and preserve the confidentiality of their records, the editorial states that mandatory or routine closures of juvenile courts from the public are not always justified. In fact, juvenile judges may be permitted to impose reasonable restrictions of access to juvenile courtrooms upon a showing that an overriding interest in the sensitivity of particular cases justifies infringing the First Amendment.

Dunn (1986) recognizes the important confidentiality function served by limiting access to juvenile courts and court records, although it is also the case that important law enforcement functions are aided and facilitated by public access and disclosures, especially where serious recidivists are involved. Although Dunn advocates a more liberal disclosure policy for juveniles, it is also recommended that juveniles should be notified whenever information about them is sought. By thus knowing the identity of persons seeking information, youthful offenders may be able to minimize any adverse effects of public disclosures.

The greater formality of juvenile proceedings, as well as their openness to others, may restrict the discretion of juvenile judges, as some writers allege, but this limitation is not necessarily an undesirable one. Juvenile judges have

The changing nature of juvenile courts is apparent through the greater use of counsel who represent juveniles charged with offenses in adversarial proceedings. (Courtesy of H. Armstrong Roberts)

been known to make decisions that only incidentally related to the alleged offense. For instance, Emerson (1969:88–89) reported that a juvenile judge once ordered physical examinations for two 15-year-old girls who had been arrested for shoplifting clothes in a department store. Among other things, he wished to determine whether they had been "sexually active." What that had to do with the case is unclear, but it was clearly unrelated to the offense of shoplifting. It is doubtful that in today's juvenile courtroom, juvenile judges would be able to get away with irrelevant directives such as the one described by Emerson. The presence of a defense counsel representing the juvenile's interests would deter judges from such conduct, although in 1969, *parens patriae* was still a strong feature of these courts, and juvenile females were particularly vulnerable to the overprotection of paternalistic juvenile court judges.

One indication that the juvenile justice process has escalated to a new level of legal formality and sophistication and has become increasingly criminalized, as Feld (1984) has suggested, is the emergence of materials about juvenile defense procedures prepared by such noted criminal defense attorneys as F. Lee Bailey. Bailey and a colleague, Henry B. Rothblatt, published *Handling Juvenile Delinquency Cases* in 1982 (Bailey and Rothblatt, 1982). This legal manual covered various important defense issues, including practical techniques for successfully representing juvenile offenders. Separate chapters included discussions of diversion and intake, plea bargaining, trial procedures, dispositional hearings, and post-dispositional and juvenile corrections issues. Subsequently, bibliographical materials about juveniles and the law have been prepared by Ream (1985). Other prepared materials include procedures developed by the Juvenile Justice Standards Project of the American Bar Association (Green, 1984), a legal reference guide for lawyers who specialize in U.S. children's law (Horowitz and Davidson, 1984), case law materials on juvenile justice (Miller, 1985), and selections of sample pleadings used by the defense in juvenile court practice (Volenik, 1986). Even juvenile judges have been targeted as recipients of data about new due process procedures that should be followed in juvenile courts (Guernsey, 1985). Much of this material, together with the growth of the adversarial system in juvenile courtrooms, indicates a more prominent role for defense attorneys in the juvenile justice process.

The Advocacy Role of Defense Attorneys

For especially serious juvenile offender cases, defense attorneys are increasingly useful and necessary as a means of safeguarding juvenile rights and holding the juvenile justice system more accountable in its treatment of juvenile offenders. Widespread abuse of discretion by various actors throughout all stages of the juvenile justice process is well documented and has been described in this and previous chapters. The intrusion of defense attorneys into the juvenile justice process, under a new "due process" framework, is a logical consequence of the expansion of juvenile rights by the U.S. Supreme Court in recent decades (Ito, 1984).

Although juveniles are entitled to the services of attorneys at all stages of juvenile proceedings, some investigators have shown that about half of all youths processed in the juvenile justice system are not represented by counsel (Feld, 1988b). Shortly after the *Gault* decision in 1967, the Minnesota legislature mandated the assistance of counsel for all juveniles in delinquency proceedings. It was believed that making provisions for defense counsel would maximize the equitable treatment of youths by Minnesota juvenile courts. However, Feld's (1988b) analysis of 17,195 cases involving adjudications of delinquency in 1986 found that only about half of all juveniles adjudicated delinquent in these Minnesota juvenile courts had had attorneys to represent them.

Analyzing adjudication data from an earlier period in five other jurisdictions besides Minnesota, Feld (1988a) discovered similar figures. Roughly half of all juveniles adjudicated delinquent in these state juvenile courts had legal representation at the time of their adjudications. It is unclear whether the juveniles who did not have defense counsel also did not request defense counsel. It would have been inconsistent with *Gault* as well as unconstitutional if these juveniles had requested defense counsel and been denied it in those jurisdictions. But Feld may have provided at least two plausible explanations for this finding. He found that juveniles who were represented by attorneys in each of these jurisdictions and who were also adjudicated as delinquent tended to receive harsher sentences and dispositions from juvenile judges compared with those juveniles who did not have defense counsel to represent them. Thus, it would seem that the presence of defense counsel in juvenile courts, at least in those jurisdictions examined by Feld, actually aggravated the dispositional outcome instead of mitigating it. An alternative explanation is that the more serious offenders in those jurisdictions were more likely to acquire counsel. Thus, they would logically receive harsher sentences compared with less serious offenders if they were ultimately adjudicated as delinquents.

The manifest function of defense attorneys in juvenile courts is to ensure that due process is fulfilled by all participants. Defense attorneys are the primary advocates of fairness for juveniles who are charged with crimes or other types of offenses. Minors, particularly those who are very young, are more susceptible to the persuasiveness of adults. Law enforcement officers, intake probation officers, and prosecutors might extract incriminating evidence from juveniles in much the same way as police officers and prosecutors might extract inculpatory information from suspects in criminal cases, if certain constitutional safeguards were not in place. For adults, a major constitutional safeguard is the Miranda warning, which, among other things, advises those arrested for crimes of their right to an attorney, their right to terminate police interrogations whenever they wish and remain silent, their right to have their attorney present during questioning, and their right to have an attorney appointed for them if they cannot afford one.

Juvenile Highlights

Should juveniles receive capital punishment when they commit capital crimes? In those states that invoke capital punishment as the maximum penalty—about two thirds of all state jurisdictions—the minimum age at which offenders can be executed is a sensitive issue. Until the 1980s, executions of juveniles in some states included no specific provisions about minimum ages. In 1988, the U.S. Supreme Court decided the case of *Thompson v. Oklahoma,* in which a youth had committed the capital crime of murder when he was 15 years of age. It was decided that the death penalty was cruel and unusual punishment for those who were 15 years of age or younger at the time they committed their capital offenses.

That year, there were 2,200 convicts on death row, and about thirty of these were offenders who were juveniles when they committed their capital crimes. In 1989, the U.S. Supreme Court heard two cases in which the death penalty had been imposed by lower courts on two youths, aged 16 and 17 respectively, in Missouri and Kentucky. Heath Wilkins, a 16-year-old from Missouri, and Kevin Stanford, a 17-year-old from Kentucky, were both convicted of brutal slayings they committed as juveniles. Both were sentenced to death and both appealed their convictions and sentences. The U.S. Supreme Court upheld the constitutionality of the death penalty in both of these cases. Thus, it is now lawful to execute offenders who were aged 16 or 17 at the time they committed their capital crimes. Of course, this applies only in states that have the death penalty. States may also raise these minimum ages for youthful executions, if the legislatures vote to do so. But the *Thompson* decision means that states are now prohibited from executing offenders who were under age 16 when their capital offenses were committed. Affected are youths such as Jesus Jimenez, 19, who was sentenced to die in Arizona State Prison for the murder of a five-year-old girl when he was 16. He killed her by strangling and repeatedly stabbing her. Percy Lee, 20, was sentenced to die in a Pennsylvania penitentiary for the murder of a mother and her teenage daughter when he was 17 years of age.

(Some factual information adapted from Alain L. Sanders, "Bad News for Death Row," *Time,* July 10, 1989, pp. 48–49.)

Normally, defense attorneys for adults charged with crimes are reluctant to have their clients say anything at all to police officers or others.

When the Miranda warning became official policy for police officers and others, the warning and accompanying constitutional safeguards were not believed applicable to juveniles. Thus, law enforcement officers continued to question youths about crimes during the post-Miranda years. Since it is generally accepted that a juvenile's understanding of the law is usually poor (Lawrence, 1984; Peterson, 1988), it might be assumed further that juveniles might be more easily manipulated by law enforcement authorities. An attempt to protect juveniles from themselves in making incriminating Fifth Amendment-type statements was the U.S. Supreme Court case of *Fare* v. *Michael C.* (1979). This case involved a juvenile who spoke to the police about his involvement in a crime. (See Chapter 10 for a more extensive discussion of the case.) The Court ruled that the "totality of circumstances" test should govern whether juveniles intelligently and knowingly waive their right to be questioned by police about crimes, and whether it is necessary first to obtain parental consent. Undoubtedly this decision had led many states to enact statutes that specifically render inadmissible any admissions juveniles might make to police in the absence of parental guidance or consent (Shaffner, 1985).

Some experts believe that the U.S. Supreme Court has always supported the *parens patriae* nature of juvenile courts, and that its purportedly liberal decisions about juvenile constitutional guarantees have been intended only to provide minimal procedural protections (Dale, 1987). Nevertheless, the possibilities of incarceration in secure juvenile detention facilities and/or transfer to criminal court jurisdiction, where harsher penalties may be administered, are sufficient to warrant the intervention of defense counsel in many juvenile cases. If anything, defense counsel may prevent some youths from being railroaded into accepting unnecessary conditional interventions from intake officers or juvenile court judges. It is not the intention of defense attorneys to aggravate matters and cause their juvenile clients to receive punishments that are proportionately more severe than they would normally receive from the same judges if defense counsel weren't present. But it is a curious paradox that those who seek justice and due process and who exercise their rights in this regard end up being penalized for these behaviors. This situation will probably exist for some years in both the juvenile and criminal justice systems.

In many respects, this paradox is similar to the disparity in sentencing among those who have similar criminal histories and are convicted for the same offenses, but who receive widely disparate sentences depending upon whether their convictions are obtained through plea bargaining or through a jury verdict in a criminal trial. There is no particular reason for judges to subject those who exercise their right to a trial to more severe punishments upon conviction than those who accept plea agreements and plead guilty, but different punishments are frequently administered (Champion, 1988). One explanation, an extralegal or nonlegal one, is that the extra punishment is the penalty for requiring the state to prove its case against the defendant in open court. Knowing about this sentencing disparity, many defense attorneys counsel their clients, especially where there is strong inculpatory evidence, to plead guilty to lesser charges and accept a lesser penalty to avoid more severe punishments that judges almost certainly will impose upon conviction through a trial. It would appear from the available evidence that juvenile judges are guilty of the same behavior when dealing with juvenile clients who are represented by counsel and those who are not. For the present, anyway, being represented by counsel in juvenile court seems more of a liability than an asset.

Toward a Unified Court System?

Presently, there are several different types of courts in every U.S. jurisdiction. Usually, these courts have general, original, and concurrent jurisdiction, meaning that some courts share adjudicatory responsibilities involving the same subject matter. In Arkansas, for example, chancery courts have jurisdiction over juvenile delinquency cases, although separate county courts may also hear cases involving juveniles. In Colorado, district courts have general jurisdiction over criminal and civil matters, probate matters, and juvenile cases. However, there are specific juvenile courts in Colorado that hear juvenile cases as well. Tennessee county courts, circuit courts, and juvenile courts have concurrent jurisdiction over delinquency and other types of juvenile cases (e.g., children in need of supervision, child custody cases).

Court unification *is a general proposal that seeks to centralize and integrate the diverse functions of all courts of general, concurrent, and exclusive jurisdiction into a more simplified and uncomplicated scheme.* One way of viewing court unification is that it is ultimately intended to abolish concurrent jurisdiction wherever it is currently shared among various courts in a common jurisdiction, although no presently advocated court unification model has been shown to be superior to others proposed (Dahlin, 1986). There are different ways of achieving unification, although not everyone agrees about which method is best. One example of court unification is in Pennsylvania.

Prior to 1969, Pennsylvania had two appellate courts and numerous local courts that functioned independently of one another (Pomery, 1982). Even the Pennsylvania Supreme Court lacked full and explicit administrative and supervisory authority over the entire judicial system. As the result of the Pennsylvania Constitutional Convention of 1967–1968, a new Judiciary Article, Article V of the Pennsylvania Constitution, was framed. Vast changes were made in court organization and operations. A Family Division was established to deal exclusively with all juvenile matters. A ten-year follow-up evaluation of Pennsylvania's court unification concluded that the present court organization is vastly superior to the pre-1969 court organization (Pomery, 1982). Efficiency and economy were two objectives sought by these court changes. Both aims were achieved.

Studies of jurisdictions representing various degrees of unification have been conducted to assess whether there is necessarily an improvement in economy, coordination, and speed associated with maintaining records and processing cases (Henderson *et al.*, 1984). Georgia, Iowa, Colorado, New

Jersey, and Connecticut were examined. Data were collected from records maintained by state administrative officials and local trial courts, and interviews were conducted with key court personnel. A total of 103 courts were selected for analysis, including 20 courts of general jurisdiction, 69 courts of limited jurisdiction, and 15 juvenile courts. More centralized organizational schemes only partially fulfilled the expectations of these researchers. Henderson *et al.* (1984) report that under centralization, poorer areas were likely to do better financially, although courts in well-off areas faced tighter budget restrictions. Greater uniformity of operations was observed in most jurisdictions. Further, centralization of court organization tended to highlight problems in previously neglected areas, including family and juvenile services. The findings relating to differences in the effectiveness and efficiency of case processing in trial courts in both decentralized and centralized systems were inconclusive, however.

At present, few states have adopted the high degree of court centralization exhibited by Pennsylvania. One explanation for the general reluctance of various jurisdictions to commit to substantial court reform is that such change threatens vested interests and has the potential for blunting judicial and political power. This phenomenon was observed, for example, in the State of Washington during the period of divestiture of status offenses from the jurisdiction of juvenile courts. The intended goals of divestiture in Washington included ridding juvenile courts of nonserious status offenders. However, divestiture was inconsistently received among Washington's juvenile court judiciary (Schneider, 1984). If such reactions to divestiture, one specific court reform, occur among juvenile court judges, what may we contemplate the reception of court unification to be among judges in general in any jurisdiction?

For juveniles, court unification poses potentially threatening consequences. For example, in those jurisdictions where considerable fragmentation exists in the processing of juvenile cases or where concurrent jurisdiction distributes juvenile matters among several different courts, juveniles, especially habitual offenders, may be able to benefit by of a general lack of centralization in record-keeping. Thus, juveniles may be adjudicated delinquent in one juvenile court jurisdiction, but this record of adjudication may not be transmitted to other courts in adjacent jurisdictions. In time, it is likely that a national record-keeping network will exist, in which all juvenile courts may access information from other jurisdictions. Currently, however, the confidentiality of record-keeping is a structural constraint that inhibits the development of such extensive record-sharing.

Those who favor a separate and distinct juvenile justice system apart from the criminal justice system contend that the primary goal of juvenile courts should be individualized treatment, with therapy and rehabilitation as dominant factors (Dwyer and McNally, 1987). However, other voices encourage perpetuating a separate juvenile justice system which not only is designed to treat and prevent delinquency but is also designed to hold juveniles strictly accountable for their actions (Springer, 1987). Thus, it is

BOX 8.2

Juvenile Highlights

Are male juvenile murderers under-achievers and high school dropouts?

Richard and Nancy Langert of Winnetka, Illinois, a suburb of Chicago, had good jobs. They were planning on moving into a larger home closer to work in the coming months. Their lives were beginning to prosper. In April, 1990, an intruder entered their home. A short while later, both Nancy, 25, and her husband, Richard, 30, would be dead.

Nancy's father found the couple after they failed to show up at church. Both bodies were in the family basement. Richard had been handcuffed and shot in the back of the head. Nancy, several months pregnant, had been shot in the elbow, side, and stomach. She had scrawled some initials in blood as she died.

At first, police believed burglary might have been the motive, but $500 in cash was found strewn about the living room floor. About to wrap up the case as another unsolved murder, police officers were contacted several months later by a high school student who informed them that one of his schoolmates had bragged about killing the Langert couple. David Biro, a 17-year-old high school honor student, was arrested and taken into custody. A search of his home uncovered a glass cutter, several sets of handcuffs, and a .357 magnum revolver believed to be the murder weapon. Biro's own statements to police and to his classmates disclosed details about the murders that only the murderer would know and that police officers had never released to the press. His parents were dumbfounded. His student friends acknowledged later that he was fascinated with power and violence, and was regarded by some as an insane genius. Some believe that Biro wanted to commit the perfect crime, reviving memories of Loeb and Leopold, the preppy, highly intelligent murderers who killed Bobby Franks in Chicago in the 1920s.

(Some factual information adapted from Civia Tamarkin, "David Biro Said He Was a Killer: Now the Police Seem to Agree," *People Weekly*, November 12, 1990, pp. 67–70.)

suggested that less use be made of detention and greater use be made of probation and parole, with the primary objectives of offering restitution to victims, compensating communities and courts for the time taken to process cases, and performing community services to learn valuable lessons (Maloney *et al.*, 1988; Rubin, 1988).

There is no question that the "get tough" movement is still strong and pervasive throughout the juvenile justice system. One indication of this is the increased use of waivers or transfers, as more juveniles are shifted to the jurisdiction of criminal courts. We have seen the implications of this for juveniles, and some of these implications are not entirely unfavorable. Increasing numbers of juvenile court judges are soliciting the involvement of members of the community in voluntary capacities to assist in monitoring adjudicated youths. Greater responsibility is being shifted to parents in many jurisdictions, particularly when their children commit crimes against property and do extensive monetary damage (National Council of Juvenile and Family Court Judges, 1986).

Public policy currently favors protecting juveniles as much as possible from the stigma of criminal labeling; part of this protective policy involves the large-scale removal of youths from jails and prisons (Georgia Commission on Juvenile Justice, 1985; Greenwood, 1986d; Mones, 1984). Recommendations from the public include greater use of nonsecure facilities and programs as opposed to detention in secure facilities (Conti *et al.*, 1984). Especially manifest is the concern for very young offenders. More children under age 10 are entering the juvenile justice system annually (Sametz, 1984). Clearly, effective programs and procedures for processing such children need to be in place and operative. Encouragement for greater use of community-based services and treatment programs, special education services, and school-based early intervention programs is apparent (Sametz, 1984; Steinhart, 1988).

There is increasing bureaucratization of juvenile courts, indicated in part by greater formality of juvenile case processing. Juvenile proceedings are increasingly adversarial proceedings similar to those in criminal courts. Almost all of the trappings found in criminal courts are found in juvenile courts, with some significant exceptions that have been noted (Feld, 1987a; Sutton, 1985). Most juvenile courts are not courts of record, and much informality exists regarding calling witnesses and offering testimony. Federal and state rules of evidence are relaxed considerably and do not apply directly to juvenile civil proceedings. However, in some jurisdictions where prosecutorial presence has been increased greatly (as one indication of greater bureaucratization of juvenile courts), little perceptible impact upon juvenile processing was observed (Laub and MacMurray, 1987).

Juvenile courts are sometimes classified as belonging either to a "traditional" or "family" model or a "due process" model (Ito, 1984; Watkins, 1987). Traditional courts tend to perpetuate the doctrine of *parens patriae,* and juvenile judges in these courts retain a good deal of discretion in adjudicating offenders. They rely more heavily on detention as a punishment. The "due process" juvenile courtroom, on the other hand, relies more heavily on pre-adjudicatory interactions between defense counsels and prosecutors, and nonjudicial handling of cases is more the rule than the exception. More frequently used in such courts are nonsecure facilities, community-based programs, probation, and diversion with conditions (Ito, 1984).

The political approach to punishing juveniles is to rely heavily on the sentiments expressed by voting constituencies. State legislators are at the helm of juvenile justice reforms currently, and several organizations are strategically positioned to offer their guidance and assistance in formulating new juvenile policies. The American Bar Association, the American Legislative Exchange Council, and the Institute of Judicial Administration have provided legislators with model penal codes and proposed juvenile court revisions to introduce consistency throughout an inconsistent juvenile justice system (American Bar Association, 1986; Orlando *et al.*, 1987; Treanor and Volenik, 1987). The federally funded Juvenile Justice Reform Project, which has reviewed existing juvenile codes and statutes in all fifty states, has conducted an extensive national opinion survey of child-serving professionals (Rossum *et al.*, 1987). Two model juvenile justice acts have been proposed— the Model Delinquency Act and the Model Disobedient Children's Act. Among other things, these acts distinguish between delinquent and status offenders and make provisions for their alternative care, treatment, and punishment. Both acts are designed to hold juveniles responsible for their acts and to hold the system accountable for its treatment of these youths as well (Rossum *et al.*, 1987).

It is debatable whether these codes are functional and in the best interests of the youths served. Some experts say that these codes will weaken the current protections extended to dependent children and children in need of supervision. Furthermore, a serious erosion of judicial discretion may occur, accompanied by increased use of pretrial detention for juveniles where serious crimes are alleged. Also, status offenders may be jailed for violating court orders (Orlando *et al.*, 1987). Indeed, it is difficult to devise a code of accountability that is founded on the principle of "just deserts" and that nevertheless performs certain traditional treatment functions in the old context of *parens patriae* (Treanor and Volenik, 1987). Additionally, codes of any kind promote a degree of blind conformity, or compliance with rules for the sake of compliance. With greater codification of juvenile procedures, less latitude exists for judges and others to make concessions and impose individualized sentences where appropriate. The very idea of "individualized" sentences, while appealing to "just deserts" interests, invites abuse through discriminatory treatment on racial, ethnic, gender, and socioeconomic grounds.

Judges themselves see the juvenile court as attempting to instill within youths a respect for the law and as helping them in assuming greater responsibility for their actions (Challeen, 1986). Interestingly, this represents a dramatic shift from the policy in which juveniles were considered victims of the system and thus less accountable for their actions. The emphasis currently is on a policy that identifies delinquents as offenders deserving of punishment (McDermott and Laub, 1987). However, the current organizational structure of juvenile courts and the prevalent rehabilitative orientation among those who work with and process juveniles presents various obstacles to prosecutorial effectiveness in ensuring that "just deserts" will be realized for youths charged with serious offenses (Laub and MacMurray, 1987). One final observation is in order before concluding this chapter. Despite the intent of juvenile sentencing reforms to create harsher sanctions as general deterrents to juvenile delinquency, the juvenile justice system continues to be viewed as a lenient system by prosecutors, legislators, and the public (Harris, 1988; Steinhart, 1988).

Summary

Juvenile courts were established first in Illinois in 1899. By 1918 all U.S. jurisdictions had courts that specialized in juvenile matters, although they were not always designated as juvenile courts *per se.* Historically, juveniles were considered as chattel or property belonging to parents. There were no specialized courts that decided cases against them. Forms of corporeal punishment were used extensively in colonial times, such as stocks and pillories. Reformatories, such as the New York House of Refuge, were established in the early 1800s as a means of providing youths with food, clothing, and shelter, although juveniles also were expected to adhere to strict disciplinary standards and follow religious principles. Child savers included philanthropists and other benefactors who sought to save juveniles from lives of crime as adults. Often, these saving efforts resulted in incarceration and dubious forms of work training. Child savers helped to define various juvenile behaviors that were eventually prohibited by statutes in different jurisdictions.

A formal juvenile justice process was not created until the early 1900s. One explanation for the slow growth of this process has to do with the types of communities that existed in the 1800s. Many small communities used social sanctions to punish those who violated the law, since social stigma was more feared than a loss of privileges through incarceration. The period of Reconstruction following the Civil War stimulated changes, including mass urbanization and the rapid rise of large cities with factories and sweatshops. These businesses often used child labor, which was an unprotected labor category then.

Early juvenile proceedings were guided by the principle of *parens patriae,* and decisions were made by judges and others presumably for the benefit of affected juveniles. The frequent arbitrariness of these decisions prompted allegations of unfairness and inequitable treatment. In time, juvenile courts came to adopt an adversarial system, where prosecutors and defense attorneys would prosecute and defend juveniles accused of crimes. This bureaucratization of the juvenile justice system has been both praised and criticized. Presently, attempts are being made to hold juveniles more accountable to others for their behavior. Punishments meted out by juvenile courts are increasingly connected with restitution or victim compensation rather than with punishment for the sake of punishment.

Because of the diversity of court organization, juvenile matters are handled in a wide variety of jurisdictions in U.S. courts. Efforts have been made to unify the different courts in each jurisdiction, in order to achieve greater control over case flow and enjoy the benefits of more economical court operations. Greater centralization of court organization, one goal of unification, would mean fuller exchange of information about cases. This outcome might have adverse implications for juveniles, who currently may offend in several different jurisdictions and not be considered recidivists. This is because the different juvenile court jurisdictions do not ordinarily exchange information about their juveniles with other courts. Confidentiality of court records is a major factor that discourages information exchanges. Court unification would encourage such information exchanges to create more efficient and economical court organization and operations and to heighten juvenile accountability.

Key Terms

Act to Regulate Treatment and Control of Dependent, Neglected, and Delinquent Children (250)
Jane Addams (249)
Adversarial systems (258)
Beyond a reasonable doubt (260)
Cesare Beccaria (250)
Charles Loring Brace (249)
Child savers (249)
Court unification (267)
Due process courts (257)

Illinois Juvenile Court Act (248)
New York Children's Aid Society (249)
New York House of Refuge (248)
Police prosecutors (261)
Preponderance of the evidence (260)
Society for the Prevention of Pauperism (248)
Standard of proof (260)
Traditional courts (257)

Questions for Review

1. What formal provisions existed during the 1800s that related to juveniles and their conduct, before the invention of juvenile courts? Give an example.

2. What was the New York House of Refuge? When was it created and what were some of its manifest goals? Was it successful at achieving its goals? Why or why not? Explain.

3. Who were child savers? What were their aims? How did they assist in the bureaucratization of juvenile courts? Give some examples.

4. What was Hull House? In what respect was it a community-based agency?

5. Did the Truancy Act in Colorado in 1899 provide for the establishment of a new juvenile court? What did this act accomplish? How did this event influence certain status offenders and the way they were treated?

6. What were some of the major provisions of the Illinois Juvenile Court Act of 1899? How were juvenile delinquents defined?

7. What were some of the punish-

ments prescribed for dependent and neglected children under the Illinois Juvenile Court Act of 1899?

8. Briefly explain the difference between the terms *gemeinschaft* and *gesellschaft*. How do these terms relate to the way juvenile offenders were originally treated in the small communities and villages of the American colonies?

9. Discuss the movement from *gemeinschaft* to *gesellschaft*. Compare this movement with the accompanying changes in social relations and modifications in how juveniles were eventually defined or conceptualized.

10. What was the basis for the closed and arbitrary nature of juvenile courts prior to the 1960s? What are some of the events that have changed these courts and the arbitrariness of juvenile judges?

11. What are two significant landmark juvenile cases that did much to vest juveniles with specific constitutional rights? Describe briefly the rights conveyed and some of the changes these cases have caused in juvenile court operations.

12. Compare and contrast *due process courts* with *traditional courts*.

13. What is the adversarial system of American justice? What significant events have occurred that have yielded an adversarial juvenile justice system? In what respects are adversarial systems advantageous for juveniles? In what respects are adversarial systems disadvantageous and even harmful to juveniles?

14. Are public defenders available for juvenile offenders in various jurisdictions? Do all juveniles seek the representation of counsel when they appear in juvenile court? What evidence can you cite here that is relevant?

15. Describe some of the research that has focused upon greater prosecutorial involvement in juvenile court action. What, if anything, have these studies shown that would lead you to believe that juvenile courts have changed the way juveniles are processed? What evidence can you cite that little, if anything, has changed in certain jurisdictions relating to juvenile processing in these courts?

16. How has the standard of proof changed in juvenile proceedings? What was the early standard of proof? What is the current standard of proof? What seems to be the factor that determines when the latter standard of proof is exercised in any juvenile's case?

17. Who are police prosecutors? How might these police prosecutors experience a conflict of interest in prosecuting juveniles?

18. How are defense attorneys for juveniles considered their advocates? In what respect is a defense counsel for a juvenile defendant harmful? Explain.

19. Compare the severity or harshness of penalties juvenile judges impose on those juveniles who have attorneys compared with those who do not have them. Compare this situation with the

way criminal court judges might tend to treat criminals who plead guilty through plea bargaining or who might be convicted through a criminal trial. What are the similarities in the two situations?

20. What is meant by court unification? How is court unification beneficial to court operations and organization generally?
21. How is court unification potentially threatening to juvenile recidivists? Explain.

Suggested Readings

HOROWITZ, ROBERT M, and HOWARD A. DAVIDSON (EDS.) (1984). *Legal Rights of Children*. Colorado Springs, CO: Shepard's/McGraw-Hill.

KRISBERG, BARRY (1988). *The Juvenile Court: Reclaiming the Vision*. San Francisco: National Council on Crime and Delinquency.

METCHIK, B. (1987). *Recommending Juvenile Offenders for Pretrial Release*. New York: New York City Criminal Justice Agency.

REED, DAVID (1983). *Needed: Serious Solutions for Serious Juvenile Crime*. Chicago: Chicago Law Enforcement Study Group.

SINGER, SIMON I. (1985). *Relocating Juvenile Crime: The Shift from Juvenile to Criminal Justice*. Albany, NY: Nelson A. Rockefeller Institute of Government, State University of New York.

CHAPTER 9

The Adjudicatory Process: Dispositional Alternatives

Introduction

An important task performed by prosecutors and others at an early stage of the juvenile justice system is to select for prosecution those cases involving the most serious offenders. Prosecutors must make assessments of probable case outcomes, weighing factors such as the dangerousness of certain youths and the probable effectiveness of various kinds of intervention that might be used in their control and management. Forecasts of dangerousness and risk are useful for anticipating the appropriate programs and interventions, and for making the proper recommendations to juvenile court judges for sanctions. Some of the fairly recent measures of risk assessment and dangerousness predictors will be described. The effectiveness of these measures will also be examined in light of prosecutorial and judicial decision making. Finally, an overview of judicial sentencing options will be presented. Each of these options will receive detailed coverage in later chapters.

276

The Nature of the Offense

In 1987, an estimated 1,145,000 delinquency cases were disposed of in the juvenile justice system. This amounts to about 44 delinquency cases per 1,000 juveniles. Only 230,000 of these cases involved some detention between the time of referral to court intake and disposition. About 30 percent of all final delinquency adjudications resulted in either nonsecure or secure detention (Snyder et al., 1990:5–6). Serious older juvenile offenders are more likely to have their cases transferred to criminal courts for processing, depending upon the jurisdiction (Fagan and Deschenes, 1990; Grisso et al., 1988). About 11,000 delinquency cases were transferred to criminal courts in 1987 (Snyder et al., 1990:6).

At least one study highlights a disturbing finding about transferred youths, however. An examination of juvenile courts in Boston, Detroit, Newark, and Phoenix during the period 1981–1984 disclosed that, for 201 youths transferred from the jurisdiction of juvenile courts to criminal courts, no strong determinants of the judicial transfer decision were identifiable (Fagan and Deschenes, 1990). Fagan and Deschenes (1990) suggest that the absence of uniform criteria for juvenile transfers is, by itself, an important finding, since it means that largely informal criteria and vague statutory language used to guide judges and prosecutors in making transfer decisions or recommendations are highly subjective and may invite inequities. Thus, we are reminded that decisions about youths at various stages of the juvenile justice process are not fixed and perfectly objective, but rather, they are often diffuse and subjective. This underscores the importance of examining any existing criteria that may be relevant in affecting a youth's life chances in the system.

Those youthful offenders who remain in juvenile courts for disposition are subject to the relatively limited range of penalties these courts can impose, from warnings or reprimands to secure detention. Delinquent acts involving physical harm to others or the threat of physical harm are considered violent offenses, in contrast to the larger category of property offenses, which encompass vehicular theft, petty larceny, and burglary. Intake officers perform the initial screening function by sending on only the more serious offenders or those who in the opinion of the intake officers should have their cases adjudicated by juvenile judges.

Juvenile court prosecutors screen those cases further by deciding which cases have the most prosecutive merit. Prosecutors are influenced by numerous factors in deciding whether to prosecute juveniles formally. Age, offense seriousness, and previous record often determine whether prosecutors move forward with cases or divert them to informal arbitration through alternative dispute resolution (Hughes and Schneider, 1989; National College of Juvenile and Family Law, 1989). Despite the potential for recidivism, over 80 percent of the juvenile cases referred to juvenile courts annually are disposed of informally, without formal adjudication by juvenile court judges (McCarthy, 1987b, 1989; Stewart et al., 1986).

An integral feature of many diversion programs is the willingness of juveniles to compensate victims for their monetary losses through a program of restitution (Bazemore, 1989). Juries comprised of a youth's peers may impose restitution as a condition of diversion, and satisfactory completion of such a diversion program will likely avoid the scars of a formal delinquency adjudication (Ervin and Schneider, 1990; Galaway and Hudson, 1990; Seyfrit *et al.*, 1987). Juvenile courts continue to view their roles as largely rehabilitative, and judges seek to assist youths in avoiding any negative consequences of secure detention (Farnworth *et al.*, 1988; Watkins, 1987). Various interventions are believed beneficial to juveniles in lieu of formal adjudicatory actions in juvenile courts (National College of Juvenile and Family Law, 1989). However, some evidence suggests that interventions involving intensive supervision of youthful offenders may not be particularly effective at reducing their rates of recidivism (Minor and Elrod, 1990).

Consideration is also given to whether juveniles are suffering from any psychiatric disorders, such as depression or anxiety, or whether they are drug/alcohol dependent (Meyers *et al.*, 1990; Shichor and Bartollas, 1990). It is not unusual to observe severe psychiatric disorders among juvenile murderers (Malmquist, 1990). Private detention facilities are often used to house youths suffering from various psychological ailments, whereas public facilities accommodate more traditional youthful offenders, or those who have more prior offenses, who are on probation, or who have had their probation revoked frequently (Shichor and Bartollas, 1990).

In many jurisdictions, secure confinement is a last resort of judges in dealing with serious juvenile offenders (Pennell *et al.*, 1990). Nevertheless, growing rates of violence among juveniles, especially for offenses such as first-degree sexual assault, aggravated robbery, and homicide, and the increasing influence of the "get tough" movement in juvenile courts, are causing juvenile judges to adopt more punitive stances in their juvenile sentencing practices (Minnesota Criminal Justice Analysis Center, 1989). Thus, the nature of the offenses alleged, together with inculpatory evidence against youths charged, weighs heavily in favor of moving certain more chronic offenders into the system toward formal adjudication. The rise of youth gangs in large U.S. cities, together with greater involvement in illicit drug trafficking, has done much to place more youths at risk in possible detention in secure facilities (Spergel, 1990; Taylor, 1989).

First Offender or Prior Offender?

Whether juveniles are first offenders or have prior juvenile records is crucial to many prosecutorial decisions. The overwhelming tendency among prosecutors is to divert petty first offenders to some conditional program. Many diversionary programs involve restitution or victim compensation in some form. Contracts are arranged between youths and their victims, whereby youths reimburse victims, either partially or completely, for their financial

Contemporary community reintegration programs for juveniles stress group therapy and counseling, where youths may acquire better self-definitions and become more productive when they subsequently re-enter society. (© Bob Daemmrich/Stock Boston)

losses. These programs often involve mediators who are responsible for securing agreements between juvenile offenders and their victims. Known as alternative dispute resolution, these mediation programs are believed to be fairly widespread and effective (Hughes and Schneider, 1989). Several diversionary programs will be described in Chapter 11.

Evidence suggests that prior offenders, even chronic and violent offenders, stand a good chance of receiving some nondetention sanction if they are eventually adjudicated as delinquent (Dobbert, 1987). However, chronic juvenile offenders also stand a greater chance of pursuing criminal careers as adults than do first offenders (Greenwood, 1986c). Currently, no uniform policies exist among jurisdictions about how chronic offenders should be identified. Because of poor record-keeping and the lack of interjurisdictional record-sharing, many youthful offenders are repeatedly diverted from formal juvenile court processing, despite their chronic recidivism. Some jurisdictions measure whether formal action against juveniles should be taken on the basis of the number of times they have been arrested. After four arrests, youths in some jurisdictions may have petitions filed against them as delinquents.

Investigations of hidden delinquency disclose that many juveniles who commit offenses are never arrested for them (Miller and Gold, 1984). Even those who are frequently arrested may be subject to the same types of dispositions as in their previous arrests. Thus, as in musical chairs, those who receive probation or diversion for earlier offenses in certain jurisdictions are likely to receive probation or diversion for their latest offenses (Thornberry and Christenson, 1984). Yet other researchers find some escalation in sentencing severity for chronic offenders processed by juvenile courts (Henretta et al., 1986).

Despite the relatively greater seriousness of violent offenses compared with property offenses, juvenile property offenders account for the majority of petitioned juveniles annually in most juvenile courts by a margin of almost 3 to 1 (Snyder et al., 1990:14). Substantial numbers of status offenders continue to be processed by the juvenile justice system as well. Thus, it is unclear who is being targeted by "get tough" policies nationwide during the 1980s and 1990s. Ideally, only the most serious, chronic, and violent juveniles should be targeted for the harshest juvenile court penalties. However, an overwhelming majority of long-term detainees in public and private secure facilities are property offenders, again by a substantial margin of 2 to 1 (Flanagan and Maguire, 1990:564).

One implication of this finding is that those most likely to be targeted for juvenile court action are chronic property offenders. They are considered the most troublesome in several respects. They clog juvenile court dockets again and again, and they are usually slow to abandon their pattern of delinquent conduct. They cost taxpayers considerable money. Comparatively fewer juveniles are violent offenders. Often, however, these violent offenders are placed in residential facilities for individual or group therapy or given psychiatric examinations and treatment. In Tennessee, for example, a 13-year-old boy plotted the murder of his 11-year-old sister for several months. One morning in 1986, he took his mother's .38 caliber revolver and shot his sister point-blank in the face, killing her. He propped her up in her bed to make the deed look like suicide. He forged a suicide note. Later, he was confronted by overwhelming incriminating evidence and confessed. He was placed in a psychiatric facility, where he was held for observation and treatment for several years. During his time spent in this facility, he openly boasted to others about his sister's murder. Further, he frequently used a video-game pistol to "shoot" other patients in the dayroom of the mental hospital. He is scheduled for release in 1994, the year he reaches the age of majority and the juvenile court loses jurisdictional control over him. Several hospital attendants believe he will kill as an adult. There is little or nothing that the system can do to keep him from reentering society.

The strong rehabilitative and reintegrative principles upon which the juvenile courts have operated for most of the twentieth century continue to influence the way violent juvenile offenders are treated. For instance, Fagan (1990) has described various reintegrative programs designed especially for violent juvenile offenders (**Violent Juvenile Offender Programs** or **VJO Programs**) that provide several positive interventions and treatments. Instead of long-term incarceration in secure detention, many violent juvenile offenders are placed in community-based secure facilities, where they remain for short periods before being reintegrated into their communities. Transitional residential programs include sustained intensive supervision as youths are gradually given freedoms and responsibilities (Fagan, 1990:238–239).

The VJO Program described by Fagan (1990:239) is based upon a theoretical model integrating strain, control, and learning theories. Four program dimensions include:

1. *Social networking:* the strengthening of personal bonds (attitudes, commitment, and beliefs) through positive experiences with family members, schools, the workplace, and nondelinquent peers.
2. *Provision of opportunities for youths:* the strengthening of social bonds (attachment and involvement) through achievement and successful participation in school, workplace, and family activities.
3. *Social learning:* the process by which personal and social bonds are strengthened and reinforced. Strategies include rewards and sanctions for attainment of goals or for contingent behaviors.
4. *Goal-oriented behaviors:* the linking of specific behaviors to each client's needs and abilities, including problem behaviors and special intervention needs (e.g., substance abuse treatment or psychotherapy) (Fagan, 1990:240).

Generally, Fagan reports that violent juvenile offenders who participate in these programs seem less inclined to recidivate. He believes that "carefully implemented and well-managed intervention programs," those that involve "early reintegration activities preceding release from secure care and intensive supervision in the community, with emphasis on gradual reentry and development of social skills to avoid criminal behavior" do much to "avert the abrupt return to criminality after release from the program" of these youths. Those youths exposed to more conventional and longer secure detention and treatment appear to recidivate at greater rates and to persist in their delinquent behaviors (Fagan, 1990:258).

It is difficult to formulate specific guidelines about how violent juvenile offenders ought to be handled in their juvenile court processing. Currently, competing philosophies of rehabilitation and "just deserts" recommend polarities in treatments, ranging from total diversion to total detention. According to the Minnesota Criminal Justice Analysis Center (1989), if courts or legislatures move to punish and incarcerate serious juvenile offenders, we can expect to see a substantial increase in the need for additional secure facilities. It is doubtful that the services provided by these facilities will be effective at reducing recidivism among these types of serious offenders. However, if the traditional treatment and rehabilitation approach of juvenile courts is used, there are strong indications that such treatments are equally ineffective.

Certain objective criteria might be applied to decision making at various points throughout the juvenile justice system. These criteria are prevalent in most state criminal codes and describe an assortment of conditions or circumstances that are more or less influential regarding juvenile offender dispositions, regardless of their seriousness. These objective criteria are called *aggravating* and *mitigating circumstances.*

Aggravating and Mitigating Circumstances

Playing an important role in determining how far any particular juvenile moves into the juvenile justice system are various *aggravating* and *mitigating circumstances* accompanying his or her acts. In the early stages of intake and prosecutorial decision making, aggravating and mitigating circumstances are often considered informally, and much depends upon the amount of detail furnished by police officers about the delinquent acts. **Aggravating circumstances** *are usually those actions on the part of juveniles that tend to intensify the seriousness of their acts.* Accordingly, where aggravating circumstances exist, one's subsequent punishment might be intensified. At the other end of the spectrum are **mitigating circumstances,** or *those factors that might weigh in the juvenile's favor. These circumstances might lessen the seriousness of the act as well as the severity of punishment imposed by juvenile judges.* Lists of aggravating and mitigating circumstances follow.

Aggravating circumstances applicable both to juveniles and adults include

1. *Death or serious bodily injury to one or more victims.* The most serious juvenile offenders are those who cause death or serious bodily injury to their victims. Homicide and aggravated assault are those offenses that most directly involve death or serious physical harm to others, although it is possible to inflict serious bodily injury or deep emotional scars through armed robbery and even some property crimes, including burglary. When death or serious bodily injury occurs as the result of delinquent acts, this weighs heavily against offenders as a strong aggravating circumstance. However, as we have seen in some jurisdictions, even death to victims may be insufficient to warrant committal of juveniles to secure detention. Instead, they may be hospitalized and treated for mental illness or psychological problems. The harshest option available to juvenile judges is direct commitment to secure detention, such as an industrial school or reform school.

One judicial consideration is whether the youth contemplated the act and its consequences in advance. Was the bodily injury or death premeditated or accidental and unintentional? Some authorities argue that if one or more deaths follow armed robbery or any other serious crime, then these deaths were premeditated to the extent that the offenders knew the risks they were taking and the potential for death or serious bodily injury to their victims. Nevertheless, judges must determine for themselves whether the youthful offenders calculated the consequences. This consideration would cause some offenders to receive treatment rather than incarcerative punishment. Some studies of juvenile murderers disclose, for example, that homicidal adoles-

BOX 9.1

Juvenile Highlights

How much difference can a year make? If you ask Richard Wershe, Jr., of Detroit, Michigan, it can mean the difference between freedom at age 21 and life imprisonment without parole. Richard, known as "White Boy Rick" by his black associates in Detroit, was arrested by FBI and DEA officials in May, 1987, and charged with possessing eight kilos of cocaine valued at about $5 million. Wershe, 18 years of age at the time, was tried in federal court. Wershe's father contended that he and his son had been working with federal drug enforcement agents in an undercover capacity when Wershe was apprehended. DEA officials denied that Wershe had been working for them. When he was convicted, in February, 1988, the judge sentenced him to a mandatory penalty of life in prison without parole. The federal judge who sentenced him, Judge William Hathaway, said that Wershe was worse than a mass murderer as far as his court was concerned.

Had Wershe been tried in juvenile court on the same charges, the maximum sentence he could have received was long-term detention in a juvenile facility until the age of his majority, or 21. Of course, he could have been transferred to the jurisdiction of criminal courts through a waiver action.

Justice is at times peculiar in its administration. At about the same time in another state, a man was given three years' probation for the murder of another man. In Knoxville, Tennessee, Steve Douglas Palmer, a 33-year-old, was sentenced to three years' probation for shooting another man, Kenneth Johnson, 35, twice in the head. Originally, first-degree murder charges were filed against Palmer, but these charges were subsequently reduced to involuntary manslaughter. Which of these crimes is more serious? How should the justice administered in each case be evaluated?

(Portions adapted from Associated Press, "City Gets Victory: Dealer, 18, Given Life Term," *Knoxville News-Sentinel*, February 21, 1988, p. A10; Staff, "Man Given Probation Term in Death," *Knoxville News-Sentinel*, December 17, 1987, p. A19.)

cents are also likely to have criminally violent family members, to participate in gangs, to abuse alcohol and drugs, to suffer severe educational difficulties including mental retardation, to have perceptual deficiencies, and to perform badly on intellectual, perceptual, and achievement tests (Busch *et al.*, 1990; Ewing, 1990). With these social and psychological antecedents, many youths appear disadvantaged at the outset by extralegal factors. Judges may consider these environmental and psychological factors in determining whether particularly serious offenders should receive enhanced sentences or more lenient treatment alternatives.

2. *An offense committed while the offender is awaiting resolution of other delinquency charges.* Are juveniles awaiting an intake hearing after being arrested for previous offenses? Many juveniles commit new delinquent acts between the time they are arrested for other offenses and the date of their intake hearing. These offenders are probably good candidates for temporary detention in secure holding facilities until their cases can be heard by intake officers and delinquency petitions can be filed. Recommendations from intake officers will likely include information about the new charges filed against them. This is an aggravating circumstance that might serve to intensify the harshness and severity of punishments imposed later by juvenile judges.

3. *An offense committed while the offender is on probation, parole, or work release.* Offenders with prior adjudications who are currently serving their sentences may reoffend during these conditional periods. Usually, a condition of diversionary and probationary programs is that youths refrain from further delinquent activity. Thus, they may be in violation of a program condition. Probation, parole, and work release program violations are separate offenses that are accompanied by harsher penalties. In effect, these are incidents of **contempt of court,** since they involve violations of direct court-ordered conditional activities. The probation, parole, or work release conditional programs have usually been granted to certain offenders because they have been deemed trustworthy by officials. Therefore, violations of the court's trust are especially serious, and it becomes less likely that these juveniles will be extended such privileges in the future. But again, jurisdictional variations in this regard suggest that some juveniles continue to receive the same types of punishments imposed in previous adjudications (Thornberry and Christenson, 1984).

4. *Previous offenses for which the offender has been punished.* Possessing a prior record is a strong indicator of one's chronicity and potential for future offending behavior. Juvenile judges may be less inclined to be lenient in sentencing those with prior records, especially where serious delinquent acts have been committed. Incarcerative punishments are imposed frequently by these judges, although as we have seen, property offenders are incarcerated more frequently than violent juvenile offenders by a margin of at least 2 to 1. Because the juvenile justice system continues to endorse rehabilitation as one of its chief aims, it is disturbing when recidivists reappear before judges facing new charges. This suggests that previous treatments and probationary programs have been less effective than anticipated, or have even been completely ineffective. Harsher handling of these offenders is indicated in future sentencing decisions.

5. *Leadership in the commission of a delinquent act involving two or more offenders.* Especially in gang-related activities, playing a leadership role is an

aggravating circumstance. Are certain youths gang leaders? Do they incite others to commit delinquent acts? Gang leaders are often targeted for the harshest punishments, since they are most visible to their peers and serve as examples of how the system deals with juvenile offenders. Those playing minor roles in gang-related activity might be treated more leniently by judges.

6. *A violent offense involving more than one victim.* As the number of victims increases as the result of any delinquent conduct, the potential for physical harm and death rapidly escalates. Robberies of convenience stores and other places where there are large numbers of customers are likely to involve multiple victims. The number of victims or potential victims aggravates the initial delinquent conduct, whatever it might be.

7. *Extreme cruelty during the commission of the offense.* Maiming victims or torturing them during the commission of delinquent acts is considered extreme cruelty and worthy of enhanced punishments by juvenile judges. The murder of Gregg Smart, a 24-year-old salesman from Derry, New Hampshire, in May, 1990, is indicative of such extreme cruelty that might be considered as an aggravating circumstance. Smart had married Pam Wojas, a college girlfriend, in May, 1989. While he took on the responsibilities of married life and attempted to provide for his wife and family, his wife rapidly became disenchanted with the boredom of her new life. She yearned for the rock and roll life of the younger set and sought the companionship of teenagers, including 16-year-old William Flynn, who became her secret lover. Later, Flynn conspired with two other teenagers to kill Gregg Smart. According to subsequent trial testimony, Smart begged for his life while being held by one of Flynn's teenaged associates. Flynn shot Smart in the head with a .38 caliber revolver. Pam Smart and her lover, Flynn, were arrested later and charged with first-degree murder. Flynn was originally scheduled to be tried as an adult in criminal court. Flynn's act would be considered especially serious and aggravated in the subsequent trial, since extreme cruelty was inflicted on Gregg Smart before he was killed, and there was a possibility that Flynn could be sentenced to death if convicted. But at trial's end in 1991, Pamela Smart stood convicted of being an accomplice to first-degree murder, and she was given a mandatory sentence of life imprisonment without parole. Flynn on the other hand was sentenced to twenty-eight years under a plea bargain agreement. His accomplices received similar sentences.

8. *Use of a dangerous weapon in the commission of the offense, with high risk to human life.* The second and third leading causes of death among juveniles under age 21 are homicides and suicides, and most of these events include the use of firearms (University of Hawaii at Manoa, 1990). The rise in the number of youth gangs in the United States, together with a rise in drug trafficking among youths, suggests a new level of juvenile violence emerging (Hagedorn, 1988; Spergel, 1990). Using firearms to commit delinquent acts greatly increases the potential harm to victims. Thus, possessing dangerous weapons, such as knives, firearms, or other instruments, will likely enhance the severity

of the sentence judges might impose in adjudicatory proceedings. Many states currently have mandatory "flat time" associated with using firearms during the commission of felonies. For example, felony offenders who use firearms and are subsequently apprehended and convicted stand a good chance of receiving an additional two years beyond the sentences imposed by judges. These are mandatory two-year incarcerative terms that cannot be reduced through parole or the accumulation of "good time" credits. For juveniles, the use of dangerous weapons is considered an aggravating circumstance. While mandatory penalties do not accompany firearms use by youths, their sentences will likely be harsher where firearms are involved compared with the sentences meted out to youths who commit the same offenses but without the use of firearms.

Mitigating circumstances include the following:

1. *No serious bodily injury resulting from the offense.* Petty property offenders who do not endanger lives or injure others may have their sentences mitigated as a result. Interestingly, however, property offenders account for a majority of long-term juvenile detainees in industrial schools or secure juvenile facilities.

2. *No attempt to inflict serious bodily injury on anyone.* Those juveniles who commit theft or burglary usually wish to avoid confrontations with their victims. While some juveniles prepare for such contingencies and therefore pose bodily threats to others, most youthful offenders committing such acts run away from the crime scene if discovered. This is evidence of their desire to avoid inflicting serious bodily harm on their victims.

3. *Duress or extreme provocation.* A compelling defense used in criminal court cases is that offenders were under duress at the time they committed their crimes. They may have been forced to act in certain ways by others. When Patricia Hearst was kidnapped by the Symbionese Liberation Army (SLA) during the 1970s, she was later rescued by the FBI and other law enforcement personnel. She claimed that her captors forced her at gunpoint to participate in bank robberies to raise funds for the SLA movement, despite photographs taken of her at the time showing her brandishing a weapon in a bank lobby. Although she alleged duress from her captors, she was nevertheless convicted later of bank robbery charges. Under certain circumstances, youths may plead that they were coerced or were acting under duress when committing delinquent acts in concert with others. Gang membership and gang violence may be precipitated to a degree because of duress. Youths may join gangs for self-protection and to avoid being assaulted by other gang members. Juvenile court judges must decide whether duress actually existed or whether the youths acted voluntarily. Also, if youths were provoked by others into fighting, their illegal behaviors might be mitigated by this finding by the court.

4. *Circumstances that justify the conduct.* Any circumstance that might serve to justify one's conduct can be a mitigating factor. If youths act to protect themselves or others, then judges may find these circumstances strong enough to justify whatever conduct was exhibited. Youths may intervene in a spousal assault, in an effort to protect one spouse from killing or seriously injuring the other spouse. Later, one or both spouses may bring assault charges against these youths. Judges would probably agree that their intervention was justified, since they believed one spouse to be in danger from the actions of the other spouse.

This particular mitigating factor usually refers to some act of necessity, such as breaking and entering to prevent a neighbor's house from burning. An automobile might be stolen, but later it might be found that an emergency existed requiring that the participating youths bring a family member or friend to the hospital for treatment. These factors are most often subjectively determined and are raised by families, defense attorneys, or the youths themselves at the time they are adjudicated. Intake officers may make their own observations and recommendations about these circumstances and pass them along to prosecutors and judges. This particular mitigating factor has been written in such diffuse language that it is subject to broad interpretation by judges.

5. *Mental incapacitation or physical condition that significantly reduced the offender's culpability in the offense.* This particular factor specifies conditions that relate to drug or alcohol dependencies or to mental retardation or mental illness. If youths are suffering from some form of mental illness or are retarded, or if they are alcohol- or drug-dependent, this may limit their capacity to understand and comply with the law.

6. *Cooperation with authorities in apprehending other participants, or making restitution to the victims for losses they suffered.* Those youths who assist police in apprehending others involved in delinquent acts are credited with these positive deeds. Also, juveniles who make restitution to victims or compensate them in part or in whole for their financial losses stand a good chance of having their cases mitigated through such restitution and good works.

7. *No previous record of delinquent activity.* First offender juveniles, particular those under age 16, are especially targeted for the most lenient treatment. These youths are frequently diverted from the system at the point of intake. Even first offender youths who have committed violent acts are often given a second chance through participation in a diversion program (McCarthy, 1989).

These lists of aggravating and mitigating circumstances are not exhaustive. Other factors may exist that impact upon the judicial decision. At each stage of the juvenile justice process, interested officials want to know with some certainty whether certain offenders will recidivate if treated leniently. No one knows for sure whether certain offenders will be more likely to recidivate than others, although certain factors appear to be correlated closely with recidivism. We will examine several attempts to assess a juvenile's dangerousness and risk to the community. Such assessments are crucial in many jurisdictions in influencing prosecutorial and judicial decision making.

Juvenile Risk Assessments and Predictions of Dangerousness

This section examines several methods whereby assessments may be made of youths in terms of their risk to communities, their **dangerousness** to themselves and others, and their diverse needs. **Risk assessment** is an element of a classification system and traditionally means the process of determining the probability that an individual will repeat unlawful or destructive behavior (Baird, 1985:34). **Risk prediction** takes several forms, including the prediction of violent behavior, predictions of new offenses (recidivism), and the prediction of technical program violations associated with probation and parole (Baird, 1985:34).

These attempts to forecast juvenile behaviors are important, because many actors in the juvenile justice system use these predictions or forecasts as the basis for their decision making. Intake officers who initially screen youthful offenders try to decide which offenders are most deserving of leniency and which should be moved further into the system for formal processing. Prosecutors want to know which juveniles are most receptive to diversion and most amenable to change. Thus, they can ensure that only the most serious and chronic offenders will be processed, while the remaining youths will have another chance to live reasonably normal lives in their communities without juvenile justice system supervision. And judges want to know which youths will likely reoffend if returned to their communities through probation or some other nonincarcerative option.

False Positives and False Negatives. There are at least two major dangers inherent in risk or dangerousness predictions. First, youths who are identified as likely recidivists may receive harsher treatment compared with those who are considered unlikely to reoffend. At the same time, many of those youths considered as good risks for probation or diversion may eventually turn out to be dangerous, although predictions of their future conduct gave assurances to the contrary. Second, those youths who receive harsher punishment and longer detention because they are believed to be dangerous may not, in fact, be dangerous. Thus, we risk *overpenalizing* those who will not be dangerous in the future, although our forecasts suggest they will be dangerous. We also risk *underpenalizing* those believed by our forecasts not to be dangerous, although a portion *will* eventually turn out to be dangerous and will kill or seriously injure others.

These two scenarios identify *false positives* and *false negatives*. **False positives** *are those persons predicted to be dangerous in the future but who turn out not to be dangerous.* **False negatives** *are those persons predicted not to be dangerous in the future but who turn out to be dangerous anyway.* False positives are those who are unduly punished because of our predictions, while false negatives are those who do not receive needed punishment or future supervision. For adult criminals, attempts to forecast criminal behaviors have led to recommendations for *selective incapacitation* in many jurisdictions. **Selective incapacitation** *involves incarcerating or detaining those persons believed to be likely recidivists on the basis of various behavioral and attitudinal criteria* (Greenwood, 1982; Van Dine *et al.*, 1977; Wolfgang *et al.*, 1972). The theory behind selective incapacitation is that if high-risk offenders can be targeted and controlled through long-term detention, then their circulation will be limited, as well as the potential crimes they might commit (Struckhoff, 1987:30).

Selective incapacitation is controversial (Gottfredson, 1984). Walker (1985) raises five general questions about the usefulness and desirability of selective incapacitation in dealing with offenders in general. They are

1. Can we correctly estimate the amount of crime reduction that will result?
2. Can we accurately identify chronic offenders and predict their future behavior?
3. Can we afford the monetary costs of implementing selective incapacitation should it involve massive construction of new detention centers?
4. Can we implement a policy of consistent selective incapacitation without violating constitutional rights?
5. What will the side effects be?

Basically, incapacitation is a strategy for crime control involving the physical isolation of offenders from their communities, usually through incarceration, to prevent them from committing future crimes (Visher, 1987:514). But Walker's questions are quite important, since there are some important implications of selective incapacitation for youthful offenders. The major harm is penalizing certain youths for acts they haven't yet committed. Can we legitimately punish anyone in the United States for suspected future criminality or delinquency? Whatever one's personal feelings in this regard, the answer is that such punishments *are* imposed each time parole boards deny parole requests or probation recommendations are rejected in favor of incarceration.

Visher (1987:514−515) describes two types of incapacitation—collective and selective. Under **collective incapacitation,** crime reduction would be accomplished through traditional offense-based sentencing and incarcerative policies, such as mandatory minimum sentences. Under **selective incapacitation,** those offenders predicted to pose the greatest risk of future crimes would become prime candidates for incarceration and for longer prison sentences (Visher, 1987:515). A major problem throughout both the criminal justice system and the juvenile justice system is that no universally acceptable implementation policies have been adopted in most jurisdictions supporting the use of such incapacitation strategies.

The quality of risk assessment devices is such that at present we cannot depend on them as absolutely perfect indicators of future conduct. Baird (1985:34) says that some of the problems associated with scales that purportedly predict risk are that they are too new to have generated much data concerning their accuracy, and that many scales used to forecast delinquency have been adapted from adult offender versions. Thus, they have questionable validity when applied to youthful offender aggregates. Also, follow-up periods have been relatively short, thus preventing researchers from validating the predictive utility of these scales over time. Despite the continuing controversy surrounding the application of risk prediction measures and the criticisms by some researchers that such predictions are either impossible or inappropriate, such predictions continue to be made (Fisher, 1984). Jesness (1987:156–157) suggests that while our predictive tools are not perfect, they are sufficiently accurate to be taken seriously and to be used in practice.

Generally, risk assessment measures are one of three types: (1) **anamnestic prediction devices;** (2) **actuarial prediction devices;** and (3) **clinical prediction devices.**

1. *Anamnestic Prediction Devices.* These types of devices use past sets of circumstances to predict future behaviors. If the current circumstances are similar to past circumstances, where previous offense behaviors were observed, then it is probable that youths will exhibit future offending.
2. *Actuarial Prediction Devices.* Actuarial prediction is an aggregate predictive tool. Those youthful offenders who are being considered for diversion, probation, or parole are compared with former offenders who have similar characteristics. Performances and records of previous conduct in view of diversion, probation, or parole decisions serve as the basis for profiling the high-risk recidivist. Certain youths may exhibit characteristics similar to previous juveniles who became recidivists. The expectation is that current youths will likely recidivate as well.
3. *Clinical Prediction Devices.* Clinical prediction involves professional assessments of diagnostic examinations and test results. The professional training of probation officers, prosecutors, and judges, as they experience working with youthful offenders directly, enables them to forecast probable behaviors of their present clients. Clinical prediction involves administration of psychological tools and personality assessment devices. Certain background and behavioral characteristics are assessed as well.

Common Elements of Risk Assessment Devices. Most risk assessment measures, both for adult and juvenile offenders, contain several common elements. Adapting these common elements to youthful offender scenarios, the following elements seem prevalent:

1. Age at first adjudication.
2. Prior criminal behavior (a combined measure of the number and severity of prior offenses).
3. Number of prior commitments to juvenile facilities.
4. Drug/chemical abuse.
5. Alcohol abuse.
6. Family relationships (parental control).
7. School problems.
8. Peer relationships.

For each of these elements, some evidence has been found to establish a definite association between them and a youth's recidivism potential. These associations are not always strong, but in an actuarial prediction sense, there is a basis for assuming that each of these elements has some causal value. For example, the earlier the age of first adjudication and/or contact with the juvenile justice system, the greater the risk of recidivism (Jesness, 1987:154). Poor school performance, family problems and a lack of parental control, drug and/or alcohol dependencies, prior commitments to juvenile facilities, and a prior history of juvenile offending are individually and collectively linked with recidivism.

The California Youth Authority includes the following variables and response weights as a means of assessing risk level:

1. *Age at first police contact:**
   9 = score 6 points
   10 = score 5 points
   11 = score 4 points
   12 = score 3 points
   13 = score 2 points
   14 = score 1 point
   15 = score 0 points
2. *Number of prior police contacts:*
   (score actual number)
3. *Aggression and/or purse snatching:*
   score "yes" = 1, "no" = 0
4. *Petty theft:*
   score "yes" = 1, "no" = 0
5. *Use of alcohol or glue:*
   score "yes" = 1, "no" = 0
6. *Usually three or more others involved in delinquent act:*
   score "yes" = 1, "no" = 0
7. *Family on welfare:*
   score "yes" = 1, "no" = 0
8. *Father main support in family:*
   score "yes" = 1, "no" = 0
9. *Intact family:*
   score "yes" = 1, "no" = 0
10. *Number of siblings:*
    3 = score 1 point
    4 = score 2 points
    5 + = score 3 points
11. *Father has criminal record:*
    score "yes" = 1, "no" = 0
12. *Mother has criminal record:*
    score "yes" = 1, "no" = 0
13. *Low family supervision:*
    score "yes" = 1, "no" = 0
14. *Mother rejects:*
    score "yes" = 1, "no" = 0
15. *Father rejects:*
    score "yes" = 1, "no" = 0
16. *Parents wanted youth committed:*
    score "yes" = 1, "no" = 0

* Adapted from the California Youth Authority, 1990.

17. *Verbal I.Q.:*
    equal to or less than 69 = 4
    70−79 = 3
    80−89 = 2
    90−99 = 1
    100+ = 0
18. *Negative school attitude:*
    score 0−3

19. *Grade level:*
    at grade level = 1
    1 year retarded = 2
    2 years retarded = 3
    3 years retarded = 4
    4 + years retarded = 5
20. *School disciplinary problems:*
    score "yes" = 1, "no" = 0

On the basis of the score obtained, youths might be assigned the following risk levels:

RISK LEVEL SCORE	DEGREE OF RISK
0−22	Low
21−31	Medium
32 +	High

Youths who receive scores of 0−22 are considered low risks, whereas those with scores of 32 or higher are considered high risks. California Youth Authority officials believe that while it is not absolutely certain that all youths with higher scores will be recidivists and all those with lower scores will be nonrecidivists, there does appear to be some indication that these categorizations are generally valid ones. Thus, these classifications might be used to segregate more serious offenders from less serious ones in secure detention facilities. Or such scores might be useful in forecasts of future performance in diversion or probationary programs.

A similar instrument has been devised for adult parolees and has been used by the U.S. Parole Commission in its early-release decision making relating to federal prisoners. Table 9.1 shows the **Salient Factor Score Index (SFS 81),** developed by Hoffman (1983).

When measures or indices such as these are examined critically, it is interesting to note how such important life-influencing decisions can be reduced to six or seven predictive criteria. In the case of the instrumentation devised by the California Youth Authority, decisions about youths made by this organization are supplemented with several other important classifying criteria, such as personality assessment tools, youth interviews, and professional impressions.

Assisting juvenile court judges in their decision making relating to sentencing juvenile offenders during adjudicatory proceedings are *predispositional reports* that are often filed by juvenile probation officers, especially in serious cases. **Predispositional reports** *contain background information about juveniles, the facts relating to their delinquent acts, and possibly probation officer recommendations for particular dispositions. They serve the function of helping judges make more informed sentencing decisions. They also serve as needs* assessment devices, helping probation officers and other juvenile authorities

TABLE 9.1   Hoffman's SFS 81 Salient Factor Score Index

The Federal Parole Board's Salient Factor Score Index

Register Number _____ Name _____

Item A: PRIOR CONVICTIONS/ADJUDICATIONS (ADULT OR JUVENILE) ....☐
None ....= 3
One...................................= 2
Two or three ....= 1
Four or more...........................= 0
Item B: PRIOR COMMITMENT(S) OF MORE THAN THIRTY DAYS (ADULT OR JUVENILE) ......☐
None ....= 2
One or two ....= 1
Three or more ....= 0
Item C: AGE AT CURRENT OFFENSE/PRIOR COMMITMENTS ....☐
Age at commencement of the current offense:
    26 years of age or more ....= 2***
    20-25 years of age....................= 1***
    19 years of age or less ....= 0
***EXCEPTIONS: If five or more prior commitments of
more than thirty days (adult or juvenile), place an "x" here
and score this item......................= 0
Item D: RECENT COMMITMENT FREE PERIOD (THREE YEARS) ....☐
No prior commitment of more than thirty days (adult or
juvenile) or released to the community from last such
commitment at least three years prior to the
commencement of the current offense............= 1
Otherwise.............................= 0
Item E: PROBATION/PAROLE/CONFINEMENT/ESCAPE STATUS VIOLATOR THIS TIME ....☐
Neither on probation, parole, confinement, or escape status
at the time of the current offense; nor committed as a
probation, parole, confinement, or escape status violator
this time..............................= 1
Otherwise.............................= 0
Item F: HEROIN/OPIATE DEPENDENCE......................☐
No history of heroin/opiate dependence...........= 1
Otherwise.............................= 0
    TOTAL SCORE ....☐
NOTE: For purposes of the Salient Factor Score, an instance of criminal behavior resulting in a judicial
        determination of guilt or an admission of guilt before a judicial body shall be treated as a
        conviction, even if a conviction is not formally entered.

Scores on the SFS 81 can range from 0 to 10 and receive the following interpretation:

Score Range	Parole Prognosis	Score Range	Parole Prognosis
0–3	Poor	5–7	Good
4–5	Fair	8–10	Very Good

to determine high-need areas for certain youths and to channel them to specific community-based organizations and agencies for particular treatments and services.

Not all juvenile courts require the preparation of predispositional reports. They take much time to prepare, and their diagnostic information is often limited, since juvenile justice system budgets in many jurisdictions are restricted. In many respects, these reports are comparable to **pre-sentence investigation reports,** or **PSIs,** filed by probation officers in criminal courts for various convicted adult offenders. Unfortunately, there is no consistent pattern regarding the use of such predispositional reports and their preparation among jurisdictions. These reports and their contents and functions will be examined in Chapter 11.

In recent years, various juvenile justice reforms have been implemented in many juvenile courts. Some of these reforms have been mandated by U.S. Supreme Court decisions extending the rights of juvenile offenders. Greater uniformity in handling and less disparity in sentencing are desirable outcomes in the aftermath of extensive informal juvenile processing that characterized the juvenile courts of previous decades (Blackmore *et al.,* 1988; Schneider and Schram, 1986). Nevertheless, there continues to exist a great deal of individualism among juvenile court judges in different jurisdictions with regard to how the various laws and decisions pertaining to juveniles should be interpreted (Farnworth *et al.,* 1988; Ito, 1984; Krisberg, 1988).

The Judicial Decision

In most jurisdictions, juvenile judges may exercise several options when deciding specific cases. They may adjudicate youths as delinquent and do no more, other than to record the event. If the juvenile appears again before the same judge, harsher sentencing measures may be taken. The judge might divert juveniles to community-based services or agencies for special treatment. Those youths with psychological problems or who are emotionally

Juvenile court judges may exercise many options when sentencing youthful offenders. Influencing their decision making are certain aggravating or mitigating circumstances as might be noted by the prosecutor or defense counsel. (©W Jim Pickerell/Stock Boston)

disturbed, are sex offenders, or have drug and/or alcohol dependencies may be targeted for special community treatments. Various conditions as punishments such as fines, restitution, or some form of community service may also be imposed by judges. The more drastic alternatives are varying degrees of custodial sentences—the placement of juveniles in foster homes, camp ranches, reform schools, or industrial schools. These nonsecure and secure forms of placement and/or detention are usually reserved for the most serious offenders. Below is a summary of judicial options. These will be explored in greater detail in subsequent chapters. For the present, one or more of the following eleven options may be exercised in any delinquency adjudication:

1. A stern reprimand may be given.
2. A verbal warning may be issued.
3. An order may be given to make restitution to victims.
4. An order may be given to pay a fine.
5. An order may be given to perform some public service.
6. An order may be given to submit to the supervisory control of some community-based corrections agency on a probationary basis.
7. A sentence may be imposed, but the sentence may be suspended for a fixed term of probation.
8. An order may be issued for the placement of the juvenile in a foster home.
9. An order may be issued for the placement of the juvenile in a residential center.
10. An order may be given to participate under supervision at a camp ranch or special school (either nonsecure or secure detention).
11. An order may be given to be confined in a secure facility for a specified period.

The verbal warnings and reprimands are classified as **nominal punishments,** whereas making restitution to victims, payment of fines, performance of community service, community-supervised probation, and suspended sentences with conditional probationary alternatives are considered **conditional punishments.** Finally, placement in foster or group homes, in camp ranches or schools, or in secure facilities such as industrial schools, are considered **custodial punishments.**

As we have seen in earlier chapters, the juvenile court is becoming increasingly an adversarial adjudicatory proceeding. While not all juvenile offenders are defended by attorneys, many youths and their families exercise their right to due process and retain a defense attorney's services (Feeney, 1987; Feld, 1988b; Ito, 1984). This formalizes juvenile court dispositions and to some extent reduces the sentencing latitude a juvenile judge may exercise. In some jurisdictions, at least, sentences imposed by judges have been harsher in those instances where juveniles have been represented by attorneys. Of course, if the greater seriousness of the offense prompted the retention of an attorney initially, then this would explain the harsher sentence imposed. In any event, juvenile proceedings have become more formal in recent years compared with earlier traditional courts. With the increase in formality, the use of nominal reprimands has perhaps declined, since juvenile judges are less inclined to moralize in the presence of defense counsels.

Implications of the Judicial Decision for Juvenile Offenders

In recent years, a considerable amount of the authority of juvenile court judges has been undermined by various reforms, including the deinstitutionalization of status offenses and automatic transfers of certain youths to criminal courts for processing. The **New York Juvenile Offender Law (JO Law),** for example, mandates the transfer to criminal court of certain youths who commit particular types of crime (Singer and McDowall, 1988). However, it is doubtful whether such reforms have accomplished their desired objectives. Singer and McDowall (1988) report, for instance, that only 14 percent of all JO Law arrestees in 1983 actually received sentences of confinement as a result of their criminal court convictions. Further, the law seemed to have little or no effect on juvenile crime rates or on New York crime patterns generally. For these and other reasons, juvenile court judges throughout the United States appear to endorse the general continuation of juvenile court jurisdiction over most juvenile offenders, even some of the most serious ones.

Many juvenile judges have expressed the view that the juvenile justice system is superior to the criminal justice system in regard to the treatment of juveniles and the protection of public safety (Rubin, 1983). Rubin says that many judges do not consider either serious or repetitive minor juvenile offenders to be an overwhelming problem. They believe that juveniles should receive the rehabilitative protection that juvenile courts can provide. Finally, they reportedly stress the importance of relying on community-based services as the major means of meeting youths' needs. Although they do not rule out secure detention, they believe it should be reserved for only the most serious and persistent offenders.

Some judges believe that the "shock value" of exposing juveniles to the prison environment can be sufficient to scare them "straight" or into conforming modes of behavior. In some jurisdictions in Colorado, for instance, judges direct certain juveniles to participate in a program known as **SHAPE-UP,** an aversion program involving two visits to the Colorado State Penitentiary and discussions with some of the prisoners confined there (Berry, 1985). Despite this exposure to prison life for certain youths, recidivism rates do not seem to be any better among program participants than among those not exposed to the SHAPE-UP program.

The implications of judicial decision making for youthful offenders are several. Depending upon a judge's philosophical stance, some juveniles may receive more lenient treatment than others charged with the same offense (Hassenfeld and Cheung, 1985). There are obvious pressures exerted on

BOX 9.2

Juvenile Highlights

When should youths become accountable for their violent acts? In 1989, a 28-year-old white female jogger was running through New York's Central Park after dark when she was accosted by 30 black teenagers and brutally bound, gagged, beaten, raped repeatedly, and left for dead, naked and bleeding in a mud puddle. Miraculously, she survived her ordeal to testify in the trial of her attackers, although she had no memory of the night.

Three youths, Antron McCray, 16, Raymond Santana, 15, and Yusef Salaam, 16, were the first three defendants charged in the case, tried as adults under the New York Juvenile Offender Law. These youths were charged with attempted murder, rape, sexual abuse, assault, robbery, and riot. Although there were racial overtones at the trial, they were overshadowed by the grotesqueness and gruesomeness of the attack as vividly described in videotaped confessions made to police officers by each of the boys charged. "The tapes are so emotionally powerful that, on the basis of them alone, the prosecution is going to get a conviction," said Timothy Sullivan of *The American Lawyer*.

It was at first considered doubtful whether the jogger would testify. However, she later testified under the condition that she would remain anonymous before the public. Although she was in a coma for a lengthy period, her recovery, considered by doctors to be miraculous, left her suffering from post-traumatic amnesia. Prosecutors believed that much would depend upon whether the jury believed that the boys' confessions were coerced in any way or were made voluntarily. Subsequently, the boys were convicted of the crimes alleged.

(Portions adapted from Bruce Frankel, "Co-worker Could Barely Identify Battered Jogger," *USA Today*, July 12, 1990, p. 3A.)

---

judges from various sectors within communities. These pressures may encourage them to impose more severe sanctions on juvenile offenders, although some of these sectors continue to promote reintegrative and rehabilitative sanctions (Arthur, 1983; Conrad, 1983; Feld, 1987a). The recent influence of the "get tough" movement on juvenile judges is apparent (Treanor and Volenik, 1987). Juvenile codes are constantly being revised in favor of sanctions that hold youths increasingly accountable for their actions (Rossum *et al.*, 1987). Some evidence suggests that our changing conceptions of adolescence have helped to shift the perspectives of certain judges from viewing juveniles as societal victims in need of treatment to seeing them as responsible offenders deserving of punishment (McDermott and Laub, 1987).

Judges are seemingly caught in the middle of the punishment dilemma. If they impose sanctions considered by juveniles themselves to be too light, they may inadvertently cause youths to become cynical about the system and the meaningfulness of sanctions. Youths may push the system to its limits through chronic recidivism, knowing that the system will not act against them and restrain their movements through long-term detention until other, more lenient measures have been exhausted. Leniency may breed greater amounts of recidivism among those treated leniently by the juvenile justice system (McCarthy, 1989). But by placing juveniles in secure detention, some degree of "criminalization" may occur, in which juveniles are socialized by their peers and emerge as more hard-core delinquents than when they entered those facilities. Various voices within communities create a degree of role conflict for judges, as they seek to appease contrary or opposing interests. Furthermore, in some jurisdictions it is doubtful whether dramatic sentencing policy shifts make much of a difference in the rate of juvenile reoffending anyway (Schneider, 1984b).

Judicial decision making and sentencing decisions depend, in part, upon the availability of programs for juveniles in their communities. If diversion programs or extensive community-based services are nonexistent or limited, this fact limits sentencing options. Not all juvenile court jurisdictions have alternative dispute resolution mechanisms, for instance (National College of Juvenile and Family Law, 1989). Even where judges are inclined to favor secure detention of juvenile offenders, chronic overcrowding of secure juvenile facilities may prevent them from imposing incarcerative sanctions for all juveniles who merit them (Krisberg *et al.*, 1985b). In those communities with extensive community-based services and resources, there is a fear among the public and even among judges that some net-widening may occur, simply because of the availability and prevalence of such services (Blomberg, 1984; Pabon, 1985). Simultaneously, a heavy reliance upon community-based services by juvenile court judges means that more juveniles will remain free to move about in their communities. Thus, there is the continuing question of whether community residents are sufficiently insulated and protected from the more dangerous youthful offenders who are selected for community-based treatments rather than secure detention (Pabon, 1985).

Because of prevalent overcrowding in many existing juvenile detention facilities, and because there are disproportionate numbers of minority youths incarcerated in such places, some institutional abuses and scandals are apparently perpetuated rather than abolished by the current emphasis on "just deserts" (Breed and Krisberg, 1986). Furthermore, it may be that incarcerated youths experience greater difficulty readjusting to school environments and having relatively normal social experiences upon their release from secure detention (Sametz and Hamparian, 1986). Even those who participate in carefully regulated, intensively supervised programs, such as **VisionQuest,** continually exhibit high recidivism rates (Greenwood and Turner, 1987). (VisionQuest is discussed at length in Chapter 12.)

Thus, although there is extensive institutionalization of delinquent youths, there are questions about the effectiveness of such institutionalization for deterrence and delinquency control. Juvenile court judges will continue to exercise a high degree of individualized sentencing for youths in the traditional context of *parens patriae,* despite the influence of "due process" reforms in juvenile courts in recent years. A middle ground regarding the treatment of juvenile offenders has not been achieved as yet, in any particular jurisdiction. Therefore, the question of whether sentencing actions by juvenile court judges are either too lenient or too harsh cannot presently be evaluated accurately. The fact is, we still do not know whether it is better to emphasize rehabilitation or punishment in the application of juvenile sanctions.

Summary

Screening of juvenile offenders occurs at various stages of juvenile justice processing. Intake officers perform initial screening functions, apart from those functions performed by law enforcement officers that have to do with deciding which juveniles should be arrested. Prosecutors later screen cases further, by targeting only the most serious juvenile offenders for prosecution. Finally, juvenile court judges make final decisions about offender dispositions in adjudication proceedings. Consideration is given to whether offenders are first-timers, or whether they have prior records of delinquent activity. Chronic violent offenders are among the most serious delinquents processed by the system, although such offenders actually account for a small proportion of all juvenile arrests. However, long-term detainees in juvenile detention facilities are predominantly less serious property offenders with extensive histories of recidivism.

Judges consider aggravating and mitigating circumstances when sentencing offenders. Aggravating circumstances result in severer punishments; these circumstances include whether death or serious bodily injury was suffered by victims, whether offenders committed their offenses while on probation or parole, whether they have prior records, whether they played leadership roles in the delinquent activity, whether weapons were used to commit their acts, and whether extreme cruelty was demonstrated toward victims. Mitigating circumstances, or those factors that lessen punishments imposed, include cooperating with authorities to apprehend other delinquents, lack of a prior record of delinquent activity, mental incapacitation or retardation, drug/alcohol dependencies, and whether youths committed their acts while under duress. It is up to each judge to establish the weights these factors should receive in deciding a youth's sentence.

Attempts to forecast delinquent conduct have been made by using various risk assessment devices and dangerousness measures. While most of these measures have not been extensively validated, some researchers believe they are of value in forecasting delinquent behavior and ought to be used. The use of such instruments has led some researchers to believe that high-risk youths may be targeted for selective incapacitation, in which their behaviors are controlled through lengthy incarceration. However, other investigators believe such selective incapacitation is fundamentally unfair, and that it is inconsistent with constitutional guarantees and safeguards to punish persons for acts they have not, as yet, committed. Other problems of such measures include false positives and false negatives, or the identification of those who are predicted to be dangerous but turn out not to be dangerous, and those who are predicted not to be dangerous, but who turn out to be dangerous anyway. Common elements of such instrumentation include age at first adjudication, number of prior offenses, alcohol and drug abuse, unstable family environments, and poor school performance.

In some jurisdictions, juvenile probation officers prepare predispositional reports for the most serious offenders. These materials contain useful information which helps judges make informed sentencing decisions. No schemes are foolproof, however. Judges experience role conflict as they attempt to balance community interests, which favor due process and "just deserts," against other traditional sentiments that favor rehabilitation and reintegration. The range of sanctions available to juvenile judges includes nominal, conditional, and custodial punishments. Depending upon the particular treatment orientation of judges, different punishments imposed can have far-reaching effects on affected juveniles.

Key Terms

Actuarial prediction devices (290)
Aggravating circumstances (282)
Anamnestic prediction devices (290)
Clinical prediction devices (290)
Collective incapacitation (289)
Conditional punishments (295)
Contempt of court (284)
Custodial punishments (295)
Dangerousness (288)
False negatives (289)
False positives (289)
Mitigating circumstances (282)
New York Juvenile Offender Law
    (JO Law) (296)

Nominal punishments (295)
Predispositional reports (293)
Pre-sentence investigation reports
    (PSIs) (293)
Risk assessment (288)
Risk prediction (288)
Salient Factor Score Index (SFS 81)
    (293)
Selective incapacitation (289)
SFS 81 (293)
SHAPE-UP (296)
Violent Juvenile Offender Program
    (VJO Program) (280)
VisionQuest (298)

Questions for Review

1. At what stages of the juvenile justice process are screening functions performed? Describe how screening is performed at the stages you have identified.
2. How are first offenders treated, compared with those with prior records, in prosecutorial and judicial decision making?
3. What might lead you to suspect that the most serious juvenile offenders are not always punished fully by the juvenile justice system?

4. What is the Violent Juvenile Offender Program and what is it designed to do? What are some of its key dimensions? Is it effective? Discuss.

5. What are aggravating circumstances? At what stages of juvenile justice system proceedings are they considered? What are some examples of aggravating factors?

6. What are mitigating circumstances? Give five examples. How are mitigating factors used by juvenile judges in their sentencing of juveniles? How much subjectivity is there in considering any given factor as either mitigating or aggravating? Explain.

7. What are risk assessment instruments or predictors of dangerousness? Give two examples.

8. What are some common criteria associated with these measures? What relation do these criteria have to delinquent conduct? Explain.

9. Differentiate between false positives and false negatives. What relevance does each have for predicting dangerousness and controlling delinquent conduct?

How does each conceivably overpenalize and underpenalize juveniles? Explain.

10. Differentiate between collective and selective incapacitation. What are the goals of each? How does each type of incapacitation achieve its goals?

11. What are three types of prediction devices? Define each and give an example. Which types of measures do you feel are most valid and why?

12. What is a predispositional report? What functions does it serve? Do all juvenile court jurisdictions use predispositional reports?

13. What are three general categories of punishments that juvenile judges might impose on youthful offenders? Describe each type of punishment briefly, noting several alternatives in each of the three categories you have listed.

14. What is the basic nature of the role conflict experienced by juvenile judges in sentencing youthful offenders? Describe this conflict and how it has occurred in view of certain juvenile justice reforms.

Suggested Readings

BAZEMORE, S. GORDON (1989). *The Restitution Experience in Youth Employment.* Washington, DC: Office of Juvenile Justice and Delinquency Prevention.

FINCKENAUER, J. O. (1982). *Scared Straight: and the Panacea Phenomenon.* Englewood Cliffs, NJ: Prentice-Hall.

MYERS, MARTHA A., AND SUSETTE M. TALARICO (1987). *The Social Contexts of Criminal Sentencing.* New York: Springer-Verlag.

ROCKELL, BARBARA A. (1988). *The Investigation and Prosecution of Crimes Against Children in New York State.* Albany, NY: New York Office of Justice Systems Analysis.

SANDBERG, DAVID N. (ED.) (1988). *The Child Abuse–Delinquency Connection.* Lexington, MA: Lexington Books.

CHAPTER 10

The Legal Rights of Juveniles

Introduction

By now, it should be apparent that juveniles in the United States have been treated as a minority class in several ways other than age. Regarding their legal rights, youths have only recently been granted selected rights commensurate with those of adults. Currently, they are denied the full range of rights available to adults charged with crimes. Even evidentiary standards (e.g., admissibility of evidence, search and seizure guidelines, probable cause, confessions) applicable to adult criminals do not apply fully to juveniles charged with delinquent conduct. Felkenes (1988:397) astutely observes that "the list of adult [constitutional] guarantees not afforded to [juveniles] is more conspicuous [than the rights they have already been extended]."

Prior to the mid-1960s, almost every juvenile court in the nation made important, life-altering decisions affecting juveniles according to what the courts believed to be in the youths' best interests. These best interests were almost always subject to court definition and interpretation. This was and continues to be the fundamental doctrine of *parens patriae*. Since the mid-1960s, juveniles have achieved several significant legal milestones, including, but not limited to, the right to be represented by counsel, the right to cross-examine their accusers, and the right against self-incrimination. This chapter examines the contemporary range of legal rights extended to juveniles.

Several landmark cases will be described in which significant rights have been established through U.S. Supreme Court decisions. Some of the more important implications of these decisions for juvenile offenders will be discussed.

Juvenile rights are best understood in the context of the traditional *parens patriae* doctrine and the way in which it has gradually been transformed by social and institutional changes. As one consequence of greater urbanization, Americans have enjoyed the advantages of greater vocational and geographical mobility. The educational level of the population has gradually increased. Today, citizens are more sophisticated than in the past, and their legal understanding and interest have greatly improved. Past chapters have described the gradual shift from *gemeinschaft* to *gesellschaft* in community life and some of the changes this shift has brought about in social relationships. The dominant *parens patriae* doctrine remained unchallenged for decades; however, a growing wave of appeals of juvenile court decisions to the U.S. Supreme Court has resulted in an extensive erosion of this doctrine.

The *parens patriae* doctrine was part of a larger policy framework in which the U.S. Supreme Court continually expressed its reluctance to intervene in juvenile court matters. This larger framework was the "hands off" policy relating to juvenile court issues as well as to the operation of correctional institutions. The "hands off" doctrine originated in the nineteenth century and prevailed until it was effectively nullified by several landmark U.S. Supreme Court cases in the 1940s and 1960s. As juvenile offenders have acquired greater numbers of constitutional rights, they have also acquired greater accountability for their actions, including the risk of the death penalty for capital offenses.

The issue of capital punishment for juveniles will also be treated briefly. This is especially important since the U.S. Supreme Court determined in 1988 that the death penalty may not be administered to any juvenile who was under the age of 16 at the time a capital crime was committed (*Thompson* v. *Oklahoma,* 1988) and upheld the executions of two other youths aged 16 and 17 respectively the following year. The application of the death penalty to juveniles is likely to generate large numbers of appeals in future years.

Original Juvenile Jurisdiction: Parens Patriae

Until the mid-1960s, juvenile courts had considerable latitude in regulating the affairs of minors. This freedom to act in a child's behalf was rooted in the largely unchallenged doctrine of *parens patriae*. When juveniles were apprehended by police officers for alleged infractions of the law, sooner or later they were turned over to juvenile authorities or taken to a "juvenile hall" for further processing. They were not advised of their right to legal representation, to have an attorney present during any interrogation, or to remain silent. They could be questioned by police at length, without parental notification or legal contact. In short, they had little, if any, protection against violations of adult constitutional rights on the part of law enforcement officers and others. They had no access to due process because of their status as juveniles. "Due process" was not given priority largely because of the benevolent approach taken by most juvenile judges. Thus, they made decisions for juveniles that were believed to be in their best interests.

When juveniles were required to appear before juvenile court judges, they seldom had an opportunity to rebut evidence presented against them or to test the reliability of witnesses through cross-examination. This was rationalized at the time by asserting that juveniles did not understand the law and had to have it interpreted for them by others, principally juvenile court judges. Subsequent investigations of the knowledge youths have of their rights seems to confirm this assertion (Lawrence, 1984). Sanborn (1990) has characterized these early adjudicatory proceedings as "informal clinic-like sessions." Despite the many recent reforms in juvenile court procedures, Sanborn believes that unfairness continues to be prevalent throughout contemporary adjudicatory hearings.

Prosecutors were seldom present in juvenile proceedings, since the proceedings were nonadversarial, and juvenile court judges handled most cases informally, independently, and subjectively, depending upon the youth's needs and the seriousness of the offense. If judges decided that secure detention would best serve the interests of justice and the welfare of the juvenile, then the youth would be placed for an indeterminate period in a secure detention facility that was similar in many ways to adult prisons or jails. These decisions were seldom questioned or challenged.

A primary reason for this silent acceptance of juvenile court judges' decisions was that the U.S. Supreme Court had repeatedly demonstrated its reluctance to intervene in juvenile matters or to question decisions made by juvenile judges. In the case of *In re Gault* (discussed shortly), Justice Stewart typified the traditional orientation of former Supreme Courts by declaring:

> The Court today uses an obscure Arizona case as a vehicle to impose upon thousands of juvenile courts throughout the Nation restrictions that the Constitution made applicable to adversary criminal trials. I believe the Court's decision is *wholly unsound* [emphasis mine] as a matter of constitutional law, and sadly unwise as a matter of judicial policy. . . . The inflexible restrictions that the Constitution so wisely made applicable to adversary criminal trials have no inevitable place in the proceedings of those public social agencies known as juvenile or family courts (387 U.S. at 78–79).

The *parens patriae* doctrine first received formal recognition in U.S. courts in 1839 in the case of **Ex parte Crouse** (1839). A youth, Mary Ann Crouse, was committed to the Philadelphia House of Refuge by her mother, because, as her mother alleged, Mary Ann was "incorrigible." Mary Ann's father opposed the commitment to the House of Refuge, and he filed a petition for her release. The petition cited the facts that she had been denied a jury trial and that the state action to incarcerate her was unconstitutional. The courts denied his petition, arguing that Mary Ann was being confined in a school, not a prison, and that reform, not punishment, was the objective. Weisheit and Alexander (1988:56) believe that the *Crouse* case was the first to spell out the legal justification for applying the *parens patriae* principle to children in the United States.

Thus, juvenile courts or "public social agencies" were given almost complete autonomy and authority to act in a juvenile's behalf, taking whatever action was deemed necessary. Usually, the "action deemed necessary" was closely aligned with some form of rehabilitation or had rehabilitation as a primary objective. However, Weisheit and Alexander (1988:56–57) note that the original meaning of *parens patriae* was connected with the need to support or care for children, and not necessarily to rehabilitate or reform them. In some respects, this **"hands off" doctrine** was similar to the "hands off" policy of the U.S. Supreme Court in relation to adult corrections policies and practices. The high court elected not to intervene in correctional matters, since they believed that prison wardens and superintendents knew what was best for their inmates and could be trusted to act responsibly in their behalf. This was the *parens patriae* doctrine applied to state and federal prisoners and exercised by prison administrators.

The "hands off" stance of the U.S. Supreme Court toward corrections lasted from 1871 until 1941, exactly 70 years. In the case of **Ruffin** v. **Commonwealth** (1871), a Virginia judge declared that "prisoners have no more rights than slaves." Thus, during the next 70 years, prisoners were used as guinea pigs in various biological and chemical experiments, particularly in the testing of gases used on the front lines in Europe during World War I. Such tests of chemical agents on prisoners were conducted at the Michigan State Prison at Jackson. Some prisons mandated inmate sterilization, because it was believed that criminal behavior was hereditary. No committees for the protection of human subjects existed to protest this kind of inmate treatment. Additionally, prisoners were subject to extensive corporeal punishment. For example, the Arkansas State Prison Farm in Tucker, Arkansas, used the "Tucker Telephone" to torture nonconforming prisoners. Electrodes from an old crank-type telephone were connected to an inmate's testicles, penis, and toes, and shocks were administered that left many prisoners crippled for life. "Long-distance calls" were made on the Tucker Telephone for especially unruly prisoners. Inmates were not permitted mail privacy, visitation, or other privileges; they had absolutely no rights other than those dispensed or withheld by prison authorities.

The U.S. Supreme Court began to change this unfortunate situation in 1941 in the case of **Ex Parte Hull** (1941). This case involved attempts by prisoners to petition the courts to hear various grievances or complaints. Prison superintendents and staff would routinely trash these petitions, contending that they were improperly prepared and hence legally unacceptable. In the *Hull* decision, the Court held that no state or its officers could deprive inmates of their right to access the federal or state courts through their petitions. This decision opened the floodgates of prison reform, and in successive years, inmate rights expanded considerably.

In many respects, juveniles were like adult inmates in prisons. Youths had no legal standing and virtually no rights other than those extended by the courts. The right to trial by jury, a basic right provided any defendant who might be incarcerated for six months or more by a criminal court conviction, did not exist for juveniles unless juvenile court judges permitted such trials. Most juvenile court judges abhor jury trials for juveniles and refuse to permit them. Even today, juveniles do not have an absolute right to a trial by jury, with few exceptions through state statutes. Thus, juveniles may be deprived of their freedom for many years on the basis of a personal judicial decision.

Because of the informality of juvenile proceedings in most jurisdictions, there were frequent and obvious abuses of judicial discretion. These abuses occurred because of the absence of consistent guidelines whereby cases could be adjudicated. Juvenile probation officers might casually recommend to judges that particular juveniles "ought to do a few months" in an industrial school or other secure detention facility, and the judge might be persuaded to adjudicate these cases accordingly.

However, several forces were at work simultaneously during the 1950s and 1960s that would eventually have the conjoint consequence of making juvenile courts more accountable for specific adjudications of youthful offenders. One of these forces was increased parental and general public recognition of and concern about the liberal license taken by juvenile courts in administering the affairs of juveniles. The abuse of judicial discretion was becoming increasingly apparent and widely known. Additionally, there was a growing disenchantment with the ideal of rehabilitation, although this disenchantment was not directed solely at juvenile courts. Rogers and Mays (1987:383) note that "disaffection during the 1960s and 1970s with the

Some critics believe that the informality of juvenile court proceedings should be preserved, since this allows judges to make decisions about juveniles on a case-by-case basis. Other critics believe that these judges have too much discretion and that juvenile court proceedings should be more formal in accordance with the "due process" model. (© Gale Zucker/Stock Boston)

juvenile court was typical of the disenchantment then with many of society's institutions."

Feld (1988a) observes that the juvenile court as originally envisioned by progressives was procedurally informal, characterized by individualized, offender-oriented dispositional practices. However, the contemporary juvenile court departs markedly from this progressive ideal. Today, juvenile courts are increasingly criminalized, featuring an adversarial system and greater procedural formality. This formality effectively inhibits any individualized treatment these courts might contemplate, and it has increased the perfunctory nature of the sentencing of juveniles adjudicated as delinquent.

Sutton (1985) aptly describes the transformation of juvenile courts into more formal proceedings as part of the national trend toward bureaucratization and as an institutional compromise between law and social welfare. Bureaucracy stresses a fixed hierarchy of authority, task specialization, individualized spheres of competence, impersonal social relationships between organizational actors, and impartial enforcement of abstract rules. Thus, in the context of bureaucracy, decision making is routinized rather than arbitrary. Personalities and social characteristics are irrelevant.

Applied to juvenile court proceedings, juvenile court decision making becomes a function of the nature and seriousness of offenses committed and the factual delinquent history of juvenile defendants. Emotional considerations in bureaucratic structures are nonexistent. The bureaucratic approach would be that juveniles should be held to a high standard of accountability for their actions. Furthermore, an individualized, treatment-oriented sanctioning system would be inconsistent with bureaucracy and violative of its general principles of impartiality. This type of system for juvenile justice seems consistent with the sentiments of a large portion of U.S. citizens and their belief that juvenile courts should "get tough" with juvenile offenders (Springer, 1987).

The primary elements of *parens patriae* that have contributed to its persistence as a dominant philosophical perspective in the juvenile justice system are summarized as follows:

1. *Parens patriae* encourages informal handling of juvenile matters as opposed to more formal and criminalizing procedures.
2. *Parens patriae* vests juvenile courts with absolute authority to decide what is best for youthful offenders (e.g., support services and other forms of care).
3. *Parens patriae* strongly encourages benevolent and rehabilitative treatments to assist youths in overcoming their personal and social problems.
4. *Parens patriae* avoids the adverse labeling effects that formal court proceedings might create.
5. *Parens patriae* means state control over juvenile life chances.

A major change from *parens patriae* state-based interests to a "due process" juvenile justice model means an abandonment of most of these elements. Decision making relative to youthful offenders is increasingly rationalized,

TABLE 10.1   Chronological Summary of Major Events in Juvenile Justice[a]

Year	Event
1791	Bill of Rights passed by U.S. Congress
1825	New York House of Refuge established
1839	*Ex parte Crouse*, established right of juvenile court to intervene in parent–child matters
1841	John Augustus initiates probation in Boston
1853	New York Children's Aid Society established
1855	Death penalty imposed on 10-year-old in Louisiana in a poorly documented case; earliest juvenile execution was Thomas Graunger, 16-year-old, for sodomizing a horse and cow in 1642
1866	Massachusetts statute passed giving juvenile court power to intervene and take custody where parents are unfit
1868	Fourteenth Amendment passed by U.S. Congress, establishing right to due process and equal protection under the law
1874	Massachusetts established first Children's Tribunal to deal with youthful offenders
1889	Indiana established children's guardians to have jurisdiction over neglected and dependent children
1889	Hull House established in Chicago by Jane Addams to assist unsupervised children of immigrant parents
1899	Compulsory School Act, Colorado; statutory regulation of truants
1899	Illinois Act to Regulate the Treatment and Control of Dependent, Neglected, and Delinquent Children; first juvenile court in United States established
1901	Juvenile court established in Denver, Colorado
1907	Separate juvenile court with original jurisdiction in juvenile matters established in Denver, Colorado
1912	Creation of U.S. Children's Bureau, charged with compiling statistical information about juvenile offenders; existed from 1912 to 1940
1918	Chicago slums studied by Shaw and McKay; delinquency related to urban environment and transitional neighborhoods
1938	Federal Juvenile Delinquency Act

and the principle of "just deserts" is operative. This means that less discretionary authority is manifested by juvenile judges, as they decide each case more on the basis of offense seriousness and prescribed punishments than according to individual factors or circumstances. Table 10.1 provides a general chronology of events relating to juvenile rights during the last 200 years.

During the mid-1960s and for the next twenty years, significant achievements were made in the area of juvenile rights. Although the *parens patriae* philosophy continues to be somewhat influential in juvenile proceedings, the U.S. Supreme Court has vested youths with certain constitutional rights. These rights do not encompass all of the rights extended to adults who are

TABLE 10.1 *continued*

Year	Event
1966	*Kent* v. *United States* case established juvenile's right to hearing before transfer to criminal court, right to assistance of counsel during police interrogations, right to reports and records relating to transfer decision, and right to know reasons given by judge for transfer
1967	*In re Gault* case established juvenile's right to an attorney, right to notice of charges, right to confront and cross-examine witnesses, and right against self-incrimination
1970	*In re Winship* case established juvenile's right to criminal court standard of "beyond a reasonable doubt" where loss of freedom is a possible penalty
1971	*McKeiver* v. *Pennsylvania* case established that juvenile's right to a trial by jury is not absolute
1974	Juvenile Justice and Delinquency Prevention Act
1974	Office of Juvenile Justice and Delinquency Prevention established; instrumental in promoting deinstitutionalization of status offenses
1975	*Breed* v. *Jones* case established that double jeopardy exists if juvenile is adjudicated as delinquent in juvenile court and tried for same offense later in criminal court; prohibits double jeopardy
1982	*Eddings* v. *Oklahoma* case established that death penalty applied to juveniles was not "cruel and unusual punishment" per se
1984	*Schall* v. *Martin* case established the constitutionality of the preventive detention of juveniles
1985	*New Jersey* v. *T.L.O.* case established lesser standard of search and seizure on school property; searches and seizures permissible without probable cause or warrant
1988	*Thompson* v. *Oklahoma* case established that death penalty applied to juveniles convicted of murder who were under age 16 at time of murder is cruel and unusual punishment
1989	*Stanford* v. *Kentucky* and *Wilkins* v. *Missouri* cases established that death penalty is not cruel and unusual punishment applied to juveniles convicted of murder who were aged 16 or 17 at the time the murder was committed

[a]Compiled by author

charged with crimes. But those rights conveyed to juveniles thus far have had far-reaching implications for the way juveniles are processed. In the following section, several landmark cases involving juvenile rights will be described.

Landmark Cases in Juvenile Justice

Regardless of the causes, several significant changes have been made in the juvenile justice system and the ways youths are processed in it in recent decades. In this section, we will examine several important rights bestowed upon juveniles by the U.S. Supreme Court during the past several decades.

Describing these rights will make clear those rights juveniles did not have until the landmark cases associated with them were concluded. Then, a comparison will be made of juvenile rights and the rights that may be exercised by adults charged with crimes. It will be seen that, despite sweeping juvenile reforms and major legal gains, there remain substantial differences between the current rights of juveniles and adults when charged with offenses.

Currently, juvenile courts are largely punishment-centered, with the justice and "just deserts" models dominating court decision making. The interests of youths are secondary, while community interests are seemingly served by juvenile court actions. Juveniles are being given greater responsibility for their actions, and they are increasingly being held accountable for their wrongdoing.

Each of the cases that follow represents attempts by juveniles to secure rights ordinarily extended to adults. Given these cases, juveniles have fared well with the U.S. Supreme Court in past years. However, there are still major differences between the juvenile justice system and the criminal justice system and in the ways offenders of different ages are processed.

Kent v. *United States*. Regarded as the first major juvenile rights case and as a prelude to further juvenile court reforms, **Kent v. United States** (1966) established the universal precedents of (1) requiring waiver hearings before juveniles can be transferred to the jurisdiction of a criminal court (except for legislative automatic waivers as discussed in this and other chapters, although reverse waiver hearings must be conducted at the juvenile's request), and (2) giving juveniles the right to consult with counsel prior to and during such hearings.

The facts in the case are that in 1959, Morris A. Kent, Jr., a 14-year-old in the District of Columbia, was apprehended as a result of several housebreakings and attempted purse snatchings. He was placed on probation in the custody of his mother. In 1961, an intruder entered the apartment of a woman, took her wallet, and raped her. Fingerprints at the crime scene were later identified as those of Morris Kent, who had been fingerprinted when apprehended for housebreaking in 1959. On September 5, 1961, Kent, 16, was taken into custody by police and interrogated for seven hours. He admitted the offense and volunteered information about other housebreakings, robberies, and rapes. Although the records are unclear about when Kent's mother became aware of Kent's arrest, she did obtain counsel for Kent shortly after 2:00 P.M. the following day. She and her attorney conferred with the Social Service Director of the Juvenile Court and learned there was a possibility that Kent would be waived to criminal court. Kent's attorney advised the Director of his intention to oppose the waiver.

Kent was detained in a receiving home for one week. During that period, there was no arraignment and no determination by a judicial officer of probable cause for Kent's arrest. His attorney filed a motion with the juvenile court opposing the waiver, as well as a request to inspect records relating to Kent's previous offenses. Also, a psychiatric examination of Kent was

BOX 10.1

Juvenile Highlights

Should juveniles be held in adult jails and lockups? This practice is against the law in most jurisdictions, although detention of juveniles for brief periods of time in jails to establish their identities and ages is considered acceptable. The deinstitutionalization of status offenders from the jurisdiction of juvenile courts has done much to prevent the entry of low-risk noncriminal juveniles into the juvenile justice system. At the same time, youthful offenders who continue to be within the jurisdictional control of juvenile courts are often channeled to adult jails or lockups, simply because there are inadequate or non-existent facilities in which to detain them. Also, it is not always easy to determine that certain youthful offenders are legally juveniles.

It has been estimated that nearly 500,000 juvenile offenders are held in adult jails and lockups annually, either as pretrial detainees or on a postadjudication basis. Disturbingly, about 20 percent of these are status offenders who have not violated any criminal laws. Furthermore, about 10 percent of these are thirteen years of age or younger. Juveniles detained in adult jails exhibit suicide rates that are eight times greater than juveniles who are held in juvenile detention centers.

In recent years, numerous lawsuits have been filed by or on behalf of children wrongfully detained in adult detention facilities. One case of significance has seemingly established a legal precedent, at least in the federal district encompassing Iowa. In the case of *Hendrickson* v. *Griggs* (No. 2C 84-3012, N.D. Iowa, April, 1987), the sheriff of Webster County, Iowa, as well as the governor of the state and other parties, were sued in a class action. It was alleged that a previous ban on contact between juveniles and adult inmates had not been enforced. Other allegations were also made pertaining to the conditions under which juveniles were confined. The federal district court found for the plaintiffs, and it ordered the Iowa jail to comply by segregating juveniles from adult inmates. Thus, the issue was not whether juveniles could be detained in such facilities, since this issue had already been decided in the case of *Schall* v. *Martin* (1984). Subsequent legal challenges may attack issues of the classification of juvenile offenders, medical screening and health services, psychological screening, visitation and counsel in the courts, and environmental issues.

(Some material adapted from Michael J. Dale, "Detaining Juveniles in Adult Jails and Lockups: An Analysis of Rights and Liabilities," *American Jails* (1988) 2:46–50.)

arranged by Kent's attorney. Kent's attorney argued that because his client was "a victim of severe psychopathology," it would be in Kent's best interests to remain within juvenile court jurisdiction, where he could receive adequate treatment in a hospital and would be a suitable subject for rehabilitation.

In a manner typical of juvenile court judges at the time, the judge failed to rule on any of Kent's attorney's motions. He also failed to confer with Kent's attorney or his parents. In a somewhat arrogant decision, the juvenile judge declared that "after full investigation, I do hereby waive" jurisdiction of Kent and direct that he be "held for trial for [the alleged] offenses under the regular procedure of the U.S. District Court for the District of Columbia." He offered no findings, nor did he give any reason for the waiver or mention Kent's attorney's motions. Kent was later found guilty by a federal jury of six counts of housebreaking, although the jury found him "not guilty by reason of insanity" on the rape charge. Because of District of Columbia law, it was mandatory that Kent be transferred to a mental institution until such time as his sanity was restored. On each of the housebreaking counts, Kent's sentence was 5 to 15 years, or a total of 30 to 90 years in prison. His mental institution commitment would be counted as time served against the 30- to 90-year sentence.

Kent's conviction was reversed by a vote of 5–4. This is significant, because it signified a subtle shift in Supreme Court sentiment relating to juvenile rights. The majority held that Kent's rights to due process and to the effective assistance of counsel were violated when he was denied a formal hearing on the waiver and his attorney's motions were ignored. It is also significant that the Supreme Court stressed the phrase "critically important" when referring to the absence of counsel and waiver hearing respectively. In adult cases, critical stages are those that relate to the defendant's potential loss of freedoms (i.e., incarceration). Because of the *Kent* decision, waiver hearings are now critical stages. Regarding the effective assistance of counsel, this was also regarded by the Court as a "critically important" decision. They observed that "the right to representation by counsel is not a formality. It is not a grudging gesture to a ritualistic requirement. It is of the essence of justice. . . . Appointment of counsel without affording an opportunity for a hearing on a 'critically important' decision is tantamount to a denial of counsel" (383 U.S. at 561).

In re Gault. The case of **In re Gault** (1967) is perhaps the most noteworthy of all landmark juvenile rights cases. Certainly it is considered the most ambitious. In a 7–2 vote, the U.S. Supreme Court articulated the following rights for all juveniles: (1) *the right to a notice of charges;* (2) *the right to counsel;* (3) *the right to confront and cross-examine witnesses;* and (4) *the right to invoke the privilege against self-incrimination.* The petitioner, Gault, requested the Court to rule favorably on two additional rights sought: (1) *the right to a transcript of the proceedings* and (2) *the right to appellate review. The Court elected* **not** *to rule on either of these rights.*

The facts in the case are that Gerald Francis Gault, a 15-year-old, and a friend, Ronald Lewis, were taken into custody by the Sheriff of Gila County,

Arizona, in the morning of June 8, 1964. At the time, Gault was on probation as the result of "being in the company of another" who had stolen a wallet from a woman's purse, a judgment entered on February 25, 1964. A verbal complaint had been filed by a neighbor of Gault, a Mrs. Cook, alleging that Gault had called her and made lewd and indecent remarks. (With some levity, the Supreme Court said that "it will suffice for purposes of this opinion to say that the remarks or questions put to her were of the irritatingly offensive, adolescent, sex variety" [387 U.S. at 4].) When Gault was picked up, his mother and father were at work. Indeed, they did not learn where their son was until much later that evening. Gault was being held at the Children's Detention Home.

Gault's parents proceeded to the Home. Officer Flagg, the deputy probation officer and superintendent of the Children's Detention Home where Gault was being detained, advised Gault's parents that a hearing would be held in Juvenile Court at 3:00 P.M. the following day. Flagg filed a petition with the court on the hearing day, June 9. This petition was entirely formal, stating only that "said minor is under the age of 18 years, and is in need of the protection of this Honorable Court; [and that] said minor is a delinquent minor." It asked for a hearing and an order regarding the "care and custody of said minor." No factual basis was provided for the petition, and Gault's parents were not provided with a copy of it in advance of the hearing.

On June 9, the hearing was held, with only Gault, his mother and older brother, Probation Officers Flagg and Henderson, and the juvenile judge present. The original complainant, Mrs. Cook, was not there. No one was sworn at the hearing, no transcript was made of it, and no memorandum of the substance of the proceedings was prepared. The testimony consisted largely of allegations by Officer Flagg about Gault's behavior and prior juvenile record. A subsequent hearing was scheduled for June 15. On June 15, another hearing was held, with all the same people present, plus Ronald Lewis and his father, and Gerald's father. What actually transpired is unknown, although there are conflicting recollections from all parties who were there. Mrs. Gault asked why Mrs. Cook was not present. Judge McGhee said "she didn't have to be present at that hearing." Furthermore, the judge did not speak to Mrs. Cook or communicate with her at any time. Flagg spoke with her once by telephone on June 9. Officially, the charge against Gault was "lewd telephone calls." When the hearing was concluded, the judge committed Gault as a juvenile delinquent to the Arizona State Industrial School "for a period of his minority" (until age 21). (Parenthetically, if an adult had made an obscene telephone call, he would have received a $50 fine and no more than 60 days in jail. In Gerald Gault's case, he was facing nearly six years in a juvenile prison for the same offense.)

A *habeas corpus* hearing was held on August 17, and Judge McGhee was cross-examined regarding his actions. After hemming and hawing, the judge declared that Gault had "disturbed the peace" and was "habitually involved in immoral matters." Regarding the judge's reference to Gault's alleged "habitual immorality," the judge made vague references to an incident two years earlier when Gault had been accused of stealing someone's baseball glove and had lied to police by denying that he had taken it. The judge also recalled, again vaguely, that Gault had testified some months earlier about making "silly calls, or funny calls, or something like that."

After exhausting their appeals in Arizona state courts, the Gaults appealed to the U.S. Supreme Court. Needless to say, the Court was appalled that Gault's case had been handled in such a cavalier and unconstitutional manner. They reversed the Arizona Supreme Court, holding that Gault did, indeed, have the right to an attorney, the right to confront his accuser (Mrs. Cook) and to cross-examine her, the right against self-incrimination, and the right to have notice of the charges filed against him. Perhaps Justice Black summed up the juvenile court situation in the United States at that time when he said, "This holding strikes a well-nigh fatal blow to much that is *unique* [emphasis mine] about the juvenile courts in this Nation."

In re Winship. **In re Winship** (1970) was a less complex case than *Gault.* But it established an important precedent in juvenile courts relating to the *standard of proof* used in establishing defendant guilt. In this case the U.S. Supreme Court held that "beyond a reasonable doubt," a standard ordinarily used in adult criminal courts, was henceforth to be used by juvenile court judges and others in establishing a youth's delinquency. Formerly, the standard used had been the civil standard of "preponderance of the evidence."

The facts in the *Winship* case are that Samuel Winship was a 12-year-old charged with larceny in New York City. He purportedly entered a locker and stole $112 from a woman's purse. Under Section 712 of the New York Family Court Act, a juvenile delinquent was defined as "a person over seven and less than sixteen years of age who does any act, which, if done by an adult, would constitute a crime." Interestingly, the juvenile judge in the case acknowledged that the proof to be presented by the prosecution might be insufficient to establish Winship's guilt beyond a reasonable doubt, although he did indicate that the New York Family Court Act provided that "any determination at the conclusion of [an adjudicatory hearing] that a [juvenile] did an act or acts must be based on a preponderance of the evidence" standard (397 U.S. at 360). Winship was adjudicated as a delinquent and ordered to a training school for 18 months, subject to annual extensions of his commitment until his eighteenth birthday. Appeals to New York courts were unsuccessful.

The U.S. Supreme Court heard Winship's case and, in a 6–3 vote, reversed the New York Family Court ruling. A statement by Justice Brennan succinctly states the case for the "beyond a reasonable doubt" standard: "In sum, the constitutional safeguard of proof beyond a reasonable doubt is as much required during the adjudicatory stage of a delinquency proceeding as are those constitutional safeguards applied in *Gault*—notice of charges, right to counsel, the rights of confrontation and examination, and the privilege of self-incrimination. We therefore hold, in agreement with Chief Justice Fuld in dissent in the Court of Appeals, that where a 12-year-old child is charged with an act of stealing which renders him liable to confinement for as long as six years, then, as a matter of due process . . . the case against him must be proved beyond a reasonable doubt" (397 U.S. at 368).

McKeiver v. *Pennsylvania.* The **McKeiver** v. **Pennsylvania** (1971) case was important because in it the U.S. Supreme Court held that juveniles are not entitled to a jury trial as a matter of right. (It should be noted that as of 1990, 12 states had legislatively mandated jury trials for juveniles in juvenile courts if they requested such trials, depending upon the seriousness of the offense[s] alleged.)

The facts are that in May, 1968, Joseph McKeiver, age 16, was charged with robbery, larceny, and receiving stolen goods. Although he was represented by counsel at his adjudicatory hearing and requested a trial by jury to ascertain his guilt or innocence, Judge Theodore S. Gutowicz of the Court of Common Pleas, Family Division, Juvenile Branch, of Philadelphia, Pennsylvania, denied the request. McKeiver was subsequently adjudicated delinquent. On subsequent appeal to the U.S. Supreme Court, McKeiver's adjudication was upheld. Again, the remarks of one of the justices are of interest. Justice Blackmun stated: "If the formalities of the criminal adjudicative process are to be superimposed upon the juvenile court system, there is little need for its separate existence. Perhaps that ultimate disillusionment will come one day, but for the moment, we are disinclined to give impetus to it" (403 U.S. at 551).

Throughout the opinion delivered in the McKeiver case, it is apparent that the Supreme Court was sensitive to the problems associated with juvenile court procedure. Since criminal courts were already bogged down with formalities and lengthy protocol that frequently led to excessive court delays, it was not unreasonable for the Court to rule against perpetuating such formalities in juvenile courts. But we must recognize that in this instance, the Court merely ruled that it is not the constitutional right of juveniles to have a jury trial upon their request. This proclamation had no effect on individual states that wished to enact or preserve such a method of adjudicating juveniles as delinquent or not delinquent. In fact, about a fourth of the states today do have legislative provisions for jury trials in juvenile courts.

Breed v. *Jones.* The case of **Breed** v. **Jones** (1975) raised the significant constitutional issue of "double jeopardy." The U.S. Supreme Court concluded that after a juvenile has been adjudicated as delinquent on specific charges, those same charges may not be alleged against that juvenile subsequently in criminal courts through transfers or waivers.

The facts of the case are that on February 8, 1971, in Los Angeles, California, Gary Steven Jones, 17 years old, was armed with a deadly weapon and allegedly committed robbery. Jones was subsequently apprehended and an adjudicatory hearing was held on March 1. A petition was filed against Jones. After testimony was taken from Jones and witnesses, the Juvenile Court found that the allegations in the petition were true and sustained the petition. A dispositional hearing date was set for March 15. At that time, Jones was declared "not . . . amenable to the care, treatment and training program available through the facilities of the juvenile court" under a

TABLE 10.2   Comparison of Juvenile and Adult Rights Relating to Delinquency and Crime[a]

Right	Adults	Juveniles
1. "Beyond a reasonable doubt" standard used in court	Yes	Yes
2. Right against double jeopardy	Yes	Yes
3. Right to assistance of counsel	Yes	Yes
4. Right to notice of charges	Yes	Yes
5. Right to a transcript of court proceedings	Yes	No
6. Right against self-incrimination	Yes	Yes
7. Right to trial by jury	Yes	No in most states
8. Right to defense counsel in court proceedings	Yes	Yes
9. Right to due process	Yes	No*
10. Right to bail	Yes	No, with exceptions
11. Right to cross-examine witnesses	Yes	Yes
12. Right to confrontation	Yes	Yes
13. Standards relating to searches and seizures:		
a. "Probable cause" and warrants required for searches and seizures by the police	Yes, with exceptions	Yes, with exceptions
b. "Reasonable suspicion" required for searches and seizures without warrant	No	Yes
14. Right to hearing prior to transfer to criminal court or to a reverse waiver hearing in states with automatic transfer provisions	NA	Yes
15. Right to a speedy trial	Yes	No
16. Right to *habeas corpus* relief in correctional settings	Yes	No, with exceptions

California statute. Jones was then transferred by judicial waiver to a California criminal court where he could be tried as an adult. In a later criminal trial, Jones was convicted of robbery and committed for an indeterminate period to the California Youth Authority. The California Supreme Court upheld the conviction.

When Jones appealed the decision in 1971, the U.S. Supreme Court reversed the robbery conviction. Chief Justice Warren Burger delivered the Court opinion: "We hold that the prosecution of [Jones] in Superior Court,

TABLE 10.2   *(continued)*

Right	Adults	Juveniles
17. Right to rehabilitation	No	No
18. Criminal evidentiary standards	Yes	Yes
19. Right to hearing for parole or probation revocation	Yes	No
20. Bifurcated trial, death penalty cases	Yes	Yes
21. Right to discovery	Yes	Limited
22. Fingerprinting, photographing at booking	Yes	No, with exceptions
23. Right to appeal	Yes	Limited
24. Waivers of rights:		
a. Adults	Knowingly, intelligently	
b. Juveniles		Totality of circumstances
25. Right to hearing for parole or probation revocation	Yes	No, with exceptions
26. "Equal protection" clause of 14th Amendment applicable	Yes	No, with exceptions
27. Right to court-appointed attorney if indigent	Yes	No, with exceptions
28. Transcript required of criminal/ delinquency trial proceedings	Yes	No, with exceptions
29. Pretrial detention permitted	Yes	Yes
30. Plea bargaining allowed	Yes, with exceptions	No, with exceptions
31. Burden of proof borne by prosecution	Yes	No, with exceptions**
32. Public access to trials	Yes	Limited
33. Conviction/adjudication results in criminal record	Yes	No

---

ªCompiled by author.
*Minimal, not full, due process safeguards assured.
**Burden of proof is borne by prosecutor in 23 state juvenile courts, while the rest make no provision or mention of who bears the burden of proof.

after an adjudicatory proceeding in Juvenile Court, violated the Double Jeopardy Clause of the Fifth Amendment, as applied to the States through the Fourteenth Amendment." The Court ordered Jones' release outright or a remand to juvenile court for disposition. In a lengthy opinion, Justice Burger defined double jeopardy in this instance as (1) being adjudicated as delinquent on specific charges in a juvenile court, and (2) subsequently being tried and convicted on those same charges in criminal court. Within the context of "fundamental fairness," such action could not be tolerated.

Schall v. *Martin.* In the **Schall** v. **Martin** (1984) case, the U.S. Supreme Court issued juveniles a minor setback regarding the state's right to hold them in preventive detention pending a subsequent adjudication. The Court said that the preventive detention of juveniles by states is constitutional if judges perceive these youths to pose a danger to the community or an otherwise serious risk if released short of an adjudicatory hearing. This decision was significant, in part, because many experts advocated the separation of juveniles and adults in jails, those facilities most often used for preventive detention. Also, the preventive detention of adults was not ordinarily practiced at that time. (Since then, the preventive detention of adults who are deemed to pose societal risks has been upheld by the U.S. Supreme Court [*United States* v. *Salerno,* 1987].)

The facts of the case are that 14-year-old Gregory Martin was arrested at 11:30 P.M. on December 13, 1977 in New York City. He was charged with first-degree robbery, second-degree assault, and criminal possession of a weapon. Martin lied to police at the time, giving a false name and address. Between the time of his arrest and December 29 when a fact-finding hearing was held, Martin was detained (a total of 15 days). His detention was based largely on the false information he had supplied to police and the seriousness of the charges pending against him. Subsequently, he was adjudicated a delinquent and placed on two years' probation. Later, his attorney filed an appeal, contesting his preventive detention as violative of the Due Process Clause of the Fourteenth Amendment. The U.S. Supreme Court eventually heard the case and upheld the detention as constitutional.

Table 10.2 summarizes some of the major rights available to juveniles and compares these rights with selected rights enjoyed by adults in criminal proceedings.

Implications for Juveniles

Some of the major implications of greater juvenile court formalization for youths include: (1) more equitable treatment because of less sentencing disparity among juvenile judges; (2) greater certainty of punishment through the new justice orientation; (3) less informality in dispositions and less individualized rehabilitative treatments; (4) greater likelihood of acquiring a juvenile offender record, since procedures from intake through adjudication are increasingly codified; and (5) greater likelihood of being transferred to criminal courts through waivers, since the most serious cases will move forward more frequently to juvenile courts.

At present, all juvenile courts in the United States are civil courts. That is, those juveniles adjudicated as delinquent do not acquire criminal records as a result of these adjudications. Once youths reach the age of majority or adulthood, their juvenile records are forgotten or sealed. They begin a new slate as adults. This works to their advantage.

However, while juveniles remain within juvenile court jurisdiction, they are subject to conceivably harsher penalties as juveniles than might be the case if they were adults. For instance, the case of *Gault* reported earlier in this chapter saw a boy sentenced to nearly six years in a state industrial school for allegedly making an obscene telephone call. Adults would not be subject to such a heavy penalty. Currently, juvenile court judges have considerable power to control a juvenile's liberty. Even now in most jurisdictions, if juvenile court judges wish, they may sentence youths to long-term detention far beyond incarcerative terms normally imposed upon adults who have been convicted of similar offenses. This unfairness is a carry-over from the *parens patriae* years of juvenile courts.

We can also view juvenile court actions as comparatively more lenient than criminal courts. The very discretion that juvenile court judges may abuse against youthful offenders can also be used to administer favorable punishments. With certain exceptions as provided by state statutes and constitutional guarantees, juvenile court judges continue to exercise considerable latitude in their dispositional decision making relative to juvenile offenders.

However, the many juvenile justice reforms that have occurred during the 1970s and 1980s have caused some experts to see little difference between the way adults are processed by criminal courts and the way juveniles are processed by juvenile courts (Feld, 1984, 1988b). However, despite the increased criminalization of juvenile courts, there *are* significant differences that serve to differentiate criminal courts and criminal processing from the way youths are treated or processed by the juvenile justice system.

Perhaps the most important fact for juveniles is that juvenile court adjudications do not result in criminal records. These courts continue to exercise civil authority. Once juveniles reach adulthood, their juvenile records are routinely expunged and forgotten, with some exceptions. But having one's case adjudicated by a juvenile court operates to a youth's disadvantage in some respects. For instance, the rules governing the admissibility of evidence or testimony are relaxed considerably compared with the rules governing similar admissions in criminal courts. Thus, it is easier in juvenile courts to admit inculpatory evidence and testimony than in criminal courtrooms. Further, cases against juveniles do not need to be as convincing as cases against criminal defendants. Lower standards of proof are operative relative to search and seizure and the degree of probable cause required. Schoolchildren are particularly vulnerable in this regard, in view of **New Jersey** v. **T.L.O.** (1985), as described earlier in Table 10.1.

On the negative side, juveniles do not always receive jury trials if they request them. Less than a fourth of all states permit jury trials for juveniles by statute. In all other states, jury trials are available to juveniles only if judges permit them. In most cases, therefore, the judgment of the juvenile court is final, for all practical purposes. Appeals of decisions by juvenile court judges are relatively rare. Long-term sentences of detention may be imposed by juvenile court judges at will, without serious challenge. Current profiles of

BOX 10.2

Juvenile Highlights

Should juveniles be deprived of their rights to cruise city streets? Whether the behavior is observed in Fort Lauderdale, Florida, or in Palm Springs or Modesto, California, teenage cruising of city streets has been a common occurrence in American cities for decades. However, in recent years, cruising has reached epidemic proportions in some jurisdictions.

Youths who cruise city streets say that they drive up and down the streets, looking for dates. They see attractive teens cruising in other cars, pull alongside, exchange telephone numbers, and go home. Some teens openly drink from beer cans, play their radios and tapes loudly, and litter the city streets with trash as a part of their nightly cruising. Cruising in some cities has reached a stage where commercial traffic is regularly inhibited or obstructed by cruisers.

Some cities have struck back at cruisers and have attempted to re-strict their movements. In Hoffman Estates, Illinois, city officials joined six other communities and switched all traffic lights in their cities to red, thus effectively stopping all cruising traffic. Such bans have been implemented in other cities, such as Modesto, California, where "repetitive driving" has been outlawed.

The American Civil Liberties Union says that such bans are unconstitutional and violate teenagers' rights to unrestricted travel around city streets. Youths say that cruising is harmless, especially compared with drug use. And some police agree. Where new laws have been passed banning cruising in certain communities, police have been forced to spend time dealing with these less-serious problems instead of combating criminals.

(Some factual information adapted from *Newsweek*, August 20, 1990, p. 45.)

long-term detainees in secure juvenile facilities suggest that judges impose sentences of detention frequently. Further, a majority of these long-term detainees are less serious property offenders with some chronicity in their rate of reoffending.

Gelber (1990) has attempted to envision the juvenile court as it might exist in the twenty-first century. He sees a **two-tiered juvenile court system,** conceivably renamed the "Juvenile Services Consortium." The first tier would be devoted to adjudicating offenders under age 14. These offenders would always receive rehabilitative sanctions, such as probation or placement in conditional, community-based correctional programs. The second tier would consist of those aged 14 to 18. For these juveniles, jury trials would be available and these offenders would be subject to the same incarcerative sanctions imposed by criminal courts.

Gelber's two-tiered juvenile court projection for the twenty-first century may not be far off the mark in relation to societal expectations for such courts in future years. The public mood seems to be in favor of "deserts-based" sentencing and toward due process for juvenile offenders. The two-tiered nature of Gelber's projected court organization would seemingly achieve this "get tough" result, although provisions would remain for treatment-centered rehabilitative sanctions for younger offenders. In a sense, this two-tiered court projection seems to amount to nothing more than lowering the age jurisdiction of criminal courts from 18 to 14. However, Gelber's intent is to preserve the jurisdictional integrity of the juvenile justice system in relation to the criminal justice system. In any case, this would be an effective compromise between those favoring the traditional rehabilitative posture of juvenile courts and those favoring a shift to more punitive court policies and practices. In a later section, we will examine the notion of court unification and how juvenile courts might be affected.

The Death Penalty for Juveniles

By the end of 1986, there were 1,772 prisoners on death row awaiting the penalty of death (American Correctional Association, 1987:xxxiv). Of these, 37 were juveniles age 15, 16, or 17 (Streib, 1987:xi). Thirty-five were male, and a majority were black. Between 1642 and 1986 in this country there were 281 executions of youths who were under age 18 when they committed capital crimes. The first execution, in 1642, was of Thomas Graunger, a 16-year-old who was convicted of bestiality. He was caught sodomizing a horse and a cow. The youngest age at which the death penalty was imposed was 10. A poorly documented case of a 10-year-old convicted murderer in Louisiana occurred in 1855. A more celebrated case, that of 10-year-old James Arcene, occurred in Arkansas in 1885. Arcene was 10 years old when he robbed and murdered his victim. He was eventually arrested at age 23 and was executed (Streib, 1987:57). Today Georgia leads all states in juvenile executions, with 41. North Carolina and Ohio follow, with 19 each. Fourteen states have never executed juveniles.

Arguments for or against the death penalty for adults pertain to juveniles as well. Those favoring the death penalty say it is "just" punishment and a societal revenge for the life taken or the harm inflicted by the offender. It is claimed to be an economical way of dealing with those who will never be released from confinement. It may be administered "humanely," say supporters, through lethal injection. Supporters claim that it functions as a deterrent, causing people to refrain from committing capital crimes. Opponents say it is cruel and unusual punishment. They claim the death penalty does not deter those who intend to take another's life. They say it is barbaric and uncivilized and point out that other countries do not impose it for any

According to a 1989 U.S. Supreme Court decision, youths who commit murder when they are age 16 or over may now receive the death penalty in those states with death penalty provisions. (© Bill Powers/Frost Publishing Group)

type of offense, regardless of seriousness. It makes no sense to kill as a means of sending messages to others not to kill, say opponents of capital punishment.

For juveniles, the argument is supplemented by the fact that age functions as a mitigating factor. In any capital conviction, the convicted offender is entitled to a bifurcated trial in which guilt is established first, and then the punishment is imposed, taking into account any prevailing mitigating or aggravating circumstances. Was the crime especially brutal? Did the victim suffer? Was the murderer senile or mentally ill? Or was the murderer a juvenile? Since age acts as a mitigating factor in cases where the death penalty is considered for adults, there are those who say the death penalty should not be applied to juveniles under any conditions. Early English precedent and common law assumed that those under age 7 were incapable of formulating criminal intent, and thus, they were absolved from any wrongdoing. Between age 7 and age 12, a presumption exists that the child is capable of formulating criminal intent, and in every jurisdiction, the burden is borne by the prosecution to establish beyond a reasonable doubt that the youth was capable of formulating criminal intent.

While each case is judged on its own merits, there are always at least two sides in an issue involving murder. The survivors of the victim demand justice, and the justice they usually seek is the death of the one who brought about the death of their own. This is a manifestation of "an eye for an eye." In many respects, it is an accurate portrayal of why the death penalty is imposed for both juveniles and adults. It is supposed to be a penalty that fits the crime committed. But family members of those convicted of capital crimes cannot help but feel compassion for their doomed relatives. Someone they love is about to lose his or her life. But hadn't that person taken someone else's life? But on the other hand, will taking another life bring back the dead victim? Does taking the life of the murderer fulfill some lofty societal purpose? The arguments about this issue are endless.

(The following account has been adapted from Streib, 1987:125–127.) In 1977 in Fort Jackson, South Carolina, a 17-year-old mentally retarded youth and a 16-year-old companion were living with a 22-year-old soldier in a rented, run-down house. Alcohol, THC, PCP, marijuana, and other drugs were readily available. On a warm Saturday, October 29, after heavy drinking and consuming drugs, the three decided to look for a girl to rape. They drove to a baseball park in nearby Columbia. They parked next to a young couple, a 17-year-old boy and his 14-year-old girlfriend. On orders from the soldier, they shot the boy three times with a high-powered rifle, killing him instantly. Then they drove off with the girl to a secluded area where each raped her repeatedly. Finally, they finished her off by shooting her and mutilating her body.

The three were soon arrested by police. The 16-year-old agreed to testify against the soldier and the 17-year-old in exchange for a lighter sentence. Both the soldier and the 17-year-old eventually entered guilty pleas and were sentenced to death. After lengthy appeals, the soldier was executed by South Carolina authorities on January 11, 1985. On January 10, 1986, James Terry Roach, the 17-year-old who killed the boy and girl and mutilated the girl's body, was executed in the South Carolina electric chair. Justice was served. Or was it? A crowd cheered outside the prison walls as the execution of Roach occurred. Roach wrote his last letter, and as he was strapped into the electric chair, he read it with shaky hands: "To the families of the victims, my heart is still with you in your sorrow. May you forgive me just as I know that my Lord has done." Two one-minute surges of electricity hit him and he was pronounced dead at 5:16 A.M.

The minimum offender age for the death penalty in those states where the death penalty is imposed for capital crimes is as outlined in Table 10.3.

Until recently, the U.S. Supreme Court has consistently refused to become embroiled in the issue of capital punishment for juveniles, although it has heard several juvenile death penalty cases in past years. One frequently cited case is *Eddings* v. *Oklahoma* (1982). The case raised the question of whether the death penalty as applied to juveniles was cruel and unusual punishment under the Eighth Amendment of the U.S. Constitution. The U.S. Supreme Court avoided the issue. The justices did *not* say it was "cruel and unusual punishment," but they also did not say that it wasn't. What they said was that the *youthfulness of the offender is a mitigating factor of great weight that must be considered*. Thus, many jurisdictions were left to make their own interpretations of the high court opinion.

If any trend is apparent among states regarding the application of the death penalty for juveniles, it is that many jurisdictions are moving away from executing juveniles under age 18. The fact of age of the offender is almost always considered to be a mitigating factor by courts and juries, and public sentiment seems to favor abolishing the death penalty for all juveniles (Streib, 1987:50−51).

All of the arguments that function as either pros or cons relative to the death penalty also apply directly to the issue of juvenile executions. However, the nature of juvenile justice reforms is such that a strong belief persists that substantial efforts must be made by juvenile courts and corrections to rehabilitate juveniles rather than incarcerate or execute them. For example, a study conducted by Amnesty International examined public attitudes toward the death penalty among a sample of 1,400 Florida residents (Cambridge Survey Research, 1986). While the survey disclosed overwhelming support for the death penalty, at least among those surveyed, it also disclosed that

TABLE 10.3   Minimum Ages for Death Penalty in Selected States in 1987 Prior to *Thompson* v. *Oklahoma* (1988), *Wilkins* v. *Missouri* (1989), and *Stanford* v. *Kentucky* (1989)[a]

Age	States
16	Alabama, Arkansas, Idaho, Indiana, Kentucky, Louisiana, Mississippi, Missouri, Montana, Nevada, North Carolina, Utah, Virginia
17	Georgia, New Hampshire, Texas
18	California, Colorado, Connecticut, Illinois, Nebraska, New Jersey, New Mexico, Ohio, Oregon, Tennessee
No minimum	Arizona, Delaware, Florida, Maryland, Oklahoma, Pennsylvania, South Carolina, South Dakota, Washington, Wyoming

[a]Compiled by author.

most respondents considered the death penalty inappropriate as the ultimate punishment for juvenile offenders convicted of capital crimes. In those states where executions are conducted, where should the line be drawn concerning the minimum age at which someone becomes liable, accountable, and subject to the death penalty?

Several U.S. Supreme Court cases have been decided in recent years involving questions of executions of juveniles. These cases have been especially significant in providing a legal foundation for such executions. These include **Eddings** v. **Oklahoma** (1982), **Thompson** v. **Oklahoma** (1988), **Stanford** v. **Kentucky** (1989), and **Wilkins** v. **Missouri** (1989). As a prelude to discussing these cases, it should be noted that until 1988, 16 states had minimum-age provisions for juvenile executions (under age 18), where the range in minimum age was from 10 (Indiana) to 17 (Georgia, New Hampshire, and Texas). When the *Thompson* v. *Oklahoma* case was decided in 1988, the minimum age for juvenile executions in all states was raised to 16. The following year, the U.S. Supreme Court upheld death sentences of a 16-year-old and a 17-year-old as well.

Eddings v. *Oklahoma* (1982). On April 4, 1977, Monty Lee Eddings and several companions ran away from their Missouri homes. In a car owned by Eddings's older brother, they drove without direction or purpose, eventually reaching the Oklahoma Turnpike. Eddings had several firearms in the car, including several rifles which he had stolen from his father. While driving on the turnpike, Eddings lost control of the car. He was stopped by an Oklahoma State Highway Patrol officer. When the officer approached the car, Eddings stuck a shotgun out the window and killed the officer outright. When Eddings was subsequently apprehended, he was waived to criminal court on a prosecutorial motion. Efforts by Eddings and his attorney to oppose the waiver failed.

In a subsequent bifurcated trial, several aggravating circumstances were introduced and alleged, while several mitigating circumstances, including Eddings's youthfulness, mental state, and potential for treatment, were considered by the trial judge. However, the judge did not consider Eddings' "unhappy upbringing and emotional disturbance" as mitigating factors significant enough to offset the aggravating ones. Eddings's attorney filed an appeal which eventually reached the U.S. Supreme Court. Although the Oklahoma Court of Criminal Appeals reversed the trial judge's ruling, the U.S. Supreme Court reversed the Oklahoma Court of Criminal Appeals. The reversal turned on whether the trial judge erred by refusing to consider the "unhappy upbringing and emotionally disturbed state" of Eddings. The trial judge had previously acknowledged the youthfulness of Eddings as a mitigating factor. The *fact* of Eddings's age, 16, was significant, precisely because the majority of justices did not consider it significant. Rather, they focused upon the issue of introduction of mitigating circumstances specifically outlined in Eddings's appeal. Oklahoma was now in the position of lawfully imposing the death penalty on a juvenile who was 16 years old at the time he committed murder.

Thompson v. *Oklahoma* (1988). In the case of William Wayne Thompson, he was convicted of murdering his former brother-in-law, Charles Keene. Keene had been suspected of abusing Thompson's sister. In the evening hours of January 22–23, 1983, Thompson and three older companions left his mother's house, saying "We're going to kill Charles." Facts disclose that in the early morning, Charles Keene was beaten to death by Thompson and his associates with fists and hand-held weapons, including a length of pipe. Thompson later told others, "We killed him. I shot him in the head and cut his throat in the river." Thompson's accomplices told police shortly after their arrest that Thompson had shot Keene twice in the head, and then cut his body in several places (e.g., throat, chest, and abdomen), so that, according to Thompson, "the fish could eat his body." When Keene's body was recovered on February 18, 1983, the medical examiner indicated that Keene had been shot twice in the head, had been beaten, and that his throat, chest, and abdomen had been cut.

Since Thompson was 15 years old at the time of the murder, juvenile officials transferred his case to criminal court. This transfer was supported, in part, by an Oklahoma statutory provision indicating that there was "prosecutive merit" in pursuing the case against Thompson. Again, the subject of the defendant's youthfulness was introduced as a mitigating factor (among other factors), together with aggravating factors such as the "especially heinous, atrocious, and cruel" manner in which Keene had been murdered. Thompson was convicted of first-degree murder and sentenced to death.

Thompson filed an appeal which eventually reached the U.S. Supreme Court. The Court examined Thompson's case at length, and in a vigorously debated opinion, it overturned Thompson's death sentence, indicating in its conclusory dicta that "petitioner's counsel and various *amici curiae* [friends of the court] have asked us to 'draw the line' that would prohibit the execution of any person who was under the age of 18 at the time of the offense. Our task, today, however, is to decide the case before us; we do so by concluding that the Eighth and Fourteenth Amendments prohibit the execution of a person who was under 16 years of age at the time of his or her offense" (108 S.Ct. at 2700). Accordingly, Thompson's death penalty was reversed. Officially, this Supreme Court action effectively drew a temporary line of 16 years of age as a minimum for exacting the death penalty in capital cases. This "line" awaited subsequent challenges, however.

Stanford v. *Kentucky* (1989). Kevin Stanford was 17 when, on January 17, 1981, he and an accomplice repeatedly raped and sodomized and eventually shot to death 20-year-old Baerbel Poore in Jefferson County, Kentucky. This occurred during a robbery of a gas station where Poore worked as an attendant. Stanford later told police, "I had to shoot her [since] she lived next door to me and she would recognize me . . . I guess we could have tied her up or something or beat [her up] . . . and tell her if she tells, we would kill her." A corrections officer who interviewed Stanford said that after Stanford made that disclosure, "he [Stanford] started laughing." The jury in Stanford's case found him guilty of first-degree murder and the judge sentenced him to death. The U.S. Supreme Court eventually heard his appeal, and in an opinion which addressed the "minimum age for the death penalty" issue, decided both this case and the case of Heath Wilkins, discussed in the paragraphs to follow.

Wilkins v. *Missouri* (1989). Heath Wilkins, a 16-year-old at the time of the crime, stabbed to death Nancy Allen Moore, a 26-year-old mother of two who was working behind the counter of a convenience store in Avondale, Missouri. On July 27, 1985, Wilkins and his accomplice, Patrick Stevens, entered the convenience store to rob it, agreeing with Wilkins' plan that they would kill "whoever was behind the counter" because "a dead person can't talk." When they entered the store, they stabbed Moore, who fell to the floor. When Stevens had difficulty opening the cash register, Moore, mortally wounded, offered to help him. Wilkins stabbed her three more times in the chest, two of the knife wounds penetrating Moore's heart. Moore began to beg for her life, whereupon Wilkins stabbed her four more times in the neck, opening up her carotid artery. She died shortly thereafter. Stevens and Wilkins netted $450 in cash and checks, some liquor, cigarettes, and rolling papers from the robbery/murder. Wilkins was convicted of first-degree murder, and the judge sentenced him to death.

The U.S. Supreme Court heard both cases simultaneously, since the singular issue was whether the death penalty was considered cruel and inhumane as it pertained to 16- and 17-year-olds. At that time, not all states had achieved consensus about applying the death penalty to persons under the age of 18 as a punishment for capital crimes. Although two justices dissented from the majority view, the U.S. Supreme Court upheld the death sentences of Stanford and Wilkins, concluding that "we discern neither a historical nor a modern societal consensus forbidding the imposition of capital punishment on any person who murders at 16 or 17 years of age. Accordingly, we conclude that such punishment does not offend the Eighth Amendment's prohibition against cruel and unusual punishment" (109 S.Ct. at 2980). Thus, this crucial opinion underscored age 16 as the minimum age at which the death penalty may be administered.

Considerable debate has been generated among professionals concerning the juvenile death penalty issue (Just, 1985; Markman and Cassell, 1988; Polen, 1987; Ricotta, 1988; Streib, 1987; Streib and Sametz, 1988; Wallace, 1989). Apart from the question of whether the death penalty should be administered at all to anyone, there is no apparent consensus concerning the application of the death penalty to juveniles convicted of capital crimes. Some of the arguments favoring the death penalty stress the accountability of these youthful offenders, the justice of capital punishment where capital crimes have been committed, and the potential deterrent value of such punishment. Some of the arguments opposing the death penalty for juveniles cite the cruel and unusual nature of the death penalty, the mitigating factor of one's youthfulness, and a youth's greater potential for rehabilitation compared with adults (Brodie, 1986; Ellison, 1987; Polen, 1987; Wilson, 1983). For instance, it is argued that juveniles are more amenable to treatment and rehabilitation, and thus, provision should be made for this rehabilitation and treatment to occur (Wilson, 1983). Whatever the appeal of such an argument, the U.S. Supreme Court has, at least for the time being, resolved the age/death penalty issue with some degree of finality. Other factors will have to be cited as mitigating in a youth's defense if a capital crime is alleged.

Currently, there are only a small number of juveniles on death row in U.S. state prisons. Because of the declining frequency with which juveniles have been executed in recent years, the death penalty issue as it applies to juveniles does not seem as strong as it once did. There will always be many persons in society who will oppose the death penalty for any reason. But it is doubtful that major changes will be made in the death penalty policy as applied to capital juvenile offenders, unless the present composition of the U.S. Supreme Court changes significantly. While public sentiment is not always easy to measure, there seems to be strong sentiment for harsher penalties meted out to juveniles. This doesn't necessarily mean the death penalty or life imprisonment, but it does mean tighter laws and enforcement of those laws where juveniles are concerned. Following are discussions of several issues related to public sentiment regarding juvenile punishment. Also assessed are political sentiments toward the juvenile punishment issue.

Views of professionals in criminal justice and criminology are not that different from the views held by the general public about juvenile delinquency and what should be done to prevent or punish it. Victor Streib (1987:189) has summarized succinctly a commonly expressed, though nebulous, feeling that "our society must be willing to devote enormous resources to a search for the causes and cures of violent juvenile crime, just as we have done in the search for the causes and cures of such killer diseases as cancer. And we must not demand a complete cure in a short time, since no one knows how long it will take." Obviously, we have not cured cancer. We are even further away from discovering the etiology of delinquent behavior in all of its diverse forms and finding one or more satisfactory cures for it.

One intervention proposed by professionals in the early identification of chronic or hard-core delinquents is a multiple gating technique (Loeber and Dishion, 1987). This technique purportedly identifies extreme cases in terms of frequency, variety, seriousness, age of onset, and the number of settings in which the behavior tends to occur. Thus, antisocial and "delinquency-prone" youths may be identified early in their delinquent careers, and appropriate intervention programs may be applied to them. This selectivity is more cost-effective in the long run than more costly programs that are applicable to youths in general, regardless of their offense behaviors or personal characteristics (Loeber and Dishion, 1987). However, a social experiment covering a two-year period and involving a small number of hard-core juvenile offenders did not give much reason for optimism concerning intensive, specialized treatment and intervention as delinquency prevention forms (Gelber, 1988). Even where high-quality staff were made available to youths on a 24-hour-a-day, seven-day-a-week basis, without limitation on time or cost, and where the family's needs (e.g., jobs, food, health care, housing, schooling) were met, a majority of these "assisted" youths reverted to criminal conduct, were convicted, and were sent to prison (Gelber, 1988). Does any form of intervention really work for most offenders? We simply don't know at this point.

Summary

Historically, the United States has been influenced by the early English doctrine of *parens patriae,* under which the king of England acted as the father of the country on behalf of minors and other dependent persons. This doctrine served to shape contemporary juvenile courts and the attitudes of court officers toward youths, as well as the sentences they receive for their delinquent acts. The basic elements of *parens patriae* include state control over children's affairs, informal processing of juveniles to avoid adverse labeling effects, and benevolent and treatment-oriented sanctions that seek to rehabilitate and reform rather than to punish. The case of *Ex parte Crouse,* decided in 1839, was the first legal recognition of this doctrine in the United States, and it effectively separated parental interests in children from the interests of the court, giving the court the final power to make decisions for juveniles.

For many decades, the U.S. Supreme Court practiced a "hands off" philosophy toward the juvenile courts, since it was believed that juvenile courts act in the best interests of children. However, numerous blatant abuses of juvenile court authority led to substantial changes in the ways juveniles would be treated in future years. The U.S. Supreme Court vested juveniles with a succession of rights, beginning with the right to a hearing prior to being waived or transferred to criminal court where potentially more severe punishments might be exacted. Subsequent rights given juveniles by the Supreme Court include the right to an attorney, the right to confront and cross-examine witnesses, the right against self-incrimination, the right to notice of charges, and the right against double jeopardy. Eventually, juveniles were given minimum due process. In about a fourth of all states, juveniles are entitled to a jury trial if one is requested. However, most other states leave this option to the discretion of juvenile court judges.

Generally, juvenile courts operate with less rigorous evidentiary standards compared with criminal courts. Juveniles may be held for preventive detention. The "beyond a reasonable doubt" standard is now used as the standard of guilt or innocence in juvenile courts where the possibility of incarceration exists. Very much in favor of juvenile offenders is the fact that juvenile courts continue to exercise civil jurisdiction. Thus, adjudicated delinquents cannot acquire criminal records as the result of their misdeeds while juvenile offenders. Of course, we have seen that juveniles may be waived to criminal courts for processing, particularly where serious offenses have been alleged. Therefore, they may be treated as adults according to statutory authority, although they may still be minors. Perhaps the most serious implication of being treated as adults for juveniles is that they may have the death penalty imposed for capital crimes. In recent years the U.S. Supreme Court has upheld the death penalty as applied to 16- and 17-year-olds, although it has ruled that the death penalty is cruel and unusual punishment if administered to youths under age 16. The death penalty is controversial per se, and its use is especially controversial where youths are concerned.

Criticisms of contemporary juvenile courts are that they are increasingly similar to criminal courts and have undergone a degree of criminalization. As juvenile courts become increasingly formalized and bureaucratic, some degree of judicial discretion is lost. This is both good and bad, since juvenile court judges may abuse this discretionary authority or they may make decisions that are quite lenient and in favor of youthful offenders. Informal adjudicatory proceedings are gradually being eliminated as the juvenile court system becomes increasingly adversarial.

Key Terms

Breed v. Jones (1975) (315)
Eddings v. Oklahoma (1982) (325)
Ex parte Crouse (1839) (304)
Ex parte Hull (1941) (305)
"Hands off" doctrine (305)
In re Gault (1967) (312)
In re Winship (1970) (314)
Kent v. United States (1966) (310)
McKeiver v. Pennsylvania (1971) (315)

New Jersey v. T.L.O. (1985) (319)
Ruffin v. Commonwealth (1871) (305)
Schall v. Martin (1984) (318)
Stanford v. Kentucky (1989) (325)
Thompson v. Oklahoma (1988) (325)
Two-tiered juvenile court system (320)
Wilkins v. Missouri (1989) (325)

Questions for Review

1. What elements of *parens patriae* seemed to dominate juvenile courts for many decades prior to the reforms of the 1970s and 1980s? Discuss each.
2. Write a short essay contrasting the *parens patriae* doctrine with offender accountability and due process.
3. Briefly describe the "hands off" policy of the U.S. Supreme Court in relation to juvenile courts. How does this "hands off" policy fit in with the U.S. Supreme Court's early position toward correctional institutions and inmate problems? Compare and contrast the Court's policies relating to juvenile courts and correctional institutions.
4. What standards exist for conducting searches of students' school lockers on high school campuses? Briefly describe this standard and discuss the relevant case.

5. Discuss briefly the significance of *Kent* v. *United States*. At the time, why was this case considered a "landmark case"?

6. How did the case of *In re Gault* expand the case for juvenile rights beyond the *Kent* case? Explain briefly.

7. What standard of proof is used in juvenile courts for determining whether a juvenile is delinquent?

8. Can juvenile offenders be adjudicated as delinquent in juvenile courts on certain charges, and then tried as adults in criminal court on those same charges? Why or why not? Cite the facts of a relevant case.

9. Can juveniles be held in preventive detention? What case is applicable here? Discuss briefly the facts of the case.

10. Does a delinquency adjudication in juvenile court result in a criminal record for any youthful offender? Why or why not? Explain.

11. What is the two-tiered juvenile court of the future projected by Gelber? Describe this court briefly.

12. Identify three major cases relating to the death penalty for juveniles. In each of these cases, discuss the significance of the U.S. Supreme Court decision for affected juveniles.

13. What are some of the major arguments favoring the death penalty for juveniles? What are some arguments opposing the death penalty?

14. How many states currently impose capital punishment? If a juvenile is convicted of a capital crime, what is the maximum age the juvenile could have been at the time the offense was committed which would prohibit use of the death penalty as a punishment?

15. What is meant by court unification? How is court unification beneficial to court operations and organization generally?

16. How is court unification potentially threatening to juvenile recidivists? Explain.

17. In what respects can juvenile court judicial discretion act both for and against juvenile offenders at the time of their adjudication as delinquents?

Suggested Readings

BERNARD, D. (1988). *Juvenile Delinquency Detention and Prevention.* Paso Robles, CA: Lantern Light Books.

DAVIS, S. M. (1983). *Rights of Juveniles: The Juvenile Justice System* (2nd ed.). New York: Clark Boardman.

GUGGENHEIM, M. (1985). *The Rights of Young People.* New York: Bantam Books.

SCHWARTZ, IRA M. (1988). *(In)justice for Juveniles.* Lexington, MA: Lexington Books.

WILBANKS, W. (1987). *The Myth of a Racist Criminal Justice System.* Beaumont, CA: Wadsworth.

The Juvenile Justice System: Corrections

Part IV consists of four chapters that examine different components of juvenile corrections. "Corrections" is actually a misnomer, since it is the opinion of many professionals that both the criminal and the juvenile justice systems do almost everything but "correct" their respective offenders and clients. Despite these experts' misgivings, this traditional appellation will be used.

It is generally recognized that the primary intent of the juvenile justice system is to help juvenile offenders and prevent them from reoffending. In most jurisdictions, elaborate efforts are undertaken to exclude them from the wheels and gears of the juvenile justice system. The rehabilitation emphasis of juvenile courts and other parts of the juvenile justice system has been dominant. Only in recent years has there been a shift to a more punitive stance in relation to youthful offenders who commit serious acts. The "just deserts" and justice models that have popularly been applied to adult offender programs are equally applicable to juvenile programs, in the view of those endorsing punishment and acceptance of responsibility for one's actions, regardless of the age factor.

Chapter 11 describes various nominal sanctions that juvenile judges can impose as one class of their sentencing options. These nominal sanctions are not limited to wrist-slaps and verbal reprimands. Judges may permit certain juveniles, particularly nonserious first offenders, to participate in diversionary programs that are often conditional and require one or more constructive actions on the part of those juveniles. Diversionary programs are designed to prevent juveniles from coming into direct contact with the trappings of the juvenile justice system and the juvenile court. Juveniles are not adjudicated as delinquent. Rather, they are often shifted to community-based agencies and programs where they may obtain practical assistance from others or treatments for chemical dependencies or psychological disturbances. The implications of such programs for youthful offenders will be examined.

Chapter 11 also describes various conditional sanctions that judges may impose. The conditional sanctions described include standard probation and foster home placement. Under certain types of conditional sanctions, juveniles work closely with probation officers. The quality of assistance rendered by these probation officers often depends on their individual commitment to their tasks, their qualifications for the job, and their caseloads. Efforts are made in many jurisdictions to recruit the best applicants for such positions. Salaries vary considerably among jurisdictions, and because of scarce resources, the turnover among juvenile probation officers in some areas is quite high. Some of the recruitment problems that are faced by juvenile probation services in various communities will be discussed. An evaluation of standard probation services will also be made.

Chapter 12 continues the description of conditional sanctions that judges may impose on those juveniles adjudicated as delinquent. The subject matter of this chapter explores many of the relatively recent innovations in juvenile probation programs that fall within the rubric of intermediate punishments. Intermediate punishments lie somewhere between secure detention and probation, and they typically reflect intensive supervision by probation officers and other adults. Intermediate punishments are also closely related to community-based juvenile services, and both public and private operations are described. Innovative programs such as home confinement and electronic monitoring are examined, as well as shock probation and wilderness experiences. One measure of the success or lack of success of these programs is offender recidivism. Recidivism figures for these different programs will be provided, together with a discussion of their relevance for program prognosis and perpetuation.

Chapter 13 looks at both secure and nonsecure juvenile correctional facilities and operations. These programs may be publicly or privately operated. Privatization of juvenile corrections has increased dramatically in recent years, as private interests contend that they can provide needed juvenile services to communities at less cost than public agencies. There are conflicting views about the legitimacy of privatization, however, and some of these views will be presented and discussed.

One of the most severe punishments juvenile judges may administer is incarceration in juvenile secure detention facilities such as industrial schools or reform schools. Usually, only the most violent and persistent offenders will be incarcerated, although there are exceptions.

Another aspect of juvenile corrections is juvenile parole, or conditional early release from incarceration. Many of the juvenile parole programs that are operated today are blended with the probation programs that already exist in most jurisdictions. Often, the same juvenile probation officers oversee and monitor the activities of juvenile parolees and juvenile probationers. Different parole programs will be described and evaluated. The measure of their success or failure—the amount of recidivism—will be assessed.

CHAPTER 11

Nominal and Conditional Sanctions: Warnings, Diversion, and Standard Probation

Introduction
Nominal Dispositions Defined
Diversion
Diversion Programs for Juveniles
Implications of Diversionary Programs for Juveniles
Standard Probation for Juveniles
Juvenile Probation Officers
The Predisposition Report and Its Preparation
The Success of Standard Juvenile Probation
Summary
Key Terms
Questions for Review
Suggested Readings

Introduction

This chapter examines the least punitive options imposed as punishments by juvenile court judges or recommended by intake officers and/or prosecutors. These options include nominal reprimands, such as *verbal warnings* and *diversion,* as well as the least punitive conditional option, *standard probation.* Both diversion and standard probation are programs that may require offenders to perform various acts, such as victim restitution or compensation, community service, and good works of various kinds, and pay fines or other monetary penalties. Several diversionary programs currently used in various U.S. jurisdictions will be described. Their effectiveness will be assessed.

336

Because standard probation means that juveniles may be required to per-form certain services, make restitution, or comply with other program re-quirements, several probation programs will be described. The role of juvenile probation officers will also be examined. These officers are important, not only because they are direct links between juveniles and juvenile courts, but because they prepare predispositional reports that may influence a youth's life chances. Such predispositional reports will be illustrated. Probation officers and other experts express mixed opinions about the value of predispositional reports in the adjudication process. This diversity of opinion will be discussed.

In many jurisdictions, high labor turnover characterizes the probation officer role. Individual probation officers report various reasons for this turnover, including dissatisfaction with caseloads and other work pressures. Other officers find their work rewarding and challenging. The activities of juvenile probation officers will be described and their role in the juvenile justice system will be illustrated. Some attention will be given to how these officers are recruited initially. Finally, the overall success of the programs presented here will be described.

Nominal Dispositions Defined

Nominal dispositions *are verbal and/or written warnings issued to low-risk juvenile offenders, often first offenders, for the purpose of alerting them to the seriousness of their acts and the possibility of their receiving severe conditional punishments if they should ever reoffend.* These sanctions are the least punitive alternatives. Nominal dispositions may be imposed by police officers in their encounters with juveniles. These verbal warnings or reprimands are often in the form of station "adjustments," in which youths are taken into custody and released to their parents later, without a record being made of the incident.

Intake officers may also use nominal dispositions against certain juveniles if it is perceived that they merit only verbal warnings instead of more punitive sanctions. If petitions against certain juveniles are filed, depending upon the circumstances, judges may find them to be delinquent as alleged in these petitions. However, these adjudications do not automatically bind judges to implement conditional or custodial sanctions. Judges may simply issue warnings to adjudicated juveniles. These warnings are serious, especially after a finding that the juvenile is delinquent. Juveniles with prior records face tougher sentencing options later if they reoffend in the same juvenile court jurisdiction and reappear before the same judges.

Diversion

The Juvenile Justice and Delinquency Prevention Act of 1974 and its subsequent amendments was intended, in part, to deinstitutionalize status offenders and remove them from the jurisdiction of juvenile courts. Another

Individualized counseling is a useful therapy for many youthful offenders. Diversion enables community-based agencies and counselors to treat youths and avoid the potentially adverse effects of labeling. (Courtesy of Oregon Children's Services Division)

provision of this act was to ensure that all other adjudicated delinquent offenders would receive the least punitive sentencing options from juvenile court judges in relation to their adjudication offenses. In fact, the National Advisory Committee for Juvenile Justice and Delinquency Prevention recommended in 1980 that juvenile court judges should select the least restrictive sentencing alternatives, given the nature of the offense, the age, interests, and needs of the juvenile offender, and the circumstances of the conduct. Therefore, judicial actions that may appear too lenient may be a result of these recommendations.

One of the earliest delinquency prevention strategies that can be implemented by juvenile court judges and other actors throughout the juvenile justice system is diversion. **Diversion** *is the temporary directing of youths away from the juvenile courts, allowing them to remain with their families or guardians, attend school, and be subject to limited supervision on a regular basis by a juvenile probation officer.*

According to some experts, a primary, intended consequence of diversion is to remove large numbers of relatively minor offenders from juvenile court processing as quickly as possible (Schwartz, 1989). However, other professionals caution that one unintended consequence of diversion is the development of "wider, stronger, and different nets" (Austin and Krisberg,

Juvenile court judges have been criticized for what some people consider excessive leniency when imposing youth punishments. However, many judges believe that their decisions are made objectively and in the best interests of both the community and the juvenile offender. (© Nancy J. Pierce/Photo Researchers, Inc.)

1982). This means in the simplest terms that those youngsters diverted from the formal juvenile justice system are captured in "nets" formed by the community-based agencies (Binder, 1989). Thus, if we view social control in its broadest terms, this means that more, not fewer, children will fall under some form of social control through diversionary programs. Some experts believe that children who are delabeled as delinquents through diversion may become relabeled as the result of being placed in community mental health centers and private psychiatric care facilities or treatment programs (Office of Juvenile Justice and Delinquency Prevention, 1980a, 1980b; Schneider, 1984a).

It is claimed by some authorities that diversion of offenders should be aimed primarily at the client population that would otherwise have received formal dispositions if diversion had not occurred (Osgood, 1983). This client population consists of youths who have committed delinquent acts and not simply status offenses. However, some critics say that status offenders "escalate" to more serious offenses if left "untreated" by the system. Therefore, intervention of some sort is necessary to prevent this escalation of offense seriousness (Rankin and Wells, 1985). On the other hand, other studies have shown that status offenders do not necessarily progress to more serious offenses. Sometimes, their apparent involvement in more serious offenses is a function of relabeling of the same acts differently by police (Datesman and Aickin, 1985; Schneider, 1984b). Regardless of whether they are status offenders or have committed serious delinquent acts, divertees often exhibit some recidivism. Therefore, it is true that at least some of these divertees do progress to more serious offenses, as some critics allege (Benda, 1987).

Functions and Dysfunctions of Diversion. Diversion has certain logistical benefits and functions. First, it decreases the caseload of juvenile court prosecutors by shuffling less serious cases to probation departments. Of course, this increases the supervisory responsibilities of probation departments, which must manage larger numbers of divertees in addition to juvenile probationers. A second function of diversion is that it seems to reduce recidivism in those jurisdictions where it has been used (McDermott *et al.*, 1985; Regoli *et al.*, 1985). A third intended consequence of diversion is to reduce the degree of juvenile institutionalization or placement in either secure or nonsecure detention facilities. A fourth function is that diversion is potentially useful as a long-range crime prevention measure. Finally, diversion reduces certain youth risks, such as suicide attempts as the result of being confined in adult jails or lockups for short periods. At the 1991 Congress of Corrections, Peter Reinharz, chief of the Family Court Division of the New York City Law Department, indicated that the increasingly disturbed and violent nature of incarcerated youths and the need for corrections professionals to examine the ways in which these cases are handled are currently key correctional priorities (American Correctional Association, 1991). Rowan (1989:218) and Smith (1991) have described the stress and anxiety generated as the result of even short-term confinement for certain juveniles, and their propensity to commit suicide. At least for some youths, diversion assists in avoiding the stresses of confinement or prosecution.

One of the dysfunctional consequences of diversion is that it may "widen the net" by including some youths who otherwise would have received station adjustments by police or warnings from juvenile judges (Decker, 1985; Polk, 1984). Much of this net-widening occurs through changes in police discretion and relabeling of juvenile behaviors as more serious, however (Klein, 1979; Schneider, 1984a). Another dysfunction is that some affected youths may be led to believe that the juvenile justice system is lenient and will tolerate relatively minor law-breaking. The fact that many juvenile offenders are not sentenced to secure detention until their fourth or fifth delinquency adjudications would provide support for these beliefs.

Diversion Programs for Juveniles

Youth Service Bureaus. Diversion programs have operated in the United States for many years. In the early 1960s, **Youth Service Bureaus (YSBs)** were established in numerous jurisdictions in order to accomplish diversions, with several objectives. While we still cannot identify precisely those youths considered delinquency-prone (rather, we refer to certain youths as "at risk"), YSBs were created, in part, as places within communities where "delinquent-prone" youths could be referred by parents, schools, and law enforcement agencies (Norman, 1970). Actually, YSBs were forerunners of our contemporary community-based correctional programs, since they were intended to solicit volunteers from among community residents and to mobilize a variety of resources that could assist in a youth's treatment. The nature of treatments for youths, within the YSB concept, originally included referrals to a variety of community services, educational experiences, and individual or group counseling. YSB organizers attempted to compile lists of existing community services, agencies, organizations, and sponsors who could cooperatively coordinate these resources in the most productive ways to benefit affected juveniles (Norman, 1970; Romig, 1978).

Norman (1970:15−19) has described five types of model YSB programs.

1. *The cooperating agencies model.* This model consists of several different community-based agencies and organizations. Each organization or agency furnishes at least one paid full-time worker to the YSB program. As a team, these workers attempt to involve citizens and youths by bringing in interested professionals and others to work with juveniles who might have poor self-concepts or social adjustment problems.

2. *The community organization model.* This model utilizes community citizens who work on a strictly voluntary basis. They are encouraged to form a board of directors who will assist them in coordinating diverse community services in ways that can benefit those juveniles serviced. Such organizations would provide temporary shelter for runaways or for those youths who are experiencing family difficulties or school problems. Thus, these agencies would function to accommodate those who need emergency treatment or assistance.

3. *The citizen action model.* As the name implies, citizen involvement in the citizen action model is intensified. Community volunteers are attracted from various types of youth services. Each youth referred to these organizations is regarded as a case, and case conferences are held to determine the best treatment approaches to assist youths in solving their problems.

A YSB patterned after this model was implemented in Wise County, Virginia, in 1979. By the mid-1980s, 22 locally operated programs had been established in Virginia, costing the state about $36,000 per program. In Wise County, in the years 1979−1984, groups of interested citizens formed a Youth Commission that initiated intensive assistance programs for troubled juveniles. During that period, the number of teenage pregnancies in the county dropped from 185 to 116, while the school dropout rate declined from 8 percent to 5.6 percent. Further, the total number of juvenile arrests in that county has steadily decreased. Virginia officials have been excited about what they consider to be the success of their YSB programs.

4. *The street outreach model.* This model provides for the establishment of neighborhood centers in business areas, where group and individual therapy

may be administered to troubled youths. The accessibility of such centers in business districts is an attractive feature, since they cater to juvenile transients who are constantly roaming those same streets.

5. *The systems modification model.* This type of model has led to the establishment of community-based facilities that function in conjunction with other agencies, schools, churches, and institutions to help these other organizations become more effective in supplying the needed youth services (Norman, 1970:15–19).

Interestingly, YSBs have been accused of contributing to the net-widening problem, since they draw in numerous youths who might otherwise have avoided prolonged contact with the juvenile justice system. Nevertheless, they have established common patterns that many community-based organizations have found useful as program guides over the years.

Generally, diversion programs operate in pretty much the same ways for juveniles as they operate for adult offenders. Diversion in the juvenile justice system has the primary objective of avoiding labeling and the stigma associated with involvement in juvenile court (Anderson and Schoen, 1985; Osgood, 1983). Diversion may be either *unconditional* or *conditional.* **Unconditional diversion** *simply means that the divertee will attend school, behave, and not reappear before the juvenile court for a specified period.* **Conditional diversion** *may require juveniles to attend lectures, individual or group psychotherapy, drug or alcohol treatment centers, police department-conducted DUI classes, and/or vocational or educational classes or programs.* Successful completion of the diversion program means dismissal of the case. These programs are of variable lengths, but most run for periods of six months to a year.

The Juvenile Diversion/Non-Custody Intake Program. Officials in Orange County, California, have implemented a diversionary program called the **Juvenile Diversion/Noncustody Intake Program (JD/NCI Program),** which was implemented in 1982. Diversionary efforts in previous years by Orange County officials had been ineffective. The JD/NCI Program was designed to target more serious juvenile offenders by giving them more concentrated attention from police, probation, community agencies, schools, and families (Binder *et al.,* 1985). The JD/NCI Program was a type of conditional diversion, because juvenile clients were required to pay restitution to their victims. In addition, the more traditional elements were required, such as school attendance, employment, and school counseling. Of those juveniles entering the program, 71 percent had prior felony arrests. Binder *et al.* reported that the program successfully diverted a large proportion of intake cases ordinarily referred to the district attorney for formal processing. Besides easing the juvenile court caseload, the JD/NCI Program clients tended to have lower recidivism rates compared with those in more traditional programs, although these differences were not substantial.

The Juvenile Diversion Program (JDP). Litton and Marye (1983) have described a reasonably successful diversion program. A **Juvenile Diversion**

Program (JDP) was established in New Orleans in 1981 by the District Attorney's Office under which youths could receive diversion before being petitioned and adjudicated delinquent. During the 1981–1983 period, 233 juveniles were accepted into the program, although the program capacity was estimated at 400. The program consisted of intensive counseling and evaluative and social services. Other elements included family and individual counseling, parent involvement, restitution to victims, and utilization of various community services. After a one-year follow-up, results disclosed only a 20 percent recidivism rate among program participants. Although the researchers complained that the program was ineffective because it did not serve the full complement of 400 juveniles as it was originally conceived, there is certainly nothing wrong with a 20 percent recidivism rate. This is even more significant when those accepted into the program were first offender felons (excluding murder, rape, and robbery) and serious misdemeanants.

The Youth at Risk Program. Significant success rates (i.e., lower recidivism) have been reported by another California program known as the **Youth at Risk Program,** which was operated in Los Angeles and Contra Costa Counties during the 1982–1984 period for youths age 13 to 19. The program consisted of a ten-day rural training course comprising classes, outdoor sites for running and other physical activities, and emphasis upon self-reliance, peer resistance, peer and staff support, and individual responsibility (MetaMetrics, Inc., 1984). A community follow-up program was implemented as a continuation of these experiences. Of the 155 youths participating in the program during the period 1982–1983, 49 were studied over a fifteen-month period and compared with a matched group of probationers with similar characteristics and delinquency histories. Youth at Risk Program participants had incident recidivism rates of 34.7 percent compared with 55.1 percent for the comparison group, and a serious offense recidivism rate of only 18.4 percent contrasted with 40.8 percent for the comparison group. These figures led program officials to conclude that their program had profound positive impact on their juvenile clients (MetaMetrics, Inc., 1984).

The See Our Side (SOS) Program. In Prince George's County, Maryland, a program was established in 1983 called **See Our Side (SOS)** (Mitchell and Williams, 1986:70). SOS is referred to by its directors as a "juvenile aversion" program, and dissociates itself from "scare" programs such as Scared Straight. Basically, SOS seeks to educate juveniles about the realities of life in prison through discussions and hands-on experience, and attempts to show them the types of behaviors that can lead to incarceration (Mitchell and Williams, 1986:70). Clients coming to SOS are referrals from various sources, including juvenile court, public and private schools, churches, professional counseling agencies, and police and fire departments. Youths served by SOS range in age from 12 to 18, and they do not have to be adjudicated as delinquent in order to be eligible for participation. SOS helps *any* youth who might benefit from such participation.

SOS consists of four three-hour phases. These are described below.

Phase I: Staff orientation and group counseling session where staff
attempt to facilitate discussion and ease tension among the
youthful clients; characteristics of jails are discussed, including age
and gender breakdowns, race, and types of juvenile behavior that
might result in jailing for short periods.

Phase II: A tour of a prison facility.

Phase III: Three inmates discuss with youths what life is like behind
bars; inmates who assist in the program are selected on the basis of
their emotional maturity, communications skills, and warden
recommendations.

Phase IV: Two evaluations are made: the first is an evaluation of SOS
sessions by the juveniles; the second is a recidivism evaluation for
each youth after a one-year lapse from the time he or she
participated in SOS. The relative success of the program can be
gauged through these evaluations.

SOS officials conducted an evaluation of the program in September, 1985.
It was found that SOS served 327 youths during the first year of operation,
and that a total of 38 sessions were held. Recidivism of program participants
was about 22 percent. Again, this low recidivism rate is favorable. Subsequent
evaluations of the SOS program showed that the average rate of client
recidivism dropped to only 16 percent. The cost of the program was
negligible. During the first year, the program cost was only $280, or about 86
cents per youth served.

Implications of Diversionary Programs for Juveniles

One result of the Juvenile Justice and Delinquency Prevention Act of 1974
was to deinstitutionalize status offenders and remove them from the
jurisdiction of juvenile courts (McNally, 1984:30). This has been done in
some jurisdictions, but not in all of them. There is now much variation among
jurisdictions in how juvenile offenders are processed and treated. In recent
years, however, an increasing number of juvenile courts have imposed
sentences according to offender needs as well as according to what is "just"
and deserved (O'Neil, 1987). Better classifications of offenders need to be
devised. More must be learned about offender characteristics, their backgrounds and specific circumstances, in order that proper punishments and
treatments can be meted out by juvenile judges. For diversion programs to be
successful, they must be targeted at the most likely juvenile candidates. Most
frequently, these are low-risk first offenders or juveniles who are quite young.

Juvenile courts have come under attack in recent years as a result of what the public considers excessive judicial leniency in dealing with youthful offenders (McCarthy, 1987b:237−238; O'Neil, 1987). Often, juvenile cases are dismissed. This occurs not only during formal adjudicatory proceedings by juvenile judges, but also by intake officers in earlier screenings of offenders, and thus it is unreasonable to identify any specific part of the juvenile justice process as unusually lenient in juvenile case processing. All phases of the system seem to be influenced by the rehabilitative philosophy. And for many people, rehabilitation is equated with leniency.

The degree of case attrition through diversion dismissals has been investigated by several researchers (Ito, 1984; McCarthy, 1987b; Sarri and Hassenfeld, 1976). In the mid-1970s, for example, a study by the National Assessment of Juvenile Corrections reported that about two thirds of all juvenile referrals were dismissed either at intake or at the judicial hearing (Sarri and Hassenfeld, 1976). Studies of juvenile case dismissal rates in later years disclosed similar results, although attrition figures were somewhat lower, ranging from 30 to 54 percent (Ito, 1984; McCarthy, 1987b:239). McCarthy (1987b:240) says that dismissal rates are influenced by the same kinds of factors that impinge on prosecutors and judges in adult criminal cases: crowded court dockets, too many cases to handle adequately, overcrowding in juvenile detention facilities, and greater concern for the due process rights of offenders.

McCarthy (1987b:248−251) found that often, case dismissals occurred at the request of the petitioner, or as a result of failure of the petitioner/victim/witness to appear, or because of the trivial nature of the case. However, dismissals are not always trivial. She also found that 35 percent of all dismissals involved violent offenses, and 44 percent of all petitions filed for violent felonies were dismissed as well. McCarthy is certainly not alone when she expresses concern that the attrition of juvenile cases involving serious crime represents a major juvenile justice problem (McCarthy, 1987:251).

In addition to charges of being too lenient with offenders and dismissing or diverting their cases, juvenile courts have been targeted for other criticisms. Critics say that juvenile courts have failed to distinguish adequately between less serious and more serious offenders; they have often ignored the victims of juvenile violence; they have often failed to correct or rehabilitate juveniles in a manner consistent with their manifest purposes; they have been unconcerned or complacent about juvenile offenders and how they should be punished; they have at times confined children in adult jails; they have often failed to protect juveniles' rights; their services have often been too thinly spread; and they have been too resistant to self-examination and to suggestions for improvement (O'Neil, 1987:189). But collectively, these criticisms do not especially apply to any single juvenile court at any particular point in time. Rather, they are loosely distributed and shared by many juvenile courts. By the same token, there are many juvenile courts operating with few serious flaws.

BOX 11.1

Juvenile Highlights

Should juvenile court judges be permitted to tell youths what to wear? The American Civil Liberties Union and other rights organizations have been critical of juvenile courts in selected jurisdictions for their apparent willingness to sanction certain youths because of the clothing they wear. It is not so much a matter of wearing clothing that is unattractive or in bad taste—sometimes the clothing prohibition is directed at youths whose lives may be jeopardized by the clothing they choose to wear.

Between October, 1989, and February, 1990, at least four Chicago youths were killed over the $75 and $100 jackets they wore. In all instances, they wore "starter jackets," or pro basketball and football jackets that are highly desired throughout the delinquent community. In Chicago more than fifty jackets a month are stolen from certain youths by other youths. Police officials say that the $170 high-tech high-top Reebok shoes known as "The Pump" will probably result in

youth deaths in future months.

Several school boards have banned certain types of shoes and jackets, simply to minimize the risks to youths' lives. In February, 1990, Calvin Wash, 19, was shot to death and his pro basketball jacket stolen. In another part of the city, a boy was slain because of his Air Jordan basketball sneakers, which were stolen. Even decorative gold-capped teeth are banned in some schools because of the violence they may precipitate. One Chicago psychiatrist, Eric Plaut, says that one explanation for this type of juvenile violence is that some youths see these jackets as symbolic and totemlike representations of the successes of black males in the athletic world, and that these successful role models are often the only ones these kids see.

(Some factual information adapted from "Your Jacket or Your Life," *U.S. News & World* Report, February 26, 1990, p. 14; and Nina Darnton, "Street Crimes of Fashion," *Newsweek,* March 5, 1990, p. 58.)

Offense seriousness is an important factor in the prosecutor's or judge's decision to divert youths, or simply to issue a warning. Sex offenders, drug and alcohol abusers, and mentally retarded juveniles may require intensive counseling and treatment. Truants may require closer supervision by their parents or school authorities. Of course, juveniles who commit violent acts and demonstrate clearly that they have vicious propensities that would likely pose public risks would be seriously considered for some type of detention.

The Use of Teen Courts, Day Treatment, and Alternative Dispute Resolution. Judges might exercise the nominal option in first-offender cases where status offenses have been committed or minor criminal statutes have been violated. As a part of diversion, conditional options such as restitution, fines, or community service may be imposed in those cases where property damage was incurred as a result of the juvenile's behavior. Juvenile judges must exercise considerable discretion and impose sentences which best meet the juvenile's needs and circumstances.

In some jurisdictions, judges may divert minor cases to be resolved by *teen courts*. **Teen courts** *are informal jury proceedings in which the jurors consist of teenagers who hear and decide minor cases.* Adults function only as presiding judges, and these persons are often retired judges or lawyers who perform such services voluntarily and in their spare time. Among the first cities to establish teen courts were Seattle, Washington, and Denver (Rothstein, 1985:18). Subsequently, teen courts have been established in many other jurisdictions, including Odessa, Texas. In Odessa, for instance, juveniles are referred to teen courts for Class C misdemeanors and minor traffic violations. Defendants range in age from 10 to 16. Traffic citation cases result in teen court referrals by municipal judges, who give youths the option of paying their fines or having their cases heard by the teen court. If youths select the teen court for adjudication, they do not acquire a juvenile record. The teen court listens to all evidence and decides the matter.

Teen court sentences usually involve community service and teen court jury service. Thus, juveniles who are found "guilty" by teen courts may, in fact, serve on such juries themselves in the future, as one of their conditional punishments. Or they may be required to perform up to 22 hours of community service, such as working at an animal shelter, library, or nursing home; picking up trash in parks or ball fields; or working with various community agencies (Rothstein, 1985:22). The teen court program in Odessa has been very successful. Before teen courts were established, the recidivism rate for all juvenile offenders in the city was between 50 and 60 percent. However, teen court adjudications all but eliminated this recidivism figure. Interestingly, juveniles who are tried by the teen court often develop an interest in the legal system. Rothstein (1985:22) says that teen courts place a high priority on educating young people about their responsibilities as individuals, family members, and citizens.

Some jurisdictions have *day treatment program* centers. In Bluegrass County, Kentucky, the day treatment program is one of thirteen community-based day treatment programs throughout the state operated by the Department of Social Services (Bowling, 1987:104). **Day treatment programs** *are community-based treatments, operated either publicly or privately, that combine counseling, education, and regular school attendance with vocational assistance and job placement.* The average cost of these programs is about $30 per day. These programs bridge the gap "for some troubled youths between parental control and round-the-clock juvenile justice supervision" (Bowling, 1987:104). Client involvement is either voluntary or results from court or school referrals. Day treatment programs have achieved a 75 percent success rate, which translates into a recidivism rate of about 25 percent. This is well under the amount of recidivism normally observed as the result of standard probation.

In New Mexico, many youths are subject to alternative dispute resolution or mediation to resolve school problems. Smith (1990:112) says that the mediation process allows people to resolve conflicts in a nonthreatening and nonpunitive atmosphere. Mediators are third-party neutrals who help people in a dispute to express their points of view, identify their needs, clarify issues, explore solutions, and negotiate satisfactory agreements.

The New Mexico Center for Dispute Resolution operates a school mediation program that trains students in grades 5 through 12 to intervene as mediators in school-based disputes among students (Smith, 1990:112). Smith describes the program as consisting of three components: (1) a conflict resolution curriculum that can be taught either in academic or residential settings; (2) a mediation program that trains residents and staff to help resolve conflicts among themselves; and (3) a reintegration component involving parents and residents developing terms of daily living for when the residents return home. She further indicates that the program's rationale is that by giving students a model for positive expression and conflict resolution, it can teach them alternatives to violent and self-destructive behavior. By using these skills within the institutional setting, students can be assisted to interact successfully with their peers and adults. A voluntary program, this mediation effort has apparently reduced juvenile deviance in the jurisdiction. Thus, it may be viewed as an early intervention for preventing juvenile delinquency.

The prevailing correctional philosophy applied to juvenile corrections today, as well as to programs for adults, is punishment/control rather than treatment/rehabilitation. But like adults, juvenile offenders differ greatly in their emotional needs, offense seriousness, educational levels, vocational skills, and honesty. Therefore, it is difficult for judges to prescribe meaningful, categorical punishments that can successfully be applied to all youthful offenders facing similar charges (Baird, 1985:32). Even if specific predictor variables could be identified, they are not always foolproof for effective program placement (Simone, 1984:110–112).

In the long run, diversion programs will tend to vary in their success, depending upon how they are established and operated. For instance, a study of 213 juvenile offenders in a midwestern city was conducted during the period 1976–1980 (Davidson *et al.,* 1987). The program provided four interventions, including behavioral contracting, advocacy and behavioral contracting only with family members, court intervention, and development of interpersonal relationships. Self-reported delinquency and recidivism were measures of program effectiveness. Recidivism rates of program participants were compared with those of another group exposed to traditional supervisory and monitoring methods. While no significant differences were reported between the two groups where delinquency self-reports were used, recidivism rates among program members were slightly lower than in the control group (Davidson *et al.,* 1987). Generally, diversion efforts have been successful in other jurisdictions, where lower recidivism has been reported (Binder and Geis, 1984; Logan, 1986; Regoli *et al.,* 1985; Williams, 1984).

Those who criticize diversion programs question whether such programs are really necessary or whether they only widen the net and draw juveniles in who otherwise would receive nominal warnings or reprimands from juvenile court judges (Blomberg *et al.*, 1986). In cities such as St. Louis, for example, substantial net-widening has occurred in the aftermath and establishment of a diversion program (Decker, 1985). Other critics cite vested political interests as interfering with diversion program goals (Wilderman, 1984). Diversion may widen the net, but it does seem to work for the 80 percent or more of juveniles who are diverted from further involvement in the juvenile justice system.

Standard Probation for Juveniles

Standard juvenile probation is more or less elaborate, depending upon the jurisdiction. Of all sentencing options available to juvenile court judges, standard probation is the most commonly used. The first probation law was enacted in Massachusetts in 1878, although probation was used much earlier. John Augustus is credited with inventing probation in Boston in 1841. **Standard probation** *is a conditional or unconditional nonincarcerative sentence of a specified period following an adjudication of delinquency.*

There are several types of standard probation programs. Like their diversion program counterparts, probation programs for juveniles are either *unconditional* or *conditional.* Again, there are many similarities between probation programs devised for adults and those structured for juvenile offenders. **Unconditional standard probation** *basically allows the juvenile complete freedom of movement within the community, perhaps accompanied by periodic reports by telephone or mail with a probation officer or the probation department.* Because a PO's caseload is often high, with several hundred juvenile clients who must be managed, individualized attention cannot be given to most juveniles on standard probation. The period of unsupervised probation varies among jurisdictions depending upon offense seriousness and other circumstances. A juvenile probation order is shown in Figure 11.1.

Conditional standard probation *programs may include optional conditions and program requirements, such as performing a certain number of hours of public or community service,* providing restitution to victims, paying a fine, employment, and/or participating in specific vocational, educational, or therapeutic programs. It is crucial to any probation program that an effective classification system be in place so that juvenile judges can sentence offenders accordingly. Baird (1985:32−34) suggests that a variation of the National Institute of Corrections' (NIC) Model Classification Project scheme, in which both risk and needs are assessed, be used for juvenile classifications.

The terms of standard probation are outlined in Figure 11.1. Although these terms may be accompanied by special conditions, known as "special conditions of probation," more often than not, no special conditions are attached. The basic terms are:

1. To obey one's parents or guardians.
2. To obey all laws of the community, including curfew and school laws.

INSTRUCTIONS:
1. Original to Probation Files
2. Pink to Parents
3. Blue to Minor
4. Goldenrod to Diversion Officer

ORANGE COUNTY PROBATION DEPARTMENT
INFORMAL PROBATION AGREEMENT

The authority for undertaking a plan of informal probation which may include the use of a crisis resolution home or shelter-care facility is contained in Section 654 of the Welfare and Institutions Code, which is printed in full on the reverse side of this form. Before signing this agreement, please read it and resolve any questions about it with the deputy probation officer.

Minor's
Initials   **GENERAL RULES AND REQUIREMENTS**

_____ 1. You are to report in person and submit written reports to your probation officer as directed.

_____ 2. You are to obey all laws, including traffic rules and regulations. You are not to operate a motor vehicle on any street or highway until properly licensed and insured. You are to report to your probation officer any arrests or law violations immediately.

_____ 3. You are to obey the curfew law of the city or county in which you live or any special curfew imposed by the Court or the probation officer; specifically: _____

_____ 4. You are not to leave the State of California or change your residence without first getting permission from your probation officer. Prior to change of residence, you are to notify your probation officer of the new address. You are not to live with anyone except your parents or approved guardian without specific permission of your probation officer.

_____ 5. You are to attend school every day, every class, as prescribed by law, and obey all school regulations. Suspension from school and/or truancies/tardiness could result in action being taken by the Probation Department. You are to notify your probation officer by 10:00 a.m. on any school day that you are absent from school. If you are home from school because of illness or suspension, you are not to leave your home that day or night except to keep a doctor's appointment.

_____ 6. You are not to use or possess any intoxicants, alcohol, narcotics, other controlled substances, related paraphernalia, poisons, or illegal drugs; including marijuana. You are not to be with anyone who is using or possessing any illegal intoxicants, narcotics or drugs. Do not inhale or attempt to inhale or consume any substance of any type or nature, such as paint, glue, plant material or any aerosol product. You are not to inject anything into your body unless directed to do so by a medical doctor.

_____ 7. You are not to frequent any places of business disapproved by your probation officer, parents or guardian, specifically: ___
    _____

_____ 8. You are not to associate with individuals disapproved by your probation officer, parents or guardian, specifically: _____
    _____

_____ 9. You may be required to participate in any program outlined in Section 654 W&I Code.

_____ 10. You are to seek and maintain counseling if and as directed by the probation officer.

_____ 11. You are not to have any weapons of any description, including firearms, nunchucks or martial arts weaponry, and knives of any kind, in your possession while you are on probation, or involve self in activities in which weapons are used, i.e. hunting, target shooting.

_____ 12. You are ordered to obey the following additional terms of probations:
    _____
    _____

Probation supervision will expire on _____ unless you fail to abide by the above terms and conditions of your probation resulting in court action.

I have personally initialed, read and understand the above rules and requirements of informal probation that apply in my particular case as explained to me by the probation officer. I understand that my failure to comply with the initialed items could result in the petition, that is pending in my case, being filed with the District Attorney.

SIGNED: _____ DATE: _____
                    (minor)

SIGNED: _____ DATE: _____
                    (parent)

SIGNED: _____ DATE: _____
                    (parent)

            MICHAEL SHUMACHER
            Chief Probation Officer

BY: _____ DATE: _____
        Deputy Probation Officer

                    INFORMAL PROBATION AGREEMENT (654 W&I Code)

FO502-5118.8

Figure 11-1   Orange County Probation Department Informal Probation Agreement.

3. To follow the school or work program approved by the probation officer.
4. To follow the instructions of the probation officer.
5. To report in person to the probation officer or court at such times as designated by the probation officer.
6. To comply with any special conditions of probation.
7. To consult with the probation officer when in need of further advice.

Thus, youths sentenced to standard probation experience little change in their daily routines. Whenever special conditions of probation are attached, they usually mean additional work for probation officers. Some of these conditions might include medical treatments for drug or alcohol dependencies, individual or group therapy or counseling, or participation in a driver safety course. In some instances involving theft, burglary, or vandalism, restitution provisions may be included, whereby youths must repay victims for their financial losses. Most standard probation programs in the United States require little if any direct contact with the probation office. Logistically, this works out well for probation officers, who are frequently overworked and have enormous client caseloads of 300 or more. Greater caseloads means less individualized attention devoted to youths by POs, and some of these youths require more supervision than others while on standard probation.

Compared with some of the intensive supervision programs for juveniles discussed in the next chapter, standard probation exhibits relatively high rates of recidivism, ranging from 40 to 75 percent. Even certain youth camps operated in various California counties have reported recidivism rates as high as 76 percent (Palmer and Wedge, 1989). Therefore, it is often difficult to forecast which juveniles will have the greatest likelihood of reoffending, regardless of the program we are examining.

Baird (1985:36) cites the following elements that appear to be predictive of future criminal activity and reoffending by juveniles: (1) age at first adjudication; (2) a prior criminal record (a combined measure of the number and severity of priors); (3) number of prior commitments to juvenile facilities; (4) drug/chemical abuse; (5) alcohol abuse; (6) family relationships (parental control); (7) school problems; and (8) peer relationships. (9) Runaway

Baird recommends that needs assessments should be individualized, based upon the juvenile's past record and other pertinent characteristics, including the present adjudication offense. The level of supervision should vary according to the degree of risk posed to the public by the juvenile. While Baird furnishes no weighting procedure for each of the risk factors just listed so that judges can use these criteria effectively at the sentencing stage, he does describe a supervisory scheme that can act as a guide for juvenile probation and aftercare. This scheme would be applied on the basis of the perceived risk of each juvenile offender. His scheme would include the following:

REGULAR SUPERVISION

1. Four face-to-face contacts per month with youth.
2. Two face-to-face contacts per month with parents.

3. One face-to-face contact per month with placement staff.
4. One contact with school officials.

INTENSIVE SUPERVISION

1. Six face-to-face contacts per month with youth.
2. Three face-to-face contacts per month with parents.
3. One face-to-face contact per month with placement staff.
4. Two contacts with school officials.

ALTERNATIVE CARE CASES

1. One face-to-face contact per month with youth.
2. Four contacts with agency staff (one must be face-to-face).
3. One contact every two months with parents.

An assignment to any one of these supervision levels should be based on both risk and needs assessments. Baird (1985:38) says that agencies often make categorical assignments of juveniles to one level of supervision or another, primarily by referring to the highest level of supervision suggested by two or more scales used. Each juvenile probation agency prefers specific predictive devices, and some agencies use a combination of them. Again, no scale is foolproof, and the matter of false positives and false negatives arises, as some juveniles receive more supervision than they really require, while others receive less than they need.

At the beginning of the twentieth century, when probation began to be used for juvenile supervision, a report was issued entitled "Juvenile Courts and Probation" (Flexner and Baldwin, 1914). Writing seven years following the establishment of the National Probation Association in 1907, Flexner and Baldwin described three important aspects of probation as it applied to juvenile offenders:

1. The period of probation should always be indeterminate because judges cannot possibly fix the period of treatment in advance.
2. To be effective, probation work must be performed by full-time, professionally trained probation officers.
3. Probation is not a judicial function (Hurst, 1990a:17).

It is interesting to see how Flexner and Baldwin openly discounted the value of the judiciary in fixing the term of probation and performing supervisory functions. They were adamant in their belief that only professional probation officers should engage in such supervisory tasks, and that the judicial function should be minimal. The strong treatment orientation of probation is apparent as well, suggesting their belief that probationer treatment programs should be tailored to fit the probationer's needs. Further, they underscored the power originally assigned to probation officers and the leverage that probation officers could exert upon their clients, including possible revocation of probation if program infractions occurred.

Juvenile court officials and other youth workers in Highfields, New Jersey, established a nonsecure program for juveniles in 1950 that was known as the **Highfields Project.** This project was used exclusively for boys. All clients were housed in large homes or estates in groups no larger than twenty. The youths experienced minimal supervision from adults and were permitted to visit their families on weekends through furloughs. The boys were obligated to work up to forty hours a week in a nearby neuropsychiatric clinic doing various chores. Peer pressure was the primary treatment technique used in the Highfields Project. The effectiveness of the program was gauged by comparing the rates of recidivism among its participants with recidivism rates of other juvenile offenders. Highfields had lower recidivism rates, although the comparisons with other groups did not provide for effective matching of juveniles (Weeks, 1956). Therefore, researchers tended to view Highfields results with caution in later years.

An effective probation program is one in which probation officers (POs) have an awareness of the juvenile offender's needs and weaknesses. One problem in many existing probation programs is that POs find it hard to establish rapport between themselves and their juvenile clients. A high degree of mistrust exists, in large part because of the age difference between the PO and the offender.

Community service and restitution are conditional sentencing options that are increasingly used by juvenile court judges. Many juvenile offenders must work in community projects and allocate a portion of their earnings to victim compensation. (© Steve Starr/Picture Group, Inc.)

Some POs have suggested an approach normally practiced by psychological counselors in developing rapport between themselves and their clients. Sweet (1985:90) suggests, for instance, that each PO should (1) thoroughly review the youth's case, including family and juvenile interviews and other background information; (2) engage in introspection and attempt to analyze his or her own reactions to adolescents and responses to verbal exchanges; (3) attempt to cultivate a relationship of acceptance rather than rejection and punitiveness; (4) react favorably to a "critical incident," in which the juvenile may "screw up" and expect reprimand or punishment but receive acceptance and understanding instead; and (5) follow through with continued support, which bolsters juvenile confidence in the PO.

Some juveniles are unreachable through any kind of effective exchange. Chronic offenders, hard-core offenders, and psychologically disturbed juveniles frequently reject any attempts by authorities to understand them or assist them in any way. However, sometimes it is POs who have lost a "clear sense of what their mission is and how it is a part of the larger juvenile justice system" (Breed and Krisberg, 1986:15). This may be one consequence of the current trend toward a more punitive approach to juvenile crime (Garrett, 1985).

Juvenile Probation Officers

Many probation officers who work with juveniles report that their work is satisfying. Many of them see themselves as playing an important part in shaping a youth's future by means of the relationship they establish between themselves and the juveniles with whom they work. James R. Davis, a probation officer with the Department of Probation in New York City for 22 years, has supervised both adults and juvenile offenders. Usually, the juveniles he supervises are those age 16 and over who have been transferred to criminal courts because of more serious offenses they have committed. He shares his experiences by noting:

> Generally, I supervise adults from the age of 16 and over who are placed on probation by the court. Sometimes, I have supervised juveniles under age 16 who are tried in adult courts under the New York State Juvenile Laws. Although I have had only a few cases of juveniles who are tried as adults, they present the worst cases to me, and I am sure, to other probation officers. This is logical, since they are accused of violent crimes. Now there is a special worker who handles these [kinds of] cases.
>
> I remember a case of a juvenile who was 15 and tried as an adult. He was charged with felonious assault. He was hostile and noncooperative when supervised by me. For example, he didn't report on time, he was verbally abusive to me, and loud and hostile. He was arrested while on probation for another felony assault charge. He was known to have beaten up his grandmother. When I initiated a violation of probation for the new arrest, he became quite hostile and wanted to know why I did this. He even followed me

one night into the street and I had to get into a cab to escape him. He beat up another probationer in the waiting area of the office and was finally transferred to an intensive probation caseload.

I was supervising another juvenile who was placed on adult probation at the age of 15 for robbery. He had an arrest prior to being placed on probation for robbery and was arrested again during supervision for another robbery. He always tried to work, and at first he was cooperative. However, during supervision he became hostile, noncooperative, failing to keep appointments, and failing to wait for his turn in the office. He was black and insisted that he wanted a black probation officer, since I was white. However, the judge incarcerated him for a few weeks because of this new robbery charge. He is now awaiting the disposition of his new robbery case. Although I am still supervising him, the relationship between him and me is tense and fragile; he is still nervous and impatient, and he doesn't keep appointments on time. He minimizes his arrest record. He claims that blacks do not receive justice with white agents of the criminal justice system. His mother absconded from the home, and he is now supervised by his grandmother.

Although I [now] supervise [primarily] adults, anyone from the age of 16 to 19 is given a youthful offender status except for a few violent offenders. However, I believe that juveniles under 16 who are tried as adults present some special problems and do need supervision in a special caseload by experienced probation officers who are trained for this type of experience (interview with James R. Davis, January, 1991).

In a technical sense, probation officers and parole officers (POs) are also *corrections officers,* because probation and parole departments are under the correctional umbrella of the criminal justice system. However, corrections or correctional officers are traditionally associated with supervisory functions in relation to inmates of prisons and jails. Prison and jail correctional officers receive a basically different type of training from POs, although there are certain aspects of their training which are shared (e.g., legal liabilities in relation to inmates and clients, firearms training, and report preparation). For clarity, we will use the PO designation rather than the correctional officer designation in our discussions of probation and parole officers in this and other chapters.

In many jurisdictions, probation and parole officers supervise both types of offenders, probationers and parolees. Further, POs in many jurisdictions supervise both juvenile and adult offenders. Depending on how their caseloads are assigned, POs may be more or less specialized, and they may deal only with clients with certain types of problems. Table 11.1 shows the distribution of the personnel in adult and juvenile probation and parole systems in the United States during 1990.

Table 11.2 shows both adult and juvenile state administrations of probation and parole programs during 1990. It is apparent from this table that considerable diversity exists among states as to who supervises juvenile offenders. The table also shows complex divisions of labor in these jurisdictions that may occasionally prove troublesome in determining an agency's jurisdiction.

TABLE 11.1   Personnel in Adult and Juvenile Corrections (as of June 30, 1990)

Adult System

State	Employees Total	White Male	White Fem	Black Male	Black Fem	Hispanic Male	Hispanic Fem	All Others Male	All Others Fem
AL	3,289	1,333	393	1,020	526			16	1
AK	1,257	670	302	66	16	17	9	117	60
AZ	5,263	2,716	1,161	182	107	763	235	77	32
AR	1,945	920	259	633	130	1		2	
CA	27,661	11,533	5,008	2,761	1,775	3,405	1,487	1,150	542
CO	2,355	1,415	489	80	14	212	79	55	11
CT	4,263	2,194	764	722	237	270	49	19	8
DE	1,458	714	267	324	124	10	3	12	4
FL	19,152	9,625	4,683	2,044	1,891	460	257	129	63
GA	9,630	4,498	2,094	1,969	952	48	15	37	17
HI	1,487	208	78	52	13	137	45	677	277
ID[1]	599	419	153	5		15	2	5	
IL	11,483	7,064	2,380	1,240	551	140	40	50	18
IN	5,829	3,965	850	675	302	28	5	3	1
IA	1,774	1,206	376	87	26	38	12	21	8
KS[1]	2,314	1,463	584	131	61	48	7	14	6
KY	2,855	1,794	817	145	89	2		7	1
LA	5,703	2,459	1,049	1,459	727	6	3		
ME	1,285	1,020	265						
MD	5,110	2,245	513	1,401	917	18	3	11	2
MA	4,977	3,326	1,098	270	141	98	17	22	5
MI	13,886	8,011	2,987	1,258	1,117	140	55	241	77
MN	2,220	1,419	652	51	14	20	8	37	19
MS	2,814	687	393	961	757	5	1	5	5
MO	5,841	3,659	1,800	186	147	15	4	22	8
MT	546	433	111			1		1	
NE	1,393	847	421	57	30	21	6	9	2
NV	1,465	921	316	86	32	49	18	33	10
NH	643	529	107	2	1	4			
NJ	10,337	4,836	1,502	2,355	971	404	117	102	50
NM	1,953	490	186	42	9	914	257	93	19

† Combined adult and juvenile departments
* Combined male/female total
— Data not available at time of publication
1. Data as of 6/30/89
2. Hispanics are included in other categories
3. Data as of 8/2/90

SOURCE: American Correctional Association, *1991 Directory* (Laurel, MD: American Correctional Association, 1991), pp. xlii–xliii.

Juvenile System								
Employees	White		Black		Hispanic		All Others	
Total	Male	Fem	Male	Fem	Male	Fem	Male	Fem
472	102	84	202	83		1		
294	151	100	12	6	3	2	7	13
860	391	224	57	38	95	41	11	3
322	61	74	128	58				1
4,135	1,351	752	642	367	549	238	143	93
579	237	163	58	27	58	25	9	2
297	149	70	40	21	10	4	3	
170	36	39	54	39	1	1		
3,189[1]								
2,105	473	476	625	515			11	5
†								
190	117	67	1	1	2		1	1
†								
†								
227	154	67	2		4			
527	388*		118*		17*		4*	
793	555	158	56	24				
†								
†								
1,465[2]	407	276	344	422			10	6
592	284	146	78	24	35	20	3	2
1,504	—	—	—	—	—	—		
†								
406[3]	76	113	105	112				
628	265	226	76	56		2	2	1
183	104	34			2			4
†								
159	103	43	1		6	1	5	
190	120	67	3					
†								
581	100	106	13	8	190	154	6	4

4. Counted in white/black columns; shown here for sex breakdown
5. Race unknown
6. Data as of 7/31/90
7. Includes 466 males, 344 females
8. Data as of 3/31/90

TABLE 11.1   (Continued)

					Adult System				
State	Employees Total	White Male	Fem	Black Male	Fem	Hispanic Male	Fem	All Others Male	Fem
NY	34,650	23,341	6,036	2,483	1,279	938	305	198	70
NC	10,446	5,728	1,619	2,325	608	20	4	111	31
ND	340	216	115	1				8	
OH	8,378	5,027	1,801	880	545	42	25	34	24
OK	4,001	2,236	1,064	221	212	23	11	160	74
OR	1,969	1,205	547	43	28	44	22	54	26
PA	6,260	4,692	887	443	183	43	3	7	2
RI	1,258	953	191	56	18	26	4	7	3
SC	5,814	1,868	1,024	1,871	978			48	25
SD	575	386	173	1	1			12	2
TN	5,180	2,903	1,172	636	438	21		10	
TX	17,960	8,594	4,149	2,328	1,256	1,235	276	88	34
UT	1,267	803	374	18	7	25	16	15	9
VT	718							491[5]	227[6]
VA[6]	8,259	3,646	1,544	1,982	1,026	31	10	13	7
WA	4,532	2,544	1,371	227	62	104	42	102	80
WV	737	523	205	7	2				
WI	4,002	2,472	1,250	60	81	49	13	56	21
WY	375	221	96	1		43	8	4	
Total	277,508	149,977	55,678	33,847	18,401	9,923	3,473	4,328	1,881
FBP	18,294	10,138	3,136	2,270	1,125	1,030	247	272	76
DC	3,876							2,702	1,174
NYC	12,983	3,026	301	4,167	3,207	1,737	423	104	18
PHL	1,750	442	105	703	375	36	6	22	61
GU	197	13	5	8			1	130	40
VI[1]	224			148	65	10	1		
CSC[1]	11,015	7,568	3,447						
AB	2,095								
MB[8]	886								
NF	303	233	70						
ON	3,538							2,913[5]	625[5]
PEI	207	151	55	1					
PQ	2,431	2,110	321						
SK[1]	999	691	308						
YU[1]	46	36	10						

	Juvenile System							
Employees Total	White		Black		Hispanic		All Others	
	Male	Fem	Male	Fem	Male	Fem	Male	Fem
3,453	1,142	799	845	435	149	57	18	8
871	442*		429*				491[4]	380[4]
†								
1,762	490	443	451	362	7	3	5	1
1,872[1]	463	1,002	131	205			27	1
536	332	160	13	4	11	7	8	1
843	408	155	190	83	3	2	1	1
239	115	71	27	15	7	3		1
995	179	265	269	279	1		1	1
119[1]	77	41						
995[2]	358	319	175	143				
1,808	563	434	312	203	172	113	10	1
466[1]	236	168	19	7	18	4	11	3
377	112	264	1					
—	—	—	—	—	—	—		
837[7]	758*		40*		21*		18*	
†								
†								
†								
34,591	10,857	7,406	5,088	3,537	1,361	678	806	576
	28	16	339	181	4	2	5	5
580	24	24	336	209	65	41	2	1
702								

TABLE 11.2   Providers of Probation/Parole/Aftercare Services (as of June 30, 1990)

	Number Board Members*	Adult Paroling Authorities	Adult Parole Services
AL	3	Bd of Pardons & Paroles	Bd of Pardons & Paroles
AK	5 (PT)	Bd of Parole	Dept of Corrections
AZ	7	Bd of Pardons & Paroles	DOC/Cmty Svcs Div
AR	7 (PT)[1]	Bd of Parole & Cmty Rehab	DOC/Div of Pardons & Paroles
CA	9	Bd of Prison Terms**	DOC/Parole & Cmty Svcs Div
CO	7	Bd of Parole	DOC/Div of Cmty Svcs
CT	11 (PT)[2]	Bd of Parole	DOC/Div of Parole**
DE	5 (PT)[2]	Bd of Parole	DOC/Div of Cmty Corr
DC	4	Bd of Parole	Bd of Parole
FL	7	Prob & Parole Cmsn	DOC/Prob & Parole Svcs
GA	5	Bd of Pardons & Parole	Bd of Pardons & Parole
HI	3 (PT)[2]	Paroling Authority	Paroling Authority/Field Svcs
ID	5 (PT)	Cmsn for Pardons & Parole	DOC/Div Field & Cmty Svcs
IL	13	Prisoner Review Bd	DOC/Cmty Svcs Div**
IN	5	Parole Bd	DOC/Parole Svcs Section
IA	5 (PT)[2]	Bd of Parole	DOC/Div Cmty Corr Svcs
KS	5	Parole Bd	DOC/Parole Svcs**
KY	7	Parole Bd	CC/Dept Cmty Svcs & Facilities
LA	5	Bd of Parole	DPSC/Div of Prob & Parole
ME	5 (PT)	Parole Bd[3]	DOC/Div of Prob & Parole
MD	7	Parole Commission	DPSCS/Div of Parole & Prob
MA	7	Parole Bd	Parole Bd
MI	7	Parole Bd	DOC/Bur of Field Svcs

*All members serve full-time unless coded "PT."
**Accredited by Commission on Accreditation for Corrections
1. AR—3 full-time, 4 part-time
2. Chairman serves full-time; members part-time.
3. ME—Parole Board hears pre-1976 cases of parole. Flat sentences with no parole under criminal code effective 5/1/76
4. MN—Executive Officer & two Deputy Executive Officers (CCA Cmty Corr Act)
5. OH—Plus 11 hearing officers
6. PA—The Board of Probation and Parole administers adult services when sentence is over 2 yrs; county courts when sentence is 2 yrs or less.

SOURCE: American Correctional Association, *1991 Directory* (Laurel, MD. American Correctional Association, 1991), pp. xvi–xvii.

TABLE 11.2 (Continued)

Adult Probation Services	Juvenile Parole/Aftercare Services	Juvenile Probation Services
Bd of Pardons & Paroles	Co Courts	Dept Youth Svcs ($ only) & Co Cts
Dept of Corrections	No Parole/aftercare	DHSS/Div Family & Youth Svcs
State Courts	DJC/Parole Admin	State Courts
Adult Prob Commission	DCFS/Courts	DCFS/Courts
Co Depts	DYA/Parole Svcs Branch	Co Depts
Judicial Districts	DOI/Div of Youth Svcs	Judicial Districts
Office of Adult Prob	Dept Children & Youth Svcs	Superior Court/Family Div
DOC/Div of Cmty Corr	DSCYF/Div Youth Rehab**	DSCYF/Div Youth Rehab**
DC Superior Ct/Social Svcs Div	DHS/Youth Svcs Admin	DC Superior Ct/Social Svcs Div
DOC/Prob & Parole Svcs	DHRS/Children, Youth & Fam Svcs	DHRS/Children Youth & Fam Svcs
DOC/Prob Div	DHR/Div of Youth Svcs & Co Courts	DHR/Div Youth Svcs & Co Courts
State Judiciary/Prob Ofc	DPS/Youth Corr Facility/ Cmty Svcs Sect	State Judiciary/Family Courts
DOC/Div Field & Cmty Svcs	Dept Health & Welfare	Dept Health & Welfare and Co Cts
Judicial Circuits	DOC/Juv Field Svcs**	Judicial Circuits
Judicial/County Courts	DOC/Parole Svcs Section	Judicial/County Courts
DOC/Div Cmty Corr Svcs	DHS/Bur Adult, Children & Family Svcs	Judicial Districts
Judicial Districts	DSRS/Youth Svcs	Judicial Districts
CC/Dept Cmty Svcs & Facilities	CHR/Div of Family Svcs	CHR/Div of Family Svcs
DPSC/Div of Prob & Parole	DPSC/Div of Youth Svcs	DPSC/Div of Youth Svcs
DOC/Div of Prob & Parole	DOC/Div of Prob & Parole	DOC/Div of Prob & Parole
DPSCS/Div of Parole & Prob	Dept of Juv Svcs	Dept of Juv Svcs
Office of Cmsnr of Prob/ Courts	DYS/Bur of Cmty Svcs	Office of Cmsnr of Prob/ Courts
DOC/Bur Field Svcs & Dist Cts	DSS/Ofc Children & Yth Svcs/Co Cts	DSS/Ofc Children & Yth Svcs/Co Cts

7. VT−No functional juvenile parole system. Children in custody go into placement and eventually return to community under supervision of caseworker.

8. WV−Under state statute, parole is considered probation.

The following states have one or more independent county, municipal or city departments: CO, GA, IN, KS, KY, LA, MO, NE, NY, OK, TN, WY.

All Boards are independent except MD, MI, MN, OH, TX, WI.

TABLE 11.2 (Continued)

	Number Board Members*	Adult Paroling Authorities	Adult Parole Services
MN	4 (PT)[4]	DOC/Office Adult Release**	DOC/Prob Par Supv Rel/ Co Cts or CCA
MS	5 (PT)	Parole Bd	DOC/Cmty Svcs Div
MO	5	Bd of Prob & Parole	DOC/Bd of Prob & Parole
MT	3 (PT)	Bd of Pardons	DVCD/Cmty Corr Bureau
NE	5	Bd of Parole**	DCS/Adult Parole Admin**
NV	5	Bd of Parole Cmsnrs	Dept of Parole & Prob
NH	5 (PT)	Bd of Parole	DOC/Div of Field Svcs**
NJ	9	Parole Bd**	Bureau of Parole**
NM	4	Adult Parole Bd	CD/Prob & Parole Div
NY	19	Bd of Parole	Div of Parole
NC	5	Parole Commission	DOC/Div Adult Prob & Parole
ND	3 (PT)	Parole Bd	DCR/Div of Parole & Prob
OH	9[5]	DRC/Div of Parole & Cmty Svcs & Parole Bd	DRC/Div of Parole & Cmty Svcs
OK	5 (PT)	Pardon & Parole Bd	DOC/Div of Prob & Parole
OR	5	Bd of Parole & Post Prison Supv	DOC/Cmty Svcs Br/Co Cts
PA	5	Bd of Prob & Parole** & Co Cts[6]	Bd of Prob & Parole** & Co Cts
RI	6 (PT)	Parole Bd	DOC/Div of Field Svcs
SC	7 (PT)	Bd Prob, Parole & Pardon Svcs	Dept Prob, Parole & Pardon Svcs**
SD	3 (PT)	Bd of Pardons & Paroles	BPParoles/Par Svcs
TN	7	Bd of Paroles	BP/Parole Field Svcs
TX	18	Bd of Pardons & Paroles	TDCJ/PPD/Parole Supv
UT	5	Bd of Pardons	DOC/Field Operations Div
VT	5 (PT)	Bd of Parole	AHS/Dept of Corrections
VA	5	Parole Bd	DOC/Div of Adult Cmty Corr
WA	5	Indeterminate Sent Review Bd	DOC/Div Cmty Svcs
WV	3	Bd of Prob & Parole[8]	Div of Corrections
WI	4	Parole Commission	DOC/Div Prob & Parole
WY	5 (PT)	Bd of Parole	Dept of Prob & Parole
US	9	Parole Commission**	Admin Ofc of US Courts

TABLE 11.2 (Continued)

Adult Probation Services	Juvenile Parole/Aftercare Services	Juvenile Probation Services
DOC/Prob Par Supv Rel/ Co Cts or CCA	DOC/Prob Par Supv Rel/ Co Cts or CCA	DOC/Prob Par Supv Rel/ Co Cts or CCA
DOC/Cmty Svcs Div	DHS/OYS/Cmty Svcs Div	DHS/OYS/Cmty Svcs Div
DOC/Bd of Prob & Parole	DSS/Div Youth Svcs & Jud Circuits	Judicial Circuits
DVCD/Cmty Corr Bureau	Dept Family Svcs	Judicial Districts
Neb Prob Admin	DCS/Juv Parole Admin**	Neb Prob Admin
Dept of Parole & Prob	DHR/YSD/Youth Parole Bureau	Districts Courts
DOC/Div Field Svcs** & Dist Cts	DHHS/DCYS/Bur of Children	DHHS/DCYS/Bur of Children
The Judiciary/Prob Div	Bureau of Parole**	The Judiciary/Prob Div
CD/Prob & Parole Div	YA/Cmty Svcs Div/JPB	YA/Cmty Svcs Div
Div Prob & CorrAlt/Co Courts	Div for Youth/Div of Parole	Div Prob & Corr Alt/Co Courts
DOC/Div Adult Prob & Parole	Admin Office of Courts/ Juv Svcs Div	Admin Office of Courts/ Juv Svcs Div
DCR/Div of Parole & Prob	DCR/Div of Juv Svcs	DCR/Div of Juv Svcs/Supr Cts
DRC/Div of Parole & Cmty Svcs & Co Courts	Dept of Youth Svcs	Co Courts
DOC/Div of Prob & Parole	DHS/Div of Children & Yth Svcs	DHS/Div of Child & Yth Svcs, Co (3)
DOC/Cmty Svcs Br/Co Cts	DHR/CSD/Ofc Juv Corr Svcs	Co Courts
Bd of Prob & Parole** & Co Cts	Co Courts (Prob & Aftercare)	Co Courts (Prob & Aftercare)
DOC/Div of Field Svcs	DCTF/Div of Juv Corr Svcs	DCTF/Div of Juv Corr Svcs
Dept Prob, Parole & Pardon Svcs**	Dept Youth Svcs/Cmty Div	Depth Youth Svcs/Cmty Div
Unified Judicial Sys/Ct Svcs Dept	Unified Judicial Sys/Ct Svcs Dept	Unified Judicial Sys/Ct Svcs Dept
DOC/Div of Prob**	DYD/Prob Div**	DYD/Prob Div**
Cmty Justice Assis Div/ Dist Cts	TYC/Cmty SVcs Div/Ofc Par Supv	Co Depts
DOC/Field Operations Div	DHS/Div of Youth Corr	Juv Courts
AHS/Dept of Corrections	AHS/DSRS[7]	DSRS/Div of Social Svcs
DOC/Div of Adult Cmty Corr	Dept Youth & Fam Svcs	Dept Youth & Fam Svcs
DOC/Div Cmty Svcs & Co Cts	DSHS/Div of Juv Rehab	Co Courts
DOC & Judicial Circuits	DOC (Compact) and DHHR	DOC (Compact), DHHR & Jud Circuits
DOC/Div Prob & Par	DHHS/Div Yth Svcs/Co Soc Svcs Depts	Co Social Svcs Depts
Dept of Prob & Parole	Dept of Prob & Parole	Dept of Prob & Parole
Admin Ofc of US Courts/ Div of Prob		

Probation Work and Professionalism. There is a keen sense of profession-alism among most probation and parole officers. The *American Correctional Association* and the *American Probation and Parole Association* are two of the most important professional organizations. They disseminate information about corrections and probation and parole programs, and they provide workshops and various forms of professional training. Many probation and parole officers attend the meetings of these and other professional organiza-tions to learn about the latest innovations and probation programs.

Sweet (1985) views probation work with juveniles as a timely opportunity to intervene and make a difference in their lives. Thus, he sees probation as a type of therapy. He divides the therapy function that probation officers can perform into five simple steps:

1. *Case review*—probation counselors need skills to interpret the behaviors of the youths they supervise and their probable antecedents.
2. *Self-awareness*—probation counselors need to inspect their own reactions to youths; are they too impatient or overly sensitive? Traditional transference–countertransference issues must be addressed.
3. *Development of a relationship*—great patience is required; children are often rejected, and probation officers must learn to accept them and demonstrate a faith in their ability to achieve personal goals.
4. *The critical incident*—the testing phase of the relationship, when juveniles may deliberately act up to test honesty and sincerity of the PO.
5. *Following through*—successive tests will be made by juveniles as they continue to verify the PO's honesty and sincerity; POs do much of the parenting that their clients' parents failed to do. Sweet considers these stages integral features of action therapy that can often be more effective than insight-oriented therapy (Sweet, 1985:90).

Because of their diverse training, POs often orient themselves toward juvenile clients in particular ways that may be more or less effective. Because many juvenile offenders are considered manipulators who might take advantage of a PO's sympathies, some POs have devised interpersonal barriers between themselves and their youthful clients. Other POs have adopted more productive interpersonal strategies. Strong (1981) has identified several types of PO orientations toward youthful offenders that might have different implications, depending upon how these orientations influence the nature of the PO–client relationship. These orientations include: (1) the **enforcer,** in which POs perceive themselves as enforcement officers who must regulate juvenile behaviors; (2) the **detector, in** which the PO attempts to identify troublesome juvenile clients in advance on the basis of probation program rule infractions; (3) the **broker,** in which POs try to refer youths to appropriate community services and treatments; and (4) the **educator, mediator,** and **enabler,** in which POs seek to instruct and assist offenders in dealing with their personal and social problems in order to fit better into their community environments.

If POs continuously check up on their youthful clients or regard them with suspicion, they inhibit the growth of a productive interpersonal relationship that might be helpful in facilitating a youth's reentry into society. Enforcement-oriented officers and those who attempt to detect rule infractions almost always create a hostile working relationship with their clients, and communication barriers are often erected that inhibit a PO's effectiveness. Educators, enablers, and mediators are perhaps most helpful to youths, although broker-oriented POs are instrumental in helping juveniles receive the treatments and services they need.

Entry-Level Requirements for Probation Officers. A survey of 676 probation and parole officers was conducted by the American Correctional Association in 1986 (American Correctional Association, 1986b). This survey revealed that the average age of those surveyed was 38. Sixty-one percent were male, and most had bachelor's degrees. They had an average of eight to ten years of experience, and their salaries ranged from $20,000 to $25,000. Most officers (83 percent) were white, 9 percent were black, and Hispanics and others accounted for the remaining 8 percent. It should be noted that generally, states have not been generous in funding probation and parole officer positions. Thus, because of low pay in many jurisdictions, there is a fairly high rate of turnover among POs. But high turnover occurs mostly in the first year or two of service as a PO. Some states pay their POs well.

POs for the federal government and attached to the U.S. Probation Office are perhaps the highest paid POs in the nation. Their fringe benefits and pay rates make their jobs especially attractive. Often, these POs are recruited from those who have performed PO work in different states. Thus, they enter their federal positions with considerable experience. Labor turnover among POs with the U.S. Probation Office is extremely low. Many officers remain with the U.S. Probation Office until retirement because of the many rewards, both financial and psychological, it offers. Rosalind Andrews, Chief Probation Officer of the U.S. Probation Office in Knoxville, Tennessee, has remarked that "Nobody quits around here. They're here for the duration. We simply pay better than most states, and our work is interesting. There is never a dull moment around here" (Excerpts from personal interview, May, 1990). Although the U.S. Probation Office performs "supervised release" functions mostly for adult probationers and parolees, it also supervises a small number of juvenile offenders who have violated federal laws.

Largely because of the relatively high turnover among POs in state probation and parole agencies, recruitment of new POs is brisk. Entry requirements in many states are not particularly demanding. Although the sample of POs surveyed by the American Correctional Association tended to have bachelor's degrees, 78 percent of all states require only a high school diploma or GED as the minimum educational level. In 12 percent of the state jurisdictions, there are no specific educational requirements for PO work (American Correctional Association, 1986b:38).

Probation Officer Functions. The functions of POs are diverse, and they include such tasks as report preparation, home and school visits, and a variety of other client contacts. They often arrange contacts between their clients and various community-based corrections agencies who provide services and specific types of psychological and social treatments. POs themselves perform counseling tasks with their clients. They also must enforce laws associated with probation or parole program conditions. Thus, if offenders have been ordered to comply with a specific curfew and/or reimburse victims for their financial losses, POs must monitor them to ensure that these program conditions have been fulfilled.

Assessment Centers. The writing dimension of PO work cannot be overemphasized. Report preparation accounts for over half of a PO's time. Therefore, writing skills are not only useful, they are necessary. Dade County, Florida, operates an **assessment center** that is used to train its correctional officers, including many probation and parole officers in the state. Assessment centers perform screening functions and administer tests and other devices to recruit new POs and train them. Law enforcement agencies in various jurisdictions utilize assessment centers similar to those existing in various Florida jurisdictions.

Assessment centers help administrators of juvenile probation programs identify various skills of prospective officers, including (1) the ability to understand and implement policies and procedures, (2) the ability to be aware of all elements in a given situation, and to use sensitivity to others and good judgment in dealing with different situations, and (3) the ability to communicate effectively. Personal and social skills are highly prized among POs, and those who appear most qualified are subjected to a further series of tests and interviews. The testing pertains to the preparation of written reports, role-playing, and acting out problem situations, and some videotaping is used to present those trained with a variety of client scenarios. Three-person teams of evaluators conduct final screenings of applicants and attempt to select those who will minimize agency liabilities arising from client lawsuits.

Some of the major PO dimensions that are deemed most important are:

1. Problem-solving (problem analysis—the ability to grasp the source, nature, and key elements of problems); judgment—recognition of the significant factors to arrive at sound and practical decisions.
2. Communication (dialogue skills—effectiveness of one-on-one contacts with youthful clients, small group interactions); writing skills—expression of ideas clearly and concisely.
3. Emotional and motivational (reactions to pressure—functioning in a controlled, effective manner under conditions of stress); keeping one's head; drive—the amount of directed and sustained energy to accomplish one's objectives.
4. Interpersonal (insight into others—the ability to proceed, giving due consideration to the needs and feelings of others); leadership—the direction of behavior of others toward the achievement of goals.
5. Administrative (planning—forward thinking, anticipating situations and problems, and preparation in advance to cope with these problems);

commitment to excellence—determination that the task will be well done.

   Probation Officer Stress and Burnout. Stress and *burnout* are two primary factors that may interfere with a PO's work and impair performance. **Stress** *is a nonspecific response to a perceived threat to an individual's well-being* (Selye, 1976). Reactions to stress might be somatic complaints of aches and pains; irritability, loss of attention span, and fatigue are other concomitants of stress. **Burnout** *is a result of stress.* Burnout conveys *work alienation, depersonalization, depression, and other job-related complaints.* Various definitions of burnout suggest emotional, mental, and physical exhaustion that might debilitate and weaken a PO's ability to work effectively with others (Whitehead and Lindquist, 1985). As more dangerous juvenile offenders are placed in probation programs, it may be anticipated that PO stress and burnout will increase. While firearms training is often required as a part of a PO's recruitment program, POs have not typically carried firearms in past years. However, there are indications that this situation is changing, particularly with growing caseloads of more serious, violent offenders to supervise (Brown, 1990:25).

   In 1990 it was estimated that there were 20,000 juvenile probation officers in the United States (Hurst, 1990a). These officers provided intake services for nearly 1.5 million juveniles, did predispositional studies of over 600,000 cases, and received over 500,000 cases for supervision (American Correctional Association, 1991). These cases are not distributed evenly throughout the various juvenile probation departments in the United States. Thus, caseloads for some POs are considerably larger than they are for others. A high caseload is arbitrarily defined as 50 or more juvenile clients, although caseloads as high as 300 or more have been reported in some jurisdictions. Hurst (1990a:19) says that a standard probation caseload recommendation of 35 has been made by the President's Crime Commission, although this figure is rarely achieved in most probation agencies today. When caseloads are particularly high, this places an even greater burden on the shoulders of POs, who must often prepare predisposition reports for youths at the juvenile court judge's direction.

   Juvenile probation officers have been guided since 1900 by their belief in the probation mission: *protecting society and acting in the best interests of children* (Hurst, 1990a:19). Although a general lack of a strong professional membership has hampered the influence of juvenile probation officers in most U.S. jurisdictions, the U.S. Supreme Court rulings of the 1960s and 1970s expanding juvenile rights has further undermined their powers. Today, the following issues have been identified that continue to be debated:

1. *Organizational sponsorship:* Should probation services be administered by executive branches of government or by judiciary branches?
2. *Local versus state administration:* Should probation services be operated by the state or by local government?

BOX 11.2

Juvenile Highlights

What should be done with chronic juvenile offenders? In November, 1986, two teenage brothers broke into a house in East St. Louis, Illinois, occupied by six children ranging in age from 4 to 14, and demanded sex from the 12-year-old girl. She refused, and one teenager cut her throat. Because there were witnesses to this deed, the two teenagers forced the remaining children onto a bed, where they methodically shot them. All the children lived. The younger of the two attackers, 14 years of age, had already compiled a long list of arrests for violent acts. Because no deaths resulted from his actions against the children in East St. Louis, he was permitted to plead guilty to "armed violence" and was sentenced to 120 years in prison in July, 1987 after a transfer to criminal court. His brother entered a guilty plea to the same charges.

According to many juvenile delinquency experts, we are not doing a particularly good job of filtering out the most serious career offenders, who often account for most of the serious juvenile crime. Some estimates suggest that about 10 percent of violent juvenile offenders commit about two thirds of all violent juvenile crime. If these youths can be effectively targeted for treatment and/or punishment, perhaps incidents such as the one occurring in East St. Louis can be minimized.

Unfortunately, widespread apathy exists among judges and prosecutors, many of whom don't want to deal with these kids. Thus, according to Old Dominion University faculty member Wolfgang Pindur, these youths wind up getting only "band-aid" treatment instead of meaningful assistance and treatment. Currently, a debate rages over whether serious juvenile offenders are better served by counseling them away from lives of crime or whether they should serve prison time. Often, it is difficult to identify the chronic juvenile offender, since the juvenile justice systems of so many jurisdictions observe such strict confidentiality laws. Information-sharing about those juveniles who reoffend with great frequency is minimized by such confidentiality restrictions. However, new programs are being devised to furnish police and others with more complete historical data about youthful offenders who are arrested for violent crimes. It is hoped that these programs will help to ensure more effective treatments or punishments, depending upon individual circumstances.

(Some factual information adapted from Ted Gest and Cynthia Kyle, "Kids, Crime, and Punishment: Police, Prosecutors, and Courts Get Tougher with Chronic Offenders," *U.S. News & World Report*, August 24, 1987, pp. 50–51.)

3. *Client caseload:* The National Probation Association standard of a maximum caseload of fifty cases was recommended in 1923, but this figure has been reduced to thirty-five at the recommendation of the President's Crime Commission in 1967; however, such numbers are seldom achieved in actual practice.

4. *Method of supervision:* Should probation officers suppress offenders and conduct extensive surveillance on them, or should they assess their needs and bring services to bear to meet these needs?

5. *Diagnosis and classification:* Are empirical classification approaches superior to qualitative assessments of client needs?

6. *Private versus public administration of probation services:* What should be the limits of privatization in juvenile probation?

7. *Performance measurement:* How can juvenile probation officers be effectively evaluated and compensated? (Hurst, 1990b:19; Torbet, 1987).

The Predisposition Report and Its Preparation

Juvenile judges in many jurisdictions order the preparation of *predisposition reports,* which are the functional equivalent of pre-sentence investigation reports for adults. **Predisposition reports** *are intended to furnish judges with background information about juveniles to enable them to make a more informed sentencing decision.* They also function to assist probation officers and others to target high-need areas for youths and specific services or agencies for individualized referrals. This information is often channeled to information agencies such as the National Center for Juvenile Justice in Pittsburgh, Pennsylvania, so that researchers may benefit in juvenile justice investigations. They may analyze the information compiled from various jurisdictions for their own research investigations (Osgood, 1983; Polk, 1984).

Trester (1981:89–90) has summarized four important reasons for the preparation of predisposition reports:

1. They provide juvenile court judges with a more complete picture of juvenile offenders and their offenses, including the existence of any aggravating or mitigating circumstances.

2. They can assist the court in tailoring the disposition of the case to an offender's needs.

3. They may lead to the identification of positive factors that would indicate the likelihood of rehabilitation.

4. They provide judges with the offender's treatment history, which might indicate the effectiveness or ineffectiveness of previous dispositions and suggest the need for alternative dispositions.

It is important to recognize that predispositional reports are not required by judges in all jurisdictions. By the same token, legislative mandates obligate officials in other jurisdictions to prepare them for all juveniles to be adjudicated. Also, there are no specific formats that are universally acceptable in these report preparations. Figure 11.2 is an example of a predisposition report.

Rogers (1990:44) indicates that predisposition reports contain insightful information about youths that can be helpful to juvenile court judges prior to sentencing. Six social aspects of a person's life are crucial for investigations, analysis, and treatment. These include: (1) personal health, physical and emotional; (2) family and home situation; (3) recreational activities and use of leisure time; (4) peer group relationships (types of companions); (5) education; and (6) work experience (Rogers, 1990:44). According to the National Advisory Commission on Criminal Justice Standards and Goals as outlined in 1973, predisposition reports have been recommended in all cases where the offenders are minors. In actual practice, however, predisposition reports are prepared only at the request of juvenile court judges. No systematic pattern typifies such report preparation in most U.S. jurisdictions. Table 11.3 shows the type of information reported in a sample of 162 predisposition reports.

Rogers (1990:46) notes that the following characteristics were included in 100 percent of cases: (1) gender, (2) ethnic status, (3) age at first juvenile court appearance, (4) source of first referral to juvenile court, (5) reason(s) for referral; (6) formal court disposition; (7) youth's initial placement by court; (8) miscellaneous court orders and conditions, (9) type of counsel retained, (10) initial plea; (11) number of prior offenses; (12) age at time of initial offense; (13) number of offenses after first hearing; (14) total number of offenses; (15) number of companions, first offense, (16) number of detentions, and (17) number of out-of-home placements.

These predisposition reports may or may not contain victim impact statements. Pre-sentence investigation reports or PSIs that are prepared on adults who are convicted of crimes in criminal courts are the adult equivalents to predisposition reports. It is more common to see such victim impact statements in PSI reports, although some predisposition reports contain them in certain jurisdictions. These statements are often prepared by victims themselves and appended to the report before the judge sees it. They are intended to provide judges with a sense of the physical harm and monetary damage victims have sustained, and thus, they are often aggravating factors that weigh heavily against the juvenile to be sentenced.

The Success of Standard Juvenile Probation

The success of standard juvenile probation as well as other probation and parole programs is measured by the rate of *recidivism* accompanying these program alternatives. Recidivism is measured in various ways, including rearrests, reconvictions, new adjudications, return to secure detention, movement from standard probation to intensive supervised probation, and simple probation program condition violations, such as drug use or alcohol

THE PREDISPOSITION REPORT

**A Model Set of Field Notes to Guide Preparation of
Juvenile Court Predisposition Reports**

COURT REPORT OUTLINE

CASE NO:_____ HEARING DATE:_____

ADDRESS:_____PHONE:_____

1.	REASON FOR HEARING:	PETITION NO.:	PETITION DATE:	W&I / SUB:
	NAME: (AKA):			AGE:
	ALLEGATION AND REFERENCE TO P.D. REPORT OR COMPLAINT:			
2.	PRESENT SITUATION	FIRST COURT WARD	REFERRAL DATE AND AGENCY:	
	PLACE AND DATE OF DETENTION OR CUSTODY:		RELEASED TO:	DATE:
3.	CITATION	SERVED / MAILED	TO:	
	SERVED BY:		LOCATION	DATE:
4.	LEGAL RESIDENCE	DETERMINING PARENT:	ARRIVED IN SAN DIEGO COUNTY:	
	VERIFICATION:		RESIDENCE OF CHILD:	
5.	PREVIOUS HISTORY:			
6.	STATEMENT OF CHILD (Description, attitude, and statements re: allegation and home):			
	RACE: / HAIR: / EYES: / HT: / WT: / MARKS:			

Figure 11-2 A Predisposition Report. (Source: Joseph W. Rogers, "The Predisposition Report: Maintaining the Promise of Individual and Juvenile Justice," *Federal Probation* 54 (1990), pp. 51–52.)

7. STATEMENT OF PARENTS (Description, attitude, and statement re: allegation and child):

8. STATEMENT OF VICTIM, WITNESSES, RELATIVES OR OTHERS (Name, Address, Date and Relation to Case):

9. FAMILY HISTORY | MARRIAGE OF NATURAL PARENTS, DATE AND PLACE:

CHILDREN AND ORDER OF BIRTH

AGE, EDUCATIONAL LEVEL AND BACKGROUND OF NATURAL PARENTS

DATE, PLACE, REASON AND EFFECTS OF SEPARATION, DIVORCE, REMARRIAGE (CUSTODY):

PREVIOUS RESIDENCE; EMPLOYMENT; DATE ARRIVED S. D. CO.; PRESENT FAMILY UNIT:

DESCRIPTION OF HOME AND FURNISHINGS:

| OWNED | | $ |
| RENTED | | $ |

COMMUNITY RELATIONSHIP AND ENVIRONMENTAL FACTORS: POLICE RECORD OF PARENT AND/OR SIBLINGS:

DISEASES IN HISTORY OF EITHER PARENT: HANDICAPS, MENTAL DISORDERS, ALCOHOLISM, SUICIDE; HEALTH INSURANCE AND HOSPITAL ELIGIBILITY:

RELIGION AND ATTENDANCE:

PARENT - CHILD RELATIONSHIP:

Figure 11-2 (cont.)

THE PREDISPOSITION REPORT

10. ECONOMIC SITUATION	PARENT(S) EMPLOYED	TYPE JOB	EMPLOYER:

HOURS OF EMPLOYMENT:	WEEKLY/MONTHLY INCOME:
OTHER SOURCES OF INCOME	HARDSHIPS (FINANCIAL STATEMENT)

11. CHILD'S HISTORY: DATE AND PLACE OF BIRTH:

	HOSPITAL	FULL TERM
	HOME	OTHER

NORMAL DELIVERY	WEIGHT:	BIRTH INJURIES:
CESAREAN OR OTHER		

MOTHER'S HEALTH AND ATTITUDE OF PARENTS:	WEANED:	TALKED:
	WALKED:	TOILET:

DATES AND AFTER EFFECTS OF CHILDHOOD DISEASES:

Diptheria: Scarlet Fever:
Chicken Pox: Whooping Cough:
Measles: Mumps or Other:

DEVELOPMENTAL HISTORY: INJURIES OR OPERATIONS:

HANDICAPS:	SPEECH:	HEARING:	SIGHT:
ENURESIS:	TEMPER TANTRUMS:		STEALING:
LYING:	RUNAWAY:		OTHER:

RELATIONSHIP WITH SIBLINGS AND PEERS:

DISCIPLINE METHODS:

CHILD'S ROOM:	ALLOWANCE:	HOBBYS, SPORTS:
CHILD'S EMPLOYER:	HOURS OF EMPLOYMENT:	WAGES:
SEX EDUCATION:		

12. SCHOOL RECORDS	PREVIOUS SCHOOL(S)	PRESENT SCHOOL AND GRADE:

SUBJECTS AND GRADE AVERAGE:

TRUANCY:	BEHAVIOR:

REFER TO SCHOOL OR GUIDANCE BUREAU REPORTS:

13. PSYCHOLOGICAL, PSYCHIATRIC, AND MEDICAL FINDINGS (REPORTS):

14. OTHER AGENCIES (CENTRAL INDEX CLEARANCE):

15. SUMMARY AND PLAN:

16. RECOMMENDATION:

TABLE 11.3   Percentage of Juvenile Case Records in Which Line Item Information
              Was Located

Variable Identification	IBM Col.	N–162
Case code number	1-3	
Sex	4	100
Ethnic status	5	100
Age, 1st juv. ct. appearance	6	100
Source of 1st referral	7	100
Reason for 1st referral/ct. hearing	8-9	100
Recoding of prior item	10	100
Formal court disposition	11	100
Youth's initial placement by court	12	100
Miscellaneous court orders	13	100
Detention prior to 1st hearing	14	100
Type of counsel retained	15	100
Initial plea	16	100
Presiding, initial ct. hearing	17	99
Number of prior offenses	18	100
Age, time of initial offense	19	100
Number of off. after 1st hearing	20	100
Youth's total offense number	21	100
Number companions, 1st offense	22	100
Usual companionship portrait	23	92
Living arrangements 1st ct. hearing	24	99
Parent's marital status	25	99
Youth's age at divorce/death	26	93
Household economic status	27	95
Public assistance recipient?	28	88
Income dependence number	29	96
Type of neighborhood	30	60
Home assessment	31	85
Parental work situation	32	94
Parental education background	33	19
Father's health	34	78
Mother's health	35	85
Youth's school academic standing	36	94
Youth's school attendance	37	94
Youth's att./perception: sch.	38	83
Parents' att. toward youth's educ.	39	59
Child's birth	40	72

SOURCE: Joseph W. Rogers, "The Predisposition Report," *Federal Probation* 54 (1990), p. 48.

and curfew violation. One of the best discussions of recidivism and its numerous definitions is *Recidivism* by Michael Maltz (1984).

The most popular measure of recidivism is a new adjudication as delinquent for reoffending. It is generally the case that, with exceptions, intensive supervision programs have less recidivism associated with them

TABLE 11.3 (Continued)

Variable Identification	IBM Col.	N– 162
Organic/emotional dysfunctions	41	85
Other educational problems	42	80
Youth's church attendance	43	28
Youth's job record	44	73
Leisure-time interests	45	64
Youth's mental health portrait	46	86
Highest IQ recorded	47	45
Psychological intervention	48	85
Community out-patient care	49	35
Residential in-patient care	50	43
Statement of juvenile	51	92
Statement of mother	52	83
Statement of father	53	56
Youth's generalized explanation	54	95
Parents' generalized explanation	55	88
JPO's generalized explanation	56	93
Alienation	57	96
Childhood rejection	58	88
Child's concept of self	59	90
Dominant manifest personality	60	97
Personality direction	61	93
Usual peer group relationship	62	89
Achievement orientation	63	77
Siblings relationships	64	74
Mother/child relationship	65	93
Father/child relationship	66	84
Principal discipline source	67	85
Quality of discipline	68	77
Family difficulty with police	69	76
Last known offense	70-71	99
Decoding of prior item	72	99
Time under JPO supervision	73	93
Number of detentions	74	100
Number of out-of-home placements	75	100
Dominant form of JPO contact	76	83
JPO home visit frequency	77	67
Overall frequency of contact	78	78
Final status of case	79	95
Judge, last court hearing	80	99

than standard probation. Over the years, a recidivism standard of 30 percent has been established among researchers as the cutting point between a successful probation program and an unsuccessful one. Programs with recidivism rates of 30 percent or less are considered successful, while those with more than 30 percent recidivism are considered not particularly successful. This is a purely arbitrary figure, although it is frequently cited in the research literature to give it some credibility as a success standard.

Standard probation, which means little or no direct and regular supervision of offenders by probation officers, has a fairly high rate of recidivism among the various state jurisdictions. Recidivism rates for juveniles on standard probation range from 30 percent to 70 percent, depending upon the nature of their offenses and prior records. Not all intensive supervision programs have low rates of recidivism, however. Clarke and Craddock (1987) report, for instance, that for samples of North Carolina probationers exposed to two types of probation programs, intensive probation and standard probation, intensive probation juveniles had a recidivism rate of 64 percent. This compared with a recidivism rate of 34 percent for standard probationers. Clarke and Craddock suggested that one reason for this unusual difference was that the intensive probationer sample consisted of high-risk juveniles with a greater likelihood of reoffending. Thus, some amount of natural selection occurred, in which the more hard-core offenders received closer probation supervision. For some juvenile clients, it matters little whether they are intensively supervised or placed under standard probation, since they will probably reoffend later anyway.

It is of interest to note that the rate of adult recidivism in the United States is approximately 60 percent (Greenfeld, 1985). This varies among jurisdictions, with some states showing lower rates of recidivism for adult probationers and some states showing higher rates. Petersilia et al. (1985) have shown, for instance, that about 70 percent of all felony probationers in California are recidivists, and that they will commit new offenses within 36 months of previous convictions.

Summary

Nominal options available to juvenile court judges include verbal warnings and diversion. Verbal warnings may be committed to writing, so that judges may refer to them if the same juveniles reappear for new offenses at a later date. Diversion is often suggested by either intake probation officers or prosecutors. More serious offenders have been targeted for more intensive supervision programs, such as the Juvenile Diversion/Noncustody Intake Program in Orange County, California, Youth at Risk programs, and See Our Side programs.

One alternative diversionary program is the teen court, where peers decide the punishment imposed in minor offense cases. Offenders tried by a teen court may be asked to serve on such a court themselves in the future, as one type of conditional punishment imposed upon them. Day treatment programs are used in some jurisdictions. These programs permit youths to attend school as well as participate in day treatment activities in late afternoon hours. Such programs provide vocational as well as educational assistance. Another option is to divert youths to alternative dispute resolution programs where mediators resolve disputes between victims and juvenile offenders.

Standard probation is a commonly used sentencing option. This type of probation may be either conditional or unconditional, with supervision by adults optional and at a judge's discretion. Conditions ordinarily include victim compensation or restitution, community service, or payment of fines. Standard probation programs include the Highfields Project, which uses peer pressure as a primary treatment technique. The aim of such a program is to help youths acquire independence and positive self-definitions.

Juvenile probation officers are drawn from diverse backgrounds, and the entry-level qualifications for such positions vary among states. A high school diploma is the minimum requirement in some jurisdictions, while other jurisdictions have no particular educational requirements. Probably a majority of those working with youths in a PO capacity have college degrees, however. Assessment centers enable states such as Florida to select the most qualified applicants through a series of interviews and the administration of personality/aptitude tests. Desirable abilities for POs include writing, communication, and human relations skills. Writing skills are important because much of PO's time is devoted to preparing predisposition reports. These reports are used by juvenile court judges in determining the most appropriate sentences for offenders. They are similar to adult pre-sentence investigation reports, and contain information about the offender as well as the offense and the circumstances under which it was committed. POs have a high rate of labor turnover, since pay scales for such positions in a majority of states are not particularly high. However, the interpersonal rewards of such work cause many POs to remain in these positions for many years. Caseloads vary among jurisdictions, and the least satisfying work is characterized by high caseloads, which prevent officers from devoting individualized attention to the most needy youthful offenders.

Key Terms

Assessment center (366)
Broker (364)
Burnout (367)
Conditional diversion (342)
Conditional standard probation (349)
Day treatment program (347)
Diversion (338)
Educator, mediator, enabler (364)
Enforcer (364)
Detector (364)
Highfields Project (353)
Juvenile Diversion/Noncustody Intake (JD/NCI) Program (342)

Juvenile Diversion Program (JDP) (342–343)
Nominal dispositions (337)
Predisposition report (369)
See Our Side (SOS) Program (343)
Standard probation (349)
Stress (367)
Teen courts (347)
Unconditional diversion (342)
Unconditional standard probation (349)
Youth at Risk Program (343)
Youth Service Bureaus (340)

Questions for Review

1. What are two types of nominal sanctions that juvenile court judges may impose? What are some of the factors that seem to contribute to the use of nominal sanctions as opposed to conditional ones? Explain.

2. What are some important functions of diversion? What are some dysfunctions of diversion? In what sense may youths acquire a cynicism about the juvenile justice system when diversion is used as a sanction?

3. What are Youth Service Bureaus and what are their functions? What are five general models that are used as patterns by Youth Service Bureaus? What evidence is there that YSBs are effective?

4. Differentiate between conditional and unconditional diversion. What are two types of conditional diversion programs? Describe each briefly.

5. What is the See Our Side program? Describe it briefly.

6. What is a teen court? How are teen courts effective in sanctioning low-risk juvenile offenders?

7. What are day treatment programs? Compare day treatment programs with alternative dispute resolution programs. Evaluate the effectiveness of each for reducing recidivism of delinquent offenders.

8. What are two types of standard probation? Describe each.

9. What are several of the special conditions of probation ordinarily imposed by juvenile court judges?

10. What is the Highfields Project? Describe the program format briefly. How does it rate regarding its influence on delinquency recidivism?

11. In what sense are POs also corrections officers? What are some entry-level requirements for persons performing PO roles in the juvenile justice system?

12. What are four types of orientations POs may use in approaching their work with juveniles? Briefly describe the implications of such orientations for interpersonal relations between POs and the youthful clients.

13. What is an assessment center? What sorts of activities does it perform? Describe a Florida assessment center.

14. What are stress and burnout, and how do these factors influence PO performance?

15. What is a predisposition report? What types of information does it contain? What are its basic functions? Discuss briefly.

16. Evaluate standard probation in terms of the recidivism rates associated with it. How does the rate of recidivism among juvenile probationers compare with adult probationer recidivism rates? Discuss briefly.

Suggested Readings

ADAMS, DENNIS (1987). *Path of Honor*. Tucson, AZ: Blue Horse Productions.

ARRIGONA, NANCY, AND TONY FABELO (1987). *A Case Study of Juvenile Probation in Texas*. Austin, TX: Criminal Justice Policy Council.

BUTTS, JEFFREY A., and SAMUEL M. STREIT (1988). *Youth Correctional Reform: The Maryland and Florida Experience*. Ann Arbor, MI: Center for the Study of Youth Policy, University of Michigan.

CHAMBERS, OLA R. (1983). *The Juvenile Offender: A Parole Profile*. Albany, NY: Evaluation and Planning Unit, New York State Division of Parole.

GREENE, JACK R., and STEPHEN D. MASTROFSKI (EDS.) (1988). *Community Policing*. New York: Praeger.

HEINZ, JOSEPH W., SUZANNE GARGARO, and KEVIN G. KELLY (1987). *A Model Residential Juvenile Sex-Offender Treatment Program: The Hennepin County Home School*. Syracuse, NY: Safer Society Press.

KLOCKARS, CARL B., and STEPHEN D. MASTROFSKI (EDS.) (1991). *Thinking about Police: Contemporary Readings*. New York: McGraw-Hill.

MILLER, ALDEN, and LLOYD OHLIN (1985). *Delinquency and Community*. Beverly Hills, CA: Sage.

ROSE, S. D., and J. L. EDLESON (1987). *Working with Children and Adolescents in Groups*. San Francisco: Jossey-Bass.

SICKMUND, MELISSA, and PHYLLIS JO BAUNACH (1986). *Public Juvenile Facilities, 1985: Children in Custody*. Washington, DC: U.S. Department of Justice.

STUMPHAUZER, J. S. (1986). *Helping Delinquents Change: A Treatment Manual of Social Learning Approaches*. New York: Haworth Press.

CHAPTER 12

Conditional Sanctions: Intensive Supervised Probation and Community-Based Correctional Alternatives

Introduction

This chapter describes several of the more intensive conditional sanctions that juvenile court judges may impose, including an array of *intermediate punishment programs* for juveniles. **Intermediate punishment** programs, according to McCarthy (1987a), are sanctions that exist somewhere between incarceration and [standard] probation on the continuum of criminal penalties. Intermediate punishments described here include *intensive supervised probation* (ISP), *community-based juvenile corrections, electronic monitoring, home confinement,* and *shock probation.*

The significance of intermediate punishment programs is that they permit a higher degree of supervisory control over juvenile offenders than nominal

Many community-based correctional programs involve juvenile offenders in productive and fulfilling activities. Youths learn to be more accountable to others as well as developing greater self-worth. (Courtesy of Harris County Juvenile Probation Department)

sanctions do. They are generally considered to be delinquency deterrents and to be repressive, in the sense that they are intended to promote a strong degree of crime or delinquency control through offender monitoring. Therefore, they deter by controlling offender behaviors and by making it increasingly difficult for individual offenders to deviate from program conditions. Offenders who are closely supervised or monitored have fewer opportunities to reoffend compared with those in traditional probationary or diversionary programs. Collectively, intermediate punishment programs are generally intended for more serious, habitual, or chronic juvenile offenders, although it is not unusual to place certain first offenders in intermediate punishment programs if the first offense is a particularly serious one.

It is not uncommon for juvenile court judges to sanction juvenile offenders with fines and restitution orders in addition to other program requirements if intermediate punishments are imposed. A brief discussion of the use of fines and victim reparations will be presented here. Each of the intermediate punishment programs presented will also be assessed in terms of its effectiveness at reducing recidivism.

Some General Goals of Intermediate Punishment Programs

There is considerable variation among intermediate punishment programs, although they tend to exhibit similar goals or objectives. These goals include, but are not limited to:

1. Provision of sanctions that are less expensive than secure detention.
2. Achievement of lower rates of recidivism as compared with standard probation.
3. Greater emphasis on reintegration into the community as the primary correctional goal.
4. Provision of a greater range of community services and organizations in a cooperative effort to assist youthful offenders.
5. Minimization of the adverse influence of labeling that might result from secure detention.
6. Improvement in personal educational and vocational skills of individual offenders, together with acquisition of better self-concepts and greater acceptance of responsibility for one's actions.

Intermediate punishment programs are operated in every state for both juvenile and adult offenders. They are sometimes referred to as **creative sentencing,** since they fall somewhere between standard probationary sentences and traditional incarcerative terms that might be imposed by judges.

Classification Criteria for Placement in ISP Programs

One problem frequently faced by judges is deciding which juveniles should be assigned to which programs. This is a classification problem involving risk prediction, and the level of accuracy associated with juvenile risk prediction instruments is about as poor as with adult risk prediction devices (Baird, 1985). This problem is considered one of correction's greatest challenges (Joyce, 1985:86). Nevertheless, judges attempt to make secure or nonsecure detention decisions on the basis of the following elements:

1. Classification based on risk of continued criminal activity and the offender's need for services.
2. A case management classification system designed to help probation and

parole officers develop effective case plans and select appropriate casework strategies.
3. A management information system designed to enhance planning, monitoring, evaluation, and accountability.
4. A work load deployment system that allows agencies to effectively and efficiently allocate their limited resources (Baird, 1985:34).

Chronic recidivists and serious offenders are prime candidates for secure detention. However, an increasing number of community-based programs are being designed to supervise such offenders closely and offer them needed services and treatments. Although classification and risk assessment were described to some extent in Chapter 9, it is helpful to review briefly some of the issues relating to the effectiveness of such instrumentation.

Classification of any offender is made difficult by the fact that the state of the art in predictions of risk and dangerousness is such that little future behavior can be accurately forecast. This holds for juveniles as well as for adults. We know that status offenders may or may not escalate to more serious offenses, with the prevailing sentiment favoring or implying nonescalation (Datesman and Aickin, 1985; McCarthy and Smith, 1986; Nagoshi, 1986). Effective classification schemes have not been devised, although we know that on the basis of descriptions of existing offender aggregates, the factors of gender, age, nature of offense, seriousness of offense, race or ethnicity, and socioeconomic status are more or less correlated.

The flaws of various classification schemes are made more apparent when program "failures" are detected in large numbers. Juvenile judges sometimes make the wrong judgments and decisions about juvenile placements. Intake officers may make similar errors of classification when conducting initial screenings of juveniles. The issues of "false positives" and "false negatives" are relevant here, because some youths may be unfairly overpenalized for what authorities believe are valid predictive criteria of their future dangerousness. Also, some youths may be wrongfully underpenalized, because it is believed that they will not commit serious offenses in the future, and they do commit such offenses (Gottfredson and Tonry, 1987; Gottfredson and Gottfredson, 1988).

Two classification instruments used for determining community-based agency and program placements are the **Delaware Initial Security Placement Instrument** and the **Florida Dangerousness Instrument.** Figures 12-1 and 12-2 show the contents of these instruments and the points assigned for various offenses and prior adjudications.

Depending upon the scores received by various juvenile clients when classified, they may or may not be entitled to assignment to intensive supervised probation or to a community-based program. Theoretically, those youthful offenders who are considered dangerous and violent are poor candidates for inclusion, because it is predicted that they might harm themselves or others, including agency staff or probation officers. Also, those considered not dangerous would be predicted to be good candidates as

---

Initial Security Placement Instrument

Date: _____

File #: _____

Score: _____

1. Name

2. D.O.B.

3. Date of Current Commitment

4. Current most serious instant offense which resulted in adjudication and present commitment.

---

5. Most serious prior adjudicated offense (against person)

6. Number of prior felony adjudications

7. Open felony charges   Yes _____   No _____   Specify _____

8. History of in-patient psychiatric hospitalization
   Yes _____   No _____

I. Severity of current offense
   Class A Felony (10 pts.)   _____
   Class B Felony (7 pts.)   _____

II. Most serious prior adjudication
   Class A Felony (5 pts.)   _____
   Class B Felony (3 pts.) (exclude escape)   _____

III. Number of prior adjudications for
felonies—three or more in last two years (5 pts.)

_____

IV. Prior out of home court ordered placement
as a result of adjudication for delinquent act
   Yes (1 Pt) _____
   No (0 Pt) _____   _____

TOTAL   _____

Figure 12-1   Delaware Initial Security Placement Instrument (*Source:* Naneen Karraker *et al., Public Safety with Care: A Model System for Juvenile Justice in Hawaii* [Alexandria, VA: National Center on Institutions and Alternatives, 1988], p. 83)

FLORIDA INSTRUMENT

Dangerousness

---

1. Present alleged offense is a:

_____ First Degree Felony   THE CHARGE IS _____

Score 6 points for first degree : SCORE = _____

_____ Second Degree Felony   THE CHARGE IS _____
_____ Third Degree Felony   THE CHARGE IS _____

Score 1 point each for second and third SCORE = _____

2. The alleged offense required the victim to receive medical

YES   NO   If yes, explain _____

_____

Score 1 point for yes, and "0" for no SCORE = _____

3. The alleged offense involved an overt THREAT of physical harm to another person.

YES   NO   If yes, explain _____

_____

Score 1 point for a yes answer and "0" for no. SCORE = _____

4. How many adjudicated felonies does the alleged perpetrator have during the last 2 years?

_____

Score 1 point for two (2) or more and "0" for less than 2 SCORE = _____

5. How many adjudicated violent felonies does the alleged perpetrator have during the last 2 years?

_____

Score 1 point for 2 or more and "0" for less than 2 SCORE = _____

TOTAL SCORE FOR DANGEROUSNESS = _____

SIx (6) or above = high dangerousness
3–5 = moderate dangerousness
below 3 = low dangerousness

Figure 12-2   Florida Dangerousness Instrument (*Source:* Naneen Karraker *et al.,* *Public Safety with Care* [Alexandria, VA: National Center on Institutions and Alternatives, 1988], p. 84)

program clients. However, classification instruments do not always discriminate effectively. Ironically, Karraker *et al.* (1988:88) report that in some jurisdictions, such as Massachusetts, secure detention has been used unsuccessfully with violent juveniles, and they appear most responsive when assigned to nonsecure programs, including ISP and community-based projects.

This finding is consistent with the work of Butts and DeMuro (1989), who caution that risk assessment instruments may suggest institutionalization for some youths who might actually be better accommodated by alternative, nonsecure programs that are a part of ISP. In their investigations of risk assessments and placements of samples of Massachusetts youths under the supervision of the Division for Children and Youth Services (DCYS), they found that most of the youths had prior delinquency adjudications, records of drug or alcohol abuse, and families that were dependent upon public assistance in the recent past. They support juvenile court actions that involve a graduated series of sanctions to handle nonviolent youths who violate their probationary conditions. They also favor the development of strong, nonresidential, alternative schools/attention centers in lieu of traditional incarceration in state facilities. However, they recognize a continuing problem that causes many juvenile court jurisdictions to incarcerate large numbers of youths who actually would be better off receiving some ISP nonincarcerative alternative. The problem is that inadequate resources in many of these jurisdictions have inhibited the development of ISP programs that would, ironically, cost less than institutionalization.

Intensive Supervised Probation (ISP) for Juveniles

Intensive supervised probation (ISP) programs, alternatively known as *intensive probation supervision* (IPS) programs, have become increasingly popular for managing nonincarcerated offender populations (Snyder and Marshall, 1990). (ISP will be used to describe the programs developed in different jurisdictions, regardless of whether the ISP or IPS designation is used by individual programs.) Since the mid-1960s, these programs have been aimed primarily at supervising adult offenders, but in recent years, ISP programs have been designed for juvenile offenders as well (Armstrong, 1988:342). **Intensive supervised probation (ISP)** *is a highly structured and conditional supervision program for either adult or juvenile offenders that serves as an alternative to incarceration and provides for an acceptable level of public safety* (adapted from a definition by Armstrong, 1988:343).

Characteristics of ISP Programs. ISP programs for juveniles have been developed and are currently operating in about one third to one half of all U.S. jurisdictions (Armstrong, 1988; Wiebush, 1990). Two popular adult ISP programs that have been copied and applied to juveniles in certain jurisdictions are the **New Jersey ISP model** (Pearson and Bibel, 1986) and the **Georgia ISP model** (Erwin, 1986). Typically, both of these programs are intended for prison-bound offenders and are perceived as one means of alleviating jail and prison overcrowding.

Drug & Alcohol Counsel — Dwi Programs

The Georgia ISP model, considered by some experts to be the toughest probation program for adults in the United States, is a three-phase enterprise and includes five face-to-face contacts per week with offenders; 132 hours of mandatory community service; mandatory curfew; mandatory employment; weekly checks of local arrest records; routine alcohol and drug screenings; a caseload of twenty-five clients for POs; and PO-determined counseling, vocational/educational offender training, and regular court reports on offender progress. Offenders are in the Georgia program for an indeterminate period, usually from six to twelve months. The New Jersey ISP model is an eighteen-month program, featuring twenty PO–client contacts during the first fourteen months (with at least twelve of these visits being face-to-face during the first six months); regular curfew checks; employment checks; payment of fines and program maintenance costs; victim restitution; drug and alcohol screenings; community service work; maintenance by clients of a daily diary of their progress and improvement; and a PO caseload of twenty-five.

Both of these programs have exhibited low rates of recidivism among adult clients, or recidivism rates of less than 30 percent. However, they have been criticized because their clients are handpicked and "creamed" from the most eligible offenders, and thus, they are among the least likely candidates to reoffend anyway.

Similar to their adult ISP program counterparts, **juvenile intensive supervised probation (JISP)** programs are ideally designed for secure detention-bound youths and are considered acceptable alternatives to incarceration. According to Armstrong (1988:342), this is what JISP programs were always meant to be. Armstrong differentiates JISP programs from other forms of standard probation by citing obvious differences in the amount of officer–client contact during the course of the probationary period. For example, standard probation normally involves no more than two face-to-face officer–client contacts per month. He says that JISP programs might differ from standard probation according to the following face-to-face criteria: (1) two or three times per week versus once per month; (2) once per week versus twice per month; or (3) four times per week versus once per week (the latter figure being unusually high for standard probation contact) (Armstrong, 1988:346).

The brokerage nature of probation officer dispositions toward their work is evident in the different types of services provided by the different JISP programs investigated by Armstrong. For example, of the fifty-five programs he examined (92 percent of his total program sample), he found that the following range of services, skills, and resources were mentioned as being brokered by POs in different jurisdictions:

1. Mental health counseling.
2. Drug and alcohol counseling.
3. Academic achievement and aptitude testing.
4. Vocational and employment training.

5. Individual, group, and family counseling.
6. Job search and placement programs.
7. Alternative education programs.
8. Foster grandparent programs.
9. Big Brother/Big Sister programs.

Wiebush (1990:26) cautions that not all ISP programs are alike. Nevertheless, many juvenile ISP programs have elements in common, including the following:

1. Recognition of the shortcomings of traditional responses to serious and/or chronic offenders (e.g., incarceration or out-of-home placement).
2. Severe resource constraints within jurisdictions that compel many probation departments to adopt agency-wide classification and workload deployment systems for targeting a disproportionate share of resources for the most problematic juvenile offenders.
3. Program hopes to reduce the incidence of incarceration in juvenile secure detention facilities and reduce overcrowding.
4. Programs tend to include aggressive supervision and control elements as a part of the "get tough" movement.
5. All programs have a vested interest in rehabilitation of youthful offenders.

From these analyses of ISP program content generally, we can glean the following as basic characteristics of ISP programs:

1. *Low officer–client caseloads* (i.e., thirty or fewer probationers).
2. *High levels of offender accountability* (e.g., victim restitution, community service, payment of fines, partial defrayment of program expenses).
3. *High levels of offender responsibility.*
4. *High levels of offender control* (home confinement, electronic monitoring, frequent face-to-face visits by POs).
5. *Frequent checks for arrests, drug and/or alcohol use, and employment/school attendance* (drug/alcohol screening, coordination with police departments and juvenile halls, teachers, family) (Armstrong, 1988:342–343; Wiebush, 1990).

The Ohio Experience. An excellent illustration of the value of JISP has been described as "the **Ohio experience**" by Richard G. Wiebush (1990). Wiebush has compared three different Ohio counties that have used different ISP programs for their juvenile offenders, as well as the Ohio Department of Youth Services (ODYS). The counties include Delaware County (predominantly rural), Lucas County (Toledo), and Cuyahoga County (Cleveland). The ODYS is state-operated and manages the most serious offenders, since these are exclusively felony offenders on parole from secure detention. In each of the county jurisdictions, most of the offenders are detention-bound, with the exception of the Lucas County juveniles, who are sentenced to ISP after having their original sentences of detention reversed by juvenile court judges. Tables 12.1 and 12.2 show the basic parameters of the different Ohio programs as well as the program sizes and staffing patterns.

TABLE 12.1 Basic Parameters of the Ohio Programs—*Models, Goals, and Client Selection*

Characteristic	Jurisdiction			
	Delaware	*Lucas*	*Cuyahoga*	*ODYS*
Agency type *Program model*	County probation Probation enhancement and alternative to incarceration	County probation Alternative to incarceration	County probation Probation enhancement	State parole Parole enhancement
Program goals	Reduced recidivism Reduced commitments Reduced O/H placement	Reduced commitments	Reduced recidivism Reduced commitments Reduced O/H placement	Reduced recidivism Reduced recommitment
Primary client selection criterion	High risk score	Post-commitment status	High risk score	High risk score
Additional criteria	Chronic felony offenders; high needs	Excluded offenses = use of weapon, victim injury, drug trafficking	Status offenders excluded	Metro area resident; 2 + violent offenders included automatically
Philosophy, supervision emphasis	All stress "balanced" approach—relatively equal emphasis on public safety and rehabilitation.			

SOURCE: Richard G. Wiebush, "Programmatic Variations in Intensive Supervision for Juveniles: The Ohio Experience," *Perspectives* 14 (1990). p. 28.

TABLE 12.2   ISP Program Size and Staffing Patterns

	Jurisdiction			
Characteristic	Delaware	Lucas	Cuyahoga	ODYS
Total agency caseload*	225	500	1,500	1,500
ISP caseload	17	60	360**	525
ISP staff/youth ratio (P/P officers)	1 : 17	1 : 15	1 : 30	1 : 13
Surveillance staff/youth ratio	2 : 17	2.5 : 60	3 : 60	2 : 39
Team configuration	Court administrator 1 ISP PO 2 surveil staff (p/t) Student interns Family advocates	1 unit supervisor 4 ISP POs 2 surveil staff (f/t) 2 surveil staff (p/t) 3 comm. service staff (p/t)	1 team leader 2 ISP POs 3 surveil staff (f/t)	3 ISP POs 2 surveil staff (p/t)
Number of teams	1	1	6	1–3 per region, 14 total
Coverage	7 days; 14 hrs/day	7 days; 14 hrs/day	7 days; 24 hrs/day	7 days; 14 hrs/day

*Caseload = cases under supervision at any one time.
**Projected figure for summer, 1989.
SOURCE: Richard G. Wiebush, "Programmatic Variations in Intensive Supervision for Juveniles: The Ohio Experience," *Perspectives* 14 (1990), p. 29.

An inspection of Table 12.1 shows the different types of agencies involved, the particular program models used by each, and the types of juvenile offender/clients served. Each of the programs uses risk scores for client inclusion, with the exception of the Lucas County program.

The Delaware County JISP program targets those juveniles with a high propensity to recidivate as well as more serious felony offenders who are detention-bound. Youths begin the program with a five-day detention, followed by two weeks of house arrest. Later, they must observe curfews, attend school and complete schoolwork satisfactorily, report daily to the probation office, and submit to periodic urinalysis. Each youth's progress is monitored by counselors and surveillance staff 16 hours a day, seven days a week. Wiebush says that although the Delaware program has a rather strict approach, it embodies rehabilitation as a primary program objective. The Delaware program has about a 40 percent recidivism rate, which is high, although it is better than the 75 percent rate among the general juvenile court population of high-risk offenders elsewhere in Ohio jurisdictions.

In Lucas County, program officials select clients from those already serving sentences of detention who are considered high-risk offenders. Lucas County officials wished to use this particular selection method, since they wanted to avoid any appearance of "net-widening" that their JISP program might reflect. Drawing from those already incarcerated seemed the best strategy in this case. The Lucas program is similar to the Delaware program in its treatment and control approaches. However, the Lucas program obligates offenders to perform up to 100 hours of community service as a program condition. House arrest, curfew, and other Delaware program requirements are also found in the Lucas program. The success of the Lucas program has not been evaluated fully, although it does appear to have reduced institutional commitments by about 10 percent between 1986 and 1987.

The Cuyahoga County program (Cleveland) was one of the first ISP programs in Ohio's metropolitan jurisdictions. It is perhaps the largest county program, with 1,500 clients at any given time, as well as six juvenile court judges and 72 supervisory personnel. One innovation of the Cuyahoga program was the development of a team approach to client surveillance and management. This program, like the other county programs, performs certain broker functions by referring its clients to an assortment of community-based services and treatments during the program duration. Currently, there are six teams of surveillance officers each of whom serves about sixty youths. These teams are comprised of a team leader, two counselors, and three surveillance staff.

The nature of contact standards for this and the other three programs are shown in Table 12.3.

Table 12.3 shows that all four programs follow a four-phase plan, in which the intensity of supervision and surveillance over offenders is gradually reduced after particular time intervals. The ODYS program reevaluates juveniles at 3-, 5-, and 7-month intervals, using a risk assessment device, rather than graduate them to new phases automatically. In 1989, Hamparian and Sametz (1989) made an interim evaluation of the Cuyahoga program.

TABLE 12.3   Contact Standards by Type and Phase*

Type of Contact	Jurisdiction			
	Delaware	Lucas	Cuyahoga	ODYS
Phase I				
PO, direct with youth	5/week	2/wk.	1/wk.	6.5/month
Family, direct	not specified (n.s.)	4/month	n.s.	2/month
Surveillance**	11 wk.	14/wk.	17/wk.	4/wk.
Duration (minimum)	21 days	30 days	30 days	90 days
Phase II				
PO, direct with youth	5/wk.	2/wk.	1/wk.	4–6/month
Family, direct	n.s.	2/month	n.s.	2/month
Surveillance**	11/wk.	10/wk.	8/wk.	4/wk.
Duration	28 days	50 days	75 days	60 days
Phase III				
(PO, direct with youth	3/wk.	1/wk.	1/wk.	2–6 month
Family, direct	n.s.	2/month	n.s.	1/month
Surveillance**	0–11/wk.	7/wk.	5/wk.	2–4/wk.
Duration	70 days	50 days	75 days	60 days
Phase IV				
PO, Direct with youth	1–3/wk.	2/month	as needed	2–6/month
Family, direct	n.s.	1/month	n.s.	1/month
Surveillance**	none	5/wk.	3/wk.	2–4/wk.
Duration	By contract	26 days	75 days	60 days

*ODYS does not use phase system to govern youth movement through the program. Youths are classified at 3, 5 and 7 months, based on reassessment of risk.

**Includes direct and telephone contacts.

SOURCE: Richard G. Wiebush, "Programmatic Variations in Intensive Supervision for Juveniles: The Ohio Experience," *Perspectives* 14 (1990), p. 30.

This evaluation showed that the rate of recidivism among Cuyahoga clients was about 31 percent during a nine-month follow-up. Additional evaluations of the program were being made at the time of this writing.

The ODYS program operates the state's nine training schools in addition to supervising the 3,000 youths each year who are released on parole. The ODYS has 93 youth counselors to staff seven regional offices. The ODYS commenced JISP in February, 1988, and supervised those high-risk offenders with a predicted future recidivism rate of 75 percent or higher. Since these clients were all prior felony offenders with lengthy adjudication records, they were considered the most serious group to be supervised compared with the other programs. Accordingly, the ODYS supervision and surveillance structure exhibited the greatest degree of offender monitoring. The team approach has been used by the ODYS, with teams consisting of three youth counselors and two surveillance staff.

Because of geographical considerations, some variations have been observed among teams regarding the numbers of offenders supervised as well as the intensity of their supervision or surveillance. Basically, the ODYS program incorporated many of the program conditions that were included in the various county programs. These conditions or components have been divided into *control* components and *treatment* components and are shown respectively in Tables 12.4 and 12.5.

Since its creation, the JISP program operated by the ODYS has exhibited a drop in its recidivism rate. On the basis of a comparison of the first year of its

TABLE 12.4   Program Components—Control Elements

	Jurisdiction			
Component	*Delaware*	*Lucas*	*Cuyahoga*	*ODYS*
Surveillance	X	X	X	X
Curfew	X	X	X	X
Front-end detention	X	—*	—	—
House arrest	X	X	X	O
Prior permission	X	—	—	—
Electronic surveillance	—	—	O	—
Urinalysis	O	X	O	O
Daily sanctioning (phase system)	X	X	X	—
Hourly school reports	X	X	X	—
Formal graduated sanction schedule	—	X	—	X

*Most Lucas ISP youth do have front-end detention, but it is not mandated.
Key: X = Mandatory component.
     — = Component not available.
     O = Component optional, varies by youth.
SOURCE: Richard G. Wiebush, "Programmatic Variations in Intensive Supervision for Juveniles," *Perspectives* 14 (1990), p. 31.

TABLE 12.5   Program Components—*Treatment Elements*

	Jurisdiction			
Component	*Delaware*	*Lucas*	*Cuyahoga*	*ODYS*
Individualized contracts	X	X	X	X
Individual counseling (non-p.o.)	O	O	O	O
Family counseling or family conferences	O	X	O	O
Group counseling	X	X	O	O
In-home family services	X	—	X	—
Community sponsors, advocates	—	—	—	—
Alternative education	O	O	O	O
Job training	O	O	O	O
Substance abuse counseling	O	O	O	O

	Jurisdiction			
Component	*Delaware*	*Lucas*	*Cuyahoga*	*ODYS*
School Attendance (or work)	X	X	X	X
Community service	O	X	O	O
Restitution	O	O	O	O

KEY: X = Mandatory component.
     — = Component not available.
     O = Component optional, varies by youth.
SOURCE: Richard G. Wiebush, "Programmatic Variations in Intensive Supervision for Juveniles," *Perspectives* 14 (1990), p. 32.

operation with recidivism figures for its clients from the previous year, the ODYS program had a 34 percent reduction in its rate of recidivism. Further, a 39 percent reduction in parole revocations occurred. This is significant, considering the high-risk nature of the offender population being managed.

Wiebush notes that all of these programs have required enormous investments of time and energy by high-quality staff. Further, each program has illustrated how best to utilize existing community resources to further its objectives and best serve juvenile clients in need. However, Wiebush says that what is good for Ohio probationers and parolees may not necessarily be suitable for offenders in other jurisdictions. Nevertheless, these programs function as potential models for other jurisdictions.

Weaknesses and Strengths of ISP Programs. An underlying weakness of most JISP programs is that local demands and needs vary to such an extent among jurisdictions that after twenty-five years, we have yet to devise a standard definition to describe what is meant by intensive supervised probation (Ellsworth, 1988:28). The dominant types of current ISP programs are (1) those that are designed as "front-end" alternatives to secure detention, (2) those that combine incarceration with some degree of community supervision (shock probation), and (3) those that follow secure detention.

Ellsworth's insightful analysis of the progress of developing ISP programs in the United States since the early 1960s highlights certain problems that JISP programs are currently facing. One of the first strategies employed by probation departments was the "numbers game" reshuffling of caseloads, in which reduced caseloads for POs were ordered to supposedly improve officer–client interpersonal contact. It was argued that reduced caseloads would necessarily intensify the supervision as well as the supervisory quality of officer–client relationships. Several recent studies have experimented with varying degrees of officer–client contact and recidivism rates (see Southeimer *et al.*, 1990 for a review of some of these studies.) PO caseload reductions were mandated by one of the recommendations of the Task Force on Corrections appointed by the President's Commission on Law Enforcement and the Administration of Justice in 1967.

However, a project investigating the different recidivism rates of probationers supervised more or less intensively and conducted subsequently in San Francisco, known as the **San Francisco Project,** did much to undermine the nation's confidence in the value of manipulating sheer caseload numbers (Banks *et al.*, 1977). The San Francisco Project compared recidivism rates of probationers supervised by POs with caseloads of twenty and forty respectively, with the former caseloads defined by probation departments as "intensive" and the latter caseloads defined as "ideal." No significant differences in recidivism rates of probationers were reported between "intensive" and "ideal" caseload scenarios. In fact, those POs with caseloads of twenty probationers reported more technical program violations (e.g., curfew violations, traveling violations, drug/alcohol violations) than those with caseloads of forty probationers. Greater offender monitoring simply made it possible for POs to spot more program violators.

Despite the methodological and theoretical flaws cited by various critics of the San Francisco Project, the study suggested that something beyond sheer numbers of cases assigned POs should be an integral part of the officer–client relationship. Ellsworth (1988:28–29) says that the next step to be taken by probation departments should be the construction of risk/needs assessment instruments and classification systems that would enable probation departments to plan their case assignments more effectively. One of these instruments was the Wisconsin Case Classification System, which introduced the idea of **case supervision planning** through the **Client Management Classification** interview. This interview purportedly enabled POs to proactively supervise their clients more effectively, since they could identify in advance certain problems that otherwise would interfere with productive officer–client relationships. Instead of reacting to client problems whenever they surfaced, POs could thereby anticipate certain client problems and take steps to deal with them in advance of their occurrence (Ellsworth, 1988:28).

Subsequently, various probation departments implemented case assignment policies employing a finer degree of specialization than case allocation procedures formerly used. Those offenders with drug abuse problems would be grouped according to this problem and assigned to POs who had acquired a drug abuse specialty. Ideally, probation departments would benefit because officers would be assigned cases they enjoyed working with and in which their particular skills could be maximized. They would be in a better position to understand client problems and could be better "enablers" and "brokers" for their clients, arranging contacts between them and existing community services.

Unfortunately, there have been unanticipated consequences arising from such case supervision planning. Intradepartmental jealousies and a lack of POs with specific competencies have made it either impossible or impractical for certain probation departments to implement case supervision planning fully. Further, specialized case allocations have at times undermined the officer–client relationship, since the enforcement nature of PO work has sometimes collapsed through changing interpersonal relationships. In short, some officers have become emotionally involved with their offender/clients to the extent that they are no longer effective enforcers of other program requirements. Ellsworth (1988:29) indicates that currently, a basic incompatibility exists between POs who favor a law-and-order approach to PO work (consistent with the "get tough" philosophy), and those who favor a rehabilitation or "treatment" approach that is closely associated with the case planning process. Case supervision planning, therefore, is considered irrelevant by some POs, since in their view, the primary function of POs is to conduct surveillance activities, control the behaviors of their clients, ensure offender accountability, and ensure offender compliance with program conditions.

Case supervision planning may be appreciated to a greater degree by considering several alternative case assignment strategies that are presently used by various probation departments. The most prevalent model is the **conventional model,** which is the random assignment of probationers to POs on the basis of their present caseload in relation to others. This is much like the **numbers game model,** in which total probationers are divided by the total POs in a given department, and each PO is allocated an equal share of the supervisory tasks. Thus, POs may supervise both very dangerous and nondangerous probationers. Another model is the **conventional model with geographic considerations.** Simply, this model consists of assigning probationers to POs who live in a common geographic area. The intent is to shorten PO travel time between clients. Again, little or no consideration is given to an offender's needs or dangerousness in relation to PO skills. The **specialized caseloads model** is the model used for case supervision planning, in which offender assignments are made on the basis of client risks and needs and PO skills and interests in dealing with those offender risks and needs (Carlson and Parks, 1979).

No doubt some of the problems of JISP have been attributable to different caseload assignment models or to other organizational peculiarities and conflicting organizational goals that interfere with the performance of juvenile PO roles. One solution is referred to as the *balanced approach,* and it has been described by Maloney *et al.* (1988). *The* **balanced approach** *to juvenile probation is neither a wholly punitive nor a wholly rehabilitative* *formulation but, rather, is a more broad-based, constructive approach. It operates on the assumption that decision making must take into consideration the converging interests of all involved parties in the juvenile justice process, including offenders, victims, the community at large, and the system itself. No party to the decision making should benefit at the expense of another party; rather, a balancing of interests should be sought.* The balanced approach, therefore, simultaneously emphasizes community protection, offender accountability, individualization of treatments, and competency assessment and development (Armstrong *et al.*, 1990:10).

Essentially, the balanced approach forces community leaders and juvenile justice system actors to examine their individual juvenile codes legally and determine whether a balance exists between offender needs and community interests. Punitive provisions of these codes should address victim needs as well as the needs of juvenile offenders, to the extent that restitution and victim compensation are a part of improving an offender's accountability and acceptance of responsibility. The fairness of the juvenile justice system should be assessed by key community leaders, and a mission statement should be drafted that has the broad support of diverse community organizations. Training programs can be created through the close coordination of chief probation officers in different jurisdictions, whereby offender needs can be targeted and addressed. All facets of the community and the juvenile justice process should be involved, including juvenile judges. The high level of community involvement will help to ensure a positive juvenile probation program that will maximize a youth's chances for rehabilitation (Armstrong *et al.* , 1990:12).

Ellsworth contends that ISP programs fail because they often neglect to address many of the problems suggested by Armstrong *et al.* According to Ellsworth (1988:29–30), the reasons case supervision planning is often unsuccessful are as follows:

1. *Purpose:* the purposes of case supervision planning have not been thought out carefully.
2. *Perceptual differences:* offenders often change only when they find it necessary to change—not because we want them to change.
3. *Resistance:* we don't always recognize that resistance to change is normal; sometimes we prematurely shift emphasis to an enforcement orientation and rules of probation; case planning starts to look more like the probation order whenever this occurs.
4. *Expectation:* desired change is sought too quickly; we sometimes expect too much from offenders or expect unrealistic changes to be made.
5. *Focus:* there is a tendency to focus on lesser problems in order to gain ''success.''
6. *Involvement:* we often fail to involve offenders in the case planning process.
7. *Stereotyping:* case supervision planning is equated with treatment and rehabilitation, and thus, it is often rejected without an adequate consideration of its strengths.

8. *Getting too close:* sometimes POs are perceived as getting too close to offenders.
9. *Perceptions of accountability:* nonspecific case plans cannot be criticized by supervisors; case plans are often too vague or so general that supervisors cannot determine if those plans are actually implemented.
10. *Use of resources:* there is a tendency to "burn out" community resources by referring involuntary offenders, those who are not ready to work on their problems.
11. *Measurement:* probation successes or failures are not measured according to some case plan but, rather, according to arrests, convictions, or numbers of technical violations.
12. *Management:* there is a general lack of understanding or support for case supervision planning by management; POs are considered exclusively officers of the court, and judges don't particularly expect offenders to change because of officer "treatments," but expect only that someone will share the blame or accountability whenever offenders commit new crimes or violate one or more of their probationary conditions.
13. *Training:* staff members have not been adequately trained in the development, implementation, and evaluation of case plans.

The principles of JISP programs are sound. Basically, implementation problems of one type or another have hindered their success in various jurisdictions (Jones, 1990). It is apparent that juvenile probation services will need to coordinate their activities and align their departmental and individual PO performance objectives with those of community-based agencies that are a part of the referral network of services and treatments in order to maximize goal attainment. Consistent with the balanced approach to managing offenders, Klein (1989:6) recommends that in order for ISP programs to maximize their effectiveness, they should be individualized to a high degree, so that a proper balance of punishment/deterrence and rehabilitation/ community protection may be attained. An offender's constitutional rights should be recognized, but at the same time, accountability to victims and the community must be ensured. In the next section, we will examine several specific ISP programs that are considered community-based alternatives in contrast with state- or locally-operated public programs.

Community-based Alternatives

Community-based corrections agencies and organizations are not new. An early community-based corrections program for adult offenders, known as the Probation Subsidy Program, was created in California in 1965 (Lawrence, 1985). Originally, these programs were intended to alleviate prison and jail overcrowding by establishing community-based organizations that could accommodate some of the overflow of prison-bound offenders. However, corrections officials soon realized that the potential of such programs was great for offender rehabilitation and reintegration, and that juveniles as well as adult offenders could profit from involvement in them. Many states subsequently passed **community corrections acts** that were aimed at funding local government units to create community facilities which could provide services and other resources to juveniles. Huskey (1984) says that the overall objective of community corrections agencies is to develop and deliver "front-end" solutions and alternative sanctions in lieu of state incarceration.

The American Correctional Association (ACA) Task Force on Community Corrections Legislation has recommended that these community corrections acts should not be directed at especially violent offenders. Rather, the states should be selective about who fits program requirements. General ACA recommendations are that (1) states should continue to house violent juvenile offenders in secure facilities, (2) judges and prosecutors should continue to explore various punishment options in lieu of incarceration, and (3) local communities should develop programs with additional funding from state appropriations (Huskey, 1984:45). The ACA Task Force identified the following elements as essential to the success of any community corrections act:

1. There should be restrictions on funding high-cost capital projects as well as conventional probation services.
2. Local communities should participate on a voluntary basis and should be able to withdraw at any time.
3. Advisory boards should submit annual criminal justice plans to local governments.
4. There should be a logical formula in place for allocating community corrections funds.
5. Only detention-bound juveniles should be targeted, rather than adding additional punishments for those who otherwise would remain in their communities (in short, avoid "net-widening").
6. Financial subsidies should be provided to local government and community-based corrections agencies.
7. Local advisory boards in each community should function to assess program needs and effectiveness, and to propose improvements in the local juvenile justice system and educate the general public about the benefits of intermediate punishments.
8. A performance factor should be implemented to ensure that funds are used to achieve specific goals of the act.

Community-based corrections agencies often utilize volunteers from the community to lower their operating costs. Besides using volunteers, community-based agencies should attempt to employ only the most qualified support personnel in order to enhance community acceptance of such programs. Local advisory boards, consisting of community residents and business persons, do much to promote community acceptance of such community-based programs. They function as liaisons and help to dispel certain myths that are associated with these agencies and programs. A good example

BOX 12.1

Juvenile Highlights

Can a privately operated marine institute rehabilitate hard-core juvenile offenders? The Fort Smallwood Marine Institute near Baltimore, Maryland, thinks so. Fort Smallwood opened its doors in 1988 as one of the newest privately operated juvenile rehabilitation facilities operated by the parent Associated Marine Institutes, Inc., a nonprofit organization founded in Florida in 1969. Corporation officials monitor all programs at least twice a year, although individual program directors have considerable autonomy in conducting the operations of their institutes.

Fort Smallwood has contracted with the Maryland Department of Juvenile Services. Maryland pays about 90 percent of the $425,000 Fort Smallwood annual budget, with the remainder obtained from grant monies and donations. Juvenile pupil costs are about $36 per day, or about $8,000 for a six- to eight-month stay. This is a relatively low figure, since there is no need for security and many youths work at Fort Smallwood and stay in their own homes during evening hours and on weekends.

The rehabilitative program operated by Fort Smallwood consists of completing 54 courses in different academic areas. Graduation is based upon completing all course requirements and having good attendance and performance records. Any youth who interferes with others or poses a risk to the program goals is ejected and must serve time in a secure Maryland juvenile facility. Among other subjects, Fort Smallwood graduates take courses in math, history, science, and English. Also, the curriculum is vocation-oriented, with an emphasis on marine-related courses and Red Cross training. A youth–staff ratio of six-to-one assists youths in learning the fundamentals of sailboating and powerboating, reading navigational charts, use of marine radios, and anchoring, docking, and repairing boats.

The Fort Smallwood program can handle thirty juveniles who are selected for participation by juvenile probation officers. All participants have been arrested several times for crimes ranging from drug dealing to auto theft and burglary. Violent offenders, including arsonists and rapists, and those with histories of mental illness, are not eligible for program participation, according to state laws. Youths who graduate gain in self-esteem, and many of them qualify for interesting and well-paying marine work with private companies. The recidivism rate is low, about 20 percent, which is far lower than in secure detention facilities.

(Some factual information adapted from Steven Mardon, "On Board, Not Behind Bars," *Corrections Today* (1991) 53:32–38.)

of a community-based corrections agency is the *Allegheny Academy* in Pennsylvania.

The Allegheny Academy. In February 1982, the **Allegheny** (Pennsylvania) **Academy** was opened by the Community Specialists Corporation, a private, nonprofit corporation headquartered in Pittsburgh and specializing in the community-based treatment of young offenders (Costanzo, 1990:114). The program's general aim is to change the negative behavior of offenders. The targets of the Allegheny Academy are those juvenile offenders who have failed in other, traditional probation programs in Pennsylvania. Thus, the youthful clients are recidivists who, Allegheny officials believe, would not particularly benefit from further institutionalization through secure detention.

The Allegheny Academy was originally designed as a facility that could provide meaningful aftercare to adjudicated offenders. Clients are referred to the Academy by juvenile court judges in lieu of incarceration. The program may be completed by clients in about six months. Youths live at home, but they must attend the Academy each day after school and also on weekends. They receive two full-course meals a day and return to their homes around 8:00 or 9:00 P.M. each evening. Follow-up calls are made to these youths' homes by supervisors, who monitor the program-imposed curfew of 10:30 P.M. The Academy offers instruction and other forms of assistance to enable participants to acquire greater responsibilities. Buses carrying fifteen passengers each pick clients up daily and return them to their homes in the evenings. After they have successfully complied with program requirements for twenty-eight days in a row, they are gradually allowed community days at home on weekends. Students' failure to attend classes or observe curfews may result in their being sent to the county juvenile detention facility for two to fourteen days (Costanzo, 1990:116).

Student activities at Allegheny Academy include woodworking, carpentry, masonry, painting, electrical and structural repair, food services, vehicle maintenance, graphic arts, and computer skills. Students also receive individual or group counseling as well as some family counseling. They are encouraged to learn about substance abuse and behaving well in their schools and homes. Between 1982 and 1990, the cost of operating Allegheny Academy has been only a fraction of what it would have cost to impose long-term detention on all of the juveniles served. Further, clients have paid out over $100,000 in restitution to various victims through earnings from summer work programs.

Two other programs that have become popular as rehabilitative strategies for dealing with youthful offenders are the Boston Offender Project and Project New Pride.

The Boston Offender Project. Sometimes, it is prudent to seek a compromise in the custody imposed in various juvenile probation programs, in which a degree of secure custody over juveniles is necessary for a short time, but where nonsecure supervision would also be permitted and desirable. One of the most frustrating aggregates of juvenile offenders is that small minority that commits violent offenses (Murphy, 1985:26). Judges and probation officers

Some youths benefit from a combination of probation and confinement. In many jurisdictions, boot camps operate to instill discipline within youths. Subsequently, a majority of boot camp participants do well in fulfilling the remainder of their probationary programs. (Courtesy of Central Oregon Youth Conservation Corps.)

are often at a loss for strategies to deal effectively with such offenders. Often, the options are secure custody in a reform school or a waiver to criminal courts, presumably for more stringent punishments and longer sentences of confinement. Some professionals in juvenile corrections have continued to believe, however, that there are other viable options, provided that the time and resources can be allocated properly.

In 1981, an experimental program was commenced in Boston to give some of these professionals their chance to put into practice what they believed could be done in theory. The Massachusetts Department of Youth Services was awarded a grant to implement what eventually became known as the **Boston Offender Project** (BOP). BOP was one of five demonstration sites selected. Its target was violent juveniles, and the program goals included reducing recidivism among them, enhancing public protection by increasing accountability for major violators, and improving the likelihood of successful reintegration of juveniles into society by focusing on these offenders' academic and vocational skills (Murphy, 1985:26).

BOP sought to improve the typical handling of a violent juvenile case in the following ways:

1. By developing three coordinated phases of treatment consisting of initial placement in a small, locked, secure-treatment program, followed by planned transition into a halfway house, and finally, a gradual return to the juvenile's home community.

2. By assuring the delivery of comprehensive services by assigning particularly experienced caseworkers who are responsible for working intensively with a caseload of not more than eight violent offenders and their families.
3. By providing services focused on increasing the educational level of offenders and tying educational programs to the marketplace, significantly increasing the prospects of meaningful employment (Murphy, 1985:26).

BOP was similar to shock probation, in that violent juvenile offenders would experience some confinement in a secure facility, but after a short time would be released to less secure surroundings. Thus, a shock element was included, at least implicitly, in the BOP structure.

The BOP has several important features that differentiate it from the treatment received by juveniles in the control group. First, diagnostic assessments of juveniles in BOP went well beyond standard psychological assessments, and these measures were administered on an ongoing basis to chart developments in psychological, vocational, and medical areas. Second, caseworkers in the BOP program were three times more experienced (in numbers of years) than standard program caseworkers. A third important difference was that BOP caseworker loads were limited to eight, while caseloads for workers in the standard program were as high as twenty-five.

A fourth feature was that BOP caseworkers were actively involved in the treatment phase, whereas the standard program caseworker involvement was passive. A fifth feature of BOP was that caseworker visits to juveniles were eight times as frequent per month as standard program visits. A sixth BOP feature was an automatic assignment to nonsecure residential facilities once the first secure phase of the program was completed. For standard program participants, this was not necessarily an option. Furthermore, in the BOP program, continued violence would subject a participant to regression, so that the offender could be placed back in secure confinement. In the standard program, there was only limited flexibility to make this program shift. Finally, the standard program was terminated for youths when they reached 18 years of age, while the BOP could be discontinued or continued before or after age 18, depending upon caseworker judgment.

Some important differences between the two groups emerged over the next several years. For instance, 79 percent of BOP clients found unsubsidized employment, compared with only 29 percent of the control group. Also, only about a third of the BOP clients had been rearrested. This was about half the rearrest rate exhibited by the control group. Thus, while the BOP may not be the perfect solution to the problem of violent juvenile offenders, it does offer a viable, middle-ground alternative which has demonstrable success, at least with some offenders. For the chronic, hard-core, and most dangerous offenders, detention is one of the last resorts as a judicial option.

Project New Pride. One of the most popular probation programs is **Project New Pride,** which was established in Denver, Colorado in 1973. It has been widely used as a model for probation programs in other jurisdictions in subsequent years (Laurence and West, 1985). New Pride is a blend of education, counseling, employment, and cultural education directed at more serious offenders between the ages of 14 and 17. Juveniles eligible for the New Pride program must have at least two prior convictions for serious misdemeanors and/or felonies, and they must be formally charged or adjudicated for another offense when referred to New Pride. There are very few females in New Pride—only about 10 or 15 percent. This is not because of deliberate exclusion, but rather because females tend to have lower rates of recidivism and commit less serious offenses compared with their male delinquent counterparts. Those who are deliberately excluded are offenders previously diagnosed as severely psychotic or who have committed forcible rape.

Project New Pride's goals include (1) *reintegrating participants into their communities through school participation or employment,* and (2) *reducing recidivism rates among offenders.* The project emphasizes schooling, employment, and closeness with families. It is a community-based project and utilizes professional probation officers as well as volunteers. The project staff offers employment counseling services and job placement, tutoring for school assignments and projects, and vocational training. Project New Pride personnel will help juveniles fill out job application forms and answer other questions relevant for effective job-hunting and success in school.

Some of the areas where New Pride programs have been established have led to juveniles' developing small businesses such as bakeries, janitorial services, and lawn and gardening services to help defray the costs of their program expenses. Taxpayer dollars finance New Pride projects in various jurisdictions. It is estimated that the cost for each juvenile serviced by Project New Pride is $4,500, compared with $28,000 to incarcerate the same offender in a reform or industrial school (Project New Pride, 1985). The goals of Project New Pride seem reachable. Over the years, recidivism rates have been low, less than 20 percent. Furthermore, nearly half the juveniles who have participated in various New Pride projects throughout the United States have returned to school to finish their high school educations or have completed the GED. Almost three fourths of all participants hold full-time jobs successfully (McCarthy and McCarthy, 1984:312; Pacific Institute for Research and Evaluation, 1985).

Community-based programs are particularly advantageous for youths because they provide opportunities for them to remain integrated with their communities. At the same time, youths receive assistance through agency referrals to available services and treatments. Altschuler and Armstrong (1990a:170) suggest that community-based correctional programs and other intensive probation supervision programs can maximize their effectiveness and assistance to youthful clients if they attempt to realize five important principles. These include:

1. Preparing youths for gradually increased responsibility and freedom in the community.
2. Helping youths become involved in the community and getting the community to interact with them.

3. Working with youths and their families, peers, schools and employers to identify the qualities necessary for success.
4. Developing new resources and supports where needed.
5. Monitoring and testing youths and the community on their abilities to interact.

In the next section, we will examine three increasingly important intermediate punishments that seem to be working well with adult and juvenile offenders alike. These include (1) *electronic monitoring*, (2) *home confinement*, and (3) *shock probation.*

Electronic Monitoring. **Electronic monitoring** *is the use of telemetry devices to verify that an offender is at a specified location during specified times* (Schmidt and Curtis, 1987:137). Electronic monitoring devices were first used in 1964 as an alternative to incarcerating certain mental patients and parolees (Gable, 1986). Subsequently, electronic monitoring was extended to include monitoring of office work, employee testing for security clearances, and many other applications (U.S. Congress Office of Technology Assessment, 1987a, 1987b).

Second Judicial District Judge Jack Love of New Mexico is credited with implementing a pilot electronic monitoring project in 1983 for persons convicted of drunk driving and certain white-collar offenses, such as embezzlement (Houk, 1984). Subsequent to its use for probationers, the New Mexico State Supreme Court approved the program, since it required the voluntary consent of probationers as a condition of their probation programs. Judge Love directed that certain probationers should wear either anklets or bracelets that emitted electronic signals that could be intercepted by their probation officers who conducted surveillance operations. After a short period of such judicial experimentation, other jurisdictions decided to conduct their own experiments for offender monitoring with electronic devices. Eventually, experiments were underway, not only for probationers, but for parolees and inmates of jails and prisons (Schmidt, 1986:56). By 1988, there were over 2,300 offenders on electronic monitoring programs in at least thirty-three states (Schmidt, 1989).

There are at least four types of electronic monitoring signaling devices. The first, a *continuous-signal device,* consists of a miniature transmitter that is strapped to the probationer's wrist. The transmitter broadcasts an encoded signal that is received by a receiver-dialer in the offender's home. The signal is relayed to a central receiver over the telephone lines. A second type of monitor is the *programmed contact device,* which is similar to the continuous-signal device. However, in this case, a central computer from the probation office is programmed to call the offender's home at random hours to verify the probationer's whereabouts. Offenders must answer their telephones, insert the wristlet-transmitter into the telephone device, and their voices and signal emissions are verified by computer. A third monitor is a *cellular device.* This is a transmitter worn by offenders that emits a radio signal that may be received by a local area monitoring system. Up to 25 probationers may be monitored at once with such a system. The fourth type of monitor is the *continuous signaling transmitter*, which is also worn by the offender. These send out continuous signals which may be intercepted by portable receiving units in the possession of probation officers. They are quite popular, since POs may conduct "drive-bys" and verify that offenders are at home during curfew hours when they are supposed to be.

These wristlet/anklet transmitters are certainly not tamper-proof. They are similar in plastic construction to the wristlet ID tags given patients at the time of hospital admissions. However, these electronic devices are somewhat more sturdy. Nevertheless, the plastic is such that it is easy to remove. It can be easily seen whether the device has been tampered with (e.g., stretched, burned, mutilated), since it is impossible to reattach without special equipment in the possession of the probation department. If tampering has occurred and probationers have attempted to defeat the intent of the device, they may be subject to probation revocation, and may be punished by incarceration.

Gradually, the use of electronic monitoring devices has been extended to include both low- and high-risk juvenile offenders. In Knoxville, Tennessee, for example, electronic monitoring is used to a limited degree with juvenile probationers, but only as a last resort. Thus, juvenile offenders who have failed in other types of probation programs or community-based agencies are placed in an electronic monitoring program prior to being placed in secure detention. If they do not comply with their electronic monitoring program conditions, they will be sent to secure detention at one of the state's several public and private secure detention facilities.

Charles (1989a) describes the implementation of an electronic monitoring program for juvenile offenders in Allen County, Indiana. Known as the *Allen County, Indiana Juvenile Electronic Monitoring Program Pilot Project*, or EMP, this program was begun as an experimental study in October, 1987 and was conducted for nine months through May, 1988. At the time the study started, the probation department had twenty-five POs who were appointed by the court and certified by the Indiana Judicial Conference. During 1987, 2,404 juveniles were referred to the probation department by the court. About 34 percent of these were female offenders. During that same year, 167 youths were incarcerated in secure facilities for delinquents at a total cost of $1.5 million.

Charles (1989b:152–153) indicates that because of fiscal constraints, Allen County agreed to place only six juveniles in the electronic monitoring program. However, two of these youths recidivated and were dropped from it shortly after it started. The remaining four youths remained in the program. The juvenile judge in these cases sentenced each youth to a six-month probationary period with electronic monitoring. Each youth wore a conspicuous wristlet, which eventually became a symbol of court sanctions. Like the proverbial string tied around one's finger, the wristlet was a constant reminder to these juveniles that they were "on probation." Further, others who became aware of these electronic devices helped these youths to avoid activities that might be considered in violation of probation program conditions.

Despite the small number of participants in Charles' research, his findings are of interest and suggest similar successful applications on larger offender aggregates. Each juvenile was interviewed at the conclusion of the program. They reported that their wristlets were continuous reminders of their involvement in the probation program. However, they didn't feel as though program officials were spying on them. In fact, one of the youths compared his experience with electronic monitoring with his previous experience of being supervised by a probation officer. He remarked that whenever he was under the supervision of the probation officer, he could do whatever he wished, and there was little likelihood that his PO would ever find out about it. However, with the wristlet he was always under the threat of being discovered by the computer or by the surveillance officer.

Another interesting phenomenon was the fact that the wristlet enabled certain offenders to avoid peer pressure and "hanging out" with their friends. Since they had wristlets, they had good excuses to return home and not violate their curfews. Also, the families of these juveniles took a greater interest in them and their program. In short, at least for these four youths, the program was viewed very favorably and was considered successful. Parents who were interviewed at the conclusion of the program agreed that the program and monitoring system had been quite beneficial for their sons. While electronic monitoring for juveniles is still in the early stages of experimentation in various jurisdictions, Charles (1989c) believes that it is a cost-effective alternative to incarceration.

Some Criticisms of Electronic Monitoring. One limitation of electronic monitoring programs is that they are quite expensive to implement initially. The direct costs associated with their purchase or lease may seem prohibitive to local jurisdictions that are used to incarcerating juveniles and defraying their maintenance costs over an extended period. However, once a given jurisdiction has installed such equipment, the system eventually pays for itself and functions to reduce overall incarcerative expenses that otherwise would have been incurred had these same youths been placed in secure detention.

Also, electronic monitoring programs require some training on the part of the users. While those using such systems do not need to be computer geniuses, some computer training is helpful. Electronic monitoring is a delinquency deterrent for many offenders. However, it is not foolproof. In spite of the fact that they may be easily tampered with, electronic wristlets and anklets only help to verify an offender's whereabouts. They do not provide television images of these persons and what they may be doing. One federal probation officer reported that one of his federal probationers on electronic monitoring was running a successful stolen property business out of his own home. Thus, he was able to continue his criminal activities unabated, despite the home confinement constraints imposed by electronics.

Electronic monitoring has also been criticized as possibly violative of the Fourth Amendment "search and seizure" provision, where, it is alleged by some critics, electronic eavesdropping might be conducted within one's home or bedroom. This argument is without serious constitutional merit, since the primary function of such monitoring is to verify an offender's whereabouts. Some sophisticated types of monitoring systems are equipped with closed-circuit television transmissions, such as those advertised by the Bell Telephone Company as viewer-phones of the future. But even if such monitoring were so equipped, this additional feature would intrude only where offenders wished it to intrude, such as their living rooms or kitchens.

The fact is that many offenders may be inexpensively tracked through these monitoring systems, and their whereabouts can be verified without time-consuming face-to-face checks. For instance, a single juvenile probation officer may conduct "drive-bys" of client residences during evening hours and receive their transmitted signals with a portable unit. This silent means of detection is intended only to enforce one program element—namely, observance of curfews. Other checks, such as those conducted for illegal drug or alcohol use, must be verified directly, through proper testing and expert confirmation. As we will see, electronic monitoring is increasingly used in tandem with another sentencing option—home confinement.

Home Confinement. The use of one's home as the principal place of confinement is not new. In biblical times, St. Paul was sentenced to house arrest in Rome for two years, and performed tentmaker services for others (Lilly and Ball, 1987:359). **Home confinement** *is a program of intermediate punishment involving the use of the offender's residence for mandatory incarceration during evening hours after a curfew and on weekends* (Lilly and Ball, 1987).

Most experts agree that Florida pioneered the contemporary use of home confinement in 1983 (Flynn, 1986:64). At that time, corrections officials considered the use of homes as incarcerative facilities acceptable alternatives to defray the high cost of traditional incarceration in prisons or jails. When Florida implemented its home confinement program, it did so under the Correctional Reform Act of 1983. This act provided that the home could be used as a form of "intensive supervised custody in the community" (Flynn, 1986:64). This highly individualized program is intended primarily to restrict offender movement within the community, home, or nonresidential placement; it is accompanied by specific sanctions such as curfew, payment of fines, community service, and other requirements. When Florida implemented it, prison costs were running almost $30 per inmate per day, while home confinement required an expenditure of only about $3 per offender per day.

Although Florida officials consider home confinement to be punitive, some people disagree. They believe that incarceration should be in a jail or prison if it is to be meaningful incarceration. But Petersilia (1986) reports that home confinement may be even worse as a punishment than prison. Her interviews with probation officers in San Diego, California, yielded a statement from one probationer to the effect that while he was on home confinement, his kids would beg him to take them to the corner store to buy them ice cream cones. It was punishment to have to refuse their requests.

BOX 12.2

Juvenile Highlights

Are there more troubled teens today than there have been in previous decades? In the blue-collar community of Bergenfield, New Jersey, one evening in March, 1987, four teenagers went on a double date. They stopped at an Amoco service station and bought $3 worth of gas. Next, Cheryl Burress, 17, and her sister Lisa, 16, drove to Garage No. 74 at the Foster Village Apartments with their boyfriends, Thomas Olton, 18, and Thomas Rizzo, 19. The garage was a well-known hangout for youths who wanted to drink and smoke marijuana in private. They drove their car into the garage and shut and locked the door. They left their car idling and opened their car windows. They sat back, inhaled the exhaust fumes, and silently died within the hour.

Police officers found suicide notes that indicated these youths had formed a suicide pact. They were depressed over the recent suicide of a friend, Joe Major, who had fallen 200 feet to his death at the nearby Palisades cliffs along the Hudson River. Subsequent investigations by police disclosed the fact that these youths had been treated for drug- or alcohol-related problems at various rehabilitation clinics. Two of the youths had slash marks on their wrists from razor blades, indicating previous suicide attempts.

About 5,000 youths committed suicide each year during the 1980s. This is well above suicide rates for youths in the 1950s and 1960s. Depression, poor school performance, inability to adjust at school or at home, and a sense that all options have been exhausted result in either suicides or suicide attempts by thousands of teenagers annually. The police chief of Bergenfield characterized the youths who committed suicide in Garage No. 74 as "pain-in-the-ass-type kids" who were just troubled losers hanging out aimlessly, drinking too much and doing a little dope, "going nowhere fast."

(Some factual information adapted from Larry Martz, Peter McKillop, Andy Murr, and Ray Anello, "The Copycat Suicides," *Newsweek*, March 23, 1987, pp. 28–30, and Amy Wilentz, "Teen Suicide," *Time*, March 23, 1987, pp. 12–13.)

In many jurisdictions, home confinement is supplemented with electronic monitoring (Schlatter, 1989). Relatively little is known about the extent to which home confinement is used as a sentencing alternative for juvenile offenders. Since probation is so widely used as the sanction of choice except for the most chronic recidivists, home confinement is most often applied as an accompanying condition of electronic monitoring. However, this type of sentencing may be redundant, since curfew for juvenile offenders means home confinement anyway, especially during evening hours. As a day

sentence, home confinement for juveniles would probably be counterproductive, since juveniles are often obligated to finish their schooling as a probation
program condition. Since school hours are during the daytime, it would not
make sense to deprive juveniles of school opportunities through some type of
home detention. *used as a plea bargain role*

   Shock Probation. **Shock probation** *is an intermediate punishment in
which offenders are initially sentenced to terms of secure detention; after a period of
time, between 90 and 180 days, youths are removed from detention and sentenced to
serve the remainder of their sentences on probation* (adapted from Vito, 1984). The
actual term "shock probation" was coined by Ohio authorities in 1964 (Vito,
1984:22).

   Sometimes, shock probation is used synonomously with combination
sentences or split sentences. Other terms, such as intermittent sentences,
mixed sentences, or jail as a condition of probation, are also used
interchangeably with shock probation, although they have somewhat
different meanings. Combination sentences or split sentences occur whenever
judges sentence offenders to a term, a portion of which includes incarceration
and a portion of which includes probation. Mixed sentences occur whenever
offenders have been convicted of two or more offenses and judges sentence
them to separate sentences for each conviction offense. Intermittent sentences
occur whenever judges sentence offenders to terms such as weekend
confinement only. Jail as a condition of probation is a sentence that prescribes
a specified amount of jail incarceration prior to serving the remainder of the
sentence on probation.

   Technically, shock probation is none of these. Youths sentenced to shock
probation don't know they have received such sentences. The judge sentences
them to incarceration. The youths have no way of knowing that within three
or four months, they will be yanked out of detention, brought before the same
judge, and sentenced to probation. This new probationary sentence is
contingent upon their good behavior while in detention. Thus, they are
"shocked" by their detention. When they are resentenced to probation later,
they should be sufficiently "shocked" to avoid further offending. But
recidivism figures suggest it doesn't always work that way.

   Yurkanin (1989:87) indicates that shock probation, at least for adult
offenders, is escalating in its use among state jurisdictions. She reports that in
mid-1988, nearly 1,100 offenders were participating in at least nine shock
probation programs in different states, including Georgia, Oklahoma, Mississippi, Louisiana, South Carolina, New York, and Florida. At least five
additional states were planning to implement shock probation programs
during the next few years.

   Shock probation is a misnomer in a sense. If we recall that probation is a
sentence in lieu of incarceration, then it doesn't make much sense to
incarcerate offenders first, then release them later and call them "probationers." Technically, it might be more accurate to refer to this type of
intermediate punishment as *shock parole,* since these are previously incarcerated offenders who are resentenced to a supervised release program. In any
case, the intended effect of incarceration is to scare offenders sufficiently so

brings kids into prison for a short period of time and scared the shit out of the kids.

that they refrain from reoffending. Simply put, their incarcerative experiences are so shocking that they don't want to face further incarceration.

Shock probation has sometimes been compared erroneously with *Scared Straight*, a New Jersey program implemented in the late 1970s. Scared Straight sought to frighten samples of hard-core delinquent youths by having them confront inmates in a Rahway, New Jersey, prison. Inmates would yell at and belittle them, calling them names, cursing, and yelling. Inmates would tell them about sexual assaults and other prison unpleasantnesses in an attempt to get them to refrain from reoffending. However, the program was unsuccessful. Despite early favorable reports of recidivism rates of less than 20 percent, the actual rate of recidivism among the participating youths was considerably higher. Furthermore, another control group not exposed to Scared Straight had a lower recidivism rate (Lundman, 1984). The Scared Straight program is perhaps closer in principle to the SHAPE-UP program implemented in Colorado and discussed as a diversionary measure earlier. However, SHAPE-UP program authorities deny any program similarities other than prisoner—client interaction for brief periods (Mitchell and Shiller, 1988).

The juvenile version of shock probation or *shock incarceration* is perhaps best exemplified by juvenile **boot camps.** Also known as the **Army Model,** boot camp programs are patterned after basic training for new military recruits. Juvenile offenders are given a taste of hard military life, and such regimented activities and structure for up to 180 days are often sufficient to "shock" them into giving up their lives of delinquency or crime and staying out of jail (Ratliff, 1988:98). Boot camp programs in various states have been established, including the **Regimented Inmate Discipline** program in Mississippi, the *About Face* program in Louisiana, and the shock incarceration program in Georgia. These are paramilitary-type programs that emphasize strict military discipline and physical training (Ratliff, 1988:98).

Two good examples of boot camp programs are the *U.S. Army Correctional Activity* (USACA) in Fort Riley, Kansas, established in 1968 (Ratliff, 1988), and the *Butler (New York) Shock Incarceration Correctional Facility* (Waldron, 1990). In both programs, inmates wear army uniforms, learn basic army drills, salute, and participate in a rigorous correctional treatment program. Ordinarily, youthful first-offender felons are targeted for involvement in these programs. The Butler Shock program, for instance, involves young offenders ranging in age from 16 to 29. They must stay in the camp for six months and comply with all program rules. About 88 percent of boot camp trainees are successful and win a parole later. The Butler facility has inmates who have been heavily involved in drug-dealing. About 90 percent of participants have been convicted of drug offenses. They have rigorous work details, must complete schoolwork, and must adhere to a highly disciplined regimen. They are given eight minutes for meals, and they must carry their leftovers in their pockets.

Their days begin at 5:30 A.M., with reveille blaring over the intercom. Immediately, drill instructors start screaming at them. Besides military drilling, all inmates must experience drug counseling and study. At the Fort

Many youthful offenders are permitted to remain at home, attend school, and work at part-time jobs. However, they must comply with certain probation conditions, such as participating in counseling or receiving group therapy. (© Mark Newman)

Riley facility, inmates may learn vocational skills and crafts. They also receive counseling and other therapy and treatment. At both camps, physicians and other support staff are ready to furnish any needed medical treatment. When they eventually leave the facility, most have changed their outlook on life and have acquired new lifestyles not associated with crime. Again, recidivism rates among these inmates are under 30 percent, which is considered an indication of program success.

Other ISP Program Conditions

Briefly reviewing judicial sentencing options: at one end of the sentencing spectrum, judges may adjudicate youths as delinquent, impose nominal sanctions, and take no further action other than to record the event. If the same juveniles reappear before the same judge in the future, sterner measures may be taken in imposing new sentences. Or the judge may divert juveniles to particular community agencies for special treatment. Juveniles with psychological problems or who are emotionally disturbed, are sex offenders, or have drug and/or alcohol dependencies may be targeted for special community treatments. At the other end of the spectrum of punishments are the most drastic alternatives of custodial sanctions, ranging from the placement of juveniles in nonsecure foster homes and camp ranches, to placement in secure facilities such as reform schools and industrial schools. These nonsecure and secure forms of placement and/or detention are usually reserved for the most serious offenders.

Probation is the most commonly used sentencing option. Probation is either unconditional or conditional. This chapter has examined several conditional intermediate punishments, including intensive probation supervision and community-based programs. A youth's assignment to any of these programs may or may not include conditions. Apart from the more intensive monitoring and supervision by POs, juveniles may be expected to comply with one or more conditions, including restitution, if financial loss was suffered by one or more victims in cases of vandalism, property damage, or physical injury. Also, fines may be imposed. Or the judge may specify some form of community service. All of these conditions may be an integral part of a juvenile's probation program. Violation of or failure to comply with one or more of these conditions may result in a probation revocation action. Probation officers function as the link between juvenile offenders and the courts regarding a youth's compliance with these program conditions. (Juvenile probation and parole revocation will be discussed in Chapter 13.)

Restitution, Fines, and Victim Compensation. An increasingly important feature of probation programs is **restitution** (Rubin, 1986; Staples, 1986). Several models of restitution have been described. These include:

1. The **financial/community service model,** which stresses the offender's financial accountability and community service to pay for damages.
2. The **victim–offender mediation model,** which focuses upon victim–offender reconciliation.
3. The **victim reparations model,** in which juveniles compensate their victims directly for their offenses (Schneider, 1985).

The potential significance of restitution, coupled with probation, is that it suggests a reduction in recidivism among juvenile offenders. In a restitution program in Atlanta, Georgia, for example, 258 juvenile offenders participated in several experimental treatment programs, one of which included restitution. The restitution offender group had a 26 percent reduction in recidivism compared with juveniles who did not have restitution included as a condition (Schneider and Schneider, 1985). But other experts caution that if restitution is not properly implemented by the court or carefully supervised, it serves little deterrent purpose (Staples, 1986).

Beyond their effects in reducing recidivism, requirements for restitution, payment of fines, and **victim compensation** also increase offender accountability. Given the present philosophical direction of juvenile courts, this condition is consistent with enhancing a youth's acceptance of responsibility for wrongful actions committed against others and the financial harm they have caused. Rubin (1988:38) suggests that an important part of the mission of probation is to increase a youth's personal accountability. He notes, for example, that the Santa Clara County (San Jose), California Probation Department says that "offenders will be held responsible to the community and to themselves through personal accountability and restitution as a part of any sanction whether or not it involves custody" (Rubin, 1988:38).

Many of the programs we have already discussed include restitution as a part of their program requirements. Restitution orders may be imposed by juvenile court judges with or without accompanying sentences of detention. The Lucas County (Ohio) Juvenile Court, highlighted earlier in this chapter because of its intensive supervision program, utilizes about $90,000 of its state monies to pay restitution-owing juveniles to perform community service for repayment to victims (Rubin, 1988:39).

However, Rubin (1988) cautions that restitution as a program condition may at times be difficult to enforce. In part because the juvenile court continues to have an informal quality, it is difficult to ensure that restitution orders have been met by youthful offenders. Youths themselves may feel that the level of restitution set by judges is excessive. If they fail to comply with court-ordered restitution, they face a contempt-of-court charge, which is a new, more serious offense. In some instances, juveniles are ordered to repay insurance companies who have reimbursed victims for their medical expenses and other losses. Juvenile court judges attempt to impose restitution based in part on the amount of a victim's loss and in part on a youth's ability to pay. Rubin (1988:42) recommends that the burden of ensuring a youth's compliance with a restitution order should be upon the supervising agency or placement facility. These institutions are in the best position to monitor a youth's performance and can measure fairly accurately a youth's earnings and restitution contributions. Restitution does seem to improve offender accountability and responsibility.

Community Service. Often connected with restitution orders is **community service.** Community service may be performed in diverse ways, from cutting courthouse lawns and cleaning up public parks to painting homes for the elderly or repairing fences on private farms. Youths typically earn wages for this service, and these wages are usually donated to a victim compensation fund. The different types of community service activities are limited only by the imagination of the juvenile court and community leaders. Similar to restitution, community service orders are intended to increase offender accountability and individual responsibility. Evidence suggests that community service achieves such objectives, although offender accountability is enhanced if offenders participate in community service programs with clear goals and guidelines.

Summary

Intermediate punishments are sanctions that juvenile court judges may impose that lie somewhere between standard probation and incarceration. Popular intermediate punishments include intensive supervised probation, community-based programs, electronic monitoring, home confinement, and shock probation. The significance of such programs is that the more intensified supervision and monitoring of juvenile offenders will deter them from committing new offenses. Generally, recidivism figures seem to show that these programs are successful in reducing delinquency.

Intensive supervised probation increases the number of PO/client contacts as well as accompanying conditions, such as payment of fines, curfew, drug and alcohol checks, restitution orders, and individual or group therapy. Georgia and New Jersey have operated ISP programs for adult offenders for many years, and juvenile authorities have experimented with programs with similar characteristics. Ohio ISP programs suggest that ISP may be implemented differently, depending upon the jurisdiction. Yet, similar results are obtained regarding offender avoidance of further offending. Ordinarily, juveniles are screened for participation through the use of dangerousness assessment instruments. Some experts suggest a balanced approach to juvenile ISP, including both punitive and rehabilitative dimensions. Overall objectives are to increase offender accountability and personal responsibility.

Community-based programs include the Allegheny (Pennsylvania) Academy, where students learn useful crafts and other skills, and the Boston Offender Project, which is aimed at reintegrating youths into their communities. Other intermediate punishments include electronic monitoring and home confinement, where offenders wear electronic bracelets or anklets that emit electronic signals which can be received by POs to verify an offender's whereabouts. Homes are used as incarcerative facilities, and PO checks verify one's presence. Both of these programs are geared toward helping cut the costs of incarcerating juvenile offenders. Shock probation is also used in some jurisdictions. In this form of punishment, offenders are initially incarcerated for a period of up to 180 days; then, depending upon their good behavior, they are removed from detention and resentenced to probation for the remainder of the terms they must serve. Accompanying these punishments are the payment of fines, restitution, and community service. It is presumed that such conditional penalties enhance accountability and improve an offender's responsibility to victims and society.

Key Terms

Allegheny Academy (401)
Army model (411)
Balanced approach (396)
Boot camp (411)
Boston Offender Project (402)
Case supervision planning (395)
Client Management Classification (395)
Community-based corrections (398)
Community corrections acts (399)

Community service (414)
Conventional model (396)
Conventional model with geographic considerations (396)
Creative sentencing (382)
Delaware Initial Security Placement Instrument (383)
Electronic monitoring (405)
Financial/community service model (413)

Questions for Review

1. What is an intermediate punishment program? Give some examples of intermediate punishments.
2. Identify five key goals of intermediate punishment programs. Which programs do you feel best achieve these goals? Why? Discuss.
3. What is meant by creative sentencing? In what respect is an intermediate punishment a creative sentence?
4. Describe two types of risk classification instruments designed to assess dangerousness. What are the criteria that both of these instruments tend to share?
5. What is an intensive supervised probation program? What are the primary characteristics of such programs?
6. What are the manifest goals of ISP programs? Give two examples of such programs and discuss the degree to which their respective goals are achieved.
7. What is meant by the Ohio experience? Discuss the four types of Ohio programs and their major differences.
8. What are the general characteristics that most juvenile ISP programs tend to share? Discuss the weaknesses and strengths of ISP programs.
9. What was the San Francisco Project? Why do you believe that probation departments might seek to criticize it?
10. Describe four different programs for assigning PO caseloads. Which ones do you feel best meet the needs of offenders? Why? Explain.
11. What is meant by the balanced approach to probation work?
12. What is a community-based intermediate punishment program? Describe the essential features of community-based programs.
13. Describe the purposes and functions of the Allegheny Academy. Was this project successful? Why or why not?
14. What is the Boston Offender Project? In what way is the BOP similar to shock probation?

15. Compare Project New Pride and the Allegheny Academy. What are the goals of each? Which program do you believe is more successful at reducing delinquent conduct? Why?

16. What is electronic monitoring? Describe four types of electronic monitoring systems.

17. How is the work of POs enhanced by electronic monitoring? What are drive-bys?

18. Write a short essay on your feelings about the constitutionality of electronic monitoring and its use in supervising juvenile offenders.

19. What is home confinement? Briefly give a history of its use in the United States. What are some accompanying punishments that might be imposed together with home confinement?

20. What is shock probation? Differentiate between split sentencing, intermittent sentencing, mixed sentences, and jail as a condition of probation.

21. What are boot camps? Describe the characteristics of boot camp experiences. What are the goals of boot camps? Do they appear to be successful? Why or why not?

22. Describe community service, payment of fines, restitution, and victim compensation as four conditions judges might impose, together with probationary sentences. Write a short essay evaluating these conditions.

Suggested Readings

BLOMBERG, THOMAS G. (1984). *Juvenile Court and Community Corrections.* Lanham, MD: University Press of America.

GREENWOOD, PETER W., and SUSAN TURNER (1987). *The Visionquest Program: An Evaluation.* Santa Monica, CA: Rand Corporation.

JENSON, JEFFREY MARK (1988). *Effects of a Skills Training Intervention with Juvenile Delinquents.* Ann Arbor, MI: University Microfilms International.

LAUGHRAN, EDWARD J., ET AL. (1986). *Reinvesting Youth Corrections Resources: A Tale of Three States.* Minneapolis, MN: Center for the Study of Youth Policy, Hubert H. Humphrey Institute of Public Affairs, University of Minnesota.

McCARTHY, BERNARD, and BELINDA McCARTHY (EDS.) (1991). *Community-based Corrections* (2nd ed.). Pacific Grove, CA: Brooks/Cole.

QUAY, HERBERT C. (ED.) (1987). *Handbook of Juvenile Delinquency.* New York: Wiley.

WIEBUSH, RICHARD G. (1989). *An Assessment of Intensive Supervision in the Delaware County Juvenile Court.* Columbus, OH: Ohio Governor's Office of Criminal Justice Services.

CHAPTER 13

Custodial Sanctions: Juvenile Correctional Systems and Parole

Introduction

The U.S. Department of Justice's Office of Juvenile Justice and Delinquency Prevention reported that by mid-February, 1989, over 56,000 juveniles were held in public correctional facilities in the United States. This was a 5 percent increase over those confined in 1987 and a 14 percent increase over those confined in 1985. Admissions and discharges of juveniles from correctional facilities during 1989 were 1.3 million, the highest number since 1970 (Allen-Hagen, 1991:1–3). Minority youths made up 60 percent of those confined, while those held for drug or alcohol offenses increased by 150 percent since 1985.

 One of the most important components of the juvenile justice system is *juvenile corrections*. **Juvenile corrections** *encompasses all personnel, agencies, and*

418

institutions that supervise youthful offenders. In Chapters 11 and 12, we examined various nominal and conditional options that related to supervising juveniles who are placed on diversion or sentenced to probation or intermediate punishment programs. This chapter describes several custodial sentencing options, the most severe sanctions that juvenile court judges may impose. These sanctions are usually administered to youths who have been adjudicated as delinquent and who are considered sufficiently serious or dangerous offenders to merit close supervision or secure detention.

First, a brief history of juvenile corrections in the United States will be presented and some of the more important goals of such corrections will be described. Next, an overview of several custodial sentencing options will be provided. This overview will be followed by a description of some of the more popular nonsecure and secure custodial alternatives. Because some juvenile offenders require greater discipline and harsher treatment than others, correctional facilities vary in the degree of supervision and control exerted over juvenile inmates. These facilities and programs will be described and assessed.

Juveniles released from nonsecure or secure custody are often placed on parole for limited periods. Those juveniles placed on parole are ordinarily expected to abide by various parole conditions in order to fulfill their parole programs successfully. Some of these conditions and parole programs will be described. If juveniles violate one or more parole conditions, their parole may be revoked. Parole revocation may mean that juveniles will be returned to their original custodial institutions. This revocation process will be described.

Finally, several key issues in juvenile corrections will be presented. These issues include the privatization of juvenile corrections, housing juveniles in adult lockups or jail facilities, classifying offenders for their subsequent placement, and offender recidivism.

The History of Juvenile Corrections

Recalling a definition of delinquency provided earlier, *juvenile delinquency is any act committed by a juvenile which, if committed by an adult, would be a crime* (Rogers and Mays, 1987:566). In the United States, especially during the 1800s and early 1900s, juvenile matters were handled by a variety of civil courts and nonlegal institutions such as welfare agencies. The doctrine under which juveniles were managed and processed was called *parens patriae,* which means "parent of the country" (Black, 1979:1003). Historically, this term was a part of English common law during the medieval period, and it meant that juvenile matters were within the purview of the king and his agents, usually chancellors and other officials in various regions. Figuratively, the king was the "father of the country" and assumed responsibility for all juveniles. Through the centuries this term was accepted by most jurisdictions. Subsequently, the United States adopted the *parens patriae* doctrine as an effective way of dealing with juvenile matters.

Arguably, one of the first correctional facilities to recognize juveniles as a category different from adult males and females was the **Walnut Street Jail** in Philadelphia. The Walnut Street Jail was constructed in 1776 to house the overflow of inmates from the High Street Jail. When the Walnut Street Jail was originally constructed, little or no thought was given to whether males, females, and minors would be housed in separate areas. Usually, inmates of all ages and genders were housed in common rooms, with straw strewn on the floors for sleeping. No attempt was made to segregate prisoners. In 1790, new policies were implemented within the Walnut Street Jail to provide for the separate confinement of prisoners according to gender and age. Further, the jail provided for segregating more dangerous prisoners from less dangerous ones through an innovation known as **solitary confinement.** Ironically, more than a few jails in the United States today house juveniles with adult inmates for various durations, despite certain regulations to the contrary. Thus, at least some jails today continue to exhibit some of congregate accommodations that typified the original Walnut Street Jail in 1776. This particular problem is an issue that will be addressed later in this chapter.

The first public reformatory for juvenile offenders was the New York House of Refuge, organized in New York City in 1825 by the Society for the Prevention of Pauperism (Cahalan, 1986:101). Since there was little central-ized organization to these houses of refuge, it is difficult to determine the impact of these facilities on delinquency (Rogers and Mays, 1987:426). The manifest goals of these houses of refuge were to provide poor, abused, or orphaned youths with food, clothing, and lodging, although in return, hard work, discipline and study were expected.

Charles Loring Brace in 1853 established the New York Children's Aid Society, which functioned primarily as a placement service for parentless children (Mennel, 1983:199). The term *juvenile delinquency* was seldom used during the early 1800s, because public authorities stressed parental control of children and regarded youthful misbehaviors as stemming from lack of discipline rather than something that should be dealt with more formally (Mennel, 1983:198). Many early institutions designed to care for and reform juveniles were operated under private, charitable, and religious sponsorship.

Subsequently, the Civil War, followed by the Reconstruction Period and vast industrialization, left many families fatherless. In the subsequent years, many of these families moved to urban areas such as Chicago, Boston, and New York, where they sought jobs in shops and factories. In the absence of child labor laws, many children were exploited as cheap labor by so-called sweatshops. In addition, large numbers of youths roamed the streets unsupervised while their parents worked at jobs for long hours. Eventually, "children's tribunals" were established in various states, including Massa-chusetts and New York, in order to punish youths charged with various offenses. The first statute authorizing such a tribunal to deal with juvenile matters was passed in Massachusetts in 1874 (Hahn, 1984). A similar statute was passed in 1892 in New York.

In 1889, **Jane Addams** established and began to operate **Hull House,** a settlement home for children of immigrant families in Chicago. Financing for this home came largely from charitable organizations and philanthropists, and it existed to provide children with activities to alleviate boredom and monotony while their parents were at work. Many children without parents were accommodated by Addams. Teaching children morality, ethics, and certain religious precepts were important components of juvenile treatment programs in Addams's day (Hahn, 1984).

The *Compulsory School Act* was passed by the Colorado State Legislature in 1899. Its goal was preventing truancy among juveniles. This act targeted youths who were habitually absent from school, who wandered about the streets during school hours, and who had no obvious business or occupation. These youths were labeled "juvenile disorderly persons." Since the act was aimed primarily at truancy, it is not considered a juvenile court act in a technical sense. The Illinois legislature created the first juvenile court act on July 1, 1899. It was called *An Act to Regulate the Treatment and Control of Dependent, Neglected and Delinquent Children.* Between 1899 and 1909, twenty states had passed similar legislation for the establishment of juvenile courts. By 1945, all states had juvenile court systems. However, these systems varied greatly among jurisdictions, and the responsibility for deciding juvenile dispositions rested with different types of court systems.

In 1880 the first census of juvenile offenders in public institutions was conducted by the U.S. Bureau of Census. This report indicated that there were over 11,000 juvenile offenders in U.S. institutions. That figure doubled by 1904, and by 1980, there were over 59,000 juveniles in various U.S. public correctional facilities (Cahalan, 1986:104). By June 30, 1990, there were over 75,000 juveniles under supervision in U.S. public and private facilities in state systems (American Correctional Association, 1991:xxxvi–xxxvii).

Goals of Juvenile Corrections

Various goals of juvenile corrections include (1) *deterrence,* (2) *rehabilitation and reintegration,* (3) *prevention,* (4) *punishment and retribution,* and (5) *isolation and control.* These goals may at times appear to be in conflict (Thornton *et al.,* 1987:350–351). For instance, some experts stress delinquency prevention through keeping juveniles away from the juvenile justice system through diversion and warnings. However, other critics say that the juvenile justice system is too lenient with offenders and must "get tough" with them through more certain and stringent penalties for the offenses they commit (Garrett, 1985). A middle ground stresses both discipline and reform.

1. *Deterrence.* According to correctional critic Robert Martinson, who has said "nothing works" in American corrections, no program has been shown to be 100 percent effective in deterring juveniles from committing delinquent acts or recidivating (Martinson, 1974). However, other researchers suggest

that significant deterrent elements of juvenile correctional programs include clearly stated rules and formal sanctions, anticriminal modeling and reinforcement, and a high degree of empathy and trust between the juvenile client and the staff (Gendreau and Ross, 1984). Traditional counseling, institutionalization, and diversion are considered largely ineffective, according to other investigators (Pabon, 1985). Also, it may be that a natural intervention occurs apart from any particular program designed to deter, simply as the result of aging. As youths grow older, their offending appears to reach a plateau and then decline. Thus, many youths may grow out of the delinquency mode as they become older.

2. *Rehabilitation and reintegration.* Community-based publicly and privately operated correctional programs for juveniles often have a strong rehabilitative orientation (Martin, 1987). Some rehabilitative and reintegrative programs stress internalizing responsibilities for one's actions, while other programs attempt to inculcate social and motor skills (Greenwood and Zimring, 1985; Goldsmith, 1987; Rousch and Steelman, 1982). Other programs are aimed at diagnosing and treating youths who are emotionally disturbed. Alternative medical and social therapies are often used (Awad, 1985; Washington State Department of Social and Health Services, 1986). For instance, Weber and Burke (1986) describe a Teaching-Family Treatment Model that has been used in 125 group homes throughout the United States. It currently contains elements such as (a) teaching delinquent youths communication skills, daily living skills, survival skills, educational advancement and study skills, and career skills; (b) breaking such skills into specific behaviorally defined components; (c) ensuring that the delinquents practice the skills in the problem setting; (d) assessing each youth's skill needs; (e) developing individualized teaching plans; and (f) teaching to the individual skill deficits.

3. *Prevention.* Delinquency prevention seems to be a function of many factors. One factor is early preschool intervention. Preschool intervention programs seem to have modest success rates (Syracuse/Onondaga County Youth Bureau, 1984). In 1962 the Perry Preschool Project was implemented in Ypsilanti, Michigan (Berrueta-Clement *et al.*, 1984). Nearly 70 percent of the children who participated in the program had no future reported offenses as juveniles and only 16 percent were ever arrested for delinquent acts. However, about half of the nonparticipants in the same school had future reported offenses as juveniles, and 25 percent were subsequently arrested for delinquency.

4. *Punishment and retribution.* Some people want to see youths, especially violent ones, punished rather than rehabilitated. The "wilding" incident involving the near-death of a female jogger by a gang of youths in New York City's Central Park is a case in point. Anthony P. Travisono, former Executive Director of the American Correctional Association (ACA), has indicated that

he has been plagued by questions from the media about the official policy of the ACA with regard to how juveniles should be treated. Travisono says that "judging from the questions[from reporters about the juvenile violence in the jogger incident], without a doubt, they wanted to see [these] teenagers treated as adults and sent straight to prison; most seemed to feel that a trial would be an unnecessary bother" (Travisono, 1989:4). However, Travisono added that currently, there is no clear correctional policy about how these and other violent youths should be processed or punished.

One major impact of the "get tough on crime" policy adopted by many jurisdictions is that the juvenile justice system seems to be diverting a larger portion of its serious offenders to criminal courts, where they may conceivably receive harsher punishments. This may be one reaction to widespread allegations that the juvenile courts are too lenient in their sentencing of violent offenders, or that the punishment options available to juvenile court judges are not sufficiently severe. For those juveniles who remain within the juvenile justice system for processing, secure custody for longer periods seems to be the court's primary response to citizen allegations of excessive leniency.

5. *Isolation and control.* Apprehension and confinement of juvenile offenders, especially chronic recidivists, is believed to be important in isolating them and limiting their opportunities to reoffend. In principle, this philosophy is similar to selective incapacitation. However, the average length of juvenile incarceration terms in public facilities in the United States is less than ten months (Cahalan, 1986). Thus, confinement by itself may be of limited value in controlling the amount of juvenile delinquency. Greenwood (1986a) says that control for the sake of control may be self-defeating as a long-range delinquency prevention strategy. Furthermore, when youths are placed in custodial settings, the emphasis of the facility is more often on control than on rehabilitation.

Current Juvenile Custodial Alternatives

The custodial options available to juvenile court judges are of two general types: (1) *nonsecure,* and (2) *secure.* Nonsecure custodial facilities are those that permit youths freedom of movement within the community. Youths are generally free to leave the premises of their facilities, although they are compelled to observe various rules, such as curfew, avoidance of alcoholic beverages and drugs, and participation in specific programs that are tailored to their particular needs. These types of nonsecure facilities include *foster homes, group homes and halfway houses,* and *camps, ranches, experience programs,* and *wilderness projects.*

Secure custodial facilities are the juvenile counterpart to adult prisons or penitentiaries. Such institutions are known by different names among the states. For example, secure, long-term confinement facilities might be called "youth centers" or "youth facilities" (Alaska, California, Colorado, District of

Columbia, Illinois, Kansas, Maine, Missouri), "juvenile institutions" (Arkansas), "schools" (California, Connecticut, New Mexico), "schools for boys" (Delaware), "**training schools** or centers" (Florida, Indiana, Iowa, Oregon), "youth development centers" (Georgia, Nebraska), "youth services centers" (Idaho), "secure centers" (New York), "industry schools" (New York), and "youth development centers" (Tennessee). This listing is not intended to be comprehensive, but it illustrates the variety of designations states use to refer to their long-term secure confinement facilities. An overview of the number of types of juvenile facilities and programs on a nationwide basis is shown in Table 13.1 (pages 426–428).

In earlier years, these facilities would have been known as "reform schools," reflecting the influence of *houses of reformation* in the United States established during the early 1850s. However, an inspection of the most recent ACA Directory listing all juvenile correctional facilities in the United States shows a conspicuous absence of the term *reform school.* Interestingly, these contemporary designations frequently imply "helping," "treatment," "rehabilitative," or "reintegrative" milieus in their names. Despite this euphemistic name-changing, designed to lend dignity to these settings and their functions, they remain principally custodial, strict, and punitive institutions, and their rehabilitative and reintegrative qualities are questionable. The distribution of juveniles under various forms of supervision among state systems in 1990 is shown in Table 13.2 (pages 430–431).

Nonsecure Confinement

Nonsecure confinement involves placing certain youths in (1) **foster homes,** (2) **group homes and halfway houses,** or (3) **camps, ranches, experience programs,** and **wilderness projects.**

Foster Homes. If the juvenile's natural parents are considered unfit, or if the juvenile is abandoned or orphaned, foster homes are often used for temporary placement. Those youths placed in foster homes are not necessarily law violators. They may be *children in need of supervision* (CHINS). Foster home placement provides youths with a substitute family. A stable family environment is believed by the courts to be beneficial in many cases where youths have no consistent adult supervision or are unmanageable or unruly in their own households. In 1990, approximately 4,000 youths were under the supervision of foster homes in state-operated public placement programs (American Correctional Association, 1991). Rogers and Mays (1987:429) indicate that many of those assigned to foster homes are dependent, neglected, or abused, and youths typically are in the 10 to 14 age range.

Foster home placements are useful in many cases in which youths have been apprehended for status offenses. Most families who accept youths into their homes have been investigated by state or local authorities in advance to determine their fitness as foster parents. Socioeconomic factors and home stability are considered important for child placements. Foster parents are often typical middle-aged, middle-class citizens with above-average educational backgrounds. Despite these positive features, it is unlikely that foster homes are able to provide the high intensity of adult supervision required by more hard-core juvenile offenders. Further, it is unlikely that these parents can furnish the quality of special treatments that might prove effective in the youth's rehabilitation or societal reintegration. Most foster parents simply are not trained as counselors, social workers, or psychologists. For many nonserious offenders, however, a home environment, particularly a stable one, has certain therapeutic benefits.

Group Homes and Halfway Houses. Another nonsecure option for juvenile judges is the assignment of juveniles to group homes and halfway houses. Placing youths in group homes is considered an intermediate option available to juvenile court judges. Group homes or halfway houses are community-based operations that may be either publicly or privately administered (Simone, 1984:110). The notion of a "halfway house" is frequently used to refer to community homes used by adult parolees recently released from prison. These halfway houses provide a temporary base of operations for parolees as they seek employment and readjustment within their communities. Therefore, they are perceived as transitional residences, halfway between incarceration and the full freedom of life "on the outside." To many ex-inmates, the transition from the rigidity of prison culture to the unregulated life in the outside world can be traumatic. Many ex-inmates need time to readjust. The rules of halfway houses provide limited structure as well as freedom of access to the outside during the transitory stage.

Usually, group homes have counselors or residents to act as parental figures for youths in groups of 10 to 20. Certain group homes, referred to as **family group homes,** are actually family-operated, and thus, they are in a sense an extension of foster homes for larger numbers of youths. In group homes, nonsecure supervision of juvenile clients is practiced. Nearly 4,000 youths were in state-sponsored group homes during 1990 (American Correctional Association, 1991).

No model or ideal group home exists in the nation to be emulated by all jurisdictions, and what works well for youths in some communities may not be effective in other jurisdictions. However, most successful group homes have strong structural elements, in which all residents are obligated to participate in certain program components, predictable consequences for rule violations are rigorously enforced, and there is constant monitoring by staff workers. Thus, juveniles have the best of both worlds—they can live in a homelike environment and visit with family and friends in a home setting; yet they must comply with strict rules governing curfew, program participation, and other court-imposed conditions (Simone, 1984:112).

Whether privately or publicly operated, group homes require juvenile clients to observe the rights of others, participate in various vocational or educational training programs, attend school, participate in therapy or receive prescribed medical treatment, and observe curfew. Urinalyses or other tests may be conducted randomly as checks to see whether juveniles are taking

TABLE 13.1   Number of Juvenile Facilities and Programs (as of June 30, 1990)

State	Institutions			Diagnostic/ Reception			Community Based			Detention Centers		
	M	F	C	M/F	C	L	M/F	C	L	M/F	C	L
Alabama	3		1		1							
Alaska			4									1
Arizona	4	1				2	1/0	1				
Arkansas	1		1			1						
California	8		1	2/0		1	3/0			2/0		
Colorado	1				1	1	15/2	1			5	
Connecticut			1									
Delaware	1										2	
Florida	2						85/7	18			20	
Georgia	3	1						23			19	
Hawaii			1			1			1			
Idaho			1		3[1]		5/3[1]	9			1	
Illinois	6	1				2						
Indiana	2	1					2/0					
Iowa[2]	1	1			1						1	
Kansas	3	1			1	1						
Kentucky	7	1	1					13				
Louisiana	2		1			1	8/2	6				
Maine			1									
Maryland			1				11/5	50		1/0	4	
Massachusetts	9	2		3/0			18/1	11		4/2		
Michigan	7		1	1/0	1		22/2	4		1/0	1	
Minnesota	1		1									
Mississippi	2		1									
Missouri	4		2									
Montana	1	1			1	2	3/1					
Nebraska	1		1									
Nevada	1		1									
New Hampshire			1				1/0				1	
New Jersey	3						41/7					
New Mexico	1	1			1		6/1					
New York	3		1				18/3	3		1		
North Carolina	2		3								4	
North Dakota			1			1						
Ohio	8	1										
Oklahoma			1	1/0			5/2					8
Oregon	1		1		1							
Pennsylvania	6		1									
Rhode Island			1		1		6/1			1/0		

C = Coed.
L = Located in other facilities.
*Combined male/female total.
[1]Privately run.
[2]Data as of 6/30/89.
[3]Two privately run marine institutes.
[4]Contract for 20 residen & 37 nonres programs.

SOURCE: American Correctional Association, *1991 Directory* (Laurel, MD: American Correctional Association, 1991), p. xxiv.

Medical Psych			Homes		Camps			Other		
M/F	C	L	M/F	C	M/F	C	L	M/F	C	L
			4/1							
		5						49/0[1]		5
			25/0		5/0	1	3			
					1/0			2/0[1]	1	
			3/0						3	
		1								
	1[1]			159						
	11		11/7		3/0				2	
			16/8	17						
	1			130	7/0				2	
			5/1			1			30	
								4/0[1]		
					1/0					
			6/1		2/1	1			2	
				2				2/1[1]		
								1/2[1]		
	1/0									
			8/2	5						
					2/[1]	2[1]				
					1/0					
			14*[1]		1/0			15*[1]		
					5/0					
					2/0					

''Other'' Includes: AZ, educa(5)/residen(37)/nonres(12):
CO, orientation; GA, MA, Day trtmt; KY, re-ed programs;
MI, private training schools; MO, outdoor education;
NH, special ed school (residen); OK, contracted residen;
SC, marine institutes(5)/chronic status offender(1);
TX, resident(13)nonres(13)medical-psych(23) homes(76)/camp(1); WV, youthful offender in-stitution; DC, prerelease.

TABLE 13.1   (continued)

State	Institutions			Diagnostic/ Reception			Community Based			Detention Centers		
	M	F	C	M/F	C	L	M/F	C	L	M/F	C	L
South Carolina	2		1		1			1				
South Dakota			1									
Tennessee	2		2	1/0			8/5					
Texas	3		3		2		8/1					
Utah			3		3			2			10	
Vermont			1		1	1		1	2		1	1
Virginia		1	5		1		27/7	27			17	
Washington	2		1									
West Virginia	1		1			1						
Wisconsin	1		1									
Wyoming	1	1										
Total	106	14	50	8/0	20	15	293/50	170	3	92	86	10

drugs or consuming alcohol contrary to group home policy. If one or more program violations occur, group home officials may report these infractions to juvenile judges, who retain dispositional control over the youths. Assignment to a group home or any other type of confinement is usually for a determinate period.

A positive element of group homes is that they provide youths with the companionship of other juveniles. Problem-sharing often occurs through planned group discussions. Staff are available to assist youths to secure employment, work out difficult school problems, and absorb emotional burdens arising from difficult interpersonal relationships. However, these homes are sometimes staffed by community volunteers with little training or experience with a youth's problems. There are certain risks and legal liabilities that may be incurred as the result of well-intentioned but bad advice or inadequate assistance. Currently, there are limited regulations among states as to how group homes must be established and operated. Training programs for group home staff are scarce in most jurisdictions, and few standards exist relating to staff preparation and qualifications. Therefore, considerable variation exists among group homes relating to the quality of services they can extend to the juveniles they serve.

Simone (1984) suggests that one way in which group homes can improve their effectiveness is for staff workers and home administrators to develop associations with various community interests. Group home workers function as resource personnel for needy youths, and networking with community residents can improve the quality of their contacts and successful placements. Furthermore, such contacts serve to alleviate possible community fears that "juvenile delinquents" are running rampant in their neighborhoods (Lauen, 1984:117). One possible reason for group home "failures" in certain

Medical Psych			Homes		Camps			Other		
M/F	*C*	*L*	*M/F*	*C*	*M/F*	*C*	*L*	*M/F*	*C*	*L*
			1/1	3				3/[1]	3[3]	
					1/0			0/1		
			1/0							
								47/16[1]	54[1]	
								57*		
			6/1	3			1			
			7/0		2/0					
									1	
1/0	13	6	94/22	319	33/1	5	4	180/20	98	5

neighborhoods is resident beliefs that property values will somehow be affected adversely, since lawbreakers are living among them. However, research, including the works of Carlson *et al.* (1977) and the State of Colorado (1980), has illustrated that such facilities in numerous communities have no effects on property values in those neighborhoods where they are placed.

Camps, Ranches, Experience Programs, and Wilderness Projects. Camps, ranches, or "camp ranches" are nonsecure facilities that are sometimes referred to as *wilderness projects* or *experience programs.* A less expensive alternative to the confinement of juvenile offenders, even those considered chronic, is participation in *experience programs. Experience programs include a wide array of outdoor programs designed to improve a juvenile's self-worth, self-concept, pride, and trust in others* (McCarthy and McCarthy, 1984:318).

Hope Center Wilderness Camp. One wilderness experiment that appears successful is the **Hope Center Wilderness Camp** in Houston, Texas (Clagett, 1989). This camp has an organized network of four interdependent, small living groups of twelve teenagers each. The camp's goals are to provide quality care and treatment in a nonpunitive environment, with specific emphases on health, safety, education, and therapy. Emotionally disturbed youths whose offenses range from truancy to murder are selected for program participation. Informal techniques are used, including "aftertalk" (informal discussions during meals), "huddle up" (a group discussion technique), and "powwow" (a nightly gathering around a camp fire). Nondenominational religious services are conducted. Participants are involved in various special events and learn to cook meals outdoors, camp out, and other survival skills. Follow-ups by camp officials show that camp participants exhibit recidivism rates of only about 15 percent (Clagett, 1989).

TABLE 13.2   Juveniles Under Supervision in State Systems (as of June 30, 1990)

State	Total	Secure Institutions Training Schools Total	M	F	Detention M	F	Diagnostic M	F	Other M	F	Day Care Foster Care M	F
Alabama	536	372	338	34			74	8	17			
Alaska	374	140	116	24	55	13					64	14
Arizona	1,003	702	646	56	20		70	10				
Arkansas	212	187	164	23			24	1				
California	8,710	8,117	7,833[1]	284[1]	123*		79[1]	3[1]	42*			
Colorado	943	363	346	17	282	48	46					
Connecticut	195	195	168	27								
Delaware	128	78	75	3	41	9						
Florida[2]	6,846	440			1,402*							
Georgia	2,868	666	614	52	566	68					104	14
Hawaii	80	73	63	10					2			
Idaho	349	110	102	8	9	2	16	3			51	64
Illinois	1,283	1,243	1,168	75								
Indiana	779	722	547	175								
Iowa	241	241	201	40								
Kansas	1,690	493	414	79	54	14	20	3	6	2	92	25
Kentucky	1,177	360	318	42					117			
Louisiana	2,058	707	678	29	206	24	131	12			63	29
Maine	375	242	217	25								
Maryland	1,764	205	189	16	244	28			1		121*	
Massachusetts	1,570	116	101	15	255	13			20		23	12
Michigan	2,900	652	612	40	106[3]	20[3]			36			
Minnesota	192	145	141	4								
Mississippi	326	326	299	27								
Missouri	581	231	210	21					108	13		
Montana	226	176	125	51			14					
Nebraska	482	200	157	43			20	7			29	6
Nevada	300	300	238	62								
New Hampshire	152	104	92	12	23							
New Jersey	1,393	682	673	9							257	52
New Mexico	450	264	233	31			78	21	3			
New York	2,882	1,580	1,424	156		6					69	40
North Carolina	897	646	565	81	47*							
North Dakota	460	98	76	22		2	22	6	1	1	20	15
Ohio	2,079	2,054	1,902	152								
Oklahoma	1,336	129	124	5	128[4]	12	1					
Oregon	524	399	359	40			3	4	118			
Pennsylvania	725	352	322	30								
Rhode Island	180	131	126	5	18		7	5				
South Carolina	1,077	558	480	78			133	33			44[3]	19
South Dakota	181	181	146	35								
Tennessee	994	638	599	39			13				162	41
Texas	2,458	1,075	1,029	46	65	4	108	8	117	20	55	14
Utah	535	71	69	2	103	11	33	2	6			
Vermont	174	9	9		10	2					48	5
Virginia	13,418	1,418[3]	1,262[3]	156[3]	8,900	2,181						
Washington	850	633	587	46								
West Virginia[2]	112	96	87	9			16					
Wisconsin	602	547	517	30					14	4	19	1
Wyoming	103	103	57	46								
Total	69,770	29,570	26,818	2,312	12,663[5] 15,102	2,439	917 1,044	127	608[5] 646	40	1,157[6] 1,452	295

Notes:
*Combined male/female total.
[1]Estimated
[2]Data as of 6/30/89.
[3]Includes diagnostic.
[4]Contracted coed.
[5]May include some females.
Average length of stay: Secure 7.69 months
Nonsecure 6.79 months
Secure "Other: AL, intensive treatment; KS, KY, OR, camps; MA, adult corrections; MI, wilderness (short term; MO, awaiting placement; NM, escapes; TX, residential treatment centers; UT, jail; DC, prerelease house.
Nonsecure "Other": GA, attention homes; HI, transition house; ID, substance abuse/residential trtmt; KY, day trtmt/re-educational programs; ME, AWOL/authorized absence; MA, AWOL/missing/out of state/DSS/DMH; MI, Home/private agency placement; MO, park camps; NE, absconders/arrest; NH, shelter/detention; NY, independent living; PA, state-operated institutions; RI, home confinement; SC, chronic status offender; UT, AWOL/out of state, etc.

SOURCE: ACA, *1991 Directory* (Laurel, MD: American Correctional Association, 1991), pp. xxxvi–xxxvii.

TABLE 13.2 (continued)

Residential Hfwy House Community M	F	Wilderness M	F	Group Homes M	F	Other M	F	(Avg) Entering Offender M & F	Under 16 Total	16 up to 18 Total	18 and Over Total
				55	10				215	294	27
72	16							15.00	165	176	33
10				47	10	113	21	15.60			
									123	89	
44*						302*		17.80	357[1]	2,230[1]	6,123[1]
144	7					37	16	16.40	260	492	138
								15.00	151	44	
								16.80	41	72	15
1,123*		20*		36*		3,825					
448	88	11		16		681	206	15.00			
						5		16.30			
				58	29	5	2	16.00			
						37	3	15.50	469	722	52
56	1							16.10	137	642	
								16.10	86	155	
12	3			228	62	540	136		625	811	204
				72	32	383	213	15.42	688	664	143
288	43			125	85	245	100	15.00	826	1,009	223
						19	114	15.70			
189*		38*		590*		348*		16.49			
613	52	16	8	183	13	188	58	15.50	399	1,142	28
83	21					1,982		16.00			
		47						16.10	15	80	50
								15.10	156	159	11
		10		75	11	89	44	15.50	258	323	
		2		9		25		16.00	46	113	17
136	26			25	5	21	5	16.00	147	291	39
								16.22	138	158	4
10							15	15.80	31	111	
374	28							16.11	95	1,095	203
67	13					4		16.00	139	265	46
152	47			213	73	535	82	15.30	1,511	1,252	119
		204*						14.50	586	103	
				79	28	122	66	15.75	176	266	14
25								15.89	725	1,242	112
		12		336	162	504	52	15.90	216	209	21
		36				310	27	15.70	289	220	15
								15.10			
				14	1	3	1	15.00	42	91	47
				25	6	194	65	15.00	551	337	
								16.25	55	96	30
75	42	15		8				16.00			
157	12			118	9	588	110	15.70	869	1,509	80
134	11					151	13				
6	1	6		19	5	55	10	15.00	59	102	13
125*				683*		184	104	15.00			
				104		109	4	15.30	231	429	200
								16.00	12	95	5
			6			11		15.90	124	293	53
								15.60	43	60	
4,343[5]	411	423[5]	8	3,110[5]	541	11,573[5]	1,448	15.72	11,056	17,441	8,063
4,754		431		3,651		13,021		Avg			

PROJECT OUTWARD BOUND. Another wilderness project, **Project Outward Bound,** is one of more than 200 programs of its type in the United States today. Outward Bound was first introduced in Colorado in 1962 with objectives emphasizing personal survival in the wilderness. Youths participated in various outdoor activities, including rock climbing, solo survival, camping, and long-range hiking during a three-week period (McCarthy and McCarthy, 1984:319). Program officials were not concerned with equipping these juveniles with survival skills per se, but rather, they wanted to instill within the participants a feeling of self-confidence and self-assurance that would help them feel better able to cope with their problems back in their communities.

HOMEWARD BOUND. A program for boys known as **Homeward Bound** was established in Massachusetts in 1970. Homeward Bound was designed to provide juveniles with maturity and a sense of responsibility through the acquisition of survival skills and wilderness experiences. In a six-week training program, 32 youths were subjected to endurance and physical fitness training and required to perform community service (McCarthy and McCarthy, 1984:318–319). Additionally, officials of the program worked with the boys to develop a release program when they completed the project requirements successfully. During the evenings, the juveniles were given instruction in ecology, search and rescue, and overnight treks.

Toward the end of the program, the boys were subjected to a test— surviving a three-day, three-night trip in the wilderness to prove that each boy had acquired the necessary survival skills. Recidivism rates among these boys were lower than for boys who had been institutionalized in industrial or reform schools (Willman and Chun, 1974). Although these programs serve limited numbers of juveniles and some authorities question their value in deterring further delinquency, some evidence suggests that these wilderness experiences generate a lower rate of recidivism among participants when compared with those youths who are institutionalized in industrial schools under conditions of close custody and monitoring (McCarthy & McCarthy, 1984:319).

VISIONQUEST. A fourth well-established wilderness program is **Vision-Quest,** a private, for-profit enterprise operated from Tucson, Arizona. Currently, VisionQuest operates in about 15 states and serves about 500 juveniles annually. Its cost is about half that of secure institutionalization (Gavzer, 1986:10). Among the various jurisdictions that have used Vision-Quest for their juvenile probationers is San Diego County, California (Greenwood and Turner, 1987).

Juvenile offenders selected for participation in the VisionQuest program in San Diego were secure incarceration–bound offenders with several prior arrests and placements with the California Youth Authority. VisionQuest staff members conducted interviews with certain juveniles who were tentatively selected for inclusion in the program. On the basis of VisionQuest staff recommendations, juvenile court judges would assign these juveniles to VisionQuest, where they would be under an indeterminate sentence of from six months to a year or more (Greenwood, 1990).

Greenwood (1990:20) describes the VisionQuest experiences of youths as follows. They immediately find themselves in a rustic type of boot-camp environment, where they live in an Indian tepee with six to ten other youths and two junior staff. They sleep on the ground and engage in a strenuous

Modern incarcerative facilities for juveniles are equipped with classrooms where youths may receive traditional instruction and continue their educational training. Youth Centers stress rehabilitation through individualized counseling and participation in vocational and educational programs. (Courtesy of the American Correctional Association, photo by Jefferson Youth Center)

physical fitness program. They complete regular schoolwork. Failure to perform their daily chores adequately results in an immediate confrontation between them and senior staff. They participate in an orientation and outdoor training program, which takes several months to complete. Eventually, they take a wagon train on the back roads of the western states to Canada, averaging about 24 miles a day, for four to six months. All the while, they are given increased responsibilities, including breaking in horses that VisionQuest acquires annually. Eventually, the attend the VisionQuest group home in Arizona where it is determined whether they can be reintegrated into their communities (Greenwood, 1990:20–21).

Greenwood and Turner (1987) have evaluated the effectiveness of VisionQuest by comparing a sample of 89 male juvenile offenders with a sample of 177 juveniles assigned to San Diego County Probation. Both the San Diego County probationers and the VisionQuest youths were tracked for one year following the completion of their programs. VisionQuest participants had a recidivism rate of 55 percent compared with 71 percent for the regular probationers. Although this rate of recidivism is high compared with many other intensive supervision probation programs, the sizable difference in recidivism for both groups means that the program is viewed as moderately successful. Other researchers in different jurisdictions where VisionQuest has been used report that average recidivism figures are about 33 percent for VisionQuest participants (Gavzer, 1986).

Secure Confinement: Variations

Persistent Problems. As was noted earlier, secure juvenile correctional facilities in the United States are known by various names. Furthermore, not all of these secure confinement facilities are alike. Many institutions provide only custodial services for chronic or more serious juvenile offenders, whereas other incarcerative facilities offer an array of services and treatments, depending on the diverse needs of the juveniles confined. Breed and Krisberg (1986:14) contend that "the history of juvenile corrections has been governed by a repetitive cycle of institutional abuses and scandals, public exposure to these problems, and spurts of reformist activity." A major factor contributing to these problems, they argue, is the fact that "juvenile corrections has not evolved from a set of rational or planned responses to explicit goals" (p. 14).

Architectural Improvements and Officer Training Reforms. In recent years, however, numerous improvements have been made in the overall quality of juvenile correctional facilities throughout the United States (U.S. General Accounting Office, 1983). Evidence of improvement in juvenile corrections is the massive effort made by authorities in numerous jurisdictions to design and build better-equipped juvenile facilities that minimize problems of idle time and overcrowding. Examples of modern facility designs and creative architectural structures that offer dormitorylike settings rather than penal ones are the Young Adult Offenders Program facility in Draper, Utah, and the Denver, Colorado Mount View School (Munyon, 1985; Sullivan, 1988). Private interests, including the Corrections Corporation of America, have assisted as well in providing more modern designs and plant operations for secure juvenile facilities in various states such as California and Tennessee.

Besides constructing more attractive physical plants in which to house hard-core offenders, juvenile corrections planners have also made efforts to improve the quality of all levels of staff who administer and supervise juvenile inmates. Entering juveniles exhibit a myriad of personal and social problems. Some youths are psychologically disturbed and suicidal. Others are distinctly antisocial and violent. Correctional officers at these facilities must be prepared for virtually any behavior that might arise. At the Taft Youth Development Center in Pikeville, Tennessee, a facility that houses felons and misdemeanants from 15 to 21, a male correctional officer was attacked by a 15-year-old. The youth lunged at the officer and bit into the officer's crotch area. Six officers were required to pull the youth away from the officer. The officer's pants had been ripped apart, and his scrotum had been bitten off by the youth. Such incidents are not limited to violent juvenile males. A 16-year-old female juvenile at the same facility attacked her female teacher during a history lesson, and portions of the teacher's blouse and breast were bitten off by the youth, who apparently didn't like the grade she received on an exam.

Admittedly, these incidents are bizarre, but they do occur. Textbook instruction cannot be extensive enough to cover all situations and to advise what to do when these and similar incidents arise. In an effort to prepare correctional officers to cope with various types of inmate problems, several local and national organizations have established training courses to heighten officers' awareness of problems and the skills needed to deal with them. Santa Clara County (San Jose), California, has one of the largest direct supervision jails in the nation. It has over 4,500 bookings per month, as well as at least 600 psychiatric referrals. A portion of these bookings and referrals are juveniles. Recognizing that staff training should be a major priority, administrators from the Custody and Mental Health services established a training experience for officers, including classes in suicide identification and intervention, psychiatric illnesses, management of assaultive behavior, and communication skills (Quinlan and Motte, 1990:22–23).

In Tacoma, Washington, Pierce County Sheriff Raymond A. Fjetland has developed a program, the Master Correctional Officer Program, which is designed to improve the performance of staff correctional officers for future roles within the corrections division (Tess and Bogue, 1988:66). The program includes three stages; entry level, senior level, and master level. Officers must accumulate points in various educational and on-the-job training areas, including weapons qualification, comprehensive written examinations, and frequent performance evaluations. Thus, Sheriff Fjetland has helped to establish a program that provides officer incentives to advance as well as to acquire more effective skills to deal with offenders of all types and ages. Greater professionalism, expertise, and productivity are the outcomes of this innovative "continuous motivator" program (Tess and Bogue, 1988:67).

Both male and female correctional officers are targeted for additional training to cope with inmate problems. Formerly, it was alleged by some critics that female correctional officers tended to lack the same degree of authority as their male counterparts when dealing with inmates. However, on-the-job training and self-improvement courses sponsored and conducted by the American Correctional Association have done much to improve correctional officer credibility and performance (Lonardi, 1987:142). According to ACA standards, correctional officers should have at least 160 hours of orientation and training during their first year of employment. Certification is awarded after satisfactorily completing the ACA training course. An analysis of female correctional officer effectiveness in relation to male officers has been made by Simon and Simon (1988). They indicate that at least for the samples they studied of 45 female officers and 115 male officers of a large state institution, gender made no difference when it came to upholding the legitimacy of sanctions imposed by these officers. Other research supports the view that female correctional officers exhibit performance levels equal to those of their male counterparts (Zimmer, 1986).

Juvenile Detention Resource Centers. The U.S. Department of Justice's Office of Juvenile Justice and Delinquency Prevention (OJJDP) promulgated specific guidelines for all juvenile correctional facilities in the early 1980s. These guidelines were published as *Guidelines for the Development of Policies and Procedures for Juvenile Detention Facilities.* The goal of the OJJDP was to establish *national juvenile detention resource centers* around the United States in various jurisdictions that would provide information, technical assistance, and training to juvenile corrections professionals who wished to participate (Criswell, 1987:22). The ultimate aim of these juvenile detention centers was to provide juveniles with better and more adequate services and assistance. These model centers would act as prototypes for other centers to be established in different jurisdictions. In 1985, the Southwest Florida Juvenile Detention Center at Fort Myers was established as the state-operated resource center. In subsequent years, numerous regional detention resource centers were created throughout Florida to provide juvenile inmates with a broader array and quality of services and personnel.

Such detention centers have done much to improve juvenile confinement standards throughout the nation. The ACA has been actively involved in assisting different jurisdictions in their efforts to establish juvenile detention resource centers and operate them successfully. Rousch (1987:33) notes that "the most striking factor is that each resource center is a model of how detention should be operated. Each center has specific strengths and different priorities regarding the use of resources . . . [the strengths of these centers include] . . . comprehensive intake screening, a wide range of effective alternatives to detention, a variety of effective programs, excellent staff, volunteer involvement, staff training, and medical and health care services."

Short-Term and Long-Term Facilities. Secure juvenile correctional facilities in the United States are either **short-term** or **long-term.** Short-term detention facilities are designed to accommodate juveniles on a temporary basis. These juveniles are awaiting a later juvenile court adjudication, subsequent foster home or group home placement, or a transfer to criminal court. Sometimes youths will be placed in short-term confinement because their identity is unknown and it is desirable that they not be confined in adult lockups or jails. Other youths are violent and must be detained temporarily until more appropriate placements may be made. The designations "short-term" and "long-term" may refer to periods from a few days to several years, although the average duration of juvenile incarceration across all offender categories nationally is about six to seven months (Bureau of Justice Statistics, 1986a). The average short-term incarceration in public facilities for juveniles is about 30 days.

Some short-term juvenile confinement is **preventive detention** or **pretrial detention,** in which juveniles are awaiting formal adjudicatory proceedings. While some authorities question the legality of jailing juveniles or holding them in detention centers before their cases can be heard by juvenile judges, the U.S. Supreme Court has upheld the constitutionality of pretrial and preventive detention of juveniles, especially dangerous ones, in

BOX 13.1

JUVENILE HIGHLIGHTS

What is wrong with juvenile corrections? According to Allen F. Breed and Barry Krisberg, the chairman and president respectively of the National Council on Crime and Delinquency in San Francisco, there are both fact and fiction surrounding public criticisms of juvenile corrections. Various scandals and abuses are highlighted by the media, and public attention is attracted to these atypical scenes. Generally, the public is relatively uninformed about various juvenile correctional dilemmas and potential remedies.

Both Breed and Krisberg believe that most juvenile correctional facilities are currently overcrowded, that residents are disproportionately minority youths, and that these youths experience longer periods of confinement than do nonminority youths. In more than a few instances, mentally ill juveniles are placed, untreated, in detention facilities, where their psychological problems are intensified.

One continuing problem is that juvenile corrections has never evolved from a rational set of explicit or planned responses to definite goals. It is difficult to pin down precisely what the goals of juvenile corrections should be. Should they be primarily rehabilitative, should they be primarily punitive, or should they be both? The California Youth Authority, cited as a model of juvenile corrections by many other states, has had more than its fair share of scandals. The *Los Ange-les Times* has reported that some youths have been leather-strapped in a spread-eagle fashion to metal beds, their wrists and ankles bound with leather cuffs, as a punishment for disruptive behavior. Other children as young as 11 years of age have been forced to march and eat their meals in silence.

A federal judge found that the McClaren School for Boys in Oregon used isolation to excess as a punishment for unruly youths. Furthermore, individual cells were dirty and unsanitary. Another federal judge found that a Florida juvenile detention facility was guilty of hogtying youths and shackling them to fixed objects as punishments for nonconforming behavior.

Breed and Krisberg believe that the treatment ideology remains strong throughout juvenile corrections, although insufficient monitoring of juvenile facilities occurs to ensure facility compliance with federal guidelines for proper treatment of youthful offenders. Currently, the political environment may be too hostile to accept reforms that would improve treatment conditions for young offenders. A desirable goal is to achieve a treatment-oriented, community-based model of juvenile corrections, although attaining such a goal may be a difficult task politically.

(Factual information adapted from Allen F. Breed and Barry Krisberg, "Juvenile Corrections: Is There a Future?," *Corrections Today* (1986) 48:14–20.)

the case of **Schall** v. **Martin** (1984) (Bookin-Weiner, 1984; Lee, 1985; Worrell, 1985). While no national policy is in place currently about the temporary jailing of juveniles together with adult offenders, various organizations and agencies have issued statements urging legislative action to formally prohibit such practices and establish separate juvenile confinement facilities in affected jurisdictions (National Council on Crime and Delinquency, 1986). In Massachusetts and several other states, juveniles may post bail for their offenses in order to avoid pretrial detention (Massachusetts Department of Youth Services, 1984). In some states such as Pennsylvania, legislative mandates have prohibited the jailing of juveniles altogether (Keve, 1984).

Because of space limitations in certain jurisdictions or the general lack of proper juvenile correctional facilities, juveniles are sometimes housed in special areas in jails. However, a movement away from confining juveniles in jails has gained momentum in recent years, under the federally funded Jail Removal Initiative. Started in 1981, this program has assisted over twenty jurisdictions in twelve states to provide alternatives to juvenile confinement in jails or other adult lockups (Brown, 1985). Huskey (1990:122) indicates that new laws enacted in various state jurisdictions such as Illinois currently mandate that no juveniles may be placed in adult jails for periods longer than six hours. Further, no child under the age of 10 may be held in an adult jail, and no juvenile can be sentenced to spend time in an adult jail. However, in 1989, 53,994 juveniles were being held in adult jails in various U.S. jurisdictions (Bessette, 1990:2).

Juvenile court judges have the authority to place certain juveniles in *long-term secure confinement facilities.* These facilities are ordinarily regional, full-service institutions, complete with restrictive construction materials and hardware, maximum-security areas, large capacities, inflexible security and program levels, classrooms, recreational areas, hospitals or infirmaries, and assorted other facilities and services, depending upon the jurisdiction and affluence of local and state budgets. A 1989 census of Children in Custody (CIC) in publicly run facilities shows that approximately 60 percent of these facilities are long-term, while about 40 percent are short-term. Table 13.3 shows the types of state and locally administered public juvenile facilities, according to the number of facilities, juvenile population counts, and juvenile admissions for 1989.

A profile of juveniles in these correctional facilities is revealing. Table 13.4 shows some selected demographic characteristics of these juvenile inmates for the years 1987 and 1989.

Between 1987 and 1989, the number of female inmates of these juvenile facilities declined by 8 percent, while the number of male juvenile inmates increased by 7 percent. Male juvenile inmates made up 88 percent of those incarcerated in public confinement facilities in 1989. Sixty percent of all juvenile inmates in public facilities in 1989 were of minority status. Incredibly, a small proportion of these juveniles were age 9 or under. Between 1987 and 1989, a 17 percent increase in admissions was observed for those youths from ages 10 to 13.

TABLE 13.3 Types of State and Locally Administered Public Juvenile Custody Facilities by Number of Facilities, Juvenile Population Counts, and Juvenile Admissions (1989)

	Total	State-Administered Facilities	Locally Administered Facilities
Facilities	1,100	529	571
Short-term	492	105	387
Institutional	422	96	326
Open	70	9	61
Long-term	608	424	184
Institutional	223	177	46
Open	385	247	138
Juvenile Residents	56,123	34,823	21,300
Short-term	19,967	4,855	15,112
Institutional	19,146	4,613	14,533
Open	821	242	579
Long-term	36,156	29,968	6,188
Institutional	25,704	23,202	2,502
Open	10,452	6,766	3,686
Juvenile Admissions	619,181	167,372	451,809
Short-term	520,949	98,132	422,817
Institutional	504,863	96,060	408,803
Open	16,086	2,072	14,014
Long-term	98,232	69,240	28,992
Institutional	61,648	48,562	13,086
Open	36,584	20,678	15,906

SOURCE: Barbara Allen-Hagen, *Public Juvenile Facilities: Children in Custody 1989* (Washington, D.C.: U.S. Department of Justice, 1991), p. 7.

TABLE 13.4 Selected Demographic Characteristics of Juveniles Held in Public Juvenile Facilities on Census Days (1987 and 1989)

	1987	1989	Percent Change
Total Juveniles	53,503	56,123	+5%
Sex			
Male	46,272	49,443	+7%
Female	7,231	6,680	−8%
Minority Status			
Nonminority[a]	23,375	22,201	−5%
Minority	30,128	33,922	+13%
Black[b]	20,898	23,836	+14%
Hispanic[c]	7,887	8,671	+10%
Other	1,343	1,415	+5%
Age on Date of Census			
9 years and under	73	45	−38%
10−13 years	2,811	3,276	+17%
14−17 years	43,898	44,894	+2%
18 years and over	6,721	7,908	+18%

[a]Includes whites not of Hispanic origin.
[b]Includes blacks not of Hispanic origin.
[c]Includes both whites and blacks of Hispanic origin.
SOURCE: Barbara Allen-Hagen, *Public Juvenile Facilities: Children in Custody, 1989* (Washington, D.C.: U.S. Department of Justice, 1991), p. 3.

As we have observed in previous chapters, the "get tough" movement has influenced decision making throughout the juvenile justice system. It might be expected that only the most violent and serious juvenile offenders would tend to be institutionalized for long periods. However, a profile of inmates, according to their offenses, suggests that just the opposite is the case. Table 13.5 shows the types of offenses for which male and female juveniles were held in public correctional facilities for the years 1987 and 1989.

There has been only an imperceptible change from 1987 to 1989 in the proportion of violent offenders or those who have been adjudicated delinquent for committing crimes against persons (e.g., homicide, aggravated assault, rape, robbery). For example, only 25 percent of all detainees in 1987 were violent offenders, whereas about 25.5 percent of all detainees in 1989 had been adjudicated for violent offenses. However, the proportion of detainees who were property offenders declined from 44 percent in 1987 to about 40 percent in 1989. A major increase in detainees adjudicated for alcohol/drug offenses was observed, from 7.8 percent in 1987 to 11.7 percent in 1989. Among other things, this changing detainee population suggests shifting judicial priorities about those who are currently being incarcerated. Not only are alcohol/drug juvenile offenders increasing annually, but judges are incarcerating them with greater frequency. The proportion of detainees who were probation violators increased several percentage points between these years as well. Finally, the proportion of detainees who were status offenders declined slightly between 1987 and 1989. Nevertheless, status offenders continue to make up about 4 percent of all those incarcerated in public detention facilities (Sweet, 1991).

Some Criticisms of Confining Juveniles. There are numerous proponents and opponents of juvenile incarceration of any kind. Those favoring incarceration cite the disruption of a youth's lifestyle and separation from other delinquent youths as a positive dimension (Lucart, 1983; Rutherford, 1986). For example, youths who have been involved with delinquent gangs or with friends who engage in frequent law-breaking would probably benefit from confinement, since these unfavorable associations would be interrupted or terminated. Of course, juveniles can always return to their old ways when released from confinement. There is nothing the juvenile justice system can do to prevent this. But at least the existing pattern of interaction that contributed to the delinquent behavior initially is temporarily interrupted (Lucart, 1983; U.S. General Accounting Office, 1985b).

Another argument favoring incarceration of juveniles is that long-term confinement is a deserved punishment for their actions. This is consistent with the "just deserts" philosophy that seems to typify contemporary thinking about juvenile punishment. There is a noticeable trend away from thinking in terms of the "best interests" of youths and toward thinking about ways to make youths more accountable for their actions (Feld, 1988a). Feld says that this shift has prompted debate among juvenile justice scholars about the true functions of juvenile courts and the ultimate aims of the sanctions they impose.

TABLE 13.5   Types of Offenses/Other Reasons for Which Male and Female Juveniles Were Held in Public Juvenile Facilities (1987 and 1989)

Total Juveniles	1987 Total	1987 Male	1987 Female	1989 Total	1989 Male	1989 Female
	53,503	*46,272*	*7,231*	*56,123*	*49,443*	*6,680*
Delinquent Offenses[a]	50,269	44,757	5,512	53,037	47,843	5,194
Offenses Against Persons	13,300	12,297	1,003	14,327	13,210	1,117
Violent—murder, forcible rape, robbery, and aggravated assault	7,943	7,438	505	8,566	7,976	590
Other—manslaughter, simple assault, sexual assault	5,357	4,859	498	5,761	5,234	527
Property Offenses	23,431	21,272	2,159	22,780	20,849	1,931
Serious—burglary, arson, larceny/theft, and motor vehicle theft	15,746	14,595	1,151	15,181	14,112	1,069
Other—Vandalism, forgery, counterfeiting, fraud, stolen property, unauthorized use of a motor vehicle	7,685	6,677	1,008	7,599	6,737	862
Alcohol/Drug Offenses	4,161	3,733	428	6,586	6,067	519
Public Order Offenses	2,380	1,864	516	2,788	2,406	382
Probation Violations	4,200	3,183	1,017	4,920	3,942	978
Other Delinquent Offenses[b]	2,797	2,408	389	1,636	1,369	267
Nondelinquent Reasons	3,234	1,515	1,719	3,086	1,600	1,486
Status Offenses[c]	2,523	1,198	1,325	2,245	1,128	1,117
Abuse/Neglect[d]	429	190	239	426	205	221
Other[e]	29	20	9	113	78	35
Voluntarily Admitted	253	107	146	302	189	113

[a]Offenses that would be criminal if committed by adults.
[b]Includes unknown and unspecified delinquent offenses.
[c]Offenses that would not be criminal for adults, such as running away, truancy, and incorrigibility.
[d]Also includes those held for emotional disturbance or mental retardation.
[e]Includes all other unspecified reasons for detention or commitment.

SOURCE: Barbara Allen-Hagen, *Public Juvenile Facilities: Children in Custody, 1989* (Washington, D.C.: U.S. Department of Justice, 1991), p. 4.

For some critics, the question of whether juvenile incarceration is rehabilitative is irrelevant. The fact is, juvenile confinement restricts a juvenile's mobility and is seen as a deterrent to delinquent conduct. We don't know for sure how much of a deterrent effect is achieved through incarcerating juveniles. But incarceration does suffice as a punishment. If juveniles break the law, they should be punished. Thus, incarceration may be viewed as a form of retribution.

Maloney (1989) summarizes the opinions of many juvenile justice experts who believe that incarceration can serve multiple ends. He says that currently, many rules of supervision in confinement facilities and other supervision programs are negatively oriented. Youths are told which rules to follow and which behaviors are prohibited. He believes that dispositions imposed by juvenile courts and implemented by the juvenile correctional system should be geared toward improving a youth's ability to perform in society. Dispositions "should be action-oriented and skill-based, supported by counseling and therapy only when necessary to help youths reach their competency goals." He recommends that "the nature of services provided at each level of the system should be consistent, and that there should be an element of accountability, a competency-building element, and a public protection element" (Maloney, 1989:34). Certainly, one major step in this direction is the development of the national juvenile detention resource centers described earlier.

Opponents of long-term incarceration of juveniles believe, among other things, that there are possibly adverse labeling effects from confinement with other offenders. Thus, juveniles might acquire concepts of themselves as juvenile delinquents and might persist in reoffending when released from confinement later. However, it could be maintained that if they are incarcerated, they know they are delinquents anyway. Will they necessarily acquire stronger self-definitions as delinquents beyond those they already possess? In some respects, it is status-enhancing for youthful offenders to have been confined in some "joint" or juvenile correctional facility, so that they may brag to others about their experiences later. No doubt, confinement of any kind will add at least one dimension to one's reputation as a delinquent offender among other offenders in the community. Furthermore, such institutions may offer an informal education, one which teaches youthful offenders the methods they'll need to know to avoid detection and apprehension. Thus, in a sense they may become schools for more advanced criminal learning.

Other arguments suggest that the effects of imprisonment on a juvenile's self-image and propensity to commit new offenses are negligible (Anson and Eason, 1986; Frazier and Bishop, 1985). Thus, confinement as a punishment may be the primary result, without any tangible, long-range benefits such as self-improvement or reduction in recidivism. At least there does not appear to be any consistent or reliable evidence that detaining juveniles automatically causes them to escalate to more serious offenses or to become adult criminals. According to some analysts, the peak ages of juvenile criminality fall between the sixteenth and twentieth birthdays, with participation rates falling off

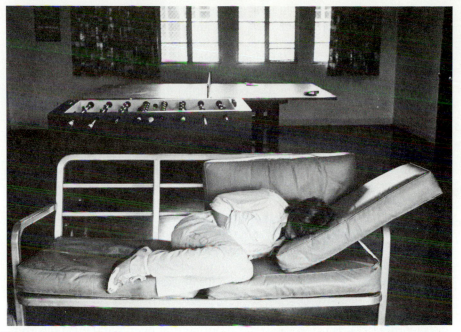

Many detention facilities, such as the one in Travis County (Austin), Texas, provide youths with a dormitory-like atmosphere. Contemporary architectural improvements and innovations in secure incarcerative facilities for juveniles seek to de-emphasize the prison-like atmosphere of cells and bars. (© Bob Daemmrich/Stock Boston)

rapidly after that (Greenwood, 1986c:151). Thus, incarceration for a fixed period may "naturally" ease the delinquency rate, at least for some of the more chronic offenders.

Juvenile Parole

Parole for juveniles is similar to parole for adult offenders. Those juveniles who have been detained in various institutions for long periods may be released prior to serving their full sentences. Generally, **parole** *is a conditional supervised release from incarceration granted to youths who have served a portion of their original sentences.*

   Purposes of Parole. The general purposes of parole are

1. *To reward good behavior while youths have been detained.*
2. *To alleviate overcrowding.*
3. *To permit youths to become reintegrated back into their communities and enhance their rehabilitation potential.*
4. *To deter youths from future offending by ensuring their continued supervision under juvenile parole officers.*

Some authorities also believe that *the prospect of earning parole might induce greater compliance with institutional rules* among incarcerated youths. Also, parole is seen by some experts as *a continuation of the juvenile's punishment,* since parole programs are most often conditional in nature (e.g., observance of curfew, school attendance, staying out of trouble, periodic drug and alcohol urinalyses, participation in counseling programs, and vocational and educational training).

How Many Youths Are On Parole? Estimates vary about how many juvenile offenders are on parole at any given time. The present lack of coordination among jurisdictions relating to juvenile offender record-keeping makes it difficult to determine the actual numbers of juvenile parolees or probationers at any given time. Furthermore, some jurisdictions continue to block public scrutiny of juvenile court adjudicatory proceedings or their results. Since one's juvenile record is expunged or sealed upon reaching adulthood, even historical research on this subject is limited by various systemic constraints. Attesting to the dearth of information about juvenile parole is the work of Knepper and Cavender (1990). They underscore the fact that juvenile parole is one of the most underresearched topics within the juvenile justice system. Nevertheless, apart from intermediate punishment programs and secure-confinement facilities, the American Correctional Association (1991:xxxvi−xxxvii) has reported that over 5,500 juveniles were in nonsecure, state-operated halfway houses in 1990, and that about another 15,000 youths were under other forms of state-controlled supervision, either as probationers or parolees.

Characteristics of Juvenile Parolees. Some of the characteristics of juvenile parolees are mirrored by the characteristics of those detained in state-operated correctional facilities illustrated in Table 13.4. Isolated studies of juvenile parolees indicate that a majority are male, black, and between 17 and 19 years of age (Chambers, 1983; New York State Division of Parole, Evaluation, and Planning, 1985). Wylen (1984) describes the characteristics of 464 juvenile offenders who were paroled to the New York State Division of Parole from 1978 through 1983. She says that 96 percent were male, 93 percent were minorities, 60 percent came from families receiving some form of public assistance, 43 percent abused drugs such as marijuana, 18 percent abused alcohol, and about 10 percent had been hospitalized for psychiatric problems. More than 75 percent of these offenders had prior records and had acted in concert with at least one other juvenile in the commission of their adjudication offenses. About 65 percent of these youths were considered supervision "successes," although a third had previously been under the supervision of the Division of Parole.

Juvenile parolees share many of the same programs used to supervise youthful probationers. Intensive supervised probation programs are used for both probationers and parolees in many jurisdictions. Furthermore, juvenile probation officers often perform dual roles as juvenile parole officers as they supervise both types of offenders. Some jurisdictions, such as New York State, have established specialized supervision units to work with juvenile parolees, who tend to be older than probationers. In a pilot project of parole work with juvenile offenders called **PARJO,** for instance, juvenile parole officers were especially effective as brokers in directing parolees to vocational training agencies where they could learn useful skills and become employed (New York State Division of Parole, Evaluation, and Planning, 1985). PARJO coupled intensive supervision through reduced caseloads with highly motivated officers who worked on the youths' behalf to match them with prospective employers. The PARJO project reported significant reductions in recidivism among those youthful clients who participated.

Generally, studies of juvenile parolees tend to show that the greater the intensity of supervisory aftercare, the lower the recidivism (New York State Division of Parole, Evaluation, and Planning, 1985; Wiederanders, 1983). Influencing the degree of success of juvenile parole is whether juveniles are successfully employed or actively involved in development or counseling programs (Chambers, 1983; Wylen, 1984). Because so many nonviolent and less serious juvenile offenders are placed in secure confinement together with more dangerous offenders, few dramatic differences are apparent between juvenile probationers and parolees to compare with the significant differences in population characteristics of their adult counterparts. For most juveniles who spend time behind bars or "industrial" school walls, the experience is traumatic. For standard juvenile parole programs, recidivism seems about the same as that for standard probation supervision. About 65 percent of the juveniles on parole refrain from committing new offenses (Wylen, 1984).

In 1990 the Office of Juvenile Justice and Delinquency Prevention (OJJDP) was conducting a research project designed to formulate guidelines for and identify favorable features of successful intensive parole supervision programs for juveniles (Altschuler and Armstrong, 1990b). Their research interests were targeted at identifying those youths who might benefit the most from a parole program, as well as the most useful methods for supervising offenders. Among their chief concerns was the reduction and potential elimination of recidivism among youthful parolees. While it is unrealistic to expect that any program will ever eliminate recidivism, it is possible to target certain program features that might serve to reduce it among specific populations, including juvenile parolees. It is hoped that the efforts of the OJJDP will eventually yield more successful strategies for managing an especially troublesome offender aggregate.

Deciding Who Should Be Paroled. The decision to parole particular juveniles is left to various agencies and bodies, depending upon the jurisdiction. Studies of the sentencing of juvenile delinquents indicate that in forty-five state jurisdictions, the sentences imposed are indeterminate (Frost *et al.*, 1985). In thirty-two states, early-release decisions are left up to the particular juvenile correction agency, whereas six states use parole boards exclusively, and five other states depend upon the original sentencing judge's decision. Only a few states had determinate sentencing schemes for youthful offenders, in which early release would be established by statute in much the same way as it is for adult offenders.

In New Jersey, for instance, a seven-member parole board appointed by the governor grants early release to both adult and juvenile inmates. In Utah, a Youth Parole Authority exists, which is a part-time board consisting of three citizens and four staff members from the Utah Division of Youth Corrections (Norman, 1986). Ideally, the Utah Youth Parole Authority utilizes objective decision-making criteria in determining which youths should be released short of serving their full sentences. Norman (1986) observes, however, that discrepancies often exist between what the Authority actually does and what it is supposed to do. Thus, some criticisms have been to the effect that the primary early-release criteria are related to behavior while in the institution rather than to other factors, such as prospects for successful adaptation to community life, employment, and participation in educational or vocational programs. Norman investigated approximately 300 juvenile parole hearings for over thirty-seven days as the basis for his observations.

The Utah Youth Parole Authority is not alone in receiving criticism about the fairness of its parole decision making. Many parole boards for both adults and juveniles are comprised of persons who make subjective judgments about inmates on the basis of many factors beyond so-called objective criteria. Predispositional reports prepared by juvenile probation officers, records of institutional behavior, a youth's appearance and demeanor during the parole hearing, and the presence of witnesses or victims may exert unknown impacts upon individual parole board members. Parole decision making is not an exact science. Where elements of subjectivity intrude into the decision-making process, a juvenile's rights are seemingly undermined. Parole board decision-making profiles in various jurisdictions may exhibit evidence of early-release disparities attributable to racial, ethnic, gender, or socioeconomic factors.

Recidivism and Parole Revocation. **Parole revocation** *is the early termination of one's parole program, usually for one or more program violations.* When an offender's parole is terminated, regardless of who does the terminating, there are several possible outcomes. One is that the offender will be returned to secure confinement. This is the most severe result. A less harsh alternative is that offenders will be shifted to a different kind of parole program. For instance, if a juvenile is assigned to a halfway house as a part of the parole program, the rules of the halfway house must be observed. If one or more rules are violated, such as failing to observe curfew, failing drug or alcohol urinalyses, or committing new offenses, a report is filed with the court or the juvenile corrections authority for possible revocation action. If it is decided later that parole should be terminated, the result may be to place the offender under house arrest or home confinement, coupled with electronic monitoring, in which the juvenile would be required to wear an electronic wristlet or anklet and remain on the premises for specified periods. Other program conditions would be applied as well. The fact is that an offender is not automatically returned to confinement following a parole revocation.

Usually, if a return to incarceration is not indicated, the options available to judges, parole boards, and others are limited only by the array of supervisory resources in the given jurisdiction. These options ordinarily involve more intensive supervision or monitoring of offender behaviors. Severe overcrowding in many juvenile incarcerative facilities discourages revocation action that would return large numbers of offenders to industrial schools or youth centers. Intermediate punishments function to accommodate larger numbers of serious offenders, including those who have their parole revoked.

Recidivism is measured in many different ways. Maltz (1984) describes at least ten different ways it can be defined. However, the more common meanings of recidivism pertain to committing new offenses, being arrested on suspicion of committing new offenses (rearrests), being convicted of new offenses (reconvictions), violating parole or probation program rules, or being returned to secure confinement (reincarceration). As we have seen in earlier chapters, recidivism is often used as the gauge of program success or failure. An arbitrary figure of 30 percent recidivism is considered by many professionals to be a "cutting point," meaning that amounts of recidivism in excess of 30 percent are regarded as evidence of program failure, whereas amounts of recidivism less than 30 percent are considered evidence of program success. Like juvenile probationers, juvenile parolees exhibit differing degrees of recidivism, depending upon the types of supervision programs to which they are assigned. Usually, though not always, the more intensive supervision programs yield lower recidivism rates. Average recidivism figures for juveniles nationally are misleading, since each jurisdiction uses different programs and assigns different caseloads to POs. But recidivism rates among juvenile parolees seem to range from 25 percent to 40 percent in various studies that have examined this phenomenon (Chambers, 1983; Palmer and Wedge, 1989; Wiederanders, 1983; Wylen, 1984). Regardless of how recidivism is measured, when it occurs while juveniles are on probation or parole, this constitutes grounds for parole or probation revocation actions.

The process of parole revocation for juveniles is not as clear-cut as it is for adult offenders. The U.S. Supreme Court has not ruled thus far concerning how juvenile parole revocation actions should be completed. Prior to several significant U.S. Supreme Court decisions, either parole or probation revocation could be accomplished for adult offenders on the basis of reports filed by probation or parole officers stating that offenders were in violation of one or more conditions of their programs. Criminal court judges, those ordinarily in charge of determining whether to terminate one's probationary status, could decide this issue on the basis of available evidence against offenders. For adult parolees, decision making relative to terminating their parole could be made by parole boards without much input from offenders. In short, parole officers and others might simply present evidence that one or more infractions or violations of probation or parole conditions had been committed. These infractions, then, could form the basis for revoking probation or parole as well as a justification for these decisions.

A probationer's or parolee's right to due process in any probation or parole revocation action was largely ignored prior to 1967. Thus, technical violations, such as failing to submit monthly reports, violating curfew, filing a falsified report, or drinking alcoholic beverages "to excess," might result in an unfavorable recommendation from one's PO that the probation or parole program should be terminated. Popular television shows sometimes portray parole officers as threatening their clients with parole revocation: "Do this or else I'll have you back in the joint!," meaning a return to prison for adult offenders. Currently, it is not so easy to accomplish either type of revocation.

For adult parolees as well as for adult probationers, revocations for either probation or parole are currently two-stage proceedings. The landmark cases that have directly affected parolees and probationers and their rights are: (1) **Mempa** v. **Rhay** (1967), (2) **Morrissey** v. **Brewer** (1972), and (3) **Gagnon** v. **Scarpelli** (1973). While these landmark cases pertain to adult probationers and parolees, they have significance for juvenile probationers and parolees as well. *The significance is that juvenile justice policies are often formulated or influenced on the basis of U.S. Supreme Court decisions about the rights of adult inmates, parolees, or probationers and the procedures involved in their processing throughout the criminal justice system. These cases are not binding on juvenile court judges or juvenile paroling authorities, but do they provide a legal basis for specific actions in pertinent juvenile cases if the juvenile justice system chooses to recognize them as precedent-setting.*

Mempa v. Rhay (1967). Jerry Mempa was convicted in criminal court of "joyriding" in a stolen vehicle on June 17, 1959, in Spokane, Washington. The judge placed him on probation for two years. A few months later, on September 15, 1959, Mempa was involved in a burglary. The county prosecutor in Spokane requested that Mempa's probation be revoked. Mempa admitted to police that he committed the burglary. At a **probation revocation hearing** conducted later, the sole testimony about his involvement in the burglary came from his probation officer, who obtained his factual information largely from police reports. Mempa, an indigent, was not permitted to offer statements in his own behalf, nor was he provided counsel, nor was he asked if he wanted counsel, nor was he permitted to cross-examine the probation officer about the officer's incriminating statements. The judge revoked Mempa's probation and sentenced him to ten years in the Washington State Penitentiary.

A short time later, Mempa filed a writ of *habeas corpus,* which essentially challenged the *fact of his confinement* and *the nature of his confinement.* He alleged that he had been denied the right to counsel in his probation revocation hearing, and thus, he claimed his due process rights had been violated in part. The Washington Supreme Court denied his petition, but the U.S. Supreme Court elected to hear it on appeal. The U.S. Supreme Court overturned the Washington Supreme Court and ruled in Mempa's favor. Specifically, the U.S. Supreme Court said that Mempa was entitled to an attorney but had been denied one. Furthermore, and perhaps most important, the Court declared that *a probation revocation hearing is a "critical stage" that falls within the due process provisions of the Fourteenth Amendment. Critical stages refer to any stages of the criminal justice process when a defendant is in jeopardy.* If defendants are accused of crimes, or arraigned, or prosecuted, their due process rights "attach" or become relevant. Thus, they are entitled to attorneys at any of these critical stages, since they are in jeopardy of losing their freedom. This ruling did not mean that Mempa would be entirely free from further court action. However, it did provide for a rehearing, and his ten-year sentence in the Washington State Penitentiary was set aside.

Morrissey v. *Brewer (1972).* In 1967, John Morrissey was convicted in an Iowa court of falsely drawing checks. He was sentenced to "not more than seven years" in the Iowa State Prison. He was paroled in June, 1968. Seven months later, his parole officer learned that Morrissey had bought an automobile under an assumed name and had operated it without permission, had obtained credit cards giving false information, and had given false information to an insurance company when he became involved in an automobile accident. Further, Morrissey had given his PO a false address for his residence. After interviewing Morrissey, his PO filed a report recommending that Morrissey's parole be revoked. The parole violations involved all of the infractions and false information noted above. In his own defense, Morrissey claimed that he had been "sick" and had been prevented from maintaining continuous contact with his PO during the car-buying, credit-card accumulating, and automobile accident period. The PO countered by alleging that Morrissey was "continually violating the rules." The Iowa Parole Board revoked Morrissey's parole, and he was returned to the Iowa State Prison to serve the remainder of his sentence.

During his parole revocation hearing, he was not represented by counsel, nor was he permitted to testify in his own behalf, nor was he permitted to cross-examine witnesses against him, nor was he advised in writing of the charges against him, nor was there any disclosure of the evidence against him. Furthermore, the Iowa Parole Board gave Morrissey no reasons for its revocation action. Morrissey appealed to the Iowa Supreme Court, which rejected his appeal. The U.S. Supreme Court decided to hear his appeal, however, and overturned the Iowa Supreme Court and the Iowa Parole Board actions. The Court did not specifically address the issue of whether Morrissey should have been represented by counsel, but it did establish the foundation for a *two-stage parole revocation proceeding.* The first or preliminary stage or hearing would be conducted at the time of arrest or confinement, and its purpose would be to determine whether probable cause exists that the parolee actually committed the alleged parole violation. The second stage or hearing would be more involved and would be designed to establish the parolee's guilt or innocence concerning the alleged violations. Currently, all parolees in all states must be extended the following rights relating to minimum due process rights:

1. The right to have written notice of the alleged violations of parole conditions.
2. The right to have disclosed to the parolee any evidence of the alleged violation.
3. The right of the parolee to be heard in person and to present exculpatory evidence as well as witnesses in his or her behalf.

4. The right to confront and cross-examine adverse witnesses, unless cause exists why they should not be cross-examined.
5. The right to a judgment by a neutral and detached body, such as the parole board itself.
6. The right to a written statement of the reasons for the parole revocation.

Thus, the primary significance of the *Morrissey* case is that *it established* **minimum due process** *rights for all parolees and created a two-stage proceeding whereby alleged infractions of parole conditions could be examined objectively and a full hearing could be conducted to determine the most appropriate offender disposition.*

Gagnon v. *Scarpelli (1973).* Because the matter of representation by counsel was not specifically addressed in the *Morrissey* case, the U.S. Supreme Court heard yet another parolee's case concerning a parole revocation action in which court-appointed counsel had not been provided. Gerald Scarpelli was convicted of robbery in July, 1965, in a Wisconsin court. At his sentencing on August 5, 1965, Scarpelli was sentenced to 15 years in prison, but the judge suspended the sentence and placed him on probation for seven years. Believe it or not, the following day, August 6, 1965, Gerald Scarpelli was arrested and charged with burglary. The judge immediately revoked his probation and ordered Scarpelli placed in the Wisconsin State Reformatory for a 15-year term.

At this point, Scarpelli's case becomes a little complicated. During his early stay in prison, Scarpelli filed a **habeas corpus petition** with the court, alleging that his due process rights were violated when his probation was revoked. He was not represented by counsel and he was not permitted a hearing. However, Scarpelli was paroled from prison in 1968. Nevertheless, the U.S. Supreme Court acted on his original *habeas corpus* petition filed earlier and ruled in his favor. The Court held that Scarpelli had indeed been denied the right to counsel and had not been given a hearing in the probation revocation action. Although this might seem to be a hollow victory, since Scarpelli was already free on parole, the case had profound significance in subsequent parole and probation revocation actions. The U.S. Supreme Court, referring to the *Morrissey* case that it had heard the previous year (1972), said that "a probation revocation, like parole revocation, is not a stage of a criminal prosecution, but does result in loss of liberty. . . . We hold that *a probationer, like a parolee, is entitled to a preliminary hearing and a final revocation hearing* in the conditions specified in *Morrissey* v. *Brewer.*"

The significance of the *Scarpelli* case is that it equated probation with parole in the matter of revocation hearings. While the Court *did not say* that all probationers and parolees have a right to be represented by counsel in all probation and parole revocation hearings, it *did* say that counsel *should be provided* in cases where the parolee or probationer makes a timely claim contesting the allegations. This U.S. Supreme Court decision has been liberally interpreted by the courts and parole boards in all jurisdictions. Thus, while no constitutional basis currently exists for providing counsel in *all* probation or parole revocation proceedings, these proceedings usually involve defense counsel if legitimate requests are made in advance by probationers or parolees.

Some persons are understandably perplexed by the seemingly excessive interval that elapses between the time questioned events occur, such as probation revocation actions which may have been unconstitutionally conducted, and the time the U.S. Supreme Court gets around to hearing such petitions or claims and deciding cases. It is not unusual for these time intervals to be five or six years, or even longer. The wheels of justice move slowly, especially the wheels of U.S. Supreme Court actions. Interestingly, of the more than 3,500 cases that are presented to the U.S. Supreme Court annually for hearing, only about 150 to 175 cases are heard in which decisions are written. Four or more justices must agree to hear any specific case, and even then, their convening time may expire before certain cases are heard. It is beyond the scope of this text to discuss the process by which U.S. Supreme Court cases are initiated and processed, but this short discussion should serve to explain the apparent slowness in rendering significant opinions in landmark cases.

For juveniles, these three cases are important because they provide juvenile courts and juvenile paroling authorities within juvenile corrections with certain guidelines to follow. These guidelines are not mandatory or binding, since these U.S. Supreme Court rulings pertain to adults rather than to juveniles. However, the law is not always abundantly clear regarding its applicability in a wide variety of different cases. While it may be anticipated that the U.S. Supreme Court will eventually address probation and parole revocation issues that pertain to juvenile offenders, for the present we can only use adult guidelines.

Currently, probation and parole revocation proceedings for juveniles differ widely among jurisdictions. Knepper and Cavender (1990), for instance, indicate that in a western state they examined, "informal hearings" were conducted by a juvenile parole board outside the presence of juveniles. In such informal settings, decisions about parole revocations were made. Subsequently, juveniles were brought before the board and advised in a more formal hearing of the "rightness" of the board's decision about the revocation action taken. This is strongly indicative of the continuation of *parens patriae* in juvenile matters. In other jurisdictions, explicit criteria exist for determining court or parole board actions relating to juvenile parolees who violate program rules or commit new offenses. Statutory constraints may or may not be in place to regulate judicial or parole board decision making in these situations. Again, the cases of *Morrissey, Scarpelli,* and *Mempa* have not yet been interpreted as binding on juvenile procedures.

Selected Issues in Juvenile Corrections

Investigations of the rate of secure confinement of juveniles during the past two centuries have disclosed that the rate of juvenile institutionalization has increased, especially during the most recent decades (Sherraden and Downs,

1984). Many of those youths detained for fairly long periods of 30 days or longer are less serious misdemeanants and status offenders (U.S. General Accounting Office, 1983). For this and other reasons, juvenile corrections has been under attack from various sectors for years (Dwyer and McNally, 1987:47; McNally, 1984). This attack comes from many quarters, and it coincides with a general attack on the criminal justice system for its apparent failure to stem the increasing wave of crime in the United States. Sentencing reforms, correctional reforms, experiments with probation and parole alternatives, and a host of other options have been attempted in an apparent effort to cure or control delinquents and criminals.

In 1985, the United Nations and the National Council of Juvenile and Family Court Judges adopted policy statements about the juvenile justice system that bear directly on juvenile corrections. The issues to be discussed in this final section may be better understood in the context of these statements. Several recommendations have been made by Dwyer and McNally (1987:50–51). The recommendations are that

1. Primary dispositions of juvenile courts should be to have a flexible range for restricting freedom, with the primary goal focused on restoration to full liberty rather than "let the punishment fit the crime"; no case dispositions should be of a mandatory nature, but rather, they should be left to the discretion of the judge based on predetermined dispositional guidelines; in no case should a juvenile under 18 years of age be subject to capital punishment.

2. Individualized treatment of juveniles should be continued, including the development of medical, psychiatric, and educational programs that range from least to most restrictive, according to individual need.

3. While being held accountable, chronic, serious juvenile offenders should be retained within the jurisdiction of the juvenile court. As a resource, specialized programs and facilities need to be developed that focus on restoration of liberty rather than on punishment.

4. Policy-makers, reformers, and researchers should continue to strive for a greater understanding as to the causes and most desired response to juvenile crime; research should be broad-based rather than limited to management, control, and punishment strategies.

5. Where the juvenile court judge believes that the juvenile under consideration is nonamenable to the services of the court, and based on the youth's present charges, past record in court, age, and mental status, the judge may waive jurisdiction; in all juvenile cases the court of original jurisdiction should be that of the juvenile court; the discretion to waive should be left to the juvenile judge; the proportionality of punishment should be appropriate in these cases, but the most high-risk offenders should be treated in small but secure facilities.

Each of the issues discussed subsequently is affected directly by these recommendations and policy statements. While these statements are not obligatory for any jurisdiction, they do suggest opinions and positions of a relevant segment of concerned citizens—juvenile court judges and juvenile corrections personnel. These issues include (1) *the privatization of juvenile corrections;* (2) *the classification of juvenile offenders;* (3) *the practice of holding juveniles in adult jails and lockups;* and (4) *recidivism among juvenile offenders.*

The Privatization of Juvenile Corrections. Juvenile corrections has many of the same problems as adult corrections. Chronic overcrowding in secure confinement facilities is extensive among jurisdictions (California Department of the Youth Authority, 1984). Furthermore, sexual assaults on juvenile inmates by others, including administrative staff and guards, are not uncommon. Existing facilities in many states are deteriorating rapidly. There are disproportionate representations of black, Hispanic, and Native American youths (Breed and Krisberg, 1986:14–15). With the current emphasis on more punitive juvenile sentencing policies, it is unlikely that significant improvements in the quality of juvenile correctional facilities will be made in the near future. Some experts are quite pessimistic about whether the current political environment is flexible enough or sufficiently willing to support a more humanistic and rational approach to juvenile corrections (Breed and Krisberg, 1986:20). **Privatization,** the management and operation of a correctional facility or agency by a private corporation or enterprise, usually for profit, is believed by some authorities to be one solution to overcrowded publicly operated facilities.

Nonsecure and secure facilities are both publicly and privately operated (Keating, 1984). However, private operations have been criticized because of the comparatively low accountability of administrators to citizens in contrast with publicly operated facilities (del Carmen, 1985). Florida is one of several states experimenting with various forms of private juvenile incarceration. Historically, Florida has sought to rehabilitate youths through confinement, including placement of serious offenders in reform or training schools (Pingree, 1984:60). The first school for male juveniles opened in Florida in 1900, and by 1972, four schools were operating in various jurisdictions throughout the state. But because of serious institutional overcrowding and the ineffectiveness of program treatments, Florida officials decided to shift their confinement priorities to the development of less secure, community-based facilities (Pingree, 1984:60).

Some of these Florida community-based facilities are currently privately operated, although some of the operators are not-for-profit organizations such as the Jack and Ruth Eckerd Foundation. This foundation sponsors various wilderness projects, seeking to provide juveniles with opportunities to develop certain skills and acquire more positive self-images (Pingree, 1984:61). Florida's objectives are (1) to reduce the number of juveniles actually placed in secure correctional facilities, and (2) to provide juveniles with a broader base of community options that will be instrumental in helping them to acquire vocational training and education. Much emphasis is placed on assisting youths with psychological problems as well. Thus, trained counselors work closely with Florida juvenile offenders to meet their psychological and social needs more effectively. The Florida model has served as an example for other jurisdictions in later years (Criswell, 1987).

Robbins (1986:29) has outlined several important issues relating to the privatization of corrections for both adult and juvenile offenders. He raises the following questions:

1. What standards will govern the operation of the institution?
2. Who will monitor the implementation of the standards?
3. Will the public still have access to the facility?
4. What recourse will members of the public have if they do not approve of the way the institution is operated?
5. Who will be responsible for maintaining security and using force at the institution?
6. Who will be responsible for maintaining security if the private personnel go on strike?
7. Where will the responsibility for disciplinary procedures lie?
8. Will the contractor be able to refuse to accept certain inmates, such as those with AIDS?
9. What options will be available to the government if the contractor substantially raises its fees?
10. What safeguards will prevent a private contractor from making a low initial bid to obtain a contract, and then raising the price after the government is no longer immediately able to reassume the task of operating the facility?
11. What will happen if the contractor declares bankruptcy?
12. What safeguards will prevent private vendors, after gaining a foothold in the corrections field, from lobbying for philosophical changes for their greater profit?

These are important questions that often impede the progress of the private sector as it insinuates itself into the correctional field. Currently, juvenile corrections seems to have the lion's share of the privatization business. The Corrections Corporation of America, headquartered in Nashville, Tennessee, currently operates numerous facilities for both adults and juveniles through-out the United States. Other private interests are increasingly entering these correctional areas to provide services and supervisory services, often at less cost to taxpayers than government-operated facilities.

On the positive side, Turner (1988) and others suggest that private interests can often cut the red tape associated with corrections operations. He and other professionals promote the idea that the private sector can work cooperatively with the public sector in providing the best of both worlds for offenders (Longmire, 1985; Ring, 1987; Springer, 1976, 1988). Turner notes that private-sector operations can reward employees more quickly for excellent service performed, and that new operational ideas may be implemented more quickly in private operations than in government organizations. Furthermore, many of those involved in private corrections operations have formerly been employed in administrative and staff capacities in public corrections agencies and institutions. Thus, they possess the experience to do the job and do it well.

Turner says that the profit motive is an issue often raised by opponents of privatization of corrections. For example, this profit motive might inspire private interests to keep inmates confined for longer periods to maximize profits. However, it is apparent that the current state of chronic overcrowding in public incarceration facilities with no relief in sight will maintain consistently high inmate populations in both juvenile and adult correctional facilities, regardless of whether they are privately or publicly operated. Also, if private interests can make a profit while providing quality services to inmates at less cost to government, this seems to be a compelling argument in favor of greater privatization.

The Classification of Juvenile Offenders. Guarino-Ghezzi (1989:112) has suggested that a systematic classification model can be devised by incorporating objective predictors of an offender's risk of recidivism into the intake assessment. She believes that an objective risk classification procedure can accomplish the following objectives:

1. Increase control over juvenile offenders who are placed in community settings.
2. Increase agency accountability for placement decisions.
3. Increase consistency in decision making.
4. Direct allocation of scarce resources.
5. Increase support for budget requests (Guarino-Ghezzi, 1989:112–114).

Table 13.6 shows an overview of possible risk, need, and control factors that might comprise a risk/need classification instrument that might be used by juvenile correctional officials.

Guarino-Ghezzi (1989:116) says that with few exceptions, administrative control factors are often given low priority whenever classification models are designed. But she encourages their adoption, since they are crucial in influencing how private vendors will react toward youths (in a privatization context, for instance), how youths will adjust to their programs, determining which youths are most likely to cause behavioral problems and assault staff, and whether gang involvement is indicated (possibly requiring a youth's separation from other gang members upon arrival at a new facility). Some results of more effective classification schemes include greater staff accountability, greater staff and inmate safety, and more effective programming relative to individual offenders and their needs.

Holding Juveniles in Adult Jails or Lockups. Estimates vary with regard to the number of juveniles who are currently detained in adult jails or lockups. Figures from Bessette (1990:2) suggest that the number of juveniles admitted into and released from adult jails during 1989 was 54,000. Other profession-

TABLE 13.6   An Overview of Possible Risk, Need, and Control Factors

Factors	Risk	Need	Control
Total offense record	X		
Recent offense record	X		
History of assaultive behavior	X		X
Commitment history (if applicable)	X		X
Family relationships		X	
Intellectual ability		X	
Learning disability		X	
Employment	X	X	
Voc/tech skills		X	
Health and hygiene		X	
Sexual adjustment		X	
AWOL record	X		X
Behavior in previous programs			X
Public perception of offender			X
Age			X
Drug/alcohol	X	X	
Educational adjustment	X	X	X
Peer relationships	X	X	X
Emotional response/attitude	X	X	X
Placement record	X		X
Parental control	X	X	X

SOURCE: Susan Guarino-Ghezzi, "Classifying Juveniles: A Formula for Case-by-Case Assessment," *Corrections Today* 51 (1989), p. 114.

als claim that the figures are actually much higher. For instance, Dale (1988:46) indicates that approximately 479,000 juveniles are locked up in adult jails annually in the United States, either on a pretrial detainee or postadjudication basis. Whichever figure is more accurate, the fact remains that large numbers of juveniles are incarcerated in adult jails and lockups annually.

Police officers frequently make arrests of juvenile suspects who may not appear to be juveniles and who do not provide police with proper identification. Later, investigations reveal the juveniles' true ages, and they are placed in juvenile detention or in some other juvenile facility for further processing. Some jurisdictions simply lack the facilities to accommodate juvenile offenders in areas separate from where adults are held. Thus, there are occasions when juveniles continue to be celled with adult inmates, although these occurrences are decreasing.

The most apparent problems with celling juveniles in adult lockups or jails are that (1) youths are subject to potential sexual assault from older inmates and (2) youths are often traumatized by the jailing experience. This latter problem leads to another one that is even more serious—jail suicides. Rowan (1989) and others indicate that juveniles are especially suicide-prone during the first 24 hours of their incarceration in jails. Thus, it is little consolation that states such as Illinois pass laws prohibiting a juvenile's confinement in adult

BOX 13.2

Juvenile Highlights

Is long-term confinement a suitable punishment for all serious juvenile offenders? J. Steven Smith at Ball State University in Muncie, Indiana, doesn't think so. He says that in 1988, Indiana had one of the worst records in the country for jailing juvenile offenders, even on a temporary basis. That year, over 7,000 juveniles were incarcerated in adult jails in direct violation of the federal Juvenile Justice and Delinquency Prevention Act and its accompanying Jail Removal mandates.

Smith describes the suicide of a 17-year-old youth in an Indiana county jail shortly after being arrested for shoplifting a tube of suntan lotion. Another youth hanged himself in a city lockup after being arrested on a minor charge. The parents of both boys have filed suits against the jail and lockup as well as the supervising authorities and local governments.

However, Smith says that with 92 counties and 92 juvenile judges, there is little, if any, agreement among juvenile court jurisdictions about how public policies relating to juveniles ought to be implemented. Nevertheless, the Indiana Department of Corrections in 1989 established an "alternatives-to-jail" program, patterned after a similar Michigan program, in collaboration with the Indiana Criminal Justice Institute and the Indiana Juvenile Justice Task Force, Inc., a private advocacy group. By the end of 1989, jailings of juveniles in Indiana adult facilities decreased to about 3,000, while the 1990 figures are expected to be under 1,000 once they have been tallied.

Smith believes that all too often, juvenile court judges act in response to apparent public sentiment favoring a "get tough" policy toward juvenile offenders, and that their typical reaction is to incarcerate them rather than to explore nonincarcerative options. Smith suggests that detention should be reserved for the most serious offenders who pose a danger to themselves or to others. This means that more effective classification measures need to be devised from the point of intake and at other critical points throughout the system.

(Some factual information adapted from J. Steven Smith, "A Lesson from Indiana: Detention Is an Invaluable Part of the System, But It's Not the Solution to All Youths' Problems," *Corrections Today* (1991) 53:56–60.)

Jail and prison overcrowding in many jurisdictions throughout the United States frequently result in celling juveniles with adult offenders. Although there is a general mandate to remove juveniles from adult jails and lockups, situations such as this continue in various jurisdictions because of physical plant limitations and overcrowding. (Courtesy of Frost Publishing Group, Ltd.)

jails for periods longer than six hours (Huskey, 1990). And Dale (1988:46) says that a juvenile's potential sexual exploitation does not always involve other, older inmates. In Ironton, Ohio, for example, Dale reports a case of sexual assault against a detained juvenile status offender by a corrections officer. Although a $40,000 judgment was subsequently awarded the youth, no amount of money can buy away the trauma to a juvenile resulting from such a violent sexual incident (**Doe** v. **Burwell,** 1981).

Currently, there are organized movements in many jurisdictions to mandate the permanent removal of juveniles from adult jails, even on temporary bases. Civil rights suits as well as class action claims are being filed by and on behalf of many juveniles currently detained in adult facilities. Dale (1988:46) cites the Iowa case of **Hendrickson** v. **Griggs** (1987) as a step in this direction. A federal district judge, Donald E. O'Brien, ruled that the Juvenile Justice and Delinquency Prevention Act could be used as the basis for a lawsuit seeking the permanent removal of juveniles from adult jails,

Presently, no nationwide precedents have been established to prevent juvenile incarcerations in adult lockups or jails in any absolute sense. Clearly, much remains to be done to rectify a situation that seems more within the purview of the juvenile justice system than of the criminal justice system.

Recidivism Among Juvenile Offenders. Because a broad range of intermediate punishments is not available to juvenile judges in certain jurisdictions, sentences are often imposed to detain youths in secure facilities for prolonged periods. Juvenile confinement, like adult incarceration, frequently fails to rehabilitate offenders, and they emerge more hardened, better-schooled delinquents than when they entered. While some highly regimented programs in certain states seem to work, many of the secure facilities for juveniles in the United States fail miserably in their rehabilitative ambitions. One problem encountered by many juvenile corrections authorities is how to deal effectively with aggressive youths. Sources of aggressiveness have often been traced to ineffective or undeveloped interpersonal skills.

One New York jurisdiction implemented an "aggression replacement training" (ART) program in 1983 to assist aggressive youths in developing more acceptable social skills. The ART program introduced juveniles to beginning social skills such as starting a conversation and listening, advanced social skills such as apologizing and asking for help, and skills for dealing with aggression and one's feelings (Goldstein and Glick, 1987:38–40). Thus far, evaluations of the ART program have been promising—participants have been less likely to engage in physical violence or aggression than nonparticipants in the control group. Thus, officials have concluded tentatively that aggression replacement training appears to have considerable potency as an intervention strategy (1987:42).

The emphasis currently seems to be upon minimizing the maximum-security nature of juvenile confinement and permitting juveniles greater freedom through the establishment of minimum-security facilities (McMillen, 1987:44). Although public support for minimum-security facilities for dangerous juvenile offenders is not particularly strong at present, there are signs of increasing receptivity to the idea. This is especially true when the costs of maximum-security incarceration of juveniles are compared with the costs of minimum-security secure confinement. Furthermore, juvenile self-concepts seem to be affected positively (McMillen, 1987:48).

Summary

Juvenile corrections encompasses all personnel, agencies, and institutions that supervise youthful offenders. Besides nominal and conditional sanctions that juvenile courts may impose, nonsecure and secure custodial sanctions may also be administered. Nonsecure confinement includes programs that permit limited access to communities, but where various conditions are imposed, including the observance of curfews, regular urinalyses for the detection of illegal drugs or alcohol, participation in individual or group therapy, and vocational or educational coursework. Secure confinement includes youth centers, industrial schools, and other prisonlike institutions where a youth's movements are confined to the premises.

The goals of juvenile corrections are rehabilitation and community reintegration, delinquency prevention, punishment and retribution, and isolation and control. Currently, the "get tough" movement is pervasive throughout the juvenile justice system, and the emphasis is on juvenile offender accountability and punishment. However, the rehabilitative aims of incarceration have not been neglected. Foster home placements, group homes, halfway houses, camps and ranches, and wilderness experiences or experience programs are considered nonsecure types of sanctions that juvenile courts can impose. Their success rates vary according to the type of program, although most authorities believe that youths tend to benefit from these experiences. VisionQuest is one of the better-known experience programs designed to provide participants with a greater degree of self-reliance and an improved self-concept. Outdoor skills are stressed, together with group discussions and activities that enable youths to function independently in a socially healthy environment.

Juvenile corrections has undergone substantial reforms in recent years. The establishment of juvenile detention resource centers has improved the quality of correctional staff and has helped to expand the service options available to detained youths. Major detention issues concern whether youths should be detained in adult jails or lockups and whether privatization should be used to accommodate growing numbers of youthful offenders. Better classification schemes are being designed to allow more accuracy in placements of juveniles in either nonsecure or secure detention institutions. Youths may be paroled from detention through informal processes in most jurisdictions. Several adult probation and parole revocation cases have been instrumental in guiding juvenile courts and juvenile corrections in establishing more objective guidelines for both early release and parole/probation revocation decision making.

Key Terms

Jane Addams (421)
Camps (424)
Doe v. *Burwell* (1981) (458)
Experience programs (424)
Family group home (425)
Foster home (424)
Gagnon v. *Scarpelli* (1973) (448)
Group home (424)
Habeas corpus petition (450)
Halfway house (424)

Hendrickson v. *Griggs* (1987) (458)
Homeward Bound (432)
Hope Center Wilderness Camp (429)
Hull House (421)
Juvenile corrections (418)
Long-term confinement (436)
Mempa v. *Rhay* (1967) (448)
Minimum due process (450)
Morrissey v. *Brewer* (1972) (448)
PARJO (445)

Parole (443)
Parole revocation (446)
Pretrial detention (436)
Preventive detention (436)
Privatization (453)
Probation revocation hearing (448)
Project Outward Bound (431)
Ranches (424)

Schall v. *Martin* (1984) (438)
Short-term confinement (436)
Solitary confinement (420)
Training school (424)
VisionQuest (432)
Walnut Street Jail (420)
Wilderness project (424)

Questions for Review

1. What is meant by juvenile corrections? Discuss several important parts or components of juvenile corrections.
2. Briefly describe the early efforts of corrections officials in the United States to accommodate juvenile offenders in secure confinement. What was the role of the Walnut Street Jail in this regard? Discuss the significance of solitary confinement pertaining to juveniles.
3. What are four major aims or objectives of juvenile corrections? Discuss each briefly.
4. What are three major types of nonsecure confinement facilities that are currently used in various jurisdictions? Describe each and indicate their potential benefits for youths.
5. Differentiate between a foster home and a family group home. What are their respective functions, and who are the intended juvenile benefactors?
6. What is a wilderness project or experience program? What are the functions of such programs? Give two examples.
7. Describe VisionQuest and some of its major strengths that might relate to juvenile rehabilitation.

8. What is a juvenile detention resource center? What are some of its important functions? Is there any evidence that such a facility is having an impact on the current state of juvenile corrections? Discuss briefly.
9. Differentiate between short-term and long-term secure confinement facilities for juveniles. What are the purposes of each?
10. What are some of the pros and cons of long-term confinement for juvenile offenders?
11. Describe some of the major demographic characteristics of long-term juvenile inmates. Are juvenile parolees similar in their characteristics?
12. What is meant by parole revocation? What circumstances might result in a juvenile's parole being terminated?
13. Identify three important landmark cases pertaining to adult probation and parole revocation hearings. Discuss the significance of each case as it might relate to juvenile corrections and juvenile parole.
14. What are some of the major problems confronted by officials who attempt to classify juvenile offenders? What factors seem to

be most predictive of one's
risk?

15. About how many juveniles
move through adult lockups
and jails annually? What legal
provisions are in place to limit

such incarcerations and admissions? Discuss some of the
problems of holding juveniles in
adult facilities, even for short
periods.

Suggested Readings

BAIRD, S. CHRISTOPHER (1987). *A Model Management System for Juvenile Corrections.*
    Madison, WI: Isthmus Associates.

BENEDEK, ELISSA P., and DEWEY G. CORNELL (EDS.) (1989). *Juvenile Homicide.* Washing-
    ton, DC: American Psychiatric Press.

GALAWAY, BURT, and JOE HUDSON (EDS.) (1991). *Criminal Justice, Restitution, and Recon-
    ciliation.* Monsey, NY: Criminal Justice Press.

KANE, THOMAS R. (1985). *Research Review: Impact of the Youth Corrections Act.* Wash-
    ington, DC: U.S. Federal Bureau of Prisons.

SHELEFF, LEON SHASKOLSKY (1991). *Ultimate Penalties: Capital Punishment, Life Imprison-
    ment, Physical Torture.* Columbus, OH: Ohio State University Press.

Comparative Juvenile Justice and the Future of the Juvenile Justice System

Part V begins with Chapter 14, which describes the juvenile justice systems of three different countries: Great Britain, Japan, and the Soviet Union. Great Britain is of interest in part because much of American jurisprudence stems from early English common law and legal precedents. Although the concept of juvenile delinquency is largely an American creation, the mechanisms for processing juvenile offenders have been influenced strongly by British antecedents. The *parens patriae* doctrine originated as a means by which chancellors or the king's representatives could oversee various matters, including dispositions of children who were either in need of care or who had violated the law. Japan has an independent juvenile justice system that is based on a different ancestry. However, greater international exchanges and cooperative professional arrangements in recent decades have brought outside influences to bear on the Japanese juvenile justice system. Criminologists of different countries have been significant in facilitating experimental programs regarding juvenile offender rehabilitation, training, and societal reintegration. The Soviet Union has traditionally dealt with juveniles under the broad rubric *hooliganism*. Hooliganism encompasses everything from prostitution, public drunkenness, and unemployment to juvenile delinquency.

These various juvenile justice systems conceptualize juvenile offenders differently, and the treatments and interventions used by these countries tend to reflect the differences in their criminological thinking. Comparative juvenile justice is intrinsically rewarding because it gives us an opportunity to compare our own system of processing juvenile offenders with the systems used in other countries. While there are common threads linking most types of juvenile offensive behaviors in these countries, procedures for dealing with offenders vary. These procedures are inevitably linked with the political systems of the respective countries.

Part V concludes with Chapter 15, which summarizes several major trends that are occurring throughout the juvenile justice system. In the last several decades, we have witnessed numerous changes regarding the legal rights of juveniles and the ways juveniles are processed in both the juvenile and criminal justice systems. Changing patterns of delinquent conduct have no doubt been factors influencing systemic changes. Because the legal rights of juveniles are rapidly becoming synonymous with the constitutional rights possessed by adults, some experts have advocated a unification of juvenile and criminal courts. Nevertheless, strong sentiment exists for preserving the paternalistic and civil nature of juvenile courts and the juvenile justice process generally. A summary of major trends is presented that includes changing codes of conduct within law enforcement relating to juvenile contact, prosecutorial and judicial decision making, and juvenile corrections. Especially targeted for experimental programs is the field of juvenile corrections, where greater privatization of management and operations is taking place. Intermediate punishments, including intensive supervised probationary programs, community-based services, home confinement, and electronic monitoring, are being implemented at a greater rate in most jurisdictions to ease the growing caseloads of juvenile probation and parole officers. Experiments are being conducted with shock probation and parole, camp ranches and group homes, and other nonsecure confinement alternatives for juvenile offenders. Finally, the future of juvenile justice is discussed especially in view of the many changes that have already taken place in the juvenile justice process.

CHAPTER 14

Comparative Juvenile Justice Systems

Introduction

Are there juvenile delinquents in other countries? Are juveniles defined in the same ways in other parts of the world as in the United States? Are the offenses juveniles commit in other countries qualitatively similar to or different from the delinquent acts committed by delinquent youths in the United States? How are juveniles punished by different cultural systems? Are these punishments effective?

This chapter is about the juvenile justice systems of other countries. Three countries have been selected for comparative purposes: England, Japan, and the Soviet Union. The choices of countries were influenced by (1) their different legal traditions, (2) their different conceptions of crime and delinquency, and (3) their different ways of dealing with juvenile offenders. Most like the United States is England. In fact, much of the common law practiced in the United States is based on early English common law. Many of our conceptions about juveniles have been influenced by the ways juveniles have been treated historically in England.

Japan is included in part because it has undergone substantial changes in its

In the Soviet Union, juvenile delinquents are called *hooligans*. This catch-all term also includes drunks, social misfits, prostitutes, and loiterers. (Reuters/Bettmann)

criminal and juvenile justice systems in the post—World War II years. The rate of juvenile delinquency in Japan is fairly high, with juveniles accounting for almost 30 percent of all Penal Code crimes annually (Yoshitake, 1989:88). Any person under age 20 in Japan is considered to be a juvenile. The Japanese juvenile justice system seeks to involve families of juveniles in significant ways in various solutions to delinquency problems. Delinquent children are viewed either as ''problem juveniles'' or as ''juveniles with problems'' (Yoshitake, 1989:97).

The Soviet Union has been included in part because it is a totalitarian state with a system of legal precedents that differs considerably from those of most Western nations. Considerable powers are vested in the people in various communities throughout the Soviet Union, and **people's courts** are commonplace for frequent adjudications of serious offenses. Punishments are often related to constructive work for most adult offenders, although juvenile offenders frequently receive compulsory educational training. Labor colonies are used extensively as punishments for various types of offenses. Offenses by juveniles make up about 12 percent of all crimes committed in the Soviet Union annually, and about 80 percent of these juveniles engage in *hooliganism* and theft. **Hooliganism** *is a catchall term referring to acts of mischief, public drunkenness, loitering, prostitution, and assorted other offenses* (Terrill, 1984).

The organization of this chapter is as follows: A brief description of the criminal justice system of each country will be presented. There is always an interface between the criminal and the juvenile justice systems in each of these countries, and it is important to know the nature of these associations. Next, a general description of the juvenile justice system of each country will be presented. Definitions of juvenile delinquency for each of the countries will also be provided.

Juvenile interactions with law enforcement officers, prosecutors, and the courts will be examined. For each country, a brief description of juvenile corrections and aftercare programs will be presented. Finally, recidivism will be described in order to assess the effectiveness of each country's juvenile justice system and how well youthful offenders are managed. A concluding section will contrast the three juvenile justice systems with the juvenile justice system of the United States in several important dimensions, including juvenile rights and processing.

Comparative Juvenile Justice Systems Defined

Whenever criminal or juvenile justice systems of other countries are examined and compared with those of the United States, such investigations are *comparative* or *cross-cultural*. Thus, **comparative or cross-cultural juvenile justice systems** *study is the study of the similarities and differences in the juvenile justice systems of other cultures, societies, and institutions* (adapted from Terrill, 1984:ix).

Every country has a different penal code, and definitions of crime vary from one nation to the next. In some countries, such as the Soviet Union, there are relatively few violent crimes committed annually compared with the rate of violent crime in the United States. There are few bank robberies in the Soviet Union. For a citizen to become instantly wealthy within any Soviet community would be too conspicuous and would attract the attention and close scrutiny of others. In fact, the Soviet government relies heavily on the reports of informants about the suspected wrongdoing of others.

Access to firearms varies considerably among countries as well. No doubt fewer violent crimes will be observed in those countries with stricter firearms laws. For example, police officers in England most often make their rounds of neighborhoods unarmed. While they stand little chance of winning a battle with armed criminals, few criminals in England use firearms to commit their crimes. The use of firearms in the commission of a crime in England is severely punished (Beynon, 1986).

In some countries, such as Nigeria, criminal offenders may be subject to corporeal punishments, such as caning or lashing, for various crimes. Drunkenness in Nigeria might be punishable by receiving 100 lashes. Other countries may mutilate offenders in certain ways. In certain Islamic nations, thieves may have their hands amputated as the prescribed punishment. Since alcoholic beverages in Islamic nations are forbidden, public drunkenness is dealt with severely.

We may gain great insight into how crimes and delinquency are defined in different countries by observing the nature of the punishments imposed. In the United States, we frequently subject convicted or adjudicated offenders to incarceration. This is considered unproductive in other countries, where offenders are sent to work colonies to work for a specified period, under a type of community service sanction. In Sweden, for instance, many convicted offenders who serve time in correctional facilities are entitled to four-week paid vacations as private citizens for each year of their incarceration. Furthermore, the government makes frequent weekend furloughs available to them so that they may visit their families. Their work in prison is of a kind which will enable them to secure employment more easily when they are released.

Juvenile Justice in England

The juvenile justice system in England is best understood as a part of the overall criminal justice system there. Official records of crime in England were not systematically compiled by the government until 1955. A comprehensive record-keeping system was devised as one result of the **Criminal Justice Act of 1948.** The British Home Secretary was vested with various powers, including discretionary authority to conduct research into the causes of delinquency and crime as well as offender treatment, and "other matters connected herewith" (Johnson, 1983:80). In 1955 there were 438,085 serious crimes reported to police. In 1970, there were 1,555,995 crimes reported, for a general crime increase of 300 percent. By 1985, this figure had risen to 3,247,030 crimes, more than double the 1970 figure (International Crime Center, 1986:56). Currently, the **British Crime Survey (BCS),** begun in 1981, is the official source of crime information in England. It is similar to the *National Crime Survey* in the United States, which reports the amount of crime on the basis of victim surveys. The *British Crime Survey* is believed by many experts to be more accurate at reflecting crime in Great Britain than official sources and Home Office and police reports. More crime is reported by the *BCS* than by other official sources of available data.

Changes in the law have produced modifications in the definition of crime. Prior to 1967, the law divided crimes into two broad classes, roughly corresponding to the U.S. crime categories of felonies and misdemeanors. As a result of the **Criminal Law Act of 1967,** three crime categories were created. These include: (1) **summary offenses,** or violations such as public drunkenness, disorderly conduct, petty theft, and solicitation for prostitution; (2) **indictable offenses,** or more serious crimes that are heard by a crown court, including, but not limited to, rape, robbery, and murder; and (3) **hybrid offenses,** or crimes that may be heard either by a magistrate or a jury; an example of a hybrid offense would be embezzlement.

The **Judicature Acts of 1873 and 1875** established a system of criminal courts that has endured to the present in England. If we begin at the "bottom" of the British court structure, we can identify various *courts of the first instance.* These include **magistrate's courts** and **crown courts.** Magistrate's courts handle about 85 percent of the serious crimes. These courts may hear summary offense charges, indictable offense charges, or hybrid offense charges. Police officers who make arrests often function as police prosecutors in these magistrate's courts, where they present evidence against the accused and other pertinent information about the crime alleged.

Duty solicitors are made available by the government to provide immediate legal advice to defendants, who must decide whether or not to plead guilty to the offenses alleged. These solicitors are comparable to public defenders in U.S. courts. Most often, guilty pleas are entered, since the incentives offered these defendants are quite favorable. They include (1) lesser penalties compared with those that might be imposed by other courts; (2) the avoidance of the stigma or embarrassment of a public trial, and (3) lighter sentences imposed by magistrates (Hughes, 1984:569). Jury trials in magistrate's courts are relatively rare. Judicial decisions are based upon the principle of **stare decisis,** which is the law of precedent wherein judges rely upon the way similar cases were decided by judges of higher courts previously.

Crown courts generally hear the more serious indictable offenses and are authorized to conduct jury trial proceedings. Judges in crown courts take an active role in the proceedings; they may interrogate witnesses and make favorable and adverse comments about them or about the defendants. Jury selection methods are similar to those used in the United States, although **voir dires** or juror challenges, cannot be made by either the prosecution or defense attorneys. *Voir dires are opportunities for both the prosecution and the defense to interview potential jurors to determine their suitability as jurors.* Without *voir dires,* it is impossible to determine the biases of any particular juror in a case. Prosecutors must prove their cases against criminal defendants beyond a reasonable doubt.

There are three appellate courts that may be accessed by lower courts. Magistrate's court decisions may be appealed directly to the crown courts we have just discussed. Crown court decisions may be appealed to **divisional courts** or **courts of appeal, criminal division.** These divisional courts and courts of appeal, criminal division would correspond roughly to civil and criminal courts of appeal in various state jurisdictions. Thus, if a civil matter was being appealed, it would be directed to the divisional court. A criminal matter decided in a crown court would be appealed to the court of appeal, criminal division. These courts of appeal consist of seventeen judges, although the judges sit in groups of three when hearing appealed cases. Finally, the highest court is the **House of Lords,** which, in addition to being the upper house of the British parliament, also serves a function equivalent to that of the United States Supreme Court.

Juvenile Delinquency. The juvenile justice system of England is much like the juvenile justice system in the United States. Presently, there are continuing debates among English juvenile justice experts about the direction to be taken by the juvenile justice system. The debate is over whether the system should be primarily rehabilitative or should be a justice-oriented system in which youths are held accountable for their acts and punished in accordance with the severity of the offenses committed. Like the United States, England attempts to divert youthful first offenders from the trappings of formal judicial systems; this reflects the influence of labeling theory in shaping juvenile justice policies. However, the juvenile justice system of England is fragmented and is not clearly coordinated with various social and correctional services (Pratt, 1986).

Many British criminologists believe that ineffective parenting is responsible for much juvenile delinquency. Punishments in England for youthful offenders are primarily rehabilitative, and thus, community-based correctional programs are growing in popularity. (© Richard Kalvar/Magnum Photos)

Early English common law provided that youths under age 7 were not to be held accountable for any of their actions, regardless of their seriousness. In recent decades, this minimum age has been raised to 10. Children between the ages of 10 and 13 may be held accountable for their actions, provided that the government can sustain the burden of proof that these youths knew the seriousness and consequences of their acts. Thus, the presence of *mens rea* must be established as in U.S. criminal courts. Prosecutions of children between ages of 10 and 13 are rare. Youths between the ages of 14 and 16 are designated as **young persons** and are considered fully responsible for their actions under criminal law (Terrill, 1984:90–91). Another category of youthful offender is a **juvenile adult,** or a person between the ages of 17 and 20. These youthful offenders are subject to special provisions when being sentenced by judges (Terrill, 1984:91).

The types of offenses committed by British youths do not differ greatly from those committed by U.S. youths. The juvenile justice system of England must deal with runaways, truants, and curfew violators, as well as with those who commit crimes (Newman, 1989). Like U.S. juvenile justice experts, British experts believe that alcoholism and drug use are closely correlated with juvenile offending (McMurran and Whitman, 1990). British criminologists also think that ineffective parenting is a contributing factor to much of the delinquency that is prevalent in England today (H. Wilson, 1987). There are youth gangs throughout England, and more than a few children are involved in illegal gambling activities and have problems with social adjustment (Hains and Hains, 1988; Heal and Laycock, 1987; Huff and Collinson, 1987). These facts lend strong support to the idea that British delinquents commit their offenses in groups rather than in isolation (Emler *et al.*, 1987).

Prosecution and the Courts. As the result of the Children and Young Persons Act of 1969, a juvenile court was created that currently has jurisdiction over youths under 17 years of age. An earlier version of the juvenile court was established in 1908, although such a court was largely a magistrate's court which was called into special session for the purpose of adjudicating juvenile offenders. Terrill (1984:91) says that despite the fact that the new version of the juvenile court has become more specialized regarding the cases it hears, it is basically the same type of court that was created in 1908. Dependent and neglected children, child abuse cases, and unmanageable and unruly children are within the jurisdiction of this court, in addition to delinquent offenses. These courts have jurisdiction over all matters involving juveniles under age 17 with the exception of murder (Terrill, 1984:92). Since the death penalty was abolished in Great Britain in the 1960s, no one is executed for capital crimes. Lengthy prison terms are imposed as the alternative.

Reports from corrections officials in Great Britain disclose the fact that the number of juveniles entering custodial institutions has increased steadily since 1983 (Pengelly, 1985). Some experts believe that this increase in the use of incarceration for youthful offenders is the result of a growing disenchantment among British authorities with the rehabilitative efficacy of the juvenile justice system (Hawkins and Zimring, 1986; Rumgay, 1990; T. Wilson, 1987).

Cases against juveniles are begun largely through police actions. Rigorous changes in the laws relating to searches of criminal suspects and seizures of property have affected law enforcement officers in every British community. Today, officers must bring forth only those cases against offenders in which their evidence is strong and meets the criteria established by district attorney generals (Giller and Tutt, 1987). Thus, in recent years, police officers have increased the amount of cautioning they use against youthful offenders. Police cautioning is the use of verbal reprimands or warnings in police encounters with low-risk youths who may not have committed any crime but may have violated curfew or some other minor infraction.

Police cautioning has increased from 47 percent in 1981 to 60 percent in 1985 (Giller and Tutt, 1987). Usually, when officers use police cautioning instead of bringing youths into custody, the attorney general's office has required that several criteria be met. These include the following: (1) when juvenile offenders are encountered and taken into custody, police officers must first obtain an admission of guilt from them relating to the alleged offense; (2) the evidence against cautioned juveniles must be particularly strong, and it must satisfy the attorney general's guidelines for evidence that could be used for a successful prosecution; and finally, (3) parents or guardians must consent to the caution being issued (Giller and Tutt, 1987).

As a general rule, there is reluctance among British police officers about bringing youths into formal custody, since it is believed that an arrest

BOX 14.1

Juvenile Highlights

When juveniles are classified, either at intake or at the time of detention as the result of a delinquency adjudication, they are ordinarily diagnosed in terms of the most appropriate means of dealing with their difficulties. The Japanese juvenile justice system uses "classification homes" to hold both juvenile delinquents and predelinquents on a temporary basis, pending their disposition to other forms of community or state care.

Juveniles in Japan are defined as any youths under the age of 20. A Juvenile Law provides that those considered delinquents or designated for education, treatment, and other forms of protection, and those believed to be at risk of becoming *future* delinquents — "predelinquents" — are subject to special procedures. In 1987, there were approximately 289,000 juvenile offenders in Japan. The Juvenile Law divides youths into three broad categories: (1) those who are aged 14–20 who violate Penal Code laws; (2) those offenders younger than 14 who do not violate Penal Code laws in a technical sense, since they are "child offenders"; and (3) predelinquents who are younger than 20 years of age and are thought because of other behaviors to be likely future delinquents.

Juvenile classification homes fulfill a dual function. First, they pro-

vide temporary housing for youths awaiting a juvenile court adjudication. Thus, this is a form of pretrial detention. Second, they provide a place of detention away from adults for particularly young offenders. The Child Welfare Law provides for child guidance centers to conduct diagnostic tests and assign child offenders to particular juvenile institutions, with or without the youth's or parent's consent. Thus, these homes are in fact diagnostic centers for the juvenile court. Japan operated 53 classification homes in 1989. The length of an average juvenile stay is fourteen days. Boys and girls are segregated by floor.

The positive benefits of these homes are that they are centralized and reflect unified policies among regions. Both delinquents and predelinquents are accommodated. Also, detention is not equated with jailing. Furthermore, adults are effectively separated from juvenile offenders or pre-offenders. Even Japan has violent juveniles; these youths are also accommodated, and special detention facilities exist for separating hard-core youths from less serious juvenile offenders and problem juveniles.

(Some factual information adapted from Mitsuyo Yoshitake, "Juvenile Classification Homes in Japan," *American Jails* (1989) 2:88–97.)

experience will result in unfavorable labeling of youthful offenders. There-fore, station adjustments in British police departments occur with great frequency, in much the same way as they occur in U.S. police departments. Juveniles who have been arrested must be brought before presiding magistrates within 72 hours of their arrest. Remand or detention orders may be issued for especially serious or violent juvenile offenders.

More serious juvenile offenders may be transferred to criminal courts or crown courts for disposition, where indictable offenses are tried. Juvenile judges in Great Britain exercise considerable discretionary powers in the way adjudicatory hearings are conducted. They may permit parents and other interested persons to testify either on behalf of or against the juvenile. Youths are entitled to be represented by **solicitors** (attorneys). Juvenile court judges determine guilt or innocence. If the verdict is "guilty," judges must provide their reasons for the verdict in writing.

Juvenile Corrections. Once youths are adjudicated as delinquent by the court, a range of options is available to British juvenile court judges that is similar to that of U.S. juvenile court judges. There are nominal, conditional, and custodial options that may be exercised as punishments. Nominal options are usually verbal reprimands, whereas conditional options include probation with or without conditions, restitution, community service, and/or victim compensation. If a custodial option is exercised by the presiding judge, there are several detention alternatives that may be chosen, depending on the seriousness of the conviction offense. Prior to 1982, there were four major custodial options. One of these, the *borstal,* was abolished by the Criminal Justice Act of 1982 (Rumgay, 1990).

Borstals provided rehabilitative services in a secure custodial environment, where youths could participate in vocational and educational training, or receive counseling or group therapy. Usually, borstal confinement was a reformative sentence which varied from six months to two years (Terrill, 1984:95). Two reasons for the discontinuation of borstals are that they reflected a high degree of recidivism and that they appeared to be ineffective as delinquency deterrents and rehabilitative agents. Some critics believe that despite high rates of recidivism, borstals offered many British delinquents opportunities to change their lives in much the same way that VisionQuest operates in the United States as a juvenile rehabilitative medium (Hawkins and Zimring, 1986).

Three remaining alternative custodial sanctions existed for six years following the Criminal Justice Act of 1982: placement in *detention centers,* placement in *community homes,* and placement in *attendance centers.* Detention centers are comparable to industrial schools used for the most hard-core offenders in the U.S. juvenile justice system. Community homes are community-based correctional facilities much like group homes in the United States—juveniles are continuously supervised and are required to engage in various rehabilitative enterprises. Attendance centers are community-based services that youths may be required to attend, usually for several hours a day, during the probationary term they serve. These attendance centers are similar to halfway houses for youthful offenders in the United States, and they provide a variety of services for their youthful clients.

In 1988, another major change in British juvenile justice occurred through the passage of the **Criminal Justice Act of 1988.** This act simplified the way youthful offenders were defined, and a new, unified custodial sentence was established. The new sentence available to convicted youths is known as "detention in a young offender institution," and it places the responsibility on the Prison Service for determining where offenders should serve their sentences. Decisions are based on age, sentence length, and other related factors. The purposes of this new detention are (1) personal development of individuals, (2) the promotion of amiable staff/inmate relations, and (3) the encouragement of links with home and community through the sentence. Thus, the use of furloughs is encouraged (*American Jails,* 1990:92).

Various strategies are currently being employed in England as ways of decreasing the rate of recidivism among both juveniles and adults (Heal and Laycock, 1987). In fact, England is experimenting with intermediate punishment programs to about the same degree as the United States. Many British criminologists share U.S. sentiments about incarcerating juvenile offenders, and feel that incarceration should be reserved for only the most serious types of offenders. In the meantime, various strategies will be employed until the most productive crime prevention solutions or interventions have been identified.

Juvenile Justice in Japan

Although small in area, Japan is one of the most densely populated countries in the world. In 1987 there were over 120 million people scattered over 234,577 square miles, an area about 1/25th the size of the United States (Nakayama, 1987:168). Despite the crowding, Japan is the only country in the industrialized world to report a decrease in its crime rate in recent years (Terrill, 1984:253). A Diet, or bicameral body consisting of representatives and councilors, is the highest authority, and the Emperor of Japan is merely a figurehead (Nakayama, 1987:253).

Statutory law under the Penal Code of Japan defines all criminal conduct. No distinctions are made between felonies or misdemeanors, but each specified statutory offense has an explicit punishment; punishments are graduated in severity according to the seriousness of the offense. Common-law interpretations of the law are prohibited, and the principle of *stare decisis* is seldom invoked, since explicit statutes and statutory punishments exist for each crime. The maximum statutory punishment is the death penalty, which is imposed only for the most serious offenses, including sabotage, homicide, and insurrection. Fewer than five persons a year are executed, typically through death by public hanging (Zenon, 1990:125). The range of punishments short of the death penalty includes imprisonment with or without labor, short-term detention, fines, and/or confiscation of property.

The most common punishment is imprisonment with labor. The minimum prison length is one month; the maximum is fifteen years. Under exceptional aggravating circumstances, sentences may be imposed of up to twenty years, although criminals may be eligible for parole after serving ten years of any longer sentence (Nakayama, 1987:175–176). Punishments for juveniles are primarily educational, although more serious juvenile offenders are often committed to the Juvenile Training School, a secure detention facility. Further descriptions of juvenile punishments will be presented later in this section.

Juvenile Delinquency. According to the Japanese Penal Code, the age of accountability for juveniles under the Juvenile Law is 14, and no one under age 14 is considered legally responsible. Youths aged 16 and older are eligible for prosecution as adults, although the Japanese system considers that juvenile court jurisdiction over youths ends at their 20th birthday. Thus, depending on the seriousness of offenses alleged, youths may be treated either as adults or as juveniles, and they may be tried in either a District Court or a Family Court. Juvenile delinquency trends in Japan vary according to different age categories. Delinquency among 14-year-olds has increased slightly since 1970, whereas delinquency among older juveniles aged 18 and 19 has decreased (Tokuoka and Cohen, 1987).

For juveniles under age 20, there are specific breakdowns in terms of ages and labels applied. Youths under the age of 14 are distinguished either as **lawbreaking children,** *or those who commit criminal offenses,* and **pre-offense juveniles,** *or those who commit status offenses, such as running away from home, violating curfew, or being truant.* Generally, juveniles between the ages of 14 and 20 who have committed criminal offenses are subject to the jurisdiction of Family Courts. Family Courts will be discussed in greater detail subsequently. Virtually all major cities in Japan have Family Courts to resolve juvenile matters.

Prosecution and the Courts. The court structure of Japan is fairly simple. The **Supreme Court of Japan** is similar in function to the U.S. Supreme Court, since it interprets the Japanese Constitution and hears appeals from lower courts. A quorum of eleven judges convenes, and a majority of eight judges must agree before any law is declared unconstitutional (Terrill, 1984:260–261). Below the Supreme Court are eight **High Courts** that are generally equivalent to the thirteen U.S. Circuit Courts of Appeal. These courts are dispersed throughout Japan, and they hear appeals from lower courts. High Courts are presided over by a president and several judges, although three judges must sit and decide cases.

Beneath the High Courts are fifty District Courts that hear both civil and criminal matters. These courts are similar to federal district courts, with the exception that in the most serious cases that might involve the death penalty, a three-judge panel must convene and decide guilt or innocence. Presently, Japan does not have a jury system; it fell into disuse in 1943 when the Jury Law was suspended (Terrill, 1984:266–267). Finally, there are **Summary Courts** and **Family Courts** that deal with minor crimes and family/juvenile matters respectively. There are about 575 Summary Courts that handle traffic matters and resolve minor disputes and petty offense cases, including public drunkenness and disorderly conduct. Summary Courts have fixed jurisdictions whereby fines and sentences cannot exceed previously specified maximums. Actions of Summary Courts are monitored closely by High Courts.

Family Courts, established under the Juvenile Law of 1948, exist in all Japanese jurisdictions and hear all matters pertaining to juvenile delinquency, child abuse and neglect, and child custody. Both status offenders and delinquents appear before Family Court judges. As with juvenile court judges in U.S. jurisdictions, Family Court judges have considerable discretionary authority. They decide cases within the *parens patriae* context. Thus, their concern is for what is best for children rather than for determining their guilt or imposing harsh punishments. For particularly serious juvenile offenders, Family Court judges may send their cases to District Courts for criminal prosecution. This is the equivalent of a judicial waiver or transfer action to criminal court jurisdiction that might occur in U.S. juvenile courts.

Terrill (1984:290) notes that about 50 percent of all juvenile cases brought before Family Court judges are dismissed outright without a hearing, and another 30 percent are dismissed after a hearing has been conducted. These high dismissal rates are often linked with a lack of evidence against alleged offenders. Furthermore, the remainder of the juveniles who appear before Family Court judges have their cases heard in a very informal atmosphere, with the press and the public barred. Photographing juvenile offenders is strictly prohibited, and any case details from Family Courts are kept confidential. It would appear that Japanese Family Court judges are interested in helping youths avoid the possible negative effects of the stigma that might result from court exposure or publicity. About 2,438 youths were referred to Family Courts as predelinquent cases in 1987; of these, about half were runaways (Yoshitake, 1989:93). Overall, about 289,169 juvenile and child offenders were cleared by police in 1987 (Yoshitake, 1989:88). Larceny or theft accounted for three fourths of these offenses, including shoplifting and bicycle theft. Almost two million youths were cited by police in 1987 for traffic violations.

Juvenile Corrections. The dispositions available to Family Court judges are much like those available to U.S. juvenile court judges. These Family Court judges may issue verbal warnings or reprimands to youths considered delinquent. Probation is also a judicial sentencing option, and about 8 percent of all youths appearing before these judges receive probation as a sentence (Japan Ministry of Justice Rehabilitation Bureau, 1985). Nearly three fifths of all offenders sentenced to probation receive community probation supervision. Youths on probation may or may not be subject to the supervision of formally trained probation officers. Often, volunteers are used to assist in monitoring a youth's activities. Also, judges may require that both youths and their families receive treatment or counseling at **Child Guidance Centers** that are located in most Japanese cities. These centers are staffed by trained psychologists, social workers, and family specialists who can provide applicable counseling and other forms of treatment to both youths and other family members.

Another possible sanction is to commit children to **Child Education and Training Homes** (Terrill, 1984:291). These are the equivalent of the group homes in the United States that are used to house youths who are neglected or dependent, or whose families have been declared unfit by the court. **Juvenile Training Schools** may also be used as secure detention facilities. These institutions offer educational and vocational training to youths in various age groups. They are divided according to age as follows: (1) *Primary Juvenile Training Schools* (ages 14 to 16); (2) *Middle Juvenile Training Schools* (ages 16 to 20); (3) *Advanced Juvenile Training Schools* (ages 16 to 20), designed for more serious habitual offenders; and (4) *Medical Juvenile Training Schools* (ages 16 to 20), for youths who are suffering from mental or physical handicaps (Terrill, 1984:291).

The most severe sentence is placement in a detention facility known as a Juvenile Prison (Zenon, 1990). One such prison is the Kawagoe Juvenile Prison. All prisons in Japan provide either for single-inmate occupancy or dormitorylike confinement, because Japanese correctional officials believe that two-person confinement poses the dangers of sexual assaults and escape planning. The Kawagoe Juvenile Prison is extremely clean and smoothly operated. This and other similar Juvenile Prisons are operated to provide vocational training and educational opportunities to offenders. Over the years, there has been a systematic decrease in the use of Juvenile Prisons for juvenile detention. In most cases, detention in such facilities is short-term, lasting an average of six months.

Japan has a rather elaborate classification system for juvenile offenders. Once juveniles have contact with police and it is decided that they should be brought before Family Court judges, public prosecutors function to screen out the least serious cases. Habitual offenders and more serious delinquents are placed for up to fourteen days in one of fifty-three **classification homes** throughout Japan. Classification homes are elaborate institutions, complete with psychological staffs, testing and diagnostic services, medical facilities, detention facilities, and observation rooms (Japan Ministry of Justice Corrections Bureau, 1985). These homes administer intelligence tests, interview youths and their parents, and make recommendations to Family Court judges about particular dispositions, which may include probation or some other type of conditional, supervised release option. About 43 percent of those juveniles who are classified by these homes are placed on probation, while about 27 percent are recommended for placement in training schools (Yoshitake, 1989:96–97). Again, the emphasis is on a youth's rehabilitation and welfare in virtually all Japanese youth agencies and court actions.

Overall recidivism rates in Japan for all criminal offenders are about 50 percent, meaning that about 50 percent of all first offenders reoffend later (Parker, 1986). But this figure is deceptive, since there are considerably fewer dangerous offenders in Japan compared with other countries, such as the

United States. Although the United States appears to be more experimental in its use of various rehabilitative practices than Japan, Japanese authorities are fairly optimistic about their existing parole and probation services, as well as their community-based correctional agencies to assist both adult and juvenile offenders (Parker, 1986). It is interesting to note, however, that Japanese officials have begun to rely more heavily on the formal controls of the legal system for containing juvenile offenders, rather than on the informal social controls of families, communities, peers, and schools, as they have in the past.

Juvenile Justice in the Soviet Union

Privileges, not money, are the most prized commodities in the Soviet Union. Therefore, there is comparatively little violent crime. Interpersonal violence, such as aggravated assault, is primarily family-related, and crimes against the person categorically account for less than 10 percent of all Soviet crime (Shelley, 1987). Almost half of all crimes in the Soviet Union are economic crimes. These economic crimes include theft, embezzlement, petty theft, misappropriation of socialist property other than petty theft, and robbery (Savitsky and Kogan, 1987:193). However, little reliable information is available about the true amount of crime in the Soviet Union. One reason for this is that regional officials often prefer to deal privately with crimes committed in their jurisdictions, without incurring criticisms from central headquarters in Moscow. Also, these officials want to give central authorities a good impression of their jurisdictions, and to appear successful in deterring criminal activity by reporting low crime rates.

Crime in the Soviet Union is broadly defined. A new Criminal Code implemented in 1960 defined crime as *socially dangerous acts (acts or omissions to act) that infringe the Soviet social or state system, the socialist system of economy, socialist property, the person, or the political, labor, property, or other rights of citizens, or any other socially dangerous act which infringes the socialist legal order.*

The Ministry of Justice in Moscow maintains records of crime, although this agency is reluctant to share its crime statistics with other countries. Some idea of the true amount of crime may be gleaned from the fact that in 1978, there were over 3,000 Soviet prisons, correctional-labor camps, and colonies. These allegedly held as many as five million prisoners (Shifrin, 1978).

There are several procedural alternatives in the Soviet Union for dealing with criminals. Local law enforcement officials can deal with petty crimes themselves, or they may hand over offenders to a court of public representatives. Local militias can handle public drunkenness cases or disorderly conduct. Private citizens may act as judicial boards and form **comrades' courts** to hear more serious offenses. Comrades' courts are comprised of private citizens in factories, organizations, collective farms, and apartment blocks, and they have jurisdiction over small property crimes, labor violations, antisocial behavior, petty hooliganism, petty speculation, petty theft, petty embezzlement of state property, minor assaults, and other minor offenses (Connor, 1972:194–195). The sanctions most often imposed by such citizens' bodies are fines, verbal reprimands, and condemnations. Restitution orders and disciplinary actions by employers may also be levied against those found guilty of minor offenses.

In most jurisdictions, there are squads of people's volunteers known as **druzhiny.** *Druzhiny* often work in collaboration with local police agencies to enforce antiparasite laws which prohibit persons from not working for long periods. Long-term unemployment in the Soviet Union is a serious offense and is punishable by different types of sanctions, including banishment.

Soviet courts use an accusatory process against offenders rather than an adversarial one. In the most serious cases, however, formal courts exist that are much like those in the United States, in that prosecutors present cases against criminal defendants, and defense attorneys attempt to free their clients from the system. Acquittals in such court proceedings are rare. Acquittals have steadily declined from over 10 percent before World War II to less than 1 percent in the 1980s (Solomon, 1987). Solomon (1987) suggests that one reason for this is that judges are cooperating to a greater degree in recent years with prosecutors, known as **procurators,** to avoid incidents of failure for which they might be held responsible. In short, if a case goes to a Soviet court, the chances of a criminal conviction are nearly 100 percent. Despite this high conviction rate, criminal defendants are presumed innocent until proved guilty.

The maximum punishment in the Soviet Union for the most serious offenses is death. No precise figures are available on the numbers of executions performed annually, but estimates are that at least five persons a day are executed, or about 1,750 per year (Connor, 1972; Zeldes, 1981). The Soviet Union leads the world in annual numbers of executions for crime violations. Punishments for less serious offenses include (1) deprivation of freedom, (2) exile, (3) banishment, (4) corrective works without deprivation of freedom, (5) deprivation of the right to occupy certain offices or engage in certain activities, (6) fines, (7) dismissal from office, (8) imposition of the duty to make amends for harm caused, (9) social censure, (10) confiscation of property, and/or (11) deprivation of military or special rank and privileges (Connor, 1972:199).

Juvenile Delinquency and Hooliganism. In May 1987, Mathias Rust, a 19-year-old student from Hamburg, West Germany, flew his light plane 500 miles from Finland across Soviet territory, undetected by the most sophisticated radar systems in the world. He landed perfectly in Red Square in Moscow, where he was immediately taken into custody by Soviet authorities. Rust's flight was done in the name of peace, since Rust was opposed to Soviet aggression and armament in Eastern Europe and elsewhere. His prank earned him four years in a Soviet labor camp after being convicted of "malicious hooliganism." Rust was not a delinquent; rather, he was a "hooligan." Hooliganism, in the Soviet definition, is a catchall term that encompasses prostitution, public drunkenness, disorderly conduct, and vagrancy. There is no "juvenile delinquency" per se in the Soviet Union.

Juveniles under age 16 are normally exempt from criminal responsibility and punishment, although those between 14 and 16 who commit violent crimes such as homicide, assault, robbery, and rape may be subject to adult punishments (Terrill, 1984:336). If we separate prostitution, public drunkenness, and other typically nonjuvenile offending behaviors from the broad hooliganism category, then some experts believe that juvenile delinquency has declined over the years in the Soviet Union. Nevertheless, delinquency (youthful offending) remains of primary concern to the Soviet government.

Soviet authorities believe that delinquency results from social causes, and they blame easy access to alcohol and drugs for much of their delinquency problem. Further, many youths drop out of school and find it difficult to find employment. Terrill (1984:368) has described various types of delinquents in the Soviet Union, suggested by an offender typology devised by Minkovsky (1976). These delinquents, as well as the estimated proportions of them, are:

1. *Career delinquents* (about 10 to 15 percent)—youths who are intent upon making a career of criminal activity.
2. *Culturally deprived youths* (about 30 to 40 percent)—youths who are disposed toward crime because they are poor, or because their environments are such that they cannot spend their leisure time constructively.
3. *Psychologically disturbed youths* (about 25 to 35 percent)—youths who suffer from various personality disorders and who often respond to peer pressure to commit crimes.
4. *Legally uninformed youths* (about 25 to 35 percent)—very young juveniles who are either ignorant of the laws or who do not understand the nature and consequences of their actions (Terrill, 1984:368) [my interpretation of Minkovsky's descriptions as presented by Terrill].

As we have seen, there is little accurate crime information available for the Soviet Union. This is because the Soviet Union regards crime statistics as "state secrets" (Terrill, 1984:365). Regarding the offensive conduct of the juvenile population, figures are even more ambiguous or elusive. Prominent Soviet criminologists can only make educated guesses, but the best estimates suggest that juvenile offending behaviors account for about 15 to 20 percent of all Soviet crime. Delinquency is lumped under the general rubric hooliganism, which is the broadest and largest crime category. About 25 percent of all Soviet crime is categorized as hooliganism (McClellan, 1987; Ostroumov, 1970:248).

Some general figures are available from previous hooliganism estimates. In 1977, for instance, about 200,000 convictions were obtained against youths and others for hooliganism (Chalidze, 1977:200–201). Juvenile offending, including hooliganism, has increased in the Soviet Union over the years, although some experts believe that certain prevention programs have effected small decreases in the rate of hooliganism. In 1984, for instance, some Soviet criminologists reported a 1.5 percent decrease in juvenile delinquency (hooliganism) (McClellan, 1987).

Prosecution and the Courts. As an important part of the Soviet Union's crime prevention efforts, especially those efforts designed to decrease the rate of juvenile offending, various grass-roots programs have been implemented to tighten control over juveniles and provide more structured daily regimens for them (Terrill, 1984:365).

As we have seen, the age of criminal responsibility varies according to the seriousness of the offense. Generally, criminal responsibility applies to those age 16 or older, although serious offenses such as murder and rape might require that 14- and 15-year-olds charged with such offenses be tried as adults instead of juveniles. Minors are those under 18 years of age, according to Soviet law. Juveniles who are alleged to have committed one or more criminal acts are investigated by police. After an investigation, the procurator (prosecutor) decides whether or not to accuse youths of crimes. If a decision is made to accuse them of crimes, they are entitled to the services of a defense counsel. During the interim between being accused of crimes and being tried, they are usually released to the custody of their parents or guardians.

There is no juvenile court per se. Rather, youths are subject to a two-track court system. One track is reserved for older, more serious offenders, those 14- and 15-year-olds who are alleged to have committed the most serious offenses. This track will lead eventually to a trial by the People's Court. People's Courts are comprised of a judge and two *lay assessors* who are private citizens. These three persons hear and decide the case on the basis of evidence presented. The second track is to have one's case heard by the **Commission on Juvenile Affairs.** This commission hears most minor cases for youths under 14 years of age. Their jurisdiction also includes child abuse and neglect cases, vocational training and educational placement, and delinquency prevention (Terrill, 1984:370).

People's Courts that try juvenile offenders are limited adversarial proceedings, since defense counsel may rebut evidence submitted by the procurator. The parents' attendance is optional, although they may be required to testify at the court's discretion. If youths are adjudicated as guilty, they are financially responsible for any damages they may have caused. If they are unable to pay their damages and/or fines imposed, their parents become financially liable to the court and victims.

The Commission of Juvenile Affairs greatly resembles traditional juvenile courts in the United States as they were in the pre-*Gault* years. They are informally conducted proceedings, and their intent is to deter youths from further offending rather than to punish juveniles through a finding of guilt. Thus, there is a strong *parens patriae* philosophy prevalent in such proceedings. Rehabilitation and education are stressed as the Commission's aims. In both People's Courts and adjudicatory hearings of the Commission of Juvenile Affairs, the proceedings may be closed to the public at the discretion of presiding authorities. Ordinarily, cases that are closed to the public are limited to sex offense cases or those connected with state secrets (Savitsky and Kogan, 1987:207).

BOX 14.2

Juvenile Justice In Norway*

What was it like for juveniles accused of crimes in the United States before *In re Gault,* the Miranda warning, and minimum due process provisions? Look at the way juveniles are processed by the Norwegian juvenile justice system for a possible answer.

An expert on Norwegian juvenile justice, Dr. Katherine van Wormer, (1990a, 1990b), has conducted an in-depth investigation of the Norwegian system for dealing with juvenile offenders. Her experience as a social worker enabled her to see many facets of the Norwegian system of juvenile justice that the general public might not see. Her observations are of interest here. Her general opinion is that while Norway leads the world in health care, social equality, and child care, much of the world leads Norway when it comes to juvenile justice. Frankly, no mechanism exists for controlling youthful lawbreaking behavior.

A brief foundation for understanding the Norwegian juvenile justice system is in order. First, Norwegians learn to trust others at an early age. Little pressure is exerted on children, who do not begin to learn to read until age 7. They have the same teacher until they are 12. Until the seventh grade, they receive no marks or grades to indicate their educational progress. Corporeal punishment or spanking has been prohibited both at home

and at school. There are no private schools in Norway; all children receive a public school education, consistent with Norway's philosophy of equality.

In this context, it is quite understandable that the doctrine of *parens patriae* is strong throughout childhood and youth. There are no punishments prescribed for youthful offenders under age 15. There are no special courts with the jurisdiction to adjudicate juvenile offenders. Teenagers age 15 or older are subject to criminal punishments and may be sent to prison. However, sentencing in Norway for most crimes is lenient; most offenders receive probation, a suspended sentence, or incarceration for a limited period in an "open" prison.

How are juveniles sanctioned, then? Ordinarily, public prosecutors representing the police will transfer most juvenile cases to a division of the *barnevern* or "social office," which oversees and ensures child protection. Older youths might be sent to the *barnevern* for processing following a criminal trial. Any police evidence is turned over to the *barnevern* and to social workers,

*Adapted with permission from Katherine van Wormer, "The Hidden Juvenile Justice System in Norway: A Journey Back in Time," *Federal Probation* (1990a) 54:57–61; and Katherine van Wormer, "Norway's Juvenile Justice System: A Journey Back in Time," *Corrections Today* (1990b) 52:106–116.

Youths in Norway have few legal rights and are often sent to youth homes such as the *Ringsaker Ungdomshjem* for offenses such as truancy, running away from home, and drug use. Although the staff—youth ratio is often one-to-one, these homes lack organized recreational and therapeutic programs, and their rehabilitative value is limited. (Courtesy of Katherine van Wormer)

who will treat offenders, not punish them. The first step taken by the *barnevern* is an emergency measure, whereby youths are placed in the custody of the *ungdomshjem* or youth home (see photo). Parental consent for this action is largely irrelevant, since a *barnevernsnemnd* or child welfare committee may convene and determine the most appropriate treatment for the juvenile. These are five-member boards elected by the municipal council to serve for periods of four years. Most board members are women and nonprofessionals, and they serve for reasons of prestige rather than because of knowledge that is functionally relevant to a child's needs. However, this board has almost absolute control over a youth's chances in life.

Many cases that come before the *barnevern* concern child abuse and neglect, and the board has the power to place children in foster homes or youth homes. The burden of proof is on parents if they want to retain custody of their children, and this burden is often an impossible one to bear. Thus, it is easy for the board to remove children from their homes, but there is an absence of provisions for parental retrieval of children taken from them. For those youths who break the law, the *barnevern* imposes appropriate treatment conditions, including foster home placements. If police officers are not satisfied with these arrangements, van Wormer says that these officers may reopen a case and have it disposed of through the criminal courts. The *barnevern*'s jurisdiction pertains to all youths under age 18.

Typically, the *barnevernsnemnd* receives a report from the child welfare office, which has examined the case during the period of the emergency foster home placement of children. A judge presides at a hearing of the *barnevernsnemnd*, although this role is strictly one of protocol. Van Wormer indicates that the social welfare office presents its one-sided evidence in the matter and the board decides the disposition of the case in advance of the hearing. Thus, any arguments raised by parents or the parents' attorney regarding child custody are largely irrelevant, since the matter has already been decided earlier. The hearing is largely for appearances, or, as van Wormer indicates, a "mere formality after the fact."

At such hearings, no transcript of the proceedings is made, and proof of a juvenile's guilt consists of a copy of the original police report. *Barnevern*-appointed psychologists and social workers also submit their reports, although these reports have already been rubber-stamped in advance by the *barnevernsnemnd*. Any institutional placement is for an indeterminate period. The press is barred from any knowledge of the proceedings, thus insulating both the board and the child from public scrutiny. Interestingly, van Wormer says that the punishment for children is often more severe than for adults charged with the same offense. Adults will ordinarily receive a suspended sentence, whereas children may "languish away in an institution for years." Even if children request to be tried as adults (similar

to a request by an American juvenile to be transferred to the jurisdiction of criminal courts), the Norwegian criminal court will turn the cases of convicted youthful offenders over to the *barnevernsnemnd* anyway.

Van Wormer cites the *Lov om Barnevern* or Law on Children's Protection, which provides for the protection of all children under age 18. One phrase of this law is particularly unclear and has led to abuses by these boards. The law says, in part, that special measures are required [for children who] "because of misdemeanors or *other behavior* show . . . poor adjustment to the surroundings or community" [emphasis mine]. This "other behavior" may be broadly interpreted to include poor motivation, lack of cooperation, a tendency to idealize and trivialize, and a lack of maturity among schoolchildren. Thus, this vague phraseology entitles the board to make institutional placements of children for any behaviors considered "other behaviors," whatever those behaviors might be. This is a dangerous amount of power to be wielded in the hands of a nonprofessional board.

Van Wormer's observations of youth homes or *ungdomshjems* indicates that they can accommodate up to ten children, and they have staffs of up to ten persons. Children can be placed in these youth homes for the remainder of their childhood for a variety of offenses, including truancy, theft, and drug use. There are no structured treatment programs or recreational activities. Children from these youth homes attend the local schools for their education, but there is widespread evidence that they are labeled as "reform school" kids. The staff is minimally trained in therapy methods, although the children receive little meaningful therapy. Rather, they receive generous amounts of clothing and other material items, including bicycles, cameras, and skis. Van Wormer says that one boy mentioned that they got a lot of expensive things, but they got no love "as in a family."

Van Wormer recommends that in order to avoid the abuses of power and the secrecy that currently characterize Norwegian juvenile justice, the following kinds of changes should be contemplated:

1. Children's rights should begin at the police station, through being informed in the parents' presence of their right to an attorney and their right to refuse to answer questions.
2. There must be no punishment for crimes without a trial.
3. Children should not be punished in the name of treatment.
4. Children should be kept at home, under supervision, whenever possible.
5. Children should not be subject to two legal systems simultaneously.

6. Children should be entitled to full constitutional rights, including the right to hear testimony against them, the right to cross-examine witnesses, and the subjection of evidence to a legal finding of guilty or not guilty.
7. Children should have access to an attorney's services at all critical stages.
8. Roles of social workers should be related to treatment, not to the prosecution of cases.
9. The *barnevernsnemnd* should be abolished altogether; it serves no useful purpose and does more harm than good.

Norwegian delinquency is not extensive, and in view of the way juveniles are processed, it is unlikely that completely reliable figures on the amount of juvenile offending can ever be produced. There are several interest groups at work currently attempting to provide youths in Norway with at least some of the legal rights commensurate with those enjoyed by U.S. youths. However, strong traditional elements persist throughout the Norwegian juvenile justice system to make such progress slow. For the present, at least, *parens patriae* is still alive and well in Norway.

Juvenile Corrections. Juveniles who are found guilty by the Commission on Juvenile Affairs are usually placed in reeducational programs, where they can learn about the goals of their socialist system and how to be productive members of society (Terrill, 1984:370–371). Those youths found guilty in People's Courts may be sentenced to up to fifteen years for their crimes. Youths under age 18 may not have the death penalty imposed, even if convicted of capital offenses. Terrill (1984:371) indicates that the maximum sentences of confinement that may be imposed are ten years for those under age 18, and fifteen years for adults. Most often, these sentences are not served in their entirety, since adults may become eligible for parole after serving about three years. Usually, these sentences are served in labor colonies where productive work is performed.

For juvenile offenders, similar sanctions of confinement are imposed. However, the most common sanction is a fine. Those juveniles who are sentenced to confinement are usually placed in juvenile labor colonies and serve about a year in productive labor before being released on parole. Terrill (1984:371–372) identifies a range of possible statutory penalties that may be imposed on juveniles, including:

1. Imposition of the duty to make an apology to the victim either publicly or in another form determined by the court.
2. Issuance of a reprimand or severe reprimand.
3. Warning.
4. Imposition on a minor who has attained 15 years of age of the duty to compensate for the damage caused, if the minor has an independent wage and the amount of the damage does not exceed 20 rubles; or imposition of the duty to make good by his or her own labor the material damage caused, not exceeding 20 rubles; upon the causing of damage in an amount of more than 20 rubles, compensation for the damage is to be carried out by way of civil judicial proceedings.
5. Transfer of the minor to the strict supervision of parents or persons substituting for them.
6. Transfer of the minor to a collective of working people or a social organization, with their consent, or to individual citizens at their request.
7. Commitment to a special medico-educational institution or educational institution for children and juveniles.
8. Assignment of the minor to an educational colony for minors.
9. A suspended sentence (ordinarily reserved for first offenders).

Relatively little is known about recidivism in the Soviet Union. It is known, however, that adult recidivists are obligated to serve a number of years in labor colonies with strict regimes, where their movements are closely monitored (Savitsky and Kogan, 1987:216–217). While reliable estimates of recidivism are unavailable, the best estimates of professionals suggest that recidivism is about 40 percent among those who have served time in labor colonies or other forms of incarceration. Recidivism among those who have been treated leniently by the system and have received early release or alternative sentencing by People's Courts is estimated to be about 15 percent.

Certainly, a country that places considerable emphasis upon acquiring a legal education and an appreciation for socialist government expects much of its citizens, even in their early years. Thus, it would be expected that recidivists would be treated especially harshly. Available evidence suggests that crime prevention programs, particularly those implemented in schools in the early grades, are exerting a noticeable influence on the decline of juvenile delinquency in almost all of the fifteen union republics in the Soviet Union.

Summary

Comparative juvenile justice is an examination of the different juvenile justice systems of various countries. These comparisons provide interesting contrasts and suggest options that might be exchanged among countries for processing juvenile offenders. Cross-cultural studies of the juvenile justice systems of other countries are perhaps best approached by paying attention first to their criminal justice systems and how adult offenders are processed in them. There is a close relationship between the adult and juvenile justice systems of each country.

Each of the countries examined here defines juvenile delinquency differently and provides an assortment of punishments in response to various types of offending behaviors exhibited by youths. Compared with the United States, which establishes the age of an offender's accountability at either 18 or 21, England's age of majority is 17, while Japan and the Soviet Union use ages 20 and 16 respectively. Of the countries examined, only England has abolished the death penalty outright as the maximum punishment for either juveniles or adults. Japan does use the death penalty—public hanging—but only rarely. Fewer than five offenders are hanged each year. The United States and the Soviet Union both use the death penalty, although the Soviet Union executes upwards of 5,000 or more offenders annually to lead the industrialized world in this particular punishment.

The Soviet Union has no formal juvenile court, although juvenile courts exist under different names in the other countries described here. All juveniles in all of these countries are entitled to counsel, may be assigned to probation, may be required to do community service, or may be subject to payment of fines, and they may appeal their sentences to higher courts. Pretrial detention of juveniles in each country is discretionary with presiding judges. Japan absolutely forbids public attendance at juvenile proceedings, although this prohibition is relaxed to varying degrees in other countries that have been examined. In all countries discussed here, the burden of proof against juveniles is on the government.

Intermediate punishment options, including parole, are used in each of these countries. Plea bargaining occurs in British and U.S. juvenile courts, but Japanese Family Courts and People's Courts in the Soviet Union do not ordinarily use plea bargaining to resolve juvenile cases. Bail is an option in all of these countries, as is the right against self-incrimination (with the exception of the Soviet Union, which may compel youths and their family members to testify). Predisposition reports are filed in many juvenile courts in these countries, with the exception of the Soviet Union. The Soviet Union

TABLE 14.1   The Juvenile Justice Systems of Great Britain, Japan, and the Soviet Union Compared with the United States in Several Salient Characteristics[a]

Characteristic	United States	Great Britain	Japan	Soviet Union
1. Age of accountability	18 or 21	17	20	16
2. Death penalty	Yes	No	Yes	Yes
3. Death penalty age minimum	16	N/A*	N/A*	18
4. Juvenile court	Yes	Yes	Yes	No
5. Right to counsel	Yes	Yes	Yes	Yes
6. Use of suspended sentences	Yes	Yes	Yes	Yes
7. Use of fines	Yes	Yes	Yes	Yes
8. Use of community service	Yes	Yes	Yes	Yes
9. Classification schemes for juvenile offenders	Yes	Yes	Yes	No
10. Nominal sanctions	Yes	yes	Yes	Yes
11. Adjudicatory proceedings closed to the public	Optional	No	Yes	Optional
12. Defense counsel available	Yes	Yes	Yes	Yes
13. Burden of proof of guilt upon government	Yes	Yes	Yes	Yes
14. Intermediate punishment options	Yes	Yes	yes	Yes
15. Electronic monitoring, home confinement	Yes	No	No	No

[a] Compiled by author.
* Not applicable.

makes no direct provisions for probation, although they do have parole programs. In the other countries discussed here, both parole and probation programs exist for most juvenile offenders. All of these countries, with the exception of the Soviet Union, provide for transfers of serious juvenile offenders to the jurisdiction of criminal courts. Pretrial detention of juveniles is used in all of these countries, although its use is most restricted in the Soviet Union. All of these countries segregate juveniles from adult offenders, although we know of many instances in U.S. jails in which juveniles are housed on a temporary basis with adult offenders.

The United States and England are perhaps the most experimental of these countries in terms of intermediate punishments, such as electronic monitor-

TABLE 14.1 (continued)

Characteristic	United States	Great Britain	Japan	Soviet Union
16. Appeal to higher courts permitted	Yes	Yes	Yes	Yes
17. Pretrial detention	Yes	Yes	Yes	Limited
18. Juveniles separated from adult offenders in pretrial detention	Yes	Yes	Yes	Yes
19. Provisions for bail	Yes	Yes	Yes	Yes
20. Plea bargaining	Yes	Yes	No	No
21. Jury trials for juveniles available	Optional	Optional	No	Optional
22. Use of police cautioning	Yes	Yes	Yes	No
23. Right to notice of charges	Yes	Yes	Yes	No
24. Right against self-incrimination	Yes	Yes	Yes	No
25. Waivers to criminal courts	Yes	Yes	Yes	N/A
26. Predisposition reports filled	Optional	Yes	Yes	No
27. Probation	Yes	Yes	Yes	No
28. Parole	Yes	Yes	Yes	Yes

ing and home confinement options. Japan relies heavily on the *parens patriae* doctrine to influence how its juveniles will be treated by the juvenile justice system. It is perhaps the least punitive in its sanctioning options against juvenile offenders. However, Japan also has one of the lowest rates of juvenile offending compared with these other countries. Police cautioning is used in all countries except the Soviet Union. In all countries, nominal, conditional, and custodial sanctions are implemented by those courts having juvenile jurisdiction. Recidivism rates are reasonably uniform among these countries. Japan also has the most elaborate classificatory system for distinguishing among various types of juvenile offenders.

Key Terms

British Crime Survey (BCS) (468)
Child Education and Training
    Homes (477)
Child Guidance Centers (476)
Classification homes (477)
Commission on Juvenile Affairs
    (481)
Comparative juvenile justice system
    (467)
Comrades' courts (478)
Courts of appeal, criminal division
    (469)
Criminal Justice Act of 1948 (468)
Criminal Justice Act of 1988 (474)
Criminal Law Act of 1967 (468)
Cross-cultural juvenile justice sys-
    tem (467)
Crown courts (468)
Divisional courts (469)
Druzhiny (479)
Duty solicitors (468)
Family Courts (475)

High courts (475)
Hooliganism (466)
House of Lords (469)
Hybrid offenses (468)
Indictable offenses (468)
Judicature Acts of 1873 and 1875
    (468)
Juvenile adult (470)
Juvenile Training Schools (477)
Lawbreaking children (475)
Magistrate's courts (468)
People's courts (466)
Pre-offense juveniles (475)
Procurator (479)
Solicitors (473)
Stare decicis (469)
Summary Courts (475)
Summary offenses (468)
Supreme Court of Japan (475)
Voir dire (469)
Young persons (470)

Questions for Review

1. What is meant by comparative juvenile justice? What are some of its primary functions and contributions? Is it the same thing as the cross-cultural study of juvenile justice systems?
2. What is the influence of access to firearms in the countries discussed here and the types of crimes committed by juveniles and others?
3. What is the *British Crime Survey?* When did Great Britain begin to keep official records of crime activity?
4. Distinguish between summary, indictable, and hybrid offenses

as specified under English law. Give examples of each.
5. Are juveniles in Great Britain entitled to an attorney if accused of a crime? Briefly describe the process of conducting cases against juveniles.
6. What is the role of juvenile judges in British juvenile courts?
7. What are three types of British correctional facilities that may be used for detaining juveniles? Differentiate among them.
8. How does the rate of juvenile delinquency in Japan compare with that of other industrialized countries?

9. Distinguish among three different kinds of juvenile offenders in Japan.
10. What are two primary detention options that may be exercised by Japanese Family Court judges?
11. What are the functions of classification homes in Japan?
12. How is crime defined in the Soviet Union? Are there specific juvenile courts in the Soviet Union? Describe briefly the process by which cases are undertaken against juvenile offenders.
13. What is hooliganism? What are some of the different kinds of offenses that might be included under hooliganism?
14. What is the juvenile offender typology described by Minkovsky? Briefly describe juveniles that might fit these categorizations.
15. What are the ages of accountability for Great Britain, the Soviet Union, and Japan respectively? Which of these countries uses capital punishment? What are the age minimums for such a penalty?

Suggested Readings

COLE, GEORGE F., STANISLAW J. FRANKOWSKI, and MARC G. GERTZ (EDS.) (1987). *Major Criminal Justice Systems.* Newbury Park, CA; Sage.

TERRILL, RICHARD J. (1984). *World Criminal Justice Systems: A Survey.* Cincinnati, OH: Anderson.

WESTERMANN, TED D., and JAMES W. BURFEIND (1991). *Crime and Justice in Two Societies: Japan and the United States.* Pacific Grove, CA: Brooks/Cole.

CHAPTER 15

The Future of the Juvenile Justice System

Introduction

This chapter summarizes several of the major trends that are occurring throughout the juvenile justice system. It is apparent that the juvenile justice system is being reformed extensively, and that proponents and opponents of reform are offering compelling arguments to further their respective interests. The major division among professionals is in how juvenile offenders ought to be viewed and treated. Two major camps can be identified. These camps are affiliated with rehabilitation and justice respectively. Those promoting the rehabilitative function of the juvenile justice system tend to favor a perpetuation of the original doctrine of *parens patriae* that influenced juvenile courts and juvenile processing for so many decades. Those promoting the justice interest believe that juveniles should be held increasingly accountable for their actions and should accept responsibility for the injuries and financial losses they cause others. Currently, the general trend is toward vesting youths with additional responsibilities and increasing their accountability to victims and to society generally.

The chapter organization is as follows. First, a review of basic philosophical changes within the juvenile justice system will be presented. These changes have occurred gradually, although U.S. Supreme Court decisions have facilitated changes in selected areas of juvenile rights more rapidly than in other areas of the juvenile justice system. Second, several important trends will be described relating to law enforcement and the changing nature of police officer–juvenile interactions. Third, major trends will be described that seem to be affecting prosecutorial and judicial decision making, as increasing numbers of juvenile offenders enter the juvenile justice system for processing. Fourth, the rapidly developing area of community-based corrections and intermediate punishments will be examined, and several important trends will be described. Finally, juvenile corrections will be examined. A number of important developments have been observed relative to the organization and operation of juvenile correctional facilities in most states. A concluding note about the future of juvenile justice will be made.

The Juvenile Justice System in a Time of Change

The twentieth century has witnessed major changes in the organization and operation of American courts. Federal and state courts have been subjected to continuing efforts to reform them. The last several decades have been characterized by numerous reforms throughout the juvenile justice system. These reforms have touched virtually every facet of this system, including law enforcement, prosecution and the courts, diversion, probation, intermediate punishments, and juvenile corrections, including juvenile parole and after-care. The general nature of these reforms has been to place more emphasis on "just deserts" and justice, and on implementing a "get tough" policy nationwide against what many citizens believe to be a rising tide of violent juvenile crime. Several by-products of this "get tough" policy have been more severe sentencing policies by juvenile judges, greater use of secure detention for the more serious and chronic juvenile offenders, and greater use of juvenile transfers to criminal courts where potentially harsher penalties can be exacted.

Since the mid-1960s, juveniles have gained substantial legal rights almost equal to those enjoyed by adults charged with crimes. While in most states, a unified court system is still a remote possibility that may or may not occur in the future, it is significant that juvenile courts have taken on more and more of the characteristics of criminal courts. These characteristics include an adversarial system, a higher standard of proof with regard to guilt or innocence, and greater formality relating to evidentiary matters.

Some experts have reason to suspect that what is occurring within the juvenile justice system is paralleling certain developments that have taken place within the criminal justice system. These developments include an overwhelming increase in the numbers of criminal court cases in recent years. In many instances, prosecutors and judges have been forced to prioritize cases according to their seriousness, and to reduce the amount of court time allocated to the more serious remaining cases. Plea bargaining has historically been used to resolve many cases and obtain convictions through negotiations in sentencing decisions, and the prospect is that plea bargaining will continue to be used with even greater frequency in future years. Diversion and alternative dispute resolution offer preconviction relief to many criminal defendants, many of whom are first offenders with no criminal history. Those who are convicted of crimes often serve no jail or prison time, since probationary options are offered to them on a conditional basis. California and several other states with extensive prison overcrowding place large numbers of more serious offenders on probation annually. Over 70 percent of all convicted felons in California, for example, are placed on probation annually, although there is a 65 percent recidivism rate among these probationers. Other schemes are invoked to cope with the crisis of overcrowding, including greater allocations of "good time" credit that may lead to early release. Greater leniency in parole decision making also provides a safety valve for chronic prison overcrowding.

The juvenile justice system is similar to the criminal justice system, particularly with regard to the large numbers of juvenile offenders who enter the system annually for processing. Many juvenile secure facilities are overcrowded, and juvenile court dockets are overloaded. Many of the programs available to adult offenders are now being used with juveniles as safety valves to decrease caseloads of courts and the sheer volume of youthful offenders who remain to be processed. Alternative dispute resolution, diversion, and various forms of probation are common sentences imposed upon youthful offenders. Some of these strategies are designed to prevent them from becoming labeled as "criminals" or "delinquents" by significant others.

Proportionately, the number of violent juvenile offenders is surprisingly low compared with serious adult offenders. However, the escalating incidence of violent youth gangs, drive-by shootings in many cities, and gang warfare conducted on a very sophisticated scale, with automatic and semiautomatic weaponry, have caused many citizens to believe that juveniles generally should receive harsher treatments than they currently receive from an apparently "too lenient" juvenile justice system. Those youths believed to pose the greatest risks to others have been targeted for special processing by juvenile courts. Automatic transfer provisions exist in many states, whereby youths charged with specific types of serious crimes are automatically transferred or waived to criminal courts. The intent of such transfers is to make it possible for more severe punishments to be imposed, beyond the limited sanctions within the jurisdiction of juvenile courts. However, evidence suggests that many transferrals of juveniles are no more than cosmetic changes designed to give the appearance that "get tough" measures have been implemented in certain jurisdictions. Furthermore, many transferred youths have their cases dropped by criminal court prosecutors, and many other juveniles are able to negotiate extremely favorable options through plea bargaining. Suffice it to say that the increased use of transfers has not been fully successful in achieving the intended aims.

Almost every jurisdiction currently has habitual offender statutes applicable to the more serious adult offenders. Life sentences are often standard provisions of such statutes. On the surface, at least, life sentencing provisions seem harsh and reflect tough penalties to be exacted from the most serious adult recidivists. However, such sentences of life imprisonment are rarely imposed, even where clear evidence exists that convicted offenders are habitual offenders. The habitual offender statute is used more often as a bargaining tool to coerce guilty pleas from criminal defendants—that is, the prosecution threatens to prosecute on habitual offender charges if defendants do not plead guilty to lesser included offenses. This type of coercion is legitimized and is not deemed coercive by the U.S. Supreme Court, since it is possible for prosecutors to bring habitual offender charges against these defendants anyway. Thus, prosecutors are not threatening to invent new charges against defendants, but rather, they are merely indicating the potential for bringing charges that are supported by clear and convincing evidence.

Despite these "get tough" policies within the criminal justice system, there is a propensity among criminal court judges to impose various nonincarcerative intermediate punishments on convicted offenders, including electronic monitoring, home confinement, intensive supervised probation, or assignment to some community-based correctional agency for management. Therefore, the "get tough" strategy has created the optimum conditions for less stringent treatment for adult offenders, as correctional professionals continually seek better ways to manage growing numbers of nonincarcerated offenders.

Applying a similar "get tough" policy toward juveniles does not seem to be targeting the most serious juvenile offenders for transfer to criminal courts. Many chronic juvenile offenders are petty property offenders, and juvenile court judges often use transfers as a means of ridding their courts of these youthful nuisances. Once these offenders are transferred to criminal courts, the nature of their chronicity is seen in a much different light, particularly when contrasted with more serious adult offenders. In many instances, youthfulness functions as a mitigating factor to lessen the severity of sentences judges might impose.

Another logistical problem is what to do with youths who deserve to be detained in long-term detention facilities. Often, there is little or no space available in juvenile detention to accommodate such youths. Faced with chronic overcrowding, juvenile court judges tend to impose similar intermediate punishments upon adjudicated youths rather than confine them for any lengthy incarcerative period. But such intermediate punishments assume that sufficient community-based agencies and organizations exist in these jurisdictions to accommodate the growing numbers of those adjudicated. Some jurisdictions are simply overworked and understaffed. Also, many intermediate punishments programs are only in experimental stages in limited numbers of communities. Thus, not all of the state-of-the-correctional-art options exist in every juvenile court jurisdiction. With limited options and resources, juvenile judges are often compelled to be lenient. Thus, the juvenile justice system is often wrongly blamed for apparent leniency, when no other course of sanctioning action is available to the decision makers.

A critic of juvenile court reform, Ted Rubin (1989:135–136), has frequently argued in favor of juvenile court retention of jurisdiction over both serious and nonserious juvenile offenders. He has suggested several alternatives to incarceration as means of retaining juvenile court control over errant youths. These alternatives include:

1. Intensive probation supervision.
2. Expanded work programs.
3. Special schooling programs.
4. Full-day school and work programs.
5. School combined with adventure programs.
6. Short-term secure residential placements.
7. Specialized foster homes combined with alternative schools.
8. Long-term residential programs.

These particular dispositions following an adjudication of delinquency are intended to replace waivers of jurisdiction to criminal courts. Juvenile courts may continually reexamine particular programs to assess whether they are having the intended effect.

The President's Commission on Law Enforcement and the Administration of Justice (1967) originally held fairly high hopes for the juvenile court and how youths would be processed. The expectations of the Commission were that the courts would offer substantial rehabilitation and other treatment services to needy youths, and that agencies and organizations would be created to meet their needs effectively. But chronic juvenile offenders have impaired the attainment of these rehabilitative objectives. Some experts believe that juvenile courts, by exercising their rights to waive jurisdiction over certain juvenile offenders, are merely passing the buck to another jurisdiction. Rather, these critics argue, the juvenile courts ought to formulate alternative helping strategies to enhance a youth's rehabilitation. They hold that the juvenile justice system is fully capable of being modified to cope with most youthful offenders, and that both treatments and punishments may be administered according to a rational scheme of juvenile accountability and need.

One general change in juvenile offender processing and treatment has been to deinstitutionalize status offenders nationwide. Not all jurisdictions have fully implemented DSO, although substantial numbers of runaways, curfew violators, and truants are now diverted to agencies other than juvenile courts for treatment and assistance. There is no such thing as DSO for adult offenders, although decriminalization of various types of activities has been proposed. Decriminalization means simply to declare certain crimes to be noncrimes. For example, the State of Washington has considered proposals to legalize the possession of small quantities of marijuana and to remove the criminal label from those charged with possession. While no state has legalized marijuana possession at this writing, there are currently diverse standards among states about how much marijuana may be possessed to qualify for crimes of various levels of seriousness. In any case, the comparable phenomenon of DSO has served to dissociate juveniles from the formal trappings of juvenile courts. This achievement has successfully removed many status offenders from any criminal or delinquent taint. Nevertheless, there continue to be substantial numbers of long-term juvenile detainees in incarcerative facilities who are status offenders. DSO has not been 100 percent effective in isolating them from juvenile corrections.

It is interesting to note that the nature of juvenile offending has gradually changed. Drug trafficking has become increasingly prevalent, and alcohol and drug use among juveniles, especially among those youths involved in most crimes of violence, have tended to aggravate existing problems of youthful offender management. Juvenile offenders do not comprise a uniform category, and the diverse needs and problems of delinquent youths means that specialized agencies and organizations must be created to supervise them most effectively. Both private and public interests have risen to the challenge and created services to fill many of these needs. In the following sections, we will examine various trends that seem apparent and have received professional attention in the research literature.

A Summary of Juvenile Justice Trends

The trends discussed in this section relate to (1) *the legal rights of juveniles*, (2) *law enforcement*, (3) *the prosecution of juveniles and juvenile courts*, (4) *diversion, probation, and intermediate punishments*, and (5) *juvenile corrections and aftercare*.

Trends in the Legal Rights of Juveniles

1. *Further reforms in the area of making juvenile rights comparable to those enjoyed by adult offenders.* We will probably see U.S. Supreme Court decisions extending to juveniles the right to a jury trial where incarceration in secure detention facilities or even nonsecure facilities of six months or more may be imposed by juvenile judges. If this event occurs, juveniles will likely be entitled to other constitutional guarantees, including the right to a court-appointed attorney if the juvenile is indigent.

2. *Attaining constitutional rights commensurate with those of adult offenders.* Currently, there are no speedy trial provisions for juvenile offenders. The matter of bail for youths eligible for bail has not been decided. In future years, the U.S. Supreme Court will no doubt rule on these and other matters relating to juvenile rights. Neither juveniles nor adults are as yet constitutionally entitled to rehabilitation through juvenile and adult corrections. Since the U.S. Supreme Court has already decided this issue for adults, it is unlikely that an extension of juvenile rights will include a particular right denied adults. Nevertheless, juvenile courts will probably retain much of their treatment philosophy, while expanding the range of alternative punishments that might be imposed on youthful offenders.

BOX 15.1

Juvenile Highlights

Is teenage violence a bigger problem today than it was in the past? A poll by *Time* in June, 1989, found that 88 percent of those surveyed agreed, based upon a telephone survey of 506 adults. FBI reports showed that between 1983 and 1987, arrests of those under 18 for murder jumped by 22 percent, while aggravated assault arrests jumped by 18.6 percent for the same age category. Rape arrests of those under 18 between these years increased by 14.6 percent as well. This is made all the more dramatic by the fact that there has been a 2 percent decline in the total number of teenagers in the United States since 1983.

Disturbing many public officials is the fact that many of those arrested for violent crimes show little or no emotion or remorse. For instance, an 11-year-old joined a 15-year-old in Detroit in April, 1989, to rape a two-year-old girl. After abusing the two-year-old, they dumped her in a garbage dumpster. In Escondido, California, a 16-year-old girl and three teenaged boys went on an arson spree, setting fires that caused $1 million in damages. In April, 1988, a 16-year-old youth drove 150 miles from his home in Princeton, Kentucky, and shot to death a woman he didn't know. Known to his classmates as "Little Rambo," he allegedly said that he wanted to "get away and kill somebody." He did.

Some officials believe that easy access to weapons leads many juveniles to commit violent acts. Others believe that music, movies, television, and comic books trigger sado-masochistic violence. Together with drugs such as crack, known to cause anger and hallucinations, these influences may lead psychologically disturbed teens to kill others. Sometimes, the most cowardly and impotent gang members will be encouraged by others to kill, so that they may feel powerful and brave.

Although citizens are demanding more stringent punishments and stronger laws to combat the rising incidence of juvenile violence, some believe that parents are to blame and should be locked up themselves. Several states currently have laws that are aimed at punishing parents for the wrongdoing of their children. In California, for instance, Los Angeles police arrested a woman whose 15-year-old son had been charged with participating in the rape of a 12-year-old girl by a dozen street gang members. Under the new parental responsibility law, the mother could be fined as much as $2,500 and sentenced to one year in jail.

(Some factual information adapted from Anastasia Toufexis, "Our Violent Kids," *Time*, June 12, 1989, pp. 52–58.)

3. *Greater accountability and responsibility expected from juvenile offenders.* Some experts believe that the juvenile justice system has failed to achieve its deep-seated objectives, including the treatment and rehabilitation of youthful offenders. High rates of recidivism among growing numbers of violent offenders suggest policies that are geared toward vesting youths with greater responsibilities and accountability. Being given greater responsibilities is not necessarily equated with harsh punishment. Conditional punishments, such as victim restitution and community service, are counted as punitive. Thus, youths may be expected to take a more active role in making up for their crimes and other delinquent conduct relative to victims and any financial damage they may inflict.

Trends in Law Enforcement

1. *The deinstitutionalization of status offenses.* As we have seen, there is a general trend toward DSO as a means of diverting less serious offenders from the jurisdiction of juvenile courts. While not all jurisdictions have been equally responsive to DSO, it does seem to be working. This means less stigmatization and labeling through less association with the juvenile justice system. Juvenile courts will no longer have responsibility for dealing with runaways, incorrigibles, or truants.

2. *Greater law enforcement selectivity.* The State of Washington and various jurisdictions, such as St. Louis, Missouri, are past sites where the deinstitutionalization of status offenses has been implemented on a large scale. Police officer response to DSO has been mixed. We have seen that some officers resent being told whom they can and cannot arrest, and they perceive DSO as an unwanted challenge to their discretionary authority. Juvenile court judges in these and other jurisdictions where DSO has occurred seem to react similarly. The backlash is that many youthful status offenders are now caught up in the net-widening phenomenon, in which officers make arrests for juvenile behaviors previously defined as status offenses. Since it is difficult to question police officers' motives when they are making arrests of juvenile suspects on city streets late at night, we don't know for sure whether this is a deliberate attempt by these officers to circumvent the system and exercise their discretionary authority anyway. The likelihood is that they do attempt to circumvent the system. Thus, DSO may not be achieving its stated objectives in various jurisdictions, depending upon the actions of police officers and their diverse interactions with juveniles. Ideally, police officers will reserve their time for only the most serious offenders who are, indeed, violating the law. The argument is that there is enough crime and delinquency "out there" without police officers having to manufacture weak cases against status offenders or reinterpret their behaviors as delinquent conduct.

3. *Greater specialty units within law enforcement agencies devoted to juvenile matters.* More police departments and law enforcement agencies generally are

Delinquency prevention is a key aim of the juvenile justice system. Certain intervention programs involve teenage inmates of secure juvenile facilities who speak to students and acquaint them with the realities of confinement and the value of obeying the law. (© Bob Daemmrich/The Image Works)

establishing special units that deal with specific types of juvenile offenders. In Long Beach, California, for example, a special unit exists as a type of task force designed to combat delinquent gang activity. Long Beach has over 100 juvenile gangs of different races and ethnic affiliations, and the incidence of gang violence is high. Other units in this and other police departments have been developed primarily to engage juveniles and relate to them in ways consistent with prevailing juvenile codes. Thus, special units for juveniles may divert juveniles to various agencies for processing rather than bringing them into custody to a police station for temporary jailing.

4. *Greater attention to preventing short-term detention of juveniles with adult offenders after arrest.* It is generally agreed that juveniles should not be jailed, even temporarily, with adult offenders. Yet a large number of juveniles, even status offenders, are housed in jails with adults on temporary bases. These "temporary" periods may last as long as a week or more. The potential for sexual exploitation of these juveniles by adult inmates is great. However, it is sometimes difficult for police officers to determine a juvenile's age at the time he or she is arrested or brought into custody. Many communities lack specialized detention facilities to house juvenile offenders apart from adult arrestees. Community-based services and agencies can conceivably perform short-term detention functions, and it is likely that we will see organizations of this type emerging to fulfill these detention roles in future years.

Trends in the Prosecution of Juveniles and Juvenile Courts

The increasingly punitive nature of the juvenile justice system, evidenced by the "get tough" movement, has generated several noticeable changes in the ways juvenile offenders are perceived and treated. Some of these trends are summarized here:

1. *Greater use of transfers and waivers to adult criminal courts.* Although there is increasing use of waivers to shift more serious juvenile cases to criminal courts for presumably more serious processing, many less serious offenders are transferred to criminal court jurisdiction as well. Thus, transfers are not necessarily accomplishing what they were intended to do—namely, cause juvenile offenders to receive harsher punishments. In many jurisdictions, nonviolent, petty juvenile recidivists are being transferred, simply to get them away from juvenile judges who see them so frequently. When these offenders reach adult courts for processing, they blend in with less serious, garden-variety adult offenders and their cases are either dismissed or they are placed on probation rather than incarcerated.

2. *The juvenile court will become increasingly adversarial, in many respects paralleling the adult system.* Plea bargaining will occur increasingly, as prosecutors and defense attorneys negotiate the best deals for their juvenile clients. Juveniles in all states are entitled to the services of an attorney to represent them in any adjudication proceeding. However, we know that only about half of all juveniles currently exercise their right to an attorney. Part of the problem is that the families cannot afford an attorney's services, and juvenile courts are generally not permitted to provide public defenders for indigent juveniles. Another problem is public apathy about juvenile affairs. Many families may believe that the nonserious nature of offenses alleged against juvenile defendants does not warrant acquiring an attorney's services. Many parents continue to rely on the *parens patriae* goodwill of juvenile court judges to decide what is best for their children.

BOX 15.2

Juvenile Highlights

To what extent is easy access to firearms related to juvenile violence? Presently, the five cities in the United States with the highest murder rates are Washington, Detroit, Atlanta, New Orleans, and Dallas. Since 1987, Washington has experienced a 65.3 percent rise in yearly homicides, while Houston has experienced a 37.6 percent increase and New York has experienced an 11.7 percent increase.

The rapid rise in youth gangs and their increased involvement in drug trafficking have led to the use of more sophisticated weaponry such as AK-47 assault rifles and automatic pistols and rifles. Washington police recently instituted Operation Clean Sweep, a $6 million project designed to attack drug traffickers. Since it was begun in 1987, over 45,000 arrests have been made and the average sentences of drug traffickers in Washington courts have doubled.

Robert Trojanowicz, director of the School of Criminal Justice at Michigan State University, has said that "there is no question that if they[drug traffickers] didn't have the guns, there would be less violence." It has been found that in most drug-related killings, the murderers know their victims. Turf battles are commonplace and result in numerous gang deaths. Most of these deaths are attributable to the possession of firearms.

One of the unfortunate by-products of gang drug trafficking and the widespread use of firearms is that "mushrooms" occur. Mushrooms are innocent bystanders who are killed during gang shootouts. One "mushroom" was 12-year-old Tiffany Moore of Boston's Roxbury ghetto. Her mother sent her to South Carolina to get her away from the gang-related violence of Boston. But on a weekend visit back in Boston, Tiffany was shot to death as she sat on a mailbox talking with friends. A passing car of teenage gang members sprayed the neighborhood with bullets in an apparent retaliation for a soured drug deal. Regulation of firearms possession has been proposed, but criminals and delinquents will acquire firearms by illegal means. In Miami, four people rammed their car through the front window of a closed gun shop and drove off with $80,000 worth of stolen firearms, including several Uzi machine guns and Chinese-made AK-47 assault rifles.

(Some factual information adapted from Larry Martz, Mark Miller, Sue Hutchison, and Tony Emerson, "A Tide of Drug Killing," *Newsweek,* January 16, 1989, pp. 44–45.)

3. *Greater formality of juvenile courts.* Greater rights extended to juvenile offenders mean that juvenile court proceedings are increasingly bureaucratic in their operations. There is much to be said in favor of informally conducted proceedings, in which judges can tailor their sentences to fit particular juveniles. But these scenarios suggest inequality of treatment, regardless of the good intentions of the particular juvenile judge and the perceived fairness of sentences imposed. Different sentences for similar offenses mean sentencing disparities, and sentencing disparities are generally considered discriminatory. In future years, there will probably be less sentencing disparity as we see juvenile courts moving to a justice model of operation in which sentences are offense-based.

4. *The increased use of transfers of juveniles to criminal courts will continue, especially for serious offenses including rape, robbery, and murder.* Already, several states, including New York and Illinois, have automatic transfer statutes that result in automatic certification of juveniles in certain offender categories to the jurisdiction of criminal courts. Juveniles transferred under these automatic waiver statutes may demand a hearing to contest the transfer. In this instance, the hearing becomes a "reverse waiver hearing" in effect, since there are certain advantages to having one's case heard by the juvenile court compared with the criminal court. It is likely that the transfer process in future years will become increasingly selective. Currently, chronic nonserious property offenders are frequently transferred to criminal court. Thus, juvenile judges get rid of troublesome juveniles, but these offenders have their cases dismissed by criminal court prosecutors or judges later.

5. *Greater concern for juvenile rights.* Finally, beginning with the *Kent* case in 1966, juveniles are increasingly successful in securing favorable U.S. Supreme Court decisions affecting their rights to equal protection and due process under the law. While juveniles do not currently enjoy the full legal status of adult citizens of the United States, they have made remarkable gains in the rights they have achieved thus far. Perhaps it is wise for juvenile courts to maintain civil jurisdiction over offenders without full adult constitutional protections. With full adult status, juveniles would stand to lose many privileges they currently enjoy. When juveniles reach their majority, their records as juveniles are closed, for the most part, and they have a chance to begin fresh lives. Furthermore, even though they may be classified as delinquents through formal adjudicatory proceedings, they are not criminals. If they were to achieve the full range of constitutional rights available to adults, it is likely they would lose this noncriminal status as well.

6. *More stringent standards relating to the admissibility of evidence in juvenile proceedings.* As juvenile adjudicatory proceedings becoming more formalized, prevailing rules by which evidence is introduced will become more stringent. The decisions rendered by juvenile court judges may have long-term consequences on the life chances of specific juvenile offenders, and they may require evidentiary standards commensurate with those applied to criminal cases by federal and state rules of evidence and criminal procedure.

7. *Greater use of plea bargaining.* Plea bargaining is useful in obtaining convictions in over 90 percent of criminal cases. Plea bargaining is conducted in some juvenile court jurisdictions, although precise figures on the extent of its use nationwide are currently unavailable. Since juvenile records are sealed once juveniles reach the age of their majority, it is difficult for researchers to investigate this phenomenon accurately. However, many features of the criminal justice system are encroaching upon the juvenile justice system, and plea bargaining is no exception. It is likely that in future years, plea bargaining will be useful in the majority of delinquency adjudications. Since plea bargaining for criminal offenders often results in probation or some nonincarcerative alternative, it is reasonable to expect that plea bargaining with juveniles will result in similar offender dispositions.

This list is certainly not exhaustive, but it does highlight some of the more important trends and developments affecting juveniles and their processing through the juvenile justice system. There are many parallels between the adult and juvenile correctional systems, and programs and program goals often overlap or are duplicated in various jurisdictions. J. Edgar Hoover was a firm believer in attacking delinquency early, because he believed that more serious crimes tended to follow delinquent careers. While we have seen that offense escalation does not occur consistently for most juvenile offenders in those jurisdictions investigated, it would seem that Hoover's rehabilitative concerns and emphases have not been abandoned entirely by juvenile corrections.

Trends in Juvenile Diversion, Probation, and Intermediate Punishments

1. *Greater use of diversion.* Diversion is being used increasingly as a preadjudicatory option by judges and prosecutors. Diversion results in keeping offenders out of the system and assists them in avoiding identification with it. This trend will coincide with increased privatization of corrections, especially community-based probation agencies and services. One diversionary option is alternative dispute resolution, or ADR. ADR is used with increasing frequency as a way of constructively bypassing the juvenile court. Believing that many youths do not require the formal adjudication such courts provide, experts feel that youths will profit more from having their cases disposed of through informal arbiters. These arbiters are often lawyers or social caseworkers who decide punishment or damages to be assessed. Usually, ADR results in a compromise between the victim and the youthful offender, and the punishment is often associated with restitution or some form of victim compensation. Both parties often consent to the punishment levied in lieu of more formal processing by juvenile judges.

2. *Greater innovations in juvenile offender management, including electronic monitoring and/or home confinement.* Although electronic monitoring is only in its infancy as a supervisory medium for both adult and juvenile offenders, it has unlimited potential as an offender management tool, especially as probation and parole officer caseloads escalate. The use of the offender's home as an incarcerative setting is not necessarily a novel idea, although it is increasingly attractive as a way of managing low-risk offenders with little likelihood of recidivating. Often, home confinement is coupled with electronic monitoring. Together, these two offender management alternatives offer a glimpse of what probation and parole supervision might be like in the future.

3. *Greater emphasis on victim restitution and community service.* There is a significant movement in juvenile courts throughout the United States to order adjudicated delinquents to repay victims for their losses through restitution and/or the performance of personal services (Rubin, 1986; Staples, 1986). There is considerable support in the research literature for the idea that obligating juvenile offenders to make restitution to victims significantly reduces their recidivism (Fishbein *et al.,* 1984; Seljan, 1983; Schneider, 1985; Schneider and Schneider, 1985).

4. *Lower probation officer–juvenile client ratios and more intensive supervised probation.* Although limited probation and parole budgets prevent many jurisdictions from lowering the caseloads of POs who supervise juvenile offenders, in many jurisdictions caseloads have been reduced to promote greater contact between juveniles and their POs. This means greater supervisory and monitoring opportunities. But it also means greater opportunities for POs to offer true constructive assistance on a one-to-one basis to juveniles in need of more personalized treatment.

5. *The development of more community-based programs.* As detention center and industrial school overcrowding becomes more problematic in various jurisdictions, nonincarcerative alternatives become more attractive to legislators as well as to juvenile corrections officials. These community-based programs are either publicly or privately operated, but they are seen as a viable means of alleviating "industrial" school overcrowding. Also, they permit juveniles greater opportunities to take advantage of community resources and helping agencies.

7. *Greater reliance on private managership of intermediate punishment programs.* The privatization of intermediate punishments, including many community-based correctional agencies and programs, offers more economical means of managing offenders. Public programs are often adversely affected by red tape and superfluous expenditures. Privatization offers a more economical means of managing offenders, by transforming facilities into

profit-making institutions. The encroachment of private interests in corrections is increasing. There are no constitutional prohibitions against private interests managing those who have committed offenses against the state. Various experts counsel that offender rights may be violated through privatization; however, no substantive basis for such charges exists.

Trends in Correctional Detention and Juvenile Offender Aftercare

The following conclusions may tentatively be made about the future of juvenile correctional detention and aftercare in the United States:

1. *More minimum-security detention facilities will be established.* In recent years, states such as Florida have created several minimum-security facilities which encourage juveniles to accept more responsibilities and develop more positive self-images. Confinement behind barbed wire and prison walls is not particularly effective at rehabilitating youths. Less threatening, minimum-security surroundings are viewed as more therapeutic by many corrections officials and by the public.

2. *A larger portion of juvenile corrections will be administered by private interests.* The private sector is experiencing the greatest gains in juvenile corrections, although adult correctional programs are also feeling the encroachment of private organizations and agencies. A critical factor is that there are growing numbers of adult and juvenile offenders to manage and that public correctional agencies have been slow to add staff adequate to deal with these offender increases.

3. *Juveniles will eventually be excluded entirely from adult facilities, including jails and lockups, even on temporary bases.* Civil rights and other interest groups are attempting to see that all states remove juveniles from adult detention facilities. While this may work hardships on some isolated jurisdictions where services are not extensive, juvenile rights changes will mandate that all jurisdictions eventually comply.

4. *Detention facilities for juveniles will increasingly emphasize vocational, educational, and employment-related services in order to assist youths in obtaining jobs when released.* This will be a general shift from a custodial to a rehabilitative and reintegrative detention philosophy on a national scale. Although public and private correctional facilities are not mandated to provide for the rehabilitation of their inmates, a moral responsibility is sensed by most organizations to provide some degree of rehabilitation. If correctional institutions can show greater numbers of "success" experiences by producing larger numbers of rehabilitated or reintegrated clientele, then such institutions may attract more funding from both the public and private sectors for their perpetuation.

5. *There will be greater consistency among states in future years concerning the definition of juveniles and greater systematization regarding their treatment and processing.* The Model Penal Code devised by the American Law Institute and other organizations is an attempt to create a high degree of uniformity in laws and regulations among the states. A similar movement is underway regarding juvenile matters.

The Future of the Juvenile Justice System

It is difficult to forecast accurately the future of the juvenile justice system. The U.S. Supreme Court has vested juveniles in all states with certain rights, and it is anticipated that more rights will be extended to them in future years. One likelihood is that juveniles will eventually enjoy *all* rights currently enjoyed by adults who are charged with criminal offenses. This doesn't mean that the juvenile justice system will disappear. A full elaboration of adult rights for juveniles will cause the juvenile justice system to emulate certain features of the criminal justice system, but juvenile court jurisdictional limits will probably continue as they presently exist.

Juvenile courts will probably eventually have to utilize the full range of procedural safeguards that exist to protect adult criminal defendants. These safeguards relate to evidentiary standards, testimony of witnesses, cross-examination procedures, selection of jurors, and other procedural matters. Such safeguards seem to be a natural consequence of a juvenile's right to due process, although the U.S. Supreme Court has earlier proclaimed that the due process rights of juvenile offenders are minimal. It remains to be seen how future courts will interpret the meaning of "minimal" due process for juveniles.

Currently, juvenile court judges continue to enjoy rather wide latitude in adjudicating juvenile cases. Their decisions about juveniles are seldom questioned, and few mechanisms are in place to challenge their decisions if parents or defense attorneys disagree with them. There is an appeals process that may be invoked, similar to the one invoked by *Gault* when the constitutionality of his sentence was challenged in the 1960s. However, the U.S. Supreme Court is not interested in differences of opinion between juvenile court judges and affected juveniles about the sentences imposed. Serious issues relating to judicial decision making, especially issues of a constitutionally significant nature, will stand the greatest chance of reaching the U.S. Supreme Court.

Significant changes in juvenile court procedures will most likely emanate from state legislatures. These bodies are vested with powers to reconcile disparities in both the criminal and juvenile justice systems of their jurisdictions. Changes will occur slowly, and it is likely that it will be many years before juveniles in all states can be assured of even-handed treatment by juvenile court judges. If the criminal court systems in the various states are any indication of improvements in the equitable treatment of criminal defendants through recent justice reforms, then the prospects for full juvenile justice reform are bleak.

For example, the U.S. Sentencing Guidelines were implemented in December, 1987, to remedy the sentencing disparity among federal district judges. However, sentencing disparities in federal courts continue to occur, despite the fact that guidelines are in place to eliminate such disparities. The main problem is that some latitude has been provided these judges within which to vary offender sentences. Even though guidelines exist, departures from these guidelines may be invoked, provided judges state their reasons for departure in writing at the time of sentencing federal offenders. It is unlikely that higher courts will overturn many of the decisions of federal district judges in any of the sentences they impose, regardless of the nature and degree of sentencing departures.

Similarly, if more equitable standards were suddenly imposed for all juvenile judges to observe, they would probably continue to have some interpretive latitude within which to exercise personal discretion. Generally, the exercise of personal discretion is arbitrary and inherently discriminatory. Yet, there is little that can be done at present to force judges into a particular mold that would obligate them to decide all cases of a particular type in a particular way.

Strong sentiments exist among juvenile justice professionals and judges against such rubber-stamp justice. While uniformity in sentencing is strictly equitable, it removes individuality from juvenile court sentencing policy. And individuality in sentencing is the bedrock of the original and traditional concept of *parens patriae* embraced by juvenile courts. Such individuality enables judges to decide cases and impose sentences according to what they believe to be the best interests of affected juveniles. For many juveniles, these sentences might be less harsh than the sentences that might be imposed under more equitable, guidelines-based plans. Thus, many judges and juvenile justice experts can argue in favor of more flexible sentencing discretion, regardless of its inherently discriminatory aspects. At the same time, many affected juveniles who receive harsher sentences than others favor a more equitable sentencing scheme.

The big question, of course, is how can juveniles receive the best dispositions that juvenile courts have to offer? Can juvenile courts be equitable in their treatment of all juvenile offenders? Can they practice fairness and assure one aggregate of citizens that the sentences they impose will have positive, treatment-oriented implications? Can they practice fairness and assure another aggregate of citizens that the sentences they impose will have positive, punishment-centered, offender accountability implications? Can both punishment/accountability interests and treatment/rehabilitation interests be effectively combined in the different stages of the juvenile justice process?

Among certain juvenile justice experts, there is a fear that the original concept of the juvenile court will be lost as the result of massive juvenile

Shock probation is used increasingly as a constructive punishment by juvenile court judges. Youths suffer confinement for periods up to 130 days, after which they serve the remainder of their terms on probation. Some of these graduates of New York's Shock Incarceration Camp Program will probably reoffend, but others will have profited from the incarcerative experience. (© Michael J. Okoniewski/The Image Works)

justice reforms. At the same time, there are those experts who look forward to these reforms and their due process results.

It might be a good idea to step back and examine briefly why we are currently in our present dilemma of finding it difficult to define the ultimate goals and objectives of the juvenile justice system. Scanning daily newspapers and viewing televised reports of juvenile violence that occurs uninterrupted on a national scale will alert us to the fact that at least some juveniles are out of control and that effective mechanisms do not presently exist to contain them. Many of these offenders are recidivists. It is not unusual to see a juvenile with lengthy prior adjudications for serious offenses being given yet another probationary sentence by a juvenile court judge. Judges themselves know that there is an element of turnstile justice taking place in their system, although they can do little about it. Current conditions of overcrowding in almost all secure and nonsecure juvenile detention facilities and community-based intermediate punishment programs make it difficult to find places for all adjudicated offenders, even the worst ones. We have seen that judges often don't take detention action against juveniles until their fifth or sixth adjudicatory appearances. It is not the fault of the juvenile judges. Rather, it is the fault of government that underfunds and understaffs the most important component of the juvenile justice system, juvenile corrections. This observation is also true of adult corrections.

Improving the staffing capabilities of secure and nonsecure facilities and making more spaces available for juvenile offenders does not mean necessarily that we are going to incarcerate more of them and for longer periods. We know that for many youthful offenders, incarceration is truly a last resort. It means that the services will exist to deal more effectively with more of their needs than at present. There is a hard-core offender aggregate existing out there that deserves long-term incarceration. These juveniles need to be targeted and managed accordingly. For some juveniles, their situations are admittedly hopeless, and long-term detention is the only answer for them. Their release from the juvenile justice system will usually signify their entry into the adult criminal world. Many of these detainees will become our future criminals and fill spaces in our jails and prisons. However, this does not mean that we should write them off and treat them like the "baddest of the bad" adult federal offenders at Marion, Illinois, where the federal government operates its maxi-maxi penitentiary on a "rehabilitation-is-irrelevant" basis. Even some of the worst juvenile offenders may be helped, provided that the facilities and staff and services exist to make a difference in their lives.

It seems to many critics of the juvenile justice system that the system has somehow failed to deliver what it promised many years ago. In the days of a strong treatment/rehabilitation orientation, it was believed that juveniles needed someone to care about them and see to their diverse needs. But the average citizen looks at the record of juvenile corrections and concludes that the results are substandard. Robert Martinson was skeptical of "helping" programs, because he saw so many persons abuse the systems that were trying to help them. Inmates would deliberately join group therapy and take educational courses for self-improvement, all the while knowing that this was what officials wanted to see. These inmates knew that their chances of "getting out" would be enhanced, provided that they could convince the parole boards and others that they truly had reformed or changed. They learned to manipulate the very systems that attempted to help them and rehabilitate them. Thus, many of these "changed" ex-cons emerged from confinement "unchanged," and recidivism figures escalated. For some reason or another, the various correctional systems have not been working. Or perhaps they have not been working the way they were originally designed to work.

There seems to be agreement among juvenile justice professionals and others that the concept of a juvenile justice system and juvenile court ought to be preserved or maintained. It is presently unclear how the juvenile justice system should gear itself up to meet the diverse needs of growing numbers of juvenile offenders, including more violent ones. Although violent juveniles are relatively few in number compared with juvenile property offenders, there is evidence of increasing juvenile violence. Further, the small core of violent juveniles apparently accounts for a disproportionately large share of criminal activity. Thus, some program of collective or selective incapacitation seems warranted for these special cases.

What is needed for these more serious offenders is some form of productive detention. The accountability issue must be resolved, and the juvenile justice system itself must have the capability of exerting a deterrent influence on juvenile offenders generally. The problem, it seems, is balancing these rehabilitative and justice interests. The highlights that we have presented from each of the major juvenile justice system components are reflective of existing trends and suggest directions in which the system may be heading. Efforts to make significant improvements within the juvenile justice system will need to be cooperative ventures, with both communities and public officials involved in achieving mutually agreed-on system goals.

Summary

The juvenile justice system is undergoing reforms at every stage of the process. Experts surmise that these reforms are due, in large part, to the perceived rise in juvenile crime, particularly violent crime. However, it is believed that violent juvenile offenders are proportionately few in number compared with other offender categories, including property crimes. Also, it is believed that the "get tough" movement apparent within the criminal justice system has filtered down to influence the juvenile justice system and the reforms that have occurred. Major problems plaguing the system include detention facility overcrowding, crowded court dockets, and insufficient staffing.

Most juvenile offenders are petty offenders. Nevertheless, their chronicity or rate of reoffending is often high. Detention facilities house mostly youths who are nonviolent but persistent or chronic offenders. Experts are divided about the goals the juvenile justice system should manifest and actively pursue. One camp suggests that traditional treatment-oriented objectives should be sought within the spirit of *parens patriae*. Other interests believe that the juvenile justice system should make provisions for maximizing youthful offender accountability. Thus, there has been a noticeable increase in community-based programs which emphasize restitution, community service, victim compensation, and the payment of fines as punishments. Conditional punishments also include participating in educational programs and individual or group therapy designed to improve self-image and social skills.

Major trends in the legal rights of juveniles include a move toward obtaining rights more in keeping with those enjoyed by adult criminals whenever they are charged with crimes, and toward developing programs and punishments that enhance personal accountability for wrongdoing. In law enforcement, the deinstitutionalization of status offenses has effectively removed many status offenders from juvenile court jurisdiction. Theoretically, this has freed the system to deal with a more serious offender class, although in actual practice, many status offenders have continued to be targeted by juvenile courts through net-widening. Accordingly, there is greater law enforcement selectivity, in which police officers exercise discretion to direct their energies toward only the most serious juvenile offenders. Police departments have established specific departments devoted exclusively to handing juvenile matters. Strong interest has been expressed in removing juveniles from short-term detention in adult jails or lockups.

In prosecution and the courts, there has been a trend toward greater use of transfers of juveniles to criminal court jurisdiction. Also, juvenile courts have become increasingly adversarial, with defense attorneys ensuring the protection of juveniles accused of serious offenses by promoting their rights to equitable treatment by judges and prosecutors. This change has generated greater juvenile court formality and the application of more stringent standards governing court procedures. Greater use of plea bargaining is anticipated as more juveniles enter the system for processing annually. Intermediate punishment trends include greater use of diversion, and conditional probationary sentences including electronic monitoring and home confinement. Greater emphasis on victim compensation and restitution has been observed, and the intensity of supervision of juveniles has increased through lower probation officer–client ratios. Private interests have increasingly been relied on to provide services for juveniles that public funds have not supported fully. The strong reintegrative policy of juvenile justice is leading to the establishment of more community-based correctional services.

More minimum-security correctional facilities are under construction, and private interests will manage such facilities to an increasing degree. Eventually, all juveniles will be diverted to exclusively juvenile facilities for short-term detention, and these facilities will provide educational, vocational, and employment-related services to assist youths in improving their employment chances. Greater consistency among the states in future years will be observed relating to juvenile offender laws and their application. It is difficult to forecast the future of the juvenile justice system, but it is clear that this future is dependent upon a cooperativeness between the public and private sectors to provide a greater range of services for youths with diverse needs and problems.

Questions for Review

1. What are some of the general philosophical contrasts that inhibit juvenile justice reforms?
2. What is the general nature of the population of juveniles currently in detention in the United States? Are most of these offenders hard-core violent offenders? Why or why not?
3. How does facility overcrowding influence a judge's options in sentencing juvenile offenders?
4. What are some programs that increase juvenile offender accountability? How do these pro-

grams function to bring about greater accountability? Explain.

5. What are three major changes that have been observed in law enforcement practices related to juvenile offenders?

6. How do police, prosecutors, and judges react to the deinstitutionalization of status offenses?

7. How has the deinstitutionalization of status offenses changed the nature of juvenile defendants entering juvenile courts? Explain.

8. What actions have many police departments taken to improve their law enforcement capabilities relating to juvenile offenders?

9. Is the growth of the adversarial system in juvenile justice always beneficial to juveniles? In what senses would an adversarial system not be beneficial to them? Discuss.

10. How can the formalization of juvenile court proceedings have both positive and negative consequences for juvenile adjudications?

11. What is projected regarding the use of plea bargaining in juvenile justice? What are some of the arguments for and against using plea bargaining to resolve juvenile cases?

12. What is projected regarding the use of alternative dispute resolution in the juvenile justice system in future years?

13. In what senses are victim compensation and community service associated with enhancing offender accountability?

14. What role will be played by private interests in juvenile correctional agencies of the future?

15. How can the juvenile justice system provide individualized justice and still remain true to its function of ensuring juveniles of their rights to due process and justice? Discuss.

Suggested Readings

BARTOLLAS, CLEMENS (1990). *Juvenile Delinquency* (2nd ed.). New York; Macmillan.

EMPEY, LaMAR T., and MARK C. STAFFORD (1991). *American Delinquency: Its Meaning and Construction* (3rd ed.). Belmont, CA: Wadsworth.

HAWKINS, J. D., and J. G. WEIS (1980). *The Social Developmental Model: An Integrated Approach to Delinquency Prevention.* Seattle; Center for Law and Justice, University of Washington.

HOLTEN, N. GARY, and LAWSON L. LAMAR (1991). *The Criminal Courts: Structure, Personnel, and Process.* New York: McGraw-Hill.

REGOLI, ROBERT, and JOHN HEWITT. (1991). *Delinquency in Society: A Child-centered Approach.* New York: McGraw-Hill.

SCHOOL OF JUSTICE STUDIES (1990). *New Directions in the Study of Justice, Law, and Social Control.* New York: Plenum.

TRACY, PAUL E., MARVIN E. WOLFGANG, and ROBERT M. FIGLIO (1990). *Delinquency Careers in Two Birth Cohorts.* New York: Plenum.

Glossary

About Face Program Georgia boot camp program; *see also* Boot camps.

Actions at Law Court litigation in which one party opposes another for a wrong allegedly committed, for the protection of a right, or for the prevention of a wrong.

Act To Regulate the Treatment and Control of Dependent, Neglected, and Delinquent Children Delinquency Act passed by Illinois legislature in 1899; established first juvenile court in the United States.

Actuarial Prediction Prediction of future inmate behavior based on a class of offenders similar to those considered for parole.

Actus Reus Criminal or overt act.

Addams, Jane Originated Hull House in Chicago during 1880s; assisted wayward and homeless youths.

Adjudication A judgment or action on a petition filed with the juvenile court by others.

Adjudication Hearing Formal proceeding involving a prosecuting attorney and a defense attorney in which evidence is presented and the juvenile's guilt or innocence is determined by the juvenile judge; about one fifth of all jurisdictions permit jury trials for juveniles under certain cir-

cumstances, with or without judicial approval.

Adjustments Informal handling of juvenile cases by intake officers, without formal court action.

Adolescent Courts Informal courts operated in New York City and elsewhere for disposing of less serious juvenile offender cases informally, usually by immediate corrective penalties, such as victim compensation or services.

Aftercare General term to describe a wide variety of programs and services available to both adult and juvenile probationers and parolees; includes halfway houses, psychological counseling services, community-based correctional agencies, employment assistance, and medical treatment for offenders or ex-offenders.

Aggravated Assault An unlawful attack by one person on another for the purpose of inflicting severe or aggravated bodily injury.

Aggravating Circumstances Factors that may enhance the severity of one's sentence; these include brutality of act, whether serious bodily injury or death occurred to a victim during crime commission, and whether offender was on probation or parole when crime was committed.

AIDS Acquired Immune Deficiency Syndrome, a deadly virus often spread through sexual contact or use of unclean needles for illegal drug use.

Alaska Judicial Council Public council that evaluates judicial sentencing practices and assesses all matters pertinent to the Alaska judiciary.

Allegheny Academy Pennsylvania probation program with general aim of changing the negative behavior of offenders; targeted for those juvenile offenders who have failed in other, traditional probation programs in Pennsylvania.

Alternative Care Cases Borderline cases where judges may sentence offenders to either incarceration or probation subject to compliance with various conditions.

Alternative Dispute Resolution (ADR) Procedure whereby a criminal case is redefined as a civil one and the case is decided by an impartial arbiter, with both parties agreeing to amicable settlement, usually reserved for minor offenses; court-approved mediation programs where civilians are selected from community to help resolve minor delinquency, status offense, and abuse/neglect cases without formal judicial hearings.

Alternative Sentencing (also called *creative sentencing*) A procedure in which judge imposes sentence other than incarceration; often involves good works such as community service, restitution to victims, and other public service activity. *See also* Creative sentencing.

American Correctional Association Established in 1870 to disseminate information about correctional programs and correctional training; designed to foster professionalism throughout correctional community.

Amicus Curiae "Friend of the Court." The term refers to individuals or groups who are not parties to a particular case but who are permitted by the court to advise it regarding some matter of law that directly affects the case in question.

Anamnestic Prediction Prediction of inmate behavior according to past circumstances.

Anomie Theory Robert Merton's theory, alleging that some persons strive to achieve culturally approved goals, but adopt innovative, sometimes deviant, means to achieve these goals; anomie implies normlessness; innovators accept societal goals but reject institutionalized means to achieve them.

Appearance One's apparent socioeconomic status as indicated by one's clothing and general demeanor; unreliable criterion of socioeconomic status.

Army Model *See* Boot camps.

Arraignment Following booking, a critical stage of the criminal justice process wherein defendants are asked to enter a plea to criminal charges, a trial date is established, and a formal list of charges is provided.

Arrest Taking persons into custody and restraining them until they can be brought before court to answer the charges against them.

Arson Any willful or malicious burning or attempt to burn, with or without intent to defraud, a dwelling house, public building, motor vehicle, or aircraft, or the personal property of another.

Assembly-Line Justice Term applied to overworked, inadequately staffed court which is unsympathetic and unfair to criminal defendants; excessive delay in court action.

Assessment Centers Centers for selecting entry-level officers for correctional work. Assessment centers hire correctional officers and probation or parole officers.

Atavism Having animal-like or subhuman qualities.

Attendance Centers British community-based services that youths may be required to attend, usually for several hours a day, during the probationary term they serve; these attendance centers are similar to halfway houses for youthful offenders in the United States, and they provide a variety of services for their youthful clients.

Augustus, John Private citizen acknowledged as formulator of probation in U.S. in Boston, Massachusetts in 1841.

Automatic Transfer (Waiver) Laws Jurisdictional laws that provide for automatic waivers of juveniles to criminal court for processing; legislatively prescribed directives to transfer juveniles of specified ages who have

committed especially serious offenses to jurisdiction of criminal courts.

Avertable Recidivist Offender who would still have been in prison serving a sentence at a time when new offense was committed.

Backdooring Cases Practice by judges of sentencing borderline (low risk) offenders to incarceration with strong admonishment that they be encouraged to apply for intensive probation supervision programs.

Bail Surety provided by defendants or others to guarantee their subsequent appearance in court to face criminal charges; bail is available to anyone entitled to bail; bail is denied when suspects are considered dangerous or likely to flee. *See also* Preventive detention.

Bail Bond A written guarantee, often accompanied by money or other securities, that the person charged with an offense will remain within the court's jurisdiction to face trial at a time in the future.

Bailiff Court officer who has charge of maintaining order in the court while it is in session; bailiff is often placed in custody of jury during a trial proceeding; sometimes the bailiff has custody of prisoners while they are in the courtroom; also known as messengers.

Balanced Approach Probation orientation that simultaneously emphasizes community protection, offender accountability, individualization of treatments, and competency assessment and development.

Baldwin v. *New York* (1970) Landmark case entitling criminal defendants to jury trials if they request one, with exceptions, provided the punishment that might be imposed from a conviction would be six months or more of incarceration.

Banishment   Sanction used to punish offenders by barring them from going within a specified number of miles from settlements or towns; often tantamount to capital punishment, since those banished could not obtain food or water to survive the isolation.

Behavioral Approach   Type of police discretion typified by a blend of sociology, psychology, and political science; a developmental scheme whereby police officers attempt to negotiate their way through each public encounter.

Bench Trial   Trial where guilt or innocence of defendant is determined by the judge rather than by a jury.

Bentham, Jeremy (1748–1832) English philosopher who believed that pursuit of pleasure, or *hedonism*, was the chief motivator underlying much social action.

Beyond a Reasonable Doubt Standard used in criminal courts to establish guilt or innocence of criminal defendant.

Bifurcated Trial   Trial in capital cases where jury is asked to make two decisions; first decision is to determine guilt or innocence of defendant; if guilty, jury meets to decide punishment, which may include the death penalty.

Bobbies   Term for British police; named after Sir Robert "Bobby" Peel, the British Home Secretary, in the 1820s.

Bonding Theory   Theory of criminal behavior implying that criminality is the result of a loosening of bonds or attachments with society; builds on differential association theory; primarily designed to account for juvenile delinquency.

Booking   Process of making written report of arrest, including name and address of arrested persons, the alleged crimes, arresting officers, place and time of arrest, physical description of suspect, photographs (sometimes called "mug shots"), and fingerprints.

Boot Camps   Also known as the Army model, boot camp programs are patterned after basic training for new military recruits. Juvenile offenders are given a taste of hard military life, and such regimented activities and structure for up to 180 days are often sufficient to "shock" them into giving up their lives of delinquency or crime and staying out of jail.

Borstals   Used in Great Britain to provide rehabilitative services in a secure custodial environment, where youths could participate in vocational and educational training, or receive counseling or group therapy; usually, borstal confinement was a reformative sentence which varied from six months to two years; abolished in 1982 by Criminal Justice Act.

Boston Offender Project (BOP) An experimental program in Boston, targeted for violent juveniles; program goals include reducing recidivism, enhancing public protection by increasing accountability for major violators, and improving the likelihood of successful reintegration of juveniles into society by focusing upon these offenders' academic and vocational skills.

Brace, Charles Loring Creator of New York Children's Aid Society in 1853; philanthropist and benefactor of wayward and dependent children.

Breed v. *Jones* Landmark 1975 juvenile rights case that established right against double jeopardy; juveniles may not be adjudicated as delinquent in juvenile courts and then tried as adults in criminal courts later on the same charges.

Bridewell Workhouse A sixteenth-century London jail established in 1557; known for providing cheap labor to business and mercantile interests; jailers and sheriffs profited from prisoner exploitation.

British Crime Survey (BCS) Begun in 1981, this is the official source of crime information in Great Britain; similar to the *National Crime Survey* in the United States, which reports the amount of crime on the basis of victim surveys.

Brockway, Zebulon First superintendent of New York State Reformatory at Elmira in 1876; arguably credited with introducing first "good time" system whereby inmates could have their sentences reduced or shortened by the number of good marks earned through good behavior.

Broken Windows Approach Form of police patrol stressing better communication with citizens; foot patrols, team policing, and other "back to the people" programs are consistent with this patrol form.

Broker Probation officer work-role orientation in which PO functions as a referral service and supplies offender-client with contacts with agencies that provide needed services.

Bureau of Justice Statistics Bureau created in 1979 to distribute statistical information concerning crime, criminals, and crime trends.

Burglary Unlawful entry of a structure to commit a felony or theft.

Burnout A disorder characterized by a loss of motivation and commitment related to task performance; burnout among police is measured by Maslach Burnout Inventory and other psychological devices which test degree of commitment to the job and the loss of motivation to be successful.

Capital Punishment Imposition of the death penalty for the most serious crimes; may be administered by electrocution, lethal injection, gas, hanging, or shooting.

Career Escalation Moving as a juvenile offender to progressively more serious offenses; for example, committing new violent offenses after adjudication for property offenses.

Caseload The number of cases a probation or parole officer is assigned according to some standard such as a week, month, or year; caseloads vary among jurisdictions.

Cellular Telephone Device Electronic monitoring device worn by offender that emits radio signal received by local area monitor.

Certification *See* Transfer.

Chancellors Civil servants who acted on behalf of king of England during Middle Ages; chancellors held court and settled property disputes, trespass cases, minor property offenses, and cases of thievery, vagrancy, and public drunkenness.

Chancery Court Court of equity rooted in early English common law where civil disputes are resolved; also responsible for juvenile matters and adjudicating family matters such as divorce; has jurisdiction over contract disputes, property boundary claims, and exchanges of goods disputes.

Charge Reduction Bargaining Type of plea bargaining in which the inducement from the prosecutor is a reduction in the seriousness of charge or number of charges against a defendant in exchange for a guilty plea.

Chicago Area Project Project commenced in 1934 by Clifford Shaw designed to establish recreational centers and counseling programs for high-risk youths; delinquency prevention program.

Child Abuse Any form of cruelty causing damage to the physical, moral, or mental well-being of a child; the sexual abuse or exploitation, negligent treatment, or maltreatment of a child under the age of 18 by a person who is responsible for the child's welfare.

Child Education and Training Homes Facilities in Japan that are the equivalent of group homes in the United States; often used to house youths who are neglected or dependent, or whose families have been declared unfit by the court.

Child Guidance Centers Located in most Japanese cities; these centers are staffed by trained psychologists, social workers, and family specialists who can provide counseling and other forms of treatment to both youths and other family members.

Children and Young Persons Act of 1969 An act that established in Great Britain a juvenile court having jurisdiction over youths under 17 years of age; earlier version of the juvenile court was established in 1908, although such a court was largely a magistrate's court which was called into special session for the purpose of adjudicating juvenile offenders.

Children At Risk Youths with social and psychological backgrounds that predispose them to delinquent conduct.

Children In Need of Supervision (CHINS) Any children determined by the juvenile court and other agencies to be in need of community care or supervision.

Children's Bureau   U.S. agency operated during the period 1912–1940, charged with compiling statistical information about children and methods whereby delinquency could be prevented and treated.

Children's Tribunal   Informal court mechanisms originating in Massachusetts to deal with children charged with crimes apart from system of criminal courts for adults.

Child-Saving Movement, Child Savers   Movement during early 1800s in United States, comprised primarily of upper- and middle-class people who sought to provide assistance to wayward youths; assistance was often food and shelter, although social, educational, and religious values were introduced to children later in compulsory schooling.

Chronic Offenders (also *habitual offenders*)   Repeat offenders; persistent offenders; youths who commit frequent delinquent acts.

Citizen Value System   Parole board decision-making model appealing to public interests in seeing that community expectations are met by making appropriate early-release decisions.

Civil Rights Act   Title 42, Section 1983 of the U.S. Code permitting inmates of prisons and jails as well as probationers and parolees the right to sue their administrators and/or supervisors under the "due process" and "equal protection" clauses of the Fourteenth Amendment.

Clark, Benjamin C.   Philanthropist and "volunteer" probation officer who assisted courts with limited probation work during 1860s; carried on John Augustus's work commenced in early 1840s.

Classical Theory (also *classical school of criminology*)   Originated by Cesare Beccaria (1738–1794); assumes that people are rational beings with free will to choose between good and evil.

Classification Homes   Elaborate institutions in Japan complete with psychological staffs, testing and diagnostic services, medical facilities, detention facilities, and observational rooms; personnel administer intelligence tests, interview youths and their parents, and make recommendations to Family Court judges about particular dispositions, which may include probation or some other type of conditional, supervised release option.

Classification System   Means used by prisons and probation/parole agencies to separate offenders according to offense seriousness, type of offense, and other criteria; no classification system has been demonstrably successful at effective prisoner or client placements.

Cleared By Arrest   Term used by FBI in *Uniform Crime Reports* to indicate that someone has been arrested for a reported crime; does not necessarily mean that the crime has been solved or that the actual criminals who committed the crime have been apprehended or convicted.

Client-Specific Plan   One alternative sentencing program involving selective tailoring of sentence (other than imprisonment) for each individual offender, depending upon offense committed; requires judicial approval.

Clinical Prediction   Prediction of inmate behavior based upon professional's expert training and experience in working directly with offenders.

Cognitive Development Theory (also called *developmental theory*)   Theory stressing stages of learning process whereby persons acquire ability to think and express themselves, respect the property and rights of others, and cultivate a set of moral values.

Collective Incapacitation   Type of incapacitation in which crime reduction is accomplished through traditional offense-based sentencing and incarcerative policies, such as mandatory minimum sentences.

Combination Sentences or Split Sentences   Occur whenever judges sentence offenders to a term, a portion of which includes incarceration and a portion of which includes probation.

Commission on Juvenile Affairs   Soviet commission that hears most minor cases for youths under 14 years of age; jurisdiction also includes child abuse and neglect cases, vocational training and educational placement, and delinquency prevention.

Common Law   Authority based on court decrees and judgments which recognize, affirm, and enforce certain usages and customs of the people; laws determined by judges in accordance with their rulings.

Community-Based Corrections Programs   Locally operated services offering minimum-security, limited release, or work release alternatives to prisoners about to be paroled; may also serve probationers.

Community-Based Supervision   Reintegrative programs operated publicly or privately to assist offenders by providing therapeutic, support, and supervision programs for criminals; may include furloughs, probation, parole, community service, and restitution.

Community Control   *See* Home incarceration.

Community Corrections Act   Statewide mechanism included in legislation whereby funds are granted to local units of government and community agencies to develop and deliver "front end" alternative sanctions in lieu of state incarceration.

Community Diversion Incentive (CDI)   Virginia diversion program established in 1981 for prison-bound offenders; participants were required to perform specified unpaid community services and make financial restitution to victims; clients were also subject to intensive supervised probation.

Community Homes   British community-based correctional facilities much like group homes in the United States; juveniles are continuously supervised and are required to engage in various rehabilitative enterprises.

Community Policing   Major police reform that broadens the police mission from a narrow focus on crime to a mandate that encourages the police to explore creative solutions for a host of community concerns, including crime, fear of crime, disorder, and neighborhood decay; rests on belief that only by working together will citizens and police be able to improve the quality of life in their communities, with the police not only as enforcers, but also as advisors, facilitators, and supporters of new community-based police-supervised initiatives.

Community Protection Program   New York State county-based program designed as an alternative to prison, in which prison-bound offenders are diverted to intensive supervision and treatment.

Community Reintegration   Process whereby offender who has been incarcerated is able to live in community under some supervision and gradually adjust to life outside of prison or jail.

Community Reintegration Model   Belief that youths who commit delinquent acts have become alienated from their communities and must be reintegrated with them; rejects institutionalization as remedy; seeks nonincarcerative alternatives, such as community-based agency supervision of youthful offenders.

Community Service   Sentence imposed by judges in lieu of incarceration whereby offenders are obligated to perform various tasks that assist the community and help to offset the losses suffered by victims or the community at large.

Comparative Juvenile Justice Systems   Analyses of criminal justice systems of other countries, studying their similarities and differences.

Complaint   Written statement of essential facts concerning the offense alleged, made under oath before a magistrate or other qualified judicial officer.

Comrades' Courts   Soviet courts that hear more serious offenses; are comprised of private citizens in factories, organizations, collective farms, and apartment blocks; have jurisdiction over small property crimes, labor violations, antisocial behavior, petty hooliganism, petty speculation, petty theft, petty embezzlement of state property, minor assaults, and other minor offenses.

Concentric Zone Hypothesis   Generated by Chicago School investigating delinquency and urban development; Robert Park and Ernest Burgess were theorists who believed that various urban zones were associated with particular types of delinquency and crime.

Concurrent Jurisdiction   The power to file charges against juveniles in either criminal courts or juvenile courts.

Conditional Dispositions (Options)   Results of a delinquency adjudication that obligate youths to comply with one or more conditions of a probation program, such as restitution, community service, work study, therapy, educational participation, or victim compensation.

Conditional Diversion Program Program where divertee is involved in some degree of local monitoring by probation officers or personnel affiliated with local probation departments.

Conflict Criminology *See* Radical criminology.

Congregate System System introduced at Auburn State Penitentiary in New York whereby prisoners could work and eat together in common work and recreational areas; prisoners segregated at night.

Consent Decrees Formal agreements that involve children, their parents, and the juvenile court, whereby youths are placed under the court's supervision without an official finding of delinquency, with judicial approval.

Containment Theory Belief that there are pushes and pulls in relation to delinquency, including hostility, anxiety, and discontent; pulls are external forces, such as delinquent subcultures; containments may be outer, including social norms, laws, and folkways, or inner, including individual or personal coping strategies to deal with stress and conflict.

Contempt of Court Any citation by a judge against anyone in court who disrupts the proceedings or does anything to interfere with judicial decrees or pronouncements.

Continuous Signaling Devices Electronic monitoring devices that broadcast an encoded signal that is received by a receiver-dialer in the offender's home. *See* Electronic monitoring.

Controller Value System Parole board decision-making system emphasizing the functions of parole supervision and management.

Conventional Model Caseload assignment model in which probation or parole officers are assigned clients randomly.

Conventional Model With Geographic Considerations Similar to conventional model; caseload assignment model is based upon the travel time required for POs to meet with offender-clients regularly.

Corporate Gangs Juvenile gangs that emulate organized crime; profit-motivated gangs that rely on illicit activities, such as drug trafficking, to further their profit interests.

Corrections The aggregate of programs, services, facilities, and organizations responsible for the management of people who have been accused or convicted of criminal offenses.

Corrective Works Productive labor in Soviet corrective-labor colonies.

Court Clerk Court officer who may file pleadings, motions, or judgments, issue processes, and keep general records of court proceedings.

Court of Equity *See* Chancery court.

Court of Record Any court where a written record is kept of court proceedings.

Court Reporter Court official who keeps a written word-for-word and/or tape-recorded record of court proceedings.

Courts Public judiciary bodies that apply the law to controversies and oversee the administration of justice.

Court Unification General proposal that seeks to centralize and integrate the diverse functions of all courts of general, concurrent, and exclusive jurisdiction into a more simplified and uncomplicated scheme.

Creaming Term to denote taking only those offenders most likely to succeed in a rehabilitative program; these offenders are low-risk, unlikely to reoffend.

Creative Sentencing A broad class of punishments as alternatives to incarceration that are designed to fit the particular crimes; may involve community service, restitution, fines, becoming involved in educational or vocational training programs, or becoming affiliated with other "good works" activity.

Crime Act prohibited by law, by one who is held accountable by that law; consists of legality, *actus reus, mens rea,* consensus, harm, causation, and prescribed punishment.

Crime Clock Graph used in *Uniform Crime Reports* to show number of specific types of crime (e.g., robbery, murder, forcible rape) committed according to some time standard such as minutes or seconds; calculated by dividing number of crimes reported annually by number of minutes or seconds in a year.

Crime Control Model A model of criminal justice that emphasizes containment of dangerous offenders and societal protection; a way of controlling delinquency by incapacitating juvenile offenders, through some secure detention or through intensive supervision programs operated by community-based agencies.

Crime Prevention The anticipation, recognition, and appraisal of crime risk and the initiation of some action to remove or reduce it.

Crimes Against Property Nonviolent or passive crimes in which no physical harm is inflicted upon victims (includes vehicular theft, burglary, and larceny).

Crimes Against the Person Violent crimes, including all crimes committed in the victim's presence (includes murder, rape, robbery, aggravated assault).

Crimes Cleared By Arrest Crimes included in the *Uniform Crime Reports* in which an arrest has been made; possible offenders have been apprehended, sufficient evidence exists to connect them with the crime, and they have been taken into custody.

Criminal Code of Soviet Union Implemented in 1960, defined crime as socially dangerous acts (acts or omissions to act) that infringe the Soviet social or state system, the socialist system of economy, socialist property, the person, or the political, labor, property, or other rights of citizens, or any other socially dangerous act which infringes the socialist legal order.

Criminal Informations *See* Information.

Criminal Investigation Division Division of any agency associated with investigating crimes; Internal Revenue Service has Criminal Investigation Division or CID to investigate taxpayers who attempt to commit crimes in avoiding the payment of their taxes.

Criminal Justice Interdisciplinary field studying nature and operations of organizations providing justice services to society; also refers to lawmaking bodies including state legislatures and Congress, local, state and federal agencies that try to enforce the law.

Criminal Justice Act of 1948 A comprehensive record-keeping system was authorized by this act; the British Home Secretary was vested with various powers, including discretionary authority to conduct research into the causes of delinquency and crime as well as offender treatment, and "other matters connected herewith."

Criminal Justice Act of 1982 Abolished borstals used for delinquency rehabilitation in Great Britain.

Criminal Justice Act of 1988 British act that simplified the way youthful offenders were defined and established a new, unified custodial sentencing system. New sentences available are known as "detention in a young offender institution"; places the responsibility on the Prison Service for determining where offenders should serve their sentences; decisions are based upon age, sentence length, and other related factors; purposes of this new detention are (1) personal development of individuals, (2) promotion of amiable staff/inmate relations, and (3) encouragement of links with home and community through the sentence; use of furloughs is encouraged.

Criminal Justice System An interrelated set of agencies and organizations designed to control criminal behavior, detect crime, and apprehend, process, prosecute, punish, and/or rehabilitate criminal offenders.

Criminal Trial An adversarial proceeding within a particular jurisdiction, at which a judicial determination of issues can be made, and a defendant's guilt or innocence can be decided impartially.

Criminology The study of crime, the science of crime and criminal behavior, the forms of criminal behavior, the causes of crime, the definition of criminality, and the societal reaction to crime.

Critical Phase or Stage Phase of investigation by law enforcement officers when case moves from investigatory to accusatory against specific suspects; any action or stage where one's freedom is in jeopardy.

Crofton, Sir Walter Director of Ireland's prison system during 1850s; considered "father of parole" in various European countries; established system of early release for prisoners; issued "tickets of leave" as an early version of parole.

Cross-Cultural Juvenile Justice Systems   *See* Comparative juvenile justice systems.

Cross-Examination   Examination of one side's witnesses by the other side, either the prosecution or defense.

Crown Courts   In Great Britain, courts that generally hear the more serious indictable offenses and are authorized to conduct jury trial proceedings. Judges in crown courts take an active role in the proceedings; they might interrogate witnesses and make favorable and adverse comments about them or about defendants.

Cultural Transmission Theory   Theory emphasizing transmission of criminal behavior through socialization.

Curfew Violators   Youths who violate laws and ordinances of communities prohibiting youths from being on the streets after certain evening hours, such as 10:00 P.M. ; curfew itself is a delinquency prevention strategy.

Custodial Options   Either nonsecure or secure options resulting from a delinquency adjudication; juveniles may be placed in foster homes, group homes, community-based correctional facilities, or secure detention facilities that are either publicly or privately operated.

Dangerousness   Defined differently in different jurisdictions; refers to prior record of violent offenses; potential to commit future violent crimes if released; propensity to inflict injury; predicted risk of convicted offender or prison or jail inmate; likelihood of inflicting harm upon others.

Day Parole   *See* Work release.

Day Pass   *See* Work release.

Deadly Force   Any force used by law enforcement officers or others, which may result in death or great bodily harm, to apprehend those suspected of or engaging in unlawful acts.

Death-Qualified Jury   Term applied to a jury which has been selected on the basis of their willingness to impose the death penalty in a capital case if the situation warrants such a decision; implies exclusion of persons from possible jury duty who could not vote for a death penalty even if defendant were guilty of capital crime.

Decarceration   Type of deinstitutionalization in which juveniles charged with status offenses are still under court jurisdiction and subject to filing of petitions, but detention of youths is prohibited; youths may be removed from their homes and placed in nonsecure facilities, put on probation, required to attend treatment or service programs, and subjected to other behavioral restraints.

Decriminalization   Legislative action whereby an act or omission, formerly criminal, is made noncriminal and without punitive sanctions; usually occurs through legislative action.

Defendant   Anyone charged with one or more crimes.

Defendant's Sentencing Memorandum   Version of events leading to conviction offense in the words of the convicted offender; version may be submitted together with victim impact statement.

Defense-of-Life Standard Standard by which law enforcement officers decide whether to use deadly force in effecting arrest of criminal suspects; involves discretion as to whether officer's life or the lives of others are in jeopardy as the result of suspect's actions.

Deinstitutionalization of Status Offenses (DSO) Eliminating status offenses from the delinquency category and removing juveniles from or precluding their confinement in juvenile correction facilities; process of removing status offenses from jurisdiction of juvenile court.

Delinquency Any act committed by a youth of not more than a specified age who has violated criminal laws or engages in disobedient, indecent, or immoral conduct, and is in need of treatment, rehabilitation, or supervision; status acquired through an adjudicatory proceeding by juvenile court.

Delinquent Child Infant of not more than a specified age who has violated criminal laws or engages in disobedient, indecent or immoral conduct, and is in need of treatment, rehabilitation, or supervision.

Demand Waiver Demands by juveniles to have their cases transferred from juvenile courts to criminal courts.

Department of Justice Organization headed by Attorney General of United States; responsible for prosecuting federal law violators; oversees Federal Bureau of Investigation and the Drug Enforcement Administration.

Desert Model *See* Justice model.

Detector Probation officer work-role orientation in which PO attempts to identify troublesome clients or those who are most likely to pose high community risk.

Detention Centers British juvenile industrial schools used for the most hard-core offenders.

Detention Hearing Judicial or quasijudicial proceeding held to determine whether or not it is appropriate to continue to hold or detain a juvenile in a shelter facility.

Determinate Sentencing Sentence involving confinement for a fixed period of time and which must be served in full and without parole board intervention, less any "good time" earned in prison.

Determinism View that a specific factor, variable, or event is a determinant of one's actions or behaviors.

Deterrence Actions that are designed to prevent crime before it occurs by threatening severe criminal penalties or sanctions; may include safety measures to discourage potential lawbreakers such as elaborate security systems, electronic monitoring, and greater police officer visibility.

Deterrence Model Model of crime control based upon the philosophy of deterrence. *See also* Deterrence.

Deviance Conduct which departs from accepted codes expected by society or by a particular group.

Differential Association Theory Edwin Sutherland's theory of deviance and criminality through associations with others who are deviant or criminal; theory includes dimensions of frequency, duration, priority, and intensity.

Differential Reinforcement Theory View that combines elements of labeling theory with conditioning; persons are rewarded during social learning for engaging in acceptable behaviors; may obtain judgments from juvenile delinquents and be adversely influenced.

Direct Examination Questioning of witnesses by prosecution or defense attorney, in which initial questioning is conducted by side calling witness.

Discovery Procedure where prosecution shares information with defense attorney and defendant; specific types of information are made available to defendant before trial, including results of any tests conducted, psychiatric reports, transcripts or tape-recorded statements made by the defendant; also known as "Brady materials" after a specific court case.

Discretionary Waivers Waivers of juveniles to criminal courts by judges, at their discretion or as a result of their judgment.

Discretion, Police Relating to the police role, police discretion is the distribution of non-negotiably coercive force employed in accordance with the dictates of an intuitive grasp of situational exigencies; police have authority to use force to enforce the law, if in the officer's opinion, the situation demands it.

Dispositions Results of a delinquency adjudication; may be nominal, conditional, or custodial.

Diversion The official halting or suspension of legal proceedings against criminal defendants after a recorded justice system entry, and possible referral of those persons to treatment or care programs administered by a nonjustice or private agency. *See also* Pretrial release.

Diversion Program One of several programs preceding formal court adjudication of charges against defendants; defendants participate in therapeutic, educational, or other helping programs; may result in expungement of criminal charges originally filed against defendant; may include participation in Alcoholics Anonymous or driver's training programs. *See also* Diversion.

Diversion to Civil Court Procedure whereby a crime is reduced in seriousness to that of a tort action and placed for disposition in civil court rather than in criminal court. *See also* Alternative dispute resolution.

Divertee Person who participates in a diversion program or who is otherwise granted diversion.

Divestiture *See* Divestiture of jurisdiction.

Divestiture of Jurisdiction Condition wherein juvenile courts cannot detain, petition, adjudicate, or place youths on probation for any status offense.

Divisional Courts and Courts of Appeal, Criminal Division Courts in Great Britain that correspond roughly to civil and criminal courts of appeal in various U.S. state jurisdictions.

Drift Theory (also called *neutralization theory*) Theory according to which some youths drift toward unlimited freedom and away from control and restraint; choices of delinquent conduct result from rationalization that society is unfair or unjust, that victims deserve to be victims.

Druzhiny Squads of peoples' volunteers in the Soviet Union that work in collaboration with local police agencies to enforce antiparasite laws which prohibit persons from not working for long periods.

Due Process Basic constitutional right to a fair trial, presumption of innocence until guilt is proven beyond a reasonable doubt, the opportunity to be heard, to be made aware of a matter that is pending, to make an informed choice whether to acquiesce or contest, and to provide the reasons for such a choice before a judicial official.

Due Process Juvenile Courts Courts characterized by more formal case dispositions, adversarial relations between prosecutor and juvenile defense attorneys, and greater rate of intake dismissals.

Due Process Model Treatment model based upon one's constitutional right to a fair trial, to have an opportunity to be heard, to be made aware of matters that are pending, to a presumption of innocence until guilt has been established beyond a reasonable doubt, to make an informed choice whether to acquiesce or contest, and to provide the reasons for such a choice before a judicial official.

Duress Affirmative defense used by defendants to show lack of criminal intent, alleging force, psychological or physical, from others as stimulus for otherwise criminal conduct.

Duty Solicitors British public defenders made available by the government to provide immediate legal advice to defendants who must decide whether or not to plead guilty to the offenses alleged.

Early Release *See* Parole.

Ectomorphs One of William Sheldon's body types; thin, submissive persons.

Eddings v. *Oklahoma* (1982) Landmark U.S. Supreme Court case holding that death penalty applied to juveniles is not cruel and unusual punishment per se.

Educator *See* Enabler.

Ego Part of Sigmund Freud's psychoanalytic theory; ego is recognition of others and a respect for their rights and interests.

Electronic Monitoring A policy or program which uses electronic devices that emit electronic signals; these devices, anklets or wristlets, are worn by offenders, probationers and parolees; the purpose of such devices is to monitor an offender's presence in a given environment where the offender is required to remain or to verify the offender's whereabouts.

Electronic Monitoring Devices Devices—the *hardware*—worn about the wrist or leg which are designed to monitor an offender's presence in a given environment where the offender is required to remain.

Enabler Probation officer work-role orientation in which PO seeks to instruct and assist offenders in dealing with problems as they arise.

Endomorphs One of William Sheldon's body types; obese persons.

Enforcer Probation officer work-role orientation in which POs see themselves as enforcement officers charged with regulating client behaviors.

Evidence Tangible or verbal materials that relate to a crime; may be eyewitness testimony, weapons used to commit crime, lab reports or tests, testimony from anyone having knowledge about crime committed.

Exculpatory Evidence Evidence considered beneficial to defendants, tending to show their innocence.

Ex Parte Crouse (1839) Landmark case in which courts removed children from their parents' jurisdictional control.

Ex Parte Hull (1941) Landmark case in which U.S. Supreme Court held that prisoners have access to courts; first ruling to effectively challenge and undermine "hands-off" doctrine.

Expungement Orders Deletion of a person's arrest record from official sources; in most jurisdictions, juvenile delinquency records are expunged when the age of majority or adulthood is reached.

Extralegal Factors Factors unrelated to the offense committed that influence intake decisions, such as juvenile offender attitudes, school grades and standing, gender, race, ethnicity, socioeconomic status, and age.

False Negative Offender predicted not to be dangerous who turns out to be dangerous.

False Positive Offender predicted to be dangerous who turns out not to be dangerous.

Family Courts Established in Japan under the Juvenile Law of 1948, these exist in all Japanese jurisdictions and hear any matters pertaining to juvenile delinquency, child abuse and neglect, and child custody matters; both status offenders and delinquents appear before Family Court judges; similar to juvenile court judges in U.S. jurisdictions, Family Court judges have considerable discretionary authority; they decide cases within the *parens patriae* context.

Federal Bureau of Investigation Established in 1908 through Department of Justice Appropriation Act; investigative agency that enforces all federal criminal laws; compiles information for the *Uniform Crime Reports* annually; acts as the enforcement arm of the Department of Justice; investigates over 200 different kinds of federal law violations; maintains extensive files on criminals; assists other law agencies.

Federal Bureau of Prisons Established in 1930; charged with providing suitable quarters for prisoners and safekeeping of all persons convicted of offenses against the United States; also contracts with local jails and state prisons for confinement of federal prisoners where there are insufficient federal facilities in the geographical area where the person has been convicted.

Federal *Habeas Corpus* Statute Title 28, Section 2241 of the U.S. Code permitting probationers, parolees, and inmates of prisons and jails to challenge the fact, length, and conditions of their confinement or placement in particular facilities or programs.

Felony Crime punishable by imprisonment in prison for a term of one or more years; a major crime; an index crime.

Felony Probation Practice of not requiring felons to serve time in jail or prison, usually because of prison overcrowding; involves conditional sentence in lieu of incarceration.

Financial/Community Service Model Juvenile offender restitution model which stresses the offender's financial accountability and community service to pay for damages.

Fine Financial penalty imposed at time of sentencing of convicted offenders; most criminal statutes contain provisions for the imposition of monetary penalties as sentencing options.

First Offenders or First-Time Offenders Criminals who have no previous criminal records; these persons may have committed crimes, but they have only been caught for the latest offense.

Force Continuum Measure of the amount of force law enforcement officers apply in making arrests; subjective measure.

Forcible Rape The carnal knowledge of persons forcibly and against their will; assaults or attempts; rape by force or threat of force is also included.

Furlough Program Program designed to permit incarcerated offenders to leave prison temporarily to visit their homes with promise to return to facility at expiration of furlough.

***Furman* v. *Georgia* (1972)** Landmark case that temporarily suspended application of death penalty; ruling was that proper procedural safeguards did not exist in Georgia to apply death penalty appropriately. This ruling did not abolish the death penalty; rather, it indicated discriminatory and arbitrary nature of death penalty being administered in Georgia.

Georgia Intensive Supervision Probation Program Program begun in 1982 that established three phases of punitive probation conditions for probationers; phases moved probationers through extensive monitoring and control to less-extensive monitoring, ranging from six to twelve months; program has demonstrated low rates of recidivism among participants.

"Getting It Together" Program
Program established in late 1970s
that emphasized a combination
of social skills training and affective or emotional therapy to assist immature personalities and
those who exhibited neurotic behaviors; designed to improve
self-esteem and foster greater
self-control and positive values.

Good Marks   Marks obtained by
prisoners in nineteenth century
England in which prisoners were
given credit for participating in
educational programs and other
self-improvement activities.

Good Time   The amount of time
deducted from the period of incarceration of a convicted offender; calculated as so many
days per month on the basis of
good behavior while incarcerated.

Graffiti Removal Community
Service Program   Community
program designed as condition of
probation in cases of vandalism,
in which youths must remove
graffiti from public buildings or
houses; used in conjunction with
other program conditions.

Grand Jury   An investigative body
whose numerical makeup varies
among states; duties include determining probable cause regarding commission of a crime and
returning formal charges against
suspects. *See* True bill and No
bill.

Gregg v. *Georgia* (1976)   Landmark case providing for lawful
application of death penalty,
where dual jury deliberation is
conducted; one stage decides
guilt, second stage decides punishment. *See also* Bifurcated trial.

Group Homes   Also known as
group centers or foster homes,
these are facilities for juveniles
that provide limited supervision
and support; juveniles live in
homelike environment with
other juveniles and participate in
therapeutic programs and counseling; considered nonsecure custodial.

Habeas Corpus   Writ meaning
"produce the body"; used by
prisoners to challenge the nature
and length of their confinement.

Habitual Offender (also *chronic
offender*)   Persistent offender;
any youth with frequent previous
adjudications as delinquent; different jurisdictions have different
standards about what constitutes
habitual offending; usually, three
or more adjudications for serious
offenses qualify offenders for
"habitual" label.

Habitual Offender Statute   Statutes vary among states; these
statutes provide for life imprisonment as a mandatory sentence
for chronic offenders who have
been convicted of three or more
serious felonies within a specific
time period.

Halfway House   Nonconfining
residential facility intended to
provide offenders with a period
of readjustment to the community after incarceration.

"Hands-Off" Doctrine   Doctrine
practiced by the federal courts
wherein official court policy was
not to intervene in matters relating to adult corrections; belief
that correctional superintendents,
wardens, and departments of cor-

rections are in best position to make decisions about welfare of inmates; applied to juvenile corrections and juvenile courts similarly.

Hedonism   Belief espoused by Jeremy Bentham that pursuit of pleasure and avoidance of pain are the chief motivating factors underlying behavior.

Heredity   Theory that behaviors are result of characteristics genetically transmitted; criminal behaviors would be explained as resulting from inherited genes from parents or ancestors who are criminal or who have criminal propensities.

Hidden Delinquency   Delinquency reported by surveys of high school youths; considered "hidden" because it most often is undetected by police officers; delinquency disclosed through self-report surveys.

High Courts   Japanese courts that are generally equivalent to the thirteen U.S. Circuit Courts of Appeal; these are dispersed throughout Japan, and they hear appeals from lower courts; presided over by a president and several judges, although three judges must sit and decide cases.

Home Confinement (also called *house arrest* or *home incarceration*)   Plan intended to house offenders in their own homes with or without electronic devices; reduces prison overcrowding and prisoner costs; intermediate punishment involving the use of offender residences for mandatory incarceration during evening hours after a curfew and on weekends.

Home Incarceration (also called *house arrest, community control,* or *home confinement*)   The use of an offender's home as the primary place of incarceration in lieu of jail or prison.

Homeward Bound   Established in Massachusetts in 1970; designed to provide juveniles with opportunity to learn responsibility through the acquisition of survival skills and wilderness experiences. A six-week training program subjected 32 youths to endurance training, physical fitness, and performance of community service.

Hooliganism   Term used by Soviets in defining a broad range of criminal conduct; included in hooliganism are disorderly conduct, alcohol or drug abuse, prostitution, and loitering.

Hope Center Wilderness Camp   *See* Wilderness Experiments.

Hospital of Saint Michael   Hospital established at request of Pope in Rome in 1704; provided for unruly youths and others who violated the law; youths were assigned tasks, including semiskilled and skilled labor, which enabled them to get jobs when released.

House Arrest   *See* Home confinement.

House of Lords   Upper house of British parliament; also functions as the British equivalent to the United States Supreme Court.

Hybrid Offense   English term for offense in which prosecutor has discretionary authority as to whether to treat offense summarily or through indictment.

ID   The "I want" part of a person, formed in one's early years; Sigmund Freud's term to depict that part of personality concerned with individual gratification.

Illinois Juvenile Court Act   Act passed by Illinois legislature in 1899 providing for the first juvenile court and treatment programs for various types of juvenile offenders.

Impeachment   Attempt by prosecution or defense to question the credibility of each others' witnesses.

Implicit Plea Bargaining   Entry of guilty plea by defendant with the expectation of receiving a more lenient sentence from authorities.

Incident   Specific criminal act involving one or more victims.

Inculpatory Evidence   Evidence considered adverse to defendants or tending to show their guilt.

Indentured Servant   Voluntary slave who entered into a contract with merchants or businessmen, usually for seven years, wherein merchants would pay their fare to the American colonies from England in exchange for their labor.

Indeterminate Punishment   *See* Indeterminate Sentencing.

Indeterminate Sentencing   Sentences of imprisonment by the court for either specified or unspecified durations, with the final release date determined by a parole board.

Index Offenses   Specific felonies used by the Federal Bureau of Investigation in the *Uniform Crime Reports* to chart crime trends; there are eight index offenses listed prior to 1988: aggravated assault, larceny, burglary, vehicular theft, arson, robbery, forcible rape, and murder.

Indictable Offenses   Offenses in Canada or Great Britain that include violations of the criminal code or federal statutes.

Indictment   A charge or written accusation found and presented by a grand jury that a particular defendant probably committed a crime.

Infant   Legal term applicable to juveniles who have not attained the age of majority; in most states, age of majority is 18.

Information   Sometimes called criminal information; written accusation made by a public prosecutor against a person for some criminal offense, without an indictment; usually restricted to minor crimes or misdemeanors.

Initial Appearance   Formal proceeding during which the judge advises defendants of the charges against them.

In re Gault   Landmark 1967 juvenile rights case that established a juvenile's right to an attorney, adequate notice of charges, right to confront and cross-examine witnesses, and right to be warned of incriminating nature of statements they might make that might be used against them.

In re Winship   Landmark 1970 juvenile rights case that changed the evidentiary standard from "preponderance of the evidence" to "beyond a reasonable doubt."

Intake Screening   A critical phase during which a determination is made by a juvenile probation officer or other official whether to release juveniles to their parent's custody, detain juveniles in formal detention facilities for a later court appearance, or release them to parents pending a later court appearance.

Intensive Supervised Probation (also known as *Intensive Probation Supervision* or *IPS*) Supervised probation under probation officer; involves close monitoring of offender activities by various means.

Intensive Supervision Program Offender supervision program with following characteristics: (1) low officer–client caseloads (i.e., thirty or fewer probationers); (2) high levels of offender accountability (e.g., victim restitution, community service, payment of fines, partial defrayment of program expenses); (3) high levels of offender responsibility; (4) high levels of control of offender (home confinement, electronic monitoring, frequent face-to-face visits by POs) (5) frequent checks for arrests, drug and/or alcohol use, and employment/school attendance (drug/alcohol screening, coordination with police departments and juvenile halls, teachers, family).

Interagency Agreement Plan Early intervention plan instituted in San Diego County, California in 1982 for the purpose of reducing delinquency; graduated sanctions used for repeat offenders; youths held accountable for their actions; gradual increase of services and punishments for repeat offenders.

Intermediate Punishments Punishments involving sanctions existing somewhere between incarceration and probation on a continuum of criminal penalties; may include home incarceration and electronic monitoring.

Intermittent Sentences Occur whenever judges sentence offenders to terms such as weekend confinement only.

Interstitial Zones (also called *zones in transition*) Slum areas associated with highest rates of crime and delinquency.

Intoxication Defense used by defendants to explain otherwise criminal conduct; does not overcome *actus reus,* but may be used as a mitigating circumstance to account for otherwise violent behavior; may be used to rebut presumption of premeditation.

Investigatory Stage The stage of a criminal investigation during which law enforcement officers are collecting information and evidence and no charges have been brought against any particular suspect.

Jail City- or county-operated and financed facilities to contain offenders who are serving short sentences; jails also house more serious offenders from state or federal prisons through contracts to alleviate overcrowding; jails also house pretrial detainees, witnesses, juveniles, vagrants, and others.

Jail As a Condition of Probation A sentence that prescribes a specified amount of jail incarceration prior to serving the remainder of the sentence on probation.

Judicature Acts of 1873 and 1875   Acts that established a system of criminal courts that has endured to the present in Great Britain.

Judicial Plea Bargaining   Type of plea bargaining in which judge offers a specific sentence.

Judicial Reprieve   Temporary relief or postponement of the imposition of a sentence; begun during Middle Ages at the discretion of judges to permit defendants more time to gather evidence of their innocence or to allow them to demonstrate that they had reformed their behavior.

Judicial (Discretionary) Waiver   Decision by juvenile judge to waive juvenile to jurisdiction of criminal court.

Judicious Nonintervention   Similar to a "do nothing" policy of delinquency nonintervention.

Jurisdiction   The power of a court to hear and determine a particular type of case; also refers to territory within which court may exercise authority such as a city, county, or state.

Jurist Value System   Category of decision making by parole boards wherein parole decisions are regarded as a natural part of the criminal justice process in which fairness and equity predominate.

Jury   See Petit jury.

Jury Trial   Trial at which guilt or innocence of defendant is determined by jury instead of by the judge.

Just Deserts Model   Philosophy that stresses offender accountabil-ity as a means to punish youthful offenders; uses victim compensation plans, restitution, and community service as ways of making offenders pay for their offenses.

Justice Model   Philosophy which emphasizes punishment as a primary objective of sentencing; includes fixed sentences, abolition of parole, and an abandonment of the rehabilitative ideal; rehabilitation is seen as functional to the extent that offenders join rehabilitative programs voluntarily.

Justice Philosophy   See Justice Model.

Juvenile   A person who has not attained his or her eighteenth birthday; varies among states, although age 18 is most commonly used.

Juvenile Adult   In Great Britain, a youth between the ages of 17 and 20. These youthful offenders are subject to special provisions when being sentenced by judges.

Juvenile Delinquency   Violation of the law by a person prior to his or her eighteenth birthday; any illegal behavior committed by someone within a given age range punishable by juvenile court jurisdiction; whatever the juvenile court believes should be brought within its jurisdiction; violation of any state or local law or ordinance by anyone who has not as yet achieved the age of majority.

Juvenile Delinquency Act of 1974   Federal act specifying that juveniles are persons who have not as yet attained their eighteenth birthday; contains provisions for defining delinquent acts and separating status offenders from delinquent offenders.

Juvenile Delinquent   Any infant of not more than a specified age who has violated criminal laws or engages in disobedient, indecent, or immoral conduct, and is in need of treatment, rehabilitation, or supervision.

Juvenile Diversion/Noncustody Intake Program   California juvenile program implemented in 1982 targeted for more serious juvenile offenders; characterized by intensive supervised probation, mandatory school attendance, employment, and counseling.

Juvenile Diversion Program   Any program for juvenile offenders that temporarily suspends their processing by the juvenile justice system; similar to adult diversion programs (*see* Diversion); also, program established in 1981 in New Orleans by District Attorney's Office whereby youths could receive treatment before being petitioned and adjudicated delinquent.

Juvenile Justice and Delinquency Act of 1974   *See* Office of Juvenile Justice and Delinquency Prevention.

Juvenile Justice System   The system through which juveniles are processed, sentenced, and corrected after arrests for juvenile delinquency.

Juvenile Offender Law   *See* New York Juvenile Offender Law.

Juvenile Prisons   Japanese secure juvenile facilities that provide either for single-inmate occupancy or dormitorylike confinement, because Japanese correctional officials believe that two-person confinement is most dangerous for sexual assaults and planning escapes; operated to provide vocational training and educational opportunities to offenders.

Juvenile Training Schools   Japanese schools used as secure detention facilities; institutions offer educational and vocational training to youths in various age groups; divided according to age as follows: (1) *Primary Juvenile Training Schools* (ages 14 to 16), (2) *Middle Juvenile Training Schools* (ages 16 to 20), (3) *Advanced Juvenile Training Schools* (ages 16 to 20), designed for more serious habitual offenders, and (4) *Medical Juvenile Training Schools* (ages 16 to 20), for youths who are suffering from mental or physical handicaps.

Kent v. *United States*   A 1966 landmark juvenile case that led to the requirement of a hearing before juveniles could be transferred summarily to criminal court by juvenile court judges.

Labeling Theory   Theory attributed to Edwin Lemert whereby persons acquire self-definitions that are deviant or criminal; persons perceive themselves as deviant or criminal through labels applied to them by others; the more people are involved in the criminal justice system, the more they acquire self-definitions consistent with the criminal label.

Larceny-Theft Unlawful taking, carrying, leading or riding away of property from the possession or constructive possession of another; includes shoplifting, pocket-picking, thefts from motor vehicles, and thefts of motor vehicle parts or accessories.

Law The body of rules of specific conduct, prescribed by existing, legitimate authority, in a particular jurisdiction, and at a particular point in time.

Law-Breaking Children Japanese designation for children who commit criminal offenses.

Law Enforcement The activities of various public and private agencies at local, state, and federal levels that are designed to ensure compliance with formal rules of society that regulate social conduct.

Law Enforcement Assistance Administration (LEAA) Program begun in 1968 and terminated in 1984, designed to provide financial and technical assistance to local and state police agencies to combat crime in various ways.

Legal Factors Factors influencing the intake decision relating to the factual information about delinquent acts; crime seriousness, type of crime committed, prior record of delinquency adjudications, and evidence of an inculpatory or exculpatory nature.

Legislative Waiver Provision that compels juvenile court to remand certain youths to criminal courts because of specific offenses that have been committed or alleged.

Libido In Sigmund Freud's psychoanalytical theory, sex drive; basic drive for sexual stimulation and gratification.

Life-Without-Parole Penalty imposed as maximum punishment in states that do not have death penalty; provides for permanent incarceration of offenders in prisons, without parole eligibility; early release may be attained through accumulation of good time credits.

Limited Risk Control Model Model of supervising offenders based on anticipated future criminal conduct; uses risk assessment devices to place offenders in an effective control range.

Long-Term Facility Any incarcerative institution for either juveniles or adults that is designed to provide prolonged treatment and confinement, usually for periods of one year or longer; prisons are considered long-term.

Maconochie, Alexander (1787–1860) Prison reformer and former superintendent of the British penal colony at Norfolk Island and governor of Birmingham Borough Prison; known for humanitarian treatment of prisoners and issuance of "marks of commendation" to prisoners that led to their early release; considered the forerunner of indeterminate sentencing in the United States.

Magistrate's Courts Courts in Great Britain that handle about 85 percent of serious crimes. These courts may hear summary offense charges, indictable offense charges, or hybrid offense charges. Police officers who make earlier arrests often function as police prosecutors in these magistrate's courts, where they present evidence against the accused and other pertinent information about the crime alleged.

Mala In Se   Crimes that are intrinsically evil or wrong, including murder, rape, or arson.

Mala Prohibita   Offenses defined by legislatures as crimes; many state and federal criminal statutes are *mala prohibita*.

Mandatory Sentencing   Law under which court is required to impose an incarcerative sentence of a specified length, without the option for probation, suspended sentence, or immediate parole eligibility.

Manifest Functions   Intended or recognized functions; when associated with probation and parole, manifest functions are to permit offender reintegration into society.

Massachusetts Prison Commission   Investigative body appointed by governor in 1817 to examine prison conditions and prisoner early release options and to make recommendations about policy issues; noted for originating concept of halfway house.

Maxi-Maxi Prison   *See* Maximum security prison.

Maximum Security Prison   Holds prisoners to a high standard of custody, including constant surveillance, often solitary confinement; limited privileges.

McKeiver v. *Pennsylvania*   Landmark 1970 juvenile rights case that established that juveniles are not entitled to a jury as a matter of right in a juvenile court proceeding; the right to a jury trial in juvenile court is discretionary with the juvenile judge.

Mediator   *See* Enabler.

Medical Model (also known as *treatment model*)   Model that considers criminal behavior an illness to be treated; delinquency is also seen as a disease subject to treatment.

Medium-Security Prisons   Inmates are given more freedom compared with maximum-security facilities; their movements are monitored; often, these facilities are dormitorylike, and prisoners are eligible for privileges.

Mens Rea   Intent to commit a crime; guilty mind.

Mesomorph   One of William Sheldon's body types; strong, muscular, athletic individuals.

Minimum Due Process   *See* Due Process.

Minimum Security Prison   Designated for nonviolent, low-risk offenders; inmates are housed in efficiency apartments, permitted family visits; considerable inmate privileges.

Minnesota Sentencing Grid   Sentencing guidelines established by Minnesota legislature in 1980 and used by judges to sentence offenders; grid contains criminal history score, offense seriousness, and presumptive sentences to be imposed; judges may depart from guidelines upward or downward depending upon aggravating or mitigating circumstances.

Miranda Warning   Warning given to suspects by police officers advising them of their legal rights to counsel, to refuse to answer questions, to avoid self-incrimination, and other privileges.

Misdemeanor   Crime punishable by confinement in city or county jail for a period of less than one year; a lesser offense.

Mistake   Affirmative defense used by defendants to account for criminal conduct, in which defense is that law violation was accidental or that knowledge of law was absent.

Mistrial   Trial ending before defendant's guilt or innocence can be established; usually results from "hung" jury in which jurors are unable to reach agreement on guilt or innocence; also can occur because of substantial irregularities in trial conduct.

Mitigating Circumstances   Factors that lessen the severity of the crime and/or sentence; such factors include old age, cooperation with police in apprehending other offenders, and lack of intent to inflict injury.

Mixed Sentence   Sentence imposed whenever offenders have been convicted of two or more offenses and judges sentence them to separate sentences for each conviction offense.

Model Penal Code   Code developed by the American Law Institute clarifying crimes and accompanying punishments; no jurisdictions are obligated to adhere to the Model Penal Code.

Modes of Adaptation   Part of Robert Merton's theory of anomie; adaptations were ways individuals coped with and achieved cultural goals by using institutionalized means; modes included conformity, innovation, ritualism, retreatism, and rebellion.

Monitoring the Future   Survey of 3,000 high school students made annually by Institute for Social Research at University of Michigan; attempts to discover hidden delinquency not ordinarily disclosed by published public reports.

Motor Vehicle Theft   Theft or attempted theft of a motor vehicle, including automobiles, trucks, buses, motorcycles, motorscooters, and snowmobiles.

Murder and Nonnegligent Manslaughter   The willful or non-negligent killing of one human being by another.

Narrative   Portion of pre-sentence investigation report prepared by probation officer or private agency in which description of offense and offender are provided; culminates in and justifies a recommendation for a specific sentence to be imposed on the offender by judges.

National Crime Information Center (NCIC)   Center established by the FBI in 1967; central information source for stolen vehicles, accident information, stolen property, arrested persons, fingerprint information, criminal offenses, and criminal offenders and their whereabouts.

National Crime Survey   Published in cooperation with the United States Bureau of the Census, a random survey of 60,000 households, including 127,000 persons 12 years of age or older; includes 50,000 businesses; measures crime committed against specific victims interviewed and not necessarily reported to law enforcement officers.

National Institute of Corrections' Model Classification Project Risk and needs assessment project established by the federal government to enable juvenile judges to make more informed sentencing decisions.

National Youth Survey   Survey of large numbers of youths annually or at other intervals to assess hidden delinquency among high school students.

Negligence   Liability accruing to prison or correctional program administrators and POs as the result of a failure to perform a duty owed clients or inmates or the improper or inadequate performance of that duty; may include negligent entrustment, negligent training, negligent assignment, negligent retention, or negligent supervision (for example, providing POs with revolvers and not providing them with firearms training).

Net-Widening   Pulling juveniles into juvenile justice system who would not otherwise be involved in delinquent activity; applies to many status offenders (also known as "widening the net").

Neutralization Theory   *See* Drift theory.

New Jersey Intensive Probation Supervision Program   Program commenced in 1983 to serve low-risk incarcerated offenders

and draws clients from inmate volunteers; program selectivity limits participants through a seven-stage selection process; participants must serve at least four months in prison or jail before being admitted to program which monitors their progress extensively; similar to Georgia Intensive Probation Supervision Program in successfulness and low recidivism scores among participants.

New Jersey v. *T.L.O.* (1985) Landmark case where court held that standard of search and seizure involving school searches of student lockers and personal effects is a lesser standard than probable cause; established reasonable suspicion and totality of circumstances as justifications for student searches.

New York Children's Aid Society Organization created in 1853 by Charles Loring Brace to find foster homes for dependent children, orphaned youths, runaways, and others.

New York House of Refuge   Established in New York City in 1825 by the Society for the Prevention of Pauperism; school managed largely status offenders; compulsory education provided; strict prisonlike regimen was considered detrimental to youthful clientele.

New York Juvenile Offender Law   Law providing for automatic transfer of juveniles of certain ages to criminal courts for processing, provided they have committed especially serious crimes.

No Bill Bill issued by grand jury indicating no basis exists for charges against defendant; charges are usually dropped or dismissed later by judge.

Nolle Prosequi Decision by prosecution to decline to pursue criminal case against defendant.

Nominal Dispositions Juvenile adjudicatory disposition resulting in lenient penalties such as warnings and/or probation.

Nonavertable Recidivist Offender whose prior sentence would not have affected the commission of new crimes.

Noninterventionist Model Philosophy of juvenile delinquent treatment involving the absence of any direct intervention with certain juveniles who have been taken into custody.

Numbers Game Model Caseload assignment model for probation or parole officers in which total number of offender/clients is divided by number of officers.

Objective Parole Criteria General qualifying conditions that permit parole boards to make nonsubjective parole decisions without regard to an inmate's race, religion, gender, age, or socioeconomic status.

Offender Rehabilitation Condition achieved when criminals are reintegrated into their communities and refrain from further criminal activity. *See also* Rehabilitation.

Offense Escalation The belief that less serious adult or juvenile offenders will eventually progress to more serious types of crimes.

Office of Juvenile Justice and Delinquency Prevention Agency established by Congress under the Juvenile Justice and Delinquency Prevention Act of 1974; designed to remove status offenders from jurisdiction of juvenile courts and dispose of their cases less formally.

Outreach Centers Substations or satellite offices of regular probation and parole agencies.

Overcharging Action by prosecutors of charging a defendant with more crimes than are reasonable under the circumstances; raising the charge to a more serious level, expecting a conviction for a lesser crime.

Overcrowding Condition that exists when numbers of prisoners exceed the space allocations for which the jail or prison is designed; often associated with double-bunking or putting two prisoners in one cell.

Paraprofessional Person who works in a community agency or public organization; has some skills relating to corrections, but is not certified or has not completed any formal course of study culminating in a corrections certificate or degree.

Parens Patriae Literally "parent of the country"; refers to doctrine whereby state oversees the welfare of youth; originally established by king of England and administered through chancellors.

Parole Conditional release of offenders from confinement facility prior to expiration of their sentences; offenders are placed under supervision of a parole agency.

Parole Board	Committee of persons who determine whether or not prisoners should be granted parole—i.e., released prior to serving the full terms prescribed by their original sentences.

Parolee	Offender who has served some time in jail or prison, but has been released prior to serving entire sentence imposed upon conviction.

Parole Officer	Corrections official who supervises parolee.

Parole Revocation	Two-stage proceeding that may result in a parolee's reincarceration in jail or prison; first stage is a preliminary hearing to determine whether parolee violated any specific parole condition; second stage is to determine whether parole should be cancelled and the offender reincarcerated.

Part I and Part II Offenses	Two major categories of offenses reported in the *Uniform Crime Reports* by the Federal Bureau of Investigation annually; Part I offenses are felonies, whereas Part II offenses are ordinarily misdemeanors.

Peer Juries	Juries that consist of youths under age 17 who make informal recommendations to judges about the dispositions of young offenders; operated in selected jurisdictions, such as Columbia County and Liberty County, Georgia.

Penal Code of Japan	Defines all criminal conduct; no distinctions are made between felonies or misdemeanors, but each specified statutory offense has an explicit punishment; punishments are graduated in severity according to seriousness of crime.

People's Courts	Soviet courts in which juvenile offenders are tried; proceedings are adversarial to a limited extent, since defense counsel may rebut evidence submitted by the procurators; parent's attendance is optional, although they may be required to testify at the court's discretion.

Persistent Offender	Same as chronic offender; repeat offender; recidivist; one who commits frequent delinquent acts.

Petition	Official document filed in juvenile court on juvenile's behalf, specifying reasons for the youth's court appearance; document asserts that juveniles fall within the categories of dependent or neglected, status offender, or delinquent, and the reasons for such assertions are usually provided.

Petit Jury	Traditional jury that hears evidence of crime in jury trial and decides a defendant's guilt or innocence.

Philadelphia Society for Alleviating the Miseries of Public Prisons	Philanthropic society established by the Quakers in Pennsylvania in 1787; attempted to establish prison reforms to improve living conditions of inmates; brought food, clothing, and religious instruction to inmates.

Plea Bargaining	A preconviction agreement between the defendant and the state whereby the defendant pleads guilty with the expectation of either a reduction in the charges, a promise of sentencing leniency, or some other government concession short of the maximum penalties that could be imposed under the law.

Police Cautioning   Verbal reprimands by police officers when confronting certain low-risk juveniles who may not be committing crimes but may be violating curfew or other minor infractions.

Police Discretion   The range of behavioral choices available to police officers within the limits of their power.

Police Prosecutors   Police officers in some jurisdictions who act as prosecutors to bring formal charges against juveniles; law enforcement officers who perform prosecutorial functions.

Poor Laws   Laws in English Middle Ages designed to punish debtors by imprisoning them until they could pay their debts; imprisonment was for life, or until someone could pay their debts for them.

Positive School   Belief that criminal conduct may be explained by biochemical and genetic factors; physical features of persons can be used to infer things about their criminal propensities.

Prediction   An assessment of some expected future behavior of a person, including criminal acts, arrests, or convictions.

Predictors of Dangerousness and Risk   Any assessment devices that attempt to forecast one's potential for violence or risk to others; any factors that are used in such instruments.

Predispositional Report   Report prepared by juvenile intake officer for juvenile judge; purpose of report is to furnish the judge with background about juveniles to make a more informed sentencing decision; similar to PSI report.

Preliminary Examination   See Preliminary hearing.

Preliminary Hearing   Proceeding in which both prosecutor and defense counsel present some evidence against and on behalf of defendants; proceeding to determine whether probable cause exists to believe that a crime was committed and that the particular defendant committed the crime.

Pre-Offense Juveniles   Japanese children who commit status offenses, such as running away from home, violating curfew, or being truant.

Preponderance of Evidence   Standard used in civil courts to determine defendant or plaintiff liability.

Pre-Sentence Investigation   Investigation of a convicted defendant conducted at the request of the judge; purpose of investigation is to determine worthiness of defendant for parole or sentencing leniency.

Presentence Investigation Report (PSI)   Document prepared, usually by a probation agency or officer, that provides background information on the convicted offender including name, age, present address, occupation (if any), potential for employment, crime(s) involved, relevant circumstances associated with the crime, family data, evidence of prior record (if any), marital status, and other relevant data; report filed by probation or parole officer appointed by court; report contains background information, socioeconomic data, and demographic data relative to defendant.

Presentment   Charge brought against a defendant by a grand jury acting on its own authority.

President's Commission on Law Enforcement and the Administration of Justice   National commission established in 1967 to establish and promote standards for the selection of police officers and correctional employees; led to the establishment of the Law Enforcement Assistance Administration (LEAA). *See also* Law Enforcement Assistance Administration.

Presumptive Sentencing   Sentence prescribed by statute for each offense or class of offense; the sentence must be imposed in all unexceptional circumstances, but where there are mitigating or aggravating circumstances, the judge is permitted some latitude in shortening or lengthening the sentence within specific boundaries, usually with written justification.

Pretrial Detention   Order by court for defendant (juvenile or adult) to be confined prior to adjudicatory proceeding; usually reserved for defendants considered dangerous or likely to flee the juris-

diction if released temporarily; *see also* ROR.

Pretrial Diversion   Diversionary measure for selected defendants prior to any formal trial proceeding; designed to provide person with counseling or other services rather than incarceration; avoids trial and record.

Pretrial Release   Freedom from incarceration prior to trial granted to defendants. *See* ROR.

Prevention/Control Model   Philosophy of attempting to repress or prevent delinquency by using early intervention strategies, including wilderness programs, elementary school interventions.

Preventive Detention   Constitutional right of police to detain suspects prior to trial without bail, where suspects are likely to flee from the jurisdiction or pose serious risks to others.

Primary Deviation   Deviation occurring when youths spontaneously violate the law by engaging in occasional pranks.

Prison   Facility designed to house long-term serious offenders; operated by state or federal government; houses inmates for terms longer than one year.

Privatization   Trend in prison and jail management and correctional operations generally in which private interests are becoming increasingly involved in the management and operations of correctional institutions.

Probable Cause   Reasonable belief that a crime has been committed and that the person accused of the crime committed it.

Probatio   A period of proving or trial or forgiveness.

Probation   Sentence not involving confinement that imposes conditions and retains authority in sentencing court to modify conditions of sentence or resentence offender for probation violations.

Probationer   Person who does not go to jail or prison after being convicted of a crime, but rather serves a term outside of prison subject to certain behavioral conditions.

Probation Officer (PO)   Corrections official who functions to monitor convict's progress outside of prison.

Procurators   Soviet prosecutors.

Project New Pride   One of the most popular probation programs, established in Denver, Colorado in 1973; a blend of education, counseling, employment, and cultural education directed at those more serious offenders between the ages of 14 and 17; juveniles eligible for the New Pride program must have at least two prior convictions for serious misdemeanors and/or felonies; goals include (1) reintegrating participants into their communities through school participation or employment, and (2) reducing recidivism rates among offenders.

Project Outward Bound   *See* Wilderness Experiments.

Prosecution   Carrying forth of criminal proceedings against a person culminating in a trial or other final disposition such as a plea of guilty in lieu of trial.

Prosecutor   Court official who commences civil and criminal proceedings against defendants; represents state or government interests; prosecutes defendants on behalf of state or government.

Prosecutorial Waivers   Transfers of juveniles to criminal courts by prosecutorial action or recommendation; transfers made at request of juvenile prosecutor.

Provo Experiment   Experiment with delinquent youths conducted in Provo, Utah during 1950s and 1960s; project directors manipulated delinquent youths through interventions that focused discussions on self-concepts and acquiring delinquent characteristics; process of introspection led to unlearning delinquent behaviors through group processes.

Psychoanalytic Theories   Theories that stress the importance of early childhood experiences as influential on adult conduct; Sigmund Freud's theory, involving the id, ego, superego, and libido as different dimensions and/or forces that inhibit or release various behaviors.

Psychological Theories   Theories that focus on the learning process, the process whereby individuals acquire language, self-definitions, and a moral sense.

Public Defender   Court-appointed attorney for indigent defendants who cannot afford private counsel.

Radical Criminology   View that crime is a product of socioeconomic factors, where more wealthy interests create and perpetuate discriminatory laws and law enforcement efforts which target persons of lower socioeconomic status.

Radical Nonintervention Similar to a "do nothing" policy of delinquency nonintervention.

Rand Corporation Private institution that conducts investigations and surveys of criminals and examines a wide variety of social issues; located in Santa Monica, California; distributes literature to many criminal justice agencies; contracts with and conducts research for other institutions.

Reality Therapy Model Equivalent of shock probation, whereby short incarcerative sentences are believed to provide "shock" value for juvenile offenders and scare them so that they avoid reoffending behaviors.

Rearrest One indicator of recidivism; consists of taking parolee or probationer into custody for investigation in relation to crimes committed; not necessarily indicative of new crimes committed by probationers or parolees; may be the result of police officer suspicion.

Recidivism New crime committed by an offender who has served time in prison or was placed on probation for previous offense; tendency to repeat crimes.

Recidivism Rate Proportion of offenders who, when released from probation or parole, commit further crimes.

Recidivist Offender who has committed previous offenses.

Reconviction Measure of recidivism whereby former convicted offenders are found guilty of new crimes by a judge or jury.

Reform Schools Different types of vocational institutions designed to both punish and rehabilitate youthful offenders; operated much like prisons as total institutions.

Regimented Inmate Discipline Program (RID) Oklahoma Department of Corrections program operated in Lexington, Oklahoma for juveniles; program stresses military-type discipline and accountability; facilities are secure and privately operated.

Rehabilitation Correcting criminal behavior through educational and other means, usually associated with prisons.

Rehabilitation Model Model of youth management similar to medical model, in which juvenile delinquents are believed to be suffering from social and psychological handicaps; provides experiences to build self-concept; experiences stress educational and social remedies.

Rehabilitative Ideal *See* Rehabilitation.

Reincarceration Return to prison or jail for one or more reasons including parole or probation violations and revocations, rearrests, and reconvictions.

Released On Own Recognizance (*See* ROR)

Restitution Stipulation by court that offenders must compensate victims for their financial losses resulting from crime; compensation for psychological, physical, or financial loss by victim; may be imposed as a part of an incarcerative sentence.

Reverse Waiver Actions (also called *reverse waiver hearings*) Formal proceedings to contest automatic transfer of juveniles to jurisdiction of criminal courts; used in jurisdictions with automatic transfer laws.

Reynolds, James Bronson Early prison reformer, established The University Settlement in 1893 in New York; settlement project was ultimately abandoned when Reynolds and others could not demonstrate its effectiveness at reform to politicians and the public generally.

Risk/Needs Assessments, Instruments Predictive devices intended to forecast offender propensity to commit new offenses or recidivate.

Role Ambiguity Lack of clarity about work expectations; unfamiliarity with correctional tasks.

Role Conflict Clash between personal feelings and beliefs and job duties as probation, parole, or correctional officer.

ROR Means "released on own recognizance"; used in connection with bail determination in initial appearance proceedings, preliminary examinations, and arraignments; defendants do not have to post bond and are released on their honor to report to court at a later date for trial.

Ruffin v. *Commonwealth* (1871) Landmark ruling by Virginia judge establishing the "hands-off" doctrine practiced by subsequent courts and applied to adult corrections for seventy years.

Rules of Criminal Procedure Formal rules followed by state and federal governments in processing defendants from arrest through trial; rules vary from state to state.

Runaway Any juvenile who leaves home for long-term periods without parental consent or supervision; may include unruly youth who cannot be controlled or managed by parents or guardians.

Salient Factor Score (SFS 81) Score which is used by parole boards and agencies to forecast an offender's risk to the public and future dangerousness; numerical classification that predicts the probability of a parolee's success if parole is granted.

Sanctioner Value System System used by parole boards in early release decision making where amount of time served is equated with seriousness of conviction offense.

San Francisco Project Project that compared recidivism rates of probationers supervised by POs with caseloads of twenty and forty respectively and found that no significant differences in recidivism rates of probationers were reported between "intensive" and "ideal" caseload scenarios.

Scared Straight Juvenile delinquency prevention program that sought to frighten samples of hard-core delinquent youths by having them confront inmates in a Rahway, New Jersey prison; inmates would yell at and belittle them, calling them names, cursing, and yelling; inmates would tell them about sexual assaults and other prison horrors in an attempt to get them to refrain from reoffending.

Scavenger Gangs Gangs formed primarily as a means of socializing and for mutual protection.

Schall v. *Martin* Landmark 1984 juvenile rights case that upheld a court's right to order the pretrial detention of juveniles deemed to be dangerous.

Screening Procedure used by prosecutor to define which cases have prosecutive merit and which do not; some screening bureaus are made up of police and lawyers with trial experience.

Sealing of Records *See* Expungement orders.

Secondary Deviation Deviation occurring whenever youths commit crimes that become a part of their behavior patterns and lifestyles.

Secure Confinement Confinement of juvenile offender in facility which restricts movement in community; similar to adult penal facility involving total incarceration.

Selective Incapacitation Selectively incarcerating individuals who show a high likelihood of repeating their previous offenses; based on forecasts of potential for recidivism; includes but is not limited to dangerousness.

Self-Report Information Surveys of youths (or adults) based upon disclosures these persons make about the types of offenses they have committed and how fre-

quently they have committed them; considered more accurate than official estimates.

Sentence Recommendation Plea Bargaining Plea bargaining wherein prosecutor recommends a specific sentence to the judge in exchange for a defendant's guilty plea.

Sentencing Disparity Any variation in severity of sentence or length of sentence imposed which might be attributable to a person's gender, race, ethnic background, or socioeconomic status.

Sentencing Memorandum Court decision that furnishes ruling or finding and orders to be implemented relative to convicted offenders; does not necessarily include reasons or rationale for sentence imposed.

SFS 81 *See* Salient Factor Score.

Shape-Up Program Diversion program in which juveniles spend two days over a two-week period at Colorado State Penitentiary to discuss confinement with prisoners; shock value of prison life seems to be therapeutic for youths and diverts them from further delinquent conduct.

Shock Parole *See* Shock Probation.

Shock Probation An intermediate punishment in which offender is initially sentenced to a term of secure detention; after a period of time, between 90 and 180 days, youth is removed from detention and sentenced to serve the remainder of sentence on probation; the term ''shock probation" was coined by Ohio authorities in 1964.

Short-Term Facility   Any incarcerative institution for either adults or juveniles in which confinement is for a period of less than one year; jails are considered short-term facilities.

Situationally Based Discretion   Confronting crime in the streets on the basis of immediate situational factors, time of night, presence of weapons, numbers of offenders; requires extensive personal judgments by police officers.

Social Control Theory (also called *bonding theory*)   Theory that stresses processual aspects of youths' becoming "bonded" or socially integrated with the norms of society; the greater the integration or bonding with teachers and parents, the less likelihood that youths will engage in delinquent conduct.

Socialization   Learning through contact with others.

Society for the Prevention of Pauperism   Philanthropic society that established first public reformatory in New York in 1825, the New York House of Refuge.

Sociobiology   Study of biological basis for social action.

Solitary Confinement   Segregation of prisoners in individual cells; originally used at Walnut Street Jail in Philadelphia, Pennsylvania, in 1790.

SOS   "See Our Side" juvenile "aversion" program in Prince George's County, Maryland, designed to prevent delinquency.

Specialized Caseloads Model   Probation officer caseload model based on POs' unique skills and knowledge relative to offender drug or alcohol problems; some POs are assigned particular clients with unique problems that require more than average PO expertise.

Specialized Offender Accountability Program (SOAP)   Program operated by the Lexington Correctional Center in Oklahoma for juveniles under 22 years of age; based upon military disciplinary model; individualized treatment is provided, although a strict military regimen is observed.

Split Sentences   *See* Combination sentences.

Standard of Proof   Norms used by courts to determine validity of claims or allegations of wrongdoing against offenders; civil standards of proof are "clear and convincing evidence" and "preponderance of evidence," while criminal standard is "beyond a reasonable doubt."

Standard Probation   In this procedure, probationers must conform to all terms of their probation program, but their contact with probation officers is minimal; often, their contact is by telephone or letter once or twice a month.

Stanford v. *Kentucky* (1989)   Landmark case decided with *Wilkins* v. *Missouri* (1989) by U.S. Supreme Court authorizing application of death penalty for juveniles aged 16 and 17 years of age respectively at time their capital crimes were committed.

Stare Decisis "To let stand." This is the principle whereby lower courts rule in specific cases consistent with similar rules of higher courts.

Station Adjustments   Decisions made by police officers about certain juveniles taken into custody and brought to police stations for processing and investigation; adjustments often result in verbal reprimands and release to custody of parents.

Status Offender   Anyone committing a status offense, including runaway behavior, truancy, curfew violation, loitering. *See* Status offense.

Status Offense   Violation of statute or ordinance by minor, which, if committed by adult, would not be considered either a felony or a misdemeanor; also, any acts committed by juveniles which would (1) bring them to the attention of juvenile courts and (2) not be crimes if committed by adults.

Stigmatization   Social process whereby offenders acquire undesirable characteristics as the result of imprisonment or court appearances; undesirable criminal or delinquent labels are assigned to those who are processed through the criminal and juvenile justice systems.

Sting Operations   Actions of law enforcement officers designed to trap criminals; usually involve undercover activities, such as buying stolen property from burglars in an attempt to apprehend them; law enforcement officers pose as dishonest persons who buy stolen merchandise knowingly.

Stop Assaultive Children Program (SAC)   Program started in Phoenix, Arizona, in late 1980s and designed for those youths who have committed serious family violence; children are detained in a juvenile facility for a short time, and their release is contingent upon being law-abiding, observing curfew, and other conditions; their prosecution is deferred; must participate in counseling; may include volunteer work.

Strain Theory   Subculture theory of delinquency focusing on stress or tension between societal values and values of subgroups of delinquent youths.

Strategic Leniency   Selective leniency with certain offenders who are believed to be nonviolent and least likely to reoffend.

Stress   Negative anxiety which is accompanied by an alarm reaction, resistance, and exhaustion; such anxiety contributes to heart disease, headaches, high blood pressure, and ulcers.

Structured Discretion   Term applied to judicial sentencing decisions in which guidelines exist to limit the severity or leniency of sentences imposed; intention of structured discretion is to standardize sentences and create greater fairness in the courts; also applies to early release parole decisions by parole boards.

Subcultures   Albert Cohen's notion of delinquent cultures within a larger culture; value systems and modes of achievement gain status and recognition apart from the mainstream culture.

Summary Courts   Minor Japanese courts having fixed jurisdictions where fines imposed or sentences cannot exceed previously specified maximums; actions are monitored closely by High Courts.

Summary Offenses   Violations of the law in Great Britain such as public drunkenness, disorderly conduct, petty theft, and solicitation for prostitution.

Superego   In Sigmund Freud's psychoanalytic theory, conscience; higher-level moral development.

Theories   Integrated explanatory schemes that predict relationships between two or more phenomena; provide rational foundation to account for or explain things; integral components include propositions and assumptions, or different kinds of statements about the real world that vary in their tentativeness or certainty.

Thompson v. *Oklahoma* (1988)   Landmark juvenile case in which U.S. Supreme Court held that executions of juveniles who committed capital crimes when they were under age 16 constitutes cruel and unusual punishment and is prohibited.

Totality of Circumstances   Sometimes used as the standard whereby offender guilt is determined or search and seizure warrants may be obtained; officers consider entire set of circumstances surrounding apparently illegal event and act accordingly.

Traditional Juvenile Courts   Courts in which proceedings are characterized by less formal adjudications and greater use of detention.

Traditional Rehabilitation Model. *See* Rehabilitation.

Traditional Treatment-Oriented Model   Model of supervising offenders that stresses traditional, rehabilitative measures that seek to reintegrate offenders into the community through extensive assistance.

Transfer   Proceeding in which juveniles are remanded to the jurisdiction of criminal courts; also known as certification and waiver.

Transfer Hearing   Also known as *certification* or *waiver*, this is a proceeding to determine whether juveniles should be certified as adults for purposes of being subjected to jurisdiction of adult criminal courts where more severe penalties may be imposed.

Treater Value System   Parole board decision making system in which emphasis is upon rehabilitation, and early release decisions are made on the basis of what will best suit the offender.

Treatment Model   *See* Medical Model.

Truants   Juveniles who are habitually absent from school without excuse.

True Bills   Indictments or charges against defendants brought by grand juries after considering inculpatory evidence presented by prosecutor.

Two-Tiered Juvenile Court System   System of juvenile court organization suggested by Gelber, wherein first tier adjudicates matters involving juveniles under 14 years of age and always involves rehabilitative, nonincarcerative sanctions; second tier involves those from 14 to 18; jury trials may be provided for those in second tier.

Unconditional Diversion Program   Program in which no restrictions are placed on offender's behavior; no formal controls operate to control or monitor divertee's behavior.

Uniform Crime Reports   Official source of crime information published by Federal Bureau of Investigation annually; accepts information from reporting law enforcement agencies about criminal arrests; classifies crimes according to various index criteria; tabulates information about offender age, gender, race, and other attributes.

University Settlement   Privately operated facility founded in New York in 1893 by James Bronson Reynolds to provide assistance and job referral services to community residents; settlement involved in probation work in 1901; eventually abandoned after considerable public skepticism, and when political supporters withdrew their support.

U.S. Army Correctional Activity (USACA)   Boot camp in Fort Riley, Kansas established in 1968. *See also* Boot camps.

U.S. Code Annotated   Comprehensive compendium of federal laws and statutes, including landmark cases and discussions of law applications.

U.S. Sentencing Guidelines   Guidelines implemented by federal courts in November 1987 obligating federal judges to impose presumptive sentences on all convicted offenders; guidelines exist based upon offense seriousness and offender characteristics; judges may depart from guidelines only by justifying their departures in writing.

Victim Compensation   Any financial restitution payable to victims by either the state or convicted offenders.

Victim Impact Statement   Statement filed voluntarily by victim of crime, appended to the presentence investigation report as a supplement for judicial consideration in sentencing offender; describes injuries to victims resulting from convicted offender's actions.

Victimization   The basic measure of the occurrence of a crime; a specific criminal act that affects a single victim.

Victim−Offender Mediation Model   Juvenile offender restitution model which focuses on victim−offender reconciliation.

Victim Reparations Model   Juvenile offender restitution model wherein juveniles compensate their victims directly for their offenses.

Violent Juvenile Offender Program (VJOP)   Program designed to provide positive interventions and treatments; reintegrative programs, including transitional residential programs, are provided for those youths who have been subject to long-term detention; provides for social networking, educational opportunities for youths, social learning, and goal-oriented behavioral skills.

Visionquest   Carefully regulated, intensive supervision program designed to provide positive social and psychological experiences for juveniles; reintegrative program to improve educational and social skills; wilderness program.

Voir Dire   A proceeding in which the defense and prosecuting attorneys may interview or examine potential jurors in open court to determine their impartiality.

Waiver   *See* Transfer.

Waiver Motion or Hearing   Motion by prosecutor to transfer juvenile charged with various offenses to a criminal or adult court for prosecution; waiver motions make it possible to sustain adult criminal penalties.

Walnut Street Jail   Reconstructed from earlier Philadelphia Jail in 1790; first real attempt by jail officials to classify and segregate prisoners according to age, gender, and crime seriousness; introduced idea of solitary confinement.

Wilderness Experiments   Experience programs that include a wide array of outdoor programs designed to improve a juvenile's self-worth, self-concept, pride, and trust in others.

Wilkins v. *Missouri* (1989)   Landmark case decided by U.S. Supreme Court, together with *Stanford* v. *Kentucky* (1989), authorizing use of death penalty for juveniles aged 16 and 17 at time they committed their capital crimes.

Workhouses   *See* Bridewell Workhouse.

Work Release   Community-based program whereby persons about to be paroled work in community at jobs during day, return to facility at night; limited supervision; any program that provides for prison labor in the community, under conditions of relaxed supervision, and for which prisoners are paid adequate wages.

Young Persons   In Great Britain, youths considered fully responsible for their actions under criminal law.

XYY Theory   Asserts that certain chromosomatic abnormalities may precipitate violence and delinquent behavior; X chromosomes are regarded as passive, while Y chromosomes are considered aggressive; some persons have two Y chromosomes, and thus, they are considered especially aggressive and inclined toward violence.

Bibliography

ACKER, JAMES R. (1987). "Social Sciences and Criminal Law: Capital Punishment by the Numbers—An Analysis of *McClesky v. Kemp.*" *Criminal Law Bulletin* 23:454–482.

AGEE, VICKIE L., and BRUCE MCWILLIAMS. (1984). "The Role of Group Therapy and the Therapeutic Community in Treating the Violent Juvenile Offender." In *Violent Juvenile Offenders: An Anthology* (Robert A. Mathias, Paul DeMuro, and Richard S. Allinson, eds.). San Francisco, CA: National Council on Crime and Delinquency.

AGNEW, ROBERT. (1984). "Appearance and Delinquency." *Criminology* 22:421–440.

AGNEW, ROBERT. (1985a). "A Revised Strain Theory of Delinquency." *Social Forces* 64:151–167.

AGNEW, ROBERT. (1985b). "Social Control Theory and Delinquency: A Test of Theory." *Criminology* 23:47–61.

AGOPIAN, MICHAEL W. (1989). "Targeting Juvenile Gang Offenders for Community Service." *Community Alternatives: International Journal of Family Care* 1: 99–108.

AKERS, RONALD L. *et al.* (1983). "Are Self-Report Studies of Adolescent Deviance Valid? Biochemical Measures, Randomized Response, and the Bogus Pipeline in Smoking Behavior." *Social Forces* 62:234–251.

ALASKA SENATE FINANCE COMMITTEE. (1986). *Running Toward Prison: Who Are Alaska's Runaways and Will They Fill Tomorrow's Prisons?* Juneau: Alaska Senate Finance Committee.

ALEXANDER, JAMES F. *et al.* (1988). *"Family Approaches to Treating Delinquents."* In *Mental Illness, Delinquency, Addictions, and Neglect* (Elam W. Nunnally, Catherine S. Chilman, and Fred M. Cox, eds.). Newbury Park, CA: Sage.

ALLEN-HAGEN, BARBARA (1991). *Public Juvenile Facilities: Children in Custody 1989.* Washington, DC: U. S. Department of Justice, Office of Justice Programs.

ALSCHULER, ALBERT W. (1979). "Plea Bargaining and Its History." *Law and Society Review* 13:211–245.

ALTSCHULER, DAVID M., and TROY L. ARMSTRONG. (1990a). "Designing an Intensive Aftercare Program for High-Risk Juveniles." *Corrections Today* 52:170–171.

ALTSCHULER, DAVID M., and TROY L. ARMSTRONG. (1990b). "Intensive Parole for High-Risk Juvenile Offenders: A Framework for Action." Unpublished paper presented at the American Society of Criminology meetings, November, Baltimore, MD.

AMANDES, RICHARD B. (1979). "Hire a Gang Leader: A Delinquency Prevention Program That Works." *Juvenile and Family Court Journal* 30:37–40.

AMERICAN BAR ASSOCIATION. (1986). *Criminal and Juvenile Justice Policies: A Roadmap for State Legislators and Policymakers.* Washington, DC: American Bar Association.

AMERICAN CORRECTIONAL ASSOCIATION. (1983). *The American Prison: From the Beginning . . . A Pictorial History.* College Park, MD: American Correctional Association.

AMERICAN CORRECTIONAL ASSOCIATION. (1985). "Special Issue: Juveniles in the Community and in Custody." *Corrections Today* 47:14–36, 78–82.

AMERICAN CORRECTIONAL ASSOCIATION. (1986). *Vital Statistics in Corrections.* College Park, MD: American Correctional Association.

AMERICAN CORRECTIONAL ASSOCIATION. (1987). *1987 Directory.* College Park, MD: American Correctional Assoication.

AMERICAN CORRECTIONAL ASSOCIATION. (1988). *1988 Directory.* College Park, MD: American Correctional Association.

AMERICAN CORRECTIONAL ASSOCIATION. (1989). *1989 Directory.* College Park, MD: American Correctional Association.

AMERICAN CORRECTIONAL ASSOCIATION. (1990). *1990 Directory.* College Park, MD: American Correctional Association.

AMERICAN CORRECTIONAL ASSOCIATION. (1991). *1991 Directory.* College Park, MD: American Correctional Association.

AMERICAN JAILS. (1990). "England and Wales." *American Jails* 4:92.

ANDERSON, DENNIS R., and DONALD F. SCHOEN. (1985). "Diversion Programs: Effect of Stigmatization on Juvenile Status Offenders." *Juvenile and Family Court Journal* 36:13–25.

ANSON, RICHARD H., and CAROL S. EASON. (1986). "The Effects of Confinement on Delinquent Self-Image." *Juvenile and Family Court Journal* 37:39–47.

ARBUTHNOT, JACK, DONALD A. GORDON, and GREGORY J. JURKOVIC. (1987). "Personality." In *Handbook of Juvenile Delinquency* (Herbert C. Quay, ed.). New York: Wiley.

ARMSTRONG, TROY L. (1988). "National Survey of Juvenile Intensive Probation Supervision. Part I." *Criminal Justice Abstracts* 20:342–348.

ARMSTRONG, TROY L., DENNIS MALONEY, and DENNIS ROMIG. (1990). "The Balanced Approach in Juvenile Probation: Principles, Issues, and Application." *Perspectives* 14:8–13.

ARRIGONA, NANCY, and TONY FABELO. (1987). *A Case Study of Juvenile Probation in Texas.* Austin, TX: Criminal Justice Policy Council.

ARTHUR, LINDSAY G. (ed.). (1983). "Dispositions." *Juvenile and Family Court Journal* 34:1–100.

AUGUST, ROBIN. (1981). *A Study of Juveniles Transferred for Prosecution to the Adult System.* Miami, FL: Office of the Dade-Miami Criminal Justice Council.

AUSTIN, JAMES, and BARRY KRISBERG. (1982). "The Unmet Promise of Alternatives to Incarceration." *Crime and Delinquency* 29:374–409.

AWAD, GEORGE. (1985). "Juvenile Delinquency." In *Clinical Criminology: The Assessment and Treatment of Criminal Behavior* (Mark H. Ben-Aron, Stephen J. Hucker, and Christopher D. Webster, eds.). Toronto: M and M Graphics.

BAILEY, F. LEE, and HENRY B. ROTHBLATT. (1982). *Handling Juvenile Delinquency Cases.* Rochester, NY: Lawyers Co-Operative Publishing Company.

BAILEY, WILLIAM C. (1983). "Disaggregation in Deterrence and Death Penalty Research: The Case of Murder in Chicago." *Journal of Criminal Law and Criminology* 74:827–859.

BAILEY, WILLIAM C. (1984). "Murder and Capital Punishment in the Nation's Capital." *Justice Quarterly* 1:211–233.

BAIRD, S. CHRISTOPHER. (1984). *Classification of Juveniles in Corrections: A Model Systems Approach.* Washington, DC: Arthur D. Little.

BAIRD, S. CHRISTOPHER. (1985). "Classifying Juveniles: Making the Most of an Important Management Tool." *Corrections Today* 47:32–38.

BAIRD, S. CHRISTOPHER. (1987). *A Model Management System for Juvenile Corrections.* Madison, WI: Isthmus Associates.

BAIRD, S. CHRISTOPHER *et al.* (1986). *Issues in Juvenile Delinquency.* College Park, MD: American Correctional Association.

BAKAL, YITZHAK, and BARRY KRISBERG. (1987). *Placement Needs Assessment for Youth Committed to Oregon Training Schools.* San Francisco, CA: National Council on Crime and Delinquency.

BAKER, WENDY, and WENDY B. NAIDICH. (1986). *Assessing the Needs of Homeless and Runaway Youth.* New York: Covenant House.

BALL, RICHARD A., and J. ROBERT LILLY. (1987). "The Phenomenology of Privacy and the Power of the State: Home Incarceration with Electronic Monitoring." In *Critical Issues in Criminology and Criminal Justice* (J. E. Scott and J. Hirschi, eds.). Beverly Hills, CA: Sage.

BALL, RICHARD A., C. RONALD HUFF, and J. ROBERT LILLY. (1988). *House Arrest and Correctional Policy: Doing Time at Home.* Beverly Hills, CA: Sage.

BANDURA, ALBERT, and RICHARD WALTERS. (1959). *Adolescent Aggression.* New York: Ronald Press.

BANKS, J., T. R. SILER, and R. L. RARDIN. (1977). "Past and Present Findings in Intensive Adult Probation." *Federal Probation* 41:20–25.

BARNUM, RICHARD. (1987). "Biomedical Problems in Juvenile Delinquency: Issues in Diagnosis and Treatment." In *From Children to Citizens* (James Q. Wilson and Glenn C. Loury, eds.). New York: Springer-Verlag.

BARTOLLAS, CLEMENS. (1990). *Juvenile Delinquency,* 2nd ed. New York: Macmillan.

BARTON, WILLIAM, and JOSEFINA FIGUEIRA-MCDONOUGH. (1985). "Attachments, Gender, and Delinquency." *Deviant Behavior* 6:119–144.

BAZEMORE, S. GORDON. (1989). *The Restitution Experience in Youth Employment: A Monograph and Training Guide to Job Components.* Washington, DC: U. S. Department of Justice.

BECCARIA, CESARE BONESANA. (1764). *On Crimes and Punishments.* (reprinted edition: Indianapolis, IN: Bobbs-Merrill, 1963).

BECK, A., S. KLINE, and L. GREENFELD. (1988). *Survey of Youth In Custody, 1987.* Washington, DC: U. S. Department of Justice, Bureau of Justice Statistics.

BECKER, HOWARD S. (1963). *Outsiders: Studies in the Sociology of Deviance.* New York: Free Press.

BEDAU, HUGO A. (1982). *The Death Penalty in America.* New York: Oxford University Press.

BEDEROW, LAURI S., and FREDERIC G. REAMER. (1981). *Treating the Severely Disturbed Juvenile Offender: A Review of Issues and Programs.* Washington, DC: Report submitted to the Office of Juvenile Justice and Delinquency Prevention (Grant 79-JN-AX-0018).

BELL, D., and K. LANG. (1985). "The Intake Dispositions of Juvenile Offenders." *Journal of Research on Crime and Delinquency* 22:309–328.

BENDA, BRENT B. (1987). "Comparison of Rates of Recidivism among Status Offenders and Delinquents." *Adolescence* 22:445–458.

BENNETT, RICHARD R., and SANDRA BAXTER. (1985). "Police and Community Participation in Anti-Crime Programs." In *Police Management Today: Issues and Case Studies* (James J. Fyfe, ed.). Washington, DC: International City Management Association.

BENTHAM, JEREMY. (1790). *An Introduction to the Principles of Morals and Legislation.* (reprinted edition: New York: Hafner, 1948).

BERG, BRUCE L. (1984). "Inmates as Clinical Psychologists: The Use of Sociodrama in a Non-Traditional Delinquency Prevention Program." *International Journal of Offender Therapy and Comparative Criminology* 28:117–124.

BERGER, RONALD J. (1989). "Female Delinquency in the Emancipation Era: A Review of the Literature." *Sex Roles* 21:375–399.

BERGSMANN, ILENE R. (1988). *State Juvenile Justice Education Survey.* Washington, DC: Council of Chief State School Offenders.

BERGSMANN, ILENE R. (1989). "The Forgotten Few: Juvenile Female Offenders." *Federal Probation* 53:73–78.

BERRUETA-CLEMENT, JOHN R. *et al.* (1984). "Preschool's Effects on Social Responsibility." In D. P. Weikart et al. (Eds.), *Changed Lives: The Effects of the Perry Preschool Program on Youths Through Age Nineteen.* Ypsilanti, MI: High/Scope Press.

BERRY, RICHARD L. (1985). *Shape-Up: The Effects of a Prison Aversion Program on Recidivism and Family Dynamics.* Ann Arbor, MI: University Microfilms International.

BESSETTE, JOSEPH M. (1990). *Jail Inmates 1989.* Washington, DC: U. S. Department of Justice.

BEYNON, HELEN. (1986). "The Ideal Civic Condition: Part 2." *Criminal Law Review,* October: 647–659.

BINDER, ARNOLD. (1982). "The Juvenile Court, the U. S. Constitution, and When the Twain Shall Meet." *Journal of Criminal Justice* 12:355–366.

BINDER, ARNOLD. (1989). "Juvenile Diversion." In *Juvenile Justice: Policies, Programs, and Services* (Albert R. Roberts, ed.). Chicago, IL: Dorsey Press.

BINDER, ARNOLD, and GILBERT GEIS. (1984). "Ad Populum Argumentation in Criminology: Juvenile Diversion as Rhetoric." *Crime and Delinquency* 30:309–333.

BINDER, ARNOLD *et al.* (1985). "A Diversionary Approach for the 1980s." *Federal Probation* 49:4–12.

BISHOP, DONNA M., CHARLES E. FRAZIER, and JOHN C. HENRETTA. (1989). "Prosecutorial Waiver: Case Study of a Questionable Reform." *Crime and Delinquency* 35:179–201.

BITTNER, EGON. (1985). "The Capacity to Use Force as the Core of the Police Role." In *Moral Issues in Police Work* (Frederick A. Elliston and Michael Feldberg, eds.). Totowa, NJ: Rowman and Allanheld.

BJERREGAARD, BETH, and PETER C. KRATCOSKI. (1987). "A Comparison of Felony-Connected and Non-Felony Connected Adolescent Homicides." Unpublished paper presented at the American Society of Criminology meetings, November, Montreal, CAN.

BLACK, DONALD J., and ALBERT J. REISS, JR. (1976). "Police Control of Juveniles." In *Readings in Criminal Justice* (Richter H. Moore, Thomas C. Marks, Jr., and Robert V. Barrow, eds.). Indianapolis, IN: Bobbs-Merrill.

BLACK, HENRY CAMPBELL. (1979). *Black's Law Dictionary.* St. Paul, MN: West Publishing Company.

BLACKMORE, JOHN, MARCI BROWN, and BARRY KRISBERG. (1988). *Juvenile Justice Reform: The Bellwether States.* Ann Arbor: University of Michigan.

BLOMBERG, THOMAS G. (1984). *Juvenile Court and Community Corrections.* Lanham, MD: University Press of America.

BLOMBERG, THOMAS G., GARY R. HEALD, and MARK EZELL. (1986). "Diversion and Net Widening: A Cost-Savings Assessment." *Evaluation Review* 10:45–64.

BLUSTEIN, JEFFREY. (1983). "On the Doctrine of *Parens Patriae:* Fiduciary Obligations and State Power." *Criminal Justice Ethics* 2:39–47.

BOOKIN-WEINER, HEDY. (1984). "Assuming Responsibility: Legalizing Preadjudicatory Juvenile Detention." *Crime and Delinquency* 30:39–67.

Bortner, M. A. (1986). "Traditional Rhetoric, Organizational Realities: Remand of Juveniles to Adult Court." *Crime and Delinquency* 32:53–73.

Bowker, Lee H., and Malcolm W. Klein. (1983). "The Etiology of Female Juvenile Delinquency and Gang Membership: A Test of Psychological and Social Structural Explanations." *Adolescence* 18:739–752.

Bowling, Linda R. (1987). "Day Treatment for Juveniles: A Book in Bluegrass County." *Corrections Today* 49:104–106.

Breed, Allen F., and Barry Krisberg. (1986). "Juvenile Corrections: Is There a Future?" *Corrections Today* 48:14–20.

Brennan, William J. (1986). "The 1986 Oliver Wendall Holmes, Jr. Lecture: Constitutional Adjudication of the Death Penalty: A View from the Court." *Harvard Law Review* 100:313–331.

Breunlin, Douglas C. *et al.* (1988). "A Review of the Literature on Family Therapy with Adolescents 1979–1987." *Journal of Adolescence* 11:309–334.

Brodie, David P. (1986). "The Imposition of the Death Penalty on Juvenile Offenders: How Should Society Respond?" *Journal of Juvenile Law* 10:117–124.

Brown, J. W. (1985). *National Program Coordinator Jail Removal Initiative.* Urbana: Community Research Center, University of Illinois.

Brown, Michael F. (1984). "Use of Deadly Force by Patrol Officers: Training Implications." *Journal of Police Science and Administration* 12:133–140.

Brown, Paul W. (1990). "Guns and Probation Officers: The Unspoken Reality." *Federal Probation* 54:21–26.

Brown, Waln K., Timothy P. Miller, and Richard L. Jenkins. (1987). "The Favorable Effect of Juvenile Court Adjudication of Delinquent Youth on the First Contact with the Juvenile Justice System." *Juvenile and Family Court Journal* 38:21–26.

Bucy, June. (1985). *To Whom Do They Belong? A Profile of America's Runaway and Homeless Youth and the Programs that Help Them.* Washington, DC: National Network of Runaway and Youth Services, Inc.

Bureau of Justice Statistics. (1986). *Children in Custody.* Washington, DC: U. S. Government Printing Office.

Burgess, Robert, and Ronald Akers. (1966). "Differential Association-Reinforcement Theory of Criminal Behavior." *Social Problems* 14:128–147.

Burris, Scott. (1987). "Death and a Rational Justice: A Conversation on the Capital Jurisprudence of Justice John Paul Stevens." *Yale Law Review* 96:521–546.

Busch, Kenneth G. *et al.* (1990). "Adolescents Who Kill." *Journal of Clinical Psychology* 46:472–485.

Butler, T. (1985). "Objectives and Accountability in Policing." *Policing* 1:174–186.

Butts, Jeffrey A., and Paul DeMuro. (1989). *Risk Assessment of Adjudicated Delinquents.* Ann Arbor: Center for the Study of Youth Policy, University of Michigan.

Cahalan, Margaret W. (1986). *Historical Corrections Statistics in the United States, 1850–1984.* Washington, DC: U. S. Department of Justice.

California Department of the Youth Authority. (1984). *Adolescent Abuse: A Guide for Custody Personnel.* Sacramento: California Department of the Youth Authority, Prevention and Community Corrections Branch.

California Department of the Youth Authority. (1985a). *Assessment of Planned Re-Entry Program (PREP).* Sacramento: California Department of the Youth Authority.

California Department of the Youth Authority. (1985b). *Youth Service Bureaus: Report to the Legislature.* Sacramento: California Department of the Youth Authority.

CALIFORNIA OFFICE OF CRIMINAL JUSTICE PLANNING. (1984). *Governor's Youth Crime Prevention Program: Training Guide.* Sacramento: California Office of Criminal Justice Planning.

CAMBRIDGE SURVEY RESEARCH. (1986). *An Analysis of Political Attitudes toward the Death Penalty in the State of Florida.* Cambridge, MA: Cambridge Survey Research.

CAMPBELL, ANNE. (1984). *The Girls in the Gang: A Report from New York City.* New York: Basil Blackwell.

CARLSON, BONNIE. (1986). "Children's Beliefs about Punishment." *American Journal of Orthopsychiatry* 56:308–312.

CARLSON, ERIC, and EVALYN PARKS. (1979). *Critical Issues in Adult Probation: Issues in Probation Management.* Washington, DC: U. S. Department of Justice.

CARLSON, E. W. *et al.* (1977). *Halfway Houses: National Evaluation Program—Phase I Summary Report.* Columbus: Ohio State University, Program for the Study of Crime and Delinquency.

CARLSON, NANCY D. (1987). "Jailing Juveniles: Impact on Constitutional Rights." *New England Journal on Criminal and Civil Confinement* 13:45–67.

CARPENTER, PATRICIA, and SALEK SANDBERG. (1985). "Further Psychodrama and Delinquent Adolescents." *Adolescence* 20:599–604.

CARPENTER, PATRICIA, and DENNIS P. SUGRUE. (1984). "Psychoeducation in an Outpatient Setting—Designing a Heterogeneous Population of Juvenile Delinquents." *Adolescence* 19:113–122.

CARTER, SUE. (1984). "Chapter 39, the Florida Juvenile Justice Act: From Juvenile to Adult with the Stroke of a Pen." *Florida State University Law Review* 11:922–947.

CHALIDZE, VALERY. (1977). *Criminal Russia: Essays on Crime in the Soviet Union.* New York: Random House.

CHALLEEN, DENNIS A. (1986). *Making it Right: A Common Sense Approach to Criminal Justice.* Aberdeen, SD: Melius and Peterson.

CHAMBERS, OLA R. (1983). *The Juvenile Offender: A Parole Profile.* Albany: Evaluation and Planning Unit, New York State Division of Parole.

CHAMPION, DEAN J. (1988). *Felony Probation: Problems and Prospects.* New York: Praeger.

CHAMPION, DEAN J. (1989a). "Teenage Felons and Waiver Hearings: Some Recent Trends, 1980–1988." *Crime and Delinquency* 35:577–585.

CHAMPION, DEAN J. (ed.). (1989b). *The U. S. Sentencing Guidelines: Implications for Criminal Justice.* New York: Praeger.

CHAMPION, DEAN J. (1990a). *Corrections in the United States: A Contemporary Perspective.* Englewood Cliffs, NJ: Prentice-Hall.

CHAMPION, DEAN J. (1990b). *Criminal Justice in the United States.* Columbus, OH: Merrill.

CHAMPION, DEAN J., and G. LARRY MAYS. (1991). *Juvenile Transfer Hearings: Some Trends and Implications for Juvenile Justice.* New York: Praeger.

CHARLES, MICHAEL T. (1989a). "The Development of a Juvenile Electronic Monitoring Program." *Federal Probation* 53:3–12.

CHARLES, MICHAEL T. (1989b). "Electronic Monitoring for Juveniles." *Journal of Crime and Justice* 12:147–169.

CHARLES, MICHAEL T. (1989c). "Research Note: Juveniles on Electronic Monitoring." *Journal of Contemporary Criminal Justice* 5:165–172.

CHEATWOOD, DERRAL. (1988). "The Life-Without-Parole Sanction: Its Current Status and a Research Agenda." *Crime and Delinquency* 34:43–59.

CHESNEY-LIND, MEDA. (1978). "Young Women in the Arms of the Law." In *Women, Crime, and the Criminal Justice System* (L. H. Bowker, ed.). Lexington, MA: Lexington Books.

CHESNEY-LIND, MEDA. (1987a). *Girls' Crime and Woman's Place: Toward a Feminist Model of Female Delinquency.* Honolulu: Youth Development and Research Center and Women's Studies Program, University of Hawaii.

CHESNEY-LIND, MEDA. (1987b). "Saving Girls: New Initiatives to Reinstitutionalize Status Offenders." Unpublished paper presented at the American Society of Criminology meetings, November, Montreal, CAN.

CHICAGO POLICE DEPARTMENT. (1988). *Collecting, Organizing, and Reporting Street Gang Crime.* Chicago, IL: Chicago Police Department, Gang Crime Section.

CHINEN, MERTON, MYRON SEU, and ERIC TANAKA. (1986). *Pre-Commitment Factors of Juveniles Incarcerated at the Hawaii Youth Correctional Facility: A Study of the 1974– 1978 Population.* Honolulu: Youth Development and Research Center, University of Hawaii-Manoa.

CLAGETT, ARTHUR F. (1989). "Effective Therapeutic Wilderness Camp Programs for Rehabilitating Emotionally-Disturbed, Problem Teenagers and Delinquents." *Journal of Offender Counseling, Services, and Rehabilitation* 14:79–96.

CLARKE, STEVENS H. (1975). "Some Implications for North Carolina of Recent Research in Juvenile Delinquency." *Journal of Research in Crime and Delinquency* 12:51–60.

CLARKE, STEVENS H., and AMY D. CRADDOCK. (1987). *An Evaluation of North Carolina's Intensive Juvenile Probation Program.* Chapel Hill: Institute of Government, University of North Carolina at Chapel Hill.

CLARKE, STEVENS, CHRISTOPHER RINGWALT, and ANDREA CIMINELLO. (1985). *Perspectives on Juvenile Status Offenders: A Report to the North Carolina Governor's Crime Commission.* Chapel Hill: Institute of Government, University of North Carolina.

CLAYTON, OBIE. (1983). "Reconsideration of the Effects of Race in Criminal Sentencing." *Criminal Justice Review* 89:15–20.

COHEN, ALBERT K. (1955). *Delinquent Boys.* New York: Free Press.

COLLEY, LORI L., and ROBERT G. CULBERTSON. (1988). "Status Offender Legislation and the Courts." *Journal of Offender Counseling, Services, and Rehabilitation* 12: 41–56.

COLLEY, LORI, ROBERT G. CULBERTSON, and EDWARD J. LATESSA. (1987). "Juvenile Probation Officers: A Job Analysis." *Juvenile and Family Court Journal* 38:1–12.

COLVIN, MARK, and JOHN PAULY. (1983). "A Critique of Criminology: Toward an Integrated Structural-Marxist Theory of Delinquency Production." *American Journal of Sociology* 89:513–551.

CONNER, G. (1986). "Use of Force Continuum." *Law and Order* 34:18–19, 60.

CONNOR, WALTER D. (1972). *Deviance in Soviet Society: Crime, Delinquency, and Alcoholism.* New York: Columbia University Press.

CONRAD, JOHN P. (1983). "Is There No Alternative to the Hard Line in Juvenile Justice?" *Judicature* 67:162–163.

CONRAD, JOHN P. (1987). "Dealing with Crime on the Streets." In *Handbook on Crime and Delinquency Prevention* (Elmer H. Johnson, ed.). Westport, CT: Greenwood Press.

CONTI, SAMUEL D. et al. (1984). *An Assessment of the Juvenile Justice System in Philadelphia.* Williamsburg, VA: National Center for State Courts.

CORNELL, DEWEY G., ELISSA P. BENEDEK, and DAVID M. BENEDEK. (1987). "Juvenile Homicide: Prior Adjustment and a Proposed Typology." *American Journal of Orthopsychiatry* 57:383–393.

CORNELL, DEWEY G. et al. (1987). "Characteristics of Adolescents Charged with Homicide: A Review of 72 Cases." Behavioral Sciences and the Law 5:11–23.

COSTANZO, SAMUEL A. (1990). "Juvenile Academy Serves as Facility Without Walls." Corrections Today 52:112–126.

CRAWFORD, J. (1988). Tabulation of a Nationwide Survey of Female Inmates. Phoenix, AZ: Research Advisory Services.

CRIMINAL JUSTICE NEWSLETTER. (1988). "Juvenile Justice." Criminal Justice Newsletter 19:1–8.

CRISWELL, JOHN E. (1987). "Juvenile Detention Resource Centers: Florida's Experience Provides a Model for the Nation in Juvenile Detention." Corrections Today 49:22–26.

CURRAN, DANIEL J. (1984). "The Myth of a 'New' Female Delinquent." Crime and Delinquency 30:386–399.

DAHLIN, DONALD C. (1986). Models of Court Management. Millwood, NY: Associated Family Press.

DALE, MICHAEL J. (1987). "The Burger Court and Children's Rights—a Trend toward Retribution." Children's Legal Rights Journal 8:7–12.

DALE, MICHAEL J. (1988). "Detaining Juveniles in Adult Jails and Lockups: An Analysis of Rights and Liabilities." American Jails, Spring:46–50.

DATESMAN, SUSAN K., and MIKEL AICKIN. (1985). "Offense Specialization and Escalation among Status Offenders." Journal of Criminal Law and Criminology 75:1246–1275.

DAVIDSON, GERALD E. (1987). "Treatment and Behavior Change in Juvenile Delinquents." In Handbook on Crime and Delinquency Prevention (Elmer H. Johnson, ed.). Westport, CT: Greenwood Press.

DAVIDSON, WILLIAM S. et al. (1987). "Diversion of Juvenile Offenders: An Experimental Comparison." Journal of Consulting and Clinical Psychology 55:68–75.

DAVIS, KENNETH C. (1969). Discretionary Justice: A Preliminary Inquiry. Baton Rouge: Lousiana State University Press.

DeANGELO, ANDREW J. (1988). "Diversion Programs in the Juvenile Justice System: An Alternative Method of Treatment for Juvenile Offenders." Juvenile and Family Court Journal 39:21–28.

DECKER, SCOTT H. (1985). "A Systemic Analysis of Diversion: Net Widening and Beyond." Journal of Criminal Justice 13:207–216.

DECKER, SCOTT H., and CAROL W. KOHFELD. (1984). "A Deterrence Study of the Death Penalty in Illinois, 1933–1980." Journal of Criminal Justice 12:367–377.

DECKER, SCOTT H., and CAROL W. KOHFELD. (1987). "An Empirical Analysis of the Effect of the Death Penalty in Missouri." Journal of Crime and Justice 10:23–46.

DEL CARMEN, ROLANDO V. (1985). "Legal Issues in Jail and Prison Privatization." Unpublished paper presented at the National Association of Juvenile Correctional Agencies, August, Las Vegas, NV.

DELORTO, THERESA E., and FRANCIS T. CULLEN. (1985). "The Impact of Moral Development on Delinquent Involvement." International Journal of Comparative and Applied Criminal Justice 9:129–143.

DEMBO, RICHARD et al. (1987). "The Nature and Correlates of Psychological/Emotional Functioning among a Sample of Detained Youths." Criminal Justice and Behavior 14:311–334.

DOBBERT, DUANE L. (1987). "Positive Contingency Probation Management." Juvenile and Family Court Journal 38:29–33.

DOERNER, WILLIAM G. (1987). "Child Maltreatment Seriousness and Juvenile Delinquency." Youth and Society 19:197–224.

DOERNER, WILLIAM G. (1988). "The Impact of Medical Resources on Criminally Induced Lethality: A Further Examination." *Criminology* 26:171–179.

DOUGHERTY, JOYCE. (1988). "Negotiating Justice in the Juvenile Justice System: A Comparison of Adult Plea Bargaining and Juvenile Intake." *Federal Probation* 52:72–80.

DOWNS, WILLIAM R., and JOAN F. ROBERTSON. (1990). "Referral for Treatment among Adolescent Alcohol and Drug Abusers." *Journal of Research in Crime and Delinquency* 27:190–209.

DRAPER, THOMAS (ed.). (1985). *Capital Punishment.* New York: H. W. Wilson.

DUNN, ALLYSON. (1986). "Juvenile Court Records: Confidentiality vs. the Public's Right to Know." *American Criminal Law Review* 23:379–398.

DURHAM, ALEXIS M., III. (1988). "Ivy League Delinquency: A Self-Report Analysis." *American Journal of Criminal Justice* 12:167–197.

DWYER, DIANE C., and ROGER B. McNALLY. (1987). "Juvenile Justice: Reform, Retain, and Reaffirm." *Federal Probation* 51:47–51.

ELLIOTT, DELBERT S. *et al.* (1983). *The Prevalence and Incidence of Delinquent Behavior, 1976–1980.* Boulder, CO: Behavioral Research Institute.

ELLIOTT, DELBERT S., FRANKLYN W. DUNFORD, and DAVID HUIZINGA. (1987). "The Identification and Prediction of Career Offenders Utilizing Self-Reported and Official Data." In *Prediction of Criminal Behavior* (John D. Burchard and Sara Burchard, eds.). Newbury Park, CA: Sage.

ELLIS, LEE. (1985). "Evolution and the Nonlegal Equivalent of Aggressive Criminal Behavior." *Aggressive Behavior* 12:57–71.

ELLISON, W. JAMES. (1987). "State Execution of Juveniles: Defining 'Youth' as a Mitigating Factor for Imposing a Sentence Less Than Death." *Law and Psychology Review* 11:1–38.

ELLSWORTH, THOMAS. (1988). "Case Supervision Planning: The Forgotten Component of Intensive Probation Supervision." *Federal Probation* 52:28–33.

EMERSON, ROBERT M. (1969). *Judging Delinquents.* Chicago, IL: Aldine.

EMLER, NICHOLAS, STEPHEN REICHER, and ANDREW ROSS. (1987). "The Social Context of Delinquent Conduct." *Journal of Child Psychology and Psychiatry* 28:99–109.

EMPEY, LAMAR T., and JEROME RABOW. (1961). "The Provo Experiment in Delinquency Rehabilitation." *American Sociological Review* 26:679–695.

ERVIN, LAURIE, and ANNE SCHNEIDER. (1990). "Explaining the Effects of Restitution on Offenders: Results from a National Experiment in Juvenile Courts." In *Criminal Justice, Restitution, and Reconciliation* (Burt Galaway and Joe Hudson, eds.). Monsey, NY: Criminal Justice Press.

ERWIN, BILLIE S. (1986). "Turning Up the Heat on Probationers in Georgia." *Federal Probation* 50:70–76.

ESKILSON, ARLENE *et al.* (1986). "Parental Pressure, Self-Esteem and Adolescent Reported Deviance: Bending the Twig Too Far." *Adolescence* 21:501–515.

EWING, CHARLES PATRICK. (1990). *When Children Kill: The Dynamics of Juvenile Homicide.* Lexington, MA: Lexington Books.

FAGAN, JEFFREY A. (1988). *The Social Organization of Drug Use and Drug Dealing Among Urban Gangs.* New York: John Jay College of Criminal Justice.

FAGAN, JEFFREY A. (1990). "Treatment and Reintegration of Violent Juvenile Offenders: Experimental Results." *Justice Quarterly* 7:233–263.

FAGAN, JEFFREY A., and ELIZABETH PIPER DESCHENES. (1990). "Determinants of Judicial Waiver Decisions for Violent Juvenile Offenders." *Journal of Criminal Law and Criminology* 81:314–347.

FAGAN, JEFFREY A., ELIZABETH S. PIPER, and YU-TEH CHENG. (1987a). "Contributions of

Victimization to Delinquency in Inner Cities." *Journal of Criminal Law and Criminology* 78:586–609.

FAMULARO, RICHARD et al. (1988). "Advisability of Substance Abuse Testing in Parents Who Severely Maltreat Their Children: The Issue of Drug Testing Before the Juvenile/Family Courts." *Bulletin of the American Academy of Psychiatry and the Law* 16:217–223.

FARNWORTH, MARGARET. (1984). "Male-Female Differences in Delinquency in a Minority-Group Sample." *Journal of Research in Crime and Delinquency* 21:191–212.

FARNWORTH, MARGARET, CHARLES E. FRAZIER, and ANITA R. NEUBERGER. (1988). "Orientations to Juvenile Justice: Exploratory Notes from a Statewide Survey of Juvenile Justice Decisionmakers." *Journal of Criminal Justice* 16:477–491.

FARRINGTON, DAVID P. (1985). "Predicting Self-Reported and Official Delinquency." In *Prediction in Criminology* (David P. Farrington and Roger Tarling, eds.). Albany: State University of New York Press.

FARRINGTON, DAVID P. (1986). "Stepping Stones to Adult Criminal Careers." In *Development of Antisocial and Prosocial Behavior: Research, Theories, and Issues* (D. Olweus, J. Block, and M. Yarrow, eds.). New York: Academic Press.

FATTAH, EZZAT A. (1985). "The Preventive Mechanisms of the Death Penalty: A Discussion." *Crimecare Journal* 1:109–137.

FEENEY, FLOYD. (1987). "Defense Counsel for Delinquents: Does Quality Matter?" Unpublished paper presented at the American Society of Criminology meetings, November, Montreal, CAN.

FELD, BARRY C. (1984). "Criminalizing Juvenile Justice: Rules of Procedure for the Juvenile Court." *Minnesota Law Review* 69:141–276.

FELD, BARRY C. (1987a). "The Juvenile Court Meets the Principle of the Offense: Changing Juvenile Justice Sentencing Practices." Unpublished paper presented at the American Society of Criminology meetings, November, Montreal, CAN.

FELD, BARRY C. (1987b). "The Juvenile Court Meets the Principle of the Offense: Legislative Changes in Juvenile Waiver Statutes." *Journal of Criminal Law and Criminology* 78:471–533.

FELD, BARRY C. (1987c). "In re Gault Revisited: The Right to Counsel in the Juvenile Court." Unpublished paper presented at the American Society of Criminology meetings, November, Montreal, CAN.

FELD, BARRY C. (1988a). "The Juvenile Court Meets the Principle of Offense: Punishment, Treatment, and the Difference It Makes." *Boston University Law Review* 68:821–915.

FELD, BARRY C. (1988b). "In Re Gault Revisited: A Cross-State Comparison of the Right to Counsel in Juvenile Court." *Crime and Delinquency* 34:393–424.

FELD, BARRY. (1988c). "The Right to Counsel in Juvenile Court: An Empirical Study of When Lawyers Appear and the Differences They Make." Unpublished paper presented at the American Society of Criminology meetings, November, Chicago.

FELD, BARRY C. (1989). "The Right to Counsel in Juvenile Court: An Empirical Study of When Lawyers Appear and the Difference They Can Make." *Journal of Criminal Law and Criminology* 79:1185–1346.

FELKENES, GEORGE T. (1988). *Constitutional Law for Criminal Justice,* 2nd ed. Englewood Cliffs, NJ: Prentice-Hall.

FERDINAND, THEODORE N. (1986). "A Brief History of Juvenile Delinquency in Boston and a Comparative Interpretation." *International Journal of Criminology* 24:59–81.

FERRI, ENRICO. (1901). *Criminal Sociology*. Boston, MA: Little, Brown.

FINCKENAUER, JAMES O., and DONNA S. KOCHIS. (1984). "Causal Theory and the Treatment of Juvenile Offenders: A Case Study." In *Advances in Forensic Psychology and Psychiatry* (Robert W. Reiber, ed.), Vol. 1. Norwood, NJ: Ablex.

FINE, KERRY KINNEY. (1984). *Alternative Dispute Resolution Programs for Juveniles*. St. Paul: Minnesota House Research Department.

FISHBEIN, DIANA, and ROBERT THATCHER. (1986). "New Diagnostic Methods in Criminology: Assessing Organic Sources of Behavioral Disorder." *Journal of Research in Crime and Delinquency* 23:240–267.

FISHBEIN, PAULA, DONNA HAMPARIAN, and JOSEPH M. DAVIS. (1984). *Restitution Programming for Juvenile Offenders: Its Use for Serious Juvenile Offenders in Ohio*. Cleveland, OH: Federation of Community Planning.

FISHER, R. B. (1984). "Predicting Adolescent Violence." In *The Aggressive Adolescent: Clinical Perspectives*. (C. R. Keith, ed.). New York: Free Press.

FLANAGAN, TIMOTHY J., and KATHERINE M. JAMIESON. (1988). *Sourcebook of Criminal Justice Statistics, 1987*. Albany, NY: The Hindelang Criminal Justice Research Center, The University of Albany.

FLANAGAN, TIMOTHY J., and KATHLEEN MAGUIRE. (1990). *Sourcebook of Criminal Justice Statistics, 1990*. Albany, NY: Hindelang Criminal Justice Research Center.

FLEXNER, BERNARD, and ROGER N. BALDWIN. (1914). *Juvenile Courts and Probation*. New York: Harcourt.

FLYNN, LEONARD E. (1986). "*House Arrest: Florida's Alternative Eases Crowding and Tight Budgets.*" *Corrections Today* 48:64–68.

FOGEL, DAVID. (1984). *Justice as Fairness: Perspectives on the Justice Model*. Cincinnati, OH: Anderson.

FOGEL, DAVID, and JOE HUDSON. (1981). *Justice as Fairness: Perspectives on the Justice Model*. Cincinnati, OH: Anderson.

FORST, BRIAN E. (1983). "Capital Punishment and Deterrence: Conflicting Evidence?" *Journal of Criminal Law and Criminology* 74:927–942.

FORST, MARTIN, JEFFREY FAGAN, and T. SCOTT VIVONA. (1989). "Youth in Prisons and Training Schools: Perceptions and Consequences of the Treatment-Custody Dichotomy." *Juvenile and Family Court Journal* 40:1–14.

FRASER, MARK, and MICHAEL NORMAN. (1988). "Chronic Juvenile Delinquency and the 'Suppression Effect:' An Exploratory Study." *Journal of Offender Counseling, Services, and Rehabilitation* 13:55–73.

FRAZIER, CHARLES E., and DONNA M. BISHOP. (1985). "The Pretrial Detention of Juveniles and Its Impact on Case Dispositions." *Journal of Criminal Law and Criminology* 76:1132–1152.

FRAZIER, CHARLES E., and JOHN K. COCHRAN. (1986). "Official Intervention, Diversion from the Juvenile Justice System, and Dynamics of Human Services Work: Effects of a Reform Goal Based on Labeling Theory." *Crime and Delinquency* 32:157–176.

FRIEDLANDER, ROBERT A. (1987). "Socrates Was Right: Propositions in Support of Capital Punishment." *New England Journal on Criminal and Civil Confinement* 13:1–9.

FROST, MARTIN L., BRUCE A. FISHER, and ROBERT B. COATES. (1985). "Indeterminate and Determinate Sentencing of Juvenile Delinquents: A National Survey of Approaches to Commitment and Release Decision-making." *Juvenile and Family Court Journal* 36:1–12.

GABLE, RALPH KIRKLAND. (1986). "Application of Personal Telemonitoring to Current Problems in Corrections." *Journal of Criminal Justice* 14:167–176.

GALAWAY, BURT, and JOE HUDSON (eds.). (1990). *Criminal Justice, Restitution, and Reconciliation.* Monsey, NY: Criminal Justice Press.

GALBO, ANDREA. (1985). "Death After Life: The Future of New York's Mandatory Death Penalty for Murders Committed by Life-Term Prisoners." *Fordham Urban Law Journal* 13:597–638.

GARBARINO, JAMES, JANIS WILSON, and A. C. GARBARINO. (1986). "The Adolescent Runaway." In *Troubled Youths, Troubled Families* (James Garbarino *et al.*, eds). Hawthorne, NY: Aldine.

GARDNER, SANDRA. (1983). *Street Gangs.* New York: Franklin Watts.

GARRETT, C. (1985). "Effects of Residential Treatment on Adjudicated Delinquents: A Meta-Analysis." *Journal of Research on Crime and Delinquency* 22:287–308.

GAVZER, B. (1986). "Must Kids Be Bad?" *Parade Magazine,* March 9, 1986, pp. 8–10.

GELBER, SEYMOUR. (1988). *Hard-Core Delinquents: Reaching out Through the Miami Experiment.* University: University of Alabama Press.

GELBER, SEYMOUR. (1990). "The Juvenile Justice System: Vision for the Future." *Juvenile and Family Court Journal* 41:15–18.

GELLER, MARK, and LYNN FORD-SOMMA. (1984). *Violent Homes, Violent Children.* Trenton: Division of Juvenile Services, New Jersey Department of Corrections.

GELSTHORPE, LORAINE R. (1987). "The Differential Treatment of Males and Females in the Criminal Justice System." In *Sex, Gender, and Care Work* (Gordon Horobin, ed.). Aberdeen, UK: Department of Social Work, University of Aberdeen.

GENDREAU, PAUL, and ROBERT R. ROSS. (1984). "Revivification or Rehabilitation?: Evidence from the 1980s." *Justice Quarterly* 4:349–408.

GEORGIA COMMISSION ON JUVENILE JUSTICE. (1985). *Strengthening Juvenile Justice in Georgia.* Atlanta: Georgia Commission on Juvenile Justice.

GILLER, HENRI, and NORMAN TUTT. (1987). "Police Cautioning of Juveniles: The Continuing Practice of Diversity." *Criminal Law Review,* June:367–374.

GILLESPIE, L. KAY, and MICHAEL D. NORMAN. (1984). "Does Certification Mean Prison: Some Preliminary Findings from Utah." *Juvenile and Family Court Journal* 35:23–34.

GIORDANO, PEGGY, STEPHEN A. CERNKOVICH, and M. D. PUGH. (1986). "Friendships and Delinquency." *American Journal of Sociology,* 91:1170–1202.

GLUECK, SHELDON, and ELEANOR GLUECK. (1950). *Unraveling Juvenile Delinquency.* New York: Commonwealth Fund.

GOFFMAN, ERVING. (1963). *Stigma.* Indianapolis, IN: Bobbs-Merrill.

GOLD, MARTIN. (1987). "Social Ecology." In *Handbook of Juvenile Delinquency* (Herbert C. Quay, ed.). New York: Wiley.

GOLDBERG, KENNETH J. (1984). "Action-Oriented Strategies with Violent Juvenile Offenders." In *Violent Juvenile Offenders: An Anthology* (Robert A. Mathias, Paul DeMuro, and Richard S. Allinson, eds.). San Francisco, CA: National Council on Crime and Delinquency.

GOLDSMITH, HERBERT R. (1987). "Self-Esteem of Juvenile Delinquents: Findings and Implications." *Journal of Offender Counseling Services and Rehabilitation* 11:79–85.

GOLDSTEIN, ARNOLD P., and BARRY GLICK. (1987). *Aggression Replacement Training: A Comprehensive Intervention for Aggressive Youth*. Champaign, IL: Research Press.

GONZALES, GIL P. (1982). *"In re Myron:* Juvenile Confessions." *Criminal Justice Journal* 5:349–358.

GOODSTEIN, LYNN, and JOHN HEPBURN. (1985). *Determinate Sentencing and Imprisonment: A Failure of Reform*. Cincinnati, OH: Anderson.

GOODSTEIN, LYNNE, and HENRY SOUTHEIMER. (1987). "Evaluating Correctional Placements Through the use of Failure Rate Analysis." Unpublished paper presented at the American Society of Criminology meetings, November, Montreal, CAN.

GORDON, ROBERT A. (1986). "IQ—Commensurability of Black-White Differences in Crime and Delinquency." Unpublished paper presented at the annual meeting of the American Psychological Association, August, Washington, DC.

GORING, CHARLES. (1913). *The English Convict*. London, UK: Her Majesty's Stationery Office.

GOTTFREDSON, DON M. (1984). "Selective Incapacitation." *Corrections Today* 46: 82–88.

GOTTFREDSON, DON M., and MICHAEL TONRY. (1987). *Prediction and Classification: Criminal Justice Decision-Making*. Chicago, IL: University of Chicago Press.

GOTTFREDSON, STEPHEN D., and DON M. GOTTFREDSON. (1988). *Decision Making in Criminal Justice: Toward the Rational Exercise of Discretion*, 2nd ed. New York: Plenum.

GOTTLIEB, BARBARA. (1984). *The Pretrial Processing of "Dangerous" Defendants: A Comparative Analysis of State Laws*. Washington, DC: Toborg Associates.

GOTTLIEB, BARBARA, and PHILLIP ROSEN. (1984). *Public Danger as a Factor in Pretrial Release: Summaries of State Danger Laws*. Washington, DC: Toborg Associates.

GOTTSCHALK, RAND et al. (1987). "Community-based Interventions." In *Handbook of Juvenile Delinquency* (Herbert C. Quay, ed.). New York: Wiley.

GOVE, W. R., M. HUGHES, and M. GEERKEN. (1985). "Are Uniform Crime Reports a Valid Indicator of Index Crimes?" *Criminology* 23:451–501.

GREEN, G. S. (1985). "The Representativeness of the Uniform Crime Reports: Ages of Persons Arrested." *Journal of Police Science and Administration* 13:46–52.

GREEN, MAURICE. (1984). "Child Advocacy: Rites and Rights in Juvenile Justice." In *Advances in Forensic Psychology and Psychiatry* (Robert W. Rieber, ed.), Vol. 1. Norwood, NJ: Ablex.

GREENFELD, LAWRENCE A. (1985). *Examining Recidivism*. Washington, DC: Bureau of Justice Statistics.

GREENWOOD, PETER (1982). *Selective Incapacitation*. Santa Monica, CA: Rand Corporation.

GREENWOOD, PETER W. (1986a). "Differences in Criminal Behavior and Court Responses Among Juvenile and Young Adult Defendants." In *Crime and Justice: An Annual Review of Research* (Michael Tonry and Norval Morris, eds.), Vol. 7. Chicago, IL: University of Chicago Press.

GREENWOOD, PETER W. (ed.). (1986b). *Intervention Strategies for Chronic Juvenile Offenders: Some New Perspectives*. Westport, CT: Greenwood Press.

GREENWOOD, PETER W. (1986c). "Predictors of Chronic Behavior." In *Intervention Strategies for Chronic Juvenile Offenders: Some New Perspectives* (Peter W. Greenwood, ed.). New York: Greenwood Press.

GREENWOOD, PETER W. (1986d). "Promising Approaches for the Rehabilitation and Prevention of Chronic Juvenile Offenders." In *Intervention Strategies for Chronic*

Juvenile Offenders: Some New Perspectives (Peter W. Greenwood, ed.). New York: Greenwood Press.

GREENWOOD, PETER W. (1990). "Reflections on Three Promising Programs." *Perspectives* 14:20–24.

GREENWOOD, PETER W., and SUSAN TURNER. (1987). *The Visionquest Program: An Evaluation*, R-3445-OJJDP. Santa Monica, CA: Rand Corporation.

GREENWOOD, PETER W., and FRANKLIN E. ZIMRING. (1985). *One More Chance: The Pursuit of Promising Intervention Strategies for Chronic Juvenile Offenders*. Santa Monica, CA: Rand Corporation.

GRENIER, CHARLES E., and GEORGE A. ROUNDTREE. (1987). "Predicting Recidivism among Adjudicated Delinquents: A Model to Identify High Risk Offenders." *Journal of Offender Counseling, Services, and Rehabilitation* 12:101–112.

GRIECO, EILEEN SPILLANE. (1984). "Characteristics of a Helpful Relationship: A Study of Empathic Understanding and Positive Regard Between Runaways and Their Parents." *Adolescence* Vol. 19:63–76.

GRIFFIN, BRENDA S., and CHARLES T. GRIFFIN. (1978). *Juvenile Delinquency in Perspective*. New York: Harper and Row.

GRIFFITH, W. R. (1983). *Self-Report Instrument: A Description and Analysis of Results in the National Evaluation Sites*. Eugene, OR: Institute of Policy Analysis.

GRIFFITHS, CURT TAYLOR. (1988). "Community-Based Corrections for Young Offenders: Proposal for a 'Localized' Corrections." *International Journal of Comparative and Applied Criminal Justice* 12:219–228.

GRISSO, THOMAS, ALAN TOMKINS, and PAMELA CASEY. (1988). "Psychosocial Concepts in Juvenile Law." *Law and Human Behavior* 12:403–438.

GRISWOLD, DAVID. (1978). "Police Discrimination: An Elusive Question." *Journal of Police Science and Administration* 6:65–66.

GROHMANN, STEPHEN W., and MELISSA BARRITT. (1987). *Secure Detentions of Juveniles in Wisconsin, 1985*. Madison: Wisconsin Statistical Analysis Center, Wisconsin Council on Criminal Justice.

GUARINO, SUSAN. (1985). *Delinquent Youth and Family Violence: A Study of Abuse and Neglect in the Homes of Serious Juvenile Offenders*. Boston: Massachusetts Department of Youth Services.

GUARINO-GHEZZI, SUSAN. (1989). "Classifying Juveniles: A Formula for Case-By-Case Assessment." *Corrections Today* 51:112–116.

GUERNSEY, CARL E. (1985). *Handbook for Juvenile Court Judges*. Reno, NV: National Council of Juvenile and Family Court Judges.

GUGGENHEIM, MARTIN. (1985a). "Incorrigibility Laws: The State's Role in Resolving Intrafamily Conflict." *Criminal Justice Ethics* 4:11–19.

GUGGENHEIM, MARTIN. (1985b) *The Rights of Young People*. New York: Bantam Books.

GUTKNECHT, BRUCE. (1988). "Improving Academic Achievement Through Success (IMPAACTS): Help for First-Time Juvenile Offenders." *Journal of Offender Counseling, Services, and Rehabilitation* 12:123–130.

HAAS, MICHAEL. (1988). "Violent Schools—Unsafe Schools." *Journal of Conflict Resolution* 32:727–758.

HAGAN, JOHN, A. R. GILLIS, and JOHN SIMPSON. (1985). "The Class Structure of Gender and Delinquency: Toward a Power-Control Theory of Common Delinquent Behavior." *American Journal of Sociology* 90:1151–1178.

HAGEDORN, JOHN. (1988). *People and Folks: Gangs, Crime and the Underclass in a Rustbelt City*. Chicago, IL: Lake View Press.

HAHN, PAUL H. (1984). *The Juvenile Offender and the Law*. Cincinnati, OH: Anderson.

HAINS, ANTHONY A., and ANN HIGGINS HAINS. (1988). "Cognitive-Behavioral Training of Problem-solving and Impulse-Control with Delinquent Adolescents." *Journal of Offender Counseling, Services, and Rehabilitation* 12:95–113.

HAIZLIP, T., B. F. CORDER, and B. C. BALL. (1984). "The Adolescent Murderer." In *The Aggressive Adolescent: Clinical Perspectives* (C. R. Keith, ed.). New York: Free Press.

HAMPARIAN, DONNA M. (1987). "Control and Treatment of Juveniles Committing Violent Offenses." In *Clinical Treatment of the Violent Person* (Loren H. Roth, ed.). New York: Guilford Press.

HAMPARIAN, DONNA M., and LYNN SAMETZ. (1989). *Cuyahoga County Juvenile Court Intensive Probation Supervision: Interim Report.* Cleveland, OH: Federation for Community Planning.

HAMPARIAN, DONNA M. et al. (1978). *The Violent Few: A Study of Dangerous Juvenile Offenders.* Lexington, MA: Lexington Books.

HANCOCK, PAULA, and KATHERINE TEILMANN VAN DUSEN. (1985). *Attorney Representation in Juvenile Court: A Comparison of Public Defenders and Privately Retained Counsel.* Washington, DC: U. S. Office of Juvenile Justice and Delinquency Prevention.

HANS, VALERIA P., and NEIL VIDMAR. (1986). *Judging the Jury.* New York: Plenum.

HARRIS, PATRICIA M. (1988). "Juvenile Sentence Reform and Its Evaluation: A Demonstration of the Need for More Precise Measures of Offense Seriousness in Juvenile Justice Research." *Evaluation Review* 12:655–666.

HARRIS, PATRICIA M., and LISA GRAFF. (1988). "A Critique of Juvenile Sentence Reform." *Federal Probation* 52:66–71.

HARTSTONE, ELIOT. (1985). "Turnstile Children." *Corrections Today* 47:78–82.

HARTSTONE, ELIOT, and KAREN V. HANSEN. (1984). "The Violent Juvenile Offender: An Empirical Portrait." In *Violent Juvenile Offenders: An Anthology* (Robert A. Mathias, Paul DeMuro, and Richard S. Allinson, eds.). San Francisco, CA: National Council on Crime and Delinquency.

HARTSTONE, ELIOT, ELLEN SLAUGHTER, and JEFFREY FAGAN. (1986). *The Colorado Juvenile Justice System Processing of Violent, Serious and Minority Youths.* San Francisco, CA: URSA Institute.

HASSENFELD, YEHESKEL, and PAUL P. L. CHEUNG. (1985). "The Juvenile Court as a People-Processing Organization: A Political Economy Perspective." *American Journal of Sociology* 90:801–824.

HASTIE, REID, STEVEN D. PENROD, and NANCY PENNINGTON. (1983). *Inside the Jury.* Cambridge, MA: Harvard University Press.

HAWAII CRIME COMMISSION. (1985). *The Serious Juvenile Offender in Hawaii.* Honolulu: Hawaii Crime Commission.

HAWKINS, GORDON, and FRANKLIN E. ZIMRING. (1986). "Cycles of Reform in Youth Corrections: The Story of Borstal." In *Intervention Strategies for Chronic Juvenile Offenders: Some New Perspectives* (Peter W. Greenwood, ed.). New York: Greenwood Press.

HAWKINS, J. DAVID, and TONY LAM. (1987). "Teacher Practices, Social Development, and Delinquency." In *Prevention of Delinquent Behavior* (John D. Burchard and Sara Burchard, eds.). Newbury Park, CA: Sage.

HAWKINS, J. DAVID, and DENISE M. LISHNER. (1987). "Schooling and Delinquency." In *Handbook on Crime and Delinquency Prevention* (Elmer H. Johnson, ed.). Westport, CT: Greenwood Press.

HEAL, KEVIN, and GLORIA LAYCOCK. (1987). *Preventing Juvenile Crime: The Staffordshire Experience.* London, UK: Home Office Crime Prevention Unit.

HEITGERD, JANET L., and ROBERT J. BURSIK. (1987). "Extracommunity Dynamics and the Ecology of Delinquency." *American Journal of Sociology* 92:775–787.

HENDERSON, THOMAS A. *et al.* (1984). *The Significance of Judicial Structure: The Effect of Unification on Trial Court Operations.* Washington, DC: U. S. Government Printing Office.

HENRETTA, JOHN C., CHARLES E. FRAZIER, and DONNA M. BISHOP. (1986). "The Effect of Prior Case Outcomes on Juvenile Justice Decision-Making." *Social Forces* 65:554–562.

HESTER, THOMAS. (1988). *Probation and Parole 1987.* Washington, DC: U. S. Department of Justice, Bureau of Justice Statistics.

HIRSCHI, TRAVIS. (1969). *Causes of Delinquency.* Berkeley: University of California Press.

HIRSCHI, TRAVIS, and MICHAEL HINDELANG. (1977). "Intelligence and Delinquency: A Revisionist View." *American Sociological Review* 42:471–486.

HOCHSTEDLER, ELLEN. (1986). "Criminal Prosecution for the Mentally Disordered." *Law and Society Review* 20:279–292.

HOFFMAN, PETER B. (1983). "Screening for Risk: A Revised Salient Factor Score (SFS 81)." *Journal of Criminal Justice* 11:539–547.

HOOTON, EARNEST A. (1939). *Crime and the Man.* Cambridge, MA: Harvard University Press.

HOROWITZ, ROBERT M., and HOWARD A. DAVIDSON (EDS.). (1984). *Legal Rights of Children.* Colorado Springs, CO: Shepard's/McGraw-Hill.

HOUK, JULIE M. (1984). "Electronic Monitoring of Probationers: A Step Toward Big Brother?" *Golden Gate University Law Review* 14:431–446.

HUFF, GRAHAM, and FRANCES COLLINSON. (1987). "Young Offenders, Gambling, and Video Game Playing." *British Journal of Criminology,* 27:401–410.

HUGHES, G. (1984). "English Criminal Justice: Is It Better Than Ours?" *Arizona Law Review* 26:507–614.

HUGHES, STELLA P., and ANNE L. SCHNEIDER. (1989). "Victim-Offender Mediation: A Survey of Program Characteristics and Perceptions of Effectiveness." *Crime and Delinquency* 35:217–233.

HUIZINGA, DAVID, FINN-AAGE ESBENSEN, and DELBERT S. ELLIOTT. (1987). "Development of Delinquency in High Risk Neighborhoods: The Denver Study." Unpublished paper presented at the American Society of Criminology meetings, November, Montreal, CAN.

HUMPHREY, JOHN A., and TIMOTHY J. FOGARTY. (1987). "Race and Plea Bargained Outcomes: A Research Note." *Social Forces* 66:176–182.

HUMPHREY INSTITUTE OF PUBLIC AFFAIRS. (1986). *The Incarceration of Minority Youth.* Minneapolis, MN: The Hubert H. Humphrey Institute of Public Affairs.

HURLEY, D. (1985). "Arresting Delinquency." *Psychology Today* 19:63–66, 68.

HURST, HUNTER. (1990a). "Juvenile Probation in Retrospect." *Perspectives* 14:16–24.

HURST, HUNTER. (1990b). "Turn of the Century: Rediscovering the Value of Juvenile Treatment." *Corrections Today* 52:48–50.

HUSKEY, BOBBIE L. (1984). "Community Corrections Acts." *Corrections Today* 46:45.

HUSKEY, BOBBIE L. (1990). "In Illinois: Law Forces Change in Juvenile Lockups." *Corrections Today* 52:122–123.

IKEDA, LISA, MEDA CHESNEY-LIND, and KEITH KAMEOKA. (1985). *The Honolulu Anti-Truancy Program: An Evaluation.* Manoa, HI: Youth Development Research Center.

INNES, CHRISTOPHER A. (1988). *Profile of State Prison Inmates, 1987.* Washington, DC: U. S. Department of Justice.

INTERNATIONAL CRIME CENTER. (1986). *International Crime Statistics, 1986.* Geneva, Switzerland: International Crime Center.

ITO, JEANNE A. (1984). *Measuring the Performance of Different Types of Juvenile Courts.* Williamsburg, VA: National Center for State Courts.

JACKSON, IRENE F. (1984). *A Preliminary Survey of Adolescent Sex Offenses in New York: Remedies and Recommendations.* Syracuse, NY: Safer Society Press.

JAMIESON, KATHERINE M., and TIMOTHY J. FLANAGAN. (1988). *Sourcebook of Criminal Justice Statistics.* Albany, NY: The Hindelang Criminal Justice Research Center, The University of Albany.

JAMIESON, KATHERINE M., and TIMOTHY J. FLANAGAN. (1989). *Sourcebook of Criminal Justice Statistics.* Albany, NY: The Hindelang Criminal Justice Research Center, The University of Albany.

JANUS, MARK-DAVID et al. (1987). *Adolescent Runaways: Causes and Consequences.* Lexington, MA: Lexington Books.

JAPAN MINISTRY OF JUSTICE CORRECTIONS BUREAU. (1985). *Correctional Institutions in Japan.* Tokyo, JAPAN: Ministry of Justice, Corrections Bureau.

JAPAN MINISTRY OF JUSTICE REHABILITATION BUREAU. (1985). *Community-Based Treatment of Offenders in Japan.* Tokyo, JAPAN: Ministry of Justice, Rehabilitation Bureau.

JEFFREY, C. RAY. (1979). *Biology and Crime.* Beverly Hills, CA: Sage.

JENSEN, GARY F., and DAVID BROWNFIELD. (1987). "Gender, Lifestyles, and Victimization: Beyond Routine Activity." *Violence and Victims* 1:85–99.

JESNESS, CARL F. (1987). "Early Identification of Delinquent-Prone Children: An Overview." In *The Prevention of Delinquent Behavior* (John D. Burchard and Sara N. Burchard, eds.). Newbury Park, CA: Sage.

JOHNSON, ELMER H. (1983). *International Handbook of Contemporary Developments in Criminology: Europe, Africa, the Middle East, and Asia.* Westport, CT: Greenwood.

JONES, BERNADETTE. (1990). "Intensive Probation Services in Philadelphia County." Unpublished paper presented at the American Society of Criminology meetings, November, Baltimore, MD.

JOYCE, NOLA M. (1985). "Classification Research: Facing the Challenge." *Corrections Today* 47:78–86.

JUST, DAVID A. (1985). "The Relationship between Delinquent Behavior and Work Values of Noninstitutionalized Youth." *Journal of Correctional Education* 36:148–154.

KAMERMAN, SHEILA B., and ALFRED J. KAHN (eds.). (1990). "Social Services for Children, Youth, and Families in the United States." *Children and Youth Services Review* 12:170–184.

KAPLAN, LISA et al. (1989). "Runaway, Homeless, and Shut-Out Children and Youth in Canada, Europe, and the United States." *Children and Youth Services* 11: 1–108.

KARRAKER, N., D. E. MACALLAIR, and V. N. SCHIRALDI. (1988). *Public Safety with Care: A Model System for Juvenile Justice in Hawaii.* Alexandria, VA: National Center on Institutions and Alternatives.

KEARNEY, WILLIAM J. (1989). "Form Follows Function—And Function Follows Philosophy: An Architectural Response." *Juvenile and Family Court Journal* 40:27–34.

KEARON, WILLIAM G. (1989). "Deinstitutionalization and Abuse of Children on Our Streets." *Juvenile and Family Court Journal* 40:21–26.

KEATING, J. MICHAEL. (1984). *Public Ends and Private Means: Accountability Among Private Providers of Public Social Services.* Pawtucket, RI: Institute of Conflict Management.

KEITH, RICHARD G. (1989). *Children and Drugs: The Next Generation.* Los Angeles, CA: Los Angeles Unified School District Police Officers Association.

KEMPF, KIMBERLY L., and R. L. AUSTIN. (1986). "Older and More Recent Evidence on Racial Discrimination in Sentencing." *Journal of Quantitative Criminology* 2:29–48.

KENNEY, JOHN P., and HARRY W. MORE. (1986). *Patrol Field Problems and Solutions: 476 Field Situations.* Springfield, IL: Thomas.

KEVE, PAUL W. (1984). *The Consequences of Prohibiting the Jailing of Juveniles.* Richmond: Virginia Commonwealth University.

KITSUSE, JOHN I. (1962). "Societal Reaction to Deviant Behavior: Problems of Theory and Method." *Social Problems* 9:247–256.

KLEIN, ANDREW R. (1989). "Developing Individualized Probationary Conditions." *Perspectives* 13:6–11.

KLEIN, MALCOLM W. (1979). "Deinstitutionalization and Diversion of Juvenile Offenders: A Litany of Impediments." In *Crime and Justice* (Norval Morris and Michael Tonry, eds.). Chicago, IL: University of Chicago Press.

KLEIN, MALCOLM W. (1984). "Offense Specialization and Versatility among Juveniles." *British Journal of Criminology* 24:185–194.

KLEIN, MALCOLM W., L. ROSENZWEIG, and M. BATES. (1975). "The Ambiguous Juvenile Arrest." *Criminology* 13:78–89.

KLOCKARS, CARL B. (1985). "The Dirty Harry Problem." In *Moral Issues in Police Work* (Frederick A. Elliston and Michael Feldberg, eds.). Totowa, NJ: Rowman and Allanheld.

KNEPPER, PAUL, and GRAY CAVENDER. (1990). "Decision-making and the Typification of Juveniles on Parole." Unpublished paper presented at the Academy of Criminal Justice Science meetings, April, Denver, CO.

KNOPP, FAY HONEY. (1985). *The Youthful Sex Offender: The Rationale and Goals of Early Intervention and Treatment.* Syracuse, NY: Safer Society Press.

KOBRIN, S., F. HELLUM, and J. PETERSON. (1980). "Offense Patterns of Status Offenders. In *Critical Issues in Juvenile Delinquency* (D. Shichor and D. Kelley, eds.). Boston, MA: Lexington Books.

KOHLBERG, L. (1981). *The Philosophy of Moral Development.* New York: Harper and Row.

KRATCOSKI, PETER C. (1985). "Youth Violence Directed Toward Significant Others." *Journal of Adolescence* 8:145–157.

KRATCOSKI, PETER C., and LUCILLE DUNN KRATCOSKI. (1986). *Juvenile Delinquency,* 2nd ed. Englewood Cliffs, NJ: Prentice-Hall.

KRETSCHMER, ERNEST. (1936). *Physique and Character.* London, UK: Kegan Paul, Trench, and Trubner.

KRIESMAN, J., and R. SIDEN. (1982). *Juvenile Homicide: A Literature Review.* Berkeley: University of California-Berkeley.

KRISBERG, BARRY. (1988). *The Juvenile Court: Reclaiming the Vision.* San Francisco, CA: National Council on Crime and Delinquency.

KRISBERG, BARRY, and JAMES AUSTIN. (1978). *The Children of Ishmael.* Palo Alto, CA: Mayfield.

KRISBERG, BARRY et al. (1985a) *Planning Study for the Colorado Division of Youth Services*. San Francisco, CA: National Council on Crime and Delinquency.

KRISBERG, BARRY et al. (1985b). *The Watershed of Juvenile Justice Reform*. Minneapolis: Hubert H. Humphrey Institute of Public Affairs, University of Minnesota.

KRISBERG, BARRY et al. (1986). *The Incarceration of Minority Youth*. Minneapolis: Hubert H. Humphrey Institute of Public Affairs, University of Minnesota.

KUFELDT, KATHLEEN, and PHILIP E. PERRY. (1989). "Running Around with Runaways." *Community Alternatives: International Journal of Family Care* 1:85–97.

KUPFERSMID, JOEL, and ROBERTA MONKMAN (eds.). (1987). "Assaultive Youth Responding to Physical Assaultiveness in Residential, Community, and Health Care Settings." *Child and Youth Services* 10:5–163.

LAB, STEVEN P. (1984). "Patterns of Juvenile Misbehavior." *Crime and Delinquency* 30:293–308.

LAB, STEVEN P., and WILLIAM G. DOERNER. (1987). "Changing Female Delinquency in Three Birth Cohorts." *Journal of Crime and Justice* 10:101–116.

LaFREE, GARY D. (1985). "Official Reactions to Hispanic Defendants in the Southwest." *Journal of Research on Crime and Delinquency* 22:213–237.

LAMSON, AMY. (1983). *Psychology of Juvenile Crime*. New York: Human Sciences Press.

LAUB, JOHN H. (1987). "Reanalyzing the Glueck Data: A New Look at Unraveling Juvenile Delinquency." Unpublished paper presented at the American Society of Criminology meetings, November, Montreal, CAN.

LAUB, JOHN H., and BRUCE K. MACMURRAY. (1987). "Increasing the Prosecutor's Role in Juvenile Court: Expectations and Realities." *Justice System Journal* 12:196–209.

LAUEN, ROGER J. (1984). "Community Corrections? Not in My Neighborhood!—Developing Legitimacy." *Corrections Today* 46:117–130.

LAURENCE, S. E., and B. R. WEST. (1985). *National Evaluation of the New Pride Replication Program: Final Report*, Vol. I. Lafayette, CA: Pacific Institute for Research and Evaluation.

LAVIN, G. K., S. TRABKA, and E. M. KAHN. (1984). "Group Therapy with Aggressive and Delinquent Adolescents." In *The Aggressive Adolescent: Clinical Perspectives* (C. R. Keith, ed.). New York: Free Press.

LAWRENCE, RICHARD A. (1984). "The Role of Legal Counsel in Juveniles' Understanding of Their Rights." *Juvenile and Family Court Journal* 34:49–58.

LAWRENCE, RICHARD A. (1985). "Jail Educational Programs: Helping Inmates Cope with Overcrowded Conditions." *Journal of Correctional Education* 36:15–20.

LEDDY, DANIEL D. (1985). "Families in Need of Supervision." *Criminal Justice Ethics* 4:19–38.

LEE, DEBORAH A. (1985). "The Constitutionality of Juvenile Preventive Detention: *Schall v. Martin:* Who is Preventive Detention Protecting?" *New England Law Review* 20:341–374.

LeFLORE, LARRY. (1988). "Delinquent Youths and Family." *Adolescence* 23:629–642.

LEMERT, EDWIN M. (1951). *Social Pathology*. New York: McGraw-Hill.

LEMERT, EDWIN M. (1967). *Human Deviance, Social Problems, and Social Control*. Englewood Cliffs, NJ: Prentice-Hall.

LERNER, STEVE. (1988). *Bodily Harm: The Pattern of Fear and Violence at the California Youth Authority*. Bolinas, CA: Common Knowledge Press.

LESTER, DAVID. (1987). *The Death Penalty: Issues and Answers*. Springfield, IL: Thomas.

LICK, NANCY, and DENNIS ROMIG. (1987). "The Search for an Identity: Juvenile Intensive Probation Services." Unpublished paper presented at the American Society of Criminology meetings, November, Montreal, CAN.

LILLY, J. ROBERT, and RICHARD A. BALL. (1987). "A Brief History of House Arrest and Electronic Monitoring." *Northern Kentucky Law Review* 13:343–374.

LIPSON, KARIN. (1982). "Cops and TOPS: A Program for Police and Teens That Works." *Police Chief* 49:45–46.

LITTON, GILBERT, and LINDA MARYE. (1983). *An Evaluation of the Juvenile Diversion Program in the Orleans Parish District Attorney's Office: A Preliminary Impact Evaluation.* New Orleans, LA: Mayor's Criminal Justice Coordinating Council, City of New Orleans.

LOCKE, THOMAS P. *et al.* (1986). "An Evaluation of a Juvenile Education Program in a State Penitentiary." *Evaluation Review* 10:281–298.

LOEB, ROGER C., THERESA A. BURKE, and CHERYL A. BOGLARSKY. (1986). "A Large-Scale Comparison of Perspectives on Parenting Between Teenage Runaways and Nonrunaways." *Adolescence* 21:921–930.

LOEBER, ROLF, and THOMAS J. DISHION. (1987). "Antisocial and Delinquent Youths: Methods for Their Early Identification." In *Prevention of Delinquent Behavior* (John D. Burchard and Sara Burchard, eds.). Newbury Park, CA: Sage.

LOGAN, CHARLES H., and SHARLA P. RAUSCH. (1985). "Why Deinstitutionalizing Status Offenders Is Pointless." *Crime and Delinquency* 31:501–517.

LOGAN, DIANNE. (1986). "Harris County Juvenile Probation Department: Growing Services; Shrinking Budgets." *Corrections Today* 48:22–26.

LOMBARDO, RITA, and JANET DiGIORGIO-MILLER. (1988). "Concepts and Techniques in Working with Juvenile Sex Offenders." *Journal of Offender Counseling Services and Rehabilitation* 13:39–53.

LOMBROSO, C. (1911). *Crime, Its Causes and Remedies.* Boston, MA: Little, Brown.

LONARDI, BARBARA M. (1987). "On-the-Job Training." *Corrections Today* 49:142–144.

LONGMIRE, DENNIS R. (1985). "In Support of Privatization of America's Penal Facilities: Experimental, Economic, and Political Considerations." Unpublished paper presented at the National Association of Juvenile Correctional Agencies, August, Las Vegas, NV.

LUCART, A. LEIGH. (1983). *Juvenile Detention: An Inquiry into Its Personal Dimensions.* Ann Arbor, MI: University Microfilms International.

LUNDMAN, RICHARD J. (1984). *Prevention and Control of Juvenile Delinquency.* New York: Oxford University Press.

MAHONEY, ANNE RANKIN. (1985). "Time and Process in Juvenile Court." *Justice System Journal* 10:37–55.

MAHONEY, ANNE RANKIN. (1989). "Nonresident Delinquents: Whose Problem Are They?" *Journal of Juvenile Law* 10:179–1972.

MALMQUIST, CARL P. (1990). "Depression in Homicidal Adolescents." *Bulletin of the American Academy of Psychiatry and the Law* 18:23–36.

MALONEY, DENNIS M. (1989). "The Challenge for Juvenile Corrections: To Serve Both Youths and the Public." *Corrections Today* 51:28–36.

MALONEY, DENNIS M., DENNIS ROMIG, and TROY ARMSTRONG. (1988). "Juvenile Probation: The Balanced Approach." *Juvenile and Family Court Journal* 39:1–63.

MALTZ, MICHAEL D. (1984). *Recidivism.* Orlando, FL: Academic Press.

MARGOLIS, RICHARD J. (1988). *Out of Harm's Way: The Emancipation of Juvenile Justice.* New York: Edna McConnell Clark Foundation.

MARKMAN, STEPHEN J., and PAUL G. CASSELL. (1988). "Protecting the Innocent: A Response to the Bedau-Radelet Study." *Stanford Law Review* 41:121–170.

MARTIN, KERRY C. (1987). "Treatment of Delinquent Youths in Residential Settings, 1975–1986." *Corrective and Social Psychiatry and Journal of Behavior Technology Methods and Therapy* 33:175–182.

MARTINSON, ROBERT. (1974). "What Works? Questions and Answers about Prison Reform." *The Public Interest* 35:22–54.

MASSACHUSETTS DEPARTMENT OF YOUTH SERVICES. (1984). *Pre-Trial Detention of Juveniles in Massachusetts: A Profile of Children Detained During a Six-Month Period.* Boston: Massachusetts Department of Youth Services.

MATHIAS, ROBERT A., PAUL DEMURO, and RICHARD S. ALLINSON (eds.). (1984). *Violent Juvenile Offenders: An Anthology.* San Francisco, CA: National Council on Crime and Delinquency.

MATZA, DAVID. (1964). *Delinquency and Drift.* New York: Wiley.

MAXSON, CHERYL L., MARGARET A. GORDON, and MALCOLM W. KLEIN. (1986). "Differences between Gang and Nongang Homicides." *Criminology* 23:209–222.

MAXSON, CHERYL L., MARGARET A. LITTLE, and MALCOLM W. KLEIN. (1988). "Police Response to Runaway and Missing Children: A Conceptual Framework for Research and Policy." *Crime and Delinquency* 34:84–102.

MAYS, G. LARRY, and JOEL THOMPSON. (eds.) (1991). *American Jails: Public Policy Issues.* Chicago, IL: Waveland Press.

McANANY, PATRICK D., DOUG THOMSON, and DAVID FOGEL (eds.). (1984). *Probation and Justice: Reconsideration of a Mission.* Cambridge, MA: Oelgeschlager, Gunn, and Hain.

McCARTHY, BELINDA R. (1985). "An Analysis of Detention." *Juvenile and Family Court Journal* 36:49–50.

McCARTHY, BELINDA R. (1987a) *Intermediate Punishments: Intensive Supervision, Home Confinement, and Electronic Surveillance.* Monsey, NY: Willow Tree Press.

McCARTHY, BELINDA R. (1987b). "Case Attrition in the Juvenile Court: An Application of the Crime Control Model." *Justice Quarterly* 4:237–255.

McCARTHY, BELINDA R. (1989). "A Preliminary Research Model for the Juvenile and Family Court." *Juvenile and Family Court Journal* 40:43–48.

McCARTHY, BELINDA R., and BERNARD J. McCARTHY. (1984). *Community-Based Corrections.* Monterey, CA: Brooks/Cole.

McCARTHY, BELINDA R., and B. L. SMITH. (1986). "The Conceptualization of Discrimination in the Juvenile Justice Process: The Impact of Administrative Factors and Screening Decisions on Juvenile Court Dispositions." *Criminology* 24:41–64.

McCLELLAN, DOROTHY SPEKTOROV. (1987). "Soviet Youth: A View from the Inside." *Crime and Social Justice* 29:1–25.

McCORMACK, ARLENE, MARK-DAVID JANUS, and ANN WOLBERT BURGESS. (1986). "Runaway Youths and Sexual Victimization: Gender Differences in an Adolescent Runaway Population." *Child Abuse and Neglect* 10:387–395.

McDERMOTT, M. JOAN, and JOHN H. LAUB. (1987). "Adolescence and Juvenile Justice Policy." *Criminal Justice Policy Review* 1:438–455.

McDERMOTT, M. JOAN et al. (1985). *PINS Intake Project: Final Report.* Albany: Office of Policy Analysis, Research and Statistical Services, New York State Division of Criminal Justice Services.

McDONALD, WILLIAM F. (1985). *Plea Bargaining: Critical Issues and Common Practices.* Washington, DC: U. S. Department of Justice, National Institute of Justice.

McKEACHERN, A. W., and R. BAUZER. (1967). "Factors Related to Disposition in Juvenile Police Contacts." In *Juvenile Gangs in Context: Theory, Research, and Action* (M. W. Klein, ed.). Englewood Cliffs, NJ: Prentice-Hall.

McMillen, Michael J. (1987). "Bringing Flexibility to Juvenile Detention: The Minimum Security Approach." *Corrections Today* 49:44–48, 105.

McMurran, Mary, and Jessica Whitman. (1990). "Strategies for Self-Control in Male Young Offenders Who Have Reduced Their Alcohol Consumption without Formal Intervention." *Journal of Adolescence* 13:115–128.

McNally, Roger B. (1984). "The Juvenile Justice System: A Legacy of Failure?" *Federal Probation* 48:102–110.

McShane, Marilyn D., and Frank P. Williams, III. (1989). "The Prison Adjustment of Juvenile offenders." *Crime and Delinquency* 35:254–269.

Menard, Scott. (1987). "Short-Term Trends in Crime and Delinquency: A Comparison of UCR, NCS, and Self-Report Data." *Justice Quarterly* 4:455–474.

Mennel, Robert M. (1983). "Attitudes and Policies toward Juvenile Delinquency in the United States: A Historiographical Review." In *Crime and Justice: An Annual Review of Research* (Michael Tonry and Norval Morris, eds.). Chicago, IL: University of Chicago Press.

Merton, Robert K. (1957). *Social Theory and Social Structure*. New York: Free Press.

Messerschmidt, James. (1987). "Feminism, Criminology, and the Rise of the Female Sex 'Delinquent' 1880–1930." *Contemporary Crises* 11:243–264.

MetaMetrics, Inc. (1984). *Evaluation of the Breakthrough Foundation Youth at Risk Program: The 10-Day Course and Followup Program: Final Report*. Washington, DC: MetaMetrics, Inc.

Meyers, Wade C. *et al.* (1990). "DSM-III Diagnoses and Offenses in Committed Female Juvenile Delinquents." *Bulletin of the American Academy of Psychiatry and the Law* 18:47–54.

Michigan Law Review. (1983). "Access to Juvenile Delinquency Hearings." *Michigan Law Review* 81:1540–1565.

Miller, A. Therese, Colleen Eggertson-Tacon, and Brian Quigg. (1990). "Patterns of Runaway Behavior with a Larger Systems Context: The Road to Empowerment." *Adolescence* 25:271–289.

Miller, Frank W. *et al.* (1985). *The Juvenile Justice Process*. Mineola, NY: Foundation Press.

Miller, M. O., and M. Gold. (1984). "Introgenesis in the Juvenile Justice System." *Youth and Society* 16:83–111.

Minkovsky, G. M. (1976). "USSR: Effectiveness of Treatment Measures and Problems of the Typology of Juvenile Delinquents." *Juvenile Justice: An International Survey*, No. 12. Rome: UNSDRI, pp. 221–241.

Minnesota Criminal Justice Analysis Center. (1989). *Violent and Chronic Juvenile Crime*. St. Paul: Minnesota Criminal Justice Analysis Center.

Minnesota Department of Human Services. (1990). *Drug Education Program for Minor Offenders: 1990 Evaluation*. St. Paul: Minnesota Department of Human Services, Chemical Dependency Program Division.

Minor, Kevin I., and H. Preston Elrod. (1990). "The Effects of a Multi-faceted Intervention on the Offense Activities of Juvenile Probationers." *Journal of Offender Counseling, Services, and Rehabilitation* 15:87–108.

Mitchell, Bill, and Gene Shiller. (1988). "Colorado's Shape-Up Program Gives Youth a Taste of the Inside." *Corrections Today* 50:76–87.

Mitchell, John J., and Sharon A. Williams. (1986). "SOS: Reducing Juvenile Recidivism." *Corrections Today* 48:70–71.

Mixdorf, Lloyd. (1989). "Pay Me Now or Pay Me Later." *Corrections Today* 51:106–110.

Mones, Paul. (1984). "Too Many Rights or Not Enough? A Study of the Juvenile Related Decisions of the West Virginia Supreme Court of Appeals." *Journal of Juvenile Law* 8:32–57.

Moore, Joan W. (1985). "Isolation and Stigmatization in the Development of an Underclass: The Case of Chicano Gangs in Los Angeles." *Social Problems* 33:1–12.

Morash, Merry. (1984). "Establishment of a Juvenile Police Record: The Influence of Individual and Peer Group Characteristics." *Criminology* 22:97–111.

Morris, Greggory W. (1985). *The Kids Next Door: Sons and Daughters who Kill Their Parents*. New York: William Morrow.

Munyon, William Harry. (1985). "Master Planning: Constructing a Juvenile Facility." *Corrections Today* 47:148–151.

Murphy, Edward M. (1985). "Handling Violent Juveniles." *Corrections Today* 47:26–30.

Nagoshi, Jack T. (1986). *Juvenile Recidivism: Third Circuit Court*. Honolulu: Youth Development and Research Center, University of Hawaii-Manoa.

Nakayama, Kenichi. (1987). "Japan." In *Major Criminal Justice Systems: A Comparative Survey* (George F. Cole, Stanislaw J. Frankowski, and Marc G. Gertz, eds.), 2nd ed. Beverly Hills, CA: Sage.

Nardulli, Peter F. (1978). *The Courtroom Elite: An Organizational Perspective on Criminal Justice*. Cambridge, MA: Ballinger.

National Advisory Committee for Juvenile Justice and Delinquency Prevention. (1980). *Standards for the Administration of Juvenile Justice*. Washington, DC: U. S. Government Printing Office.

National Advisory Committee on Criminal Justice Standards and Goals. (1976). *Task Force Report on Juvenile Justice and Delinquency Prevention*. Washington, DC: Law Enforcement Assistance Administration.

National Center for Juvenile Justice. (1988). *Court Careers of Juvenile Offenders*. Pittsburgh, PA: National Center for Juvenile Justice.

National Center for Juvenile Justice. (1989). *Guide to the Data Sets in the National Juvenile Court Data Archive*. Pittsburgh, PA: National Center for Juvenile Justice.

National College of Juvenile and Family Law. (1989). "Court-approved Alternative Dispute Resolution: A Better Way to Resolve Minor Delinquency, Status Offense, and Abuse/Neglect Cases." *Juvenile and Family Court Journal* 40:51–98.

National Conference of State Legislatures. (1988). *Legal Dispositions and Confinement Policies for Delinquent Youth*. Denver, CO: National Conference of State Legislatures.

National Council of Juvenile and Family Court Judges. (1986). "Deprived Children: A Judicial Response—73 Recommendations." *Juvenile and Family Court Journal* 37:3–48.

National Council on Crime and Delinquency. (1986). "National Council on Crime and Delinquency Policy Statement on Children in Jails." *Crime and Delinquency* 32:395–396.

New Jersey Division of Criminal Justice. (1985). *Juvenile Waivers to Adult Court: A Report to the New Jersey State Legislature*. Trenton: New Jersey Division of Criminal Justice.

Newman, Cathy. (1989). *Young Runaways . . . Findings From Britain's First Safe House*. London, UK: Children's Society.

Newsweek. (1990). "Judgment for the 'Wilders': A Rape Verdict in the Central Park Jogger Trial." *Newsweek,* August 27, 1990, p. 39.

Newton-Ruddy, Lara, and Mitchell M. Handelsman. (1986). "Jungian Feminine Psychology and Adolescent Prostitutes." *Adolescence* 21:815–825.

New York State Division of Parole, Evaluation, and Planning. (1985). PARJO III: *Final Evaluation of the PARJO Pilot Supervision Program.* Albany: New York State Division of Parole, Evaluation, and Planning.

Nimick, Ellen H., Linda Szymanski, and Howard Snyder. (1986). *Juvenile Court Waiver: A Study of Juvenile Court Cases Transferred to Criminal Court.* Pittsburgh, PA: National Center for Juvenile Justice.

Norman, Michael D. (1986). "Discretionary Justice: Decision-making in a State Juvenile Parole Board." *Juvenile and Family Court Journal* 37:19–25.

Norman, Sherwood. (1970). *The Youth Service Bureau—A Key to Delinquency Prevention.* Hackensack, NJ: National Council on Crime and Delinquency.

O'Connor, Roderick et al. (1984). *New Directions in Youth Services: Experiences with State-Level Coordination.* Washington, DC: U. S. Government Printing Office.

Office of Juvenile Justice and Delinquency Prevention. (1980a) *Children in Custody: Advance Report on the 1979 Census of Private Juvenile Facilities.* Washington, DC: U. S. Government Printing Office.

Office of Juvenile Justice and Delinquency Prevention. (1980b) *Children in Custody: Advance Report on the 1979 Census of Public Juvenile Facilities.* Washington, DC: U. S. Government Printing Office.

O'Neil, Carle F. (1987). "Somebody Blew It: And We Let 'Em." *Corrections Today* 49:140–192.

Orlando, Frank A., Allen F. Breed, and Robert L. Smith. (1987). *Juvenile Justice Reform: A Critique of the A.L.E.C. Code.* Minneapolis: Hubert Humphrey Institute of Public Affairs, University of Minnesota.

Osbun, Lee Ann, and Peter A. Rode. (1984). "Prosecuting Juveniles as Adults: The Quest for 'Objective' Decisions." *Criminology* 22:187–202.

Osgood, D. Wayne (1983). "Offense History and Juvenile Diversion." *Evaluation Review* 7:793–806.

Osgood, D. Wayne et al. (1987). "Time Trends and Age Trends in Self-Reported Illegal Behavior." Unpublished paper presented at American Society of Criminology meetings, November, Montreal, CAN.

Osgood, D. Wayne et al. (1988). "The Generality of Deviance in Late Adolescence and Early Adulthood." *American Sociological Review* 53:81–93.

Ostroumov, S. S. (1970). *Sovetskaia Sudebnaia Statistika.* Moscow: Izdatel-stvo Moskovskogo Universiteta.

Pabon, Edward. (1985). "A Neighborhood Correctional Program for Juvenile Offenders." *Juvenile and Family Court Journal* 36:43–47.

Pacific Institute for Research and Evaluation. (1985). *National Evaluation of the New Pride Replication Program: Final Report.* Lafayette, CA: U. S. Office of Juvenile Justice and Delinquency Prevention.

Packer, Herbert L. (1968). *The Limits of the Criminal Sanction.* Stanford, CA: Stanford University Press.

Palenski, Joseph E. (1984). *Kids Who Run Away.* Saratoga, CA: R & E Publishers.

Palmer, Ted, and Robert Wedge. (1989). "California's Juvenile Probation Camps: Findings and Implications." *Crime and Delinquency* 35:234–253.

Parker, L. Craig, Jr. (1986). *Parole and the Community-Based Treatment of Offenders in Japan.*

Pearson, Frank S., and Daniel B. Bibel. (1986). "New Jersey's Intensive Supervision Program: What Is It Like? Is It Working?" *Federal Probation* 50:25–31.

PENGELLY, HILARY. (1985). *Juvenile Justice Under the Tories: The Example of Oxford.* Norwich, UK: University of East Anglia.

PENNELL, SUSAN, CHRISTINE CURTIS, and DENNIS C. SCHECK. (1990). "Controlling Juvenile Delinquency: An Evaluation of an Interagency Strategy." *Crime and Delinquency* 36:257–275.

PETERSILIA, JOAN M. (1983). *Racial Disparities in the Criminal Justice System.* Washington, DC: U. S. Department of Justice, National Institute of Corrections.

PETERSILIA, JOAN M. (1986). "Exploring the Option of House Arrest." *Federal Probation* 50:50–55.

PETERSILIA, JOAN M., SUSAN TURNER, JAMES KAHAM, and JOYCE PETERSON. (1985). *Granting Felons Probation: Public Risks and Alternatives.* Santa Monica, CA: Rand Corporation.

PETERSON, MICHELE. (1988). "Children's Understanding of the Juvenile Justice System: A Cognitive-Developmental Perspective." *Canadian Journal of Criminology* 30:381–395.

PILIAVIN, IRVING, and SCOTT BRIAR. (1964). "Police Encounters with Juveniles." *American Journal of Sociology* 70:206–214.

PINGREE, DAVID H. (1984). "Florida Youth Services." *Corrections Today* 46:60–62.

PIPER, ELIZABETH S. (1985). "Violent Recidivism and Chronicity in the 1958 Philadelphia Cohort." *Journal of Quantitative Criminology* 1:319–344.

PLATT, ANTHONY N. (1969). *The Child Savers: The Invention of Delinquency.* Chicago, IL: University of Chicago Press.

POLEN, CHARLES A. (1987). "Youth on Death Row: Waiver of Juvenile Court Jurisdiction and Imposition of the Death Penalty on Juvenile Offenders." *Northern Kentucky Law Review* 13:495–517.

POLK, KENNETH. (1984). "Juvenile Diversion: A Look at the Record." *Crime and Delinquency* 30:648–659.

POMERY, THOMAS W. (1982). *Pennsylvania's Unified Judicial System: An Analysis with Recommendations.* Harrisburg, PA: The Committee to Study Pennsylvania's Unified Judicial System.

POPE, CARL E. (1988). "The Family, Delinquency, and Crime." In *Mental Illness, Delinquency, Addictions, and Neglect* (Elam W. Nunnally, Catherine S. Chilman, and Fred M. Cox, eds.). Newbury Park, CA: Sage.

PRATT, JOHN D. (1983). "Law and Social Control: A Study of Truancy and School." *Journal of Law and Society* 10:223–240.

PRATT, JOHN D. (1986). "A Comparative Analysis of Two Different Systems of Juvenile Justice: Some Implications for England and Wales." *Howard Journal of Criminal Justice* 25:33–51.

PRESIDENT'S COMMISSION ON LAW ENFORCEMENT AND THE ADMINISTRATION OF JUSTICE. (1967). *President's Commission on Law Enforcement and the Administration of Justice.* Washington, DC: U. S. Government Printing Office.

PROJECT NEW PRIDE. (1985). *Project New Pride.* Washington, DC: U. S. Department of Justice.

QUINLAN, JUDITH, and ELAINE MOTTE. (1990). "Psychiatric Training for Officers: An Effective Tool for Increased Officer and Inmate Safety." *American Jails* 4:22–25.

RADELET, MICHAEL R. (ed.). (1989). *Facing the Death Penalty: Essays on Cruel and Unusual Punishment.* Philadelphia, PA: Temple University Press.

RANKIN, J. H., and L. E. WELLS. (1985). "From Status to Delinquent Offenses: Escalation?" *Journal of Criminal Justice* 13:171–180.

RAPOPORT, ROBERT N. (1987). *New Interventions for Children and Youth: Action Research Approaches*. New York: Cambridge University Press.

RATLIFF, BASCOM W. (1988). "The Army Model: Boot Camp for Youthful Offenders." *Corrections Today* 50:90–102.

REAM, R. D. (ed.). (1985). "The Child and the Law: Special Bibliography Issue." *Children's Legal Rights Journal* 6:1–70.

RECKLESS, WALTER. (1967). *The Crime Problem*. New York: Appleton-Century-Crofts.

REED, DAVID. (1983). *Needed: Serious Solutions for Serious Juvenile Crime*. Chicago, IL: Chicago Law Enforcement Study Group.

REGOLI, ROBERT, ELIZABETH WILDERMAN, and MARK POGREBIN. (1985). "Using an Alternative Evaluation Measure for Assessing Juvenile Diversion Programs." *Children and Youth Services Review* 7:21–38.

REUTERMAN, NICHOLAS A., and THOMAS R. HUGHES. (1984). "Developments in Juvenile Justice During the Decade of the 70s: Juvenile Detention Facilities." *Journal of Criminal Justice* 12:325–333.

RICOTTA, DOMINIC J. (1988). "Eighth Amendment—the Death Penalty for Juveniles: A State's Right or a Child's Injustice?" *Journal of Criminal Law and Criminology* 79:821–852.

RING, CHARLES R. (1987). *Contracting for the Operation of Private Prisons—Pros and Cons*. College Park, MD: American Correctional Association.

RITTER, BRUCE. (1987). *Covenant House: Lifeline to the Street*. New York: Doubleday.

ROBBINS, IRA P. (1986). "Privatization of Corrections: Defining the Issues." *Federal Probation* 50:24–30.

ROBERTS, ALBERT R. (1989). *Juvenile Justice: Politics, Programs, and Services*. Chicago, IL: Dorsey Press.

ROGERS, JOSEPH W. (1990). "The Predisposition Report: Maintaining the Promise of Individualized Juvenile Justice." *Federal Probation* 54:43–57.

ROGERS, JOSEPH W., and G. LARRY MAYS. (1987). *Juvenile Delinquency and Juvenile Justice*. New York: Wiley.

ROGERS, RICHARD, and ROBERT M. WETTSTEIN (eds.). (1987). "Death Penalty." *Behavioral Sciences and the Law* 5:381–494.

ROMIG, DENNIS A. (1978). *Justice for Our Children*. Lexington, MA: Lexington Books.

ROSENBAUM, JILL LESLIE. (1987). "Family Dysfunction and Female Delinquency." Unpublished paper presented at the American Society of Criminology meetings, November, Montreal, CAN.

ROSNER, LYDIA S. (1988). "Juvenile Secure Detention." *Journal of Offender Counseling, Services, and Rehabilitation* 12:77–93.

ROSSUM, RALPH A., BENEDICT J. KOLLER, and CHRISTOPHER MANFREDI. (1987). *Juvenile Justice Reform: A Model for the States*. Claremont, CA: Rose Institute of State and Local Government and the American Legislative Exchange Council.

ROTHSTEIN, NATALIE. (1985). "Teen Court." *Corrections Today* 47:18–22.

ROUSCH, DAVID W. (1987). "Setting the Standard: National Juvenile Detention Resource Centers." *Corrections Today* 49:32–34.

ROUSCH, DAVID W., and B. THOMAS STEELMAN. (1982). *The Intensive Learning Program: A Comprehensive Approach to the Institutional Treatment of Juvenile Offenders*. Marshall, MI: Calhoun County (MI) Juvenile Court.

ROWAN, JOSEPH R. (1989). "Suicide Detection and Prevention: A Must for Juvenile Facilities." *Corrections Today* 51:218–223.

ROWE, DAVID C., and D. WAYNE OSGOOD. (1984). "Heredity and Sociological Theories of Delinquency: A Reconsideration." *American Sociological Review* 49: 526–540.

Rowley, John C., Charles Patrick Ewing, and Simon I. Singer. (1987). "Juvenile Homicide: The Need for an Interdisciplinary Approach." *Behavioral Sciences and the Law* 5:3–10.

Rubin, H. Ted. (1983). *Juvenile Justice and Delinquency Prevention: Viewpoints of Five Juvenile Court Judges.* Washington, DC: U. S. Office of Juvenile Justice and Delinquency Prevention.

Rubin, H. Ted. (1985). *Behind the Black Robes: Juvenile Court Judges and the Court.* Beverly Hills, CA: Sage.

Rubin, H. Ted. (1986). "Communtiy Service Restitution by Juveniles: Also In Need of Guidance." *Juvenile and Family Court Journal* 37:1–8.

Rubin, H. Ted. (1988). "Fulfilling Juvenile Restitution Requirements in Community Correctional Programs." *Federal Probation* 52:32–42.

Rubin, H. Ted. (1989). "The Juvenile Court Landscape." In *Juvenile Justice: Policies, Programs, and Services* (Albert R. Roberts, ed.). Chicago, IL: Dorsey Press.

Rudman, Cary et al. (1986). "Violent Youth in Adult Court: Process and Punishment." *Crime and Delinquency* 32:75–96.

Rumgay, Judith. (1990). "Taking Rehabilitation Out of After-Care? The Post-Release Supervision of Young Offenders." *British Journal of Criminology* 30:36–50.

Rush, George E. (1990). *The Dictionary of Criminal Justice,* 3rd ed. Guilford, CT: Dushkin.

Rutherford, Andrew. (1986). *Growing Out of Crime.* New York: Penguin.

Rydell, Peter C. (1986). "The Economics of Early Intervention Versus Later Incarceration." In *Intervention Strategies for Chronic Juvenile Offenders: Some New Perspectives* (Peter W. Greenwood, ed.). New York: Greenwood Press.

Sagatun, Inger J., and Leonard P. Edwards. (1988). "The Disposition of Juvenile Records: An Interagency Comparison." *Juvenile and Family Court Journal* 39:37–45.

Sagatun, Inger J., Loretta L. McCollum, and Leonard P. Edwards. (1985). "The Effect of Transfers from Juvenile to Criminal Court: A Log-Linear Analysis." *Journal of Crime and Justice* 8:65–92.

Samenow, Stanton E. (1989). *Before It's Too Late: Why Some Kids Get into Trouble— And What Parents Can Do About it.* New York: Times Books.

Sametz, Lynn. (1984). "Revamping the Adolescent's Justice System to Serve the Needs of the Very Young Offender." *Juvenile and Family Court Journal* 34: 21–30.

Sametz, Lynn, and Donna Hamparian. (1986). *School Reintegration of Previously Incarcerated Youths in Cleveland, 1983–1984.* Cleveland, OH: Research Division, Federal Office for Community Planning.

Sampson, Robert J. (1985). "Structural Sources of Variation in Age-Race Specific Rates of Offending Across Major U. S. Cities." *Criminology* 23:647–673.

Sampson, Robert J. (1986). "Effects of Socioeconomic Context on Official Reaction to Delinquency." *American Sociological Review* 51:876–885.

Sanborn, Joseph B. (1990). "Remnants of *Parens Patriae* in the Adjudicatory Hearing: Can a Defendant Get a Fair Trial In Juvenile Court?" Unpublished paper presented at the American Society of Criminology meetings, November, Reno, NV.

Sandberg, David N. (1989). *The Child-Abuse-Delinquency Connection.* Lexington, MA: Lexington Books.

SANDERS, WILEY B. (1945). *Some Early Beginnings of the Children's Court Movement in England.* New York: National Council on Crime and Delinquency.

SARRI, R. C. (1983). "Gender Issues in Juvenile Justice." *Crime and Delinquency* 29:381–397.

SARRI, R. C. (1988). "Keynote Remarks." Conference on Increasing Educational Equity for Juvenile Female Offenders. Washington, DC: Council of Chief State School Officers.

SARRI, R. C., and Y. HANSENFELD (EDS.). (1976). *Brought to Justice? Juveniles, the Courts, and the Law.* Ann Arbor, MI: National Assessment of Juvenile Corrections.

SAVITSKY, VALERY M., and VICTOR M. KOGAN. (1987). "The Union of Soviet Socialist Republics." In *Major Criminal Justice Systems: A Comparative Survey* (George F. Cole, Stanislaw J. Frankowski, and Marc G. Gertz, eds.). Beverly Hills, CA: Sage.

SAVITZ, LEONARD. (1982). "Official Statistics." In *Contemporary Criminology* (Leonard Savitz and Norman Johnston, eds.). New York: Wiley.

SCHACK, ELIZABETH T., and HERMINE NESSEN. (1984). *The Experiment that Failed: New York Juvenile Offender Law—A Study Report.* New York: Citizen's Committee for Children of New York, Inc.

SCHARF, P., and A. BINDER. (1983). *The Badge and the Bullet: Police Use of Deadly Force.* New York: Praeger.

SCHLATTER, GARY. (1989). "Electronic Monitoring: Hidden Costs of Home Arrest Programs." *Corrections Today* 51:94–95.

SCHLESINGER, STEVEN R. et al. (1990). *Juvenile and Adult Records: One System, One Record?—Proceedings of a BJS/Search Conference.* Washington, DC: U. S. Bureau of Justice Statistics.

SCHMIDT, ANNESLEY K. (1986). "Electronic Monitors." *Federal Probation* 50:56–59.

SCHMIDT, ANNESLEY K. (1989). *Electronic Monitoring of Offenders Increases.* Washington, DC: National Institute of Justice, Office of Justice Programs.

SCHMIDT, ANNESLEY K., and CHRISTINE E. CURTIS. (1987). "Electronic Monitors." In *Intermediate Punishments* (Belinda R. McCarthy, ed.). Monsey, NY: Criminal Justice Press.

SCHNEIDER, ANNE L. (1984a) "Deinstitutionalization of Status Offenders: The Impact of Recidivism and Secure Confinement." *Criminal Justice Abstracts,* September:410–432.

SCHNEIDER, ANNE L. (1984b). "Divesting Status Offenses from Juvenile Court Jurisdiction." *Crime and Delinquency* 30:347–370.

SCHNEIDER, ANNE L. (1985). *Guide to Juvenile Restitution.* Washington, DC: National Institute of Justice.

SCHNEIDER, ANNE L., and PETER R. SCHNEIDER. (1985). "The Impact of Restitution on Recidivism of Juvenile Offenders: An Experiment in Clayton County, Georgia." *Criminal Justice Review* 10:1–10.

SCHNEIDER, ANNE L., and DONNA D. SCHRAM. (1986). "The Washington State Juvenile Justice System Reform: A Review of Findings." *Criminal Justice Policy Review* 1:211–235.

SCHNEIDER, ANNE L., JILL G. MCKELVEY, and DONNA D. SCHRAM. (1983). "Diverstiture of Court Jurisdiction Over Status Offenders." *The Assessment of Washington's Juvenile Code.* Eugene, OR: Institute of Policy Analysis.

SCHNEIDER, PETER R., and ANN L. SCHNEIDER. (1985). "A Comparison of Programmatic and 'Ad Hoc' Restitution in Juvenile Courts." *Justice Quarterly* 1:529–548.

SCHRAM, DONNA D., and WENDY E. ROWE. (1987). *Juvenile Sexual Offender Treatment Evaluation: Final Research Report*. Olympia, WA: Governor's Juvenile Justice Advisory Committee.

SCHULMAN, RENA, and BERYL KENDE. (1988). "A Study of Runaways from a Short-Term Diagnostic Center." *Residential Treatment for Children and Youth* 5: 11–31.

SCHUR, EDWIN. (1973). *Radical Nonintervention: Rethinking the Delinquency Problem*. Englewood Cliffs, NJ: Prentice-Hall.

SCHWARTZ, IRA M. (1989). In *Justice for Juveniles: Rethinking the Best Interests of the Child*. Lexington, MA: Lexington Books.

SCHWEITZGEBEL, RALPH K. *et al.* (1964). "A Program of Research & Behavior Electronics," *Behavioral Science* 9:233–238.

SCOVILLE, JAMES C. (1987). "Deadly Mistakes: Harmless Error in Capital Sentencing." *University of Chicago Law Review* 54:740–758.

SELJAN, B. J. (1983). *Juvenile Justice System Professional Survey: A Description of Results in the National Evaluation Sites*. Eugene, OR: Institute of Policy Analysis.

SELLERS, CHRISTINE. (1987). "Juvenile Dispositions: How Far Does Legalism Go?" Unpublished paper presented at the Academy of Criminal Justice Sciences meetings, March, St. Louis, MO.

SELYE, HANS. (1976). *The Stress of Life*, 2nd ed. New York: McGraw-Hill.

SEYFRIT, CAROLE L., PHILIP L. REICHEL, and BRIAN L. STUTTS. (1987). "Peer Juries as a Juvenile Justice Diversion Technique." *Youth and Society* 18:302–316.

SHAFFER, DAVID, and CAROL L. M. CATON. (1984). *Runaway and Homeless Youth in New York City*. New York: Division of Child Psychiatry. New York State Psychiatric Institute and Columbia University College of Physicians and Surgeons.

SHAFFNER, PAULA D. (1985). "Around and Around on Pennsylvania's Juvenile Confession Carousel: This Time the Police Get the Brass Ring." *Villanova Law Review* 30:1235–1266.

SHANE, PAUL G. (1989). "Changing Patterns among Homeless and Runaway Youth." *American Journal of Orthopsychiatry* 59:208–214.

SHANNON, LYLE W. (1982). *Assessing the Relation of Adult Criminal Careers to Juvenile Careers*. Washington, DC: U. S. Department of Justice.

SHAW, CLIFFORD R., and HENRY D. MCKAY. (1972). *Juvenile Delinquency and Urban Areas* (rev. ed.). Chicago, IL: University of Chicago Press.

SHELDEN, RANDALL G. (1987). "The Chronic Delinquent: Gender and Race Differences." Unpublished paper presented at the American Society of Criminology meetings, November, Montreal, CAN.

SHELDEN, RANDALL G., and JOHN A. HORVATH. (1987). "Intake Processing in a Juvenile Court: A Comparison of Legal and Nonlegal Variables." *Juvenile and Family Court Journal* 38:13–19.

SHELDEN, RANDALL G., JOHN A. HORVATH, and SHARON TRACY. (1989). "Do Status Offenders Get Worse? Some Clarifications on the Question of Escalation." *Crime and Delinquency* 35:202–216.

SHELDON, WILLIAM H. (1949). *The Varieties of Delinquent Youth*. New York: Harper.

SHELLEFF, LEON SHASKOLSKY. (1987). *Ultimate Penalties: Capital Punishment, Life Imprisonment, Physical Torture*. Columbus: Ohio State University Press.

SHELLEY, LOUISE I. (1987). "Inter-Personal Violence in the U. S. S. R." *Violence, Aggression, and Terrorism* 1:41–67.

SHERMAN, LAWRENCE W., and BARRY D. GLICK. (1984). "The Quality of Arrest Statistics." *Police Foundation Reports* 2:1–8.

SHERRADEN, MICHAEL W., and SUSAN WHITELAW DOWNS. (1984). "Institutions and Juvenile Delinquency in Historical Persepctive." *Children and Youth Services Review* 6:155–172.

SHICHOR, DAVID, and CLEMENS BARTOLLAS. (1990). "Private and Public Juvenile Placements: Is There a Difference?" *Crime and Delinquency* 36:286–299.

SHIFRIN, A. (1978). "How Many Concentration Camps are There in the U.S.S.R.?" *Novoe Russkoe Slovo* #24656:3.

SIEGEL, LARRY J., and JOSEPH J. SENNA. (1988). *Juvenile Delinquency: Theory, Practice, and the Law*, 3rd ed. St. Paul, MN: West Publishing Company.

SIMCHA-FAGAN, ORA, and JOSEPH E. SCHWARTZ. (1986). "Neighborhood and Delinquency: An Assessment of Contextual Effects." *Criminology* 24:667–703.

SIMON, RITA J., and JUDITH D. SIMON. (1988). "Female COs: Legitimate Authority." *Corrections Today* 50:132–134.

SIMONE, MARGARET V. (1984). "Group Homes: Succeeding by Really Trying." *Corrections Today* 46:110–119.

SINGER, SIMON I. (1985). *Relocating Juvenile Crime: The Shift from Juvenile to Criminal Justice*. Albany, NY: Nelson A. Rockefeller Institute of Government.

SINGER, SIMON I., and DAVID McDOWALL. (1988). "Criminalizing Delinquency: The Deterrent Effects of the New York Juvenile Offender Law." *Law and Society Review* 22:521–535.

SKOLNICK, JEROME H., and DAVID H. BAYLEY. (1986). *The New Blue Line: Police Innovation in Six American Cities*. New York: Free Press.

SLOANE, DOUGLAS M., and RAYMOND H. POTVIN. (1986). "Religion and Delinquency: Cutting Through the Maze." *Social Forces* 65:87–105.

SMITH, DOUGLAS, and CHRISTY VISHER. (1981). "Street-Level Justice: Situational Determinants of Police Arrest Decisions." *Social Problems* 29:167–177.

SMITH, GEORGE C. (1986). *Capital Punishment 1986: Last Lines of Defense*. Washington, DC: Washington Legal Foundation.

SMITH, J. STEVEN. (1991). "A Lesson From Indiana: Detention Is an Invaluable Part of the System, But It's Not the Solution to All Youths' Problems." *Corrections Today* 53:56–60.

SMITH, MELINDA. (1990). "New Mexico Youths Use Mediation to Settle Their Problems Peacefully." *Corrections Today* 52:112–114.

SMITH, M. DWAYNE. (1987). "Patterns of Discrimination in Assessments of the Death Penalty: The Case of Louisiana." *Journal of Criminal Justice* 15:279–286.

SMYKLA, JOHN ORTIZ. (1987). "The Human Impact of Capital Punishment: Interviews with Families of Persons on Death Row." *Journal of Criminal Justice* 15:331–347.

SNELLENBURG, SIDNEY C. (1986). "A Normative Alternative to the Death Penalty." Unpublished paper presented at the Southern Association of Criminal Justice Educators, October, Atlanta, GA.

SNYDER, HOWARD N. (1988). *Court Careers of Juvenile Offenders*. Pittsburgh, PA: National Center for Juvenile Justice.

SNYDER, HOWARD N. et al. (1985). *Juvenile Court Statistics*. Pittsburgh, PA: National Center for Juvenile Justice.

SNYDER, HOWARD N. et al. (1989). *Juvenile Court Statistics*. Pittsburgh, PA: National Center for Juvenile Justice.

SNYDER, HOWARD N. et al. (1990). *Juvenile Court Statistics*. Pittsburgh, PA: National Center for Juvenile Justice.

SNYDER, KEITH B., and CECIL MARSHALL. (1990). "Pennsylvania's Juvenile Intensive

Probation and Aftercare Programs." Unpublished paper presented at the American Society of Criminology meetings, November, Baltimore, MD.

SOLOMON, PETER H., JR. (1987). *The Case of the Vanishing Acquittal: Informal Norms and the Practice of Soviet Criminal Justice.* Urbana-Champaign: Soviet Interview Project, University of Illinois.

SOUTHEIMER, HENRY, LYNNE GOODSTEIN, and MICHAEL KOVACEVIC. (1990). "An Experimental Evaluation of an Aftercare Program for Chronic Delinquents." Unpublished paper presented at the American Society of Criminology meetings, November, Baltimore, MD.

SPECK, NAN B., DEAN W. GINTHER, and JOSEPH R. HELTON. (1988). "Runaways: Who Will Run Away Again?" *Adolescence* 23:881–888.

SPERGEL, IRVING A. (1986). "The Violent Gang Problem in Chicago: A Local Community Approach." *Social Service Review* 60:94–131.

SPERGEL, IRVING A. (1990). "Youth Gangs: Continuity and Change." In *Crime and Justice: A Review of Research* (Michael Tonry and Norval Morris, eds.), Vol. 12. Chicago, IL: University of Chicago Press.

SPOHN, CASSIA, SUSAN WELCH, and JOHN GRUHL. (1985). "Woman Defendants in Court: The Interaction Between Sex and Race in Convicting and Sentencing." *Social Science Quarterly* 66:178–185.

SPRINGER, CHARLES E. (1987). *Justice for Juveniles.* Rockville, MD: U. S. National Institute for Juvenile Justice and Delinquency Prevention.

SPRINGER, MERLE E. (1976). "A Framework for the Public-Voluntary Collaboration in the Social Services—The Role of the Governmental Sector." *The Social Welfare Forum.* New York: National Association of Social Welfare Organizations.

SPRINGER, MERLE E. (1988). "Youth Service Privatization: The Experience of a Provider." *Corrections Today* 50:88–93.

STAPLES, WILLIAM G. (1986). "Restitution as a Sanction in Juvenile Court." *Crime and Delinquency* 32:177–185.

STATE OF COLORADO. (1980). *Correctional Options for the 80's.* Denver, CO: Division of Criminal Justice.

STEINHART, DAVID. (1988). *California Opinion Poll: Public Attitudes on Youth Crime.* San Francisco, CA: National Council on Crime and Delinquency.

STEWART, C. S., and M. ZAENGLEIN-SENGER. (1984). "Female Delinquency, Family Problems, and Parental Interactions." *Social Casework* 65:428–432.

STEWART, MARY JANET, EDWARD I. VOCKELL, and ROSE E. RAY. (1986). "Decreasing Court Appearances of Juvenile Status Offenders." *Social Casework* 67:74–79.

STITT, B. GRANT, and SHELDON SIEGEL. (1986). "The Ethics of Plea Bargaining." Unpublished paper presented at the Academy of Criminal Justice Sciences meetings, March, Orlando, FL.

STOUTHAMER-LOEBER, MAGDA, and ROLF LOEBER. (1988). "Parents as Intervention Agents for Children with Conduct Problems and Juvenile Offenders." *Child and Youth Services* 11:127–148.

STRASBURG, PAUL A. (1984). "Recent National Trends in Serious Juvenile Crime." In *Violent Juvenile Offenders: An Anthology* (Robert A. Mathias, Paul DeMuro, and Richard S. Allinson, eds.). San Francisco, CA: National Council on Crime and Delinquency.

STREIB, VICTOR L. (1983). "Death Penalty for Children: the American Experience with Capital Punishment for Crimes Committed while Under Age Eighteen." *Oklahoma Law Review* 36:613–641.

STREIB, VICTOR L. (1987). *The Death Penalty for Juveniles.* Bloomington: Indiana University Press.

STREIB, VICTOR L., and LYNN SAMETZ. (1988). "Capital Punishment of Female Juveniles." Unpublished paper presented at the American Society of Criminology meetings, November, Chicago.

STRONG, ANN. (1981). *Case Classification Manual, Module One: Technical Aspects of Interviewing.* Austin: Texas Adult Probation Commission.

STRUCKHOFF, DAVID R. (1987). "Selective Incapacitation." *Corrections Today* 49:30–34.

STUTT, HOWARD (ed.). (1986). *Learning Disabilities and the Young Offender: Arrest to Disposition.* Ottawa: Canadian Association for Children and Adults with Learning Disabilities.

SULLIVAN, PATRICK M. (1988). "Juvenile Facility Design: Unique Needs, Unique Construction." *Corrections Today* 50:38–44.

SUTHERLAND, EDWIN H. (1939). *Principles of Criminology.* Philadelphia, PA: Lippincott.

SUTHERLAND, EDWIN H. (1951). "Critique of Sheldon's Varieties of Delinquent Youth." *American Sociological Review* 16:10–13.

SUTTON, JOHN R. (1985). "The Juvenile Court and Social Welfare: Dynamics of Progressive Reform." *Law and Society Review* 19:107–145.

SWEET, JOSEPH. (1985). "Probation as Therapy." *Corrections Today* 47:89–90.

SWEET, ROBERT W., JR. (1991). *Public Juvenile Facilities: Children in Custody 1989.* Washington, DC: U. S. Department of Justice.

SYRACUSE/ONONDAGA COUNTY YOUTH BUREAU. (1984). *Onondaga County Interagency Coordination Project: Alternatives for Youths at Risk: A Final Report—Recommendations and Community Action Plan.* Syracuse, NY: Office of the Onondaga County Executive.

TAKATA, SUSAN R., and RICHARD G. ZEVITZ. (1987). "Youth Gangs in Racine: An Examination of Community Perceptions." *Wisconsin Sociologist* 24:132–141.

TAYLOR, CARL S. (1986). "Black Urban Youth Gangs: Analysis of Contemporary Issues." Unpublished paper presented at the American Society of Criminology meetings, November, San Francisco, CA.

TAYLOR, CARL S. (1989). *Dangerous Society.* East Lansing: Michigan State University Press.

TERRILL, RICHARD J. (1984). *World Criminal Justice Systems: A Survey.* Cincinnati, OH: Anderson.

TESCHNER, DOUGLAS F., and JOHN J. WOLTER (eds.). (1984). *Wilderness Challenge: Outdoor Education Alternatives for Youth in Need.* Hadlyme, CT: Institute of Experiential Studies.

TESS, GENE, and KATHRYN BOGUE. (1988). "Master Correctional Officer Program: An Idea with a Future." *American Jails* 1:66–67.

THOMAS, CHARLES W., and SHAY BILCHIK. (1985). "Prosecuting Juveniles in Criminal Courts: Legal and Empirical Analysis." *Journal of Criminal Law and Criminology* 76:439–479.

THOMAS, ROBERT H., and JOHN D. HUTCHESON. (1986). *Georgia Residents' Attitudes toward the Death Penalty, The Disposition of Juvenile Offenders, and Related Issues.* Atlanta: Center for Public and Urban Research, Georgia State University.

THOMSON, DOUG, and PATRICK D. MCANANY. (1984). "Punishment and Responsibility in Juvenile Court: Desert-based Probation for Delinquents." In *Probation and Justice: Reconsideration of a Mission* (Patrick D. McAnany, Doug Thomson, and David Fogel, eds.). Cambridge, MA: Oelgeschlager, Gunn, and Hain.

THORNBERRY, TERENCE P. (1979). "Sentencing Disparities in the Juvenile Justice System." *Journal of Criminal Law and Criminology* 70:164–171.

THORNBERRY, TERENCE P. (1987). "Toward an Interactional Theory of Delinquency." *Criminology* 25:863–891.

THORNBERRY, TERENCE, and R. L. CHRISTENSON. (1984). "Juvenile Justice Decision-making as a Longitudinal Process." *Social Forces* 63:433–444.

THORNTON, WILLIAM E., JR., LYDIA VOIGT, and WILLIAM G. DOERNER. (1987). *Delinquency and Justice.* New York: Random House.

TIFFANY, LAWRENCE P., YAKOV AVICHAI, and GEOFFREY W. PETERS. (1975). "A Statistical Analysis of Sentencing in Federal Courts: Defendants Convicted After Trial, 1967–68." *Journal of Legal Studies* 4:369–380.

TITTLE, CHARLES R., and ROBERT F. MEIER, (1990). "Specifying the SES/Delinquency Relationship." *Criminology* 28:271–299.

TOKUOKA, HIDEO, and ALBERT K. COHEN. (1987). "Japanese Society and Delinquency." *International Journal of Comparative and Applied Criminal Justice* 11:13–22.

TOLAN, PATRICK. (1988a). "Socioeconomic, Family, and Social Stress Correlates of Adolescent Antisocial and Delinquent Behavior." *Journal of Abnormal Child Psychology* 16:317–331.

TOLAN, PATRICK. (1988b). "Delinquent Behaviors and Male Adolescent Development: A Preliminary Study." *Journal of Youth and Adolescence* 17:413–427.

TOMSON, BARBARA, and EDNA R. FIELDER. (1975). "Gangs: A Response to the Urban World." In *Gang Delinquency* (Desmond S. Cartwright, Barbara Tomson, and Hershey Schwartz, eds.). Monterey, CA: Brooks/Cole.

TONRY, MICHAEL, and NORVAL MORRIS (eds.). (1986). *Crime and Justice: An Annual Review of Research,* Vol. 7. Chicago, IL: University of Chicago Press.

TORBET, PATRICIA McFALL. (1987). *Organization and Administration of Juvenile Services: Probation, Aftercare, and State Delinquent Institutions.* Pittsburgh, PA: National Center for Juvenile Justice.

TRACY, PAUL, JR., M. WOLFGANG, and R. FIGLIO. (1985). *Delinquency in Two Birth Cohorts: Executive Summary.* Washington, DC: U. S. Department of Justice.

TRASLER, GORDON. (1987). "Biogenetic Factors." In *Handbook of Juvenile Delinquency* (Herbert C. Quay, ed.). New York: Wiley.

TRAVISONO, ANTHONY P. (1989). "Juvenile Corrections: What Road to the Future?" *Corrections Today* 51:4.

TREANOR, WILLIAM W., and ADRIENNE E. VOLENIK. (1987). *The New Right's Juvenile Crime and Justice Agenda for the States: A Legislator's Briefing Book.* Washington, DC: American Youth Work Center.

TRESTER, HAROLD B. (1981). *Supervision of the Offender.* Englewood Cliffs, NJ: Prentice-Hall.

TROJANOWICZ, ROBERT, and BONNIE BUCQUEROUX. (1990). *Community Policing: A Contemporary Perspective.* Cincinnati, OH: Anderson.

TURNER, BOB. (1988). "Cutting Red Tape: How Privatization Can Help the Public Sector Perform More Efficiently." *Corrections Today* 50:74–87.

TURNER, CHARLES W., ALLEN M. COLE, and DANIEL S. CERRO. (1984). "Contributions of Aversive Experiences to Robbery and Homicide: A Demographic Analysis." In *Aggression in Children and Youth* (Robert M. Kaplan, Vladimir Konecni, and Raymond W. Novaco, eds). The Hague, Netherlands: Martinus Nijhoff.

TWAIN, DAVID, and LAURA MAIELLO. (1988). "Juvenile Conference Committees: An Evaluation of the Administration of Justice at the Neighborhood Level." *Journal of Criminal Justice* 16:451–461.

TYGART, CLARENCE E. (1988). "Strain Theory and Public School Vandalism: Academic Tracking, School Social Status, and Students' Academic Achievement." *Youth and Society* 20:106–118.

UNITED STATES CODE. (1990). *United States Code Annotated.* St. Paul, MN: West.

UNIVERSITY OF HAWAII AT MANOA. (1990). *Gun Control: A Youth Issue.* Honolulu: University of Hawaii at Manoa, Social Science Research Institute, Center for Youth Research.

UNIVERSITY OF PENNSYLVANIA. (1985). *Longitudinal Study of Biosocial Factors Related to Delinquency and Crime: Final Report.* Philadelphia: University of Pennsylvania Center for Studies in Criminology and Criminal Law.

U. S. CONGRESS OFFICE OF TECHNOLOGY ASSESSMENT. (1987a). *The Electronic Supervisor: New Technology, New Tensions.* Washington, DC: U. S. Government Printing Office.

U. S. CONGRESS OFFICE OF TECHNOLOGY ASSESSMENT. (1987b). *Defending Secrets, Sharing Data: New Locks and Keys for Electronic Information.* Washington, DC: U. S. Government Printing Office.

U. S. DEPARTMENT OF JUSTICE. (1976). *Two Hundred Years of American Criminal Justice: An LEAA Bicentennial Study.* Washington, DC: Law Enforcement Assistance Administration.

U. S. DEPARTMENT OF JUSTICE. (1988). *Report to the Nation on Crime and Justice.* Washington, DC: U. S. Department of Justice, Bureau of Justice Statistics.

U. S. GENERAL ACCOUNTING OFFICE. (1983). *Federally Supported Centers Provided Needed Services for Runaways and Homeless Youths.* Washington, DC: U. S. Government Printing Office.

U. S. GENERAL ACCOUNTING OFFICE. (1985). *Juvenile Justice: Detention Using Staff Provision Rather than Architectural Barriers.* Washington, DC: U. S. General Accounting Office.

U. S. SENATE JUDICIARY COMMITTEE. (1984). *Deinstitutionalization of Juvenile Nonoffenders: Hearing . . . June 21, 1983.* Washington, DC: U. S. Government Printing Office.

VAN DEN HAAG, ERNEST. (1986). "On Sentencing." In *Punishment and Privilege* (W. Bryon Groves and Graeme Newman, eds.). Albany, NY: Harrow and Heston.

VAN DEN HAAG, ERNEST, and JOHN P. CONRAD. (1983). *The Death Penalty: A Debate.* New York: Plenum.

VAN DINE, STEPHEN *et al.* (1977). "The Incapacitation of the Dangerous Offender: A Statistical Experiment." *Journal of Research on Crime and Delinquency* 14:24–34.

VAN WORMER, KATHERINE. (1990a). "The Hidden Juvenile Justice System in Norway: A Journey Back in Time." *Federal Probation* 54:57–61 [reprinted from *Corrections Today* 52:106–116 (1990)].

VAN WORMER, KATHERINE. (1990b). "Norway's Juvenile Justice System: A Journey Back in Time." *Corrections Today* 52:106–116.

VARLEY, W. H. (1984). "Behavior Modification Approaches to the Aggressive Adolescent." In *The Aggressive Adolescent: Clinical Perspectives* (C. R. Keith, ed.). New York: Free Press.

VISHER, CHRISTY A. (1987). "Incapacitation and Crime Control: Does a 'Lock 'Em Up' Strategy Reduce Crime?" *Justice Quarterly* 4:513–543.

VITO, GENNARO F. (1984). "Developments in Shock Probation: A Review of Research Findings and Policy Implementations." *Federal Probation* 48:22–27.

VOLENIK, ADRIENNE E. (1986). *Sample Pleadings for Use in Juvenile Delinquency Proceedings.* Washington, DC: American Bar Association.

VOLLMANN, JOHN J., JR. (1987). "Neutering Homicidal Recidivists in Jurisdictions without Capital Punishment." Unpublished paper presented at the American Society of Criminology meetings, November, Montreal, CAN.

WADLINGTON, W. *et al.* (1983). *Children in the Legal System.* Mineola, NY: Foundation Press.

WAHLER, ROBERT G. (1987). "Contingency Management with Oppositional Children: Some Critical Teaching Issues for Parents." In *From Children to Citizens.* Vol. III. *Families, Schools, and Delinquency Prevention* (James Q. Wilson and Glenn C. Loury, eds.). New York: Springer-Verlag.

WALDORF, DAN *et al.* (1990). "Needle Sharing Among Male Prostitutes: Preliminary Findings of the Prospero Project." *Journal of Drug Issues* 20:309–334.

WALDRON, THOMAS W. (1990). "Boot Camp Offers Second Chance to Young Felons." *Corrections Today* 52:144–169.

WALKER, SAMUEL. (1984). "'Broken Windows' and Fractured History: The Use and Misuse of History in Recent Patrol Analysis." *Justice Quarterly* 1:75–90.

WALKER, SAMUEL. (1985). *Sense and Nonsense About Crime.* Pacific Grove, CA: Brooks/Cole.

WALKER, SAMUEL. (1989). *Sense and Nonsense About Crime,* 2nd ed. Pacific Grove, CA: Brooks/Cole.

WALLACE, DONALD H. (1989). "Bloodbath and Brutalization: Public Opinion and the Death Penalty." *Journal of Crime and Justice* 12:51–77.

WALSH, ANTHONY. (1987). "Cognitive Functioning and Delinquency." *International Journal of Offender Therapy and Comparative Criminology* 31:285–289.

WALSH, ANTHONY, THOMAS A. PETEE, and ARTHUR J. BEYER. (1987). "Intellectual Imbalance and Delinquency: Comparing High Verbal and High Performance IQ Delinquents." *Criminal Justice and Behavior* 14:370–379.

WARR, MARK, and MARK STAFFORD. (1984). "Public Goals of Punishment and Support for the Death Penalty." *Journal of Research in Crime and Delinquency* 21:95–111.

WASHINGTON STATE DEPARTMENT OF HEALTH AND SOCIAL SERVICES. (1986). *Special Offenders Issue Analysis: Task Force Report.* Olympia, WA: Division of Juvenile Rehabilitation.

WATKINS, JOHN C., JR. (1987). "The Convolution of Ideology: American Juvenile Justice from a Critical Legal Studies Perspective." Unpublished paper presented at the American Society of Criminology meetings, November, Montreal, CAN.

WEBB, DAVID. (1984). "More on Gender and Justice: Girl Offenders on Supervision." *Sociology* 18:367–381.

WEBER, DONALD E., and WILLIAM H. BURKE, (1986). "An Alternative Approach to Treating Delinquent Youth." *Residential Group Care and Treatment* 3:65–86.

WEEKS, H. ASHLEY. (1956). *Highfields.* Ann Arbor, MI: University of Michigan Press.

WEICHMAN, DENNIS, and JERRY KENDALL. (1987). "A Longitudinal Analysis of the Death Penalty." *Justice Professional* 2:100–109.

WEIS, JOSEPH, and J. DAVID HAWKINS. (1981). *Report of the National Juvenile Justice Assessment Centers, Preventing Delinquency.* Washington, DC: U. S. Department of Justice.

WEISHEIT, RALPH A., and DIANE M. ALEXANDER. (1988). "Juvenile Justice Philosophy and the Demise of *Parens Patriae.* "*Federal Probation* 52:56–63.

WERNER, EMMY E. (1987). "Vulnerability and Resiliency in Children at Risk for Delinquency: A Longitudinal Study from Birth to Adulthood." In *Prevention of Delinquent Behavior* (John D. Burchard and Sara Burchard, eds.). Newbury Park, CA: Sage.

WHITAKER, GORDON *et al.* (1985). "Aggressive Policing and the Deterrence of Crime." *Law and Policy* 7:395–416.

WHITAKER, J. MICHAEL, and LAWRENCE J. SEVERY. (1984). "Service Accountability and Recidivism for Diverted Youth: A Client- and Service-Comparison Orientation." *Criminal Justice and Behavior* 11:47–74.

WHITEHEAD, JOHN T., and CHARLES LINDQUIST. (1985). "Job Stress and Burnout among Probation/Parole Officers: Perceptions and Causal Factors." *International Journal of Offender Therapy and Comparative Criminology* 29:109–119.

WIATROWSKI, MICHAEL, and KRISTINE L. ANDERSON. (1987). "The Dimensionality of the Social Bond." *Journal of Quantitative Criminology* 3:65–81.

WIDOM, CATHY SPATZ et al. (1983). "Multivariate Analysis of Personality and Motivation in Female Delinquents." *Journal of Research in Crime and Delinquency* 20:277–290.

WIEBUSH, RICHARD G. (1990). "The Ohio Experience: Programmatic Variations in Intensive Supervision for Juveniles." *Perspectives* 14:26–35.

WIEBUSH, RICHARD, DONNA HAMPARIAN, and JOE M. DAVIS. (1985). *Juveniles in the Ohio Department of Youth Services Institutions, 1982–1984. Part I. Juveniles.* Cleveland: Ohio Serious Juvenile Offender Project.

WIEDERANDERS, MARK R. (1983). *Success on Parole: The Influence of Self-Reported Attitudes, Experiences, and Background Characteristics on the Parole Behaviors of Youthful Offenders—Final Report.* Sacramento, CA: Department of the Youth Authority.

WILBANKS, WILLIAM. (1987). *The Myth of a Racist Criminal Justice System.* Monterey, CA: Brooks/Cole.

WILDERMAN, ELIZABETH. (1984). "Juvenile Diversion: From Politics to Policy." *New England Journal of Human Services* 3:19–23.

WILKINSON, CHRISTINE, and ROGER EVANS (1990). "Police Cautioning of Juveniles: The Impact of Home Office Circular 14-1985." *Criminal Law Review* (March 1990), pp. 165–176.

WILLIAMS, J. SHERWOOD et al. (1983). "Situational Use of Police Force: Public Reactions." *American Journal of Police* 3:37–50.

WILLIAMS, LEVI. (1984). "A Police Diversion Alternative for Juvenile Offenders." *Police Chief* 51:54–57.

WILLIS, CECIL L., and RICHARD H. WELLS. (1988). "The Police and Child Abuse: An Analysis of Police Decisions to Report Illegal Behavior." *Criminology* 26:695–716.

WILLMAN, HERB C., JR., and RON Y. CHUN. (1974). "Homeward Bound: An Alternative to the Institutionalization of Adjudicated Juvenile Offenders." In *Alternatives to Imprisonment: Corrections and the Community* (George C. Killinger and Paul F. Cromwell, Jr., eds.). St. Paul, MN: West.

WILSON, E. O. (1975). *Sociobiology: The New Synthesis.* Cambridge, MA: Harvard University Press.

WILSON, HARRIET. (1987). "Parental Supervision Re-Examined." *British Journal of Criminology* 27:275–301.

WILSON, JAMES Q., and RICHARD J. HERRNSTEIN. (1985). *Crime and Human Nature.* New York: Simon & Schuster.

WILSON, THELMA (ed.). (1987). *Penal Services for Offenders: Comparative Studies of England and Poland 1984/1985.* Brookfield, VT: Gower.

WILSON, WILLIAM. (1983). "Juvenile Offenders and the Electric Chair: Cruel and Unusual Punishment or Form of Discipline for the Hopelessly Delinquent?" *University of Florida Law Review* 35:344–374.

WINDLE, MICHAEL, and GRACE M. BARNES. (1988). "Similarities and Differences in Correlates of Alcohol Consumption and Problem Behaviors Among Male and Female Adolescents." *International Journal of the Additions* 23:707–728.

WITKIN, HERMAN. (1976). "Criminality in XYY and XXY Men." *Science* 193:547–555.

WOLFGANG, MARVIN, and FRANCO FERRACUTI. (1967). *The Subculture of Violence.* London: Tavistock.

WOLFGANG, MARVIN, ROBERT M. FIGLIO, and THORSTEN SELLIN. (1972). *Delinquency in a Birth Cohort.* Chicago, IL: University of Chicago Press.

WOLFGANG, MARVIN E. *et al.* (1986). *Violent Juvenile Crime: What Do We Know About It and What Can We Do About It?* Minneapolis: Center for the Study of Youth Policy, Hubert H. Humphrey Institute of Public Affairs, University of Minnesota.

WORRELL, CLAUDIA. (1985). "Pretrial Detention of Juveniles: Denial of Equal Protection Masked by the *Parens Patriae* Doctrine." *Yale Law Review* 95:174–193.

WYLEN, JANE. (1984). *A Descriptive Study of Juvenile Offenders Released to State Parole Supervision.* Albany: New York State Division of Parole.

YABLONSKY, LEWIS, and MARTIN R. HASKELL. (1988). *Juvenile Delinquency,* 4th ed. New York: Harper & Row.

YOSHITAKE, MITSUYO. (1989). "Juvenile Classification Homes in Japan." *American Jails* 2:88–97.

YOUTH POLICY AND LAW CENTER, INC. (1984). *Violent Delinquents: A Wisconsin Study.* Madison, WI: Youth Policy and Law Center, Inc.

YURKANIN, ANN. (1989). "Trend toward Shock Incarceration Increasing Among the States." *Corrections Today* 50:87.

ZASLAW, JAY G. (1989). "Stop Assaultive Children—Project SAC Offers Hope for Violent Juveniles." *Corrections Today* 51:48–50.

ZELDES, ILYA. (1981). *The Problem of Crime in the USSR.* Springfield, IL: Thomas.

ZENON, CARL. (1990). "Journey to Japan." *Corrections Today* 110:118–127.

ZIGLER, EDWARD, and NANCY W. HALL. (1987). "The Implications of Early Intervention Efforts for the Primary Prevention of Juvenile Delinquency." In *From Children to Citizens.* Vol. III. *Families, Schools, and Delinquency* (James Q. Wilson and Glenn C. Loury, eds.). New York: Springer-Verlag.

ZIMMER, LYNN E. (1986). *Women Guarding Men.* Chicago, IL: University of Chicago Press.

ZIMRING, FRANKLIN E. (1984). "Youth Homicide in New York: A Preliminary Analysis." *Journal of Legal Studies* 13:81–99.

ZIMRING, FRANKLIN E., and GORDON HAWKINS. (1986). *Capital Punishment and the American Agenda.* Cambridge, UK: Cambridge University Press.

Index of Cases

Name Index

Subject Index